Almanac of African Peoples & Nations

Mohamad Z. Yakan

Transaction Publishers
New Brunswick (U.S.A.) and London (U.K.)

Copyright © 1999 by Transaction Publishers, New Brunswick, New Jersey.

All rights reserved under International and Pan-American Copyright Conventions. No part of this book may be reproduced or transmitted in any form or by any means, electronic or mechanical, including photocopy, recording, or any information storage and retrieval system, without prior permission in writing from the publisher. All inquiries should be addressed to Transaction Publishers, Rutgers—The State University, 35 Berrue Circle, Piscataway, New Jersey 08854-8042.

This book is printed on acid-free paper that meets the American National Standard for Permanence of Paper for Printed Library Materials.

Library of Congress Catalog Number: 98-54917
ISBN: 1-56000-433-9
Printed in the United States of America

Library of Congress Cataloging-in-Publication Data

Yakan, Mohamad Z.
    Almanac of African peoples and nations / by Mohamad Z. Yakan.
        p. cm.
    Includes bibliographical references and index.
    ISBN 1-56000-433-9 (alk. paper)
    1. Ethnology—Africa. 2. Languages—Africa. I. Title.
DT15.Y35   1999
305.8'096—dc21   98-54917
                                                         CIP

TABLE OF CONTENTS

ACKNOWLEDGMENTS

Almanac of African Peoples and Nations is the culmination of phase one of an ongoing project that started in 1991. In the process of its development and completion many important references and other published works were utilized and/or consulted, the most helpful of which were: *The New Encyclopædia Britannica* (Encyclopædia Britannica, 1988); *Encyclopedia of World Cultures, Africa and the Middle East* (G.K. Hall, 1995); David H. Price's *Atlas of World Cultures* (Sage, 1990); miscellaneous publications by the Royal Anthropological Institute of Great Britain and Ireland; Basil Davidson's works on Africa's history and current Affairs, including *Africa in History* (Macmillan, 1974), *The African Genius* (Little, Brown & Company, 1969), and *The Lost Cities of Africa* (Little, Brown & Company, 1987); and Robert W. July's classic, *A History of the African People* (Charles Scribner's Sons, 1970 and 1974, and Waveland Press, Inc., 1998). July's work was especially important not only as resourceful reference, but also as an exemplar of fine scholarship, sound analysis, and balanced and objective information on the history of the African peoples.

The *Almanac of African Peoples and Nations* represents the summation of eight years of extensive research. It could not have been led to a successful conclusion without the help of several of my graduate students at the United States International University (U.S.I.U.), notably Rachel Cook, David Threats, Octavio Ramirez, and Aliza D. Carpio; the invaluable comments and reviews of many colleagues, especially Professors Karl Magyar, Rolin G. Mainuddin, Paul J. Magnarella, F. Wafula Okumu, and Stephen Sylvester; the continued encouragement of Dr. Garry Hays, President of the U.S.I.U., Dr. Althia deGraft-Johnson, former VP for Academic Affairs, Dr. Ramona Kunard, Dean of Arts and Sciences, and former and present Chairs of the Department of Global Liberal Studies, Drs. Al Zolynas and Linda Swanson; and the patience and sustained support of my beloved wife, Sibylle Faye Nickel Yakan.

PART ONE

INTRODUCTION

INTRODUCTION

Contrary to popular perceptions, the peoples of Africa constitute neither one nation nor a few nations. Like the peoples of other continents, those of Africa are neither ethnically nor religiously homogeneous. This is especially true within the territories of the political entities which since the 16th century have been subjected to a carving process by European colonial powers along European colonial interests with no regard to peoples' wishes, aspirations, and ethnic or religious ties.

The end result of the scramble for the African continent was a multitude of states, few of which could be described as nation-states with rational bonds that make up nations and distinguish one people from another. In fact, most African states are ethnically heterogenous, comprised of minorities with extensions in neighboring states. The civil wars that are currently being witnessed on the African continent are a function of European legacy in Africa.

It was not Africans who determined the boundaries of their respective states, nor did Africans determine the socio-economic composition of their respective societies. Both the boundaries and composition of African societies were determined by European powers to serve the particular economic and hegemonical interests of these powers. European decisions in this respect were implemented as if Africa was a terra nullius with no people, no societies, and no indigenous institutions. Hence, the boundaries and societal composition of African states are contrived phenomena imposed by Europeans. They are not natural phenomena. They are not a product of gradual, natural, historical processes or developments nor do they reflect the genuine aspirations of African peoples. Certainly, as long as the African status quo does not correspond to African realities in general, and the real wishes of the African peoples in particular, the continent will continue to suffer from socio-economic imbalances, if not chronic civil wars and tribal conflicts.

The path to stability on the African continent is through its people: their wishes and ultimate goals. It is not through forcing a status quo improvised by Europe which continues to serve as a means to perpetuate European zones of influence, interests, and prestige.

3

Helping Africa to reach a level of relative stability may require a Wilsonian remedy–a remedy that calls for the application of the principle of self-determination wherever and whenever a civil war occurs in the African continent. This remedy, may help the African people tailor their own destiny, rather than try to fit themselves into what has been created for them by foreign powers.

Additionally, the path to stability on the African continent is through federalism, whereby different ethnic and religious groups can live together in pluralistic societies where minority rights are duly observed, respected, and legally sanctioned.

In most African states, the unitary and highly centralized systems of government are replicas of colonial administrations, which were based on compulsion and force rather than on due processes of law. The driving interest of European powers was that of exploiting the natural and human resources of Africa. To this end, they utilized all sorts of devious and humanly dishonorable means.

The path to stability on the African continent is through the recognition of tribalism as a major, if not the major, political force in African states. Tribalism in Africa is what nationalism is in the countries of the First World. In fact, it is a stronger form of nationalism than what is experienced in a host of European states. It rests more on objective than subjective bonds. Moreover, it reflects Africa's genuine historical experiences and cultural heritages; it represents Africans' ideals, values, and aspirations; and it provides the basis for loyalties which, if properly utilized, can contribute to the development of African states. African tribalism is an indigenous rather than an alien ideology. Other things being equal, this ideology may be utilized to support the cause of development in Africa in a manner no different from kibbutzim in Israel or family-based businesses in Asian countries. Without recognizing the role of African tribalism and giving it its due regard and credit, and possibly utilizing it to support African development, of African states will continue to be alienated.

A pragmatic approach to development in Africa calls for a positive use of whatever bonds Africans together so that each member of a tribe joins forces with other members of his/her tribe for the common good of the whole tribe, and consequently, the whole society..

The Western European models of development, both in their liberal and Marxist manifestations, have so far failed to meet African developmental goals. Probably, it's time to recourse back to African models of development. African development may be more viable if it employs rather than shuns tribalism.

African societies do not support industrial economies where the individual is regarded as a unit of production and/or an economic unit (and later political) of value. Moreover, urbanization is still a weak feature of African societies. Urbanization did not phase out traditional tribal loyalties. It is going to be a while before both phenomena can transform African societies into industrial and urbanized societies such as those of the West. Hence, it is realistic to look for remedies in African societies and whatever helps to incite African societies to struggle for higher levels of productivity and achievement.

Noting the fact that both industrialization and urbanization are prerequisites of Western democracies, it is futile to propose remedies to the current African condition models that do not correspond to or reflect African realities. At this juncture, models of Western democracies do not appear to be compatible with African realities. What appears to be more promising at this juncture is representation based on the actual realities of African societies, that is, representation that recognizes both the tribe and the individual as the basic constituents of society. In other words, the remedy for the present African condition lies more in consensual rather than Western models of democracy. The latter models regard the individual, rather than any other entity, as the basic unit of political society. Obviously, African societies do not cherish such a value and it is going to be a while before industrialization, urbanization and integration popularize it. Eventually, this will establish it as a cornerstone of African political systems.

Finally, unlike Western counterparts, African societies are not highly integrated societies. As long as they lag in this respect, African societies will continue to support multitudes of influential sub-societies with claims over their constituents that at times are stronger than those of their central governments. It is only natural that sub-societies try to resist whatever leads to their loss of stature and influence, especially when these societies are ethnically or religiously different from those having command over central governments. A healthy resolution to this problem, however, is not through repression, but rather through consociational democracy, proportional representation, federalism, or one form or the other of autonomous rule. These applications provide good grounds for a modus vivendi in any state which is lagging in terms of integration or which is ethnically and/or religiously heterogeneous.

Essentially, it is because of the above considerations, as well as the belief that African peoples are entitled to their own, rather than to borrowed identities that prompted this research.

The Almanac of African Peoples and Nations is important in several respects. Apart from surveying the major ethnic groups of the African continent, it highlights the major contribution of many of these groups and the basic features of their respective cultures. Moreover, it identifies the ethnic groups that are currently partitioned by two or more states, their percentage shares of the total populations of their respective countries, and their impact on the internal political stability within their states, as well as on regional inter-African politics. Further, it points out those groups that support revisionist political aspirations and tries to show how these groups are being subjected to various centripetal and centrifugal forces.

Certainly, this almanac is a first interdisciplinary attempt at understanding African pluralism, past and present, and based on its findings, tries to forecast possible inter-ethnic conflicts in the future. It represents a preliminary effort towards a more in-depth study of African peoples and nations.

The Almanac is comprised of eight main parts.

Part One covers the introduction of the study, and moreover, it outlines its purpose and its importance to specialists, students of African affairs, and general readers.

Part Two reviews Africa's language families and their respective concentrations. This part is deemed imperative to proper classification of many African peoples and nations. Obviously, ethnic differences are based on essentially linguistic differences. In some cases, however, this general rule does not apply.

Part Three lists African languages by country. The languages that are covered in this part cover essentially the official languages that are spoken in Africa, both indigenous and non-indigenous.

Part Four profiles major African peoples and nations by country. It lists the major ethnic groups in every African country and moreover, it provides information on their respective shares of the total populations in these countries.

Part Five profiles the various African peoples and nations in an alphabetical order. Reference is made to groups that are known by more than one name and readers are directed to the name used as the group's main entry. It represents the contents of the Almanac.

Part Six covers the endnotes of the Almanac. It lists the various the references that were cited in the Almanac.

Part Seven provides a selected bibliography on African peoples and nations. In other words, it lists the main titles that were used in the development of the Almanac.

Finally, Part Eight contains an index of all entries. It lists the names of all African peoples and nations that were covered in the Almanac, as well as the pages of their respective entries.

PART TWO

AFRICAN LANGUAGE FAMILIES

AFRICAN LANGUAGE FAMILIES

AUSTRONESIAN

The Austronesian languages include the Malagasy languages of the people of Madagascar and adjacent islands. They are closely related and support numerous dialects. They contain words of Arab, Bantu, English, French and Swahili origin. The Merina dialect of the Malagasy languages has been Madagascar's official language since 1820. It is written in the Roman alphabet.

EUROPEAN

Languages falling within this group include Dutch, English, French, Portuguese and Spanish. These languages spread in Africa as a result of colonial rule. Many African states have adopted one or more of these languages as their own official languages, either with or without other indigenous languages.

HAMITO-SEMITIC

Languages belonging to this group are spoken across North Africa from Western Sahara to Somalia, stretching as far as Southern Asia.

Saho – also Afar-Saho, Sao, Shaho, Shiho and Shoho – belongs to this group. It is an Eastern Cushitic branch of the Hamito-Semitic (or Afro-Asian) family of African languages. The language is spoken by several peoples of the coastal plains of Eritrea.

The Somali language is a Cushitic language, which also includes the Afar and Galla. It has several dialects and is spoken in East Africa, particularly in Somalia, Djibouti, parts of Ethiopia and the Wajir District of Kenya.

KHOISAN

Languages of the Khoisan or San family are spoken in southern Africa and Tanzania. This family supports about 90 languages, which contain distinctive consonantal sounds, notably their four clicks.

NIGER-CONGO

The Niger-Congo or Niger-Kordofanian languages are spoken from Mauritania to Kenya and southwardly into South Africa. This family supports about 900 languages. It is subdivided into six subfamilies, including the well-known Bantu languages.

Mande languages belong to this family of African languages. They are widely spoken in Ghana, Guinea, Guinea-Bissau, Ivory Coast, Mali, Nigeria and Senegal. They comprise many sub-groups, including Malinke, Mende, Kpelle and Vai. Malinke is the most used of them. The Mande languages are tonal, using pitch levels to differentiate words.

The Voltaic languages, also called Gur, are also a branch of the Niger-Congo languages. They are spoken in Burkina Faso, Benin, Ghana, Ivory Coast, Mali and Togo. Of all Voltaic languages, Mossi (or Mosi) is the most widely used language.

Another group of the Niger-Congo family is that of the Kwa languages, which are spoken by the peoples of the area stretching from western Liberia into Nigeria, including the southern parts of the Ivory Coast, Ghana, Togo and Benin. They include Yoruba, Igbo (or Ibo), Ewe, Bini, Igala and the languages of the Akan subgroup, which include Twi, Anyi, Baule, Guang, Metyibo and Abure.

The Kwa languages are tonal. They use pitch levels to differentiate words that are otherwise pronounced identically.

The Xhosa language is a member of the Southeastern, or Ngoni (Nguni), subgroup of the Bantu group of the Benue-Congo branch of the Niger-Congo family of African languages. Other languages falling within the subgroup include Basuto (or Sotho), Ndebele, Swazi, Tswana (or Bechuana), Venda and Zulu. The language uses a system of tones to differentiate between words which would otherwise sound the same.

Swahili, properly Kiswahili, is an essentially Bantu-language. It is built out of essentially Arab words on a Bantu grammar. This language is the lingua franca of East Africa. It contains an enormous Arabic vocabulary, with some Portuguese, Hindi and English loanwords.

Makua is also a Bantu language. It is spoken in a few northern provinces in Mozambique.

NILO-SAHARAN

Languages falling within this family are spoken in central interior Africa. This family of African languages is spoken by the Nilotes, as well as by many groups in western Sudan and the area of the middle Niger River.

PART THREE

AFRICAN LANGUAGES BY COUNTRY

AFRICAN LANGUAGES BY COUNTRY

ALGERIA

Arabic is the official language, but French and Berber dialects are widely used.

ANGOLA

Portuguese is the official language, but various Bantu dialects are popular.

BENIN

French is the official language. However, Fon and Yoruba are widely spoken in the south and six major languages are used in the northern regions of the country.

BOTSWANA

English is the official language. However, the native's popular language is Setswana.

BURKINA FASO

French is the official language, but tribal languages are widespread and are spoken by the great majority of the people.

BURUNDI

Kirundi and French are the official languages, but Swahili is widely spoken along Lake Tanganyika and in the Bujumbura region.

CAMEROON

Both English and French are the country's official languages. However, some 24 major African language groups are also used.

CAPE VERDE

Both Portuguese and Crioulo are widely used. The latter language is a blend of Portuguese and West African dialects.

CENTRAL AFRICAN REPUBLIC

French is the official language. However, Sangho is the country's lingua franca and is spoken by a majority of the people. Other popular languages include Arabic, Hausa and Swahili.

CHAD

Arabic and French are the official languages. However, over one hundred different languages and dialects are used in the country, including Sara and Sango in the southern regions.

COMOROS

Arabic is the official language but Comoran, a blend of Swahili and Arabic, is most popular. However, Malagasy and French are also used by segments of the population.

CONGO

French is the official language. It is used together with many native languages, especially Lingala and Kikongo.

DEMOCRATIC REPUBLIC OF THE CONGO (formerly ZAIRE)

French is the official language of the country in which over 200 languages and dialects are spoken. The four major native languages include: Swahili, Tshiluba (Kiluba), Lingala and Kikongo.

DJIBOUTI

Arabic and French are the official languages, but Somali and Afar languages are in wide use.

EGYPT

Arabic is the official language and is spoken by the great majority of Egyptians. English and French, however, are widely understood by educated classes in the country.

EQUATORIAL GUINEA

Spanish is the official language, but pidgin English, Fang, Bubi and Ibo languages are widely used.

ERITREA

The languages of this country are Tigre, Kunama, Nora Bana and Arabic.

ETHIOPIA

The official language is Amharic but Tigrinya, Orominga, Guaraginga, Somali and Arabic are used by different segments of the population.

GABON

French is the official language, but several major native languages are widely used, particularly Fang, Myene, Bateke, Bapounou/Eschira and Bandjabi.

GAMBIA, THE

English is the official language of the country. However, several major native languages are widely used, including Fula, Mandinka and Wolof.

GHANA

English is the official language but several major native languages are widely used, including Akan, Ewe, Ga and Dagbane (or Moshi-Dagomba).

GUINEA

French is the official language of the country. However, native tribal languages are widely used.

GUINEA-BISSAU

Portuguese is the official language. However, several native languages are widely used, including Criolo.

IVORY COAST

French is the official language. Numerous native languages are used in the country, the most important of which is Dioula.

KENYA

Swahili and English are the official languages. Numerous indigenous languages, however, are also widely used.

LESOTHO

Sesotho and English are the official languages. However, both Zulu and Xhosa are widely used by segments of the country's population.

LIBERIA

English is the official language. Numerous native languages are also used by segments of the Liberian population.

LIBYA

Arabic is the official language. It is the language of the great majority of the Libyan population.

MADAGASCAR

Malagasy and French are the official languages of the country.

MALAWI

Chichewa and English are the official languages of the country, but Chilomwe, Chiyao and Chitumbuka (Tombuka) are also spoken.

MALI

French is the official language of the country. However, Bambara (Bamana, Nammana) is spoken by the great majority of the Malian population.

MAURITANIA

Hasaniya Arabic and Wolof are the official languages. However, Fula, Sarakole and Toucouleur are popular among segments of the Mauritanian population.

MAURITIUS

English is the country's official language but Bojpoori, Creole, French, Hakka, Hindi and Urdu are widely used.

MAYOTTE

French is the official language, but Mahorian, a Swahili dialect, is widely used by the natives.

MOROCCO

Arabic is the official language, but different dialects of Berber are spoken by segments of the country's population, the most popular of which is tamazight.

MOZAMBIQUE

Portuguese is the official language of the country but native languages are also spoken.

NAMIBIA

Afrikaans, German and English are official languages. Afrikaans is spoken by about 60 percent of the population, German by 33 percent and English by 7 percent. Several native languages are also widely used.

NIGER

French is the official language of the country but Hausa and Djerma are widely spoken by segments of the population.

NIGERIA

English is the official language. However, numerous native languages are widely used, especially Fulani, Hausa, Ibo and Yoruba.

REUNION

French is the official language but Creole is also widely used by the natives of the island.

RWANDA

Both Kinyarwanda and French are official languages but Kiswahili is also widely used as the country's language of commerce.

SAO TOME AND PRINCIPE

Portuguese is the official language.

SENEGAL

The official language is French but several major native languages widely used by the Senegalese include: Diola, Mandingo, Pulaar and Wolof.

SEYCHELLES

Both English and French are the official languages but Creole is widely used throughout the country.

SIERRA LEONE

English is the official language of the country, but Krio, Mende and Temne are also popular native languages. Krio is a lingua franca and is widely used in Freetown, especially by the ex-slave population. Mende is popular in the southern regions of the country and Temne in the northern ones.

SOMALIA

Somali is the official language but Arabic, Italian and English are also widely used.

PART FOUR

AFRICAN PEOPLES AND NATIONS BY COUNTRY

ALGERIA

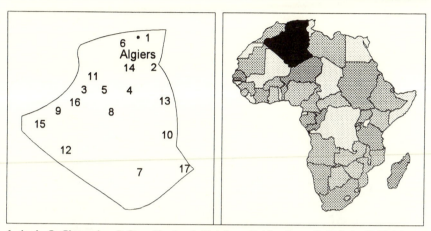

1. Arab, 2. Chaamba, 3. Dou Menia, 4. El Arbaa, 5. Hamiyan, 6. Kabyle, 7. Kel Ajjer (Taureg), 8. Mzab, 9. Nsula, 10. Ouarseni, 11. Oulad Djerir, 12. Regeibat, 13. Said Atba, 14. Shawiya, 15. Tekna, 16. Ulad Yihya, 17. Uraren (Taureg)

Algeria's population of 30,200,000 (mid-1998 PRB est.) consists of essentially four major ethnic groups, namely, Arab and Arabized Berber (77%), Berber (22%), and European and other (1%). The Arab and Arabized Berber peoples are concentrated in the country's coastal and urbanized centers, whereas the Berber population is located in the two Atlas Mountain ranges of the country especially in the vicinity of Djurdjura mountain, as well as, in the Algerian Sahara regions. The largest Berber groups include the Kabyle, the Mzabite (Mzab), and the Tuareg.

The Kabyle people are concentrated in the vicinity of the Djurdjura mountain, the Mzabite in cities south of the capital Algiers, and the Tuareg in the southern areas of the country. The European population is primarily of French background and is concentrated in the country's urbanized centers.

Other ethnic groups and/or subgroups include the Reguibat (Regeibat) and Tekna who are found in Algeria's southwestern regions. The Tekna include such subgroups as the Ait Atman, Ait Jmel, and Izarguien. Smaller groups include the Chaamba, Dou Menia, El-Arbaa, Hamiyan, Kel Ajjer, Nsula, Quarseni, Oulad Djerir, Said Arba, Ulad Yihya, and Uraren.

ANGOLA

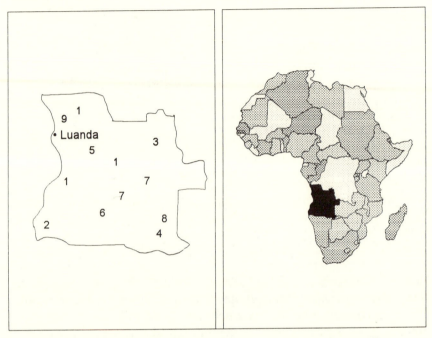

1. Bakongo, 2. Bakorocas, 3. Cokwe, 4. Herero, 5. Kimbundu, 6. !O!Kun,
7. Ovimbundu, 8. Songo, 9. Sorongo, etc.

Angola supports an ethnically heterogeneous population of about 12,000,000 (mid-1998 PRB est.). The Ovimbundu, Kimbundu (Mbundu), and Bakongo (Bacongo, Bandibu, Congo, Kongo, Koongo) are the largest of its many ethnic groups, accounting for 37%, 25% and 13% of the country's total population, respectively. Other groups, such as the Bakorocas, Herero (Ovaherero), and !O !Kun, represent 25% of the population. Finally, the Mestiços and Europeans, especially Portuguese, represent 2% and 1% of the country's population, respectively.

The Ovimbundu, the largest group, are concentrated in the central highlands of the country, the Kimbundu in its north-central areas, the Bakongo in its northern regions, and the Bakorocas in its southwestern lands. The Herero are found in Angola's southeastern territories, whereas the !O!Kun in areas along the country's southern borders with Namibia, and the Mestiços and Europeans in urbanized centers.

Smaller Angolan ethnic groups and/or subgroups include the Ambo, Ashiluanda, Avico, Bailundu, Bambeiro, Bangala, Bembe, Bie (Bié, Bihe, Viye), Caconda, Camochi, Cari, Chicuma, Chiyaka (Kikaya), Cisama, Chokwe (Cokwe, Kioko, Quioco, Tschokwe), Dembo, Dombe, Dondo (Badondo), Donguena, Ekekete, Esela, Gambo, Ganda, Gengista, Haco (Hako), Handa, Hanha (Hanya), Herero, Himba, Hinga, Holo, Huambo, Hum (Humbe), Hungo (Hungu), Imgangala, Jinga, Kakonda (Kakonde), Kakongo, Kalukembe, Kamba, Kaokabander, Kavanga, Kibala, Kibula, Kilengi, Kingolo, Kipungu, Kisama, Kissanje, Kitata, Kiyaka, Kongo-Sundi, Kougni, Kwankua, Kwanyama, Lali (Balili, Lari), Libolo, Luchazi (Lutchaze), Luango, Luimbe, Lumbo, Lunda (Alund, Arunde, Balonde, Lounda, Luntu, Malhundo, Ruund, Valunda), Luvale (Lovale, Lubale, Luena), Luwena, Luyana, Mai, Maligo, Mambari, Mashi, Mataba, Mbaka, Mbandero, Mbane, Mbondo, Mbui, Mbukushu (Hambukushu), Mbunda, Mbundu, Mbwela, Mdaka, Munungo (Minungo), Mushikongo, Mwila, Ndembu (Dembo, Mdembu, Ndembo), Ndongo, Ndulu, Ngala, Ngalangi, Ngangela, Nkangala, Ngonyelo, Ngongeiro, Ntema, Nyaneka, Nyaneka-Humbe (Haneca-Nkumbi), Nyemba, Nyembe, Nyengo, Pombo, Puna, Salampaso, Sambu, Sele, Sende, Shanjo, Shikongo (Bashikongo), Shinje, Solongo (Basolongo, Basorongo), Songo, Sorongo, Subi, Suku, Sumbe, Sundi, Vili, Woyo, Yahuma, Yaka, Yombe, and Zombo peoples.

BENIN

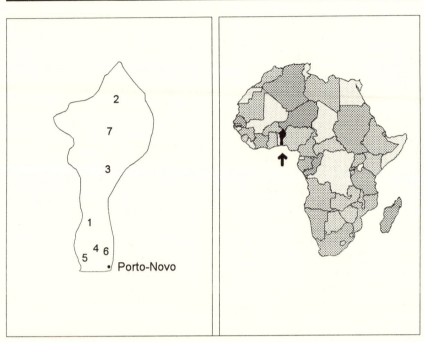

1. Adja, 2. Bariba, 3. Esan, 4. Fon, 5. Gu, 6. Ijebu, 7. Yoruba, etc.

Benin has a population of 6,000,000 (mid-1998 PRB est.) 99% of which is African and 1% European and non-European, notably people of French and Lebanese background. The African population is composed of 42 major ethnic groups. These include the Adja (Aja) and Fon (Dahomean, Fonn), two groups of the Ewe cluster, Bariba (Batonu, Bargu, Barba, Borgowa, Borgan, Batomba, Botombu, Batonun), Esan (Anwain, Ishan), and Yoruba.

The Adja and Fon people are concentrated in the central and southwestern areas of Benin, the Bariba in its north-central and northeastern regions, and the Esan and Yoruba in its eastern parts.

Smaller Beninian ethnic groups and/or subgroups include the Agonlinu, Aizo, Ana, Anago, Anlo, Ayigbé, Bade (Bedde, Bede), Berba,

Boko (Bokko), Bugabi, Busa, Chabe, Dassa, Dendi (Dandi, Dandawa), Dompago, Dye, Egun (Alada, Gu), Eachi, Ehoué, Egba, Eibe, Ephe, Fakkawa, Ga (Gamashie), Ge, Goun, Guemenu, Ho, Holli, Hyam (Ham, Hum, Jaba), Ife, Ifonyim, Ilesha, Isa, Janji, Ketu, Kilinga, Kourtey, Krepe (Krepi), Kudawa, Kwatama, Lela (Cala-Cala, Chilala, Clela, Dakarkari, Dakkarari, Kolela, Lalawa), Mahi, Maxe, Méti (Metisse), Mina (Popo), Mossi (Molé, Moshi), Nagot (Nago), Natimba, Niendé, Nikki, Ninzo, Pedah (Houéda), Pila-Pila (Yao, Yowa), Ohori, Ouatchi, Pla, Sabe, Sohanti, Somba (Tamberma), Soruba, Taneka (Tongba), Tenkodogo (Tengkedogo), Tofinu, Woaba, and Zerma (Dyarma, Dyerma, Zabarma, Zaberma, Zabarima, Zabermawa, Zarma) peoples.

BOTSWANA

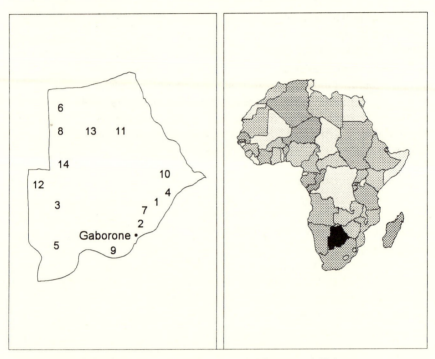

1. Batswana (Western Sotho), 2. European, 3. Hereros, 4. Kalanga,
5. Kgalagadi, 6. Kgatala, 7. Kwena, 8. Malete, 9. Ngwaketse, 10. Ngwato,
11. Rolong, 12. Sarwa, 13. Tawana, 14. Tlokwa, etc.

The Republic of Botswana supports a population of about 1,400,000 (mid-1998 PRB est.) 95% of which are Western Sotho (Batswana, Tswana), 4% Kalanga (Bakalanga, Kalaka, Vakalanga), Sarwa (Basarwa and Bushman), Hereros, and Kgalagadi (Bakgalagadi), and 1% European and Asian.

The Tswana (Batswana) people are concentrated in the eastern regions of the country; the Sarwa and Hereros in its western regions along the northern edge of the Kalahari desert; the Kalanga in the eastern regions along the country's border with Zimbabwe; and the Kgalagadi in its southwestern lands, notably in the Kgalagadi administrative district.

Peoples of European (especially English) or Asian (Indian or Malay) background are concentrated in the urban centers of the country.

The Batswana are composed of eight tribal groups, namely the Tawana (Batawana), Ngwato (Bamangwato), Kwena (Bakwena), Ngwaketse (Bangwaketse), Kgatla (Bakgatla), Malete (Bamalete), Rolong (Barolong), and Tlokwa (Batlokoa, Batlokwa, Tlokoa).

The Batawana are concentrated in the north central regions of the country in what is known as Ngamiland, wehreas the Ngwato are settled in the south central regions; the Kwena and Ngwaketse in southeastern regions; the Kgatla and Malete in the northwestern regions along the border with Namibia; the Rolong in northeastern, southern and western regions; and the Tlokwa along the border with Namibia.

Smaller Botswanian ethnic groups and/or subgroups include the Auni, Bakalahari, Bamangwato, Batlard, Birwa (Babirwa), Bolaongwe (BaLaongwe), Fokeng, Gana, Gwi, Hiechware, Hukwe, Hurutshe (Barutshe), Imilangu, Kaa (Bakaa), Kgafela Kgatla, Kgatla, Kgwatheng (Bakgwatheng), Khurutshe (Bakhurutshe), Khute, Kololo (Bakololo), Koma, Kua, Kung (Zhu, Xhu), Kung San, Kavanga, !Khara, !Ke, Kwandi, Kwangwa, Kwena (Bakuena, Bakwena, Kuena), Lete (Balete, Bamalete), Lilima, Lozi (Balozi, Barotse, Barutze, Marotse, Rotse, Rozi), Luyana, Lyuwa, Mahura, Malete (Bamalete), Tannekwe, Mashi, Mbukushu (Hambukushu), Mmanaana Kgatla, Nama (Hottentot, Khoi Khoi, Khoisan), Nanzwa, Naron, Ndebele, Ndundulu, Ngologa (Bangologa), Ngwaketse, Ngwato, Mwenyi, Nukhi, Nyengo, Phaleng (Bapheleng), Rolong, San, Shaga (Bashaga), Shona (Chona, Karanga, Mashona, Vashona), Simaa, Subiya (Subia), Talaote (Batalote, Batalowta, Talaota, Talowta), Tannekwe, Tawana (Batawana), Tlokwa (Batlokoa, Batlokwa, Tlokoa), Tsaukwe, Tserekwe, Tshe-Kwe (Tshu-Kwe), Tshidi Rolong, Twanana, Xam, Xegwi, Xo, and Yei (Bayei) peoples.

BURKINA FASO

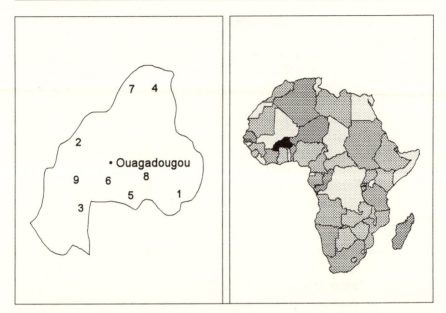

1. Bariba, 2. Bobo, 3. Brong, 4. Fulani, 5. Gurunsi, 6. Lobi, 7. Mande,
8. Mossi, 9. Senufo, etc.

The population of Burkina Faso is about 11,300,000 (mid-1998 PRB est.).
It consists of more than 50 ethnic groups, the largest ones of which are the
Mossi (Molé, Moshi), Bariba (Batonu, Bargu, Barba, Borgowa, Batomba,
Botombu, Batonun), Bobo, Fula (Foula, Foula, Foulbe, Fula, Fulani,
Fulata, Fulbe, Fulfulde, Fullah, Hilani Djallon, and Peul), Grusi (Awuma,
Gorise, Gourounsi, Grunshi, Grunsi, Grussi, Guense, Gurinse, Gurunshi,
Gurunsi, Western Kasena, Nankansi), Lobi (Lo, Lober), Mande (Manding)
and Senufo (Bamana, Sene, Senefo, Senoufo, Siena, Syénambélé).

The Mossi who represent about 25% of the population are
concentrated in the area between the Red Volta and the White Volta rivers
in the country, the Bariba in its southeastern regions, the Bobo in its
northwestern areas along its border with Mali, the Lobi in areas between
the Black Volta River and the White Volta River, the Senufo in the vicinity

of the Black Volta River, primarily in its western and southwestern regions, the Brong and Gurunsi in its southern regions along the country's border with Ghana, and the Fula and Mande in its northern and western regions, notably along Burkina's border with Mali.

Smaller ethnic groups and/or subgroups include the Aculo, Awuna, Bade, Banun, Barka, Basari (Basare), Bella (Bellah), Beng (Ben, Gan, Ngan, Ngen, Nguin), Berifor (Birifor), Bimoba (Bimawba, Bmoba, Moab, Moba), Ble, Brong (Abron, Abrong, Bobo-Fing (Boua), Bobo-Gbé (Kian, Tian), Bobo-Oulé (Tara), Bobo, Bolon, Boron, Bron, Bono, Dom, Tchaman), Builsa (Builse, Bulse, Cobiana, Kangyaga, Kanjaga), Busansi (Bisa, Bissa, Boussansé, Bussansi, Busanga, Bouzantchi, Bousanou), Cassanga, Dafi, Dagari (Dagara, Dagarte, Dagarti, Dagate, Dagati), Deforo, Dogamba, Dogon, Dorosie (Dorobe, Dorossie), Dyan (Dian, Dianne, Janni), Fakkawa, Fera, Fulse (Foulse), Gouin (Guin, Kpen, Mbwen), Gurma (Gourmantché), Grusi, Habé, Jula (Dyula, Diula, Joola, Juula, Kangah, Va, Wangara), Kado, Karaboro (Karakora), Kasena (Kassena), Kibsi, Kipirsi (Ko), Kisi, Komono, Konkomba (Komba), Kulango (Babé, Koulango, Kulano, Lorhon, Ngwela, Nkoramfo), Kurumba (Akurumba, Kouroumba), Kusasi (Koussassi, Kusae, Kusai, Kusase), Kyamba (Tchamba), Lela (Cala-Cala, Chilala, Clela, Dakarkari, Dakkarari, Kolela, Lalawa), Landoma (Cocoli, Kokoli, Landouman, Landouma, Landuma, Tiapi, Tyopi), Lele, Lilse (Lyela), Liptako (Libtako), Lo Dagara, Mamprusi (Mampruli, Mampruse, Mamprussi), Maransi, Masina, Méti (Metisse), Miwo, Mo, Nafana, Nagwa, Nakomsé, Namnam, Nanerge (Nanèrègè, Nanergue), Nankana, Niénigé (Niéniégue, Nienigue, Niniga), Ninisi (Tinguimbissi, Children of the Earth), Nioniosse, Nunuma, Ouagadougou, Pana, Pila-Pila, Quin, Rimibe, Samo, Samogho (Don, Sambla, Samoro), Sasala (Isala, Pisala, Sissala, Sisala), Sia (Sya), Sohanti, Soninké (Marka, Sarakolé, Saraxole, Serahuli, Serakhulle, Soninke), Talensi, Tengabissi (Tinguimbisi), Tenkodogo (Tengkedogo), Téuessué, Tiefo (Tyéfo), Tombo, Toro, Touna, Tounbé, Tourka (Turka, Turuka), Tusyan (Tousia, Toussian), Vagala (Vagele, Vigala), Vigye (Vigne), Wala, Wara Wara (Ouara), Yagala, Yarsé, Yatenga, Zandamo, Zaose, and Zerma (Dyarma, Dyerma, Zabarma, Zaberma, Zabarima, Zabermawa, Zarma) peoples.

BURUNDI

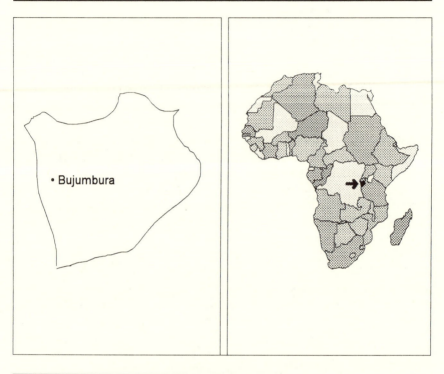

The Republic of Burundi has a population of about 5,500,000 (mid-1998 PRB est.) of which 85% is Hutu (Abahutu, Bahutu, Wakhutu), 14% Tutsi (Batutsi, Tussi, Watusi, Watutsi), 1% Twa, Rwandans, Zairians, Europeans, and South Asians. The Hutu are of Bantu origin, whereas the Tutsi are of Hamitic-Nilotic background. The Twa (Cwa) are a pygmy group.

Hutu and Tutsi peoples are spread throughout the country. The Tutsi, however, are more concentrated in the west central areas to the west of Lake Kivu. The Twa people are concentrated in the northwestern regions.

Smaller Burundian ethnic groups and/or subgroups include the Abahanza, Abajiji, Abanyaruguru, Abavuma, Gesera, Hima (Bahima), Jita, and Zigaba peoples.

CAMEROON

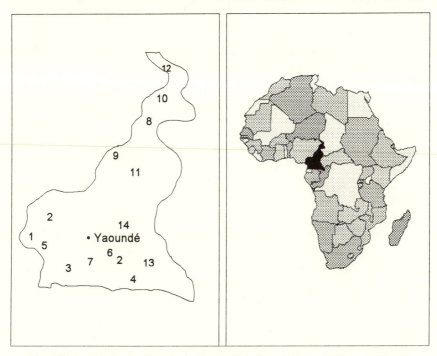

1. Bamiléké, 2. Bamum (Mum), 3. Bassa-Bakoko, 4. Bulu, 5. Douala (Duala), 6. Ewondo, 7. Fang, 8. Fulani, 9. Hausa, 10. Kanuri, 11. Kirdi, 12. Shuwa, 13. Pygm, 14. Tigar, etc.

Cameroon's population of about 14,300,000 (mid-1998 PRB est.) is ethnically heterogenous. It is composed of over 200 tribes and divided into the following groups: Cameroon Highlanders (31%), Equatorial Bantu (19%), Kirdi (11%), Fulani (10%), Northwestern Bantu (8%), Eastern Nigritic (7%), other African (13%), and non-African (less than 1%).

The Highlanders constitute the largest ethnic group in the Cameroon. They include the Bamiléké of the five Bamiléké departments, the Tigar (Tikar), also known as "grassfielders," of the Bamenda plateau, and their neighbors, the Bamum (Bamoum, Bamun), a Muslim people.

The Equatorial Bantu and the Eastern Nigritic peoples are concentrated in East Cameroon, specifically in the western hills of the Logone. The Equatorial Bantu, known as Beti-Pahouin and Fang-Pahouin, are concentrated in the Yaoundé area and include such peoples as the Ewondo, Bulu, and Fang (Fan, Fanwe, Mfang, Mpangwe). The Kirdi (Fulah name for "pagan") people are concentrated in northeastern Cameroon, notably in the hills and plains of the Logone. The Northwestern and Coastal Bantu include the Douala (Duala), the first Cameroonians to be exposed to European influences, and the Bassa-Bakoko, who are concentrated in the Sanaga River Valley. The Fulani (Foula, Foula, Foulbe, Fula, Fulani, Fulata, Fulbe, Fulfulde, Fullah, Hilani Djallon, and Peul people) are concentrated in the northern regions of the country, especially in and around Maroua, Garoua and Ngaoundéré, capitals of Fulani chiefdoms.

Other African Cameroonian groups and/or subgroups include the Shuwa (Choa) Arabs and the Chadic (Kanuri and Hausa) who live near Lake Chad, the Ejagham (Ekoi) who are concentrated in western Cameroon, and the Pygmies who are presently located in the equatorial forest of southeast Cameroon. Non-African Cameroonians include a small minority of Europeans of English, French, and German backgrounds, as well as of Asians, mainly Lebanese expatriates.

Smaller Cameroonian ethnic groups and/or subgroups include the Akunakuna, Akwa, Amasi, Arago, Assumbo, Adamana, Babanki, Babimbi, Babinki-Tungo, Babole, Bafia, Bafreng, Bafut (Bute, Bafute, Wute, Mfute), Baia, Bakoko, Bakota (Kota), Bakossi, Bakweri (Bakwiri), Bali, Bambill, Babimbi, Bamboko (Bambuko), Bambui, Bamend, Bamendankwe, Bamiléké, Bana (Fali), Bandze, Bane (Banen), Basakomo, Basho, Bassa, Bassosi, Bata, Batanga, Batu, Bayele (Gelli), Bayang, Beké, Bekpak, Beti, Bitare (Njwande, Yukutare), Bitieku, Bodiman, Bokoko, Bolewa, Bombo, Bomitaba, Bondjo, Bondongo, Bonguili, Bororo, Boulou (Bulu), Bum, Chamba (Chamba-Daka, Daba, Daka, Deng, Ewala, Jama, Nakanyare, Sama, Samba, Tchamba, Tsamba), Choa, Dari, Denya (Anyang), Djem, Dogo, Dourou, Doyayo (Dowayo), Ejagham, Eton, Ewondo, Fali, Fond, Fugon, Gbaya (Baja, Baya), Gbaya Bodomo, Gbaya Bokoto, Gbaya Bouli, Gbaya Dooka, Gbaya Kaka, Gbaya Kara, Gbaya Lai, Gbaya-Mbun, Gbaya Yaiyuwe, Gelli (Badjelli, Bagielli, Baguielli), Guidar, Guiziga (Guizaga),

Ibibio, Idoma, Igbo, Isuwu, Jukun, Kabongo, Kaka, Kamkam, Kamwe (Higi, Hiji), Kapsiki (Kapsigi), Kedjim, Kendem, Kenyang, Kilang, Kole, Kom, Koto (Bakota, Bandjambi, Ikota), Kotoko, Kotopo, Kpe, Kukele (Bakele, Ukele), Laamang, Laka (Lao Habe, Lau), Limba, Loumbou (Baloumbou), Mahongwe (Mahongwé), Mahouin, Maka, Mako, Makoula, Mambila (Bang, Mambere, Mambilla, Nor Tagbo, Tongbo), Mandara (Ndara, Wandala), Mang, Marba, Massa (Banana), Matakam, Mbam, Mbaoua, Mbedi, Mbeur, Mbo, Mbun, Menka, Meta, Moboko (Mboko), Mofu, Moussey, Mundang (Moundang), Mundani, Mungo, Musgu (Mousgoum, Musgum), Mvaé (Mvae), Namchi, Ndop, Ndoro, Ngambaye, Ngwoi (Ingwe, Ngwe, Nkwoi, Ungwe), Ninzam, Njabeta, Nkukoli (Ekuri, Lokukoli, Nkokolle), Nso, Ntumu (Ntoumou, Ntum), Nyamnyam (Bari, Niamniam, Nimbari), Nzagi (Jeng, Jenge, Njai, Njanyi, Njei, Zany), Okak, Omand, Pahouin (Beti-Pahouin, Fang, Pamue, Pangwe), Pande (Pende), Ponek, Pongo, Sanga, Sara, Séké (Boulou, Shékiani), Takamanda, Tang, Tanga, Tikar, Tiv, Tuki, Tupur (Toupouri, Tupuri), Udam, Vute (Bute, Mbute, Mbutere), War, Widekum, Wokumbe, Wiya, Wom (Pereba), Wouri (Oli), Wovea, Wum, Wute, Yako (Ekoi), Yambessa, and Yeskwa peoples.

CAPE VERDE

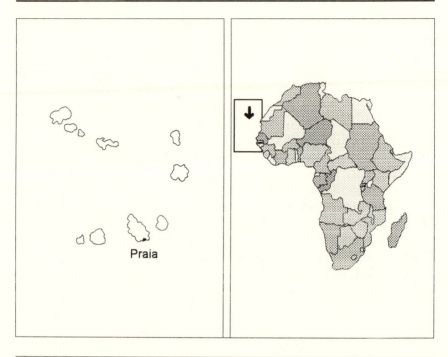

The Republic of Cape Verde supports a population of about 400,000 (mid-1998 PRB est.) which is 71% Creole (Mulatto), 28% African, and 1% European. The Cape Verde Creole are a people of mixed African and Portuguese descent. The African groups are of mixed backgrounds and are essentially descendants of peoples brought to the islands of Cape Verde to work on Portuguese plantations. They include such groups as the Badiu who live on the São Tiago island. The European minority is composed essentially of persons of Portuguese background.

CENTRAL AFRICAN REPUBLIC

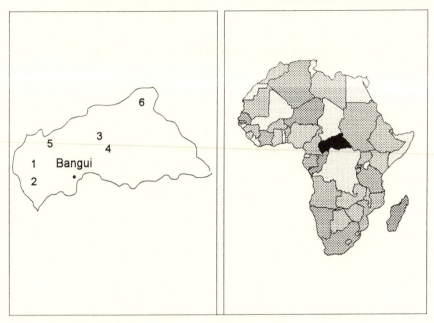

1. Banda, 2. Baja (Baya), 3. Mandjia, 4. M'Baka, 5. Mboum, 6. Sara, etc.

The Central African Republic has an ethnically diverse population of about 3,400,000 (mid-1998 PRB est.) made up of about 80 different ethnic groups, the major ones of which are the Baya (Baja, Gbaya) (34%), Banda (27%), Sara (10%), Mandjia (Mandija, Mandja, Manja) (21%), Mboum (Mbun) (4%), and M'Baka (Bwaka, Ngbaka) (4%). Like other African states, the Central African Republic has a small European minority, notably of French background.

The Banda and Baya are concentrated in the western and southwestern regions of the country, the Mandjia and M'Baka in its central regions in and around the prefecture of Lobaye, the Mboum in its western regions, and the Sara in its northern areas.

Smaller Central African ethnic groups and/or subgroups include the Aka, Ali, Azande (Azandé, Zande), Babole, Baka, Banda, Bangou, Banziri,

Basiri, Binga (Babenga, Babinga, Bambenga), Biri, Boffi, Bolgo, Bombo, Bomitaba, Bondjo, Bondongo, Bongo, Bonguili, Bororo, Bouaka, Boubangul (Bobangi, Bobangui), Bouraka, Challa (Caala), Dakpa, Dendi (Dandi, Dandawa), Dogo, Dokoa (Doko), Gbanziri, Gbaya (Baja, Baya), Gbaya Bodomo, Gbaya Bokoto, Gbaya Bouli, Gbaya Dooka, Gbaya Kaka, Gbaya Kara, Gbaya Lai, Gbaya Yaiyuwe, Gula (Goula), Gula Koumra, Gula Médé, Hausa, Issongo, Kaba, Kabongo, Kaka, Kara, Kare, Kilang, Kirdi, Kreich, Konambembe, Langba, Mandija, Laka (Lao Habe, Lau), Langba, Linda, Makoula, Mang, Mbaka, Mbaka-Mandija, Mbaoua, Mbeur, Mbimou, Méti (Metisse), Mondjombo, Namchi, Ndere, Ngambaye, Ngbaga, Ngbandi, N'di, N'gao (Ngao), Ngoundi, Nzakara, Pande (Pende), Patri (Kpatili), Runga, Sabanga, Sanga (Bosango, Sangha, Sango), Togbo, Ubanguian, Vidri, Vute, Yakoma, Yakpa, and Yanghere peoples.

CHAD

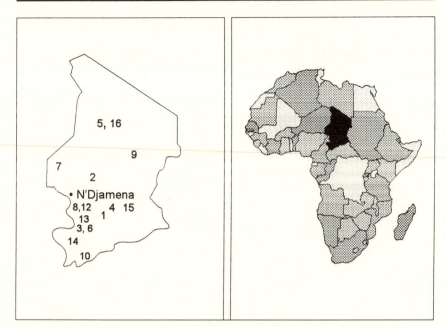

1. Baguirmi, 2. Boulala, 3. Fulbe, 4. Goulaye, 5. Hassauna, 6. Hausa,
7. Kanembou, 8. Kotoko, 9. Maba, 10. Massa, 11. Mbaye, 12. Moudang,
13. Moussei, 14. Ngambaye, 15. Sara, 16. Toubou, etc.

The Republic of Chad has a population of about 7,400,000 (mid-1998 PRB est.). This population consists of about 200 distinct ethnic groups, the major ones of which in the northern and central regions of the country are the Toubou (Tbou, Tébou, Tebu, Tibbu, Toubbou, Toubou), Fulbe (Fula, Fulani), Kotoko, Hausa, Kanembou (Berberi, Boro, Bornu, Kanembu, Kanuri), Baguirmi (Bagirmi, Barma), Boulala (Bilala, Bulala), and Maba (Fertit, Mandala, Wadain), and in the southern regions the Sara (Sar), Ngambaye, Mbaye (Mbai), Goulaye, Moudang (Moundang, Mundang), Moussei (Moussey, Musey), and Massa (Banana). In addition, Chad supports large Arab nomadic groups such as the Hassauna (Shuwa), as well as a small minority of Europeans, notably of French background.

The Baguirmi are concentrated in the lands between Bahr Ergig River and Chari River, the Boulala in the vicinities of Lake Fitri and the city of Yao, and the Fulbe and Hausa in the western and southwestern regions of the country. The Goulaye people live primarily in the Moyen-Chari prefecture, whereas the Kanembou in the Kanem prefecture on the northern shore of Lake Chad, the Kotoko and Moudang in the southwestern areas along Chad's border with Cameroon and Nigeria, and the Maba in the Wadai prefecture. The Massa and Mbaye concentrations are in Chad's southern regions, notably along the country's border with Cameroon and Central African Republic. Finally, the Moussei live in the Bongor region in the prefecture of Mayo-Kebbi; the Sara and Ngambaye along the Chari and Logone rivers, especially in the prefectures of Logone Orientale, Logone Occidentele, and Mayo-Kebbi; and the Toubou in the central Saharan region in northern Chad, notably in the Tibesti region.

Smaller Chadian groups and/or subgroups include the Abissa, Abu Semen, Abu Sharib (Abu Charib), Amdang, Anakaza (Annakaza), Aozouya, Arna, Artaj (Unay), Asungor (Asongori, Asungor, Sungor), Assale, Aungor, Awlad Jema, Awlad Sulayman, Awra, Aza, Babalia, Baggara (Baqqarra, Beni Rashid, Habiniya, Hawazma, Humr, Mesiriya, Rashaida, Rizeiqat, Seleim, Ta'aisha), Barain, Baraya, Bardoa, Barma, Batuma, Bedjond, Bellerama, Ben Wail, Beri, Bideyat, Bidio (Bidyo), Birked, Bodalla, Bolgo, Bororo, Boua, Budjia, Buduma (Boudouma, Yedina), Bulala, Bulgeda, Cerdegua, Charfarda, Daba, Dagana, Dagel, Dagila, Daju, Dalatawa (Dalatoa), Dalla, Dangaleat, Daramdé (Kultu), Dari, Daye, Daza, Dazaga, Debba, Dekker, Dindje, Dionkor (Junkun), Dirong, Dirsina, Djadne, Djagada, Djema, Djioko, Djoheina, Doba, Dogo, Dogorda, Doria, Dowaza, Doza, Dungal, Ederguia, Ennedi, Erdiha, Erenga, Factoa, Fali, Fanian (Mana), Fetra, Fongoro (Gelege), Fortena, Gablai, Gabri, Gaeda, Gala, Gallao, Garap, Gezira, Gimr, Girga, Gor (Gore), Gouboda, Goulaye, Gounda, Guérep, Guidar, Guiziga (Guizaga), Gula (Goula), Gula Koumra, Gula Médé, Guria, Gurut, Haddad, Hadjeray, Hassauna, Hemat, Issia, Jamala, Jellaba, Juhayna, Junkun (Diongor, Dionkor, Djongor), Kaba, Kabka, Kadianga, Kadjiji, Kalia, Kallameida, Kallamia, Kamadja, Kamaya, Kanoa, Kapsiki, Karanga (Vakaranga), Kara, Karbo, Karia, Kashméré, Kecherda, Kera, Keressa, Khozzam, Kibet, Kige (Kigé), Kilang, Killakada, Kim, Kinga (Kenga), Kirdi, Kobe (Kobé), Kodoi (Kodoy), Koke, Kokorda,

Kola, Kolobo, Kolop, Kongurama, Koniéré, Kosseda, Kossop, Kotoko, Kouka (Kuka), Kouri, Kreda, Kubri, Kumra, Kura, Kuri, Kwallia, Laka (Lao Habe, Lau), Lele, Lisi, Maba, Mada, Madaba, Madjigodjia, Madjingaye (Madjingayé), Magimi, Maibuloa, Makoula, Malanga, Mallumia, Mandaga, Mandala, Mandara, Mang, Manga, Maradalla, Marari, Marait (Mararit), Marba, Marcudia, Marfa, Masalat, Masalit, Matakam, Mbaoua, Mbaye (Mbayé), Mbeur, Mboun (Mbun), Medi, Media, Medogo, Mesmedjé, Méti (Metisse), Midogo, Mileri (Jebel), Miltou, Mima, Mimi, Mogode, Mogoum, Moubi, Mouloui, Mourdia, Mouroum, Mourro, Moussey (Musey), Mullumtchilloum, Mundang (Moundang), Musgu (Mousgoum, Musgum), Myssirie, Nachéré, Nar, Ndam, Nduka, Neilliam (Niellim), Ngadji, Ngama, Ngambaye, Ngaltuku, Ngigim, Noarma, Mofu, Noi, Odobaya, Oulad Mansour, Oulad Mehareb, Ounia, Rachid, Rizegat (Mahamid, Maharge, Mararit), Runga, Saba, Salamat, Sanga (Bosango, Sangha, Sango), Sara-Kaba, Saraoua, Shali, Siginda, Sinyar, Sokoro, Somrai, Soungor, Taizera, Tameurtioua, Tama, Tarsoa, Tcharigiria, Tchioda, Tchukulia, Teda, Tegua, Terintere, Tojima, Tomaghera, Torom, Toumak, Toundjour (Tunjur), Tounia, Tozoba, Tuer, Tumagri, Tupur (Toupouri, Tupuri), Ursawa, Wadjirima, Wajunga, Yakudi, Yalna, Yerima, and Zaghawa peoples.

COMOROS

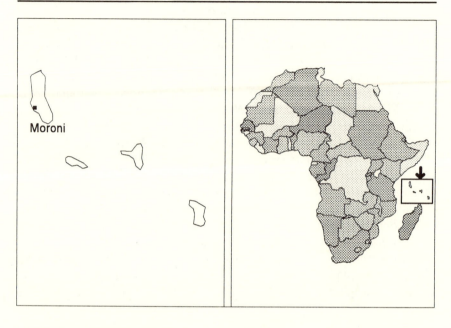

The population of the Federal Islamic Republic of the Comoros is about 500,000 (mid-1998 PRB est.). It is essentially a mixture of African, Arab and Malayo-Indonesian groups. Aside from the African Bantu and Arabs, its major ethnic groups include the Antalote, Cafre, Makoe, Oimatsaha, and Sakalava peoples.

CONGO

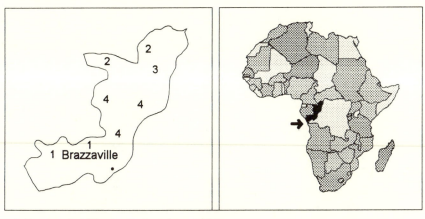

1. Kongo, 2. M'Bochi, 3. Sangha, 4. Teke, etc.

The Republic of the Congo has a population of about 2,700,000 (mid-1998 PRB est.) This population consists of about 15 ethnic groups which in their turn are divided into some 75 subgroups, almost all Bantu. The major ethnic groups include the Kongo (48%) in the south; the Sangha (Sanga) (20%) and M'Bochi (12%) in the north, and the Téké (Bateke, Batéké) (17%) in the center. The Congo also supports a small minority of Europeans, mostly French or of French background.

Smaller groups and/or subgroups include the Achikouya, Ali, Ambamba, Babole, Babuissi, Baduma, Bakamba, Bakota (Koto), Bakouélé (Bakwele), Bakoukouya, Balali, Bali, Bambana, Bangala (Bangi, Bongala), Batsangul (Tsangui), Bembe, Binga (Babenga, Babinga, Bambenga), Bombo, Bondjo, Bondongo, Bongo, Bonguili, Dondo (Badondo), Eshira, Fumbu, Furu, Irébu, Kabongo, Kamba, Konambembe, Kougni, Kuyu (Kouyou), Lali (Balili, Lari), Likouala (Likwala), Likuba, Linga, Lobala, Loi, Maku, Makwa, Mbaka, Mbata, Mbete, Mbimou, Mboko, Mfunu, Mondjombo, Mpama, Mdibu, Ngbaga, Nge-Nge, Ngiril, Nku, Mzabi (Bandjabi), Pande (Pende), Sanga (Bosango, Sangha, Sango), Sise, Sundi, Tanda, Tio, Vili, and Yombe peoples.

DJIBOUTI

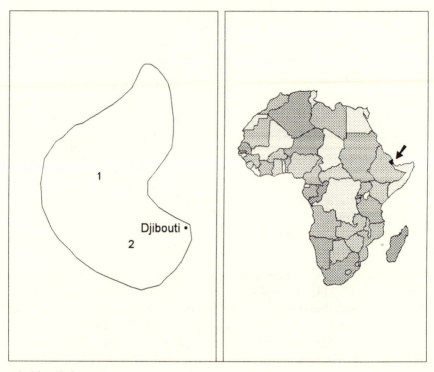

1. Afar, 2. Issa, etc.

Djibouti is a small country with a population of about 700,000 (mid-1998 PRB est.). Its people are 60% Somali, known as Issa, 35% Afar, known as Danakil, and 5% Arab and other Asian, Ethiopian, French, and Italian. The Issa are concentrated in the southern areas of the country, whereas the Afars in its northern regions. Other groups live primarily in the urban centers, notably in the capital Djibouti, the country's principal city.

Smaller groups and/or subgroups in Djibouti include such peoples as the Abgal, Dalol, Sab, and Samale (Samaale) peoples.

EGYPT

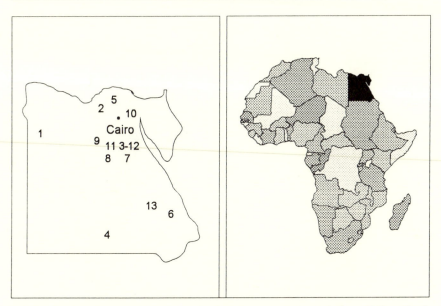

1. Aulad Soliman, 2. Awlad Ali, 3. Ayaida, 4. Baggara, 5. Beheria, 6. Beja, 7. Beni Suef, 8. Fawayid, 9. Harabi, 10. Haweitat, 11. Jawabis, 12. Maiaza, 13. Nubians, etc..

Egypt is an Arab country with a population of about 65,500,000 (mid-1998 PRB est.). Its people are 99% Arab of Eastern Hamitic stock and Nubian of Sudanic origin, and 1% Armenian, Greek, Turkish, French, Italian, and other Arab, notably Lebanese and Syrian. Religiously, about 94% of its population are Muslim and 6% Coptic Christian and other. Non-Arab Egyptian ethnic groups include the Ababda, a Beja subgroup, who live in southeastern Egypt, notably between the Nile River and the Red Sea and the Nubians who in the 1960s were relocated from their traditional lands in Aswan in southern Egypt to New Nubia north of the city of Aswan to allow for the construction of the Aswan Dam. Smaller Egyptian groups and/or subgroups include the Aulad Soliman, Awlad Ali, Ayaida, Baggara, Barabra, Beheria, Beni Suef, Fawayid, Fedija, Harabi, Haweitat, Jawabi, Kenuze (Beni Kanz), Maiaza, Maha, Qireijab, and Sukkot peoples.

EQUATORIAL GUINEA

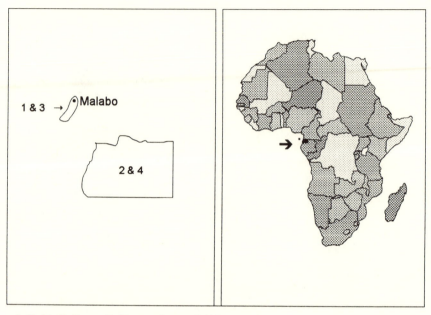

1. Bubi, 2. Fang, 3. Fernandinos, 4. Ndowe, etc.

Equatorial Guinea's population is about 400,000 (mid-1998 PRB est.). In Bioko (formerly Fernando Po), the major groups include the Bubi and the Fernandino, and in Rio Muni, the Fang (Fan, Fanwe, Mfang, Mpangwe) and Ndowe (Los Playeros/Beach People). A small minority of Europeans especially of Spanish background live in the country.

Smaller ethnic groups and/or subgroups in Equatorial Guinea include the Asangon, Balenke (Balenki), Bane, Bapuku, Baseke, Bayele (Bako), Benga (Bakota, Banga, Bonkoro), Beti, Bomoudi, Bongue, Boulou (Bulu), Boumba, Bujeba, Esangui, Eton, Gelli (Badjelli, Bagielli, Baguielli), Kombe, Maka, Muika (Muiko), Mvaé, Ntumu (Ntoumou, Ntum), Okak, Oyek, Pahouin (Beti-Pahouin, Fang, Pamue, Pangwe), Séké (Boulou, Shékiani), Wouri (Oli).

ERITREA

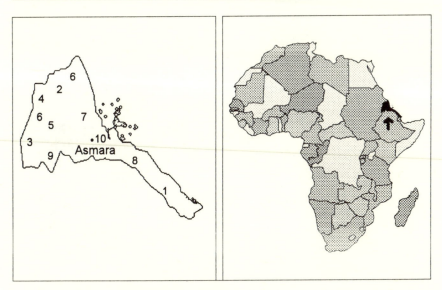

1. Afar, 2. Beja, 3. Besharin, 4. Hadendowa, 5. Halenga, 6. Kunama, 7. Mansa, 8. Saho, 9. Shamkella, 10. Tigre, etc.

The State of Eritrea has an ethnically heterogenous population of about 3,800,000 (mid-1998 PRB est.). Its major groups include the Tigrays 50%, Tigre (Tegre, Tigray, and Kunama 40%, Afar 4%, and Saho 3%). The Afar are concentrated in the southern regions of Eritrea, whereas the Kunama in the Barentu region along the country's border with Sudan, the Saho in its coastal regions, and the Tigre in its northern and western regions.

Smaller Eritrean ethnic groups and/or subgroups include the Ad Tekles, Ad Temaryam, Agaw (Agew), Agon, Asawerda, Barya (Barea), Beja, Beni Amer, Bet Asgede, Bilin, Bisharin, Erob, Hadendowa, Halenga, Ilit, Jabarti (Djeberti, Jabara, Jeberti, Jiberti), Kunama (Kunema), Marya, Mansa (Mensa), Mini Fere, Shamkella, and Tigrinya peoples.

ETHIOPIA

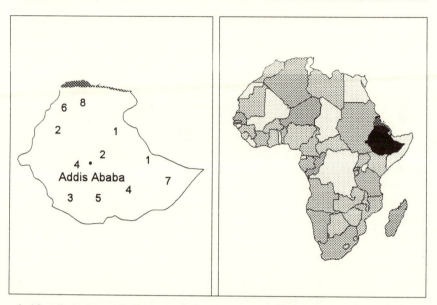

1. Afar, 2. Amhara, 3. Gurage, 4. Oromo, (Galla), 5. Sidamo, 6. Shankella, 7. Somali, 8. Tigrean, etc.

Ethiopia has an ethnically diverse population of about 58,400,000 (mid-1998 PRB est.). Of its over forty ethnic groups, the major ones are the Oromo (40%), Amhara and Tigrean (32%), Sidamo (9%), Shankella (6%), Somali (6%), Afar (4%), Gurage (2%), and other (1%). The Oromo, also known as Galla, are concentrated in the subtropical central and southern highlands of the country, whereas the Agaw, Amhara (Abyssinians), and the Tigrean (Tegre, Tigray, Tigre) in its central and northern regions. The Sidamo, also known as Sadama and Sidama, and Gurage peoples are concentrated in the southwestern regions of Ethiopia; the Afar, also known as Danakil (in Arabic) and Adal (in Amharic), in its central and southern-eastern areas; the Somali in its southern and southeastern regions, notably in the Ogaden region; and the Shankella (Shamkella) in the northwestern regions along its borders with Sudan.

Smaller Ethiopian ethnic groups and/or subgroups include the Ad Tekles, Ad Temaryam, Afran Qalla (Afran Qallo), Agaw (Agew), Agon, Ajuran, Alaba, Aleta, Alla, Anniya, Anuak (Annuak, Anyuak), Arbore, Argobba, Ari, Arssi (Arsi, Arisi, Arusi), Asawerda, Awi, Baaka, Babile, Bako, Bale, Banna, Baria, Basketo, Bayso, Begemder, Beir, Beja, Beni Amer, Beni Shangul, Berta (Berti), Bet Asgede, Bilin, Bodi, Boran (Borana, Borena), Borodda, Burji, Burun, Bussa, Chara, Daarod (Darod), Dassanetch (Dasenech), Deresa (Darasa), Dime, Dizi, Dizu, Dorze, Erob, Falasha (Bete Israel, Felasha, Kayla), Gabre (Gabbra, Garre), Gamu (Gamo, Gamu-Gofa), Garo, Gawwada, Gera, Gibi, Gidichosa, Gidole, Gimira, Gobeze, Gobeze, Gofa (Gemu-Gofa), Goma, Gosha, Guji (Gugi), Guma (Gumma), Gumuz, Gurage (Gerage, Gerawege), Gurreh, Habab (Hadendowa), Hadiya (Haddiya, Hidiya), Hamer, Harari (Hareri), Ingassana, Ittu, Jabarti (Djeberti, Jabara, Jeberti, Jiberti), Jamjam, Janjero, Jima, Kachama, Kafa, Kafa-Sadama, Karo, Keficho (Kefa), Kembatta (Kambata, Kambatta), Kemnant, Kiskena, Koma, Konso, Konta, Kosa, Koyra, Kullo, Kunfel, Kwara, Langa, Libide, Maale, Majang, Maji, Male, Malo, Mao, Marta, Meban, Mech'a, Me'en, Meni Fere, Mesengo, Mocha (Shekatcho), Murle, Mursi (Mun), Nao, Nara, Nole, Nuer, Nyangatom, Obora, Ometo, Orma, Oyda, Qimant, Raya (Azebo), Sab, Saho, Samale (Samaale), Shangama, Sheko, Shinasha, Surma, Tamboro, Tigrinya, Timbara, Tirma, Tiskena, Tolu, Tsamay, Tsemai, Tulama (Tulema), Turkana, Uduk, Walla, Wayto, Welamo (Walamo, Wolayta), Wellega, Weriza (Werize), Watawit (Wetawit), Wollo (Wello), Xamtanga, Yamarico, Yejju (Yaju), Zaghawa, Zayze (Zayze), Zergula, and Zilmanu peoples.

GABON

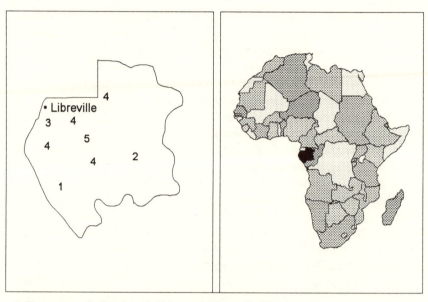

1. Bapounou, 2. Bateke, 3. Eshira, 4. Fang, 5. Okande, etc.

The Republic of Gabon has a population of about 1,200,000 (mid-1998 PRB est.). Its people belong to more than 40 ethnic groups most of which, however, are Bantu. Its major ethnic groups include the Bapounou (Mapounou, Pounou), Bateke (Batéké, Téké), Eshira (Echira, Shira), Fang (Fans, Fanwe, Mfang, Mpangwe), Mbédé, Mbete (Mbeti), and Okande (Okandé). Gabon also supports a large minority of expatriate Africans and French and other European nationals.

The Bapounou people are concentrated in the southwestern regions of Gabon, notably in the lands surrounding the N'Gounié and Nyanga rivers; the Bateke in its eastern regions, especially in the province of Haut-Ogooué; the Eshira and Fang in its coastal areas; the Mbete in its southeastern lands; and the Okande in its central regions, particulary along the banks of the Middle Ogooué River.

Smaller Gabonese ethnic groups and/or subgroups include the

Adouma, Adyumba, Ambamba, Apindji, Awandji, Babuissi, Baduma, Bakaniqui, Bakèlè (Akèlè), Bakere, Bakota (Kota, Koto), Bakouélé (Bakwele), Balèlè, Baloumbou, Bambana, Bandjabi, Bane (Banen), Banga, Bangala (Bangi), Bapounou (Bayaka, Pounou), Bassimba, Batsangul (Tsangui), Bavarma, Baveya, Bawandji, Bayaka, Benga (Bakota, Bonkoro), Beti, Binga (Babenga, Babinga, Bambenga), Bongom (Bougom), Bosyeba, Boulou (Bulu), Chiwa (Bichiwa), Dambomo, Enenga, Eton, Evéla, Fond, Furu, Galoa (Galwa), Irébu, Kanigui (Akanigui, Bakaniki), Kele, Koto (Bakota, Bandjambi, Ikota, Kota), Kuyu (Kouyou), Linga, Loi, Loumbou (Baloumbou), Mahongwe (Mahongwé), Mahouin, Maka (Makaa), Maku (Makou), Massango (Sango, Sangou), Mberenzabi, Mbete, Mbochi, Méti (Metisse), Mindassa, Mindoumou, Mitsogo (Mitshogo, Tshogo), Mpongwe, Mvaé (Mvae), Ndoumou (Mindoumou), Ngiril, Ngowé (Ngove), Ngumba, Nkomi, Ntumu (Ntoumou, Ntum), Nzabi (Bandjabi), Obamba (Mbamba), Okak, Okandé, Orungu (Ombéké, Orungou), Pahouin (Beti-Pahouin, Fang, Pamue, Pangwe), Pove (Pubi), Séké (Boulou, Shékiani), Shaké, Shamai (Shamaye), Shimba (Simba), Varama, Vili, Voungou (Voumbou, Woumbou), and Wouri (Oli) peoples.

GAMBIA, THE

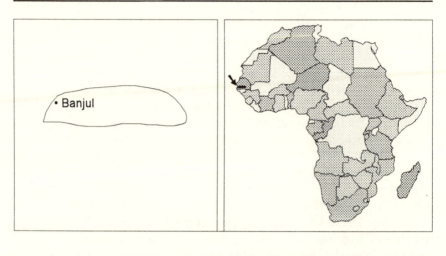

The Gambia supports a population of about 1,200,000 (mid-1998 PRB est.) 99% of which is African. Its people belong to the following major ethnic groups: Mandinka (42%); Fula, also known as Foulbe, Fulbe, Fulfulde, Fullah, Fulani, Fulata, Hilani, (18%); Wolof (16%); Dyola, called also Diola, Diula, Dyula, Jola, and Yola, (10%); Serahuli, known also as Marka, Sarakolé, Saraxole, Serakhulle, Soninke, and Soninké, (9%); other groups (4%); and, African and European (notably English) expatriates (1%). The Mandinka (Malinké, Mandinko, Mandingo, Maninka), the largest group, are spread throughout the country.

Smaller Gambian ethnic groups and/or subgroups include such peoples as the Aku, Baga, Bagafore, Balante (Balanté, Balanti), Banun (Banhun, Banyun), Bassari, Bedik, Bijago, Dorobe (Loobo), Firdus (Firdos), Fulbe Ladde, Fulbe Na'i, Fulbe Siire, Jahanka (Diakhanké, Jahaanké, Jahanke, Jaxanke, Tubacaye), Koniagui, Landoma (Cocoli, Kokoli, Landouman, Landouma, Landuma, Laube, Mandinke-Mori, Manjaca (Mandyako, Manjaco, Manjago), Mnami (Mmani), Moor, Nalu (Nalou), Niuminko (Nyoominkoo), Padjadinca, Serer, Tiapi (Tyopi), and Toroobe peoples.

GHANA

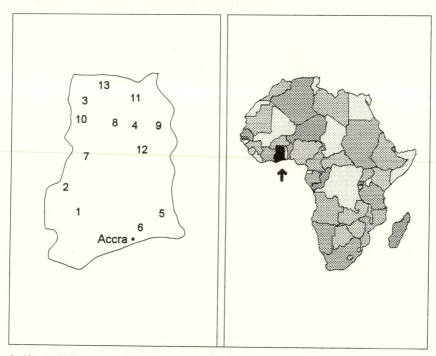

1. Akan, 2. Brong, 3. Dagaba, 4. Dagomba, 5. Ewe, 6. GA, 7. Gonja, 8. Grusi, 9. Konkomba, 10. Lobi, 11. Mamprusi, 12. Nanumba, 13. Sisala, etc.

Ghana has a population of about 18,900,000 (mid-1998 PRB est.) which is presently 99.8% African and 0.2% British, Lebanese, Syrian, Indian and other. The African population is divided into numerous ethnic groups, the major ones of which are the Akan (Akani, Akanny, Asante, Ashanti), Dagaba, Dagomba (Dogamba, Molé-Dagbane, Moshi-Dagomba), Ewe (Ehoué, Eibe, Ephe, Krepe, Krepi), Fanti (Fante, Fantyn), GA (Gamashie), Gonja, Grusi (Awuma, Gorise, Gourounsi, Grunshi, Grunsi, Grussi, Guense, Gurinse, Gurunshi, Gurunsi, Western Kasena, Nankansi), Guan (Guang, Gwan), Konkomba (Komba), Lobi (Lo, Lober), Mandinka (Malinke, Malinké, Mandinga, Mandinko, Mandingo, Maninka), Mamprusi (Mampruli,

Mampruse, Mamprussi), Nanumba, and Sisala. The Akan are the largest group representing 44% of the population. Second to the Akan in size are the Moshi-Dagomba, the Ewe and the Ga (Gamashie) who account for 16%, 13% and 8% of the country's population, respectively.

The Akan are concentrated in the southwestern, the Brong in its west central, and the Grusi in its north central regions of the country. The Ewe and Ga are situated in Ghana's southeastern areas and the Dagaba and Lobi in the northwest. The Fanti live primarily in the coastal area of the Central Region, the Mamprusi and Sisala in the northern regions of the country, and the Gonja in the central areas. Finally, the Dagomba and Konkomba are concentrated in Ghana's north-central and northeastern territories, and the Mandika in the southern areas.

Smaller Ghanian ethnic groups and subgroups include the Aburé, Abora (Abura), Abron (Abrong, Anlo, Boron, Bron, Brong, Bono, Dom, Tchaman), Abuakwa Akyem (Abuaswa Akim, Akim), Aculo, Ada, Adangbe (Adangme, Adampa, Dangme), Adansi, Adele, Agave (Crophy), Agnagan, Ahafo, Ahanta, Ahlon, Ahoulan, Aizo, Akebou, Akpafu, Akposo, Akuapem, Akwamu (Aquamboe), Akyem, Alfanema, Amanfi, Ané (Mina), Anlo, Anum (Anum-Boso), Anyi, Aowin (Awowin), Apemanim (Apimenem), Asokori (Asokore), Assin (Asen), Assumigya, Atwode (Achode, Atyoti), Attendansu (Atandanso), Avatime (Afatime), Awuna, Awutu, Ayigbé, Bagre, Basari (Bassari, Basare, Kyamba, Tchamba), Bassila, Bekwai, Bimoba (Bimawba, B'Moba, Moab, Moba, Mwan), Birifor, Bole, Bonwire, Bosume Akyem, Bowiri, Brong (Abron), Bowli, Buem (Boem), Builsa (Builse, Bulse, Kangyaga, Kanjaga), Busansi (Bisa, Bissa, Boussansé, Bussansi, Busanga, Bouzantchi, Bousanou), Chokossi (Chakossi, Kyokosi, Kyokoshi, Tschokossi, Tyokossi), Chumburung, Dagari (Dagara, Dagarte, Dagarti, Dagate, Dagati), Daza, Denkyira (Dankyira, Denkera, Denkyera, Kankyira), Deno (Bure), Dera (Deru, Kanakuru), Dghwede (Azaghwana, Dehoxde, Hude, Johode, Tghuade, Toghwede, Traude, Wa'a, Zaghmana), Dogon, Dumpo (Kaala, Kugulo), Dwaben (Juaben), Effiduase, Efutu (Afutu, Fetu, Futu), Eguafo, Ehotile (Mekyibo), Ejiso (Edwiso), Ekumfi, Etsu (Ati, Atti), Evalue, Fera, Fiaso, Fon, Fra-Fra (fra), Ga-An-Andangme, Ge, Gomoa (Gomua), Gonja (Gongya), Guemenu, Gurma (Gourmantché), Gyamen (Gyaamen, Gyaman, Jaman), Hausa, Ho, Jula (Dyula, Diula, Joola, Juula, Kangah, Va, Wangara), Kabré, Kasena (Kassena), Kilanga, Kinkomba,

Kokofu, Komono, Konkomba (Komba), Kotokoli (Chaucho, Cotocoli, Tem, Temba), Kotoku Akyem, Kpesi (Kpeshi), Kpong, Krakye (Krachi), Krepi (Krepe, Peki), Krobou (Klobi, Krobo), Kumasi (Kumase), Kusasi (Koussassi, Kusae, Kusai, Kusase), Kwahu (Akwahu, Kwawu, Quahoe), Kyamba (Tchamba), Kyerepong (Cherepong, Kyerepon), Larte (Larteh, Late), Ligbi (Ligby), Likpe, Logba, Lolobi, Lowiili, Mampong, Mandinke-Mori, Manya Krobo, Maxe, Mina (Ané), Miwo, Mo, Mossi (Molé, Moshi), Nabdam, Nagwa, Nambali, Namnam (Nabdam), Nanumba, Ningo, Nkonya, Nsuta, Ntrubu (Ntruber), Ntwumuru (Nchumbulung, Nchumuru), Nunuma (Nanoumba, Nanum, Nanune, Nibulu, Nouna, Nounouma, Nourouma), Nyangbo (Nyanga, Nyango, Yagbum), Nzima (Nzema, N'zima, Amanya, Appolo, Appolonian, Assoko, Zéma), Osudoku, Ouatchi, Pila Pila (Yao, Yowa), Pla, Prampram (Gbugbla), Salaga, Santrofoki, Sasala (Isala, Pisala, Sissala, Sisala), Sefwi (Encassar, Inkassa, Sahwi, Sehwi), Sefwi Anwiawso, Sefwi Bekwai, Sefwi Wiawso, Senfi, Senya (Beyna Bereku), Shai (Siade), Somba (Tamberma), Tafi, Talensi (Tale, Talen, Talene, Tallensi), Tampolense, Téuessué, Tofinu, Touna, Tounbé, Twifu (Twifo), Vagala (Vagele, Vigala), Wala (Oule, Walba, Walo, Wilé), Wassa (Warsha, Wasa, Wasaw, Wassaw), Wiawso, Yagala, Yendi, and Zerma (Dyarma, Dyerma, Zabarma, Zaberma, Zabarima, Zabermawa, Zarma) peoples.

GUINEA

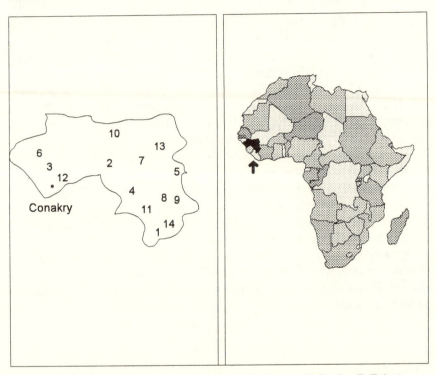

1. Baga, 2. Balante, 3. Banyun, 4. Biafada, 5. Dyalonke, 6. Dyola, 7. Fulani,
8. Kisi, 9. Landuma, 10. Malinke, 11. Nalu, 12. Pepel, 13. Tenda, 14. Sousou, etc.

Guinea's population of about 7,500,000 (mid-1998 PRB est.) consists of 18 ethnic groups, the principal ones of which are three: the Fulani (Fula, Foula, Foula, Foulbe, Fulbe, Fulfulde, Fullah, Fulata, and Hilani Djallon), the Malinke, and the Soso (Soosoo, Sosso, Sousou, Soussou, Susu). Other groups include the Baga, Balante, Banyun, Biafada, Dyalonke, Dyola (Diola, Jola, Yola), Kisi (Kissi), Landuma, Nalu (Nalou), Pepel, and Tenda (Tanda).

The Fulani people are concentrated in the northwestern parts of the country, the Malinké (Mandinka, Mandinko, Mandingo, Maninka), in its northern and northeastern regions, and the Soso in its western coastal plain and northwestern areas. The Baga, Biafada, Dyola, Pepel, and Nalu live along Guinea's coastal areas, the Balante and Landuma in the mountains that oversee the Atlantic Ocean, the Dyalonke in the central eastern parts of the country, the Tenda in the central regions, and the Kisi in the southeastern areas.

Smaller ethnic groups and/or subgroups include the Badyaran (Badyaranké, Bajaranke, Badiaranke), Bagafore, Basari, Bedik, Boin (Boeni), Jahanka (Diakhanké, Jahaanké, Jahanke, Jaxanke, Tubacaye), Kissi (Kisi), Konagi (Coniagui), Konianke, Kono, Koranko (Kouranko, Kuranko), Kpelle (Guerzé, Ngere, Nguerze, Pele), Lele, Limba, Loma (Buzzi, Lorma, Toma), Ma (Mano), Mnami (Mmani), Manyanka, Mayo, Mikifore, Pouli (Foulacounda), Soninké (Marka, Sarakolé, Saraxole, Serahuli, Serakhulle, Soninke), Temne (Timne, Timmance), Tiapi (Tyapi, Tyopi), Toucouleur (Futankobe, Takarir, Takruri, Tekarir, Tokolor, Torodo, Toncouleur, Tukri, Tukulor), Vai (Mande-tan, Vei, Vey), Wasulunka (Ouassoulounke, Wassalunke), Yalunka (Dialonke, Djalonke, Dyalonké, Jalonca, Jalonké, Jallonké, Jalunka) peoples.

GUINEA-BISSAU

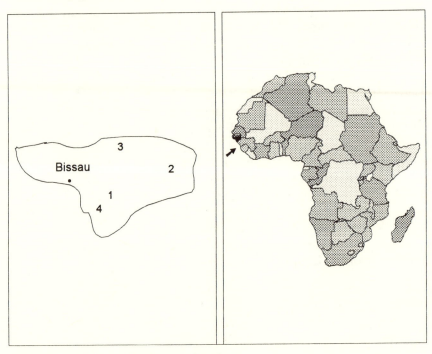

1. Balanta, 2. Fula, 3. Mandinga, 4. Papel, etc.

Guinea-Bissau's population of about 1,100,000 (mid-1998 PRB est.) is divided into numerous ethnic groups. Presently, 30% of its people are Balanta (Balanta-Brassa, Balante, Balanté), 20% Fula, 14% Manjaca (Mandyako, Manjaco, Manjago), 13% Mandinga, 7% Papel, 14% other, and less than 1% European and Mulatto.

The Balanta and the Papel are concentrated in the coastal areas of Guinea-Bissau, whereas the Fula and Mandinga (Malinké, Mandinka, Mandinko, Mandingo, Maninka) in its northern and eastern regions, respectively.

Smaller ethnic groups and/or subgroups include the Badyaran (Badyaranké, Bajaranke, Badiaranke), Bagafore, Bambara (Bamana,

Banmanan, Bamanakan), Banun (Banhun, Banyun), Basari, Bayot (Baiote), Beafada (Biafada), Bedik, Bijagó (Bissago, Bojago, Bujago), Boin (Boeni), Brame, Cassanga, Dyola (Diola, Jola, Yola), Felup (Felupe), Jula (Dyula, Diula, Joola, Juula, Kangah, Konagi (Coniagui), Konhaque (Conhaque), Landoma (Cocoli, Kokoli, Landouman, Landouma, Landuma, Tiapi, Tyopi), Loma (Buzzi, Lorma, Toma), Ma (Mano), Mayo, Va, Wangara), Mancanha, Mane, Méti (Metisse), Mnami (Mmani), Nalu (Nalou), Padjadinca, Papei, Quissinga, Soninké (Marka, Sarakolé, Saraxole, Serahuli, Serakhulle, Soninke), Soso (Soosoo, Sosso, Soussou, Susu), Tenda (Tanda), Timene, and Yalunka (Dialonke, Djalonke, Dyalonké, Jalonca, Jalonké, Jallonké, Jalunka).

IVORY COAST (CÔTE D'IVOIRE)

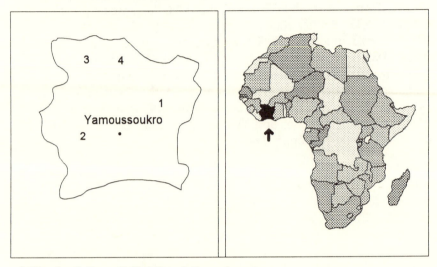

1. Baoule, 2. Bete, 3. Malinke, 4. Senoufou, etc.

The Ivory Coast has a highly heterogeneous population of about 15,600,000 (mid-1998 PRB est.). Its people are divided into over 60 ethnic groups, the major ones of which are the Baoulé (23%), Bété (18%), Senoufou (15%), and Malinke (11%). In addition, the Ivory Coast supports sizable groups of African and non-African expatriates, notably Burkinabes, French and Lebanese.

The Baoulé (Baba, Baule, Po, Ton, Kotoko, Bawle) are concentrated in the central regions of the country, notably in the areas between the Comoé and Bandama rivers; the Bété (Bete, Beti, Bokya, Kpwe, Magwe, Tsien) in its west-central regions; the Malinké (Mandinga, Mandinka, Mandinko, Mandingo, Maninka) in its northwestern lands; and the Senoufou (Bamana, Sene, Senefo, Senoufo, Senufo, Siena, Syénambélé) in its northern regions.

Smaller Ivorian ethnic groups and/or subgroups include such peoples as the Abé (Abbe, Abbey), Aburé (Abouré, Agoua, Abonwa, Compa), Abron, Adjukru (Adjoukrou, Adiourkrou, Adyukru, Boubouri, Odjukru),

Aizi, Akuri (Agru), Alagya, Alladian, Amanfi, Anyi, Aowin (Awowin), Ari (Abidji), Assini, Attie (Akié, Akyé, Atié), Avikam (Brignan, Gbanda, Lahou), Aware, Bakwe (Bakwé, Srigbé, Touwé), Bambara (Bamana, Banmanan, Bamanakan), Beng (Ben, Gan, Ngan, Ngen, Nguin), Béttié, Biai, Bini, Birifor, Blio-Gbalu, Bona, Brong (Abron), Dagari (Dagara, Dagarte, Dagarti, Dagate, Dagati), Dan (Gio, Gyo, Mebe, Samia, Yacouba), Dégha (Buru, Déya, Dyoma, Mofo), Dida, Djimini, Divo, Dorosie, Ebrie (Ebrié, Ebu, Gbon, Kyaman, Tchrimbo), Ega (Die), Ehotile (Mekyibo), Essouma, Eton, Evalue, Fiaso, Gagu (Gagon), Gan, Gbaboh, Gbagbo, Gbilibo, Gbo, Gbohbo-Niabo, Godié, Gonja (Congya), Gouin (Guin, Kpen, Mbwen), Grebo, Guéré (Gewo, Wé), Guin, Guro, Gyamen (Gyaamen, Gyaman, Jaman), Jaublin, Juarzon, Jula (Dyula, Diula, Joola, Juula, Kangah, Va, Wangara), Karaboro (Karakora), Karbardae, Komono, Kono, Konyaka, Kotoko, Kotrohou (Kodia), Kouya, Kouzié, Kovu, Kpiarplay, Krazohn-Plo, Krobou (Klobi, Krobo), Kru (Crau, Grebo, Krao, Krou, Krumen, Wané), Kulango (Babé, Koulango, Kulano), Kwaya, Kweni (Dipa, Gouro, Guro, Kouen, Koueni, Lo), Lorhon, Ngwela, Nkoramfo), Lo Dagara, Lobi (Lo Lober), Lozoua, Mahon, Maké, Manyanka, Mauka, Mbatto (Gwa), Mdenye, Mekyibo (Byetri, Ehotile, Eotile, Eoutilé, Ewutre, Mekibo, Vétéré), Méti (Metisse), Minianka, Miwo, Mona (Ganmu, Mwa, Mwanu), Moronou, Mossi (Molé, Moshi), Nafana, Ndenye, Neyo, Niaboua, Niédéboua, Nizohni, Nzima (Nzema, N'zima, Amanya, Appolo, Appolonian, Assoko, Zéma), Samogho (Don, Sambla, Samoro), Sanwi, Sapo, Seekon, Siti (Kira, Konosarala, Paxala, Sitigo), Soninké (Marka, Sarakolé, Saraxole, Serahuli, Serakhulle, Soninke), Taguana, Tchien Menyon-Kana, Tchien Menzon-Gbohbo, Téuessué, Tiefo (Tyéfo), Touna, Tounbé, Toura, Tourka (Turka, Turuka), Ubi (Oubi), Wan (Ouan, Ngwano), Wara, Wassa (Warsha, Wasa, Wasaw, Wassaw), Wasulunka (Ouassoulounke, Wassalunke), Wee (Kran, Krahn), Wedjah, Wobé (Ouobe, Wé), Yagala, Yokoboué, and Zerma (Dyarma, Dyerma, Zabarma, Zaberma, Zabarima, Zabermawa, Zarma) peoples.

KENYA

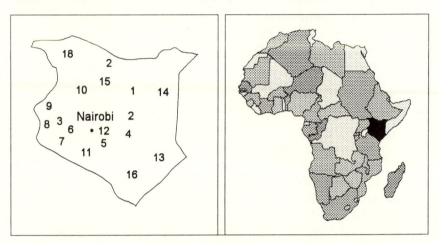

1. Boran, 2. Galla, 3. Kalenjin and Nandi, 4. Kamba, 5. Kikuyu, 6. Kipsigi,
7. Kisii, 8. Luo, 9. Luhya, 10. Marakwet, 11. Masai, 12. Meru, 13. Mijikenda,
14. Somali, 15. Sumburu, 16. Taita, 17. Tugen, 18. Turkana, etc.

Kenya supports a population of about 28,300,000 (mid-1998 PRB est.). This population is 99% African and 1% Asian and European. Its African population is divided into many ethnic groups, the major ones of which are the Galla (Oromo), Boran (Borana), Kalenjin, Kamba, Kikuyu (Gikikuyu), Kipsigi, Kisii (Gusii), Luo, Marakwet, Masai (Maasai), Meru (Ngaa), Mijikenda, Somali, Samburu (Sumburu), Taita, Tugen, and Turkana. Of these groups, the Kikuyu represent about (21%) of the total population, the Luhya (14%), the Luo (13%), the Kalenjin (11%), the Kamba (11%), the Kisii (6%), and the Meru (6%). The Asian population is essentially composed of Arabs, Malagasy and Indian sub-continent peoples, whereas the European population is made up notably of people of British, Dutch and German backgrounds.

The Boran people are concentrated in the north along Kenya's border with Ethiopia and Somalia, whereas the Galla in its east-central regions, the Kalenjin and Nandi in its Rift Valley Province, the Kamba (Akamba) in its Eastern Province, and the Kikuyu in its highlands north of the capital

Nairobi. Of other major Kenyan ethnic groups, the Kipsigi live in the western highlands of the country, the Kisii and Luo (Lwoo) in its southwestern areas, especially in the Nyanza Province, the Marakwet in its southwestern highlands in the vicinity of Lake Victoria, the Luhya (Abaluyia, Luyia) in its Western Province, the Masai and Meru in its southern regions, the Mijikenda along its southeastern coast, and the Somali people in the northeast along its border with Somalia. Finally, the Samburu people live in the Samburu District south and southeast of Lake Turkana, the Taita in the Taita Hills of the Coast Province, the Tugen in the Rift Valley Province, and the Turkana in the northwestern areas of the country near the Ugandan-Kenyan border line.

Smaller African Kenyan groups and/or subgroups include the Abasuba, Acoli, Ajuran, Alur, Bajuni (Tikuu), Bakhayo, Bukusu, Bungomek, Bura, Burji, Chawia, Chonyi, Chuka, Daarod (Darod), Dabida, Dahalo, Dambi, Digo, Dodo (Dodoth, Dotho), Dorobo (Nderebe, Ndorobo), Duruma, Elmolo, Embu, Gabre, Gaki, Ganda, Giguchi, Gimba, Giriyama (Giriama, Giryama), Gosha, Gurreh, Gwere (Bagwere, Lugwere), Idakho, Igembi, Igoji, Imenti, Issuka, Iteso (Elgumi, Itesyo, Wamia), Jaluo, Jibana, Jomvu, Jonam, Kabra, Kakelelwa, Kamba, Kambe, Karimojon, Karura, Kasigau, Kauma, Kedi, Kenyi, Keyo (Elgeyo, Keiyu), Khayo, Kipsigi, Kisa, Kishamba, Kony, Kuman, Kuria (Kulya, Tende), Laikipia Masai, Lake Nyala, Logoli, Lokoya, Manyema, Marach, Maragoli, Marakwet, Marama, Margoli, Mbale, Mbeere (Mbere), Mbololo, Mbwere, Meru, Metume, Mijikenda, Mintini, Miutini, Muganga (Mugange), Munyo Yaya (Korokoro), Murle, Muthambi, Mvita, Mwanda, Mwimbi, Nandi, Ndia, Ngare, Njemp (Tiamu), Nyala, Nyika, Nyole (Lunyole), Nyore, Okiek, Oromo, Padhola, Paluo, Pate, Pok, Pokomo, Pokot, Rabai, Rendille, Ribe, Sab, Sabaot, Sakuye (Sakakuye), Samale (Samaale), Samburu (Burkeneji, Loikop), Samia, Sanye (Ariangulu, Asi, Laa, Langulo, Liangulu, Waat, Waatha, Wasi), Sebei (Sapei), Shilluk, Shisa, Soni, Tachoni, Taita, Taveta, Tepeth, Teso, Terik (Nyang'oris), Tharaka, Tigania, Tiriki, Tsotse (Tsotso), Tugen, Turkana, Vumba, Wanga, Welwan (Malakote), Werugha, and Yaku (Mogogodo) peoples.

LESOTHO

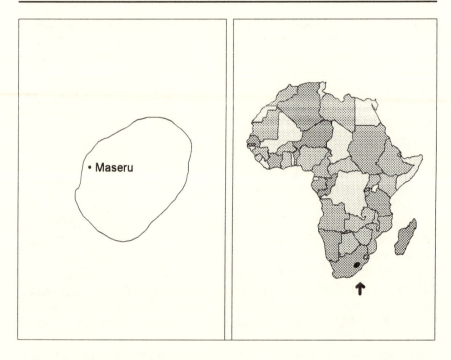

Lesotho has a population of about 2,100,000 (mid-1998 PRB est.) the great majority of which is Southern Sotho, also known as Basuto. The Sotho represent 99.7% of the population. The rest, 0.3%, are peoples of European or Asian background.

Smaller ethnic groups and/or subgroups include the Bataung, Fokeng (Bafokeng), Kwena (Bakuena, Bakwena, Kuena), Mapolane, Ngwato, Ngwaketse, Phetla (formerly Zili, Baphetla, Maphetla), Phuthi, Pondo, Thembu, Thepu, Tlokwa (Batlokoa, Batlokwa, Tlokoa), Twanana, and Vundle (Ama Vundle) peoples.

LIBERIA

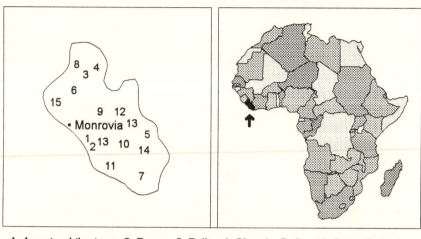

1. Americo-Liberians, 2. Bassa, 3. Bella, 4. Gbandi, 5. Gio, 6. Gola, 7. Grebo, 8. Kissi, 9. Kpelle, 10. Krahn, 11. Kru, 12. Loma, 13. Mano, 14. Ngere, 15. Vai, etc.

Liberia's population is presently about 2,800,000 (mid-1998 PRB est.) with 95% of it made up of indigenous African ethnic groups, and 5% of descendants of repatriated Africans known as Americo-Liberians and Congoe (Congoe Recaptives) peoples. Because of the civil war that erupted in 1990, its foreign community has shrunk significantly. The country's major ethnic groups include the Bassa (Basa, Basso, Gbassa), Bella, Chan, Gbandi (Bande, Gbande), Gio (Dan, Gyo), Gola, Grebo, Kissi, Kpelle (Guerzé, Ngere, Nguerze, Pele), Krahn (Kran), Kru Kru (Crau, Grebo, Krao, Krou, Krumen, Wané), Loma, Mano (Ma), Ngere, and Vai (Mande-tan, Vei, Vey).

America-Liberians and Congoes are concentrated along the Liberian coast, notably on the lands that stretch from Robertsport to Harper, the Bassa in the Grand Bassa County as well as in Marshall and River Cess territories, and the Bella in Liberia's notheastern regions. The Gbandi people live in the northwestern areas of Liberia along the country's border with Sierra Leone, the Gio, Mano and Ngere in its northeastern regions, primarily in the Nimba County, the Gola in its western counties (Bomi, Grand Cape, Lofa, and Montserrado) near the country's border with Sierra Leone, the Grebo in its southeastern counties, namely, Grand Gedeh, Maryland and Sinoe, and the Kissi and Loma in its northwestern regions close to its border with Sierra Leone and Guinea. Finally, the Kpelle are concentrated in the north central parts of Liberia, especially in the counties of Bomi, Bong, and Gibi, the Krahn in the central eastern areas close to the Liberian-Ivorian border, the Kru in the southern coastal regions, and the Vai in the northern coastal areas near the Liberia-Sierra Leone border.

Smaller Liberian ethnic groups and/or subgroups include Bandi (Gbandi), Bakwé, Batti, Bété, Biai, Bio-Wor, Biokwia, Bio-Wor, Blio-Gbalu, Boe, Boe-Glyn, Bulugba, Butulu, Chan, Dan (Gio, Gyo, Mebe, Samia, Yacouba), Dei (Dey), Deigbo, Dida, Doe, Doe-Doe, Doe-Gbahn, Dorgbor, Doru, Dorzohn Goryah, Dowein, Faah, Fenwein, Ganio, Gbaavon, Gbaboh, Gbagbo, Gbao, Gbarwein, Gbaryah, Gbear, Gbehlay, Gbi, Gbilibo, Gblor, Gbo, Gbohbo-Niabo, Gbor, Gborwein, Gbuizohn, Giah, Gianda, Gogwein, Goingbe, Gola, Gorbli, Grand Kola, Guéré (Gewo, Kran, Wé), Hasala, Hoegbahn, Jibehgbo, Jowein, Juarzon, Kaba, Kabli, Kafia, Karbadae, Kissi (Kisi), Ko-Mende, Kola, Konianke, Kono, Koranko (Kouranko, Kuranko), Kotrohou, Kouzié, Kpa-Mende, Kpay, Kpiarplay, Kploh, Kporwein, Kran, Krazohn-Plo, Kuwaa (Belle), Kwaya, Little Kola, Lobaizu, Loma (Buzzi, Lorma, Toma), Lukasu, Ma (Mano), Mambahn, Mandinka (Malinke, Malinké, Mandinga, Mandinko, Mandingo, Maninka), Marbli, Marloe, Mehwen (Mehwein), Mendé (Mendi, Kossa), Mikifore, Moweh, Neegban, Neekreen, Neekrum, Neepu, New Cess, Neyo, Niaboua, Niédéboua, Nizohni, Nyonniwein, Peter Harris, Quella, Sapo, Seekon, Seeya, Sewa Mende, Sewein, Slalay, Solay, Soniwein, Tahamba, Tchien Menyon-Kana, Tchien Menzon-Gbohbo, Timbo, Ubi (Oubi), Varmbo, Wanwuma, Wee, Wein, Wedjah, Wen-Gba-Kon, Wein, Wensohn, Wobé (Ouobe, Wé), Wrogba, Wulukoha, Yarlay, Yawiyasu, Zahr-Flahn, Zeewein, Zoduan, Zoe, Zoo, and Zor peoples.

LIBYA

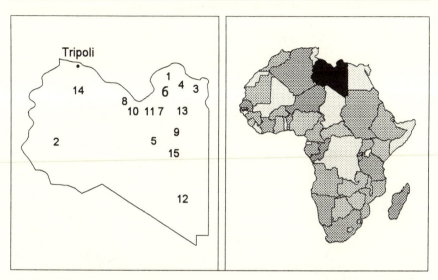

1. Abaydat, 2. Ajjers, 3. Alamamra, 4. Alharaba, 5. Almajabra, 6. Arafah, 7. Awagir,
8. Dars, 9. Fawakhir, 10. Megarha, 11. Mugharba, 12. Teda Toubou, 13. Sanusi,
14. Zentan, 15. Zuwayah, etc.

Libya's population of over 5,700,000 (mid-1998 PRB est.) is 92% Arab, 5% Berber (Taureg) and Teda Toubou (Tbou, Tébou, Tebu, Tibbu, Toubbou, Toubou), and 3% peoples from different countries, including Egypt, Greece, India, Malta, Italy, Pakistan, and Turkey.

The Arab peoples of Libya are concentrated in the northern and central regions of the country, the Berber in its western and southern regions, the Teda Toubou in its southern areas along the country's borders with Chad and Niger, and the foreign expatriates in its coastal and urbanized centers.

Smaller Libyan groups and/or subgroups include Abaydat, Ajjer, Alamamra, Alharaba, Almajabra, Arafah, Awaqir, Awlad Sulayman (Awlad Soliman), Baggara, Berti, Dar, Duwud, Fawakhir, Gezira, Gounda, Harratine, Jamala, Juhayna, Megarha, Mugharba, Qulaughli, Teda, Sanusi, Zentan, and Zuwayah peoples.

MADAGASCAR

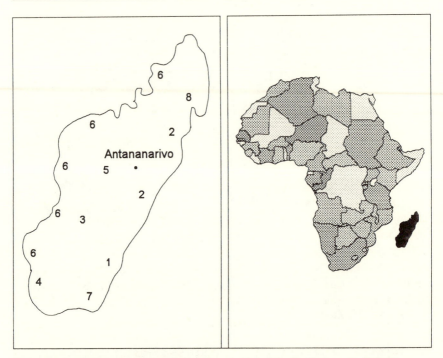

1. Antaisaka, 2. Betsimisaraka, 3. Betsileo, 4. Mahafaly, 5. Merina, 6.. Sakalava,
7. Tandroy, 8.Tsimihety, etc.

Madagascar's population of about 14,000,000 (mid-1998 PRB est.) is split between Highlanders and coastal groups. The Highlanders are predominantly of Malayo-Indonesian origin. Their major groups include the Merina (Antimerina, Hova, Imerina, Ovah) and related Betsileo. Both groups live in the Central Highlands of the country. The coastal group, known as Côtiers, comprises peoples with mixed African, Malayo-Indonisian and Arab ancestry. Their major groups include the Antaisaka (Taisakas, Tesakis), Betsimisaraka, Tsimihety, and the Sakalava.

The Antaisaka are concentrated in Madagascar's southeastern regions. The Betsimisaraka are the second largest group on the island. They live along the eastern coast, notably in areas between the Bay of Antongil and the Manjary River. The Sakalava are found along the west coast. Their concentrations are in areas between Nosy Be and Tulear. Finally, the Tsimihety are located in the island's northwestern regions, especially in the Diégo-Saurez and Majunga provinces.

In addition to the Highlanders and the Côtiers, Madagascar also supports a small minority of Europeans, especially French, Indians of French nationality, and Creoles who include persons of European parentage born in the country and/or their descendants.

Smaller ethnic groups and/or subgroups in Madagascar include the Antaifasy (Antifasy), Antaimoro, Antambahaoka, Antandroy (Tandruy), Antankarana, Antanosy, Antiboina, Antifiherena, Antimailaka, Antimaraka, Antimena, Antimilanja, Antisihanaka (Sihanaka), Arindrano, Bara, Barobe, Betanimena (Betanmena), Bezanozano, Fotsy, Halangina, Ikongo, Ilalangina, Imamono, Isandra, Mainty, Makoa, Manadriana, Mehafaly (Mehafali), Menabe (Antaiva, Tankay), Sahafatra, Sautsauta, Sihanaka, Taimoro, Tambahoaka, Tanala, Tanalana, Tandroy, Tankarana, Tanosy, Timanambondro, Timonjy, Vezu (Veso), Vinda, and Zafisoro peoples.

MALAWI

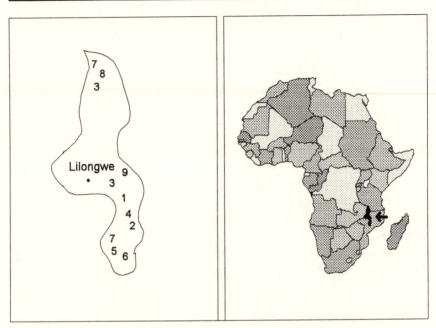

1. Chewa, 2. Lomwe, 3. Ngonde, 4. Ngoni, 5. Nyanja, 6. Sena, 7 . Tonga, 8. Tumbuka, 9. Yao, etc.

Malawi's population is about 9,800,000 (mid-1998 PRB est.). It consists of numerous African ethnic groups, the major ones of which are the Chewa (Achewa, Ancheya, Cewa, Chua, Masheba), Lomwe (Acilowe, Alomwe, Nguru), Ngonde, Ngoni (Angoni, Anguni, Mangoni, Wangoni), Nyanja, Sena, Tonga (Batonga), Tumbuka (Tumbuko), and Yao (Achawa, Adjao, Ajaua, Veiao, Wahyao, Wayao). Other ethnic groups include peoples of Asian and European background.

The Chewa people are the largest ethnic group in Malawi. Together with the Lomwe, Nyanja, and Sena, they are highly concentrated in the southern regions of the country, whereas the Ngonde, Tonga and Tumbuko in its northern regions. Another group of Tonga, however, is also found in southern Malawi. Finally, the Ngoni and Yao people are concentrated in the central and eastern parts of the country, respectively.

Smaller African Malawian ethnic groups and/or subgroups include the Ajaua (Adjao), Ambo, Chipeta (Achipeta), Chiwere, Chiwere Ngoni, Fulilwa, Fungwe, Gomani, Gomani Ngoni, Henga, Kamanga, Kiturika, Machinga, Maganga (Makanga), Maganja, Makonde (Maconde), Makoa (Makua), Maravi, Matambwe, Mawia, Mbelwe Ngoni, Mwera (Mwere), Ngindo, Ngonde, Nthali, Nyanja (Anyanja, Nianja, Niassa, Wanyanja), Phoka, Songo, Tsaw, Wenya.

MALI

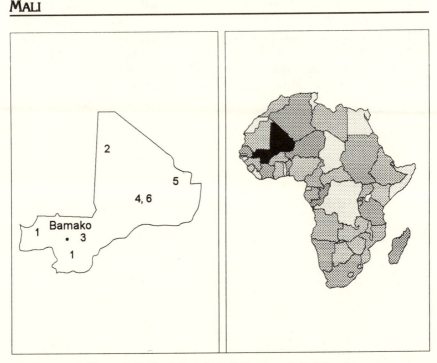

1. Mande, 2. Moor, 3. Peul, 4. Songhai, 5. Tuareg, 6. Voltaic, etc.

Mali has a population of about 10,100,000 (mid-1998 PRB est.) 50% of which are Mande peoples (Bambara, also known as Bamana, Banmanan, and Bamanakan, Malinké, Sarakolé), 17% Peul (Foula, Foula, Foulbe, Fula, Fulani, Fulata, Fulbe, Fulfulde, Fullah, and Hilani Djallon), 12% Voltaic, 6% Songhai (Songhay, Songhoi, Sonhrai, Sonhray), and 5% Tuareg and Moor.

The Mande and Peul are found throughout Mali, the Taureg in the country's northern, western and central regions, and the Songhai and Voltaic peoples along the banks of the Niger River. The Moor live primarily in the northwestern areas of the country.

Smaller Malian ethnic groups and/or subgroups include such peoples as the Amo, Arma, Azura, Bambara, Bobo, Bobo-Fing (Boua), Bobo-Gbé

(Kian, Tian), Bobo-Oulé (Tara), Boza (Bozo), Chawa, Chawai, Deforo, Dendi, Dialonke (Yalunka), Diawara, Dogon (Habé, Cadau), Fono, Gabibi (Arbi), Gow, Imajeren, Imouzourag, Imrad, Inadin, Ineslemen, Jula (Dyula, Diula, Joola, Juula, Kangah, Va, Wangara), Kado, Katab, Khasonka (Khassonké), Kiballo (Kiwollo), Kono (Konu, Kwono), Kosanke, Kurama (Tikurimi), Kourtey (Kurtey), Lisawan, Mandinka (Malinke, Malinké, Mandinga, Mandinko, Mandingo, Maninka), Mahon, Marka, Mayga (Askia), Méti (Metisse), Minianka, Nafana, Nanerge (Nanèrègè, Nanergue), Nono, Reguibat (Regeibat), Rukuba, Samo, Senoufou (Bamana, Sene, Senefo, Senoufo, Senufo, Siena, Syénambélé), Sia (Sya), Sohanti, Somono, Sorko, Tiefo (Tyéfo), Tourka (Turka, Turuka), Wasulunka (Ouassoulounke, Wassalunke), Wogo, Yatenga, and Zandamo peoples.

MAURITANIA

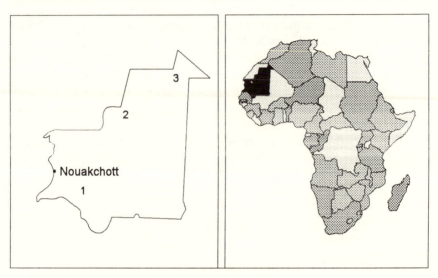

1. Imraguen, 2. Moor , 3. Regeibat, etc.

Mauritania supports a population of about 2,500,000 (mid-1998 PRB est.) 40% of which is mixed Moor-African (Maur-African), 30% Moor (Maur), and 30% African. Peoples belonging to these groups are found throughout the country. Groups of the Murd Guachey people of the Canary Islands can also be found in Mauritania.

Smaller Mauritanian groups and/or subgroups include Ahel Berikallah, Ahel Cheikh Ma el-Ainin, Ahl-Massin, Aswanik, Azarzir, Azor Diakhande, Duaish, Dyankanke, Harratine, Imraguen, Khasonka (Khassonké), Lemtouma, Ligbe, Maaquil, Masoufa, Nemadi, Ouadane, Ouakore, Oulad Tidrarin, Reguibat (Regeibat), Soninké (Marka, Sarakolé, Saraxole, Serahuli, Serakhulle, Soninke), Tekna, Tolba, Tubakai (Jahanka, Tubacaye), Wangarawa, Wangarbe, Wankore and Zenaga peoples.

MAURITIUS

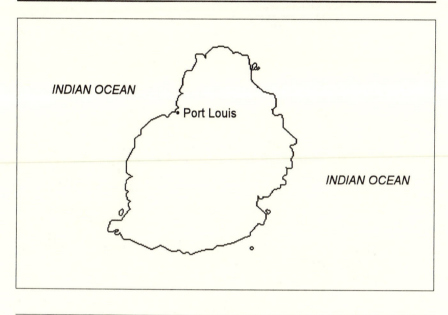

Mauritius has a population of 1,200,000 (mid-1998 PRB est.) 68% of which is Indo-Mauritian, 27% Creole, 3% Sino-Mauritian, and 2% Franco-Mauritian. Peoples of these groups are found throughout the country.

MAYOTTE

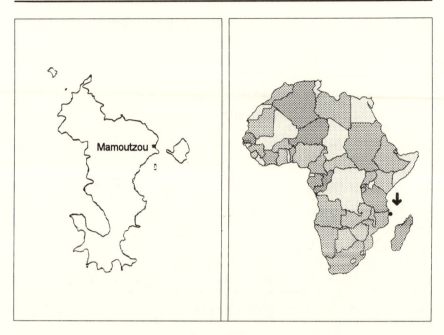

Mayotte is a "territorial collectivity" of France. Ethnically, its population is similar in its composition to that of the Comoros of which it used to be an integral part. Its population of 93,468 (July 1994 WFB est.) is divided into five major ethnic groups, namely, Antalote, Cafre, Makoe, Oimatsaha, and Sakalava. Collectively, they are known as Mahorais. Members of these groups are found throughout the collectivity.

MOROCCO

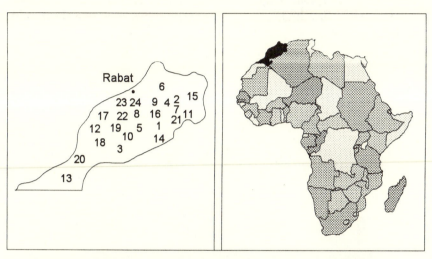

1. Ait Atta, 2. Ait Idrassen, 3. Ait Kebache, 4. Ait Oumalou, 5. Ait Walnzgit,
6. Ait Waryaghar, 7. Ait Yafelman, 8. Beni Amer, 9. Beni Guil, 10. Darwa,
11. Dou Menia, 12. Dukkala, 13. Moor, 14. Nsula, 15 Oulad Djerir, 16. Sanhaja,
17. Shawya, 18. Shluh and Berraber, 19. Sraghna, 20. Tekna, 21. Ulad Yihya,
22. Werigha, 23. Zayr, 24. Zemmur, etc.

The Kingdom of Morocco has a population of 27,700,000 (mid-1998 PRB est.) 65% of which is Arab and Arabized Berber, 34% Berber, and 0.8% European (including French and Spaniards), and 0.2% Jewish. The Arab and Arabized Berber as well as the European and Jewish populations live in the northern coastal areas of the country, whereas the Berber population in the Atlas and southern regions of the country. The Berber population is divided into numerous groups and subgroups. Its largest groups include the Ait Waryaghar (Ait Waryaghat) who live in the Rif region of northwestern Morocco, and the Berraber and the Shluh who are concentrated in the western High Atlas and Sous regions.

Smaller Moroccan ethnic groups and/or subgroups include Ahel Cheikh Ma el-Ainin, Ait Atta, Ait Idrassen, Ait Jmel, Ait Kebache, Ait Oumalou, Ait Said, Ait Walnzgit, Ait Yafelman, Beni Amer, Dou Menia,

Beni Guil, Darwa, Dukkala, Echtouka, El-Faaris, El-Guerah, Harratine, Izarguien, Moor, Nsula, Oulad Tidrarin, Reguibat (Regeibat), Sanhaja, Shawya, Shilha, Sraghna, Susi, Tekna, Ulad Yihya, Werigha, Zayr, and Zemmur peoples.

MOZAMBIQUE

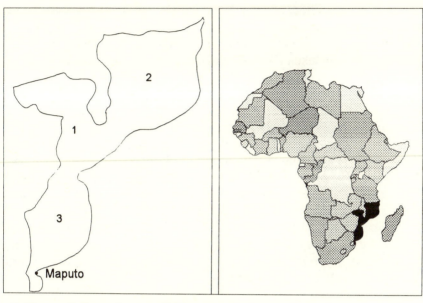

1. Chewa, 2. Macua-Lomwe, 3. Shona, etc.

The population of Mozambique is 18,600,000 (mid-1998 PRB est.). It is composed of numerous indigenous African ethnic groups, as well as of a non-African minority of Europeans, Euro-Africans, and Indians. Its major African groups include the Chewa, Macua-Lomwe (Acilowe, Alolo, Alomwe, Lomwe and Lomue, Makwa, Makua, Mukwa, Nguru), and Shona (Chona, Karanga, Mashona, Vashona).

The Chewa people are concentrated in the central regions of Mozambique; the Macua-Lomwe, the largest ethnic group in the country, in its northeastern coastal areas and the lower areas of the Zambezi River Valley and Niassa and Cabo Delgafo regions; and the Shona in its Zambezi Valley.

Smaller ethnic groups and/or subgroups in Mozambique include the Abarue, Ajaua, Ambo (Ovambo), Anyungwe, Atande, Atewe, Banda, Bande, Barwe (Barue, Bargwe), Bitonga, Boror, Botha, Budjga, Chawu,

Chifungo, Chikunda (Bachikunda, Chicunda, Cikunda), Chilendje, Chimahuta, Chinde, Chipeta (Achipeta), Chire, Chirumba, Chiware, Chiwawa, Choko, Choa, Chuabo (Maganja), Danda, Dema, Dwanwo, Gova, Hera, Hlengwe (Bahlengue, Hlengue), Kalanga, Karanga (Vakaranga), Kiturika, Korekore, Lilima, Machinga, Maganga (Makanga), Mahindo, Makat (Makate), Makoa (Makua), Makonde (Maconde), Makua, Malunga, Mamvu, Manyica (Manhica, Manyika), Maravi (Marave), Marunga, Matambe, Mavonde, Mawia (Mavia), Mbadzo, Mbire, Mestiço, Mucatu, Muera, Mutarara, Muwera, Mwanya (Mwenyi), Mwere (Mwera), Nanzwa, Ndau (Buzi, Vandau), Ngindo, (Angoni, Anguni, Mangoni, Wangoni), Njanja, Nsenga (Senga), Nyagombe, Nyampisi, Nyanguru, Nyanja (Anyanja, Nianja, Niassa, Wanyanja), Nyantaza, Nyasa, Nyungwe (Nhungwe, Nyunwe), Pande, Pembe, Pfungwe, Phodzo (Chipango, Marromeu), Ronga (Rhonga, Rsonga), Sase, Sena, Shangaan (Changane, Machangana), Shangana, Shangwa (Bashangwe, Shangwe, Shankwe, Vashangwe), Shavasha, Shope (Chope, Chopi, Chopi-Bitonga), Simboti, Songo, Tande, Tarawa, Tawara (Tavara), Tembo, Tewe, Tonga, Tsenga, Tsaw, Tswa, Tsonga, Valenge, Watombodji, Wazamoi, Yao, Zezuru (Vazezuru), Zimba, and Zinjo peoples.

NAMIBIA

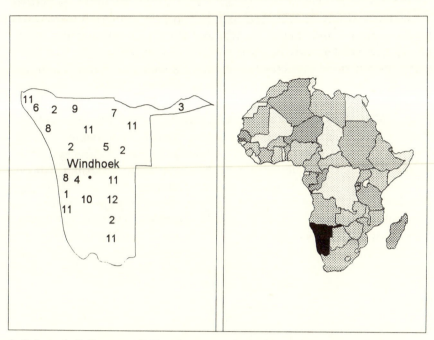

1. Coloured, 2. Damara, 3. East Caprivians (Makololo), 4. Europeans, 5. Herero, 6. Kaokovelders, 7. Kavango, 8. Nama and Ovango, 9. Ovambo, 10. Rehoboth Basters, 11. San, 12. Tswana, etc.

Namibia's population is composed of many ethnic groups. Of its total population of about 1,600,000 (mid-1998 PRB est.), 86% represent African groups, 6.5% European groups, and 7.5% mixed groups. The major African groups include the Bushman (Bushmen) or San (3%), East Caprivians (3%), Damara (9%), Herero (7%), Kaokovelders (1%), Kavango, also known as Kavanga, (6%), Nama (4%), Ovambo (47%), Tswana (1%), and other (5%). The mixed groups include such peoples as the Coloured and the Rehoboth Basters (mixed Nama/Afrikaner ancestry) who account for about 4% and 3% of the country's population, respectively. The European groups consist of Afrikaner, German and English peoples.

European, Coloured and Rehoboth Baster peoples are concentrated in the coastal areas and urbanized centers of Namibia; the Nama (Hottentots, Khoisan) in its southern regions; the Herero, Kaokovelders and Ovambo (Ambo, Huambo, Wambo) in its northern regions, notably along the border with Angola; the East Caprivians (Caprivi) in its northeastern areas, particularly along the Namibian-Zambian border; the San, also known as Sarwa, in the Kalahari Desert; and the Tswana in the country's eastern lands along the country's border with Botswana.

Smaller Namibian African ethnic groups and/or subgroups include the Ambo, Auni, Aunin, Bergdama, !Gami, Ganin, Gei-Khauan, Geinin, Geiriku, Haboben, Himba, Heiom, Huinin, Kaokabander, Kavanga, Khau-Goan, Khoikhoi, Kualuthi, Kuambi, Kuanyama, !Kung, Kung, Kauen, Kwangali, Kwangari, Lozi (Balozi, Barotse, Barutze, Marotse, Mbukushu, Rotse, Rozi), Mbalantu, Mbandero, Mbunza, Mbukushu, Ngandjera, Nkolonkati-Eunda, Nuen, Rehobath Baster, Sambyu, Subiya (Subia), Tjimba, and Witboois peoples.

NIGER

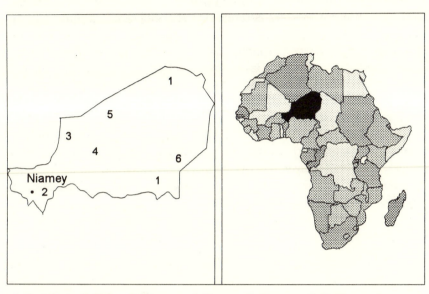

1. Beri Beri, 2. Fula, 3. Djerma, 4. Hausa, 5. Taureg, 6. Toubou, etc.

Niger's population of 10,100,000 (mid-1998 PRB est.) is ethnically heterogenous. Its major groups include the Beri Beri (4.3%), Fula (8.5%), Djerma (22%), Hausa (56%), Tuareg (8%), and Toubou, Gourmantche and other (1.2%). The country also supports a small community of European expatriates, notably from France.

The Beri Beri (Bornuan, Kanouri, Kanuri) are concentrated in the southeastern regions of Niger, whereas the Djerma (Dyarma, Dyerma, Zabarma, Zaberma, Zabarima, Zabermawa, Zarma, Zerma), a Songhai group, in the Zaberma Valley region and in areas along the banks of the Niger River, notably in the vicinity of Zermaganda. The Fula (Foula, Foula, Foulbe, Fulani, Fulata, Fulbe, Fulfulde, Fullah, Hilani Djallon, and Peul), Gourmantche (Gurma), and Hausa are found primarily in the southern areas of the country; the Taureg in its Saharan areas; and the Toubou (Tbou, Tébou, Tebu, Tibbu, Toubbou, Toubou) in its Sahel region.

Smaller ethnic groups and subgroups of Niger include the Abua,

Adarawa, Ader, Anakaza, Anoufo, Arewa, Arna, Aulliminden, Aza, Azna, Bade, Bella (Bellah), Benu, Bornuan (Berberi, Boro, Bornu, Kanembou, Kanembu, Kanuri), Bororo, Boza (Bozo), Braouia (Teda group), Bugabi, Charfarda, Daza, Dazaga, Dendi (Dandi, Dandawa), Djagada, Dowaza, Doza, Erdiha, Fakkawa, Ferouan, Gaeda, Ganda, Gbari, Gobirwa (Gober, Gobir), Golle, Gounda, Gubawa, Hyam (Ham, Hum, Jaba), Igdalen, Illabakan, Imajeren, Imouzourag, Imrad, Inadin, Ineslemen, Janji, Kado, Kalle, Kaoular, Kamadja, Kamberi (Kambari), Kanembu, Katab, Kecherda, Kel Tamajaq, Kokorda, Kourtey (Kurtey), Koyam, Kreda, Kurama, Kurfey, Kwatama, Lela (Cala-Cala, Chilala, Clela, Dakarkari, Dakkarari, Kolela, Lalawa), Lisawan, Magorawa (Magori), Manga, Mangueni, Maouri, Méti (Metisse), Mobeur (Mavar, Mober), Ninzo, Noarma, Nupe, Ounia, Tyenga, So, Sohanti, Soudié, Sorko, Teda, Tegama, Tenere, Tessellaman, Tigueddi, Wajunga, and Wogo peoples.

NIGERIA

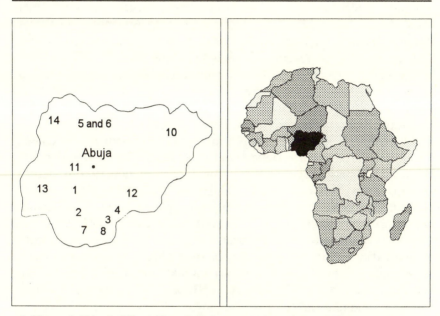

1. Ebira, 2. Edo, 3. Efik, 4. Ekoi, 5. Fulani, 6. Hausa, 7. Ibo, 8. Ibibio, 9. Ijaw, 10. Kanuri, 11. Nupe, 12. Tiv, 13. Yoruba, 14. Zerma, etc.

Nigeria supports more than 250 ethnic groups, the major ones of which are the Ebira (Edbira, Egbura, Igbira, Igbirra), Edo (Benim, Bini, Oviedo, Oviobo), Efik, Ekoi (Ejagham), Fulani (Foula, Foula, Foulbe, Fula, Fulata, Fulbe, Fulfulde, Fullah, Hilani Djallon, and Peul), Hausa, Ibo (Igbo), Ibibio, Ijaw (Ijo), Kanuri (Beriberi, Borno, Bornu, Kanembou, Kanembu), Nupe, Tiv, and Yoruba. The Hausa and Fulani of the north, the Yoruba of the southwest, and the Ibo of the south east make-up 65% of the country's population of 121,800,000 (mid-1998 PRB est.). Aside from these groups, it also supports a small non-African minority consisting of peoples of Indo-Malagasian, English and Lebanese background.

Smaller Nigerian ethnic groups and/or subgroups include the Abadja, Abaja, Abakwariga, Abam, Abanyom, Abon (Abong), Abu'a, Adarawa, Affade, Afo, Afunu, Afusare (Afusari), Agois (Wa Bambani), Agwagwune,

Akassa, Ake (Akye, Aike), Akoko, Akpa-Yache, Akpe, Akpet-Ehom, Akuku, Akunakuna, Alago (Alagoa, Arago, Idoma-Nokwus), Alege, Alensaw, Amap (Amo, Amon, Among, Ba, Timap), Anang (Anaang, Annang), Anga (Nnga, Kerang), Aniguta, Apoi, Aro, Arum, Assumbo, Auyokawa, Awak, Awhawfia, Awhawzara, Awori, Awtanzu, Ayadeghe, Ayas (Ayus), Azura, Bade, Bakpinka (Iyongiyong, Uwet), Bali, Bandawa-Minda (Jinleri, Minda), Banga (Benga), Bangwinji (Banunji), Bankal, Bantoid, Barawa, Bariba (Batonu, Bargu, Barba, Bashar, Bata, Batau, Beni, Bete, Borgowa, Batomba, Botombu, Batonun), Barke, Basan, Basho, Bassa, Bassa-Kaduna, Bassa-Kwomu (Abacha, Abatsa, Bassa-Komo), Bassa-Nge, Batu, Baushi (Bauci, Chonge, Kushi), Bekwarra, Bena, Benu, Bette-Bendi (Dama, Bete-Demdi), Bile (Bille), Binawa (Bogona), Bini, Birom (Aboro, Afango, Berom, Berum, Borom, Gbang, Kibbo, Kibo, Kibyen), Biseni, Bitare (Njwande, Yukutare), Bitieku, Boghom (Bogghom, Boghorom, Bohom, Bokhiyim, Borrom, Burom, Burrum, Burma), Boki, Boko (Bokko), Bokyi (Boki, Nfua, Nki, Okii, Uki, Vanneroki), Bole (Ampika, Borpika), Bolewa, Borgu, Bororo, Buduma (Boudouma, Yedina), Bugabi, Bugi, Buji, Bumaji, Bumo, Buno, Bura (Babir, Babur, Kwojeffa, Pabir), Burak, Burum, Busa (Busagwe, Busanse), Busawa, Buta-Ningi, Butawa, Bwal (Bwoll), Chakfem-Mushere, Chamba (Chamba-Daka, Daka, Nakanyare, Sama, Samba, Tchamba, Tsamba, Chamba-Leko), Cham-Mwana (Cham-Mwona), Charra (Nfachara), Chawa, Chawai (Atsam, Chawe, Chawi), Chessu, Chip (Ship), Choa, Chokfiem (Chakfem-Mushere), Chokobo (Azora, Cikobu, Izora), Choma-Karim (Karim, Kirim, Kiyus, Nuadhu, Shomoh, Shomong), Daba, Dadiya (Boleris, Nda Dia), Daffo-Batura, Dakarkari, Danshi, Dass (Dasse), Dassa, Daurawa, Defaka (Afakani), Degema (Atala, Attala), Dendi (Dandi, Dandawa), Deng, Denya (Anyang), Dimmuk (Doemak), Dirya (Diriya, Sago, Tsago), Dogo, Doka, Doko, Doko-Uyanga (Basanga, Dokl-Uyanga, Dosanga, Iko), Dong, Dorai, Duguza (Dugusa), Duka (Ethun, Hune), Dukkawa, Dulbu, Dungu (Dingi, Dungi, Dunjawa, Dwingi), Duru-Verre (Vere, Verre, Were), Ebe, Edda, Ediene, Ediong, Efutop (Agbaragba, Ofutop), Egba (Egbado), Eggan (Eggon, Egon, Mada, Megong), Eghagi, Egun (Alada, Gu), Etsako, Ekajuk (Akajuk), Eket (Ekit), Ekiti, Ekkpahia, Ekpetiama, Eleme, Eloyi (Afo, Afao, Aho, Afu, Epe), Emai, Emane (Amana), Enwan, Epie, Eruwa (Arokwa, Erakwa, Erohwa), Esa, Esan (Anwain, Ishan), Etche, Etsako, Etulo (Eturo, Turumawa, Utor), Evant

(Avande, Balegete, Belegate, Ovande), Eziama, Ezza, Fali, Fon, Fyam, (Fem, Gyem, Paiem, Pem, Pyam, Pyem), Fyer (Fier), Ga'anda (Mokar), Ga-Andangme, Gade (Gede), Gbagyi (Bagyi, Gwari), Gbanrai, Gbari (Agbari, Bari, Gbagyi, Gwali, Gwari, Gwarri), Gbaya (Baja, Baya), Gbaya Bodomo, Gbaya Bokoto, Gbaya Bouli, Gbaya Dooka, Gbaya Kaka, Gbaya Kara, Gbaya Lai, Gbaya Yaiyuwe, Galambi (Galambe, Galembe), Ganawuri (Aten, Etien, Jal, Niten, Ten), Gbagyi, Gbanrain, Gbaya, Geeri, Gengle (Wegele), Gera, Gerawa, Gerkawa, Geruma (Gerema, Germa), Gewara, Gezawa (Zarandawa), Ghotuo, Glavuda (Gelebda, Glanda, Glavda), Gobirwa (Gobir), Gokana, Gomei (Ankwai, Ankwe, Goemai, Groemai), Gongla (Bajama, Gomla, Jareng), Gubi (Guba), Gude (Cheke, Guduf (Afkabiye, Gudupe, Yaghwatadaxa, Yawotataxa), Guiziga (Guizaga), Gure-Kahugu (Agari, Agbiri, Anirago, Gura, Kafugu, Kagu, Kapugu), Gurmana, Gurrum, Guruntum-Mbaaru (Gurutum), Gusu, Gwa, Gwandara (Gwandari), Gwantu, Gwomu, Haddad, Higgi (Kipsiki), Horom, Hwana (Hona, Hwona), Hyam (Ham, Hum, Jaba), Ibani (Bonny), Ibarapa, Ibesikpo, Ibiaku, Ibie, Ibino (Ibeno, Ibuno), Ibiono, Ibolo, Icen (Etkywa, Ichen, Itchen, Kentu, Kyato, Nyidu), Icheve (Bacheve, Becheve, Utse, Utser, Utseu), Idaisa, Idere, Idesa, Idoma (Alago, Alagoa, Arago, Idoma-Nokwus), Idon (Idong, Igong), Iduwini, Ife, Ifonyim, Igala (Igara), Igbirra, Igbede, Igbomina, Igede (Egede, Eggede, Igedde), Igwe, Ihe, Ijebu, Ijemu, Ijesu, Iji, Ika, Ikale, Ikibiri, Ikiri, Ikono, Ikpa, Ikpanja, Ikpe, Ikpeshi, Iku-Gora-Ankkwa, Ikulu, Ikwerri, Ikwo, Ilaje, Iman, Irigwe (Aregwe, Kwal, Kwan, Kwoll, Miango, Nnerigwe, Nyamgo), Ishan, Ishielu (Eshielu), Isoko (Biotu, Igabo, Urhobo, Sobo), Isu, Isu-Ochi, Itak, Itam, Itsekiri (Chekiri, Ichakiri, Ijekiri, Irhobo, Isekivi, Iselema-Otu, Ishekiri, Iwere, Jekiri, Jekoi, Shekiri, Warri), Ivbie, Iwawa, Izon, Jaba, Jaghnin, Jaku, Jama, Janji, Janjo (Dza, Gwomo, Jen, Jenjo, Karenjo), Jara (Jera), Jarawa, Jarawan, Jen, Jerawa, Jere, Jidda-Abu (Ibut, Nakare), Jimbin, Jimi, Jiru-Kir, Jortu (Jorto), Jsoko, Ju, Jubu, Jukun, Kabou, Kadara, Kadjidi, Kafanchan, Kagoma (Agoma, Gwong, Gyong), Kagoro, Kaivi (Kaibi), Kaje (Baju, Jju, Kache, Kajji), Kalabari, Kam, Kamantam (Angan, Kamanton), Kamberi (Kambari), Kamkam, Kamo (Kamu), Kamuku, Kamwe (Higi, Hiji), Kana (Khana, Ogoni), Kanam, Kanawa, Kanembou (Berberi, Boro, Bornu, Kanembu, Kanuri), Kaninkwom, Kantana, Kanufi, Kapsiki, Karekare (Karaikarai, Kerekere), Karfa (Kerifa), Kariya (Kanyawa, Lipkawa), Katab (Atyab), Katsenawa,

Kayauri, Keaka, Kebbawa, Kendem, Kengawa (Kiengawa, Kyengawa, Tienga), Kere, Keri, Ketu, Kiballo (Kiwollo), Kila, Kilang, Kilba (Chobba, Heba), Kinuku (Kinugy, Kinuka), Kiong (Akayon, Akoiyang, Okonyong, Okoyong), Kir-Balar, Kirdi, Kirfi, Kitimi, Kobchi, Koenoem (Kanam), Kofyar, Kohumono (Bahumono, Ediba, Ekumuru), Kolokuma, Koma, Kono (Konu, Kwono), Koro, Korop (Durop, Ododop), Kotoko, Kotopo, Kouri, Koyam, Kpan (Abakan, Akpanzhi, Hwaso, Hwaye, Ibukwo, Ikpan, Kpanten, kpwate, Nyatso, Nyonyo, Yorda), Kpashan, Kubi (Kuba), Kuda-Chamo, Kudawa, Kugama (Wegam), Kugbo, Kulere (Korom Boye, Tof), Kulung (Bakulung, Bambur, Wurkum), Kukele (Bakele, Ukele), Kukuruku, Kumba (Sate, Yofo), Kumbo Mein, Kupto, Kurama (Tikurimi), Kurfei, Kuted (Kutep, Kutev, Jompre, Mbarike, Zumper), Kutin, Kutumbawa, Kuturmi (Ada), Kuzamani (Rishuwa), Kwa, Kwalla, Kwami (Kwom), Kwanka, Kwatama, Kyedye, Kyibaku (Chibak, Chibbuk, Icibak, Kikuk), Laamang, Laka (Lao Habe, Lau), Lame, Lamja, Laru (Laro), Legbo (Agbo, Igbo Imaban, Higidi), Lela (Cala-Cala, Chilala, Clela, Dakarkari, Dakkarari, Kolela, Lalawa), Lelau, Lemoro (Anemoro, Anowuru, Emoro, Limorro), Lenyima (Anyima, Inyima), Leyigha (Asiga, Ayiga, Yigha), Libo, Lo, Loke (Loko, Yako, Yakurr, Ugep), Longuda (Languda, Nunguda, Nungura, Nunguraba), Lopa, Lopawa, Lotsu-Piri (Kitta), Lubila (Kabila, Ojor), Lungu (Adong, Ungu), Luri, Mabo-Barkul, Mada (Yidda), Magu (Mvanip), Maguzawa, Maha (Maga, Maka), Makoula, Mama (Kantana, Kwarra), Mambila (Bang, Mambere, Mambilla, Manga, Mangbetu, Nor Tagbo, Tongbo), Mandara (Ndara, Wandala), Mang, Manga, Mapodi, Mapuda, Margi, Massa, Matakam, Mauri, Mbaoua, Mbembe (Ekokoma, Ifunubwa, Ofunobwan, Tigong), Okam, Oderiga, Wakande), Mbeur, Mboi (Mboire, Mboyi), Mboum, Mbula-Bwazza, Megili (Migili), Mini, Mirriam, Miya (Muya), Mofu, Montol (Baltap, Teel), Moroa, Mubi, Mundang, Mumbake (Mubako, Nyongnepa), Mundang (Moundang), Mundat, Munga, Musgu (Mousgoum, Musgum), Mwahavul (Mupun, Sura), Mwona, Namu, Nandu-Tari, Naraguta (Anaguta, Iguta), Nde-Nsele-Nta, Ndikpo, Ndoe (Anep), Ndokki, Ndorawa, Ndoro, Nemba (Brass), Nga, Ngan (Beng), Ngambaye, Ngamo (Gamo), Ngbo, Ngenge, Nggwahyi (Ngwaxi, Ngwohi), Ngizim, Ngoshe Ndhang (Ndaghan, Ngweshe, Ngoshe Sama), Ngwa, Ngwoi (Ingwe, Ngwe, Nkwoi, Ungwe), Nikim, Nikki, Ninzam (Gbhu), Ninzo, Nkalu, Nkanu, Nkem-Nkum, Nkim, Nkoro, Nkukoli (Ekuri, Nkokolle), Nnam (Ndem), Nsit, Numana,

Nung Ndem, Nunku (Nungu, Lindiri, Rendre, Rindiri, Rindre, Wamba), Nyamnyam (Bari, Niamniam, Nimbari), Nzagi (Jeng, Jenge, Njai, Njanyi, Njei, Zany), Obanliku, Obolo (Andoni), Obulom, Odot, Odual (Saka), Odut, Offot, Ogbia (Obginya), Ogbogolo, Ogboin, Ogbronuagum (Bukuma), Ogoni, Ogori-Magongo, Ohori, Oiyakiri, Okoba (Okogba), Okodia, Okpamhevi (Opameri), Okpe, Okrika, Oku, O-Kun, Olodiama, Oloma, Olulumo-Ikom, Onatshi, Ondo, Oniong, Onitsha, Oporoma, Ora, Oratta, Oring (Koring, Orri), Oron (Oro), Oru, Oruma, Ososo, Otank (Utanga), Owan, Owerri, Owo, Oyo, Pa'a (Afa, Fa'awa, Foni, Pala), Pabir, Pangu, Pai (Dalong), Panyam, Passam (Nyisam), Pero (Filiya, Pipero), Piapung, Piti (Abisi, Bisi, Pitti), Piya (Pia, Wurkum), Polci, Pongu (Arringeu), Puku, Pyapun, Remo, Reshawa (Bareshe, Gunganci, Gungawa, Jas, Reshe, Tsureshe), Ribam, Ribina, Roba (Lala, Lalla, Gworam), Ron, Rukuba (Bache, Inchazi, Kuche, Sale), Rumaya (Rumaiya), Sabe, Sanga, Sasaru, Saya, Sha, Shagawu (Maleni, Nafunfia, Shagau), Shall-Zwall, Shangawa (Kenga, Kyenga, Shanga, Shonga, Tyenga), Shani (Asennize, Shaini, Sheni), Shede (Tchade), Siginda, Siri, Sobo, Sukur (Adikummu, Gemasakun, Sugur), Surubu (Fiti, Skrubu, Srubu), Takamanda, Tal (Amtul, Kwabzak), Tala, Tamba (Tembi), Tangale (Biliri, Tangle), Tapshin, Tarakiri, Tarok (Appa, Yergam, Yergum), Tazarawa, Teme, Tera, Tienga, Tinga, Tita, Tula (Ture), Tulai, Tungbo, Tupur (Toupouri, Tupuri), Turkwan (Turkwam), Ubaghara, Ubang, Ubani, Ubium, Uhami-Iyayu, Ukaan (Anyaran, Auga, Ikan), Ukpe-Bayobiri, Ukpum, Ukue-Ehuen (Ekpenni), Ulukwumi, Umon (Amon), Uneme (Ileme, Ineme, Uleme), Upila (Okpella, Ukpila), Ura (Ula), Urhobo, Ursawa, Uruan, Utugwang (Mbe Afal, Obe, Putukwam), Ututu, Uzekwe, Vute, Waja (Wagga), Waka, Warji (Sar), Widekum, Wimtim (Vimtim, Yimtim), Wipsi, Wogo, Wurkum, Yagba, Yaki, Yako, Yala, Yamma, Yandang (Hendang, Nyandang, Yendam, Yundum), Yashi, Yekhee (Afemmais, Etsako, Iyekhee), Yergan (Yergam, Yergum, Yergun), Yeskwa (Yasgua), Yiwom (Gerka, Gurka), Yukuben (Ayikiben, Balaabe, Boritsu, Nyikobe, Nyikuben, Oohum), Yungur (Bena, Binna, Ebena, Ebina), Zamfara, Zanga, Zazzagawa, Zari, Zeem, Zerma (Dyarma, Dyerma, Zabarma, Zaberma, Zabarima, Zabermawa, Zarma), and Zul peoples.

RÉUNION

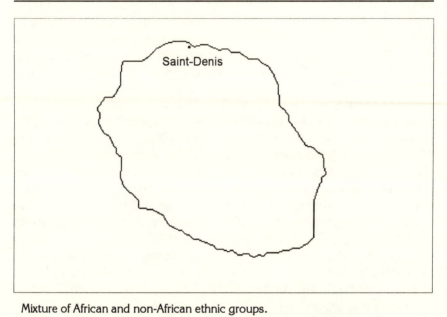

Saint-Denis

Mixture of African and non-African ethnic groups.

Réunion's population of 700.000 (mid-1998 PRB est.) is a mixture of French, African, Malagasy, Chinese, Pakistani, and Indian peoples.

RWANDA

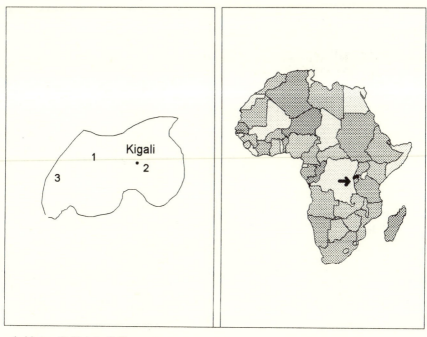

1. Hutu, 2. Tutsi, 3. Twa, etc.

The Republic of Rwanda has a population of about 8,000,000 (mid-1998 PRB est.) of which 90% is Hutu (Abahutu, Bahutu, Wakhutu), 9% Tutsi (Batutsi, Tussi, Watusi, Watutsi), 1% Twa (Gwa), Burundians, Zairians, Europeans, and South Asians. The Hutu are of Bantu origin, whereas the Tutsi are of Nilotic background. The Twa are a pygmy group who live north of Lake Leopold.

Smaller Rwandese ethnic groups and/or subgroups include the Bagogwe, Bakiga, Banyombo, Gesera, Hima (Bahima), Kiga (Rukiga), and Zigaba peoples.

SAINT HELENA

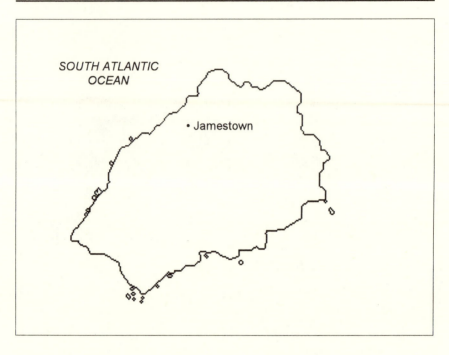

This island has a population of 6,741 (July 1994 WFB est.) made up of essentially St. Helenians.

SÃO TOMÉ AND PRINCIPÉ

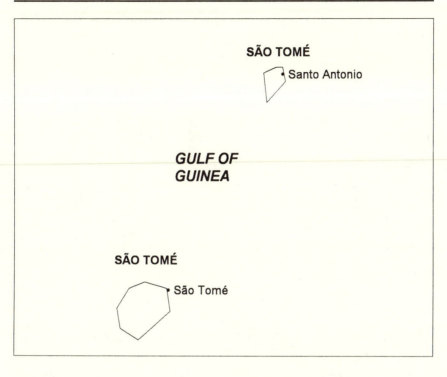

São Tomé and Principé has a population of approximately 200,000 (mid-1998 PRB est.) which consists of Mestiço, African descendants (Angolares, Forros, Servicais, Tongas), and Portuguese. The Angolare people are descendants of Angolan slaves, the Forros of freed slaves, the Servicais of African contract laborers, and the Tonga of children of Servicais born in São Tomé and Principé.

SENEGAL

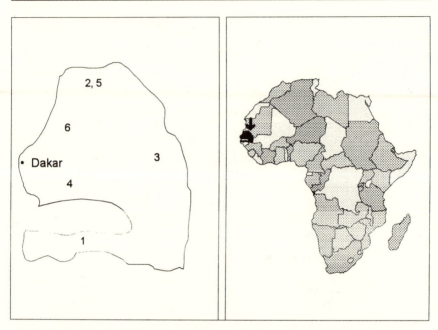

1. Diola, 2. Fulani, 3. Mandingo, 4. Serer, 5. Toucouleur, 6. Wolof, etc.

Senegal's population of 9,000,000 (mid-1998 PRB est.) consists of numerous ethnic groups, the major ones of which are the Diola (9%), Fulani (17%), Mandingo (9%), Serer (17%), Toucouleur (9%), Wolof (36%), and 1% European and Lebanese.

The Dyola (Diola, Diula, Jola, Yola) people are concentrated in the southwestern regions of the country, the Serer (Sarer, Serère, Kegueme) in its western and southern regions, and the Fulani (Fula, Fulbe) in its northern and eastern regions, notably in the Senegal River Valley. The Toucouleur (Takruri, Tekarir, Tokolor, Torodo, Toncouleur, Tukri, Tukulor, Tukylor), also known as Futankobe and Takarir, are primarily located along the banks of the Dagana River, neighboring the Fulani people; the Mandingo (Mandinka Malinke, Malinké, Mande, Manding, Mandinga, Mandinko, Mandingo, Maninka) in the eastern regions along the country's border with Mali especially in the Casamance region; and the Wolof (Jolof, Ouolof, Wollof) in the areas between the Senegal River and the Gambia River. Members of the European and Lebanese communities are located in the urbanized centers of the country.

Smaller ethnic groups and/or subgroups in the Senegal include Ahl-Massin, Aswanik, Azor, Badyaran (Badyaranké, Bajaranke, Badiaranke), Baga, Bagafore, Balante (Balanté), Banun (Banhun, Banyun), Basari, Bayot (Baiote), Bedik, Bijago, Boin, Brin-Seleki, Cangin, Gelowar, Jahanka (Diakhanké, Dyankanke, Jahaanké, Jahanke, Jaxanke, Tubacaye, Tubakai), Jamat, Jola-Haer, Khasonka (Khassonké), Konagi (Coniagui), Kujamaat (Fogny), Landoma (Cocoli, Kokoli, Landouman, Landouma, Landuma), Lebu (Lebou), Ligbe, Mandinke-Mori, Manjaca (Mandyako, Manjaco, Manjago), Méti (Metisse), Mnami (Mmani), Moor, Nalu (Nalou), Ndut, Ndyegem, Non, Nyominka, Ouadane, Ouakore, Padjadinca, Safen, Soninké (Marka, Sarakolé, Saraxole, Serahuli, Serakhulle, Soninke), Tenda (Tanda), Tiapi (Tyapi, Tyopi), Wangarawa, Wangarbe, Wankore peoples.

SEYCHELLES

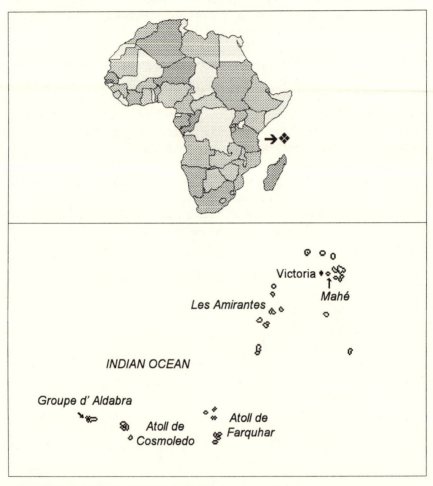

An admixture of African, Asian, and European peoples.

Seychelles has a population of about 100,000 (mid-1998 PRB est.) which is essentially an admixture of Africans, Asians, and Europeans.

SIERRA LEONÉ

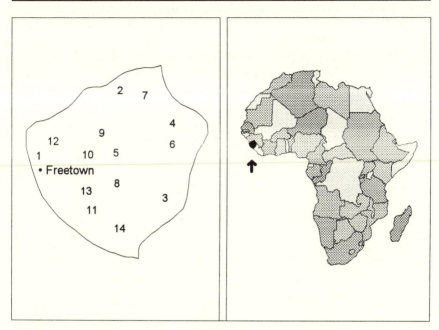

1. Bulom, 2. Dyalonke, 3. Gola, 4. Kissi, 5. Kono, 6. Kuranko, 7. Malinke,
8. Mende, 9. Limba, 10. Loko, 11. Sherbro, 12. Susu, 13. Temne, 14. Vai, etc.

Sierra Leoné has a population of 4,600,000 (mid-1998 PRB est.) 99% of which is composed of native African ethnic groups, notably the Mendé (Kossa, Mendi) and Temne (Timne, Timmance), each of which represents about 30% of the country's total population.

Other groups include the Aku, Bulom (Bullom), Dyalonke, Gola, Kissi (Kisi), Kono, Kuranko (Kouranko, Kuranko), Malinke, Limba, Loko, Gola, Sherbro, Susu (Soosoo, Soso, Sosso, Soussou), Vai (Gallina, Mande-tan, Vei, Vey), and others. Jointly, they account for 39% of the population. The non-African groups (1%) consist of the Creole, as well as European, Lebanese and Asian expatriates.

The Kissi, Kono, Kuranko, and Malinke peoples live in the northern areas of the country; the Aku, a Yoruba group, in the capital Freetown; the

Bulom, Sherbro, and Vai in the country's southern regions; the Gola, Loko, and Mendé in its central forest and coastal areas; the Susu in its western areas; the Limba in its northern and western regions; and the Temne in its central and southern lands.

Smaller ethnic groups and/or subgroups include the Aku, Biriwa, Boj, Bullom, Dablo, Dagole, Dazambo, Ding, Fanse, Gallina, Gbama, Gbande, Gboda Nenge, Gbor, Gobla, Kholifa, Ko-Mende, Konianke, Kono, Kpa-Mende, Kpo, Kposo, Krim (Kim), Krio (Creole), Kunike, La, Mana, Markoi, Mein, Mikifore, Nyein, Plimu, Safroko, Sanda, Sela, Semavule, Senje, Sokpo, Te, Tonko, Tungele, Wara Wara, Yalunka (Dialonke, Djalonke, Dyalonké, Jalonca, Jalonké, Jallonké, Jalunka), Kholifa, Kpelle (Guerzé, Méti (Metisse), Ngere, Nguerze, Pele), Loko (Lokko), Manyanka, Sanda, Sewa Mende, Sherbro, Yangaya, Yoni, and Zui peoples.

SOMALIA

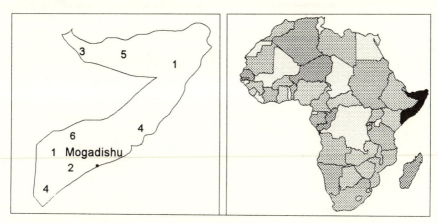

1. Daarood, 2. Digil, 3. Dir, 4. Hawiye, 5. Issaq, 6. Rahanwayn, etc.

Somalia's population of 10,700,000 (mid-1998 PRB est.) is relatively homogenous. It is 85% Somali, 14% Bantu, and 1% Asian, especially Arabs, and European.

The Somali people belong to one of six major clans, namely, the Daarood (Darod), Digil (Dighil), Dir, Hawiye, Issaq (Ishaak, Ishaaq, Ishak), and Rahanwayn (Rahanwein). Lineagewise, however, they belong to one of two groups, namely, Sab and Samale.

The Dir are concentrated in the northwestern areas along the country's border with Djibouti, the Issaq in the northern regions, the Daarood in the northern, eastern and southern regions, and the Hawiye in the central and southern regions. Finally, the Digil and the Rahanwayn are located in northwestern Somalia, notably in the country's inter-riverain lands between Shebelle and Juga rivers.

Smaller ethnic groups and/or subgroups in Somalia include the Abgal, Ajuran, Amarani, Bajuni, Bimal, Boni, Boran (Borana), Dalol, Eyle, Fourlaba, Geledi, Gobaweyn, Gosha, Gurreh, Habash, Horoneh, Issa, Mamassan, Mobilen, Ourweiné, Rendille, Sab, Saad-Moussa, Samale, Shebelle, Shidle, Siu, Wa-Boni, Wa-Gosha, Walaldon, Wardick, Wa-Ribi, Yonis-Moussa peoples.

SOUTH AFRICA

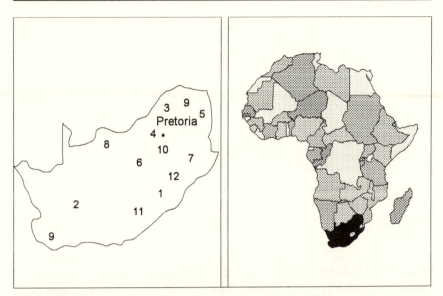

1. Asians, 2. Coloured, 3.Ndebele, 4. North Sotho (Pedi), 5. Shangana (Shangaan)-Tsonga, 6. South Sotho (Basuto), 7. Swazi, 8. Western Sotho (Tswana), 9. Venda, 10. European (White), 11. Xhosa, 12. Zulu, etc.

South Africa's population is about 38,900,000 (mid-1998 PRB est.). It consists of four major groups, namely, Africans (75.2%), people of European descent (13.6%), Coloured (8.6%), and Asians (2.6%). Africans are essentially Bantu-speaking peoples. Culturally and ethnically, however, they are diverse. They belong to one of four major ethnic groups, namely the Ngoni, Sotho, Venda, and Shangana-Tsonga. The Ngoni, the largest of these groups, includes the Zulu, Xhosa, Ndebele, and Swazi peoples. The Sotho group, the second largest, includes the Tswana (Western Sotho), Pedi (Northern Sotho), and Basuto (Southern Sotho). The Venda and the Shangana (Shangaan)-Tsonga are relatively smaller groups. The highest concentrations of these groups are in the northern and eastern regions of the country. The Zulu, for example, are concentrated in Natal east of the Drakensberg Escarpment, the Xhosa in the Transkei of the

---

eastern Cape, and the Venda and the Shangana-Tsonga in northern Transvaal.

Like Africans, peoples of European descent are also culturally and ethnically diverse. They belong to several major groups, namely, the Afrikaners who are of Dutch background, the English who are descendants of English immigrants and settlers, the French who are descendants of French Huguenots, and Germans who are descentants of German immigrants. Peoples of European descent, known as Whites, are presently concentrated in the urban centers of the country. The Coloured people are concentrated in the western Cape, notably in the Cape Province and speak either Afrikaan or English. They include people of mixed white and African blood as well as people of mixed intermarriages between European and/or African and Asian, notably Malay, persons.

Finally, the Asian people are essentially descendants of laborers from the Indian sub-continent who were brought by the British in the 1860s to work in the sugar plantations of Natal. They continue to be highly concentrated in Natal, especially in Durham. Asians are ethnically and religiously heterogenous. Aside from English, their lingua franca, they speak a variety of Indian languages and are affiliated with the Indian sub-continent religious beliefs, including Hinduism and Islam.

Smaller South African ethnic groups and/or subgroups include the Birwa (Babirwa), Bolong, Cape Nguni, Fokeng (Bafokeng), Gcaleka, Griqua, Hurutshe (Barutshe), Kaa, Kgafela Kgatla, Kgatla, Khoi khoi (Hottentot), Khurutshe, Kung, Kwena (Bakuena, Bakwena, Kuena), Lete, Lovedu, Mfengu (Fingoe), Mmanaana Kgatla, Mpondo, Natal Nguni, Nguni, Ngwato, Ngwaketse, Pedi (Bapedi), Rharhabe, Rolong, San (Sarwa, Twa), Shangaan (Changane, Machangana), Talaote, Taung, Tawana, Thembu, Tlokwa (Batlokoa, Batlokwa, Tlokoa), Tshdi Rolong, Tsonga (Tonga), Twa (Gwa), Twanana, and Xesibe peoples.

SUDAN

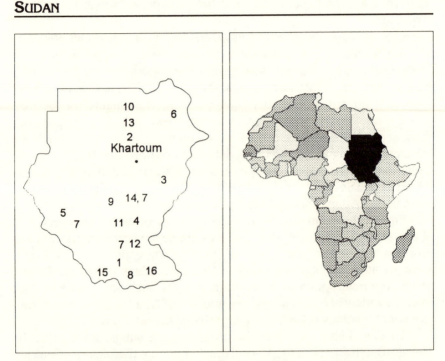

1. Acholi, 2. Jaialiyyin, 3. Anuak, 4. Azandé, 5. Baggara, 6. Beja, 7. Burun,
7. Dinka, 8. Madi, 9. Nuba, 10. Nubian and Danagla, 11. Nuer, 12. Oromo (Galla),
13. Shakiyya, 14. Shilluk, 15. Toposa, 16. Turkana, etc.

The Sudanese population of 28,500,000 (mid-1998 PRB est.) is an admixture of Arab, Afro-Arab, African, and foreign groups. The Arab and Afro-Arab peoples account for 91% of the population, whereas the Beja for 6%, the non-Arab and non-Africans for 2%, and other groups for 1%. Broadly speaking, the Arab groups are concentrated in the northern regions of the country, the Afro-Arab in its central regions, and the African ones in its southern parts.

Sudan's major ethnic groups include the Acholi (Acoli), Anuak (Annuak, Annuk, or Anyuak), Azandé, Baggara (a Juhayna Arab subgroup who are also known as Beni Rashid, Habiniya, Hawazma, Humr, Mesiriya,

Rashaida, Rizeiqat, Seleim, Ta'aisha), Beja, Dinka, Jaaliyin (Gaalin), Madi, Moru, Nuba, Nubian, Nuer, Oromo (Galla), Shilluk (Collo), Taposa (Toposa, Topoza), and Turkana.

The Anuak people are concentrated along the Blue Nile River in the eastern parts of Sudan; the Acholi and Madi along its southern border with Uganda; the Azandé in its southwestern regions; the Baggara in its Darfur and Kordofan regions, especially along the country's border with Chad; the Beja in its eastern parts near the Eritrean and Ethiopian borders; the Dinka and Nuer in the Upper Nile River Valley of the country; the Nuba in the Nuba Mountains of the Kordofan Province; the Nubians in its northern areas close to the Egyptian-Sudanese border; the Oromo in its southern regions, notably along the Sudanese-Ethiopian borders; the Shilluk in the areas between the White and Blue Nile rivers, notably on the west bank of Bahr al-Ghazal river; the Taposa in the country's Equatorial (Istiwā'i) region; and the Turkana along its southern border with Kenya and Uganda.

Smaller Sudanese groups and/or subgroups include the Ababda (Ababa), Abdallab, Abu Sharib, Abyor, Acak, Acueng, Akot, Alei, Amarar, Anag, Anyiel, Apak, Artaj (Unay), Artiqa, Ashraf, Asungor, Atuot (Attuots, Atwat), Avukaya, Awlad Jema (Awlad Jum'a), Awlad Sulayman, Aza, Baka, Bakhat, Baggara, Barabra, Barea (Barya), Bari, Bedeiriya, Beigo, Beir (Murle), Beni Amer, Beni Shangul, Beri, Berti, Bideyat, Bilin, Biri (Bviri), Birked, Bisharin, Boma-Murle, Bongo, Bor Belanda, Borno, Burun, Dair (Koska), Daju, Danagla, Daramdé, Darfur, Dazaga, Didinga, Diil, Dilling, Dirong, Djema, Dodo (Dodoth, Dotho), Dongiro (Donyiro), Dowaza, Ennedi, Erenga, Fellata, Fungor (Fung), Fur (For, Keira), Gala, Garjak, Garjok, Gawama'a, Gaweir, Gezira, Ghulfan, Gima, Gimr, Gula (Goula), Gula Koumra, Gula Médé, Gule, Gulud, Gumuz, Gurut, Haddad, Hadendowa (Hadendiwa), Halanga, Halfawi, Hamaj, Hamar, Hamid, Hamran, Hassanab, Hassaniya, Hausa, Hawara, Hawawir, Heibab, Husaynat, Ilit, Ingessana, Ja'aliyyin, Jaluo, Jamala (Kababishe, Shukriya), Jekiang, Jellaba, Jikany Nuer, Jilek, Jiye, Juhayna, Jur (Ju Luo), Kababishe, Kabka, Kadaru, Kadianga, Kadugli, Kaduru, Kakwa, Kao, Karanga, Karimojon, Kashaf, Kashméré, Katla, Kawahla (Fezara), Keiga-Girru, Kenuze, Kige (Kigé), Kobe (Kobé), Koma, Koniéré, Korobat, Kreich, Krong, Kuek, Kuku, Kumailab, Kunama (Kunema), Lak, Latuka, Lau, Leek Nuer, Lendu, Logit, Lokoya, Luac, Lugbara, Luluba, Luo (Lwoo), Maba

(Fertit, Mandala, Wadain), Madaba, Madanga, Madi, Mahasi (Maha), Malakal, Malanga, Mamar, Mamvu, Manasir, Mandari, Mangutu, Mannyuar, Marari (Marait, Mararit), Mardola, Marenga, Marfa, Masalat, Masalit, Meban, Meidob (Tiddi), Mileri (Jebel), Mima, Mimi, Mirifab, Missiriyya, Moru, Mubi, Mundu (Mundo), Murle, Ndogo, Ngok, Nubian, Nyama, Nyangbara, Nyeyu, Okebu, Otman, Palwol, Qireijab, Pari, Pojulu (Fajelu), Rorkec, Rubatab, Sere, Sinyar, Shaiab, Shalkota (Kargeddi), Shakiyya, Shukriya (Shukriyya), Sukkot, Surma, Talodi, Tama, Taqali (Taqwe, Taqili, Teqale), Temein, Thiang, Toposa, Torti, Toubou (Tbou, Tébou, Tebu, Tibbu, Toubbou, Toubou), Tuer, Tunjur, Uduk, Um Ali, Um Nagi, Urrti, Wajunga, Zabaydiya, and Zaghawa peoples.

SWAZILAND

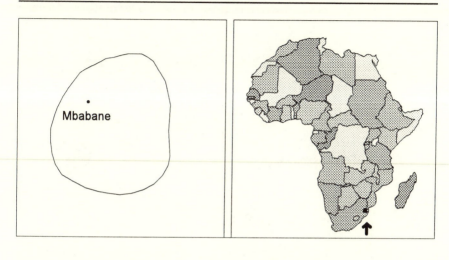

Swaziland supports a population of 1,000,000 (mid-1998 PRB est.) 97% of which is Swazi African and 3% European, notably English. The Swazi people are divided into three major groups, namely, the Bemdzabuko (Bomdzabuko), the Emafikamuva, and the Emakhandzambili.

Other ethnic groups and/or subgroups in Swaziland include the Bembo, Bhembe, Dladla, Fakude, Gama, Gwebu, Hlatshwako, Hlophe, Kubonye, Mabuza, Madonsela, Magagula, Mhlanga (Mahlangu), Makhubu, Malindza, Manana (Manama), Manyatsi, Maphosa, Mashinini, Masilela, Masuku, Matsebula, Mavuso, Maziya, Mhlanga (Mhlangu), Mncina, Mnisi, Motsa, Msimango, Mtsettfwaa, Ndwandwe, Ngcomphalala, Nguni, Ngwenya, Ngcomphalala, Nhlengetfwa, Nkambule, Nkonyane, Pedi (Bapedi), Shabalala, Shabanga (Shabangu), Shangaan (Changane, Machangana), Shongwe, Sifundza, Sihlongonyane, Simelane, Tabetse, Thabede, Tsela, Twala, Vilakati, and Zwane peoples.

TANZANIA

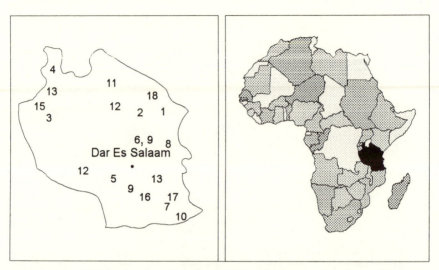

1. Chagga, 2. Gogo, 3. Ha, 4. Haya, 5. Hehe, 6. Kaguru, 7. Kutu, 8. Kwere, 9. Luguru, 10. Makoa and Makonde, 11. Masai, 12. Ngulu, 13. Sagara, 14. Shirazi (Zanizbar), 15. Sukuma, 16. Vidunda, 17. Zaramo, 18. Zigula and Kamba, etc.

Tanzania has a population of 20,600,000 (mid-1998 PRB est.) spread over the mainland and the Islands of Zanzibar and Pemba. The population of the mainland is 99% native African belonging to over 100 ethnic groups and 1% Asian, especially Arab and Persian, and European. Zanzibar's and Pemba's population, however, is mixed comprised of African, Arab, Indian, Persian, European and Somali minorities.

Tanzania's mainland major groups include the Chagga (Chaga), Gogo, Ha, Haya, Hehe, Kaguru (Kagulu), Kutu, Kwere (Mwere), Luguru, Makoa (Makua), Makonde (Maconde), Masai (Maasai/Maasi), Mbugwe, Ngulu (Nguru), Sagara (Saghala), Sukuma, Zaramo (Zalamo), and Zigalu (Zigula). Its islands, however, support one major ethnic group, namely, the Shirazi (Mbwera) people who are of Persian background.

The Chagga people live in Tanzania's northeastern regions, notably on the slopes of Mt. Kilimanjaro; the Gogo and Mbugwe east and south of

Lake Manyara in the central highlands of the country; the Ha in the areas between Lake Tanganyika and Lake Victoria; the Haya in the areas west of Lake Victoria; the Hehe in the Iringa region in the south-central parts of the country; the Kaguru, Luguru and Ngulu in the coastal mountainous areas; the Kutu, Kwere, Sagara, Zaramo, and Zigalu in the coastal lowlands; the Makoa and Makonde in the southeastern areas; the Sukuma in its northern and western lands; and the Masai in the Great Rift Valley in the northern regions of the country.

Smaller Tanzanian ethnic groups and/or subgroups include the Alagwa, Anza, Arusha, Iambi, Iramba, Isanzu, Barabaig (Datog), Baraguyu (Kwavi, Lumbwa, Liokpoli), Baturi, Bemba, Bena, Bende, Biru, Bondei, Burunge (Burungi), Chonyi, Chuka, Digo, Doe, Dorobo (Nderebe, Ndorobo), Duruma, Fipa, Fungwe, Gala, Galaganza, Ganda, Giriyama (Giriama, Giryama), Gorowa, Guruka, Ha, Hadimu, Hadza (Hadsa, Hadzapi, Hatsa, Kambe, Kauma, Kindiga, Tindiga), Hangaza, Haya, Hemba (Bahemba), Henga, Holoholo, Iambi, Igembi, Igoji, Ihanzu, Ikizu, Ikoma, Imenti, Iramba, Irambi, Irangi, Iraqw, Irwana, Isanzu (Izansu), Issenye, Jibana, Jiji, Jita, Kaguru, Kamanga, Kamba, Kami, Kara, Kauma, Kerere (Kerewe), Kilinde, Kimbu, Kinga, Kiturika, Konongo (Kinongo), Kukwe, Kuria (Kulya, Tende), Kutu, Lambya, Lomwe (Acilowe, Alomwe, Nguru), Luguru (Lugulu), Machinga, Makua, Malila, Manyima, Matambwe (Matumbi), Matengo, Mwamba, Mawanda (Mwanda), Mawia (Mavia, Mawi), Mbugu, Mbunga, Mbwila, Meru (Ngaa), Mijikenda, Mintini, Muthambi, Mwamba, Mwani, Mwera (Mwere), Mwimbi, Nankwili, Nata, Ndali, Ndamba, Ndendeule, Ndengereko (Ndengeleko), Ndonde, Ngindo (Ngindu), Ngonde, Ngoni (Angoni, Anguni, Mangoni, Nguni, Wangoni), Nguruimi, Nilyamba, Nthali, Nwenshi, Nyagtwa, Nyakyusa (Niabiussa, Sochile, Sokile), Nyambo, Nyamwanga, Nyamwezi (Banyamwezi, People of the Moon), Nyasa, Nyaturu, Nyiha, Nyika, Panga, Pare (Asu), Pemba, Pempa, Pimbwe, Pogoro (Pogolu), Poroto, Rabai, Rangi (Rongo), Redi, Ribe, Rufiji, Rukwa, Rungu, Rungwa, Ruri, Rwanda, Safwa, Sagara (Saghala), Sandawe, Sangu, Segeju, Selya, Shambaa (Sambaa, Shambala), Sisya, Songo, Songwe, Sonjo, Sowe, Suba, Subi (Shubi), Sukwa, Sumbwa, Tabwa, Tambo, Tatoga, Taveta, Tigania, Tongwe, Tumbatu, Turu (Rimi), Vemba, Vidunda, Vinza, Wandya (Wanda), Wanji, Wenya, Winamwange, Wiwa, Wungu, Yanzi, Zanaki, Ziba, Zigua, and Zinza peoples.

TOGO

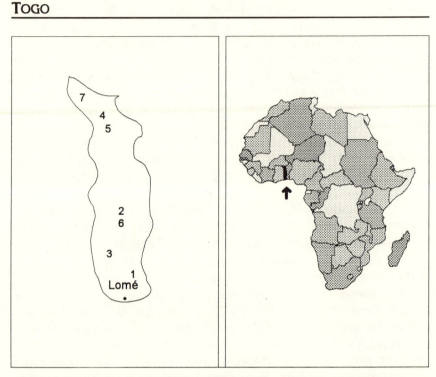

1. Aizo, 2. Akposo, 3. Ewe, 4. Dogamba, 5. Kilanga, 6. Mina, 7. Kabre, etc.

The Republic of Togo supports an ethnically heterogeneous society. Over 99% of its population of 4,900,000 (mid-1998 PRB est.) is made-up of 37 African ethnic groups the major ones of which are the Dogamba (Dagomba), a Molé-Dagbane group, Kilanga, Ewe (Ehoué, Eibe, Ephe, Krepe, Krepi), Mina (Ana, Ané, or Fante-Ane), an Ewe group, and Kabré (Cabrai, Kabure, Kaure). The rest of the population (less than 1%) represents non-African communities, especially expatriates of European and Syrian-Lebanese background.

The Ewe are concentrated in the southern regions of the country; the Aizo, a Fon subgroup, in its southeastern regions; the Akposo and Mina in its central regions; and the Dogamba and Kabre in its northern ones.

Smaller ethnic groups and/or subgroups in Togo include the Adele, Adja (Aja), Agnagan, Ahoulan, Aizo, Akebou, Akpafu, Akposo (Akposso), Anlo, Atwode (Achode, Atyoti), Avatime, Bago, Bariba (Batonu, Bargu, Barba, Borgowa, Batomba, Botombu, Batonun), Basari (Bassari, Basare, Kyamba, Tchamba), Bassila, Berba, Bimoba (Bimawba, B'Moba, Moab, Moba, Mwan), Bowli, Buem (Boem), Calo, Chokossi (Chakossi, Kyokosi, Kyokoshi, Tschokossi, Tyokossi), Dagari, Delo, Dendi (Dandi, Dandawa), Dompago, Dye, Fon, Ga (Gamashie), Ge, Gonja, Guemenu, Gurma (Gourmantché), Ho, Ife, Isa, Kabiye, Kebu, Kilanga, Konkomba (Komba), Kyamba (Tchamba), Kotokoli (Chaucho, Cotocoli, Tem, Temba), Lama, Lan-mba (Lamba), Likpe, Lobi, Logba, Lolobi, Losso, Lukpa, Mahi, Maxe, Mina (Popo), Mossi (Molé, Moshi), Nagot, Nambali, Nankana, Natimba, Naudeba, Ngangan, Niendé, Nkonya, Nyangbo (Nyanga, Nyango, Yagbum), Ouatchi, Pila-Pila, Pla, Similsi, Somba (Tamberma), Soruba, Tafi, Tenkodogo (Tengkedogo), Wala (Oule, Walba, Walo, Wilé), and Woaba peoples.

TUNISIA

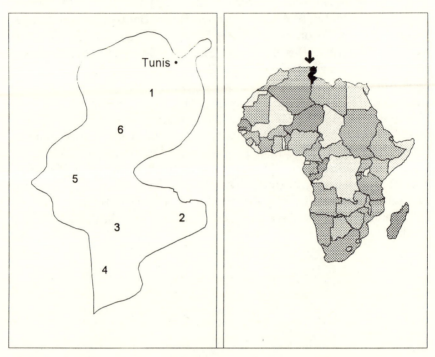

1. Arab, 2. Berber, 3. Iforas, 4. Kel Ahaggar, 5. Marazig, 6. Nemenche, etc.

Tunisia's population consists of essentially four major ethnic groups, namely, Arab, Berber, mixed Arab-Berber or Arabized Berber, and European. It has a population of 9,500,000 (mid-1998 PRB est.) of which 98% is Arab, 1% Berber, and 1% European and other. The Arab population is highly concentrated along the coastal areas of the country, whereas the Berber population in its western and southern areas. Europeans – who are essentially of French, Italian and/or Maltese background are found in the country's coastal cities and other urbanized centers.

UGANDA

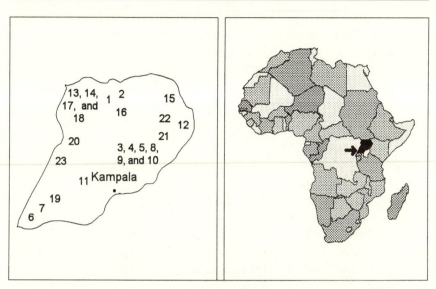

1. Acholi, 2. Alur, 3. Baamba, 4. Bagisu, 5. Bagwere, 6. Bakiga, 7. Bakonjo,
8. Banyoli, 9. Basamia, 10. Bagwe, 11. Ganda, 12. Gisu, 13. Jonam,
14. Kakwa, 15. Karamojong, 16. Lango (Langi), 17. Lugbara, 18. Madi,
19. Nkole, 20. Nyoro, 21. Soga, 22. Teso (Iteso), 23. Toro, etc.

The Ugandan population of about 21,000,000 (mid-1998 PRB est.) is 99% African and 1% Arab, Indian, and European, notably of the United Kingdom. Its African population supports many ethnic groups, including the Acholi (Acoli), Alur, Baamba, Bagisu, Bagwere, Bakiga, Bakonjo, Banyoli, Basamia, Bagwe, Ganda, Gisu (Bageshu, Bagish, Bagisu, Geshu, Gishu, Lamasaba, Masaba, Sokwia), Jonam, Kakwa, Karamojong (Karimojon), Lango (Langi), Lugbara, Madi, Nkole (Nyankole, Nyankore, Runyankore), Nyoro (Banyoro, Runyoro), Soga (Basoga, Lusoga), Teso (Elgumi, Iteso, Itesyo, Wamia), and Toro (Rutooro, Rutoro). Of these, the Ganda is the largest group followed by the Teso, Nkole and Soga, respectively.

The Acholi, Alur, Jonam and Lango people are concentrated in the north-central and northwestern areas of the country; the Karamojong and Teso in its eastern regions; the Kakwa, Lugbara and Madi in the areas north of the West Nile province as well as those along its borders with the Sudan and Zaire; the Bagisu, Bagwere, Banyoli, Basamia, and Bagwe in its southeastern regions; the Bakiga in its southwestern regions; and the Baamba and Bakonjo in its western regions.

Smaller Ugandan ethnic groups and/or subgroups include the Alur, Baka, Bakhayo (a Luhya subgroup), Bakiga, Balese, Bari, Bokora, Bongo, Budu, Bukusu, Bwisi (Lubwisi), Dodo (Dodoth, Dotho), Dongiro (Donyiro), Eyan, Gwere (Bagwere, Lugwere), Hima, Ik (Tueso), Iru, Issuka, Jaluo, Jie, Jiji, Jonam, Kabra, Kakwa, Kebu, Kedi, Kenyi (Lukenyi), Khayo, Kiga (Rukiga), Kisa, Kuku, Kuman (Kumam), Kupsabiny, Labwor, Latuka, Logit, Logo, Luluba, Luo (Lwoo), Mamvu, Mandari, Mangbetu, Mangutu, Marach, Maragoli, Marama, Matheniko, Mbo, Mening, Moyo, Mundu (Mundo), Ndaka, Nubian, Nyakwai, Nyala, Nyeyu, Nyole (Lunyole), Nyore, Nyuli, Ogoko, Okebu, Okollo, Oyuwi, Padhola, Paluo, Palwol, Pei, Pere, Pokot (Suk), Rwanda, Samia, Sebei, Shilluk, Shisa, Tepeth, Teuso, Tiriki, Tachoni, Tsotse, Turkana, and Wanga peoples.

WESTERN SAHARA

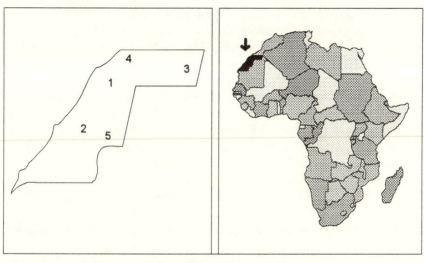

1. Imraguen, 2. Nemadi, 3. Regeibat, 4. Tekna, 5. Tiris, etc.

The population of Western Sahara is about 200,000 (mid-1998 PRB est.). Ethno-culturally, it is made up of Sahrawis, a sub-group of the *Beidan*, or Moors, a people of mixed Berber, Arab and black African groups. The Reguibat people represent the largest Berber group in Western Sahara.

Smaller Sahrawi ethnic groups and/or subgroups include Ahel Abdahou, Ahel Ahmed Ben Lahsen, Ahel Ali Oulad Soueied, Ahel Ali Ben Salem, Ahel Amar Barka, Ahel Atzman, Ahel Baba Ali, Ahel Baba Ammi, Ahel Ben Mehdi, Ahel Belal, Ahel Beilal, Ahel Bellao, Ahel Brahim Ou Daoud, Ahel Cheheb, Ahel Cheikh Mokhtar, Ahel Cheikh Ma El-Ainin, Ahel Daddah, Ahl Dekhil, Ahl Delimi, Ahel Dera, Ahel El-Hadj, Ahel Esbweir, Ahel Faki Ben Salah, Ahel Faqir Breika, Ahel Haioun, Ahel Lagoueyed, Ahel Lemjed, Ahel Meiara, Ahel Mohammed Ben Brahim, Ahel Mohammed Ben Sied, Ahel Qadi, Ahl Rachid, Ahl Salem, Ahel Sidi Abdallah Ben Mousa, Ahel Sidi Ahmed Ben Yahya, Ahel Sidi Amar, Ahel Taleb Hamad, Ahl Tenakha, Ait Atman, Ait Jmel, Ait Lahsen, Ait Ould Said, Ait Oussa, Arosien, Ait Said, Asi Moussa ouled Ali, Azouafid,

Chehagfa, Echtouka, El-Amamria, El-Beyed, El-Gherraba, El-Grona, El-Guerah, Embouat, Filala (Chorfa, Shurafa), Foqra, Fouikat, Id Ahmed, Id Brahim, Id Daoud Ou Abdallah, Injouren, Izarguien, Jenha, Khanoueh, Laouaid, Lahouareth, Lahseinat, Laiaicha, Lebouihat (El-Boihat), Lemiar, Lemnasra, Lemouissat, Lemrasguia, Lidadsa, Mejat, Menasir (Lemanisir), Mesida, Nemadi, Oulad Ali, Oulad Ali Serg, Oulad Assouss, Oulad Ba Aaisha, Oulad Ba Amar, Oulad Ba Brahim, Oulad Ba Moussa, Oulad Baggar, Ouled Ben Hossein, Oulad Borhim, Oulad Bou Sbaa, Oulad Brahim, Oulad Cheikh, Oulad Daoud, Oulad Delim, Oulad El-Hadj Ben Demouiss, Oulad El-Qadi, Oulad Hameida, Oulad Hossein, Oulad Khalifa, Oulad Khaliga, Oulad Khelaif, Oulad Lahsen, Oulad Mohammed Aidi, Oulad Moueya, Oulad Moumen, Oulad Sidi Ahmed Filali, Oulad Sidi Bou Mehdi, Oulad Sidi Djemma, Oulad Sidi Mohammed Ben Demouiss (Demouissat), Oulad Moussa, Oulad Souleiman, Oulad Taleb, Oulad Tegueddi, Oulad Tidrarin, Reguibat (Regeibat), Rema, Rouimiat, Seddagha, Selalka, Serahena, Souāid, Tekna, Taoubalt (Chorafa), Thaalat, Tiris, and Yagout peoples.

TANZANIA

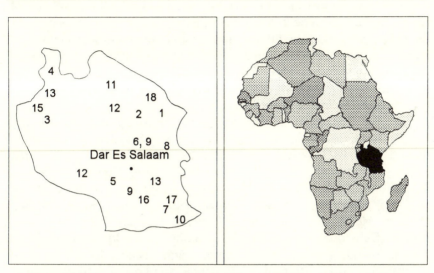

1. Chagga, 2. Gogo, 3. Ha, 4. Haya, 5. Hehe, 6. Kaguru, 7. Kutu, 8. Kwere, 9. Luguru, 10. Makoa and Makonde, 11. Masai, 12. Ngulu, 13. Sagara, 14. Shirazi (Zanizbar), 15. Sukuma, 16. Vidunda, 17. Zaramo, 18. Zigula and Kamba, etc.

Tanzania has a population of 20,600,000 (mid-1998 PRB est.) spread over the mainland and the Islands of Zanzibar and Pemba. The population of the mainland is 99% native African belonging to over 100 ethnic groups and 1% Asian, especially Arab and Persian, and European. Zanzibar's and Pemba's population, however, is mixed comprised of African, Arab, Indian, Persian, European and Somali minorities.

Tanzania's mainland major groups include the Chagga (Chaga), Gogo, Ha, Haya, Hehe, Kaguru (Kagulu), Kutu, Kwere (Mwere), Luguru, Makoa (Makua), Makonde (Maconde), Masai (Maasai/Maasi), Mbugwe, Ngulu (Nguru), Sagara (Saghala), Sukuma, Zaramo (Zalamo), and Zigalu (Zigula). Its islands, however, support one major ethnic group, namely, the Shirazi (Mbwera) people who are of Persian background.

The Chagga people live in Tanzania's northeastern regions, notably on the slopes of Mt. Kilimanjaro; the Gogo and Mbugwe east and south of

Lake Manyara in the central highlands of the country; the Ha in the areas between Lake Tanganyika and Lake Victoria; the Haya in the areas west of Lake Victoria; the Hehe in the Iringa region in the south-central parts of the country; the Kaguru, Luguru and Ngulu in the coastal mountainous areas; the Kutu, Kwere, Sagara, Zaramo, and Zigalu in the coastal lowlands; the Makoa and Makonde in the southeastern areas; the Sukuma in its northern and western lands; and the Masai in the Great Rift Valley in the northern regions of the country.

Smaller Tanzanian ethnic groups and/or subgroups include the Alagwa, Anza, Arusha, Iambi, Iramba, Isanzu, Barabaig (Datog), Baraguyu (Kwavi, Lumbwa, Liokpoli), Baturi, Bemba, Bena, Bende, Biru, Bondei, Burunge (Burungi), Chonyi, Chuka, Digo, Doe, Dorobo (Nderebe, Ndorobo), Duruma, Fipa, Fungwe, Gala, Galaganza, Ganda, Giriyama (Giriama, Giryama), Gorowa, Guruka, Ha, Hadimu, Hadza (Hadsa, Hadzapi, Hatsa, Kambe, Kauma, Kindiga, Tindiga), Hangaza, Haya, Hemba (Bahemba), Henga, Holoholo, Iambi, Igembi, Igoji, Ihanzu, Ikizu, Ikoma, Imenti, Iramba, Irambi, Irangi, Iraqw, Irwana, Isanzu (Izansu), Issenye, Jibana, Jiji, Jita, Kaguru, Kamanga, Kamba, Kami, Kara, Kauma, Kerere (Kerewe), Kilinde, Kimbu, Kinga, Kiturika, Konongo (Kinongo), Kukwe, Kuria (Kulya, Tende), Kutu, Lambya, Lomwe (Acilowe, Alomwe, Nguru), Luguru (Lugulu), Machinga, Makua, Malila, Manyima, Matambwe (Matumbi), Matengo, Mwamba, Mawanda (Mwanda), Mawia (Mavia, Mawi), Mbugu, Mbunga, Mbwila, Meru (Ngaa), Mijikenda, Mintini, Muthambi, Mwamba, Mwani, Mwera (Mwere), Mwimbi, Nankwili, Nata, Ndali, Ndamba, Ndendeule, Ndengereko (Ndengeleko), Ndonde, Ngindo (Ngindu), Ngonde, Ngoni (Angoni, Anguni, Mangoni, Nguni, Wangoni), Nguruimi, Nilyamba, Nthali, Nwenshi, Nyagtwa, Nyakyusa (Niabiussa, Sochile, Sokile), Nyambo, Nyamwanga, Nyamwezi (Banyamwezi, People of the Moon), Nyasa, Nyaturu, Nyiha, Nyika, Panga, Pare (Asu), Pemba, Pempa, Pimbwe, Pogoro (Pogolu), Poroto, Rabai, Rangi (Rongo), Redi, Ribe, Rufiji, Rukwa, Rungu, Rungwa, Ruri, Rwanda, Safwa, Sagara (Saghala), Sandawe, Sangu, Segeju, Selya, Shambaa (Sambaa, Shambala), Sisya, Songo, Songwe, Sonjo, Sowe, Suba, Subi (Shubi), Sukwa, Sumbwa, Tabwa, Tambo, Tatoga, Taveta, Tigania, Tongwe, Tumbatu, Turu (Rimi), Vemba, Vidunda, Vinza, Wandya (Wanda), Wanji, Wenya, Winamwange, Wiwa, Wungu, Yanzi, Zanaki, Ziba, Zigua, and Zinza peoples.

TOGO

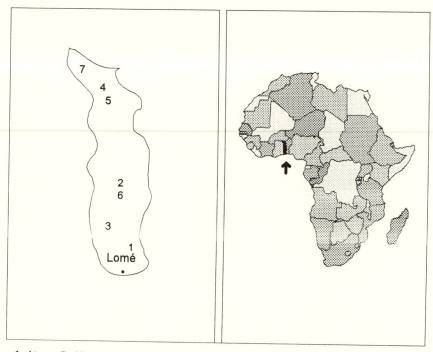

1. Aizo, 2. Akposo, 3. Ewe, 4. Dogamba, 5. Kilanga, 6. Mina, 7. Kabre, etc.

The Republic of Togo supports an ethnically heterogeneous society. Over 99% of its population of 4,900,000 (mid-1998 PRB est.) is made-up of 37 African ethnic groups the major ones of which are the Dogamba (Dagomba), a Molé-Dagbane group, Kilanga, Ewe (Ehoué, Eibe, Ephe, Krepe, Krepi), Mina (Ana, Ané, or Fante-Ane), an Ewe group, and Kabré (Cabrai, Kabure, Kaure). The rest of the population (less than 1%) represents non-African communities, especially expatriates of European and Syrian-Lebanese background.

The Ewe are concentrated in the southern regions of the country; the Aizo, a Fon subgroup, in its southeastern regions; the Akposo and Mina in its central regions; and the Dogamba and Kabre in its northern ones.

Smaller ethnic groups and/or subgroups in Togo include the Adele, Adja (Aja), Agnagan, Ahoulan, Aizo, Akebou, Akpafu, Akposo (Akposso), Anlo, Atwode (Achode, Atyoti), Avatime, Bago, Bariba (Batonu, Bargu, Barba, Borgowa, Batomba, Botombu, Batonun), Basari (Bassari, Basare, Kyamba, Tchamba), Bassila, Berba, Bimoba (Bimawba, B'Moba, Moab, Moba, Mwan), Bowli, Buem (Boem), Calo, Chokossi (Chakossi, Kyokosi, Kyokoshi, Tschokossi, Tyokossi), Dagari, Delo, Dendi (Dandi, Dandawa), Dompago, Dye, Fon, Ga (Gamashie), Ge, Gonja, Guemenu, Gurma (Gourmantché), Ho, Ife, Isa, Kabiye, Kebu, Kilanga, Konkomba (Komba), Kyamba (Tchamba), Kotokoli (Chaucho, Cotocoli, Tem, Temba), Lama, Lan-mba (Lamba), Likpe, Lobi, Logba, Lolobi, Losso, Lukpa, Mahi, Maxe, Mina (Popo), Mossi (Molé, Moshi), Nagot, Nambali, Nankana, Natimba, Naudeba, Ngangan, Niendé, Nkonya, Nyangbo (Nyanga, Nyango, Yagbum), Ouatchi, Pila-Pila, Pla, Similsi, Somba (Tamberma), Soruba, Tafi, Tenkodogo (Tengkedogo), Wala (Oule, Walba, Walo, Wilé), and Woaba peoples.

TUNISIA

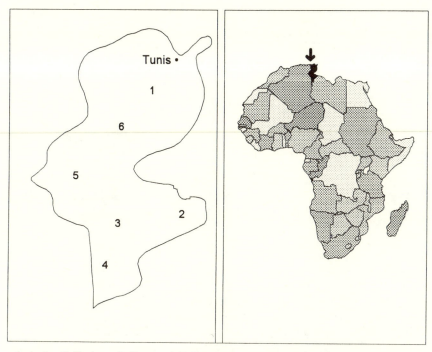

1. Arab, 2. Berber, 3. Iforas, 4. Kel Ahaggar, 5. Marazig, 6. Nemenche, etc.

Tunisia's population consists of essentially four major ethnic groups, namely, Arab, Berber, mixed Arab-Berber or Arabized Berber, and European. It has a population of 9,500,000 (mid-1998 PRB est.) of which 98% is Arab, 1% Berber, and 1% European and other. The Arab population is highly concentrated along the coastal areas of the country, whereas the Berber population in its western and southern areas. Europeans – who are essentially of French, Italian and/or Maltese background are found in the country's coastal cities and other urbanized centers.

UGANDA

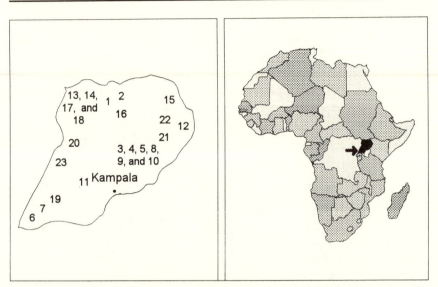

1. Acholi, 2. Alur, 3. Baamba, 4. Bagisu, 5. Bagwere, 6. Bakiga, 7. Bakonjo,
8. Banyoli, 9. Basamia, 10. Bagwe, 11. Ganda, 12. Gisu, 13. Jonam,
14. Kakwa, 15. Karamojong, 16. Lango (Langi), 17. Lugbara, 18. Madi,
19. Nkole, 20. Nyoro, 21. Soga, 22. Teso (Iteso), 23. Toro, etc.

The Ugandan population of about 21,000,000 (mid-1998 PRB est.) is 99% African and 1% Arab, Indian, and European, notably of the United Kingdom. Its African population supports many ethnic groups, including the Acholi (Acoli), Alur, Baamba, Bagisu, Bagwere, Bakiga, Bakonjo, Banyoli, Basamia, Bagwe, Ganda, Gisu (Bageshu, Bagish, Bagisu, Geshu, Gishu, Lamasaba, Masaba, Sokwia), Jonam, Kakwa, Karamojong (Karimojon), Lango (Langi), Lugbara, Madi, Nkole (Nyankole, Nyankore, Runyankore), Nyoro (Banyoro, Runyoro), Soga (Basoga, Lusoga), Teso (Elgumi, Iteso, Itesyo, Wamia), and Toro (Rutooro, Rutoro). Of these, the Ganda is the largest group followed by the Teso, Nkole and Soga, respectively.

The Acholi, Alur, Jonam and Lango people are concentrated in the north-central and northwestern areas of the country; the Karamojong and Teso in its eastern regions; the Kakwa, Lugbara and Madi in the areas north of the West Nile province as well as those along its borders with the Sudan and Zaire; the Bagisu, Bagwere, Banyoli, Basamia, and Bagwe in its southeastern regions; the Bakiga in its southwestern regions; and the Baamba and Bakonjo in its western regions.

Smaller Ugandan ethnic groups and/or subgroups include the Alur, Baka, Bakhayo (a Luhya subgroup), Bakiga, Balese, Bari, Bokora, Bongo, Budu, Bukusu, Bwisi (Lubwisi), Dodo (Dodoth, Dotho), Dongiro (Donyiro), Eyan, Gwere (Bagwere, Lugwere), Hima, Ik (Tueso), Iru, Issuka, Jaluo, Jie, Jiji, Jonam, Kabra, Kakwa, Kebu, Kedi, Kenyi (Lukenyi), Khayo, Kiga (Rukiga), Kisa, Kuku, Kuman (Kumam), Kupsabiny, Labwor, Latuka, Logit, Logo, Luluba, Luo (Lwoo), Mamvu, Mandari, Mangbetu, Mangutu, Marach, Maragoli, Marama, Matheniko, Mbo, Mening, Moyo, Mundu (Mundo), Ndaka, Nubian, Nyakwai, Nyala, Nyeyu, Nyole (Lunyole), Nyore, Nyuli, Ogoko, Okebu, Okollo, Oyuwi, Padhola, Paluo, Palwol, Pei, Pere, Pokot (Suk), Rwanda, Samia, Sebei, Shilluk, Shisa, Tepeth, Teuso, Tiriki, Tachoni, Tsotse, Turkana, and Wanga peoples.

WESTERN SAHARA

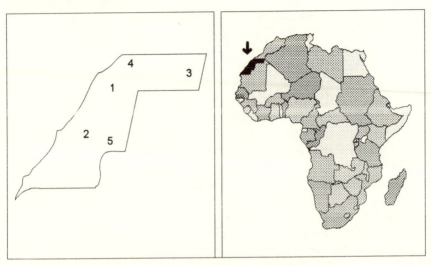

1. Imraguen, 2. Nemadi, 3. Regeibat, 4. Tekna, 5. Tiris, etc.

The population of Western Sahara is about 200,000 (mid-1998 PRB est.). Ethno-culturally, it is made up of Sahrawis, a sub-group of the *Beidan,* or Moors, a people of mixed Berber, Arab and black African groups. The Reguibat people represent the largest Berber group in Western Sahara.

Smaller Sahrawi ethnic groups and/or subgroups include Ahel Abdahou, Ahel Ahmed Ben Lahsen, Ahel Ali Oulad Soueied, Ahel Ali Ben Salem, Ahel Amar Barka, Ahel Atzman, Ahel Baba Ali, Ahel Baba Ammi, Ahel Ben Mehdi, Ahel Belal, Ahel Beilal, Ahel Bellao, Ahel Brahim Ou Daoud, Ahel Cheheb, Ahel Cheikh Mokhtar, Ahel Cheikh Ma El-Ainin, Ahel Daddah, Ahl Dekhil, Ahl Delimi, Ahel Dera, Ahel El-Hadj, Ahel Esbweir, Ahel Faki Ben Salah, Ahel Faqir Breika, Ahel Haioun, Ahel Lagoueyed, Ahel Lemjed, Ahel Meiara, Ahel Mohammed Ben Brahim, Ahel Mohammed Ben Sied, Ahel Qadi, Ahl Rachid, Ahl Salem, Ahel Sidi Abdallah Ben Mousa, Ahel Sidi Ahmed Ben Yahya, Ahel Sidi Amar, Ahel Taleb Hamad, Ahl Tenakha, Ait Atman, Ait Jmel, Ait Lahsen, Ait Ould Said, Ait Oussa, Arosien, Ait Said, Asi Moussa ouled Ali, Azouafid,

Chehagfa, Echtouka, El-Amamria, El-Beyed, El-Gherraba, El-Grona, El-Guerah, Embouat, Filala (Chorfa, Shurafa), Foqra, Fouikat, Id Ahmed, Id Brahim, Id Daoud Ou Abdallah, Injouren, Izarguien, Jenha, Khanoueh, Laouaid, Lahouareth, Lahseinat, Laiaicha, Lebouihat (El-Boihat), Lemiar, Lemnasra, Lemouissat, Lemrasguia, Lidadsa, Mejat, Menasir (Lemanisir), Mesida, Nemadi, Oulad Ali, Oulad Ali Serg, Oulad Assouss, Oulad Ba Aaisha, Oulad Ba Amar, Oulad Ba Brahim, Oulad Ba Moussa, Oulad Baggar, Ouled Ben Hossein, Oulad Borhim, Oulad Bou Sbaa, Oulad Brahim, Oulad Cheikh, Oulad Daoud, Oulad Delim, Oulad El-Hadj Ben Demouiss, Oulad El-Qadi, Oulad Hameida, Oulad Hossein, Oulad Khalifa, Oulad Khaliga, Oulad Khelaif, Oulad Lahsen, Oulad Mohammed Aidi, Oulad Moueya, Oulad Moumen, Oulad Sidi Ahmed Filali, Oulad Sidi Bou Mehdi, Oulad Sidi Djemma, Oulad Sidi Mohammed Ben Demouiss (Demouissat), Oulad Moussa, Oulad Souleiman, Oulad Taleb, Oulad Tegueddi, Oulad Tidrarin, Reguibat (Regeibat), Rema, Rouimiat, Seddagha, Selalka, Serahena, Souāid, Tekna, Taoubalt (Chorafa), Thaalat, Tiris, and Yagout peoples.

ZAIRE

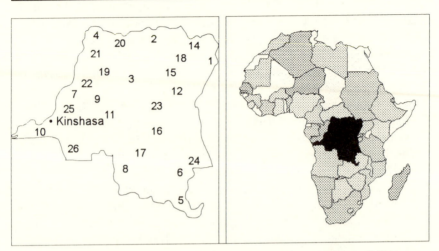

1. Alur, 2. Azende, 3. Bambole, 4. Banda, 5. Baushi, 6. Bemba, 7. Boma,
8. Chokwe, 9. Ekonda, 10. Kongo, 11. Kuba, 12. Kumu, 13. Kwese, 14. Logo,
15. Lombi, 16. Luba, 17. Lunda, 18. Mangbetu, 19. Mongo, 20. Ngbandi,
21. Ngombe, 22. Sangele, 23. Suku, 24. Tabwa, 25. Teke, 26. Yaka, etc.

Zaire, now the Democratic Republic of The Congo, supports over 200
African ethnic groups, the majority of which are Bantu. Of these groups,
the Bantu Kongo (Bacongo, Bakongo, Bandibu, Congo, Koongo), Luba
(Baluba, Baluba-Hemba, Baluba-Samba), Lunda (Alund, Arunde, Balonde,
Balunda, Lounda, Luntu, Malhundo, Valunda), and Mongo (Mono-
Nkundo), together with the Hamitic Azende (Azandé, Zande) and
Mangbetu peoples comprise about 45% of the country's total population
of 49,000,000 (mid-1998 PRB est.).

The Kongo are Zaire's largest group, but also live in the southern
regions of both the Congo Republic and the Central African Republic as
well as in northern Angola. The Luba are concentrated in the areas
between the Kasai River and Mbuji-Mayi in the west to the Lualaba and
Luffira rivers in the southeast, whereas the Mongo live south of the Middle
Congo River, notably between the Lulonga River in the north and the

Sankuru River in the south. The Azende and Mangbetu peoples are concentrated in the northern and northeastern regions of the country. The Lunda are concentrated in the Shaba region of the country, whereas the Chokwe (Batshokwe) in its southeastern regions.

Smaller African Zairian ethnic groups and/or subgroups include the Abarambo, Aka, Alur, Amba, Anza (Asalampasu), Babole, Bakiga, Bakonjo, Bakuba (Kuba), Balese, Bali, Bambala, Bambole, Bandia (Bandiya), Bangala (Bangi), Bangou (Bango), Bangu-Bangu, Banziri, Bashi, Baushi, Bemba, Bembe, Bena, Binga, Binji (Mbagani), Binza, Bira, Boa, Boma (Baboma), Bombo, Bomitaba, Boshongo (Bushong), Bouraka, Boyo, Budu, Bwile, Chisinga, Chokwe (Batshokwe, Cokwe, Kioko, Quioco, Tschokwe), Dendi, Djatsi, Dokoa (Doko), Dondo (Badondo), Efe, Ekonda, Fuleru, Furiiru, Furu, Ga'anda (Mokar), Gbanziri, Gesera, Havu, Hemba (Bahemba), Hima, Hlophe, Hum (Humbe), Hunde, Hutu, Irébu, Iyembi, Kakwa, Kala, Kalundwe, Kamba, Kanioka, Kaonde (Bakahonde, Bakaonde, Kaundi, Kunda), Kasai Luba, Katanga, Kazembe, Kete, Kivu, Kiyaka, Komo, Konambembe, Konda, Kongo-Lali, Kongo-Sundi, Kote, Kougni, Kuba (Bakuba), Kumu (Bakumu), Kunda, Kusu (Bakusu), Kuyu (Kouyou), Kwese (Bakwese), Laka (Lao Habe, Lau), Lakundwe, Lali (Balili, Lari), Lamba, Langa, Leele, Lega, Lele, Lemba, Lembwe, Lendu (Lendo), Lengola, Lese, Lia, Linga, Lobala, Logo, Loi, Lokele, Lomatwa, Lombi, Luapala, Luba-Kasai, Luba-Shaba, Lugbara, Luimbe, Lulua (Luluwa), Lungu, Lunto, Luvale (Lovale, Lubale, Luena), Makere, Maku, Malele, Mamvu, Mangbetu, Mangutu, Maweka (Mawika), Mayombe (Maiombe), Mba, Mbaka, Mbala, Mbanza (Mbandja, Mbanja), Mbesa, Mbo, Mbochi, Mboli (Mbole), Mbowe, Mbuja, Mbun (Mboun), Mbuti (Bambuti), Metoko (Mitoko), Mfunu, Moma, Mpama, Mpasu, Mputu, Mundu (Mundo), Mushikongo (Muskikongo), Mvuba, Ndaka, Ndembu (Dembo, Mdembu, Ndembo), Ndengse, Ngala, Ngambaye, Ngandu, Ngbaga, Ngbandi, Nge-Nge, Ngengelle, Ngii, Ngiril, Ngombe, Ngongo (Bangongo), Njembe, Nkoye, Nku, Nkundo, Nkutshu, Ntandu, Ntomba (Ntombe), Nwenshi, Nyamwezi (Banyamwezi, Nyamwesi, People of the Moon), Nyanga, Nyindu, Okebu, Ooli, Padhola, Pande (Bapende, Pende), Panga (Pangwa), Pere, Pitsi, Poi, Pombo, Rwanda, Sabanga, Saka, Sakata, Salampaso, Sambala, Sanga (Basanga, Bosango, Sangha, Sango), Sengele (Basengele), Shi, Shikongo, Shila, So, Solongo (Basolongo, Basorongo), Songola, Songye,

Sosso, Sua, Suku (Basuku), Sundi, Tabwa (Batawa), Tanda, Tatsi, Teke (Bateke, Téké), Tetela (Batetela), Tio, Titu, Tumbwe, Tutsi, Twa, Tyo, Vili, Vungara, Wazimba, Woyo, Yaka (Bayaka), Yakoma, Yanzi (Yan), Yeke, Yela (Boyela), Yira (Nande), Yombe, Zela, Zigaba, Zimba (Wazimba), and Zombo peoples.

ZAMBIA

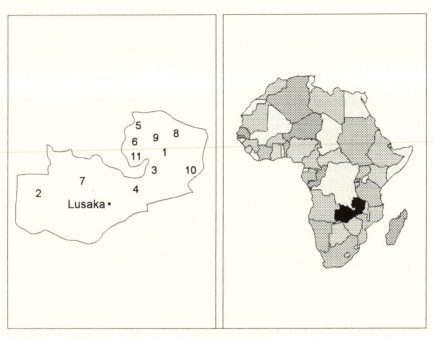

1. Ambo, 2. Anza, 3. Bemba, 4. Balamba, 5. Kaonde, 6. Luba, 7. Lunda,
8. Luvale, 9. Mambwe, 10. Tonga, 11. Tabwa, etc.

Zambia supports a population of 9,500,000 (mid-1998 PRB est.) 98.7% of which is African, 1.1% European, and 0.2% other. Its major African groups include the Ambo, Anza, Bemba (Awemba, Babemba, Wemba), Luba (Baluba), Lunda (Alund, Arunde, Balonde, Lounda, Luntu, Luvale (Lovale, Lubale, Luena), Malhundo, Valunda), Mambwe, and Tonga (Batonga).

The Ambo (Ovambo) people, a subgroup of the Chewa (Achewa, Ancheya, Cewa, Chua, Masheba), are concentrated in the eastern regions of Zambia; the Anza in its northwestern regions; the Luvale in its western and northwestern regions; the Bemba and Mambwe in its northeastern regions close to the country's borders with Tanzania and Zaire; the Luba and Lunda in its northern regions along the country's border with Zaire;

and the Tonga in its Northern Region, primarily in the vicinity of Lake Malawi.

Smaller Zambian ethnic groups and/or subgroups include the Aushi, Bisa, Botatwe, Bwile, Chikunda (Bachikunda, Chicunda, Cikunda), Chipeta (Achipeta), Chisinga (Cishinga), Chokwe (Cokwe, Kioko, Quioco, Tschokwe), Fipa, Fokeng, Fungwe, Hemba (Bahemba), Gowa (Goba), Gwembe, Henga, Ila, Imilanga Imilangu), Iwa (Mashukulumbwe), Kabende, Kamanga, Kaonde (Bakahonde, Bakaonde, Kaundi, Kunda), Katanga, Kazembe, Kololo, Koma, Kunda, Kwandi, Kwanga (Kwangwa, Makwanga), Lala, Lamba, Lambya, Lemba, Lenje (Lenge), Leya, Lima, Lozi (Balozi, Barotse, Barutze, Marotse, Mawika, Rotse, Rozi), Lunda, Luano, Luchazi (Lucazi, Luchatze), Lumbu, Lunda, Lundwe, Lungu, Luvale, Luyana, Lyuwa, Maganga (Makanga), Makoma, Malila, Mambari, Maravi (Marave), Mashashe (Mashasha), Mashi, Mbowe, Mbukushu, Mbunda, Mbwela (Lukolwe), Muemba, Mukulu, Mwanya (Mwenyi), Namwanga (Inamwanga), Ndali, Ndembu (Dembo, Mdembu, Ndembo), Ndundulu, Ngangela, Ngonde, Ngoni (Angoni, Anguni, Mangoni, Wangoni), Ngumbo, Nkoya (Mankoya), Nsenga, Nthali, Nwenshi, Nyanja (Anyanja, Nianja, Niassa, Wanyanja), Nyengo, Nyiha, Phoka, Sala, Senga, Shanjo, Shila, Shona (Chona, Karanga, Mashona, Vashona), Simaa, Sisya, Soli, Subiya (Subia), Swaka, Tabwa, Tambo, Toka, Totela, Tsaw, Tumbuka (Batumbuka, Matumboka, Tumbukwa), Unga, Ushi, Wandya (Wanda), Wenya, Winamwange, Wiwa, Yeke, and Yombe peoples.

ZIMBABWE

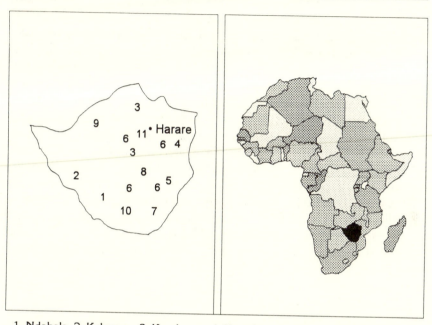

1. Ndebele, 2. Kalanga, 3. Korekore, 4. Manyika, 5. Ndau, 6. Rozwi,
7. Shangaan, 8. Shona, 9. Tonga, 10. Venda, 11. Zezuru, etc.

Zimbabwe has a population of 11,000,000 (mid-1998 PRB est.) of which 98% is African, 1% European, and 1% coloured (mixed race) and Asian. The African population belongs to a number of ethnic groups the most important of which are the Ndebele (17%); Shangaan (1%); Shona (77%); Tonga, also known as Batonga and Tsonga, (2%); Venda (1%); and other, including people of European background and Coloured.

The Shona (Chona, Karanga, Mashona, Vashona) people include such subgroups as the Abarue, Atewe, Banda, Chilendje, Chirumba, Chirware, Choa, Kalanga, Karanga, Korekore, Makate, Manyika (Manhica, Manyica), Marunga, Mavonde, Mucatu, Mwanya, Ndau, Nyampisi, Nyatanza, Rozwi (Rodzi), Tembo, and Zezuru. Likewise, the Ndebele (Amandebele, Matabele) people are concentrated in the southwestern regions of

Zimbabwe, the Shona in its central and central-eastern regions, the Tonga in its west-central areas, and the Venda and Shangaan in its southeastern lands along the country's border with South Africa.

Smaller groups and/or subgroups in Zimbabwe include the Abarue, Atewe, Banda, Barwe (Barue, Bargwe), Birwa (Babirwa), Budjga (Budga, Budja, Budya), Chilendje, Chirumba, Chive, Chiware, Chiwawa, Choa, Choko, Danda, Duma (Vaduma), Dumbuseya, Mfengu (Fingoe), Fwe, Gova, Govera, Griqua, Hera (Vahera), Hlengwe (Bahlengue, Hlengue), Jena, Kalanga (Bakalanga, kalaka, Vakalanga), Karanga (Vakaranga), Korekore, Lemba, Lilima, Makat (Makate), Manyica (Manhica, Manyika), Manzwa, Marunga, Maungwe, Mavonde, Mbire, Mucatu, Mwanya (Mwenyi), Ndau (Buzi, Vandau), Ngoni, Ngwato, Nhowe (Nhohwe, Vanhowe, Wanoe), Njanja (Vanjanja), Nyai (Banyai, Manyai, Vanyai), Nyampisi, Nyangurus, Nyanja (Anyanja, Nianja, Niassa, Wanyanja), Nyantaza, Nyubi, Nyungwe, Pfungwe, Rozvi (Barozwi, Rozvi, Varozvi, Varozwi), Shanga (Machangana), Shavasha, Talaote (Batalote, Batalowta, Talaota, Talowta), Tande, Tawara (Tavara), Tembo, Tsaw, Watombodji, Wazamoi, and Zezuru (Vazezuru) peoples.

PART FIVE

AFRICAN PEOPLES AND NATIONS

AFRICAN PEOPLES AND NATIONS

AATHI

The Aathi are an East African hunting people. Historical accounts suggest that they used to live in the Kiambu vicinity in what is presently modern Kenya. Also, they suggest that the ancestors of the Kikuyu people acquired land from the Aathi in exchange for goats sometime during the eighteenth century. The acquired properties were helpful to the gradual transformation of the Kikuyu from hunter-gatherers into horticultural people.[1]

ABA, see IBIBIO

ABABA, see ABABDA

ABABDA, see also BEJA

The Ababda (Ababa, 'Ababda) are an East African Muslim people. They are concentrated in the Eastern Desert of Egypt and northeastern regions of Sudan. The 'Ababda speak Arabic, and are one of the four main Beja groups.

ABABEMBA, see BEMBA

ABADJA

One of West Africa's Igbo subgroups. The Abadja, also spelled Abaja, are concentrated in the southern and southeastern regions of Nigeria, notably in the Gongola State.

ABAGISU, see LUHYA

ABAGUSII, see GUSII

ABAGWE, see LUHYA

ABAHANZA

One of East Africa's Hutu subgroups. The Abahanza are concentrated in Burundi. Groups of them, however, can also be found in adjoining countries.

ABAJA, see ABADJA

ABAJIJI

An East African Hutu subgroup. The Abajiji are concentrated in Burundi. Groups of them can also be found in neighboring countries.

ABAK, see IBIBIO

ABAKABRAS, see LUHYA

ABAKALIKI, see IGBO

ABAKAN, see KPAN

ABAKHAYO, see LUHYA

ABAKISA, see LUHYA

ABAKWARIGA

The common name of the Hausa-speaking Kutumbawa, Maguzawa and Gwandari peoples. The Aakwariga are a West African people. They are concentrated in the northwestern regions of Nigeria. Groups of them, however, can also be found in neighboring states.

ABALOGOLI, see LUHYA

ABALUHYA, see LUHYA

ABALUHYIA, see LUHYA

ABALUYIA, see LUHYA

ABAM

One of West Africa's Igbo subgroups. The Abam are concentrated in the southern and southeastern regions of Nigeria, notably in the Gongola State.

ABAMARACHI, see LUHYA

ABAMARAMA, see LUHYA

ABAM-OHAFFIA, see IGBO

ABANYALA, see LUHYA

ABANYOLE, see LUHYA

ABANYOM

One of West Africa's Bantu-speaking peoples. The Abanyom, also known as the Befun, live in Nigeria, primarily in the Cross River State.

ABANYORE, see LUHYA

ABANYULI, see LUHYA

ABARAMBO

These are one of the non-Bantu Sudanese ethnic minorities in Democratic Republic of the Congo (Zaire). Their main concentration is in the northern areas of the country, close to the border of Sudan. Their traditional religious beliefs of a supreme being and the power of ancestors and spirits within nature have been greatly affected by the introduction of Christianity and Islam. The exact numbers of Abarambo are not known, but they are believed to make up approximately 5-10% of Democratic Republic of the Congo (Zaire's) population. The Abarambo are an agriculturalist people.

ABARUE

The Abarue are one of Southern Africa's Shona subgroups. Their main concentrations are in Zimbabwe and Mozambique.

ABASAMIA, see LUHYA

ABASONGA, see LUHYA

ABASUBA

The Abasuba are an East African Bantu-speaking people. They live primarily in Kenya. Their neighbors are the Luo people.

ABATACHONI, see LUHYA

ABATSOTSO, see LUHYA

ABATUTSI, see TUTSI

ABAVUMA

An East African Hutu subgroup. The Abajiji live in Burundi and adjoining countries.

ABAWANGA, see LUHYA

ABBE

The Abbe, also known as the Abé and Abbey, are part of the Lagoon Cluster of peoples in the Ivory Coast. They are concentrated in the southwestern portion of this West African state and number over 85,000 people. Their neighbors include the Anyi, Ari, Attie, Baule and Ebrie peoples. The Abbe speak Kwa and their social organization is patrilineal. Fishing and agriculture are the main methods of subsistence among the Abbe and other peoples of the Lagoon Cluster.

The Abbe are divided into four tribes, each of which is governed by a chief who rules with the advice of a council of elders. None of the four tribes recognizes an overarching political authority for all groups. However, a class structure based on age was developed for the sole purpose of propagating a warrior class.

Traditional beliefs of the Abbe, as well as other peoples of the Lagoon Cluster, are extremely similar to those of the Akan peoples. There is a sky-god, similar to the Akan high god, and an earth god. An ancestor cult exists with greater emphasis on sorcery and shamanism. Shamans are well respected and even feared among the Lagoon peoples. They are attributed the power to heal, to have clairvoyant power and to predict the future.

ABBEY, see ABBE

ABDALLAB

An East African Arab people. The Abdallab live primarily in the central regions of the Republic of Sudan.

ABE, see ABBE

ABÉ, see ABBE

ABESUKHA, see LUHYA

ABETAKHO, see LUHYA

ABGAAL, see also SOMALI

An East African Somali group. The Abgaal (Abgal) are a subgroup of Hawiya, a major Somali tribe. The Hawiya groups are concentrated around Mogadishu, Somalia's capital, as well as in Somalia's southern and Kenya's northeastern regions.

ABGAL, see ABGAAL

ABIDJI

The Abidji, or Ari, which is what they call themselves, live northwest of the capital city of the Ivory Coast, Abidjan. They speak Agni and are a patrilineal tribe who, unlike other peoples of the Lagoon Cluster, concentrate only on farming. Exact numbers of the Abidji are not known. Their neighbors include the Abbe (Abe), Ajukru, Baule, Dida and Ebrie peoples.

Traditional religion of the Abidji is very similar to those other tribes in the Lagoon Cluster. It focuses on shamanism and sorcery with ancestor worship. Political power in Abidjii society lies with the chief, similar to that of the Akan peoples. No direct social hierarchy is known. Laws are made and enforced by the chief with direct cooperation from a council of elders.

ABINO, see ABINU

ABINU

One of West Africa's Yoruba subgroups. The Abinu, also spelled Abino, are concentrated in the western regions of Nigeria.

ABISSA

The Abissa are one of Chad's Bora Mabang-speaking peoples. They are a Maba subgroup. Like other Maba groups, they live primarily in the south-central Ouaddai region of the country.

ABO, see TOPOSA

ABON

The Abon, also known as the Abong, are a West African people. They are concentrated in the southeastern regions of Nigeria, notably in the Gongola State.

ABONG, see ABON

ABORA

The Abora, also spelled Abura, are a West African Twi-speaking people. They are a Fanti (Fante) subgroup in Ghana.

ABOU TELFAN

The Abou Telfan are one of Chad's ethnic groups in the Guera-Massif area. They reside in very mountainous terrain and have survived many violent invasions in the past. Their territory is a center of Christian missionary work.

ABRIWI

The Abriwi are a West African people. They are concentrated in the southern coastal areas of the Ivory Coast. Their neighbors include the Gagu, the Plawi and Tewi peoples.

ABRON, see AKAN

ABRONG, see AKAN

ABU'A

The Abu'a, also known as Abu'an, are a West African people. They are concentrated in the southernmost part of Nigeria. Their neighbors include the Edo, Efik-Ibibio, Igbo, Ijaw and Ogon peoples. Their language belongs to the Benue-Congo group of the Niger-Congo family of African languages.

ABU'AN, see ABU'A

ABU CHARIB, see ABU SHARIB

ABURA, see ABORA

ABU SEMEN

One of Chad's many ethnic groups. The Abu Semen are a Nilotic-speaking people.

ABU SHARIB

The Abusharib, also spelled Abu Charib and Abu Sharib, are a Central and East African Muslim people. They are concentrated in Chad and Sudan. The Abu Sharib are essentially pastoralists. They engage in raising livestock, including cattle, camels and goats.

ABUTIA, see EWE

ACERA, see KIKUYU

ACHIKOUYA

The Achikouya are a West Central African Bantu-speaking people. They are concentrated in the central areas of the Republic of Congo to the west of the Congo river. Their neighbors include the Fumbu, Sise and Teke peoples.

ACHOLI

The Acholi, also spelled Acoli and Acooli, are one of Uganda's and Sudan's ethnic minorities. In Uganda, they are concentrated in the north-central regions along the Ugandan-Sudanese borders, notably in the Gulu and Kitgum districts. In Sudan, they live primarily in the southern regions of the country. Their neighbors include the Alur, the Jie, the Karamoja (Karamojong), the Lango, the Madi, the Nyoro and the Paluo peoples. The Acholi speak Luo, a western Nilotic language, as well as Kiswahili and English. Their economic activity focuses on mixed farming, ironworking, animal husbandry and trade.

The Acholi society is patrilineal with a territorial aspect. The senior member of a patrilineage is regarded as the leader of the lineage. Traditionally, he exercised great control over all lineage land and other property. Marriage within a lineage was not permitted and the transfer of cattle from the groom's family to the bride's family was strictly practiced. This transfer of property reinforced the paternity of the children born to the wife. The exchange of property also included the practice of formal rituals.

Acholi political structure continues to be characterized by weak chiefships, the responsibilities of which are discharged with cooperation from lineage heads. Localized lineages continue to serve as the basic units of their society.

Formerly, the Acholi religious beliefs centered on three types of spirits (jogi; singular jok). "There were the spirits of known relatives, especially lineage ancestors; a second type was the nonancestral jok of the chiefdom as a whole. Spirits of both these types were generally beneficent... The third group of spirits were those of unknown persons and dangerous beasts; these were hostile, personified as ghosts, believed to cause sickness and other misfortunes, and dealt with by means of spirit possession."[2] Though Christianity has attracted converts, many Acholi continue to be impacted by these traditional beliefs. "Traditional beliefs... still persist, often meshed with Christian doctrine in complex ways."[3]

ACOLI, see **ACHOLI**

ACOOLI, see **ACHOLI**

ADA, see **KUTURMI**

ADAL, see **AFAR**

ADAMAUA

The Adamaua people are one of the Central African ethnic groups. They are concentrated in the north central regions of Cameroon. Their neighbors include the Chamba, Jukun, Kirdi, and Tang peoples.

ADANGME

A West African people. The Adangme, also known as Adampa, Adangbe and Dangme, are concentrated in the southern coastal regions of Ghana. Groups of them are also located in Togo. They speak the Kwa language. Their neighbors include the Akyem, Gã and Ewe peoples.

ADARAWA

The Adarawa are a West African Hausa people. They are concentrated in Niger and speak an Afro-Asiatic language. Their neighbors include the Fula, Hausa, Kurfei and Tazarawa peoples.

ADARE, see HARARI

ADDA, see IGBO

ADELE

The Adele are a West African people and one of Ghana's and Togo's ethnic minorities. They speak the Kwa language and live primarily in the southern regions of both countries. Their neighbors include the Akpose (Akposo), Atyuti, Kebu, Krachi, Tribu and Yoruba peoples.

ADHOLA, see PADHOLA

ADIOUKROU

The Adioukrou are also known as the Dabu or Bubari. They number about 30,000 and reside in the western regions of the Ivory Coast. The social structure, religion, and politics of the Adioukrou are quite similar to other groups of the Lagoon Cluster of West Africa. The Adioukrou are renowned for their extensive exploitation of the Ivory Coast's palm tree plantations.

ADJA, see also EWE and FON

These are one of the four major ethnic groups in Benin. The Adja, also known as the Aja, are related to Benin's largest group, the Fon, and are second largest group in the country after the Fon. Linguistically and culturally, they are also considered an Ewe group. The Adja are concentrated in the southern areas of Benin.

Prior to the colonial era, the Adja had a prosperous kingdom of their own which was renowned for its metal crafts. Subsequently, they got involved in the capture and sale of slaves to Europeans. Prior to falling to European rule, many of them were also sold into slavery.

ADRAR, see **TAUREG**

ADYUMBA

The Adyumba people are a West Central African ethnic group. They live in the Republic of Gabon, primarily in its western coastal regions. Their neighbors include the Mpongwe and Nkomi peoples.

AEMBA, see **BEMBA**

AFANGO, see **BIROM**

AFAR

The Afar, also called Adal, Danakil or Danaqla, are an East African people. They are concentrated in the Horn of Africa, especially in northeastern and southern Ethiopia, northwestern areas of Djibouti, and northern Somalia. In Ethiopia, they represent the sixth major ethnic group, accounting for 4% of the country's total population. In Djibouti, they are the second largest ethnic group after the Somali Issa people (60%), accounting for about 35% of the country's total population. Their neighbors include the Ittu, the Galla, the Saho, the Somali, the Wallo and the Yaju peoples. The Afar language is a northeastern African language akin to the Somali. It is a part of the Cushitic branch of the Hamito-Semitic family of African languages.

The Afar are predominantly a Muslim nomadic pastoralist people and their society is tribally organized along patrilineal kin groups. They are extremely proud of their cultural heritage and are highly individualistic.

Politically, the Afar people belong to three sultanates, each of which is headed by a sultan whose power is shared by a vizier and a tribal council. Economically, their main economic activities focus on herding, fishing and mining salt off the coast of the Red Sea. Their basic food comes from the animals that they herd and vegetables that are grown in small plots of fertile land or acquired through trade with their neighbors. Women are active in their society. They tend the sheep, cows and goats and look after the camp, whereas men attend to camels and donkeys, building tasks and dismantling the camp when moving to another grazing area.

The Afar society is divided into two main classes; the *Asaimara* (*Asahyammaras*) or red men and the *Adoimara* (*Adoyammaras*) or white men.[4] The *Asaimara* (reds) are "Descendants of the Yemenite Har-El-Mass," and the *Adoimara* (whites) are believed to be descendants of Arab patriarchs, the Halbay and the Ankala.[5] The former group comprises the landowning and titled nobles, whereas the latter is made up of tenants. In their turn, both groups are sub-divided into tribes and sub-tribes.

Traditional clothing includes a single white cloth that is wrapped around the waist and tied at the right hip. Called *sanafil*, this cloth stretches to the knee. The colors include white for men and brown for women.

The Afar love to adorn themselves with dye. Men cover their beards with *ghee* (butter), and women wear on their heads amulets and *sashes*.[6]

The Afar have a long history. Their ancestors migrated from Southern Arabia around 4000 B.C. In the course of their historical development, they had prosperous kingdoms that were able to defy Ethiopian attempts to subdue them, especially those of the Zagwe dynasty of the Agau in the late 13th century. In the 16th century, they were able not only to contain, but also to pose a serious threat to the very existence of the Ethiopian empire.[7] Under the leadership of Ahmad ben Ghazi (1506-1543), for example, in 1529, they not only succeeded in defeating the forces of the Ethiopian emperor, Lebna Dengel (1508-1540), but also placed most of the territory of the Ethiopian empire under Muslim control.[8]

The Afar's victory, however, ended in 1541, when the new Ethiopian emperor, Galawdewos (1540-1559) succeeded, with the help of the Portuguese, to defeat the Afar and to neutralize their threats for a long period of time.

AFATIME, see AVATIME

AFAWA

The Afawa people are one of the West and Central African ethnic groups. They are concentrated on the southwestern shores of Lake Chad. Their neighbors include the Kanuri, Shuwa, and Warjawa peoples.

AFENMAI, see ETSAKO

AFIPA, see FIPA

AFNU, see HAUSA

AFO

A West African people. The Afo are concentrated in central Nigeria. They speak a language that belongs to the Benue-Congo branch of the Niger-Congo family of African languages. Their neighbors include the Arago, Gbari, Gili, Gwandara, and Idoma peoples.

AFRIKANERS

Afrikaners are a white population of South Africa. They are descendants of Dutch farmers and German and French Huguenot settlers that colonized South Africa from the seventeenth century onward.[9] The first white settlement was established by the Dutch East India Company in the Cape of Good Hope in 1652 to provide a way station for its trading ships en route to and from Asia. By the end of the eighteenth century, the Afrikaners' colony supported about 15,000 people.

The Afrikaners, known also as Boers and Trekkers, tried to establish an independent republic of their own as early as 1705. Their effort was thwarted by British occupation of the colony in 1795 and Britain's subsequent permanent possession of the colony in 1814. From the 1830s to 1850s, conflict with the British led about 12,000 Boers to stage the 'great trek' north and east, which brought them into direct conflict with native African peoples.[10] There, they established their own independent republics, the Orange Free State and Transvaal. The Afrikaners were motivated by the belief that they were a "chosen people fleeing the world's corruption to follow God's will in a new land. "[11] This belief, which was articulated by Paul Kruger, later became the general foundation of Afrikaner nationalism. In particular, this belief also established the notion of separate development of races, known as apartheid. In the last quarter of the nineteenth century, the Boer republics were threatened by an influx of British immigrants. "These uitlanders, as the Boer called them,... were attracted to the northeastern part of South Africa by the discovery of diamonds at Kimberley in 1869 and of gold on the Witwatersrand in 1886."[12]

Conflict between the British and the Boer republics culminated in the Boer War of 1899, which ended in a British victory and the conclusion of the Peace of Vereeniging in 1902. It also established the Union of South Africa and its membership in the British Commonwealth of Nations in 1910. Henceforth, the relations between the Boers and the British continued to be colored by mistrust and bitterness.

In December 1931, the Union of South Africa achieved independence within the Commonwealth. In 1961, it withdrew from the Commonwealth and became the Republic of South Africa, with the Afrikaners constituting the majority among the European population and having virtually full control over the country's economic and political affairs. Their policies were racial, supporting segregation and separate development of the races (apartheid). In pursuance of their policies, the black population of the Republic of South Africa continued to be barred from exercising economic or political rights until March 1992, at which time the white population of the country (including a majority of Afrikaners) agreed, in a referendum, to introduce constitutional reforms that would end their previous racial policies. This was followed by the establishment of a multiracial and multiparty Transitional Executive Council (TEC), which effectively superseded the parliament following the adoption of a five-year interim constitution on November 18, 1993, and its ratification by the country's tricameral parliament on December 22, 1993. Subsequently, multiracial and multiparty elections were held on April 27, 1994. All these developments constituted major shifts in Afrikaners's racial policies in favor of transforming South Africa into a multiracial democracy. Under their terms, the Afrikaners conceded to the relinquishment of their control over the country to majority rule, and accepted the status of a minority with recognized constitutional rights.

The Afrikaners are agrarian in their social traditions and outlook. They speak a Dutch dialect known as Afrikaans. The great majority of them are affiliated with the Dutch Reformed Church, a Calvinist Christian sect that was brought by their ancestors to South Africa.

Currently, the Afrikaners are almost totally concentrated in the Republic of South Africa. They account for some three-fifths of the total white population of the Republic and together with other whites (especially people of British ancestry), represent about 15% of the country's total population of about 41.5 million (1995).

AFUNU, see HAUSA

AFUSARE

The Afusare are a West African people. They are concentrated in the central regions of Nigeria and speak a language that belongs to the Benue-Congo branch of the Niger-Congo family of African languages. Their neighbors include the Birom, Jarawa, Jerawa, Katab and Kurama peoples.

AGACIKU, see KIKUYU

AGAR, see DINKA

AGAU

The Agau, also Agaw and Agew, are an ancient Cushitic-speaking people that lived in the northern and central regions of the Ethiopian Plateau, especially around the Amhara, Gojjam and Shoe regions. Over the years, the bulk of these people merged with other groups that presently constitute only a small ethnic minority in modern Ethiopia.

Historical evidence suggests that the Agau people were subdued by the Semitic Coptic Christian Axumites during the ninth and tenth centuries and that slowly and gradually they were integrated in the Axumites' society and Christianized.[13] As a consequence to the fusion of Agau and Axumite, the Zagwe, an Agau Christianized family, was able to gain control of the Ethiopian monarchy during the 12th century and to continue its reign over Ethiopia for about 150 years. This contributed to the development of the country and to the shaping of the religious and cultural character of its civilization.

According to July, the physical expression of the contribution of the Agau people in general, and the Zagwe dynasty in particular, to the Ethiopian civilization "was projected most eloquently by the [eleven] monolithic churches built in the highland fastness of Lasta during the reign of King Lalibela (c. 1181-c. 1221)." [14]

In his view, these churches "were more than an architectural triumph... [They] represented the emergence of the unique Christianity of Ethiopia...," as well as "the close relationship of church and state," which was characteristic of Ethiopian society until modern times.[15]

The Zagwe dynasty of the Agau continued to rule Ethiopia until 1270, at which time the Solomonids (the descendants of Menelik I, the son of King Solomon and the Queen of Sheba, and founder of the Ethiopian Empire) were able to regain the kingdom and to rule it since the military coup of 1974. The coup resulted in the deposition of Haile Selassie I and the transformation of the country into a republic on September 12, 1974. Since the Solomonids regained control of the dynasty, the role of the Agau people has diminished.

According to The New Encyclopaedia Britannica, the "Jewish Falasha (or 'Black Jews') are believed to have descended from the Agau, and they retain some of the old Agau words in their religious vocabulary."[16] According to the same source, Agau dialects are spoken in the mountainous region of Simen northeast of the City of Gonder and in the area southeast of Gonder."[17]

The New Encyclopaedia Britannica also notes that "Awiya, a dialect spoken south of Lake Tana, is believed to contain the strongest similarities of any of the dialects to the ancient Agau language."[18] Furthermore, it maintains that "Amharic also has many Agau elements and influences."[19]

AGAW, see AGAU

AGAW, see AWI

AGEKOYO, see KIKUYU

AGEW, see AGAU and AWI

AGIKUYU, see KIKUYU

AGIRYAMA, see also GIRIAMA

The Agiryama, also known as Giriama, are an East African people. They are concentrated in the southeastern regions of Kenya.

AGNI, see ANUI

AGOI

The Agoi are a West and Central African people. They are concentrated in the southeastern border areas of Nigeria, notably in the Cross River state. Groups of them, however, can also be found in Cameroon. Their neighbors include the Kole and Udam peoples.

AGON

The Agon are an East African people. They are concentrated in Eritrea. Groups of them, however, are also found in Ethiopia. Their neighbors include the Afar, Saho, Tigrays, Tigre and Kunama peoples.

AGROU, see ALLADIAN

AHAGGAR, see TAUREG

AHLO, see AHOLE

AHOLE

The Ahole people, also known as Ahlo, are one of Togo's ethnic minorities. They are Kwa-speaking people who live primarily in the southwestern regions of the country. Most Ahole adhere to traditional animistic beliefs.

AïR, see TAUREG

AIT 'ALI, see also BERBER

A North African Berber-speaking group. The Ait 'Ali people are concentrated in the Ishilhayen region of Morocco, namely in the Western High Atlas, the Sus Valley, and the Anti-Atlas areas of the country.

AIT 'ATTA, see also BERBER

The Ait Atta are a West Saharan North African Berber-speaking people. They are concentrated in central eastern Morocco and central western Algeria.

AIT 'AYYASH, see BERBER

The Ait 'Ayyash are a Moroccan Berber-speaking group. They are concentrated in the Imazighen region of the country which includes the Middle Atlas and Central High Atlas chains, the Saghro massif, and the Presaharan oasis regions of the country.

AIT BA 'AMRAN, see also BERBER

A North African Berber-speaking people. The Ait Ba 'Amran are concentrated in the Ishilhayen region of Morocco which contains the Western High Atlas, the Sus Valley, and the Anti-Atlas areas of the country.

AIT HADIDDU, see also BERBER

A North African Berber-speaking group. The Ait Hadiddu people are concentrated in the Imazighen region of Morocco which includes the Middle Atlas and Central High Atlas chains, the Saghro massif, and the Presaharan oasis regions of the country.

AIT IDRASSEN

The Ait Idrassen are a North African Berber-speaking people. They are highly concentrated in the northeastern mountainous regions of Morocco.

AIT IMYILL, see also BERBER

A North African Berber group. The Ait Imyill are concentrated in the Middle Atlas and Central High Atlas, the Saghro massif, and the Presaharan oasis regions of the country. They speak Berber.

AIT IZDIG, see also BERBER

A North African Berber-speaking group. The Ait Izdig are concentrated in the Imazighen region of Morocco, notably in the Middle Atlas and Central High Atlas chains, the Saghro massif, and the Presaharan oasis regions of the country.

AIT KHEBACHE

The Ait Khebache people are a North African Berber-speaking group. They are concentrated in southeastern Morocco and southwestern Algeria.

AIT LAHSEN, see MOOR and SAHRAWIS

AIT MASSAD, see also BERBER

A North African Berber group. The Ait Massad are concentrated in the Imazighen region of Morocco, notably in the Middle Atlas and Central High Atlas chains, the Saghro massif, and the Presaharan oasis regions of the country.

AIT MHAND, see also **BERBER**

A North African Berber-speaking group. The Ait Mhand people are concentrated in the Imazighen region of Morocco which contains the Middle Atlas and Central High Atlas chains, the Saghro massif, and the Presaharan oasis regions of the country.

AIT MURGHAD, see also **BERBER**

A North African Berber-speaking group. The Ait Murghad are concentrated in the Imazighen region of Morocco, notably in the Middle Atlas and Central High Atlas chains, the Saghro massif, and the Presaharan oasis regions of the country.

AIT N-NUSS, see also **BERBER**

A North African Berber-speaking group. The Ait N-Nuss are concentrated in the Ishilhayen region of Morocco which contains the Western High Atlas, the Sus Valley, and the Anti-Atlas areas of the country.

AIT NDHIR, see also **BERBER**

A North African Berber group. The Ait Ndhir people are concentrated in the Imazighen region of Morocco which consists of the Middle Atlas and Central High Atlas chains, the Saghro massif, and the Presaharan oasis.

AIT OUMALOU

A North African Berber-speaking group. The Ait Oumalou are concentrated in the north-eastern mountainous regions of Morocco.

AIT SAGHRUSHSHN, see also **BERBER**

A North African Berber-speaking people. The Ait Saghrushshn are concentrated in the Imazighen region of Morocco which contains the Middle Atlas and Central High Atlas chains, the Saghro massif, and the Presaharan oasis.

AIT SIDDRAT, see also BERBER

A North African Berber-speaking group. The Ait Siddrat are a Berber people. They are concentrated in the Imazighen region of Morocco which consists of the Middle Atlas and Central High Atlas chains, the Saghro massif, and the Presaharan oasis.

AIT SUKHMAN, see also BERBER

A North African Berber people. The Ait Sukhman are concentrated in the Imazighen region of Morocco, notably in the Middle Atlas and Central High Atlas chains, the Saghro massif, and the Presaharan oasis areas of the country.

AIT WALNZGIT

The Ait Walnzgit people are a North African Berber group. They are concentrated in the eastern mountainous regions of Morocco close to the Algerian-Moroccan borders.

AIT WARAYIN, see also BERBER

A North African Berber group. The Ait Warayin are concentrated in the Imazighen region of Morocco which consists of the Middle Atlas and Central High Atlas chains, the Saghro massif, and the Presaharan oasis.

AIT WAWZGIT, see also BERBER

A North African Berber-speaking people. The Ait Wawzgit are concentrated in the Ishilhayen region of Morocco which contains the Western High Atlas, the Sus Valley, and the Anti-Atlas areas of the country.

AIT YAFEMAN

A West Saharan North African Berber group. They are concentrated in the eastern mountainous regions of Morocco close to the Algerian-Moroccan borders. The Ait Yafeman people speak a dialect of the Berber language.

AIT YUSI, see also **BERBER**

A North African Berber group. The Ait Yusi are concentrated in the Imazighen region of Morocco, notably in the Middle Atlas and Central High Atlas, the Saghro, and the Presaharan oasis areas of the country.

AITH 'AMMARTH, see also **BERBER**

The Aith 'Ammarth are a Moroccan Berber people. They are concentrated in Morocco's Rif region, notably in the provinces of El Hoceima, Nador and Taza.

AITH ANGA, see **KIKUYU**

AITH IEGENI, see **KIKUYU**

AITH IRANDU, see **KIKUYU**

AITH SA'ID, see also **BERBER**

A Moroccan Berber group. The Aith Sa'id are concentrated in the country's Rif region, notably in the provinces of El Hoceima, Nador and Taza. They speak Berber.

AITH WARYAGHAR, see also **BERBER**

A Rifian Berber group. The Aith Waryaghar are concentrated in Morocco's Rif region, notably in the provinces of El Hoceima, Nador and Taza. They are a Berber-speaking people.

AITH WURISHIK, see also **BERBER**

The Aith Wurishik are a Berber group. They are concentrated in Morocco's Rif region, notably in the provinces of El Hoceima, Nador and Taza. They are a Berber-speaking people.

AIZO

The Aizo people are one of Benin's many ethnic minorities. They are related to the country's largest ethnic group, the Fon, and are concentrated in the southern regions of the country.

AJA

These are a West African people who were linguistically and culturally influenced by the Yoruba. During the seventeenth century they established several kingdoms of their own, with Allada as their capital. In 1698, their capital, Allada, was subdued by the Kingdom of Oyo and in the 1720's by the Kingdom of Dahomey.

AJIBBA, see MURLE

AJJER, see TAUREG

AJUKRU

The Ajukru are a West African people and one of the ethnic minorities of the Ivory Coast. They speak the Kwa language and live primarily in the southern regions of the country. Their neighbors include the Ari, Avikam, and Dida peoples.

AKA, see also PYGMY

The Aka, also known as Tara-Baaka and Mbaka, are a Central and East African Bantu-speaking people. They comprise several related groups, including the Babinga, Bayaka, Biaka, and Mbenzele. They are highly concentrated in the southeastern regions of the Central African Republic.

The Aka are one of the many Pygmy people of equatorial Africa. Originally, they inhabited the tropical rain forest, in what is now within the Republic of Congo. Subsequently, they moved to other areas and settled in countries neighboring the Congo Basin, including the Central African Republic. The Aka are essentially hunters, foragers and potters.

AKAMBA, see KAMBA

AKAN

The Akan are a giant West African people of the Guinea Coast. They speak Twi (Akan) languages and comprise numerous groups, including the Abron (Abrong, Boron, Bron, Bono, Dom, Tchaman), Akyem, Anyi, Ashanti, Attie, Baule (or Baoule), Brong, Fanti, Guang and Nzima. The Akan languages are of the Kwa branch of the Niger-Congo family of African languages. The Akan people are the largest ethnic minority in Ghana and one of the ethnic minorities of both the Ivory Coast and Togo. They are concentrated in the Ahafo, Ashanti, Brong, Central, Eastern, Greater Accra and Western regions in Ghana, and the eastern areas of the Ivory Coast. In Ghana, they constitute 44% of the country's total population.

The Akan settled in their present-day countries in successive waves of migration which took place between the eleventh and eighteenth centuries A.D. As their tribes moved from south of the savanna to the forest area located between the coastal areas of the Gulf of Guinea (Atlantic ocean) and the lower reaches of the Volta river, they mixed with indigenous people and established a series of village communities. The most important of these were the Ashanti, Assin, Denkyira, Fanti (Fante), Sefwi and Wassa. Eventually, they secured their preponderance in the region, freed themselves from tribute subjection to their neighbors and through trading activities among themselves and with their neighbors, they spread their economic and political influence throughout the Volta river valley and as far as the Ivory Coast and east to Benin. By the time Portuguese traders arrived towards the end of the fifteenth century, they were already a group of powerful states.

The Akan's trading activities were further expanded upon the arrival of European traders. As a consequence, the Akan engaged themselves in both hinterland and Atlantic-oriented trade that involved among other things salt, gold, kola nuts, slaves, manufactured goods and firearms. This growing trade, directed both north and south and east and west, played an important role in articulating the political organization of the Akan people.

Prior to colonial rule, the Akan peoples developed highly organized states with governments comprised of rulers who governed with the help of ministers.[20] The most important of their states were Bono, Denkyira (Denkyera), the Akwamu, the Fanti (Fante), and the Ashanti (Asante). Because of growing trade and contact with Europeans, especially in the period between the sixteenth and seventeenth centuries, all these states experienced basic transformations. In time, they were consolidated in fewer imperial states, namely that of the Ashanti and the Fanti.

The Bono state, established around 1450, was one of the Akan's earliest states. Its territory covered what is presently the Brong-Ahafo region in Ghana. The rise of this state was "undoubtedly connected with the developing gold trade of Bighu, a Malian Muslim or Dyula commercial center 40 miles (64 kilometers) to the northwest. From there Muslim traders came to Bono soon after its foundation and many members of the royal household were later converted to Islam."[21]

The contribution of this Akan kingdom to trade and gold mining is renowned. Its kings, especially Obunumankoma (fl. c. 1450-75), 'Ali Kwame (fl. c. 1550-60), and Owusu Aduam (fl. c. 1650), not only organized the gold industry, but also introduced new mining techniques to it and oversaw arrangements of shipping gold and other exports "through the entrepôts of the Western Sudan along the trade routes of the Sahara to the terminal ports of North Africa and from there to Europe and elsewhere."[22]

The state of Bono engaged in a number of wars with the Jackpa of Gonja. It collapsed following its subjugation by Opoku Ware, the king of a rival Akan imperial state, Ashanti (Asante), in 1722-23.

Denkyira (Denkyera) is also one of the earliest Akan kingdoms. Like the Bono, it thrived on agriculture, mining and trade. Moreover, it exercised control over the Ashanti and other smaller Akan kingdoms. Denkyera's powerful status saw an abrupt end in the 1670s when it was defeated by the Ashanti Oyoko kings. Henceforth, it became one of the Ashanti tributary states.

The Akwamu state was established early in the seventeenth century in what is presently southern Ghana. Aside from agriculture, it engaged in mining and selling gold. As it grew richer, it ventured to expand its territory.

Between 1677 and 1681, it conquered the states of Ladoku, Agona and Whydah, as well as the Ewe people of the Ho region. It collapsed following its conquest by the state of Akim, an ally of the Ashanti, in 1731.[23]

The Fanti states were established in the southern regions of what is presently modern Ghana. Towards the end of the seventeenth century, their kingdoms decided to form a confederacy to provide for their joint defense against the Ashanti's rising power, as well as to protect their own trading interests, especially with European powers.

The confederacy of Fanti states was headed by both a high king, called *Brafo*, and a high priest. As a littoral country located at the Gulf of Guinea (Atlantic Ocean), it served as an intermediary in the trade between the Ashanti and the Europeans, selling Ashanti gold to Europeans and European firearms to the Ashanti. Its strategic geopolitical position invited the envy of both the Ashanti, as well as the Europeans, especially of the British and Dutch powers. In 1806, the confederacy fell to the Ashanti and hence became a tributary of the Ashanti state. In 1831, however, the British government negotiated a treaty with the Fanti and the Ashanti that provided for Fanti independence and Ashanti use of trade routes to the Atlantic. In so doing, the British government extended an informal protectorate over the Fanti confederacy.

In an effort to concert their power, the Fanti Kingdoms, Denkyira, and other southern Akan states tried to establish a strong self-governing state free from European domination. In 1868, their representatives met at Mankessim and agreed to form a new confederation with an executive council, a judiciary, and a standing army. The new Fanti confederation was supported by a written constitution and empowered to raise taxes.

The new confederation was strong enough to dissuade the Dutch government from pursuing its imperial ambitions in the Fanti kingdoms, but proved incapable of halting those of the British government. By exploiting the rivalries among members of the Confederation, the British government succeeded in its disbandment in 1873. In 1874, it "annexed the whole region south of the Ashanti empire as the Gold Coast crown colony."[24]

The Ashanti kingdom started its ascent to an imperial status when the Ashanti people, under the leadership of the Oyoko clan and its first three kings (Obiri Yeboe, Osei Tutu and Opoku Ware) rose against the Denkeyera state. In a series of campaigns in the 1670s, they succeeded in not only crushing the Denkeyera state, but also in establishing their control over the area between the Komoé river in the west to the Togo mountains in the east. In no time, the Ashanti kingdom rose to an imperial status becoming the paramount military and commercial power in the whole region. Moreover, the supremacy of the Oyoko clan was recognized by Akan and non-Akan peoples in the Kumasi region, as well as by other Akan ruling lineages. Obiri Yeboe, the first of the Oyoko kings, was killed in battle during the campaigns of the 1670's, placing the foundation of the Amanto states of Ashanti-Kumasi, Bekwai, Juaben, Kokofu and Nsuta under Osei Tutu, the second Oyoko king. Osei Tutu is credited not only for establishing the spiritual unity of the Ashanti by adopting "the Sacred Symbol of the Golden Stool," but also for establishing Kumasi as its capital and introducing a constitution that recognized "the supremacy of the *kumasihene*, or king of Kumasi, who would henceforth be known as the *asantehene*, or head of the Ashanti state."[25]

In further consolidation measures, member kingdoms were integrated into the new union by having their respective kings serve as commanders of the army of the Ashanti state, as well as members in a council of advisers to the *asantehene*. Also, member kingdoms were required to supply the Ashanti army with troops as needed and to participate in Ashanti state celebrations. Responsibility over kingdoms' domestic affairs was retained in the hands of their respective kings.

Upon these achievements, the newly structured state embarked on expanding its territory and incorporating defeated kingdoms (such as Denkyira, Akyem, Akwapim, and Akwamu) within the Ashanti union. By 1750, the year in which Opoku Ware (the third Oyoko king) died, the Ashanti empire became virtually an unchallenged power in the whole Gold Coast region. It maintained its supremacy until the middle of the nineteenth century, at which time it started to decline. Several factors contributed to the decline, including internal divisions and revolts and failures to thwart repeated British campaigns against its territory. On

January 1, 1902, the British government formally declared Ashanti a crown colony, and in a separate declaration, established the Northern Territories of the Gold Coast as a British Protectorate. Ashanti King Prempeh I had no choice but to accept the partition of his country and direct British rule. In the 1930's, however, the British government established an Ashanti Confederacy Council, and more importantly, restored the position of *asantehene*, but only as a symbolic figurehead.

Currently, the Akan are essentially an agricultural people. Their economic activity centers on producing and trading of yams, plantain, taro, cocoa and palm oil.

The Akan live in compact villages that are divided into wards and family compounds. Their family structure is strictly matrilineal. In their turn, their families are grouped into matrilineal clans, the members of which trace their descent from a common ancestress. Each clan is organized hierarchically and further subdivided into narrower lineages which represent their basic political and social units.

The head of a particular lineage serves as custodian of the lineage. He is entrusted with "the lineage's stools, the symbols of unity between the spirits of the ancestors and the living members of the lineage; every lineage also has its own god or gods."[26]

The village represents a basic political unit in Akan society. It is managed under the authority of a chief and a council of elders. The chief is elected from one the lineages, whereas the members of councils of elders are elected representatives of the respective lineages within the village. The council of elders reflects Akans' deep respect for older individuals, a feature which is inherent in their culture.

Matrilineal descent constitutes the basis of many of Akan rules and regulations and governs questions relating to marriage, inheritance, succession and land tenureship within their society. Traditionally, every Akan belonged to one of eight exogamous matrilineal clans, each of which was associated with a totemic animal connected with the first emergence of the clan ancestress on earth.[27] Paternal descent is also recognized in Akan society. Patrilineal descent, however, "determines membership in the *ntoro*, a group sharing certain taboos, surnames, forms of etiquette and ritual purification ceremonies."[28]

Though Christianity and Islam have won many Akan converts, a great majority of the Akan people continue to profess commitment to, or practice, their traditional religious beliefs – beliefs that rest on an ancestor cult, a supreme God, known as *Onyame* and *Onyankopon*, who created the universe, and lesser deities and spirits, including *Asase Yaa*, the goddess of the earth.[29]

The Akan culture supports many legends regarding life and creation. According to one legend,

> God lived on earth or at least was very near to us. But there was a certain old woman who used to pound her *fufu* [cassava meal], and the pestle used to break up against God. So God said to the old woman, 'why do you always do that to me? Because of what you are doing I am going to take myself away up into the sky.' And of a truth he did so.[30]

According to the same legend, evil may always have existed, but "its eyes were not yet open." Its eyes opened when God separated himself from mankind. "The trouble began when God separated himself from men."[31]

The Akan are noted for their high sense of realism. In their value system, a human being can control or influence his or her own destiny.[32]

AKAYON, see **KIONG**

AKEBU, see **KEBU**

AKEROA, see **TOPOSA**

AKIE, see also **OKIEK** and **KALENJIN**

An East African Okiek group, a Kalenjin people. The Akie, also spelled Akiy, are concentrated in Kenya, Tanzania and Uganda. They speak a dialect of Kalenjin, a Southern Nilotic language of the Eastern Sudanic family of African languages. The Akie are a semi-pastoralist people.

AKIY, see AKIE

AKOA

The Akoa are one of the many Pygmy people of equatorial Africa. Originally, they inhabited the tropical rain forest, in what is now within the Republic of Congo. Subsequently, however, they moved to other areas neighboring the Congo Basin, including Burundi, Cameroon, Central African Republic, Equatorial Guinea, Gabon, Central African Republic, Democratic Republic of the Congo (Zaire), Rwanda, Sudan, and Uganda. The Akoa are essentially hunters, foragers and potters.

AKOIYANG, see KIONG

AKOKO

The Akoko are a West African Yoruba people. They constitute one of Nigeria's many ethnic groups. The Akoko live in the northeastern areas of the country and are concentrated in the Ondo state. Their neighbors include the Igbira, Ora, Upila, and Yoruba peoples.

AKOKOLEMU, see KUMAN

AKOSA, see LUNDA

AKOURI, see ALLADIAN

AKPANZHI, see KPAN

AKPOSE

The Akpose, also spelled Akposo, are a West African people and one of Togo's ethnic minorities. They are Kwa-speaking people and are concentrated in the southwestern regions of the country. Their neighbors include the Ana, Fon, Ewe, Lefana, Kebu and Tribu peoples. Most Akpose still adhere to their traditional animistic beliefs.

AKPOSO, see **AKPOSE**

AKPOSSO, see **AKPOSE**

AKUM, see **KUMAN**

AKURUMBA, see **KURUMBA**

AKURUMI, see **KURAMA**

AKWA, see **NYAKWAI**

AKWAHU, see **KWAHU**

AKWALUANDA, see **MBUNDU**

AKYEM

A West African people. The Akyem are concentrated in the southern regions of Ghana. Groups of them, however, are also located in Togo. They speak the Kwa language. Their neighbors include the Adangme, Asante, Avatime, Ewe, Fanti, Gā and Krachi peoples.

ALA

The Ala are an East African people. They are concentrated in the northern regions of Kenya along the Kenyan-Ethiopian and Kenyan-Sudanese borders.

ALABA, see also **SIDAMO**

The Alaba are an East African non-Galla Cushitic-speaking Muslim people. They live chiefly in southwestern Ethiopia, particularly in the Omo river and Rift Valley regions of the country. The Alaba are a Sidamo group, and hence, are related to other Sidamo peoples such as the Garo, Hadya and

Tambaro.

The Alaba established a kingdom of their own between the tenth and twelfth centuries. During the same period they absorbed Islam from coastal Arabs. Subsequently, their kingdom, like those of other Sidamo peoples, became a tributary of the Abyssinians (Amhara and Tigre), as well as the Galla.[33]

The Alaba are essentially an agricultural people. They specialize in the production of grains, cereals, fruits and spices, as well as in animal husbandry.

ALAGIA, see ALLADIAN

ALAGYA, see ALLADIAN

ALANTE, see BALANTE

ALHAUSI, see HAUSA

ALIAB, see DINKA

ALLADIAN

The Alladian, also known as Alagia or Alagya, are a West African people. Known as the Jack-Jack by the English, the Alladian are part of the Lagoon Cluster of peoples in West Africa. They speak a language of the Akan-East Atlantic Complex and reside in the southwestern Ivory Coast. Their culture is similar to other groups of the Lagoon Cluster, and have a matrilineal social organization. The Alladians comprise several groups, the most important of which are the Aware, the Kovou (Kovu) and the Agrou (Akouri).

ALMOHADES, see ALMOHADS

ALMOHADIS, see ALMOHADS

ALMOHADS

Almohads, also Almohades and Almowahids, are a Muslim Berber people who established a powerful dynasty between the twelfth and the middle of the thirteenth century in both Morocco and Spain. The dynasty was based on a puritanical militant reformist movement of Islam that was founded by Muhammad ibn Tumart (c. 1120). Almohads overthrew Almoravids' dynasty in 1174. They reigned over Morocco and Spain until they were overtaken by the Merenide dynasty in 1269.

ALMORABIDES, see ALMORAVIDS

ALMORABIDS, see ALMORAVIDS

ALMORAVIDS

Almoravids, also Almoravides and Almurābids, are a Muslim Berber people who established a powerful dynasty between the eleventh and twelfth century in both Morocco and Spain. The dynasty was based on a puritanical militant reformist movement of Islam that was founded by Abdullah ibn Yassin (d. 1095). His successors founded the city of Marrakesh.

In 1086, the Almoravids helped Spanish Moors curb Christian campaigns to reconquer Muslim Spain, and thereupon they assumed power over the country. In 1174, their dynasty was overthrown by Almohades (Almohads or Almuwahīdūn), another Muslim puritanical militant movement.

Almoravids' movement spread throughout the northern and western regions of Africa. Adherents of the movement, for example, recaptured Awdoghast and Kumbi in what is presently modern Sudan and Ghana, respectively.

ALMOWAHEDS, see ALMOHADS

ALMOWAHIDS, see ALMOHADS

ALOLO, see MACULA

ALOMWE, see also **LOMWE**

A Southeast and East African people. The Alomwe, also known as the Lomwe, are concentrated in Malawi, Mozambique and Tanzania. They speak Chilmwe and are closely related to the Yao people.

ALUUNDA, see **LUNDA**

ALUR

The Alur are one of Uganda's, Sudan's and Democratic Republic of the Congo (Zaire's) ethnic minorities. They are part of the Nilotic-speaking groups, and are related to the Luo people of Kenya. Their language, DhuAlur, is a Western Nilotic language of the Luo (Lwo) group. The Alur are concentrated in the northwestern regions of Uganda, and the northeastern regions of Zaire. They live primarily on the northwestern shores of Lake Albert. Their neighbors include the Acholi, the Lango, the Madi, the Jie and the Paluo peoples. They support an agricultural society with the family as its basic unit. "The family is polygynous, patrilineal, and patrilocal, based economically on the house-property complex."[34]

Historical evidence suggests that the Alur people used to live in what is presently modern Sudan. Also, it suggests that they migrated to where they are presently located sometime during the seventeenth century. The Alur developed a kingdom of their own, but unlike other kingdoms in the area, it was highly decentralized and segmentary in nature.

ALUYI, see **LOZI**

AMANDEBELE, see **NDEBELE**

AMAHUMBU

The Amahumbu are a Southwest African people. They are concentrated in north central Zambia. Their neighbors include the Akosa, Ayisenga, Luena and Lunda.

AMAKWAYA

A southern African people. The Amakwaya are concentrated in the Republic of South Africa.

AMAKWENKWE

A southern African people. The Amakwenkwe are concentrated in the Republic of South Africa.

AMANGBETU, see MANGBETU

AMAR, see HAMER

AMARA, see AMHARA

AMAXOSA, see also XOSA

The Amaxosa are a South African Bantu-speaking people. They are concentrated in the Republic of South Africa, notably in its southeastern regions.

AMAZIGH, see BERBER

AMAZULU, see ZULU

AMBA

The Amba, also known as Bulebule, Hamba, Kibera and Kukamba, are an East African Nilo-Hamitic ethnic group. Their main concentrations are in the southwestern regions of Uganda and the northeastern regions of the Democratic Republic of the Congo (Zaire), notably south of Lake Albert Nyanza. The Amba are an agricultural people. They engage in farming and livestock economic activities. Their traditional society was "organized on a segmentary lineage and age-set basis."[35]

AMBO

The Ambo, also known as Ovambo, are a Western Bantu-speaking people living primarily in Angola and Namibia. In Angola, they are called Ambo and they live in the southern regions of the country. In Namibia, they are called Ovambo and live primarily in the northern regions of the country. They speak Kwanyama. The Ambo comprise a number of groups, including the Ndonga and the Kwanyama. Originally, they enjoyed highly centralized states which were ruled by hereditary royalty and aristocracy. Currently, the Ambo (Ovambo) people constitute about 50% of Namibia's population, and one of Angola's important ethnic minorities.

AMBOMU, see AZANDE

AMBUELLA

The Ambuella are a Southwest African people. They are concentrated in Zambia, primarily in its northwestern regions. Their neighbors include the Lubale, Luchazi, and Ovimbundu peoples.

AMBUI, see KIKUYU

AMBUNDU, see MBUNDU

AMERICAN-LIBERIANS

These people are the descendants of early Afro-Americans who opted to settle in Liberia. Their main concentration is along the Liberian coast. Until recently, they were virtually in full control of Liberia's political and economic life.

AMHARA

Amhara, also called Amara, are one of the main ethnic groups of central and northern highlands of Ethiopia. Their name is derived from the word *amari*, meaning "one who is pleasing, agreeable, beautiful, and gracious."[36] The territory of the Amhara is geographically diverse, stretching from Ethiopia's capital, Addis Ababa, to Lake Tana. Together with the southern Tigre (Tigrai or Tigreans), the Amhara were known as Abyssinians. The latter people are culturally different from the Tigre of the north. They speak Trigrinya, whereas the Tigre of the north speak Tigré. Amharic, also called Amarinya, Amharinya or Kuchumba, is the language of the Amhara. Like Trigrinya of the Tigre, it is related to Ge'ez (or Ethiopic), the liturgical language of the Ethiopian Orthodox Church and one of the official languages of Ethiopia.

The history of Ethiopia has always been associated with that of the Amhara and Tigre peoples. Both are descendants of Semitic Arab peoples who migrated from southern Arabia between the 6th century B.C. and the 1st century A.D. Between the 2nd and 9th centuries A.D., they established the kingdom of Aksum (Axum), which subsequently became an empire lasting until 1974. All the emperors of the kingdom of Aksum except one were Amhara, and all of them claimed divine rights as the direct descendants of King Solomon and Queen Sheba. The fall of Emperor Haile Selassie in 1974 marked the end of this long line of imperial rule.

The Amhara are an agrarian people and currently are concentrated in the Gegemdir, Gojam, Shewa (Shoa), Simen and Welo provinces of Ethiopia. Their society is patriarchal and moreover, it is based on a strict social structure that includes a landed aristocracy at the top, followed by clergy, merchants and farmers. The *shamma*, a shawl draped over the arm and shoulder, is their traditional attire. It is worn by both men and women.

Amhara live in separate villages that are governed by a chief or *cheqa sum*. The chief's power is checked by a village council or *kebeke*. The Coptic Church dominates the religious life of the Amhara. Divorce is frowned upon and a great percentage of men are lay priests.

Together with the Tigre, the Amhara constitute the second largest ethnic group in Ethiopia, accounting for 32% of the population. The Oromo are the largest group, amounting to over 44% of Ethiopia's population.

AMMELN, see also BERBER

The Ammeln are a Moroccan Berber group. They are concentrated in the Ishilhayen region of Morocco, notably in the Western High Atlas, the Sus

Valley, and the Anti-Atlas areas of the country. The Ammeln are a Berber-speaking people.

AMRAAL HOTTENTOTS

The Amraal Hottentots are a Southwest African people. They are concentrated in the central-eastern regions of Namibia. Their neighbors include the Herero, Khara (!Khara), Naron, and Witboois peoples.

ANA, see also MINA

A West African people. The Ana are concentrated in Togo and the Ivory Coast and speak a language that belongs to the Kwa branch of the Niger-Congo family of African languages. Their neighbors include the Akpose (Akposo), Ewe, Fon, and Yoruba peoples.

ANAKAZZA, see ANAKAZA

ANANG, see also IBIBIO

The Anang, also called Western Ibibio, are one of the main subgroups of the West African Ibibio people. They are concentrated in the southeastern areas of Nigeria, especially in the Cross River State. Together with other Ibibio subgroups (Andoni-Ibeno, Efik, Eket, and Ibibio proper), they represent one of the ten largest ethnic minorities of Nigeria. With other Ibibio, their population ranks after those of the Hausa, Fulani, Yoruba, Ibo, Kanuri, Tiv, Edo and Nupe peoples.

The Anang speak a Kwa language of the Niger-Congo family of African languages and share many common traits with the Igbo, one of Nigeria's major ethnic groups.

A great majority of Anang people are engaged in agriculture and trade and live in villages that are built around central courtyards. Their produce includes palm oil and kernels and one of their current main trade centers is at Ikot Ekpene, located between Calabar and Aba.

The Anang villages are governed by councils representing the heads of their various households. In their turn, villages are bonded together by descent from the same ancestors, as well as by their common tutelary spirits and totems. Socialization of men and women within villages is furthered through the initiation ceremonies and activities of secret societies. These entail religious rituals, exaltation of ancestral spirits and practice of magic, sorcery and various forms of wizardry.

The Anang are a patrilineal people. In their society, questions relating to descent, succession and inheritance are based on patrilineal lineages. The heads of their households continue to have ritual responsibilities, including the protection of ancestral shrines.

Like other West African peoples, the Anang are renowned for their wood carving skills, as well as their cane furniture and basket handicrafts.[37]

ANDONI-IBENO, see also IBIBIO

The Andoni-Ibeno, also called Delta Ibibio, are one of the main subgroups of the West African Ibibio people. They are concentrated in the southeastern areas of Nigeria, especially in the Cross River State. Together with other Ibibio subgroups (Anang, Efik, Eket and Ibibio proper), they represent one of the ten largest ethnic minorities of Nigeria. With other Ibibio groups, their population ranks after those of the Hausa, Fulani, Yoruba, Ibo, Kanuri, Tiv, Edo and Nupe peoples. The Andoni-Ibeno speak a Kwa language of the Niger-Congo family of African languages and share many common traits with the Igbo, one of Nigeria's major ethnic groups.

A great majority of Andoni-Ibeno people are engaged in agriculture and trade and live in villages that are built around central courtyards. Their produce includes palm oil and kernels.

The Andoni-Ibeno villages are governed by councils representing the heads of their various households. In their turn, villages are bonded together by descent from the same ancestors, as well as by their common tutelary spirits and totems. Socialization of men and women within villages is furthered through the initiation ceremonies and activities of secret societies which entail religious rituals, exaltation of ancestral spirits and practice of magic, sorcery and various forms of wizardry.

The Andoni-Ibeno are a patrilineal people. In their society, questions relating to descent, succession and inheritance are based on patrilineal lineages. The heads of their households continue to have ritual responsibilities, including the protection of ancestral shrines. Like other West African people, the Andoni-Ibeno are renowned for their wood carving skills.

ANÉ, see MINA

ANGARI, see KIKUYU

ANGA

A small West African ethnic group. The Angas, also known as the Kerang and Nnga, are concentrated in Nigeria, notably in the Plateau State, and speak an Afro-Asiatic language. Their neighbors include the Arago, Birom, Burum, Fulani, Gili, Hausa, Jarawa, Jukun, Mada, Mama, Yergum and Tiv peoples.

ANGICA, see BANTU

A Western Bantu-speaking people. The Angica are a Teke (Téké) group. They are concentrated in the Republic of Congo and neighboring states.

ANGOLARES

Angolares are direct descendants of Angolan slaves brought to Sâo Tomé and Principé by Portuguese slave traders. They now constitute the second largest ethnic group of the country.

ANGONI, see NGONI

ANIA

The Ania are an East African people. They are concentrated in southwestern Ethiopia and northwestern Kenya. Their neighbors include the Ala, Arusi, Ittu, and Nole peoples.

//ANIKHOE, see also SAN

These are a southern African San-speaking people. Known also as Swamp

Bushmen, the //Anikhoe are concentrated in the Okavango Delta flood plain in Botswana. Like other San groups, they are essentially foragers, hunters and gatherers.

ANJIRU, see **KIKUYU**

ANKAZA, see also **TEDA**

The Ankaza, also spelled Annakaza, Anakazza and Annakoza, are a Central and East African Teda group. They are concentrated in western Sudan. Groups of them, however, live in neighboring countries. The Ankaza are a Teda Toubou group.

ANKOLE, see **NKOLE**

ANKORE, see **NKOLE**

ANKWE

The Ankwe are a West African people. They are concentrated in the central regions of Nigeria, notably in the Plateau State.

ANLO, see also **EWE**

The Anlo are part of the Ewe group of peoples in the Volta region of Ghana, notably in its southeast corner. They maintain many traits of the greater Ewe group of peoples. In addition, they speak a dialect of Ewe, a language of the Kwa branch of the Niger-Congo family of African languages.

Historical evidence suggests that the Anlo were involved in the capture and sale of slaves to Europeans during the seventeenth and eighteenth centuries, as well as that "many were themselves sold into slavery and taken to the New World."[38]

ANNAKAZA, see **TEDA** and **TOUBOU**

ANNAKOZA, see **TEDA** and **TOUBOU**

ANNUAK, see **ANUAK**

ANNUK, see **ANUAK**

ANOUFO

These are a West African people. They are concentrated in northern Togo, especially in and around the town of Mano (formerly Sansanné-Mango). They are agriculturalists and cattle raisers.

ANSASA, see **TEMNE**

ANTAISAKA, see also **MALAGASY**

The Antaisaka, or Antesaka, are one of Madagascar's ethnic groups. They are of a mixed African, Malayo-Indonesian and Arab ancestry. They speak a dialect of Malagasy, which is an Austronesian language. Currently, the Antaisaka account for about 3.5% of the country's population.

ANTALOTE

The Antalote people are one of the five major ethnic groups of the Federal Islamic Republic of the Comoros. The other groups include the Cafre, Makoa, Oimatsaha and the Sakalava. They speak Comoran (a blend of Swahili and Arabic), a dialect of Malagasy, and French.

ANTEMORE, see also **MALAGASY**

The Antemore are one of Madagascar's ethnic groups. They speak a dialect of Malagasy, which is an Austronesian language.

ANTESAKA, see **ANTAISAKA**

ANUAK

A Western Nilotic Sudanese and Ethiopian people. The Anuak, also spelled Annuak, Annuk, and Anyuak, are a farming and pastoral people of the White Nile and the Sobat river basins. They share the basins with other groups, including the Shilluk, and are highly concentrated along the southern borders of both Ethiopia and Sudan. Historical evidence suggests that they migrated from the north to their present areas during the seventeenth century. The Anuak speak a Nilotic language closely related to Shilluk.

The Anuak society is bonded together through patrilineal kinship relations traced back to their ancestors. It is governed by a noble clan through a decentralized network of headmen of their respective hamlets. Religiously, they continue to cherish their traditional beliefs which center on the worship of a variety of good and bad spirits. Only a few Annuak are Christian or Muslim.

ANUI

The Anui, Anyi or Agni, are a West African ethnic group. They speak a language of the Twi branch of the Kwa. The Anui people are one of the main ethnic minorities of the Ivory coast. They are located in the southern parts of this country, but have tribal affiliations with more numerous groups living outside the Ivory Coast. Their neighbors include the Abe, Ajukru, Asante, Assini, Attie, Baule, Brong and Kulango peoples.

ANYANA

The Anyana are a West African people. They represent one of Togo's many smaller ethnic groups.

ANYUAK, see ANUAK

'ANZA

An Equatorial, Central, and East African people. The 'Anza are concentrated in the Democratic Republic of the Congo (Zaire). Groups of them, however, can also be found in Tanzania and Zambia.

ANZIQUES, see BANTU

A Western Bantu-speaking people. The Anziques are a Teke (Téké) group.

They live in Gabon, the Republic of Congo, and the Democratic Republic of the Congo (Zaire).

APPA, see YERGAM

AQBAAT, see COPTS

ARAB

Today, "Arab" refers to the Arabic language these peoples speak or to persons and groups whose native language is Arabic. Yet, in ancient times, prior to the advent of Islam in the 7th century, it referred to Semitic nomadic and sedentary tribes that lived or originated from the Arabian Peninsula. Currently, it comprises any of the Arabic-speaking peoples in the area lying between Western Sahara, Mauritania and Morocco on the Atlantic Ocean, to southwestern Iran. This includes North Africa, Djibouti, The Sudan, the Arabian Peninsula and Fertile Crescent countries. This area is known as the "Arab World."

Arab minorities are found in countries adjacent to the Arab World. Also, several peoples, especially in East, Central and West Africa, are descendants of an Arab ancestry or were subject to the cultural influence of the Arabs, which have spawned dialects that are very close to the Arabic language or speak languages that carry many Arabic words.

Currently, about one-third of all Arabs in the world live in North Africa. Additionally, Arabic-influenced peoples in Africa include East and West Africans, notably the Chadians, Somalis, Amharis, Tigres and Afars.

ARAGO

The Arago are a West African people. They are concentrated in Nigeria and speak a Kwa language of the Niger-Congo family of African languages. Their neighbors include the Afo, Gili, Gwandara, Idoma, Igede, Iyala and Tiv peoples.

AREOUA

The Aréoua are one of Niger's ethnic minorities. They live along the Niger river, but have close cultural contact with the Zerma people.

ARGOBBA

The Argobba, also known as Argobbinya, are a Muslim East African people. They are concentrated in southern Ethiopia and north-central regions of Kenya. The Argobba are essentially an agricultural people.

ARGOBBINYA, see ARGOBBA

ARI, see ABIDJI

ARMA

Descendants of Moroccan armies who occupied the Niger river bend areas, including Timbuktu, during the sixteenth century. They were overpowered by the Tuareg towards the end of the eighteenth century.

ARMENIAN

Descendants of Armenian immigrants who settled in Africa during and after World War I. These people are found in a number of African states. Their largest African community is in Egypt.

ARNA, see HAUSA and TEDA

ARO, see EGBO and IBIBIO

AROSIEN, see SAHRAWIS

AROU, see DOGON

ARUM

A West African Bantu-speaking people. They are concentrated in central

Nigeria, notably in Plateau State. The Arum are part of the Mama cluster of peoples.

ARUSHA

The Arusha are an East African people. They are concentrated in the north-central regions of Tanzania, notably on the lower southwestern slopes of Mt. Meru. Historical evidence suggests that they settled in this area in the second quarter of the nineteenth century. The Arusha are related to the Masai people. They speak a dialect of Maa (Maasai), the Masai language, which belongs to the Nilo-Hamitic group of African languages. Their economic activities focus on farming and herding.

The Arusha society places "a cultural premium on individualism," and moreover, it is highly egalitarian and pluralistic. In this society, social, political and legal functions are not concentrated in one or a few hands but rather "distributed among a wide variety of groups."[39] Along with these features, the Arusha society also recognizes age groups, which traditionally "consisted of youths, junior warriors, senior warriors, junior elders, senior elders, and retired elders."[40] These age groups "provided a set of roles whereby the functions of public labor, war, dispute settlement, and other matters of governance were performed."[41]

Lineage relationships in Arusha society are patrilineal. They are based on descent from a common patrilineal ancestor. In this society, each individual was traditionally born "into membership of the whole tribe, a moiety of it, one of four clans, a clan section, a sub-clan, and a lineage."[42]

The Arusha people recognize polygamy, and traditionally, the polygynous family constituted the basic unit in their society. Religiously, many of them continue to adhere to their traditional beliefs which rest on the worship of a supreme god, *Engai*, and to perform rituals to him.

ARUSI, see **OROMO**

ARUUND, see **LUNDA**

ASANTE, see **ASHANTI**

ASAORTA, see **SAHO**

ASBEN, see **TAUREG**

ASHANTI, see also **AKAN**

A famous West African Akan people. Like other Akan groups, the Ashanti, also known as Asante, speak Twi, a Kwa language. They are highly concentrated in Ghana and the Ivory Coast. In Ghana, they live in the Ahafo, Ashanti, Brong, Central, Eastern and Western administrative regions. Their neighbors include the Anyi, Assini, Brong, Ewe, Fanti, Gā, Guang, Gonja and Krachi peoples.

Historical evidence suggests that the Ashanti moved to their present locations sometime before 1600. Their migration occurred when the Oyoko, an Akan clan, settled near Lake Basumtwi and successfully engaged themselves in producing and trading gold and kola nuts to northern merchants, as well as merchants along the coast. There, they were joined by other clans which were easily assimilated into the Oyoko's thriving community. Eventually, all these groups banded together to become the Ashanti. This occurred following their war against the Denkyira of 1669. Prior to this war, the "Ashanti were a people of separate tribes, sharing a common culture and acting under the headship of chiefs and elders."[43] Their unity was entrenched when Osei Tutu assumed their leadership, established the Oyoko lineage of Ashanti rulers, and claimed that a golden stool had fallen from the sky into his lap – a sign of divine election. Thus, "all Ashanti rulers, or Asantehene as they were called, were 'enstooled' on this golden throne, which became a powerful symbol of the unity and spirit of the Ashanti people."[44]

The legacy of Osei Tutu was kept up and even furthered under the leadership of his successors, especially his son and next Ashanti ruler, Opoku Ware. Henceforth, Ashanti-Kumasi, the seat of the new state and its kingdom, became a great center of political, religious and intellectual life. The Golden Stool continues to represent the highest symbol of authority in the Ashanti society. In villages, it is represented by wooden stools, which symbolize the authority of Ashanti chiefs. The stool is not only a symbol of power, but also "the soul of the nation." To Ashanti people, it represents the symbol of their permanence and continuity as a nation.[45]

Currently, the Ashanti are partly sedentary and partly rural. Nevertheless, they continue to identify themselves with their respective clans, *abusu*. Their clans are comprised of groups of families that are based on matrilineal descent. Though Christianity has won converts, many Ashanti continue to cherish their traditional religious beliefs. The worship of one supreme being, provider and creator, *Onyame*, as well as veneration to ancestral spirits are the most important expressions of their faith. These are followed by reverence to the Golden Stool, "the spirit not only of Ashanti union, but also of the entire Ashanti people."[46]

ASHILUANDA, see KONGO

ASH-TUKEN, see also BERBER

The Ash-Tuken are a Moroccan Berber group. They are concentrated in the Ishilhayen region of Morocco, notably in the Western High Atlas, the Sus Valley, and the Anti-Atlas areas of the country.

ASIAN

Asian, or more properly Asian Africans, are people of Asian ancestry, especially from the Indian sub-continent. They are concentrated in East and South Africa, notably in the Republic of South Africa, where they constitute 2.8% of the total population.

The presence of Asians in African countries is traced back to the colonial era, at which time their immigration was facilitated by the British colonial authorities to help build railway networks in British colonies and protectorates, as well as to overcome what they believed to be shortage in reliable African labor. In time, their numbers grew significantly, and more importantly, they managed to acquire influential positions in the trading and services sectors of the countries in which they, or their descendants, were residing. In the late sixties, there were about 350,000 Asians in the East African states of Kenya, Malawi, Tanzania, Uganda and Zambia, and nearly 800,000 in South Africa. Though their numbers have dropped considerably in the post-independence era, Asian influence in East and South Africa continues to be felt until today.

ASONGORI

These are sedentary Muslim people numbering over 50,000. They are concentrated in north-central Africa, especially in Chad, and speak a particular Sudanic dialect of the Nilo-Saharan language family. The Asongori are essentially agrarian people, but are also small-scale pastoralists.

ASSINI

The Assini are a West African people and one of Ivory Coast's ethnic minorities. They speak the Kwa language and live primarily in the southern coastal regions of the country. Their neighbors include the Alagya, Anyi, Ebrie and Mekyibo peoples.

ASUA

The Asua are a Central and East African Sudanic-speaking people. They comprise several related groups, including the Aka and Bambuti, and are concentrated in the Ituri Forest of northeastern Zaire.

The Asua are one of the many Pygmy people of equatorial Africa. Originally, the Aka inhabited the tropical rain forest, in what is now the Republic of Congo. Subsequently, they moved to other areas and settled in countries neighboring the Congo Basin, including the Democratic Republic of the Congo and Central African Republic. The Asua are essentially hunters, foragers and potters.

ATAM

The Atam are a West African Bantu-speaking people. They speak a language belonging to the Benue-Congo branch of the Niger-Congo family of African languages and are related by language to the Ekoi people of southeastern Nigeria and western Cameroon.

ATBARA

The Atbara are an East African people. They are concentrated in the northeastern regions of the Sudan. Groups of them, however, can also be found in northwestern Ethiopia and Eritrea. Their neighbors include the Besharin people.

ATESO, see TESO

ATEWE

The Atewe are a Southern African Shona people. They live in Zimbabwe and Mozambique.

ATHI, see OKIEK

ATIE, see ATTIE

ATIÉ, see ATTIE

ATTAQUA

An extinct southern African people. The Attaqua used to live in the southern regions in what is now the Republic of South Africa.

ATTIE

The Attie, also spelled Atie and Atié, are a West African people. They are highly concentrated in the Ivory Coast and speak the Kwa language. Their neighbors include the Abe, Anyi, Ebrie and Mekyibo peoples. The Attie engage in coffee and cocoa growing.

ATUOT, see NUER

ATWOT, see DINKA and NUER

ATYAB, see KATAB

ATYUTI

The Atyuti are a West African people and one of Togo's ethnic minorities. They speak the Kwa language and live primarily in the central regions of the country. Their neighbors include the Adele, Dagomba, Kebu, Krachi, Tem and Yoruba peoples.

AUEN, see KOISAN and SAN

AULLIMINDEN, see TAUREG

AUNI

A southwestern African people. They are concentrated in the eastern regions of what is now the Namibia and the southwestern regions of Botswana.

AUNIN, see also KOISAN and SAN

A southwestern African people. They are concentrated in the western regions of what is now the Republic of Namibia.

AUSHI

The Aushi, also known as Baushi, are a Southwest Central African people. They are a Western Bantu-speaking Luba-Lunda group. They live in the Democratic Republic of the Congo (Zaire) and Zambia, notably in the southeast corner of Zaire. Their neighbors include the Balamba and Bempa peoples.

AUSSA, see HAUSA

AUYOKAWA

These are West African peoples and one of Nigeria's Hansa groups. The Auyokawa are concentrated in northeastern parts of Nigeria in what is presently the state of Borno (formerly Bornu). Their neighbors include the Bade, Fula (Fulani), Gerawa, Hausa, Maguzawa, Ngizim and Warjawa peoples. They are essentially an agricultural people.

AVATIME

A West African people. The Avatime, also known as the Afatime, speak a Kwa language. They live in both Togo and Ghana. Their neighbors include the Adangme, Akposo, Akyem, Ewe, Krachi and Lefana peoples.

AVIKAM

The Avikam, also known as Brignan, Gbanda, Kwaka, Lahou, and Lahu, are a small West African ethnic group. They live in the Ivory Coast, notably in the southern coastal areas of the country at the mouth of the Bandama river, and speak the Kwa language. Their neighbors include the Ajukru, Alagya, and Dida peoples. The Avikam engage in miscellaneous agricultural, fishing and trading pursuits.

AVUKAYA

The Avukaya are an Equatorial, Central and East African people. Their main concentrations are in the Sudan, Uganda and the Democratic Republic of the Congo (Zaire).

AWARE, see ALLADIAN

AWE

The Awe, also Awi, are a Central and East African Agwe-speaking people. The Agwe-speaking people comprise several groups including the Awngi, Agwa, Damot, Falasha and Yihudi. They are concentrated in Ethiopia.

AWEERA, see BONI

AWEMBA, see BEMBA

AWI, see AWE

AWNGI, see AWE

AXT-TUZIN, see also BERBER

The Axt-Tuzin are a Moroccan Berber group. They are concentrated in the northern Rif region, notably in the provinces of El Hoceima, Nador and Taza.

AYISENGA

The Ayisenga are a Southwest and Central African people. They live in the Democratic Republic of the Congo (Zaire) and Zambia.

AZA, see AZZA

AZANDE

Azande, also called Zande, Nzakara and Niam-Niam, are one of the Sudanese ethnic groups of the Central African Republic, Sudan and Democratic Republic of the Congo (Zaire). Their population is estimated at nearly one million, with over 500,000 of them in northwestern Zaire. They are concentrated along the shores of the Ubangi river and in Mbomou prefecture of the Central African Republic. Their environment varies from grasslands in the Sudanese area to rain forest in Zaire, and their subsistence pattern includes farming and hunting. The Azande are essentially a tribal agriculturalist people but also engage in trading and fishing.

The Azande are ethnically a mixed people and evidence suggests that they mingled with other peoples, especially the Ambomu. They speak a Sudanic language of the Adamawa-Eastern branch of the Niger-Congo family of African languages. They are renowned as great iron and wood carvers, as well as superb clay artisans.

The Azande support a society which is politically highly centralized. Their chiefs have firm control over their peoples. Normally, they govern with the advice of village councils. In important matters, however, the advice of all members of a village are elicited. Their most important aristocratic clans include the Vungara and the Bandia.

The Azande practice polygamy and their nobles are renowned for having many wives. They support a patrilineal social structure and live in widely scattered family homesteads.

Though they believe in a high God, *Mbori (Mboli)*, who is involved with all aspects of life, their religion is basically an ancestor cult. Hence, the concept of God in their religion is very weak and appears unimportant to their religious devotion.

The Azande have a strong tradition in witchcraft. Though seen as evil, it is widely practiced in their society. In their belief system, "at a man's death the body-soul, one of the two souls the Azande credit themselves with, becomes a totemic animal of his clan."[47]

AZJER, see TAUREG

AZNA, see HAUSA

AZZA

The Azza, also spelled Aza, people are one of the Central, East and West African ethnic groups. They are a Dagaza subgroup, and hence, a Tabou people. They live in Chad, Niger, and Sudan.

BAAMBA

A Bantu-speaking people. The Baamba are concentrated in the western regions of Uganda. They support a non-centralized type of society. Their neighbors include the Bakonjo people.

BABALIA, see BABELYIA

BABÉ, see KULANGO

BABELYIA

An East African people. The Babelyia, also spelled Babalia, are concentrated in the east-central regions of Sudan. Groups of them, however, live in Chad. They are one of the Bulala subgroups.

BABEMBA, see BEMBA

BABESUKHA, see LUHYA

BABETAKHO, see LUHYA

BABINDA, see also BABINGA

Babinda is the local name given to the Pygmies in the United Republic of Cameroon. The Babinda are a relatively small ethnic minority. They are concentrated in the southern forests of the country.

BABINGA

The Babinga are one of the many Pygmy people of equatorial Africa. Originally, they inhabited the tropical rain forest, in what is now within the Republic of Congo. Subsequently, however, they moved to other areas neighboring the Congo Basin, including Burundi, Cameroon, Central African Republic, Equatorial Guinea, Gabon, Central African Republic, Democratic Republic of the Congo (Zaire), Rwanda, Sudan, and Uganda. The Babinga are essentially hunters, foragers and potters.

BABOUTE

The Baboute, also known as Bute, Nbule, Voutere and Vute, are a West and West Central African people. The Babouti are concentrated in the southern forest region of the Cameroonian republic.

BABUKUSU, see LUHYA

BABUR

The Babur are a West African people and one of Nigeria's ethnic minorities. They live in the hills south of the Kanuri state of Borno (formerly Bornu). The Babur are a Muslim people who were impacted by various aspects of Kanuri culture. They speak Kanuri and are essentially an agricultural people.

BABWA

These are one of Democratic Republic of the Congo (Zaire's) ethnic groups. The Babwa are a Bantu-speaking people.

BACHAMA

A West African people. The Bachama speak an Afro-Asiatic language and are concentrated in western Cameroon and eastern Nigeria. Their neighbors include the Dera, Jen, Longuda, Mbula, Mumuye and Wurkum peoples.

BACHE, see RUKUBA

BACONGO, see KONGO

BADE

These are a West African people and one of Nigeria's ethnic minorities. The Bade, also called Bedde or Bede, are concentrated in northeastern parts of Nigeria, notably in Gashua in what is presently the state of Borno (formerly Bornu). Their neighbors include the Auyokawa, Hausa, Kanuri, Manga and Ngizim peoples. The Bade are a Muslim people who were impacted by various aspects of Kanuri culture. They speak Kanuri, a language that belongs to the Afro-Asiatic family of African languages, and are essentially agriculturalists. Their economic activities focus on agriculture, livestock and fishing.

The history of the Bade people is traced to the fourteenth century at which time they established their own emirate. Subsequently, their emirate became a tributary of the Bornu kingdom and in the eighteenth century, their dynasty evolved into the Gidgid family.

In 1808, the Bade were attacked by the Fulani *jihad* warriors. In the 1820's, Lawan Babuje (d. 1842), their *mai*, organized a Bade federation, fortified Gorgoram and established it as the seat of the dynasty. He also defended his emirate against the encroachments of both the Kanuri and the Fulani kingdoms. His policies were fostered by his son *Mai* Alhaji, who reigned between 1842 and 1893. During the reign of *Mai* Duna (1893-97), however, the emirate fell to the Sudanese warrior Rabih Al-Zubayr, following the British conquest of what is presently the northeastern region of modern Nigeria. In 1902, the emirate resurged with British recognition under *Mai* Salih (1897-1919). Subsequently, the Bade emirate was incorporated in the modern state of Nigeria, with Gashua as its seat.

BADEN, see KUNEMA

BADHA, see LENDU

BADONDO, see KONGO

BADUTU

The Badutu are an East African people. They are concentrated in the southern regions of Ethiopia, as well as in northern Kenya.

BADYARANKE

The Badyaranke, also known as Gola, Gula and Pajade, are a West African Tenda group. They are concentrated in the border areas between Guinea and Senegal, as well as in Liberia and Sierra Leone. They are linguistically related to the Kissi people.

BAFIA

The Bafia are a Central African people. They live in the Cameroon, and speak a Bantu language known as Rikpack. Their neighbors include the Bali, Mum, and Ndop peoples.

BAFOKENG, see FOKENG

BAGA

The Baga, also known as Baga-Binari, Baga-Koga, Barka and Kalum, are one of West Africa's smaller ethnic groups. They live in the coastal areas of Guinea, Guinea Bissau and Sierra Leone where they engage in miscellaneous fishing and trading activities. Their neighbors include the Landuma, Nalu and Susu peoples. The Baga speak a West Atlantic language that belongs to the Niger-Congo family of African languages.

BAGA-BINARI, see **BAGA**

BAGA-KOGA, see **BAGA**

BAGANDA, see **GANDA**

BAGGARA

Located in Sudan and Chad between the Nile River and Lake Chad, the Baggara (Baqara, Baqqara, Baqqarah) number approximately 6,000,000. The word baqara in Arabic means "cow." The Baggara are the results of massive unions between Arabs arriving from Arabia, Egypt and Sudan on the one hand, and Black indigenous inhabitants on the other. Their concentration is in the Darfur region, their traditional homeland, in western Sudan. The language of the Baggara is Arabic.

The Baggara are a pastoralist people, supporting a primarily nomadic lifestyle. Their society is highly tribal, with the tribe serving as the highest form of social organization. In its turn, the tribe is subdivided into smaller clans, each of which is led by the leader of the patrilineage. Their society is patrilineal with no centralized political structure. Currently, the Baggara belong to one of five major tribes, namely, the Habbania, the Hawazma, the Humr, the Messiriya and the Reizegat, or one of their subgroups such as Beni Helba, Beni Husayn, Beni Khuzam, Beni Selim, Oulad Hamayd, Salamat and Ta'aisha.

Originally, the Baggara were camel herders, but in time, they became cattlemen, stock-raisers and hunters. Because of the influence of Sudanic farmers, however, they are engaged in small-scale agriculture. Hence, their economy is a mixture of cattle and camel raising and small-scale agriculture. Men are responsible for moving the herds during the appropriate seasons, while women and children are responsible for the small gardens that make up Baggara agriculture. Baggara are renowned for traveling constantly from their settlements to markets where they sell their cattle products (particularly milk) and buy whatever goods they may need.

The great majority of the Baggara people are devout Muslims. In the 1880's, they provided substantial support to the Mahdist Islamic movement which flourished in eastern Sudan. They engaged the Egyptian Khedive authorities (then rulers of Sudan also), and later the British government, in a bitter war. This support was exemplified in the assumption of Abdallahi ibn Muhammad, a Baggara fellow, to the leadership of the movement in June 1885 (upon the sudden death of Muhammad Ahmad Al-Mahdi (its founder), until it was crushed by the British forces in a decisive battle in Omdurman on September 1, 1898.

The Baggara's Muslim faith, however, is markedly influenced by local customs. Religious ceremonies are presided over by a recognized shaykh, a person who is knowledgeable of Qura'nic sciences, the traditions of Prophet Muhammad, and Muslim laws and moral codes.

Polygamy is practiced in Baggara society within the limits set by Muslim *shariah*. A man may marry up to four wives, provided he treats them fairly and equally. Among other things, in a Baggara context, this condition calls on a man to provide each wife a tent of her own. Both parents are responsible for their children. Fathers, however, tend to devote greater attention to the upbringing of their sons, leaving the responsibility for upbringing and socializing the daughters to the mothers.

Baggara men wear long white cotton robes called *jibbas* and pantaloons to protect them from insects during the wet seasons. The men also are known to shave their heads and adorn them with headgear made of cotton. Women wear long blue clothes that cover the length of their bodies, and "adorn themselves with thick gold and ivory bracelets, amber necklaces, nose jewelry, rings, and silver anklet chains."[48]

Illiteracy is high among the Baggara and only those who receive religious instruction in Islamic studies can read and write. On the whole, their society relies on massive conversation, which includes story telling and narrations.

BAGIRMI

The Bagirmi, or Baguirmi, Barma and Bauirmi, are a people of mixed Arab, Berber and Negro origin. They live in the southern areas of the Sahara Desert close to the Bornu region. They speak Fulfulde, a dialect of the Fulani language, which is a branch of the Chari-Nile language family. They comprise several groups, the most important of which are the Barma. Currently, the Bagirmi constitute one of Chad's major ethnic groups. Together with the related Sara and Bongo, they live in the central parts of the Chari and Logone river basins.

The Bagirmi people enjoy a stratified social and political society with a privileged nobility headed by a royal family. They support an old kingdom that was founded in 1522, in the region situated southeast of Lake Chad, or what presently corresponds to the prefecture of Chari-Baguirmi in the Republic of Chad. The city of Massenya was its seat and remained the capital of the kingdom until 1894, when it was destroyed by an army of Rabih az-Zubayr, a Sudanese adventurer.

The kingdom was a buffer zone between the rival Muslim empires of Bornu to the west and Wadai to the east. It was under constant pressures by both empires and was forced to pay tribute to both of them. Thus, around 1600, during the reign of its fourth sultan Mbang (king) Abdullah, it was conquered by King Idris Alawma of Bornu and thereupon remained a vassal of Bornu throughout the 17th and 18th centuries.

In 1830, an exiled Bagirmi prince founded the Dar al-Kuti reign with the help of warriors of the Kingdom of Wadai and the Runga, of the Banda peoples. As a consequence, the kingdom became a vassal of the Wadai empire for a long portion of the 19th century.

BAGISU, see also GISU and LUHYA

The Bagisu, also known as Abagisu, Bamasaba, Gisu and Masaba, are one of Uganda's Bantu-speaking Luhya peoples. They are concentrated in the eastern regions of the country. Their social and political structures are not highly centralized. The Bagisu's neighbors include the Basoga, the Bagwere, the Banyoli, the Basamia and the Bagwe peoples.

BAGUIRMI, see BAGIRMI

BAGWAMA, see KURAMA

BAGWE

A Bantu-speaking people. The Bagwe live in the southeastern regions of Uganda. Their social and political structures are not highly centralized.

BAGWERE

The Bagwere are one of Uganda's Bantu-speaking peoples. They are concentrated in the southeastern regions of the country. Their society is not highly centralized. The Bagwere's neighbors include the Basoga, the Bagisu, the Banyoli, the Basamia and the Bagwe peoples.

BAGYELI, see KOLE

BAHAYA

An East African people. The Bahaya people are found throughout East Africa, especially in its urban centers.[49]

BAHIMA

A Bantu-speaking pastoralist people. The Bahima are concentrated in Uganda.

BAHLENGWE, see HLENGWE

BAHUMONO, see KOHUMONO

BAHURUTSHE, see TSWANA

BAHUTU, see HUTU

BAIA

The Baia are a Central African ethnic group. They are concentrated in the north central areas of the Central African Republic. Their neighbors include the Kake and Pande peoples.

BAILE, see ILA

BAIRU

A Bantu-speaking people. The Bairu are concentrated in Uganda. Like the Bahutu, they are essentially agriculturalists and jointly with Bahutu are called Banyankole.

BAKA

The Baka, also known as Tara-Baaka and Mbaka, are a Central and East African Oubanguian-speaking people. They comprise several related groups, including the Bangombe people. Their main concentrations are in southern Sudan, northeastern Zaire and southwestern Cameroon.

The Baka are one of the many Pygmy people of equatorial Africa. Originally, they inhabited the tropical rain forest, in what is now within the Republic of Congo. Subsequently, however, they moved to other areas and settled in countries neighboring the Congo Basin, including Cameroon, Central African Republic, Democratic Republic of the Congo (Zaire) and Sudan. The Baka are essentially hunters, foragers and potters.

BAKAA, see TSWANA

BAKAHONDE, see KAONDE

BAKALAGADI, see also SAN

A Southwest African people. The Bakalagadi are a San group. They are concentrated in the Kalahari Desert. Their neighbors include the Basarwa and Batswana peoples. The Bakalagadi speak Sekgalagadi, a language similar to Setswana, the language of the Batswana people.

BAKALAHARI

The Bakalahari are a Southwest African people. They are concentrated in the east-central regions of Botswana. Their neighbors include the Naron and the Masarwa peoples.

BAKALANGA, see KALANGA

BAKAMBA

The Bakamba are a West Central African people. They are concentrated in the Republic of Congo and Gabon.

BAKAONDE, see KAONDE

BAKÈLÈ, see BAKELE

BAKELE, see also KUKELE

The Bakele are a West Central African people. They are concentrated in Gabon, primarily in its western regions. Their neighbors include the Adyumba, Fang, and Nkomi peoples.

BAKERE

The Bakere are a West Central African people. They are concentrated in the Republic of Gabon, primarily in its central regions. Their neighbors include the Mberenzabi and Shake peoples.

BAKGATLA, see also TSWANA

A southern African Tswana group that shares the historical and cultural heritage of the Tswana people. They are concentrated in the Republic of Botswana, notably on the Namibian border. The Bakgatla have their own separate territory within Botswana as well as their own traditional chiefs.

In addition, they retain an inalienable communal ownership over their tribal lands. Presently, the Bakgatla represent one of Botswana's eight major tribal groups. The other main groups include the Bamangwato, Bakwena, Bamalete, Bangwaketse, Barolong, Batawana and Batlokwa.

BAKGWATHENG, see **KGALAGADI**

BAKHAYO, see **LUHYA**

BAKHURUTSHE, see **KHURUTSHE**

BAKIGA

A Bantu-speaking people. The Bakiga are concentrated in the southwestern regions of Uganda. Their society supports decentralized social and political institutions.

BAKISA, see **LUHYA**

BAKOLOLO, see **KOLOLO**

BAKONGO, see **KONGO**

BAKONJO

A Bantu-speaking people. The Bakonjo are concentrated in the western regions of Uganda. They support a non-centralized type of society. Their neighbors include the Baamba people.

BAKOROCAS

A southwestern African people. They are concentrated in the southwestern regions of Angola and the northwestern regions of Namibia, notably north of Kunene river.

BAKOTA, also see **KOTO**

A Central African people. The Bakota are concentrated in the Republic of

Congo. Groups of them, however, are also located in Gabon and Chad.

BAKUBA, see **KUBA**

BAKUENA, see **KWENA**

BAKULUNG, see **KULUNG**

BAKUTU

A Central African people. The Bakutu are concentrated in the Democratic Republic of the Congo (Zaire), notably in its equatorial forest region. They speak Lingala, a lingua franca that is known over wide areas in the country, and practice polygamy.

BAKWE (Central Africa)

A Central African people. The Bakwe are concentrated in the Sudan, Uganda and the Democratic Republic of the Congo (Zaire).

BAKWE (West Africa)

The Bakwe are a West African people. They are highly concentrated in the Ivory Coast, notably in its southern coastal regions, and speak the Kwa language. Their neighbors include the Bete, Dida, Grebo, Kran and Ngere peoples.

BAKWENA, see also **KWENA** and **TSWANA**

These are one of the Bantu-speaking group of the Republic of Botswana in southern Africa. The Bakwena are a Tswana group, and hence, share the historical and cultural heritage of the Tswana people. The Bakwena have their own separate territory within Botswana, situated in the southeast area of the country, near Gaborone. Moreover, they have their own traditional chiefs and retain an inalienable communal ownership over their tribal lands. The Bakwena represent one of Botswana's eight main tribal groups. The other main groups include the Bamangwato, Bakgatla, Bamalete, Bangwaketse, Barolong, Batawana and Batlokwa.

BALALI

These are a Congo people who were renowned for their passive resistance to French colonial administration. André Matswa was one of their prominent leaders during the first half of the twentieth century. Matswa formed an Association of Natives of French Equatorial Africa in 1926, the objectives of which called for ending racial discrimination and administrative injustices, as well as for granting French citizenship to Africans. In the 1930's, Matswa tried to form a trade union – a factor that led to his detainment by the French colonial authorities in Brazzaville, imprisonment, and eventually – after his escape from prison and recapture – to his exile to Chad where he died in 1942.[50] After the Second World War, an anti-colonial messianic cult bearing his name appeared in Brazzaville.

BALANTA, see BALANTE

BALANTE

The Balante (Balanté), also known as Alante, Balanta, Bulanda, Brassa and Frase, are a major West African ethnic group.   They are highly concentrated in Guinea, Guinea-Bissau and Senegal. In Guinea-Bissau they account for about 30% of the total population.   Their neighbors include the Banyua (Banyun), Biafada, Dyola, Malinke and Pepel peoples. The Balante society is centered on the family.

BALAONGWE, see KGALAGADI

BALE, see also LENDU and SURI

The Bale are an East African people. Their main concentrations are in the northeastern regions of the Democratic Republic of the Congo (Zaire), southeastern regions of Sudan and the southwestern areas of Ethiopia. The Bale are a Suri group. They speak Surmic (formerly Surma), an East Sudanic language of the Nilo-Saharan family of African languages.

BALESE NDAKE

The Balese Ndake people are one of Central and East African ethnic groups. Their main concentrations are in the northeastern regions of the Democratic Republic of the Congo (Zaire).

BALI

A West Central African people and one of Cameroon's more than 100 ethnic groups. The Bali are Bantu-speaking people. They are concentrated in the Bamenda region of the country. The Bali are a small but well-organized martial people.[51] Originally, they migrated from the north and settled in a territory belonging to the Widekum people. Much to the dislike of the Widekum, they were later confirmed by the German colonial authorities in their newly acquired land.

BALLOUK

The Ballouk are a West African people. They are concentrated in Guinea Bissau and neighboring countries, notably in Guinea Bissau's northwestern coastal areas. Their neighbors include the Diola and Koniagui peoples.

BALOULOU

The Baloulou are a West Central African people. They are a Mongo group. The Baloulou are concentrated in the Democratic Republic of the Congo (Zaire).

BALOUNDOU-MBO

The Baloundou-Mbo are a West Central African people. They are concentrated in the Cameroon, notably in its southern forest region.

BALUA

The Balua are a Central African people. They are concentrated in Angola, the Democratic Republic of the Congo (Zaire), and Zambia.

BALUBA

The Baluba are a Central African people. They are concentrated in Angola, the Democratic Republic of the Congo (Zaire), and Zambia. In the Democratic Republic of the Congo, the Baluba support a kingdom of their own with a dynasty that goes back at least three hundred years, and moreover, are famous for their "works of art–masks, fetishes, and other sculpture–of the most astonishing beauty."[52]   The Baluba practice polygamy.

BALUYIA, see LUHYA

BAMAKOMA, see MAKOMA

BAMALETE, see also TSWANA

These are one of Botswana's eight main tribal groups. The Bamalete are a Tswana group, and hence, share the historical and cultural heritage of the Tswana people. They have their own separate territory within Botswana, situated on the Namibia border. Moreover, they have their own traditional chiefs and retain an inalienable communal ownership over their tribal lands.

BAMANA, see BAMBARA and MANDE

BAMANGWATO

A southern African Bantu-speaking people. The Bamangwato, also known as Bangwato, are a Tswana group. They are concentrated in what is now modern Botswana. Their main political and economic center is at Serowe. The Bamangwato have their own chiefdom which is governed along lines similar to those of direct democracies. Under their political system, decisions involving critical issues are determined by the *Kgotla* or tribal assembly. Their economic activities focus on raising cattle. Presently, the Bamangwato represent one of Botswana's eight largest tribal groups. The other main groups include the Bakwena, Bakgatla, Bamalete, Bangwaketse, Barolong, Batawana and Batlokwa.

BAMARAKI, see LUHYA

BAMARAMA, see LUHYA

BAMASABA, see LUHYA

BAMBARA, see also MANDE

The Bambara people are the most numerous ethnic group in the Republic of Mali, comprising about one third of the population. They are concentrated in west central Mali along the Middle and Upper Niger river regions, notably between the Banifing river to the east and the Baule river to the west. Their neighbors include the Bobo, Bozo, Dogon (Dogan), Fula, Kagoro, Malinke, Minianka, Nono, Soninke and Senufo peoples. Together with other Mande (Malinke and Sarakole), they account for 50% of the country's total population. The Bambara speak Bambara, also known as Bamana, Bamanan Kan and Bammana, a language that belongs to the Mande branch of the Niger-Congo family of African languages. Their language is the common market language of the Malian people.

Prior to the colonial era, the Bambara developed two West African kingdoms. One kingdom was seated in Segu (Segou), between the Sénégal and Niger rivers. It was founded by two brothers, Barama Ngolo and Nia Ngolo before 1650. This state expanded into an empire under Kaladian Kulibali (1652-1682) and reached its zenith under Mamari Kulibali (1712-1755), covering the area from Bamako in the southwest and Djénné and Timbuktu in the northeast. Under Kulibali, the empire was supported by a professional army and navy. His successors extended the empire to the region of the Black Volta in the south. The Bambara empire fell in 1818, upon its conquest by Shekhu Ahmadu Lobbo of the Peul Empire of Macina.

The other kingdom, the Kaarta, was founded by rivals of Mamari Kulibali in 1753. It covered most of the area known as the Middle Niger. It collapsed when its capital, Nioro, was captured by the Muslim Tukulor warrior, El-Hadj Omar Tall in 1854.

The Bambara are predominantly Muslim. Prior to becoming Muslim in the early nineteenth century, they supported animist beliefs. In their legends "'the earth [was] divided into seven parts corresponding to seven heavens'." It was "so arranged by Faro, the agent of creation."[53] This legend corresponds to those of the Sumerians who believed in "a 'universe of seven', counting the seven steps of their ziggurats by the names of the seven planets corresponding to seven great gods, seven gates to the underworld, seven winds, seven days of the week."[54]

The main economic activities of the Bambara center on farming, animal husbandry, crafts and trade. Historical evidence suggests that during the Neolithic period their ancestors and those of the Hausa and Mandinka, succeeded in adopting and/or improvising a plowing technique which helped to transform their economies into food-producing economies.[55] The Bambara are still recognized as expert farmers, many of whom live in small towns and villages.

BAMBO, see LUBA

BAMBUR, see KULUNG

BAMBUTI, see ASUA and MBUTI

BAMILEKE

The Bamileke (Bamiléké) are a Bantu-speaking people. Currently, they constitute one of the major ethnic minorities in the Republic of Cameroon, accounting for about one-fifth of the total population. They are highly concentrated on the slopes of lush grassland valleys of western Cameroon, notably in the Adamawa Plateau and Cameroon Mountain region.

BAMOUN, see BAMUM

BAMUM

The Bamum, also known as Bamoun, Bamun and Mum, are a West African people. They are one of Cameroon's more than 100 ethnic groups, and are concentrated in the Bamenda region of the country. The Bamum speak a language that belongs to the Benue-Congo branch of the Niger-Congo family of African languages.

The Bamum are presumed to have migrated to their present territory from that of the Tikar people sometime during the eighteenth century. They first settled among their new neighbors, the Bamileke, and eventually established their own kingdom with Foumban as its seat. Their first king, or *mfon*, was Nchare.

The Bamum kingdom witnessed its first expansion during the reign of *Mfon* Mbuembue. This king was also famous for repelling a Fulani attack early in the nineteenth century, as well as for fortifying "Foumban with a surrounding wall and ditch."[56] The Kingdom's glorious period, however, was attained during the reign of *Mfon* Nijoya (1895-1923) who invented a system of writing based on pictographic characters plus ten numerals, and with "the help of his scribes prepared a book on the history and customs of the Bamum," developed a map of his country, and wrote a book on medicine and local pharmacopoeia.[57] In addition, in 1912, he founded "the first of 47 schools to teach the Bamum reading and writing in his [revised and simplified] script," and in 1913, commissioned a member of his court to prepare a printing press using it."[58] Njoya's reforms put him in conflict with the French colonial administration that was entrenching its power in the Cameroon. In 1923, he was deposed.

Currently, the Bamum people are essentially sedentary farmers and predominantly Muslim. Like other West African peoples, they are renowned for their wood and ivory carving, and metalwork. They are also famous for their embroidery, weaving and leatherwork.

BAMUN, see BAMUM

BANDA

The Banda, also known as Togbo, are Sudanese people. They are one of the ethnic groups of the Central African Republic, Cameroon, the Sudan and Democratic Republic of the Congo (Zaire). The Banda are concentrated in the Central African Republic where they live in the highlands lying between Bria, Bambari and Sibut, and account for about 27% of the total population, constituting the second largest minority after the Baya of the country's six major ethnic minorities. Their language belongs to the Adamawa-Eastern subgroup of the Niger-Congo family of African languages.

The Banda societies are patrilineally based and they presently live in small groups, each of which is governed by a headman. Their oral history, however, tells of "mountain kings" and a great leader called "Ngakola."

Early in the 18th century, Banda peoples occupied what presently constitutes southern Chad. Other Banda peoples established relations with the Muslim Kingdom of Wadai. They converted to Islam and became known as Runga.

In 1830, Banda peoples, known as Marba, joined Wadai warriors in helping an exiled Bagirmi (Baguirmi) emir (prince) establish the vassal kingdom of Dar al-Kuti. Upon that, they tried to rally other Banda peoples to their cause.

In the 1880s, some Banda peoples got into a conflict with al-Mahdi movement warriors of Sudan, which continued through the Belgian occupation in 1892 and during the French occupation of Oubangui (Ubangi) in the early 20th century in what is now Central African Republic.

BANDI

The Bandi, also called Gbunde, are a West African people. They live in the northwestern areas of the Republic of Liberia.

BANDIA, see AZANDE

BANDIBU, see KONGO

BANDJA

A West Central African people. The Bandja, also called Bandza, are concentrated in the Republic of Gabon.

BANDJAMBI, see **KOTO**

BANDZA, see **BANDJA**

BANEN

The Banen people are one of the Central African ethnic groups. They are concentrated in the eastern areas of Cameroon. Groups of them, however, are found in Equatorial Guinea and Gabon. Their neighbors include the Fang, Mbaru, Mungo, and Tanga peoples.

BANG, see **MAMBILA**

BANGALA

The Bangala are a West Central African people. They are concentrated in Angola and the Democratic Republic of the Congo (Zaire).

BANGBA

A Central African people. The Bangba are concentrated in the Democratic Republic of the Congo (Zaire), notably in its northeastern regions. Their neighbors include the Madi, Mangbetu, Mayogo, Mayvu, Makango and Barambo peoples.

BANGOMBE

The Bangome are one of the many Pygmy people of equatorial Africa. Originally, they inhabited the tropical rain forest, in what is now within the Republic of Congo. Subsequently, however, they moved to other areas neighboring the Congo Basin, including Burundi, Cameroon, Central African Republic, Equatorial Guinea, Gabon, Central African Republic, Democratic Republic of the Congo (Zaire), Rwanda, Sudan, and Uganda. The Bangombe are essentially hunters, foragers and potters.

BANGWAKETSE, see also TSWANA

These are one of the Bantu-speaking peoples of the Republic of Botswana.

The Bangwaketse are a Tswana group, and hence, share the historical and cultural heritages of the Tswana people. They have their own separate territory within Botswana, which is situated in the southeast area of the country, near Gaborone. Moreover, they have their own traditional chiefs and retain an inalienable communal ownership over their tribal lands. Currently, the Bangwaketse represent one of the eight main tribal groups in Botswana. The other main groups include the Bamangwato, Bakwena, Bakgatla, Bamalete, Barolong, Batawana and Batlokwa.

BANGWATO, see BAMANGWATO

BANKAL, see JARAWA

BANTU

The Bantu are a mixture of peoples, belonging predominantly to Central and Southern Africa. They account for more than 60 million of Africa's population and occupy about one third of the continent's land and support over 200 distinct languages which are a subgroup of the Niger-Congo family. Their languages are spoken in most areas falling below the fifth parallel of the north latitude to Cape Province in the south. In other words, Bantu-speaking peoples predominate in that territory of Africa that stretches "roughly from a line a few hundred miles above the Equator all the way to the Cape."[59] Rwanda, Makua, Xhosa and Zulu are four major Bantu languages.

According to The New Encyclopædia Britannica, "Bantu nouns usually consist of a stem preceded by a prefix that changes according to number. Nouns are grouped into categories (genders) on the basis of these prefixes. All or almost all the words in a Bantu sentence are usually marked by a prefix indicating the category to which the noun used as subject of the sentence belongs. Suffixes are also used, especially in the formation of verb stems and verb forms."[60]

Probable evidence suggests that Bantu-speaking peoples have originated in the modern Cameroon-Niger area, and from there, they migrated to other areas in Africa which about 2000 years ago were inhabited essentially by Pygmies and San (Bushmen). "Bantus are a mixture...made thousands of years ago when pools of the two basic African stocks, Hamite and Negro, began to flow into one another."[61] Out of this fusion of peoples came the Nilotic peoples of the Sudan and the Bantus.

The link between the Bantu peoples, however, is a linguistic one. It is not a racial term, nor is it a term that suggests a racial linkage between Bantu-speaking peoples.[62] This phenomenon explains why Bantu peoples are extremely diverse in terms of their economic, social and political institutions. More importantly, it explains the difference in the physical features between Bantu and Negroid peoples. "Bantus are, by and large, lighter-skinned than their parent Negroes (and lighter than some Hamites)."[63]

Historical evidence suggests that Bantus were not pastoral nomads. It suggests rather that they were originally forest people who later evolved into agriculturalists and then into cattle people. "What distinguishes them chiefly is that they became cattle people after clearing plots in the forest; cattle are vital to their whole life."[64]

Broadly speaking, almost all Bantu-speaking peoples "are held together by kinship, and have a strong clannishness and cohesiveness, under a chief or chiefs;" revere ancestors and ancestral spirits; and, base their economy on land (which is considered a communal property) and cattle.[65]

Geographically, the Bantu people belong to one of three main groups: Southern, Eastern and Western. Southern Bantus include the following peoples: Ambo, Herero, Kalanga, Karanga, Korekore, Manyika, Natal Nguni or Zulu of Natal and their offshoots (Ndebele, also Tebele, Swazi, Transvaal or Ndebele), Ndau, Ngoni (Cape Nguni of the Ciskei and Transkei-Xhosa, Thembu, Mponde, etc.), Shona, Southern Sotho, Tsonga (Tsonga, Ronga, Tswa), Tswana (Horutshe, Kgatla, Kwena, Ngwaketse, Ngwato, Rolong, Tlhaping), Venda, Zezuru, etc.. Eastern Bantu include the following people: Chagga, Gogo, Hehe, Kikuyu, Konde, Makua, Ngonde, Nyakyusa, Nyanja (Nsenga, Sena, Chewa), Nyika, Pokomo, Sagara, Sambara, Sango, Taita, Yao, etc.. These peoples are located in East Africa. Finally, Western Bantus include: Chokwe, Congo, Ila, Lozi, Luba-Lunda (Aushi, Bemba, Bisa, Luba-Hemba, Luluwa, Shila, Songe), Ogowe,

Pangwe (Fang), Songo-Meno, Teke (Angica, Anziques, etc.), Wongo-Lele-Bushongo, etc. Western Bantus are concentrated in the western areas of southern Africa.

BANYALA, see LUHYA

BANYAMWEZI, see NYAMWEZI

BANYANHKOLE, see BANYANKOLE

BANYANKOLE

The Banyankole, also spelled Banyanhkole, are an East African Ankole group. Their main concentrations are in the northwestern regions of Tanzania, as well as neighboring countries especially Uganda, Rwanda and Burundi. In Uganda, the term is used to refer to the Bahima and Bairu, two of the country's agriculturalist people.

BANYARUANDA, see NYARUANDA

BANYARWANDA, see also NYARUANDA

A term used to refer to both the Tutsi (Batutsi) and Hutu (Bahutu) peoples in Uganda. In Uganda, the Tutsi people are essentially specialized pastoralists, whereas the Hutu are essentially agriculturalists.

BANYOLI

A Bantu-speaking people. The Banyoli are concentrated in the southeastern regions of Uganda together with other related groups, including the Basoga, the Bagisu, the Bagwere, the Basamia and the Bagwe peoples. Their society supports decentralized social and political institutions.

BANYORE, see LUHYA

BANYORO, see NYORO

BANYUA

The Banyua people are a West African people. They are concentrated in Guinea and speak a West Atlantic language that belongs to the Niger-Congo family of African languages. Their neighbors include the Balante, Dyola and Pepel peoples.

BANYUN, see BANYUA

BANYYAMWESI, see NYAMWEZI

BANZIRI

The Banziri people are one of the ethnic minorities of the Central African Republic and Democratic Republic of the Congo (Zaire). Their language belongs to the Adamawa-Eastern subgroup of the Niger-Congo family of African languages.

The Banziri are essentially a tribal agriculturalist people, but also engage in trading and fishing. They are concentrated in the Upper Ubangi (Oubangui) river region of southern Central African Republic and northern Democratic Republic of the Congo (Zaire).

BANZIRTI, see BANZIRI

The Banzirti, also called Banziri, are a small Central African people. Their main concentrations are in Chad, Central African Republic, and the Democratic Republic of the Congo (Zaire).

BAOL, see BAULE

BAOULE, see BAULE

BAPEDI, see also SOTHO

The Bapedi are a Sotho people. Also known as Suthu, Suto or Basuto, the Sotho are a southern African group of peoples who are linguistically and culturally similar. They occupy the high grasslands of the region and speak Sesotho, a Bantu language. They comprise three major groups: northern (or Transvaal), western (or Tswana), and southern (or Basuto, Lesotho) Sotho peoples. They are concentrated in the Kingdom of Lesotho, as well as in Lebowa and QwaQwa, which until recently represented two of the black homelands in the Republic of South Africa.

The Sotho comprise numerous groups, the most important of which are: Pedi, Lovedu and Kanga-Kone in Lebowa, and Kwena in Lesotho. The Kwena subgroup comprises such tribes as Molibeli, Monaheng, Hlakwana, Kxwakxwa (Qwagwa) and Fokeng.

The Pedi of the Sotho, also known as Bapedi, Northern Sotho and Transvaal Sotho, were originally from Central Africa. Their ancestors who settled in the Bopedi region developed several kingdoms of their own which flourished during the seventeenth and eighteenth centuries, some of which were destroyed by Mzilikazi, a Zulu leader.

Between the 1850's and the 1870's, Sekhukhune, one of the Pedi kings, successfully resisted Afrikaner attempts to subdue them. In 1879, however, the Pedi were defeated by the British assisted by Swazi warriors and contestants to Pedi's throne. In 1896, the British divided Bopedi, their territory, into two parts, which placed them under rival rulers. The Natives' Land Act of 1913 and the Natives' Trust and Lands Act of 1936 designated Bopedi exclusively for them. Now, they are an integral part of the Republic of South Africa.

The great majority of Sotho are agricultural, relying both on cultivation and animal husbandry. But males among them often seek work outside their villages, as laborers. Their settlements are characterized "by scattered hamlets of circular huts with mud and wattle or stone walls surmounted by a conical, thatched roof."[66] In their social patterns, most Pedi recognize patrilineal lineages. Though Christianity has won many converts, Pedi people continue to practice elements of their traditional religious beliefs.

BAPHELENG, see KGALAGADI

BAPO

A West African Krou group. They are concentrated in the Ivory Coast.

BAPOTO

The Bapoto are a Central and West Central African people. Their main concentrations are in Chad, the Central African Republic and the Democratic Republic of the Congo (Zaire).

BAPOUNOU

The Babounou are the third largest ethnic group in the Gabonese Republic after the Fang and Eshira. They are essentially a tribal people. They are Bantu-speaking people. They speak Bapounou.

BAQARA, see BAGGARA

BAQQARA, see BAGGARA

BARA, see also MALAGASY

The Bara are a Malagasy East African Tandroy people. They are concentrated on the Island of Madagascar, notably in its southern regions. Groups of them, however, are found along the coastal areas of East Africa. The Bara speak a dialect of Malagasy and are closely related to other Tandroy peoples, including the Mahafale, Sakalave, and Tanosy.

BARAAWE, see BRAVA

BARABAIG

The Barabaig are an East African group. Their main concentrations are in Tanzania, primarily in the vicinity of Lake Manyara in the north central regions of the country. Their neighbors include the Burungi, Iramba, Irangi, and Iraqw peoples.

BARAMBO

A Central African people. The Barambo are concentrated in the Democratic Republic of the Congo (Zaire), notably in its northeastern regions. Their neighbors include the Bangba, Madi, Mangbetu, Mayogo,

Mayvu, and Makango.

BARAYA

The Baraya are one of the Chadian Kuri subgroups. They speak Yedina, a Buduma dialect. Like other Kuri groups, they live along the eastern shores of Lake Chad.

BAREA, see NARA

BARGU, see also BARIBA

The Bargu are a West African Voltaic-speaking people comprised of three major subgroups, namely the Borgo, Bariba and Borgenci. They are found in several states of West Africa, especially in Nigeria and Benin. They live in an area which consists of both plains and wooded savanna and is characterized by poor soil and little rainfall. Their lands, however, are drained by several small tributaries of the Niger river.

The Bargu were part of the renowned Oyo empire which flourished in West Africa, especially between the fourteenth and eighteenth centuries. They asserted the independence of their own Borgu kingdom during the latter part of the eighteenth century. Their kingdom (emirate), also known as Kwara State, was in an inland region of West Africa, northeast and east of the Niger river. Its territory covered parts of what are now the modern states of Benin and Nigeria. The political capital of the Borgu kingdom was at Nikki (now in Benin). Its spiritual capital was at Bussa, which was evacuated in 1968 to allow for the construction of the artificial Kainji Lake.

Until 1898, the tribes of the Borgu region gave their allegiance to the Sultan of Borgu and the chief of the Busa (Bussa). Competition between British and French interests in West Africa led to a territorial conflict over the region. This conflict continued even more so when Captain Frederick Lugard, acting on behalf of the Goldie's Royal Niger Company, occupied the Borgu in 1894, thwarting a French advance towards the region. Eventually, the Anglo-British conflict over the Borgu region was resolved by the conclusion of the convention of 1898, which partitioned the Borgu into two parts, an eastern and a western. Eastern Borgu, which supported the Bussa, Kaiama and Illo chiefdoms, was declared British, and became a British sphere of interest. On the other hand, western Borgu was declared French, and consequently, was placed under French control. Two years later, the British established the reorganized Eastern Borgu. They created the Borgu Province, recognized the Bussa chiefdom and gave the chiefdom Kaiama an emirate status. In 1905 and 1907, parts of the Borgu region were transferred to other provinces. In 1954, the Bussa and Kaiama emirates were merged to form the Emirate of Borgu.

BARI

One of Democratic Republic of the Congo's (Zaire's) and Sudan's ethnic groups.

The Bari are Nilotes people. They speak Bari, an Eastern Sudanic (Eastern Nilotic) language of the Chari-Nile branch of the Nilo-Saharan family of African languages. In Zaire, they are located in the north eastern parts of the country. In the Sudan, they are concentrated in the Gondokoro area, near Juba, in the southwestern region of the country.

The Bari support a relatively sedentary type of society. They live in scattered villages and their main economic activities center on farming, cattle raising and hunting.

The social organization of the Bari people is tribal, patrilineal and class-based.

The Bari people are divided into some 150 patrilineal clans and their people are divided into essentially two classes, freemen and serfs. Individuals with occupations involving hard manual labor, such as "Blacksmiths, professional hunters, and similar groups form inferior castes."[67]

Tribal initiation exercises are still being practiced among the Bari and involve both men and women. These exercises take place by extracting the lower incisors, as well as by scarring. Upon initiation, the initiated "enter age sets that have distinctive names and ornaments."[68]

In their society, authority is diffused, rather than centralized. The Bari "have many 'big men' rather than a single chief." The "big men" include the "ritual functionaries" who bring rain and the "fathers of the earth" who, through magic, "ensure successful cultivation, hunting, and warfare."[69] The positions of "big men" are patrilineally inherited.

The Bari people continue to adhere to their traditional religious faiths, which center on the belief "in a god who has two aspects: a benevolent god who dwells in the sky and produces rain and a malevolent god who lives in the earth and is associated with cultivation."[70] Additionally, they believe in the ancestor cult, which requires them to make sacrifices "to the spirits of the dead."[71]

BARIBA, see also BARGU

The Bariba are a West African Voltaic-speaking people. They are one of the three major subgroups of the Bargu people, which aside from the Bariba also include the Borgo and Borgenci. They are found in several states of West Africa, especially Nigeria and Benin. In Nigeria, they are concentrated in the west-central parts of the country, particularly in the state of Kwara. They constitute the fourth largest Nigerian ethnic group after the Fon, Adja and Yoruba. In Benin, they account, together with the Somba and other related groups, for about one-fifth or 19.5% of the country's total population. They are concentrated in the northern parts of Benin.

BARKA, see BAGA

BARMA, see BAGIRMI

BARMPE, see MENDE

BAROLONG, see also TSWANA

A Bantu-speaking people of the Republic of Botswana. The Barolong are historically and culturally a Tswana people. They have their own separate territory within Botswana as well as their own traditional chiefs. In addition, they retain an inalienable communal ownership over their tribal lands. Currently, the Barolong represent one of Botswana's eight main tribal groups. The other main groups include the Bamangwato, Bakwena,

Batawana, Bangwaketse, Bakgatla, Bamalete and Batlokwa.

BAROTSE, see **LOZI**

BAROZI, see **LOZI**

BARRKU

A West African people. They are concentrated in central Nigeria. The Barrku are one of the groups in the Mama cluster.

BARUTSE, see **LOZI**

BARUTSHE, see **LOZI**

BARYA, see also **NARA**

The Barya are a Nilotic-speaking people. They live along the Blue Nile River Valley in eastern Sudan and the Barentu region of Eritrea. Their neighbors include the Anuak, Berti, Gumuz and Kunama peoples. The Barya are semi-nomadic postarolists.

BASAKOMO

The Basakomo people are one of Central African ethnic groups. They are concentrated in the west central regions of Cameroon. Their neighbors include the Bali and Mungo peoples.

BASALAMPASU

The Basalampasu are a Central African people. They are concentrated in the Democratic Republic of the Congo (Zaire), notably in the vicinity of Lualaba.

BASAMIA, see also **LUHYA**

A Bantu-speaking Luhya people. The Basamia are concentrated in the eastern regions of Uganda, as well as in the western provinces of Kenya.

Their society supports decentralized social and political institutions. The Basamia's neighbors include the Basoga, the Bagisu, the Bagwere, the Banyoli and the Bagwe peoples.

BASARI (Guinea and Senegal)

The Basari people are one of the Tenda groups of West Africa. They live in northwestern Guinea and southeastern Senegal.

BASARI   (Togo and Ghana)

These are one of the ethnic minorities of Togo. The Basari, also known as the Kyamba and Tchamba, are a Gur-speaking Voltaic peoples. They live in the northern areas of the country, especially in la Kara western region. Groups of them, however, can also be found in Ghana. Their neighbors include the Atyuti, Dagomba, Kabre, Konkomba and Tem peoples. The Basari are predominantly agriculturalists.   They are part of the Gurma cluster of peoples.

BASARWA, see SAN

BASHAGA, see KGALAGADI

BASHIKONGO, see KONGO

BASHILANGE

The Bashilange are a West Central African people. They are concentrated in the Democratic Republic of the Congo (Zaire), notably in its east central regions. Their neighbors include the Bahavu, Bukavu, Wabembe, and Walega peoples.

BASHILELE

The Bashilele are a West Central African people. They are concentrated in the Democratic Republic of the Congo (Zaire), primarily in its east central regions. Their neighbors include the Bunda, Lulua, and Tukkongo peoples.

BASILA

A West African people. The Basila are concentrated in the northern regions of Togo and Benin. They speak a Voltaic language. Their neighbors include the Kabre, Kilinga, Tem and Yoruba peoples.

BASIRI

The Basiri are a Central and East African people. Their main concentrations are in Chad, the Central African Republic, and Sudan.

BASKETO

The Basketo are an East African Omotic-speaking people. They are concentrated in the southwestern regions of Ethiopia, primarily north of Lake Rudolf. Their neighbors include the Chara, Kambatta, and Wolamo peoples.

BASOGA

The Basoga are one of Uganda's Bantu-speaking peoples. They are concentrated in the southeastern regions of the country and support a society which is not highly centralized. The Basoga's neighbors include the Bagisu, the Bagwere, the Banyoli, the Basamia and the Bagwe peoples.

BASONGA, see LUHYA

BASS NKOME, see also IGALA

The Bass Nkome are one of Nigeria's ethnic minorities. They are concentrated in the west-central areas of the country, particularly in the state of Kwara. They recognize the Igala's king, *ata*, as their own king.

BASSA (Liberia), see also MANDE

These are one of Liberia's Mande groups. The Bassa people are the second largest group after the Kpelle. They speak Mande, a language belonging to the Niger-Congo group of African languages. Their neighbors include the Kpelle, Gola, Kran, Kru, Loma, Mano, Mende, Ngere, Sapo and Vai peoples. The Bassa engage in miscellaneous economic pursuits such as farming, fishing and trading.

BASSA (Nigeria), see also IGALA

The Bassa are a West African people and one of Nigeria's ethnic minorities. They are concentrated in the west-central areas of the country, particularly in the state of Kwara. The Bassa speak a language that belongs to the Benue-Congo family of African languages. Their neighbors include the Bassa-Nge, Gbari, Idoma, Igala and Igbirra peoples. They recognize the Igala's king, *ata*, as their own king.

BASSA-NGE

The Bassa are a West African people and one of Nigeria's ethnic minorities. They are concentrated in the west-central areas of the country, particularly in the state of Kwara. The Bassa-Nge speak Kwa. Their neighbors include the Bassa, Edo, Igala and Igbirra peoples.

BASSARI

These are one of Senegal's small, but ancient ethnic groups. They are located in the rocky highlands of Fouta Djallon.

BASSI, see GUSII

BASTER(S)

The Baster(s), also known as Rehoboth Baster(s), are a Southwest African people. They are concentrated in Namibia, notably in Rehoboth. The Basters are a people of mixed Khoi/European ancestry "who learned to speak Dutch (later Afrikaans) and were educated in Christianity."[72] Currently, they account for nearly 3% of Namibia's total population.

BASUA

The Basua are one of the many Pygmy people of equatorial Africa. Originally, they inhabited the tropical rain forest, in what is now within the

Republic of Congo. Subsequently, however, they moved to other areas neighboring the Congo Basin, including Burundi, Cameroon, Central African Republic, Equatorial Guinea, Gabon, Central African Republic, Democratic Republic of the Congo (Zaire), Rwanda, Sudan, and Uganda. They are essentially hunters, foragers and potters.

BASUKU, see **SUKU**

BASUKUMA, see **SUKUMA**

BASUNDI, see **KONGO**

BASUTO, see also **SOTHO**

The Basuto are Sotho people, also called Suthu, or Suto. They are a southern African group of peoples who are linguistically and culturally similar. They occupy the high grasslands of the region and speak Sesotho (also Sotho), a Bantu language. The Sotho comprise three major groups: northern (or Transvaal), western (or Tswana) and southern (or Basuto, Lesotho) Sotho peoples. They are concentrated in the Kingdom of Lesotho, as well as in Lebowa and QwaQwa, which until recently represented two of the black homelands in the Republic of South Africa.

The Sotho population in Lebowa is over 2.6 million, growing at the rate of 3.9% per year, whereas in QwaQwa it is about 0.8 million, growing at the rate of 2.5%. In Lesotho, the Sotho constitute about 99.7% of the country's population, growing at the rate of 2.7% per year.

The modern history of the Basuto (Sotho) people could be traced back to the early part of the nineteenth century, at which time they settled in an upland called Butha Buthe, west of the Drakensberg scrap opposite Natal. Realizing that this land did not avail safe protection to his people and their belongings, one of the young princes of an obscure Sotho sub-tribe, Moshesh, decided to move elsewhere. Hence in 1824, the Basuto settled in Thaba Bosiu. Through diplomacy, utilization of European military tactics and invitation to missionaries to settle in Thaba Bosiu, Moshesh managed to safeguard part of his people's new land and settlements against intrusions of more powerful neighbors, including the Zulus, Ndebeles, Tlokwas, Boers and British.

Moshesh's peaceful diplomatic means, however, did not spare him existential wars with the Boers who were trying to expand their territory into Basutoland for the purpose of establishing their fee states. In the 1850's and 1860's, his wars with the Boers cost the Basuto most of their fertile land and, moreover, it impoverished many of them. In order to counteract the Boers' mounting power, protect his people and safeguard the remaining free parts of Basutoland (which did not fall to the Boers), Moshesh sought British protection. His request was formally approved in 1868, at which time Sir P. Wodehouse, the then governor of the Cape, declared the annexation of Basutoland to Cape Colony. Henceforth, Basutoland remained under British protection until October 4, 1966, when it acquired its independence as the Kingdom of Lesotho with Moshesh's direct descendant, Moshoeshoe, as its constitutional monarch.

The great majority of Basuto (Sotho) are agricultural, relying both on cultivation and animal husbandry. But males among them often seek work outside their villages, as laborers. Their settlements are characterized "by scattered hamlets of circular huts with mud and wattle or stone walls surmounted by a conical, thatched roof."[73] In their social patterns, most Basuto recognize patrilineal lineages and traditionally, they allowed polygamy. Though Christianity has won many converts, many of the Basuto people still practice elements of their traditional religious beliefs.

BASUTOLAND BUSHMEN

An extinct southern African people. The Basutoland Bushmen used to live in what is now the Republic of South Africa.

BATA

A West African Afro-Asiatic-speaking people. They are concentrated in northeastern Nigeria. Groups of them, however, are also located in Cameroon. Their neighbors include the Fula, Fali, Gude, Hona, Margi, Mbula, Vere and Yungur peoples.

BATACHE, see NUPE

BATACHI, see NUPE

BATAHIN

One of Central African ethnic groups. They are concentrated in western Sudan. Their neighbors include the Hawawir and Kawahla peoples.

BATAKI, see TEKE

BATATELA

The Batatela are a West Central African people. They are concentrated in the Democratic Republic of the Congo (Zaire).

BATAWANA, see also TSWANA

The Batawana are one of Botswana's Tswana groups. They are a Bantu-speaking people and share the same historical and cultural heritages of other Tswana peoples. Presently, they represent one of Botswana's eight main tribal groups. The other main groups include the Bamangwato, Bakwena, Bangwaketse, Bakgatla, Bamalete, Barolong and Batlokwa.

BATEKE, see TEKE

BATIRIKI, see LUHYA

BATLARO, see also TSWANA

The Batlaro are a southern African Bantu-speaking Tswana group. They are concentrated in the southern regions of Botswana. Their neighbors include the Barolong who are also a Tswana people.

BATLHAPING, see TSWANA

A southern African Bantu-speaking Tswana group. The Batlhaping are concentrated in the southern regions of Botswana. Their neighbors include the Barolong who are also a Tswana people.

BATLHARO, see also TSWANA

The Batlharo are one of Botswana's Tswana groups. They are a Bantu-speaking people and live in the southern regions of the country. Their neighbors include the Barolong who are also a Tswana people.

BATLOKWA, see also TSWANA, PEDI and SOTHO

These are one of the Sotho (formerly Pedi) groups. They are concentrated in Botswana and are historically and culturally related to the Tswana people. The Batlokwa have their own separate territory within Botswana, situated on the Namibia border. Moreover, they have their own traditional chiefs and retain an inalienable communal ownership over their own tribal lands. Presently, the Batlokwa represent one of Botswana's eight main tribal groups. The other main groups include the Bamangwato, Bakwena, Batawana, Bangwaketse, Bakgatla, Bamalete and Barolong.

BATORO, see TORO

BATSOTSO, see LUHYA

BATSWANA, see TSWANA

BATTI

The Batti are a West African Kraun-speaking people. They live in Liberia, primarily in the Lofa County. The Batti are a Kuwaa subgroup.

BATUSI, see TUTSI

BATWA, see also TWA

An extinct southern African people. The Batwa used to live in what is presently the Republic of South Africa to the west of Swaziland.

BAUIRMI, see BAGIRMI

BAULE, see also BAOULE and AKAN

The Baule (Baulé), also called Baol or Baoule, are one of West Africa's ethnic groups. They speak a Twi branch of the Kwa branch of the Niger-Congo family of African languages. The Baule people are concentrated in the central region of the Ivory Coast, especially in the southern areas between the Komoé and Bandama rivers. Currently, they constitute the largest single ethnic minority in the Ivory Coast, accounting for 23% of the total population of the country. As an Akan group, they have tribal affiliations with numerous groups outside the Ivory Coast, especially the Akan people of Ghana. Their neighbors include the Abbe (Abe), Anyi, Ari, Dida, Gan, Guro and Senufo peoples.

In the 14th century they founded a state of their own, which was a satellite state of the Wolof empire of West Africa. Their state covered the area along the coast and inland to the south of Dakar, the capital of the present Republic of Sénégal.

The Baule state fell to the neighboring state of Cayor around 1556, and remained under the latter's control until 1686. In the later part of the 17th century, Cayor fell to the Wolof empire.

In 1730, the Baule people refused to be part of the Ashanti confederacy in what is presently the Republic of Ghana. Around 1750, they emigrated to their present location. Under the leadership of Queen Awura Pokou, who led the exodus, they consolidated their power and ruled a great part of what is presently modern Ivory coast.

The Baule resisted repeated European attempts to control their kingdom and lands. Towards the middle of the nineteenth century, however, they were conquered by the French, and hence, placed under French colonial rule.

While under French colonial rule, the Baule produced several prominent leaders, including Félix Houphouet-Boigny, who prior to the independence of the Ivory Coast on August 7, 1960, was elected representative of Ivory Coast and Upper Volta (now Burkina Faso), to the French Constituent Assemblies in 1945 and 1946. He was then elected to the French National Assembly in 1951 and again in 1956. Between 1956-1959, Houphouet-Boigny served as minister in the French government, and in 1960, he became president of Ivory Coast – a position which he continued to hold until his death on December 7, 1993.

The Baule people are essentially agriculturalists. Their main economic activities focus on agriculture, animal husbandry and fishing. Their agricultural products include yam, coffee, cocoa, animal husbandry and fishing. Their villages are relatively small in size and are generally composed of quarters that surround a central courtyard. Additionally, each village has its own chief and council of elders, the members of which represent various lineages. In their society lineages are matrilineal.

Traditionally, the Baule believed in the ancestor cult and a world of spirits. Like other West Africa peoples, they are renowned for their splendid wood sculpture, which illustrates their traditional beliefs.

BAUSHI, see **AUSHI**

BAVENDA, see **VENDA**

BAWANGA, see **LUHYA**

BAYA, see also **GBAYA**, or **GBEYA**

The Baya are a Central African ethnic minority who are especially concentrated in southwestern Haute-Sangha and Lobaye prefectures of the Central African Republic, as well as in the eastern and central areas of the United Republic of Cameroon. They speak a language of the Adamawa-Eastern subgroup of the Niger-Congo family and observe patrilineal descent. They live in villages headed by chiefs, who enjoy nominal power and serve essentially as arbitrators.

Originally, the Baya lived in the northern areas of Nigeria in what is now Hausa domains. In the 19th century they migrated southward to avoid a holy war launched against them by Usman dan Fodio, but were not able to stop continuous Fulani attacks against them in what is currently northern Cameroon.

Though they did not develop a state of their own, the Baya opposed colonial encroachments and to this end, they resisted the French throughout the colonial period. Early in the 1920s, they staged a revolt against the French colonial power for being forced to serve as porters and laborers. In 1929, they revolted again, protesting their conscription for the Congo-Ocean railway. The latter revolt lasted for three years and, as a consequence, many of their rebels were exterminated. Later, the French colonizers incorporated some of their chiefs as administrative magistrates.

The Baya peoples are currently divided into several subgroups, the most important of which are the Bokoto, the Buli, the Bwaka and the Kaka. They constitute the largest single ethnic group of the Central African Republic. They account for 34% of the country's total population.

BAYAKA, see also AKA, YAKA and SUKU

The Bayaka, also known as Yaka and Biaka, are a Central African people. They are concentrated in Angola and the Democratic Republic of the Congo (Zaire). Currently, however, they are called Suku. The name Yaka was used just before and after 1900 in reference to the title of the Suku king, namely, "Yaka of Mini Kongo."[74]

The Bayaka are one of the many Pygmy people of equatorial Africa. Originally, they inhabited the tropical rain forest, in what is now within the Republic of Congo. Subsequently, however, they moved to other areas neighboring the Congo Basin, including Burundi, Cameroon, Central African Republic, Equatorial Guinea, Gabon, Central African Republic, Democratic Republic of the Congo (Zaire), Rwanda, Sudan, and Uganda. The Bayaka are essentially hunters, foragers and potters.

BAYNAWA, see GUIDAR

BAYOMBI

A West Central African people. The Bayombi are concentrated in the Gabon, the Central African Republic and Chad.

BAYOT

The Bayot people are one of Guinea-Bissau's ethnic groups. They live close to the coastal areas of the country.

BAZA, see **KUNEMA**

BAZIMBA

The Bazimba are one of the many Pygmy people of equatorial Africa. Originally, they inhabited the tropical rain forest, in what is now within the Republic of Congo. Subsequently, however, they moved to other areas neighboring the Congo Basin, including Burundi, Cameroon, Central African Republic, Equatorial Guinea, Gabon, Central African Republic, Democratic Republic of the Congo (Zaire), Rwanda, Sudan, and Uganda. The Bazimba are essentially hunters, foragers and potters.

BE, see **EWE**

BECHUANA, see **TSWANA**

BEDAYRIA

A Central and East African people. The Bedayria are concentrated in both Chad and Sudan. They are primarily settled agriculturalists.

BEDDE, see **BEDE**

BEDERIAT

One of Central African people. They are concentrated in the west central areas of Sudan.

BEDE, see **BADE**

BEDIK

The Bedik people are a West African ethnic group. They are concentrated in Mali and Senegal.

BEDOUIN

An Arabic word that refers to non-sedentary and non-rural people, notably to the nomadic people who live in deserts. The term applies to many groups in Africa such as the nomads of the Egyptian desert.

BEIDAN, see MOOR

BEIR, see MURLE

BEJA

Beja are a group of East African nomadic tribes "that inhabit the Red Sea Hills and parts of the plains sloping down to the main Nile," notably the area between southeastern Egypt (the Eastern Desert) through Sudan and Eritrea into Ethiopia.[75] Their main concentrations, however, are in the Sudan, where they constitute about 6% of the country's total population, which is estimated at a little over 30 million. These people speak a Hamitic language known as Beja (also called Ta Bedawie or To Bedawi), and some Tigre, but many also speak Arabic. The Beja comprise four main groups: The 'Ababda, the Bisharin, the Hadendowa, and Beni Amer.

The Beja are the descendants of peoples that lived in the described area since 4000 B.C., if not before. Historical evidence of the fifth and fourth centuries before Christ suggests that they often raided surrounding kingdoms, including that of Kush. Also, it suggests that King Ezana of Axum had subdued them during the middle of the fourth century A.D.[76] Further, it notes that the Beja occupied the Eriterian plateau in the later part of the seventh century – a factor that contributed to the downfall of the Axomite kingdom.[77]

Prior to the thirteenth century, the Beja were Christian and continued to adhere to Christianity until the thirteenth century, at which time they became Muslim. This change of heart, however, did not significantly affect their Hamitic ethnic legacy, their tribal culture or their way of life.

In their modern history, the Beja supported the Mahdiyyah movement of the latter part of the nineteenth century. With the quelling of the movement on September 1, 1898, the Beja, like other peoples of the Sudan, fell formally to the rule of a joint Anglo-Egyptian condominium and practically to British rule. The seizure of some of their richest grazing lands in the 1950's for the purpose of implementing governmental projects (such as the Gash scheme and the Gebeit gold mines project) provoked Beja leaders to demand a form of regional rule to help address the development issues of their region, and eventually to actively engage in Sudanese politics.[78]

The social and political structures of the Beja society are based on patrilineal lineages and their kinship relations are similar to those of the Arabs.

The Beja are essentially pastoralists. They specialize in camel and cattle herding and depend on their produce to meet their subsistence needs. Aside from this specialty, however, they are also engaged in trading. In fact, prior to the opening of the Suez Canal, they supported a long tradition of commercial enterprise that involved Indian Ocean, Persian Gulf and Red Sea trading activities, as well as transportation of received goods by caravans to the Sudan hinterland, as well as to Egypt and beyond.[79] Under the impact of modernization, some Beja are being drawn to the labor market.

BELGIAN

People of Belgian background and/or Belgian expatriates or settlers who live in African countries that formerly fell to Belgium's rule and/or influence. These people and/or their descendants are unevenly distributed in the following countries: Burundi, the Democratic Republic of the Congo (Zaire), and Rwanda.

BELLA

The Bella people are one of the ethnic groups of the Republic of both Liberia and Burkina Faso. They are related to the Taureg.

BELLE

The Belle are one of West Africa's ethnic groups. They are concentrated in Liberia. Their neighbors include the Gbande and Mandingo (Malinke) peoples.

BEMBA

The Bemba, also called Awemba, Babemba, Chibemba, Chiwemba, Ichibemba, or Wemba, are a Western Bantu-speaking Luba-Lunda group who live in parts of Zambia, Democratic Republic of the Congo (Zaire) and Zimbabwe. They are concentrated in the northeastern regions of Zambia, constituting its largest ethnic group. The Bemba's language, Cibemba, is widely spoken in Zambia and is considered the lingua franca of the country.

Bemba people trace their origin to the Luba empire, a royal clan of which migrated with followers from their original lands in the Congo (southern Zaire) to their new lands at the southern end of Lake Tanganyika some time in the eighteenth or early nineteenth century. In their new lands, they organized a kingdom of their own, headed by a paramount chief, the *Chitimukulu*, who was a member of the royal clan. The Bemba considered the members of the *Chitimukulus'* clan as divine, all-powerful and intermediaries between them and their ancestral spirits.

The *Chitimukulus* engaged in the trade of ivory, copper, and slaves. Slaving was especially gainful to them. It not only contributed to their enrichment, but also to the enhancement of their power. This explains why they lost their political power when the slave trade came to an end in the late nineteenth century.

The traditional society of the Bemba is matrilineal. Moreover, it allowed polygamy but gave primacy to the first wife. Though Christianity has won converts, many Bemba continue to be impacted by their traditional belief systems.

Currently, the Bemba are sedentary people, relying essentially on staple crops for sustenance. They live in compact villages, each village of which is comprised of the matrilineal relatives of the headman. Poor soil has incited some male Bemba to work as laborers in Zambia's copper mines.

BEMBE, see KONGO

BEN GUIL

These people are a North African group. They are concentrated in the north central regions of Morocco.

BENA

The Bena are an East African Bantu-speaking people, and one of Tanzania's ethnic groups. Together with their neighbors, the Sangu and Hehe, they live north of Lake Malawi (formerly Nyasa).

Prior to colonial rule, the Bena supported a strong kingdom that was able to withstand encroachments by the Ngoni people and Arab traders on their lands. Additionally, they mastered the Ngoni superior military tactics, adopted firearms and centralized political authority. This way they managed to sustain their independence until the later part of the 1880's, at which time they fell to German rule. After World War I, they fell to British rule, under a League of Nations mandate.

BENDE

The Bende people are an East African group. They are concentrated in the southwestern regions of Tanzania.

BENE, see **FANG**

BENGA, see **FANG**

BENI, see **NUPE**

BENI AMER (Morocco)

These are a West Saharan North African people. They are named after one of their founding ancestors, Amer. The word *beni* in Arabic means sons and daughters or offsprings of, pointing to Amer. Beni Amer are concentrated in the central mountainous regions of Morocco.

BENI AMER (Ethiopia and Sudan), see also **BEJA**

These are an East African people. They are concentrated in the eastern regions of Sudan along the Sudanese borders with Ethiopia and Eritrea. Beni Amer are one of the Beja groups. They are a pastoralist people.

BENI HASSAN, see **SAHRAWIS**

BENI HELBA, see **BAGGARA**

BENI HILLAL

An Arab tribe that settled in Libya in the eleventh century. Originally, Beni Hillal used to live in the vicinity of the upper Nile Valley in Egypt.

BENI HUSAYN, see **BAGGARA**

BENI KANZ, see **KENUZ**

BENI KHUZAM, see **BAGGARA**

BENI MERZOUG, see **CHAAMBA**

BENI SELIM, see **BAGGARA**

BENI SHANGUL, see **BERTA**

BENI SULEIM

The Beni Suleim are an Arab tribe that settled in Libya in the eleventh century. Like the Beni Hillal, they originally lived in the vicinity of the upper Nile Valley in Egypt.

BERABICHE

The Berabiche are a West African people. Their concentrations are in both Mali and Nigeria. In the latter country, they live in the southern coastal areas, especially west of Niger Delta. Their neighbors include the Ijo and

Jekri peoples. In Mali, they live north of the Niger river, neighboring the Kel Antessar people.

BERBER

The Berber are the native peoples of North Africa. In ancient times, their tribes spread throughout the areas that currently constitute the states of Morocco, Algeria, Tunisia, Libya and Egypt, as well as the states in the Central Sahara and north of the Niger river. Although many were Arabized after the seventh century, Berber peoples are plentiful in the mountainous regions, especially of Morocco and Algeria. They are pastoralists, agriculturalists and hunters.

The Berber people speak Berber – languages that belong to the Hamito-Semitic language family. The Berber languages differ from one another in their sound systems but are very similar in their grammar and vocabulary. They include: Tamashek or Tuareg; Shawia or Chaouia; Rif; Tamazight; Shluh, Tashelhayt or Chleuch; Zenaga; and Numidian.

Tamashek is spoken by the Tauregs in the central Sahara and north of the Niger river; Shawia by the Shawia and Kabyle (Zouaouah or Zwawah) in Algeria; Rif and Tamazight by Moroccan Berbers; Shluh by the Shluhs in Morocco and Mauritania; and Zenaga by the Berbers of Sénégal. Numidian is extinct but used to be spoken by the Berbers of Libya. Excepting the Tamashek, Berber languages do not have scripts of their own. They use the Arabic script.

The Berber people comprise several major groups, the most important of which are the Amazigh, Rifian, Shleuh (Chleuh, Chleuch, Shluh), Swasa, Kabyle, Shawia (Shawiya), Imzabiyen and Ahaggar. The Amazigh, also called Imazighen, are a Moroccan group. They are concentrated in the middle Atlas of central and southeast-central Morocco. The Rifian, also called Irifeyen, are Moroccan Berbers. They live in the Rif Atlas region in northeastern Morocco. The Shleuh and Swasa, jointly known as Ishilhayen, inhabit the High Atlas and Sous region of southwestern Morocco. The Kabyle, also known as Iqba'iliyen, are one of Algeria's largest Berber tribes, numbering about 2.0 million. Its people are concentrated in the Grande Kabylie mountains, notably in the Tizi Ouzou and Jurjura regions of

Algeria. They are often described as one of three major groups of blond Berbers.[80] The Shawiya, also referred to as Ishawiyen, are concentrated in the Algerian Aurès. The Imzabiyen are the oasis dwellers of the Algerian Mzab. Finally, the Ahaggar, also known as the Imajeghen, are the Taureg group of the southern Algerian Sahara.[81]

In their turn, the main Berber groups are made up of numerous subgroups, including the Ait 'Ali, Ait 'Atta, Ait 'Ayyash, Ait Ba 'Amran, Ait Hadiddu, Ait Imyill, Ait Izdig, Ait Massad, Ait Mhand, Ait Murghad, Ait n-Nuss, Ait Ndhir, Ait Saghrushshn, Ait Siddrat, Ait Sukhman, Ait Warayin, Ait Wawzgit, Ait Yusi, Aith 'Ammarth, Aith Sa'id, Aith Waryaghar, Aith Wurishik, Ammeln, Ash-Tuken, Axt Tuzin, Ibuqquyen, Id aw-Kansus, Id aw-Ltit, Id aw-Tanan, Id aw-Zaddagh, Id aw-Zkri, Idemsiren, Igedmiwen, Iglawn, Igundafen, Igzinnayen, Ihahan, Ihansalen, Illalen, Imsfiwen, Imtuggan, Ind aw-Zal, Iqar'ayen, Isaffen, Iseksawen, Isuktan, Iziyyan, L-Akhsas, Mjjat, Thimsaman, and Zimmur.

Broadly speaking, the political and social organization of the Berbers is relatively democratic. With the exception of the Taureg who support aristocratic-nomadic institutions, "the essential feature of their society being the existence of a great number of small democratic communities, each entirely independent and governed solely by the will of the people."[82] The *jemâa*, an assembly or council of adults in a village attend to common political, economic and social concerns. Broadly speaking, general tribal councils do not interfere in local village affairs. Their responsibilities are restricted to addressing issues of war and peace, as well as to arbitrating disputes between villages. The Berber are Muslim peoples. They provided support to the Arabs in their conquest of the Iberian Peninsula, and subsequently developed several powerful kingdoms and empires, the most important of which were those of the Almoravids, Almohads, Almarinids and Alsa'dis.

BERBERINE, see NUBIAN

BERGDAMA, see also DAMARA

A southwestern Bantu-speaking people. The Bergdama are concentrated in the north-central regions of what is presently the Republic of Namibia.

BERI

The Beri, also known as the Kige, are an East African people. They are concentrated along the Chadian-Sudanese borders. They are divided into two major groups, namely the Bideyat and Zaghawa.

BERI BERI, see also KANURI

These are a West African people and one of Nigeria's ethnic minorities. The Beriberi are a Kanuri people. They are concentrated in northeastern parts of Nigeria in what is presently the state of Borno (formerly Bornu). They are essentially an agriculturalist and trading people.

BERIFOR

The Berifor, also spelled Birifor, are a West African people. They are concentrated in Burkina Faso, Ivory Coast, Mali and Niger. Their neighbors include the Dagari, Diam, Kulango, Lobi and Wala peoples. The Berifor speak Dagara, a Voltaic language that belongs to the Voltaic branch of the Niger-Congo family of African languages.

BERSEBA HOTTENTOS, see also HOTTENTOS

A Southwest African people. They are concentrated in the southeastern regions of the Republic of Namibia.

BERSEBA HOTTENTOTS

The Berseba Hottentots are a Southwest African people. They are concentrated in the south-east region of Namibia.

BERTA

The Berta, also known as Beni Shangul and Wetawit, are an East African agricultural people. They are highly concentrated in Ethiopia.

BERTI, see also ZAGHAWA

An East African Zaghawa Muslim group. The Berti are an agricultural people. They are concentrated in the northern regions of Sudan.

BESHARIN

The Besharin people are an East African ethnic group. They are concentrated in the southeastern regions of the Sudan. The Berti are a Beri group.

BETA ESRÁEL, see FALASHA

BETA ISRAEL, see FALASHA

BETE

The Bete people are one the major ethnic groups in West Africa. They are Bantu-speaking people. They speak a language of the Kru branch of the Kwa linguistic subfamily. Originally, they lived in Equatorial Africa.

The Bete people account for 18% of the population in the Ivory Coast and constitute the second largest ethnic group after the Baoule (Baule). They are highly concentrated in the southern parts of the country, but have tribal affiliations with more numerous groups living outside the Ivory Coast, notably in the Cameroon. Their neighbors include the Bakwe, Dida, Gagu, Guro, Ngere and Wobe.

BETHANIE HOTTENTOTS

The Bethanie Hottentots are a Southwest African people. They are concentrated in the south-central regions of Namibia.

BETI-PAHOUIN, see PAHOUIN

BETSILEO

This is one of Madagascar's ethnic groups. The Betsileo are believed to be a mixture of Bantus and Malayo-Indonesian seafarers who settled in the island at the beginning of the Christian era. They are related to the Merina, another Malayo-Indonesian group on the island and the largest ethnic group on the Island. Their language is Malagasy, which is of Malayo-

Polynesian origin. French, however, is understood and spoken by the educated among them. Together with the Merina, the Betsileo are concentrated on the central highlands of the island.

Due to their high education standards, the Betsileo are one of the most modernized peoples on Madagascar. Their old hierarchical caste system has been replaced by a capitalist system based on wealth. Also, many Betsileo still consult ancient diviners called *ombiasi*, in matters of great importance.

Betsileo can be observed wearing Western clothing, but what makes them stand out is their traditional shawl, or *lamba*, that is worn over the shoulder. All Betsileo are seen in this article of clothing but are differentiated by the material of the *lamba*. People of greater economic wealth have *lambas* made of more impressive material like silk.

Betsileo religion is a mixture of traditional faith with Christian faith. Like other Malagasy people, they "practice a form of animism combined with an almost religious respect for ancestors. They believe that upon death, people join their ancestors in the ranks of divinity and that ancestors are intensely concerned with the fate of their living descendants."[83] This explains why Betsileo highly revere their ancestors and why the tombs of their ancestors are extremely well-kept. Also, it explains the celebration of the Betsileo (and the Merina) famadihana, or the "'turning over the dead', a ceremony of exhuming their long-dead relatives, rewrapping them in new, colorful, fine silk, and carrying the remains through the streets in a joyful reunion before they are reburied."[84] On the whole, their beliefs link their kin with the Betsileo supreme God named Zanahary.

Currently, the Betsileo are the second largest ethnic group on the island of Madagascar, accounting for about 7% of the total population or what amounts to approximately 1.5 million.

BETSIMISARAKA

The Betsimisaraka are a Malagasy people living along the eastern coast of Madagascar. They are of African, Malayo-Indonesian and Arab ancestry. They speak a dialect of the West Austronesian language. Historically, they were known as fishermen, whalers, sailors and pirates. Early in the 18th century, Ratsimilaho united the Malagasy chiefdoms of Madagascar and surrounding islands, establishing the Betsimisaraka kingdom from which the Betsimisaraka acquired their name. After the collapse of the Betsimisaraka kingdom in 1791, the Betsimisaraka fell to the Merina kingdom and subsequently to the French in the 1890s.

Currently, they account for about 8% of Madagascar's population of over 11.4 million, and hence, constitute the second largest ethnic minority in the country after the Merina.

BEZANOZANO

The Bezanozano are a Southeast African-Malagasy people. They are concentrated on the Island of Madagascar, primarily in its east central coastal areas. Their neighbors include the Betsileo and Sihanaka peoples.

BHACA

The Bhaca are a Southern African people. They are concentrated in South Africa, notably in its eastern coastal areas. Their neighbors include the Khuze, Makhanya, and Mpondomise peoples..

BHELE, see MFENGU

BIAFADA

A West African people and one of Guinea's and Guinea-Bissau's ethnic groups. They live close to the coastal areas of both countries. The Biafada speak a West Atlantic language of the Niger-Congo family of African languages. Their neighbors include the Balante, Fula, Nalu, Pepel and Susu peoples.

BIAKA, see BAYAKA

BICHI

These are one of Zambia's ethnic minorities. The Bichi are a Bantu-speaking people and are related to the Ila people.

BIDEYAT

One of the ethnic groups of Central and East Africa. They are concentrated in western Sudan and northeastern Chad. Their neighbors include the Mourdia and Zaghawa peoples.

BIJAGOS

These are one of Guinea-Bissau's ethnic minorities. The Bijagos live in areas close to the sea.

BIDEYAT, see ZAGHAURA

BILALA

The Bilala, also called Boulala or Bulala, are sedentary people centered around Lake Fitri in Central Chad, making up less than 2% of the population of the Republic of Chad. They are predominantly Muslim and live primarily in the northern parts of the country. They speak a Central Sudanese language, "sometimes designated as Lisi."[85]

According to Nelson et al., the Bilala believe they all descended from a common ancestor named Bilal (probably the first *mu'azin*, prayer caller in, and African convert to, Islam, and hence, one of the early companions of prophet Muhammad) whose "descendants mixed with the Arabs."[86] They, in turn, founded a Sultanate, which is still operational today.

Late in the 14th century, the Bilala forced *Mai* Umar ibn Idris of the Sef (Sayf) dynasty of the Kanem-Bornu empire (9th century-1846) to abandon the Kanem's old capital at N'jimi and to move to Birni Ngazargamu in Bornu. The Sef dynasty was not able to retake Kanem until the 16th century. This was done under the rule of Ali Ghaji (1472-1504) and that of his son, Idris Katakarmabi (1504-1526), who had dealt heavy blows to the Bilala people.

The Bilala's economic activity centers on raising herds, as well as on trading with their Arab and Muslim neighbors. Their education is conducted by Qur'anic schools.

BILEN

An East African sedentary people. The Bilen, also called Bogos, are concentrated in the northern highlands of Ethiopia. They are predominantly farmers.

BINGA, see also PYGMY

The Binga are a Pygmy people. They constitute one of Congo's ethnic minorities. Groups of them, however, can also be found in the Cameroon, Central African Republic, Democratic Republic of the Congo (Zaire), and Gabon.

BINI, see EDO

BINNA, see YUNGUR

BIRA

These are one of Democratic Republic of the Congo's (Zaire's) ethnic groups. The Bira are a Bantu-speaking people.

BIRI

The Biri people are one of Central Africa's ethnic groups. Their main concentrations are in southeastern Chad, northeastern Central African Republic, and southwestern Sudan. Their neighbors include the Gabou, Kare, and Nzakara peoples.

BIRIFOR, see BERIFOR

BIROM

The Birom, also known as Afango, Gbang, Kibyen, Kibbo, and Kibo, are a West African people. They are highly concentrated in central Nigeria. Their neighbors include the Angas, Jarawa, Jerawa, Katab, Mada and Mama peoples. The Birom's language belongs to the Benue-Congo group of the Niger-Congo family of African languages.

BISA, see also LUNDA

These are a Central African Bantu-speaking people whose history is traced to the Lunda empire. Discontented with the conditions in their original homeland in the Lunda kingdom, they migrated to the area below Lake Tanganyika. At their new homeland east of Lake Bangweulu, they spread the Lunda culture, and moreover, engaged in internal and external trading activities with the Yao and Katanga, as well as with Kilwa and Zanzibar.

BISHARIN, see also BEJA

The Bisharin are an East African Muslim people. They are concentrated in the Eastern Desert of Egypt and northeastern regions of Sudan. The Bisharin speak Arabic, and are one of the four main Beja groups.

BITO

One of Uganda's ethnic minorities. The Bito are Luo-speaking Nilotic people. In pre-colonial times they established a powerful kingdom of their own known as the Bunoro kingdom. Located in northern Uganda, their kingdom survived until 1966, at which time it was abolished by the Ugandan government.

BNGALA

A West Central African people. The Bngala, also spelled Bangala, are one of the Mboshi cluster of peoples in the Republic of Congo. Groups of them, however, can also be found in the Democratic Republic of the Congo (Zaire).

BOB, see BOBO

BOBO, see also MOSSI

The Bobo, also known as Bob and Bwa, are one of the important ethnic minorities of Burkina Faso, Ivory Coast and Mali. They speak a language of the Voltaic (Gur) branch of the Niger-Congo family and are essentially a sedentary agricultural people. The Bobo are highly concentrated in the northeastern part of the Ivory Coast. In Mali, they constitute together with other Voltaic peoples, about 12% of the total population and live in the eastern and the southeastern areas of the country. In Burkina Faso, they form a sizable minority. Their neighbors include the Bambara, Dagari, Diam, Dogon, Dyula, Lilse Minianka, Nono, Nunuma, Sia and Tusyan peoples.

BODALLA

The Bodalla are one of the Chadian Kuri subgroups. They speak Yedina, a Buduma dialect. Like other Kuri groups, they live along the eastern shores of Lake Chad.

BOER, see AFRIKANER

BOFI

The Bofi, also known as Babinga, are a West and West Central African people. They are one of the many Pygmy people of equatorial Africa. Originally, they inhabited the tropical rain forest, in what is now within the Republic of Congo. Subsequently, they moved to other areas. Of these groups, the Bofi among them eventually settled in the southeastern regions of Central African Republic, notably in its forest-savanna areas. The Bofi are essentially hunters, foragers and potters.

BOGOS, see BILEN

BOK, see also KONY and KALENJIN

An East African Kony people, a Kalenjin group. The Bok people are concentrated in Kenya, Tanzania and Uganda. They speak a dialect of Kalenjin, a Southern Nilotic language of the Eastern Sudanic family of African languages. They are a semipastoralist people.

BOKI

These are a West African people. The Boki speak a language that belongs to the Benue-Congo branch of the Niger-Congo family of African languages. They are related in their language to the Ekoi (Ekoid) people of southeastern Nigeria and western Cameroon. Their neighbors include the Ekoi, Iyala, Mbembe, Tiv and Yako peoples.

BOKO

The Boko, also called Bokoboro, are one of West Africa's ethnic groups. Their main concentration is in the west central areas of Nigeria, particularly in the state of Kwara. Their major neighbors include the Bargu, Busa, Reshe, Fulani, Kamberi and Yoruba peoples.

BOKOBORO, see BOKO

BOKOTO, see BAYA and MONGO

BOLA, see MANCAGNE BRAME

BOLE, see BOLEWA

BOLEWA

The Bolewa are a West African people and one of Nigeria's ethnic minorities. The Bolewa, also known as Bole and Fika, are concentrated in northeastern parts of Nigeria in what is presently the state of Borno (formerly Bornu). The Bolewa are a Muslim people who were impacted by various aspects of Kanuri culture. They speak Kanuri and are essentially agriculturalists. Their neighbors include the Auyokawa, Fula, Kanuri, Kare-kare and Tera peoples.

BOLIA, see MONGO

BOMA-KASAI, see BOMA-SAKATA

BOMA-MURLE, see MURLE

BOMA-SAKATA

The Boma-Sakata, also Boma-Kasai and Kiboma, are a West Central African cluster of peoples. Their main concentration is in the lower part of the Kasai river.

BOMBESA

The Bombesa are a West Central African people. They are concentrated in the Democratic Republic of the Congo (Zaire).

BOMVANA

The Bomvana are a southern African group. They are concentrated in South Africa, primarily in the southwestern coastal regions of the country. Their neighbors include the Gcoika and Mpondomise peoples.

BONA

The Bona are a West African people. They are an Anyi subgroup and are concentrated in the west central regions of the Ivory Coast. Their neighbors include the Birifor, Dagaba, and Gonja peoples

BONDEI

The Bondei are an East African people. They are one of the Shirazi groups, and hence, are presumed to be of Persian descent. They are concentrated in southeastern Kenya and northeastern Tanzania.

BONGA, see also UBANGI

The Bonga are an Ubangi people. They live in the Republic of Congo and the Central African Republic.

BONGANDU, see MONGO

BONI

The Boni, also known as Aweera, are a Cushitic East African people. They are concentrated in the eastern regions of Kenya along the Kenyan-Somali border.

BONGO (Chad)

The Bongo are one of the many ethnic groups of which Chad is composed. Their language belongs to the Chari-Nile family. Together with the related Sara and Bagirmi, they live in the central parts of the Chari and Logone river basins.

BONGO (Gabon)

The Bongo are one of the many Pygmy people of equatorial Africa. Originally, they inhabited the tropical rain forest, in what is now within the Republic of Congo. Subsequently, they moved to other areas. Of these groups, the Bongo among them eventually settled in western Gabon. The Bongo comprise several groups, including the Akoa and Bazimba. They are essentially hunters, foragers and potters.

BONG'OM, see also KONY and KALENJIN

An East African Kony people, a Kalenjin group. Their main concentrations are in Kenya, Tanzania and Uganda. The Bong'om speak a dialect of Kalenjin, a Southern Nilotic language of the Eastern Sudanic family of African languages. They are a semipastoralist people.

BONO

The Bono are a West African people. They constitute one of Ghana's ethnic minorities. The Bono are an Akan subgroup. They live in the central areas of Ghana. Their neighbors include Kana and Wala peoples.

BOONGA, see UBANGI

BOR, see DINKA and NUER

BORAN, see also OROMO

A seminomadic people of East Africa, the Boran, also called Borana and

Borena, are one of the major subgroups of the Oromo, also known as Galla, the largest ethnic minority in Ethiopia. They are related to other Oromo subgroups, including the Arusi, the Gudji, the Macha and the Tulama.

The traditional lifestyle of the Boran is essentially pastoral and they are currently concentrated along the frontier areas of Ethiopia, Kenya and Somalia.

Like other Oromo peoples, the Boran are descendants of Cushite invaders of the 1500s, who overran the Amhara and Tigre. Now, they adhere to the Amhara and Tigrayan Christian and Muslim religions and hold a decisive place in Amharan-Tigrayan Ethiopian society.

BORANA, see **BORAN** and **OROMO**

BORENA, see **BORAN** and **OROMO**

BORGENCI, see also **BARGU** and **BARIBA**

The Borgenci are one of the three major subgroups of the Bargu people of West Africa, which apart from them, also include the Bariba and the Bargu. They are a Voltaic-speaking people and are located in several states of West Africa, especially Nigeria and Benin. In Nigeria, they are concentrated in the west-central parts of the country, particularly in the state of Kwara. Together with other Bargu people, they constitute the fourth largest Nigerian ethnic group after the Fon, Adja, and Yoruba. In Benin, they account, together with the Somba and other related groups, for about one fifth or 19.5% of the country's total population. They are concentrated in the northern parts of Benin.

BORGU, see also **BARGU** and **BARIBA**

The Borgu are a West African Voltaic-speaking people. They are one of the three major subgroups of the Bargu people, which, aside from the Borgu, also include the Bariba and Borgenci. They are found in several states of West Africa, especially Nigeria and Benin. In Nigeria, they are concentrated in the west central parts of the country, particularly in the state of Kwara. Together with other Bargu people, they constitute the fourth largest Nigerian ethnic group after the Fon, Adja, and Yoruba. In Benin, they account, together with the Somba and other related groups, for about one-fifth or 19.5% of the country's total population. They are concentrated in the northern parts of Benin.

BORNU, see KANEMBA

BORO, see KANEMBA

BORODDA, see WOLAYTA

BORON, see AKAN

BORORO, see also FULANI

The Bororo are a nomadic Pygmy Fulani (Peul) people. They constitute one of the ethnic minorities of the Central African Republic. They live around Bouar and Bambari and are essentially cattle herders.

BORORO'EN, see FULANI

BOSYEBA

The Bosyeba are a West Central African people. They are concentrated in the south central regions of Cameroon. However, some groups can be found in Gabon and the Central African Republic. Their neighbors include the Fang, Komke, and Makka peoples.

BOTSWANA, see TSWANA

BOUDOUMA

The Boudouma people are located in the states of Chad, Nigeria, Cameroon and Niger. They speak Kanembou, as well as Arabic, and live a sedentary lifestyle. The Boudouma are fishermen as well as pastoralists. Also, during the dry seasons of northern Africa, they are involved with small-scale agriculture. Most Boudouma people are Muslim. They were converted to Islam by their neighbors, the Kanembou, with whom they maintain good relations.

BOUROUBA, see CHAAMBA

BOULAIDA, see BLIDA

BOULALA, see BILALA

BOYA, see LONGARIM

BOYELA, see MONGO

BOZO, see also MANDE

The Bozo are a West African Mande group. They speak Mande and are concentrated in the Republic of Mali where they constitute one of its major ethnic minorities. The Bozo neighbors include the Bambara, Bobo, Dogon, Fula, Minianka, and Nono peoples.

BRAM

A West African people. The Bram people are one of Guinea-Bissau's ethnic groups. They are concentrated in the coastal areas of the country.

BRAME, see MANCAGNE

BRAOYA

The Braoya people are one of the Central African ethnic groups. They live in northwestern Chad and northeastern Niger. Groups of them, however, can also be found in the south central areas of Libya. Their neighbors include the Gounda and Toubou peoples.

BRASSA, see BALANTE

BRAVA

These are a small ethnic minority in Somalia. The Brava, also known as Baraawe, claim descent from Portuguese settlers.

BRIGNAN, see AVIKAM

BRITISH

People of British background and/or British expatriates or settlers who live in African countries that formerly fell to Britain's rule and/or influence. These people and/or their descendants are unevenly distributed in the following countries: Benin, Botswana, Egypt, Gambia, Ghana, Kenya, Malawi, Mauritius, Nigeria, Saint Helena, Seychelles, Sierra Leone, Somalia, South Africa, Sudan, Swaziland, Tanzania, Uganda, Zambia, and Zimbabwe.

BRON, see AKAN

BRONG, see also AKAN

The Brong are a West African Akan group. They speak Twi, an Akan language of the Kwa branch of the Niger-Congo family of African languages, and are concentrated in Ghana and the Ivory Coast, notably in the Brong region in Ghana. Their neighbors include the Anyi, Asante, Guang, Krachi, Kulango and Nafana peoples.

BUA

The Bua are a Central African people. They are concentrated in the southern regions of the Republic of Chad.

BU-BANKAM

These are one of Togo's ethnic groups. The Bu-Bankam are Voltaic (Gur)-speaking people. They are located in the northern areas of the country.

BUBARI, see ADIOUKROU

BUBI

The Bubi are one of the ethnic minorities of Equatorial Guinea. They are concentrated in the island of Bioko. Historical evidence suggests that they were among the first African people to meet the Portuguese mariners in 1472.[87]

BUDJA

These are one of Democratic Republic of the Congo's (Zaire's) ethnic groups. The Budja are a Bantu-speaking people.

BUDU

The Budu are a Central African people. They are concentrated in the Democratic Republic of the Congo (Zaire), notably in its north eastern regions. Their neighbors include the Bangba, Barambo, Mabisanga, Madi, Makango, Mangbetu, Mayogo and Mayvu peoples.

BUDUM

The Budum are a West African people and one of Nigeria's ethnic minorities. They live in the vicinity of Lake Chad. The Budum are a Muslim people who were impacted by various aspects of Kanuri culture. They speak Kanuri and are essentially an agricultural people.

BUDUMA, see also KANURI

The Buduma are a Kanuri group who live in Cameroon, Chad, Niger and Nigeria. Their language belongs to the Saharan group of languages. In Chad, they are concentrated around Lake Chad and in the Kanem region. Their neighbors include the Kanembu, Kanuri, Kwayam, Mabar and Shuwa peoples.

BUGISU, see GISO

BUGUSU, see LUHYA

BUHA

The Buha are an East African group. Their main concentrations are in the southwestern regions of Tanzania, primarily on the northeastern banks of Lake Tanganyika. Their neighbors include the Ha and Jijii peoples.

BUILSA

A small West African people. They are concentrated in northern Ghana. Their neighbors are the Mamprusi people.

BUJAH, see BEJA

BUKALA

The Bukala is one of the many ethnic groups of which Chad is composed. Their language belongs to the Saharan group of languages, and they are concentrated in the plains of the Guéra-Massif. They are sedentary people.

BUKEDI

The Bukedi are a Ugandan people. They are concentrated in the southeast region of the country along the Ugandan-Kenyan borders. Their neighbors include the Busoga, the Sebei and the Teso peoples.

BUKULI

The Bukuli are an East African people. They are concentrated in Uganda, notably on the northeastern shores of Lake Victoria. Their neighbors include the Bugusu (Lubya), Ganda, Sese, and Soga peoples.

BUKOMBONG

This is one of Togo's ethnic groups. The Bu-Kombong are Voltaic (Gur)-speaking people. They are located in the northern areas of the country.

BUKUSU, see LUHYA

BULALA, see BILALA

BULANDA, see BALANTE

BULDOK, see NUER

BULEBULE, see AMBA

BULI, see BAYA

BULIBUZI, see AMBA

BULOM, see BULLOM

BULLOM

The Bullom, also Bulom, are a small West African ethnic group. They are located primarily in the coastal areas of Sierra Leone and speak a language that belongs to the West Atlantic branch of the Niger-Congo family of African languages. They are renowned for their secret initiation of their youths, as well as for being the alleged founders of the powerful Poro Society.[88] Their neighbors include the Limba, Loko, Kono, Kuranko, Mende, Sherbro, Susu and Temne peoples.

BULU, see FANG

BUM

The Bum people are one of the Central African ethnic groups. They are concentrated in the west central region of Cameroon. Their neighbors include the Fugon, Kom, and Wiya peoples.

BUMBU

The Bumbu are a West African people. They are concentrated in the northern regions of the Ivory Coast. Groups of them, however, can also be found in Burkina Faso and Ghana. Their neighbors include the Baule, Wala, and Wangara peoples.

BUNDA

The Bunda are a West Central African people. They are concentrated in the Democratic Republic of the Congo (Zaire).

BUNGORO

Ugandan agriculturalist people. The Bungoro are concentrated in the uplands in the western regions of the country. Their neighbors include the Ankole and Toro peoples.

BUNGU

The Bungu are an East African people. They are concentrated in the southwestern regions of Tanzania, particularly in the eastern vicinity of Lake Ruwa. Their neighbors include the Manda, Nyiha, and Safwa peoples.

BUNJAWA, see HAUSA

BUNU

The Bunu people, also known as Kabba, are one of Nigeria's ethnic minorities. They are concentrated in the west central areas of the country, particularly in the state of Kwara. The Bunu are a predominantly Muslim people who engage in farming.

BUNYORO, see NYORO

BURA

These are a West African people and one of Nigeria's ethnic minorities. The Bura, also known as Pabir, are concentrated in northeastern parts of Nigeria in what is presently the state of Borno (formerly Bornu). Their neighbors include the Hona, Kanuri, Margi and Tera peoples. The Bura are essentially an agricultural people.

BURAKA

These are one of the ethnic minorities of the Central Republic of Africa. They are concentrated in the Ubangi region of the country. They are essentially a tribal people engaged in trading and fishing.

BURENEJI, see SAMBURU

BURJI

A Southern Ethiopian people. The Burji are concentrated in the Rift Valley region. Their neighbors include the Konso, Borana, Gauwada and Gidole peoples.

BURRUZA

A West African people. They are concentrated in central Nigeria. The Burruza are one of the groups in the Mama cluster.

BURULI

The Buruli are an East African people. They are concentrated in the Republic of Uganda, primarily in the western vicinity of Lake Kyoga. Their neighbors include the Bugusu (Luhya), Nyoro, and Ssingo peoples.

BURUM

The Burum are a West African people. They are highly concentrated in central Nigeria. Their neighbors include the Angas, Fula, Jarawa and Yergum peoples. The Burum's language belongs to the Benue-Congo group of the Niger-Congo family of African languages.

BURUN, see also BURUNGI and UDUK

The Burun people are one of the ethnic groups of Sudan. They are concentrated southwest of the Blue Nile. Their neighbors include the Nuer, the Koma, the Galla, the Malakal, the Shilluk, the Anuak, and the Dinka.

BURUNGI

The Burungi, also known as Burun, are an East African Uduk group. Their main concentrations are in Ethiopia, Sudan and Tanzania, primarily in the vicinity of Lake Manyara in north central Tanzania. Their neighbors include the Barabaig and Irangi peoples.

BUSA

The Busa, also called Bussa or Bussangi, are one of Nigeria's ethnic minorities. They are concentrated essentially in the west central areas of the country, particularly in the state of Kwara. The Busa are also located in Burkina Faso and surrounding countries. Their major neighbors in Nigeria include the Bargu (Borgo), Dendi, Fula (Fulani), Kamberi, Nupe, Reshe, Tienga and Yoruba peoples.

In Burkina Faso and Niger, their neighbors include the Gurensi, Grunshi, Moba, Mossi and Nunuma peoples. The Busa speak Mande, a language that belongs to the Niger-Congo family of African languages.

The Busa developed their own chiefdom in the 1730s, with Bussa as its center. During the eighteenth century, their chiefdom was prominent enough to exact tributes from neighboring kingdoms and emirates. Like other peoples of the Borgu region, they fell to the British in 1894 and in 1900, their chiefdom was recognized as an emirate. In 1954, their emirate joined with that of the Kaiama and their Amir, Muhammadu Sani, who became the first amir of Borgu. In 1968, Bussa was evacuated to New Bussa (built in 1966) to allow for the construction of the artificial Kainji Lake. The New Bussa is located 24 miles (39 kilometers) south of old Bussa.[89]

The Busa are a Muslim people. Their affairs are overseen by their Amir, who combines both political and religious responsibilities.

BUSANSI, see also MANDE

A West African people. The Busansi are a Voltaic people of the Mande group of peoples. They are concentrated in the north central regions of Burkina Faso. Their neighbors include the Anoufo, Gurma, and Tallensi

peoples.

BUSHONGO, see also KUBA

Western Bantu-speaking people. They are concentrated in Angola and the Democratic Republic of the Congo (Zaire), primarily in the south central regions of the latter country.

BUSOGA, see SOGA

BUSSA, see BUSA

BUSSANGI, see BUSA

BUTAWA

A West African people. The Butawa are concentrated in northern Nigeria. Their neighbors include the Gerawa, Hausa, Maguzawa and Warjawa peoples. The Butawa's language belongs to the Benue-Congo group of the Niger-Congo family of African languages.

BUTE, see BABOUTI

BWA, see BOBO

BWAKA, see BAYA

BWAL

One of West Africa's peoples. The Bwal live primarily in the Plateau State in Nigeria. They are closely related to the their neighbors the Dimmuk, Kwalla, and Namu peoples.

BWILE

The Bwile are a West Central and East African people. They are concentrated in the southeastern regions of the Democratic Republic of the Congo (Zaire) and the northeastern regions of Zambia.

BUZI, see also MANDE

The Buzi, also known as Loma and Toma, are Mande people. They are located in several West African states, primarily in the southwestern Burkina Faso and northern Ivory Coast where their neighbors include the Gbandi and Kissi peoples.

C-GROUP

The C-Group are a race of pastoralist people of obscure origin who occupied ancient Nubia.[90] Historical evidence suggests that these people were in control of the areas between Nubia and the Red Sea, as well as of areas south of the Nile's First Cataract during the reign of the Middle Kingdom in ancient Egypt.[91]

CAFRE

The Cafre people are one of the five major ethnic groups of the Federal Islamic Republic of the Comoros.

CALABAR, see IBIBIO

CAMEROON HIGHLANDERS

Cameroon highlanders constitute the largest ethnic minority in the United Republic of Cameroon. They account for 31% of the country's population.

CAPE COLOURED, see COLOURED

CAPRIVIAN

A Southwest African people. The Caprivian people, also known as East Caprivians, are concentrated in Namibia where they represent nearly 4% of the country's population.

CAZEMBE, see LUNDA

CEWA, see MARAVI

CHAAMBA

These people are a northwestern Saharan Arab nomads. They are an Arab people and speak Arabic. They are concentrated in the vicinity of Metlili, their political and commercial center, as well as in El Goléa, Ouargla, El Oued and Erg. The Chaamba comprise numerous groups and subgroups such as the Mouadhi, Bou Rouba, Ouled Allouch, Ouled Touameur, Ouled Abd-el-Kader, Ouled Hanich, Ouled Aicha, Ouled Fredj and Beni Merzoug. Their economic activities focus on raising livestock, especially camels and goats, limited farming, and trading with neighboring peoples.

The Chaamba are presumed to have moved to their present location from Syria in the early part of the fourteenth century. It is also presumed that "their initial impetus carried them as far west as the Piedmont country on the southern slope of the Atlas mountain complex south of Oran, and that they later moved from there southeastward to Metlili, probably about the middle of the fourteenth century."[92]   Prior to the colonial era and subsequently the partitioning of the Saharan region among the modern states of Algeria, Chad, Libya, Morocco, Tunisia, Sudan and Western Sahara, "the Chaamba used to have full control of all caravan trade passing over the central section of the north-south route that connected the Algerian coast with Timbuctoo and the western Sudan."[93] Their own caravans "used to go regularly as far north as the high plateau country of the Atlas Mountain complex south of Oran and southward to the western Sudan."[94]   Now, their mobility in the Saharan desert has been highly curtailed.

Patrilineal clans constitute the basic units of the Chaamba society. Each clan is made up of one or more extended family whose members are the descendants of one male ancestor. In their turn, clans are grouped into one of four categories in light of their ranking in the class structure of the society. The first group is that of warrior and shurafa, that is noble, clans. The second group is that of nomadic common and vassal clans. The third group is that of sedentary clans. Finally, the fourth is that of auxiliary groups and aliens. All clans, however, are united in a loosely structured confederation headed by the Ouled Allouch clan and subclans, notably Ouled Touameur, Ouled Abd-el-Kader and Ouled Hanich. Chieftainship in Chaamba clans and subclans is hereditary in the male line.

CHAGA, see CHAGGA

CHAGGA

The Chagga (Chaga), also known as Dschagga, Haya, Haya Chaga, Jagga, Wa-caga, Wachagga or Waschagga, are an East African Bantu-speaking people. They speak Kichagga, an Eastern Bantu language. The Chagga, originated in the Taita region, and eventually settled on the eastern, southern and western slopes of Mt. Kilimanjaro in northern Tanzania.[95] They are famous coffee growers. Currently, they represent one of Tanzania's large ethnic groups. The Chagga people are essentially agriculturalists and farmers. Their economic activities focus on growing coffee.

CHAI

The Chai are an East African Suri group. They speak Surmic (formerly Surma) and are concentrated in southwestern Ethiopia and southeastern Sudan, notably in the Kefa region of Sudan.

CHAINOQUA

An extinct southern African people. The Chainoqua used to live in the southwestern regions of what is now the Republic of South Africa.

CHAKOSSI

The Chakossi are one of the ethnic minorities of the Republic of Ghana. They are highly concentrated in the Northern Region, where they live in the chiefdom of Dagbon. The latter chieftainship also comprises several subject tribes or clans, including the Chakossi. Groups of Chakossi people are also found in Togo. The Chakossi speak a language of the Voltaic (Gur) branch of the Niger-Congo family of African languages. Their neighbors include the Dagomba, Gurensi, Kabre, Konkomba, Moba, Konkomba, Mamprusi (Manprusi) and Somba peoples.

CHAMBA

The Chamba are a West African people. They are concentrated in eastern Nigeria and Western Cameroon. Their language belongs to the Adamawa branch of the Niger-Congo family of African languages. The Chamba neighbors include the Daka, Fula, Kotopo, Mumuye and Vere peoples.

CHARA

The Chara are an East African people. They are concentrated in southeastern Sudan, primarily north of Lake Rudolf. Groups of them, however, can also be found in southwestern Ethiopia. Their neighbors include the Basketo, Kambatta, Mazhi, and Toposa peoples.

CHARFARDA, see TOUBOU

CHARIGURIQUA

An extinct southern African Hottentot group. The Chariguriqua used to live in the western regions of what is now the Republic of South Africa.

CHAUCH, see KOTOKOLI

CHAWAI

The Chawai are a West and Central African people. They are concentrated in the northeastern regions of Nigeria. Their neighbors include the Birom, Hausa, Jerawa, Mada, and Yeskwa peoples.

CHEBLENG, see also ENDO and KALENJIN

An East African Endo people, a Kalenjin group. Their main concentrations are in Kenya, Tanzania and Uganda. They speak a dialect of Kalenjin, a Southern Nilotic language of the Eastern Sudanic family of African languages. The Chebleng are a semipastoralist people.

CHEKE, see GUDE

CHEMWAL, see also NANDI and KALENJIN

An East African Nandi people, a Kalenjin group. Their main concentrations are in Kenya, Tanzania and Uganda. They speak a dialect of Kalenjin, a Southern Nilotic language of the Eastern Sudanic family of African languages. The Chemwal are a semipastoralist people.

CHERANG'ANY, see also MARAKWET and KALENJIN

The Cherang'any are an East African Marakwet people, a Kalenjin group. They are concentrated in Kenya, Tanzania and Uganda, notably in the Rift Valley region. The Cherang'any speak a dialect of Kalenjin, a Southern Nilotic language of the Eastern Sudanic family of African languages. They are a semipastoralist people.

CHERANGANI, see also TUGEN and KALENJIN

An East African Tugen people, a Kalenjin group. They are concentrated in Kenya, Tanzania and Uganda, notably in the Rift Valley region. The Cherangani speak a dialect of Kalenjin, a Southern Nilotic language of the Eastern Sudanic family of African languages. They are a semipastoralist people.

CHEREPONG, see KYEREPONG

CHEWA, see also MARAVI

An east African Bantu-speaking people. The Chewa are related to the Nyanja people. They are concentrated in Zambia and Malawi, primarily west of Lake Nyasa. Their neighbors include the Chikunda and Senga peoples.

CHIBEMBA, see BEMBA

CHIGA

The Chiga, also known as Kiga and Rukiya, are a Bantu-speaking people. They are one of Uganda's ethnic minorities. The Chiga are concentrated in the western areas of Uganda along the country's border with Rwanda and the Democratic Republic of the Congo (Zaire). Their society is highly segmentary in its structure. It is based on segmented clans and lineages.

CHIKUNDA

The Chikunda are a Southeast African-Malagasy people. They are concentrated in Zambia north of Lake Kariba. Groups of them, however, can also be found in Zimbabwe. Their neighbors include the Angoni, Bisa, Chewa, and Nsenga peoples.

CHILALA, see KOLELA

CHILENDJE

One of Southern Africa's peoples. The Chilendje are a subgroup of the Abarue, a Shona people. They live in Zimbabwe and Mozambique.

CHIMATENGO, see MATENGO

CHIMAVIHA, see MAWIA

CHIMWERA, see MWERA

CHIPOLGOLO, see POGORO

CHISHINGA

The Chishinga are a Southwest African people. They are concentrated in the north central regions of Zambia. Their neighbors include the Aushi and Nukulo peoples.

CHIWARE

One of Southern Africa's peoples. The Chiware are a subgroup of the Abarue, a Shona people. They live in Zimbabwe and Mozambique.

CHIWEMBA, see BEMBA

CHLEUH (CHLEUCH), see BERBER

CHOA

The Choa is an Arab tribe of the northern regions of Cameroon. They are also found in Nigeria, especially in its northeastern regions, along the southern shores of Lake Chad. Their neighbors include the Afawa, Kanum, Koto, Mandara, and Warjawa peoples.

CHOBBA, see KILBA

CHOCHOQUA, see also KHOISAN

An extinct southern African Khoisan people. The Chochoqua used to live in the southwestern regions of what is presently the Republic of South Africa.

CHOKO

One of Southern Africa's peoples. The Choco are a subgroup of the Abarue, a Shona people. They live in Zimbabwe and Mozambique.

CHOKWE, see also LUNDA

The Chokwe, also known as Lunda-Chokwe, are a Lunda group of people of Central Africa. They are among the ethnic minorities of the states of Angola, Democratic Republic of the Congo (Zaire), and Zambia. The majority of them are concentrated in Angola, where their population is estimated at about 1.5 million. The Chokwe are a Bantu-speaking people. Their language, Chokwe, is a mixture of Ruund and Lunda.

Originally, the Chokwe were a small group of seminomadic hunters and part of the great Lunda kingdom. They collaborated with Ovimbundu traders in collecting and marketing ivory. With the aid of firearms, they slowly spread their control, absorbing local people within their society. In the seventeenth century, they split from the Lunda kingdom, establishing their own trading empire that resisted a number of European incursions on their newly acquired territory. In the late nineteenth century, they staged a series of assaults on the Lunda empire, contributing to its weakening and eventual downfall in face of Portuguese and Belgian encroachments.

Politically, the Chokwe support highly decentralized institutions. The political structures of their villages vary greatly. Some are self-governed, while others are part of vast chiefdoms. Chiefs are chosen due to their wisdom and overall intelligence. Economically, a great majority of them are agriculturalists. Some of them, however, work as miners in the diamond mines of the Lunda Norte province in Angola.

Though predominantly Catholic, the Chokwe people continue to be impacted by their traditional religion, which rested on the belief in an all-powerful yet disinterested god, as well as in nature spirits and spirits of ancestors. Chokwe villages continue to have special areas recognized as sacred grounds where ancestors are worshiped and the nature spirits are revered. Additionally, sorcery is very influential in their society and is seen as the main cause of death in their villages.[96]

The Chokwe are known to be great artisans. They were the main artisans of the Lunda kingdom and after the separation, they continued to produce carvings of ivory, bone, wood and clay. They also excelled in producing jewelry and ornaments made of copper and bronze. Many of their carvings and sculptures involve their ancestors.

CHONYI

The Chonyi people are an East African Mijikenda group. They are concentrated in Kenya, notably along its coast. Their economic activities focus on agriculture, fishing, and trading. The Chonyi speak a dialect of Mijikenda, a language that belongs to the Northeast Coastal Bantu languages.

CHOPI

The Chopi are a Southeast African-Malagasy people. They are highly concentrated in the southern coast of Mozambique.

CHUABO

The Chuabo are a Southeast African-Malagasy people. They are concentrated in the eastern regions of Mozambique. Their neighbors include the Podzo, Sena, and Yao peoples.

CHUKA

The Chuka are an East African Bantu-speaking people. They are concentrated in the Eastern Province of Kenya. The Chuka are a Meru people.

CHWEZI, see also HIMA

One of the Hima clans, the leaders of which developed their own dynasty and centralized state, the kingdom of Kitara, sometime during the fifteenth century. The kingdom was located between Lake Victoria and Lake Albert. Towards the end of the century, however, they were overwhelmed by the Nilotic Luo people of the Bahr al-Ghazal region. Upon reorganizing the kingdom of Kitara as the kingdom of Bunyoro, they established their own Bito dynasty. As a result, some Chwezi–namely the Hima–moved southward, where they established a new ruling clan–the Hinda–under the leadership of which several kingdoms and principalities were founded in the areas between Lake Victoria and Lake Tanganyika.[97]

Like the Hima, the Chwezi are essentially a cattle-keeping pastoralist people. Currently, they are located in a number of East African states, especially Uganda.

CIPUNGU

The Cipungu are a Southwest African people. They are concentrated in Angola, notably in its west central regions. Their neighbors include the Cisanji peoples.

CISAMA

The Cisama are a West Central African people. They are concentrated in the western regions of Angola.

CISANJI

The Cisanji are a Southwest African people. They are concentrated in Angola's west central coastal areas. Their neighbors include the Cipungu, Esele, Hanya, and Ndombe peoples.

CLELA, see KOLELA

COKWE

A West Central African Western Bantu-speaking people. The Cokwe are concentrated in Angola and the Democratic Republic of the Congo (Zaire). In Zaire, their neighbors include the Pende people of the Bandundu and Kasai administrative provinces.

COLLO, see SHILLUK

COLOURED

Coloured, formerly Cape Coloured, are people of mixed indigenous African, European and East Indian blood who live mainly in the southwestern portion of the Republic of South Africa. They originated primarily from unions between men and women of different races. Their main concentrations are in Cape Town and its suburbs and Port Elizabeth, as well as in the rural areas of the western Cape of Good Hope province. They constitute about 8.6% of South Africa's total population and speak Afrikaans and English.

Many coloureds are spread across the South African economic spectrum. Some survive in ghettos as low-paid domestics, while others work as shopkeepers, artisans, skilled workers, teachers or policemen.

During the apartheid era of South Africa the Coloured were allowed to engage in political activities through a chamber of their own representatives in the country's tricameral parliament.

Cape Coloureds have spawned their own arts and culture. They are known for their traditional music that harkens back to a time of racial unity before the apartheid system. Also many Coloured writers have been noted in

Afrikaans, as well as in English South African literature.

Many Coloureds are members of the Dutch Reformed Church or the English Anglican Church; yet, there is a small minority of them that recognize their Malaysian roots or adhere to Islam.

CONGO, see BANTU and KONGO

CONIAGUI

The Coniagui, also known as Duka and Tenda, are a West African Tenda people. They live in the border region between Guinea and Senegal.

COPIERS, see also MALAGASY

The Copiers are one of Madagascar's ethnic groups. They are of a mixed African, Malayo-Indonesian and Arab ancestry. They speak a dialect of Malagasy, which is an Austronesian language.

COPTS

The Copts, known in Arabic as *al-Aqbāt*, are an ancient Christian people of eastern and northeastern Africa whose ethnic identity is derived primarily from the doctrines of the Coptic Church. They are highly concentrated in Egypt. Their language is a Hamito-Semitic language that was spoken in Egypt from about the second century A.D. Subsequently, it was written essentially in the Greek alphabet. As a consequence of the Arabization and Islamization of Egypt in the seventh century, the term Copt was used to designate Egyptian Christians, notably those who identified themselves with the Coptic Church and the Monophysite Doctrine. Also, it was used to identify Christians of Eritrea, Ethiopia, and Sudan who adhered to the beliefs of the Coptic Church.

Originally, the Coptic Church was called the Egyptian Church. In the 19th and 20th centuries, however, it started to acquire the name of Coptic Orthodox Church to distinguish Copts of the Eastern Orthodox rite from those who converted to Roman Catholicism.

Currently, Copts are concentrated in the central and northern regions of Egypt, notably in Alexandria, Cairo, Asyuut, Luxor, and other urban centers of the country. In Sudan, they are concentrated in Khartoum, whereas in Ethiopia, they are concentrated in the capital, Addis Ababa, and Christian areas of the country. In Eritrea, Eritrean Copts are concentrated in Asmara, the capital.

COTOCOLI, see KOTOKOLI and TEM

CREOLE

The Creole peoples are descendants of ex-slaves of varied origins who had been freed and settled essentially by former colonial powers in more than one African country. As a result, the settlers provides cores for the growth of Creole communities, the peoples of which had some European or Asian admixture, if not significant exposure to European culture. In Africa, the centers of these communities were in such cities as St. Louis (Senegal), Ouidah (Benin), Lagos (Nigeria), Libreville (Gabon), Freetown (Sierra Leone), and Monrovia (Liberia); or islands such as Fernando Po, the Comoros, São Tomé, Mauritius, Principé, Réunion, and Seychelle.

CUSH

Cush, also Kush, a Nubian people of East Africa in general and ancient Egypt, the Sudan and Ethiopia in particular. They speak Cush, a language that belongs to the Cushitic group of the Hamito-Semitic family of African languages.

The history of the Cush people is traced back to the Stone Age, at which time they herded cattle and grew cereal crops.[99] Their ancient kingdom was seated in a city called Napata in what is now modern Sudan. Although not much is known about the Cush or their culture, many "historians believe [that] they were a wealthy and powerful people as far back as the ninth century B.C. The [Cushite] civilization thrived for almost 1,000 years, leaving extensive but largely unexcavated ruins of its monuments and villages."[100]

In the eighth century B.C., the Cush armies conquered Egypt, establishing the renowned Cushite dynasty, also called Napata dynasty, Ethiopian dynasty, or the 25th dynasty of ancient Egypt. The dynasty was founded by Shabaka after his father, Kashta, upon annexing Upper Egypt to Cush, which "was the southern portion of the region known as Nubia."[101] The Cushite dynasty spanned from 716 to 656 B.C.

During their reign over Egypt, the Cush people also managed to dominate much of the African continent. In the seventh century B.C., however, they were forced by invading Assyrian armies "to retreat up the Nile River and resettle in the ancient city of Meroë."[102] There, they succeeded in establishing a new empire that was renowned for its iron tools and weapons. This empire, however, started to lose its influence and power after A.D. 200, and by the year 700 it collapsed in the face of the rising power of its neighbors.

According to Jim Haskins and Joann Biondi, "[historians] believe that the [Cush] had a great influence on the developments of civilization in other parts of Africa. Some Ashanti and Yoruba legends refer to [Cush] ancestors who migrated from [Cush] territory to create new empires in West Africa."[103]

CUSSU

A Southwest African Bantu-speaking people. The Cussu live in the southeastern regions of Angola.

DAAROOD, see DAROD

DABA

The Daba are a West and West Central African people. They are concentrated in the northern regions of Cameroon.

DABU, see ADIOUKROU

DADJO, see DAJU

DAGAA WIILI, see LOBI-DAGARTI

DAGABA, see also LOBI-DAGARTI

The Dagaba, also known as Dagarti, are a West African people. They are concentrated in the Northern and Upper administrative regions of Ghana adjacent to the Ghanian northwestern borders with Burkina Faso and the Ivory Coast. Groups of them, however, are also located in Burkina Faso and the Ivory Coast. The Dagaba neighbors include the Grusi, Gonja, Lobi and Sisala peoples.

DAGARA, see LOBI-DAGARTI and KANURI

DAGARA-LOBR, see LOBI-DAGARTI

DAGARI, see DAGARTI

DAGARTI, see also LOBI-DAGARTI

These are a West African people. The Dagarti, also called Dagari, are concentrated in the Ivory Coast and adjoining countries. They are culturally related to the Lobi people. Like the Lobi, they speak a language that belongs to the Voltaic branch of the Niger-Congo family of African languages. The Dagarti neighbors include the Berifor, Bobo, Diam, Grunshi, Lobi, Nunuma and Wala peoples.

DAGBAMBA, see MAMPRUSI

DAGILA, see KURA

DAGOMA, see DAGOMBA

DAGOMBA

The Dagomba people, also known as Dagoma, Weiya (Wiya) and Yooba, are one of the ethnic communities of the Republic of Ghana, where they are known as Moshi-Dagomba and account for 16% of the country's total population. Second to the Akan (44%), they constitute the largest ethnic minority in Ghana. They are highly concentrated in the Northern Region, where they live in the chiefdom of Dagbon. The latter chieftainship also comprises several subject tribes or clans, the most important of which are the Komkombo (Komkomba, Konkomba) and the Chakossi. The Dagomba people are also one of the ethnic minorities of Togo, where they have a large concentration especially in la Kara.

The Dagomba people speak Dagbane, a language of the Voltaic (Gur) branch of the Niger-Congo family of African languages. Their neighbors include the Atyuti, Basari, Builsa, Gonja, Grusi, Konkomba, Krachi, Mamprusi (Manprusi), Nanumba and Tem peoples. In the 14th century, they developed their own kingdom and managed to extend its control south to the Black Volta. The kingdom's size, however, was reduced in the mid-seventeenth century, as a result of the Conja's conquests. Subsequently, it fell to the Ashanti towards the end of the seventeenth century and then to the British in 1874.

The Dagomba are essentially a patrilineal people. Patrilineages are the basis of their society and are hierarchically arranged into several segments. On the whole, however, their society is made up of two major groups, the chiefly and the commoners.

DAHOMEANS, see EWE and FON

DAHOMEY, see EWE and FON

DAJU

The Daju people are one of Chad's ethnic groups. They are concentrated in the Ouaddai region. They are Muslim people who developed an independent sultanate of their own in the past. The Daju are presently settled agriculturalists.

DAKA

The Daka are a West African people. They are concentrated in eastern Nigeria and Western Cameroon. Their language belongs to the Adamawa branch of the Niger-Congo family of African languages. The Daka neighbors include the Chamba, Fula, Jukun and Mumuye peoples.

DAKARKARI, also see DAKKARARI and KOLELA

The Dakarkari, also called Kolela, Lalawa and Lela, are a West African people. They are concentrated in the northwestern regions of Nigeria.

DAKKARARI, see DAKARKARI and KOLELA

DAKHO, see LUHYA

DAKWA

The Dakwa are a Central African people. Their main concentrations are in Chad and Central African Republic. The Dakwa's neighbors in both countries include the Banzirti and Ngapou peoples.

DALALEKUTUK, see MASAI

DALLA, see MEDI

DAMA (East Africa), see DASANEC

DAMA (Southwest Africa), see HERERO

DAMAQUA

An extinct southern African people. The Damaqua used to live in the southern regions of what is presently the Republic of South Africa.

DAMARA, see also HERERO

The Damara people, also known as Bergdama and Haukhoin, are one of Namibia's Herero groups. They are Khoisan-speaking people and live primarily in the southern regions of the country. The Damara are a very dark skinned group who live by hunting and on the wild vegetable produce. Their society is patrilineal with the family as its basic unit. They believe in a supreme spiritual being, *Ilgauab*, the same deity of northern Bushmen and the Hottentots. Originally, the Damara were a mountain people. In time, however, they were driven into the hills by their neighbors the Herero and the Hottentots.[104] Currently, they represent about 8% of Namibia's population.

DAMAT, see **MASAI**

DAMBOMO, see **KOTO**

DAMERGU

A West African ethnic group. The Damergu are concentrated in Niger, notably in its eastern regions. Their neighbors include the Air and Gounda peoples.

DAMOT, see **AWI**

DAN, see also **MANDE**

The Dan, also called Gio or Yakuba, are a Mande (Mende) people. They constitute one of the major ethnic minorities of the Ivory Coast and a significant ethnic minority in Liberia. In the Ivory Coast, they are highly concentrated in the Dang (Dans) and Toura mountains of the west central regions of the country, as well as in contiguous areas within Liberia. The Dan have tribal affiliations with numerous groups outside these two countries and are closely related to the Gere (Ngere, or Guere) to the south of their current concentrations. They speak the Southern branch of the Mande linguistic family. The Dan neighbors include the Guro, Konyanke, Kpelle, Malinke, Ngere and Wobe peoples.

Though known as Yakuba, a Semitic name stemming from the name of Prophet Jacob, the Dan do not appear to be related to Dan, one of the twelve tribes of Israel, which is assumed to have been lost after the Assyrian conquest of the Kingdom of Israel in 721 B.C.

In their social and political organization, the Dan are subdivided into numerous clans, which are not socially or politically linked to a central authority or a single paramount chief. They continue to live in villages of varying sizes, observe bilateral kinship relationships based on fathers' and mothers' patrilineages and practice their traditional religious beliefs. Most of their marriages are monogamous.

The Dan people are predominantly agriculturalist. Currently, they engage in growing rice, cassava, rubber and coffee.

Like other West African peoples, the Dan are renowned for their splendid wood sculpture, especially the hardwood masks and the large wooden spoons which represent first wives of important men. Also, they are famous for their murals which they paint on exterior house walls.[105]

DANAKIL, see AFAR

DANAQLA, see AFAR

DANDA

The Danda are a Southeast African-Malagasy people. They are concentrated in the southern coastal areas of Mozambique. Their neighbors include the Manyika and Ndau peoples.

DARASA

The Darasa are an East African people. They are concentrated in the southern regions of Ethiopia, primarily in the estern vicinity of Lake Abaya. Groups of them, however, can also be found in northern Kenya. Their neighbors include the Batutu and Sidamo peoples.

DAROD, see also SOMALI

A Somali clan. The Darod live in the northwestern regions of Somalia. They also have extensions in both Kenya and Ethiopia.

DARWA

The Darwa are a North African people. They are concentrated in the east central mountainous regions of Morocco. Their neighbors include the Ait Walnzgit and Sraghna peoples.

DASANEC

The Dasanec, also known as Dama, Gelleba (Gelubba), and Merile, are an East African pastoralist and agricultural people. They are concentrated in Ethiopia and Kenya.

DATOG, see TATURU

DAZA, see also TOUBOU

The Daza, also called Dazaga, are a Central African people. They are concentrated in the northwestern regions of Chad. Their neighbors include the Anakazza, Noarma, and Zaghawa peoples. The Daza are a nomadic Arab group.

DAZAGA, see DAZA

DE, see also KRU

The De are one of the Kru peoples. They are concentrated in Liberia and the Ivory Coast, primarily in their coastal areas. Their neighbors include the Bassa and Vai peoples.

DEBRI-MELA, see SAHO

DEFORO

A West African people of the Middle Niger lands. The Deforo are concentrated in Burkina Faso, Mali and Niger. Their neighbors include the Fula, Dogon, Mossi, Songhai and Taureg peoples. They speak a language that belongs to the Voltaic branch of the Niger-Congo family of African languages.

DEGHWEDE

The Deghwede, also called Hude, Wa'a and Zaghvana, are a West African people. They are concentrated in the northeastern regions of Nigeria.

DEMBO, see MBUNDU

DENDI

A West African people and one of Benin's ethnic minorities. The Dendi are associated with the Niger Valley. They are concentrated in the northern regions of Benin and speak a Nilo-Saharan language. Their neighbors include the Busa, Borgu, Fula, Tienga and Zerma peoples.

DERA

A West African Nigerian people. The Dera are concentrated in the northeastern regions of Nigeria. Their neighbors include the Hona, Longuda, Mbula, Tangale, Tera and Yungur peoples. They speak a language that belongs to the Afro-Asiatic family of African languages.

DERDEKISHIA, see TEDA

DETI, see also SAN

These are a southern African San-speaking people. The Deti are concentrated along the Botletli river in Botswana. Like other San groups, they are essentially foragers, hunters and gatherers.

DEY

A small West African ethnic group. The Dey people, also known as Dewoi and Dewoin, are concentrated in Liberia, especially in the Montserrado County and the capital Monrovia.

DHOLUO, see LUO

DHOPADHOLA, see PADHOLA

DHULBAHANTE, see also SOMALI

An East African Somali group. The Dhulbahante are an Harti clan. They are part of the Darod tribe, one of the major tribes in Somalia.

DIAKHANKE

The Diakhanke, also called Diakkane, Diankhanke, Jahanka and Janhanka, are a West African Soninke Muslim farming people. They are concentrated in Gambia, Mali and Senegal. Their economic activities focus on farming, stock raising, and trading.

DIAKKANE, see DIAKHANKE

DIALONKE

The Dialonke, also known as Djallonke and Dyalonke, are a West African people. They are concentrated in the savanna areas surrounding the Fouta Djallon plateau, near the source of the Gambia river, west-central Guinea. Groups of them are also located in Sierra Leone and other West Atlantic states. The Dyalonke speak a language that belongs to the Mande branch of the Niger-Congo family of African languages. Their neighbors include the Fula, Limba, Malinke, Susu and Tenda peoples.

DIAM, see also LOBI-DAGARTI

These are a West African people. The Diam, also called Dian, are concentrated in the Ivory Coast and adjoining countries. They are linguistically related to the Lobi-Dagarti peoples. They speak Lobi, a language that belongs to the Voltaic branch of the Niger-Congo family of African languages. The Diam neighbors include the Bobo, Dagari, Dorossié, Guin, Karaboro, Komono, Lobi, Sia and Tusyan peoples.

DIAN, see LOBI-DAGARTI

DIANKHANKE, see DIAKHANKE

DIDA, see also KRU

The Dida are a West African people and one of the Kru (Krou) groups. They are concentrated in the Ivory Coast and speak the Kwa language. Their neighbors include the Ajukru, Ari, Bakwe, Baule, Bete, Gagu and Guro peoples. The Dida engage in miscellaneous economic activities such as farming, fishing and trading.

DIDINGA

An East African people of southern Ethiopia and Sudan. The Didinga speak Didinga, a Surmic (formerly Surma) language which belongs to the East Sudanic group of the Nilo-Saharan family of African languages. They are related to the Suri, Me'en, Mursi and Murle peoples of the Kefa region in Ethiopia and Sudan.

DIETKO

These are a West and Central African people. They are concentrated in the northeastern regions of Nigeria, notably along the western shores of Lake Chad. Their neighbors include the Kanuri people.

DIKGALE, see PEDI

DIGHIL, see also SOMALI

One of the main Somali clans. The Dighil, also spelled Digil, live in the southern regions of Somalia between the Shibel (Shabeelle) and Juba rivers.

DIGIL, see DIGHIL

DIGIRE, see OKIEK

DIGO

The Digo, also Kidigo, are an East African Mijikenda group. They are concentrated in Kenya, notably along its coast. Their economic activities focus on agriculture, fishing, and trading. The Digo speak Mijikenda, a language that belongs to the Northeast Coastal Bantu languages.

DIILA, see KUNEMA

DIMMUK

One of West Africa's peoples. The Dimmuk, also known as the Doemak, live primarily in the Plateau State in Nigeria. They are closely related to the their neighbors the Bwal, Kwalla, and Namu peoples.

DINKA

Dinka, also called Jieng and Moinjaang, are an East African Nilotic people. They are concentrated in the rich savannah lands enveloping the central Nile River basin and its tributaries in southeast Sudan and southwest Ethiopia. They are latter-day descendants of Ethiopians and speak Dinka, which is part of the Eastern Sudanic languages of the Chari-Nile branch of African languages. The Dinka are predominantly semi-nomadic, pastoralist and agriculturalist people whose main economic activity focuses on cattle raising. Their population is estimated at over 2 million people.

The Dinka are closely related to other East African groups, especially the Nuer. Their society is subdivided into relatively small and autonomous groups, the most important of which are the Agar, Aliab, Atwot, Bor, Rek, Malual and Ngok. In their turn, these are subdivided into smaller units, each unit of which enjoying a high degree of autonomy. "Because of the vast geographical area they occupy, the Dinka exhibit great diversity of dialect, although they value intra-group unity in the face of enemies."[106]

The Dinka are a very independent and proud people and are highly attached to their lands, traditional laws and customs. To a Dinka, Dinkaland, with all its deprivations and troubles, is the best land in the world. "Until very recently, going to a foreign land was not only a rarity, but a shame. For a Dinka to threaten his relatives with leaving Dinkaland was seen as little short of suicide."[107]

The cultural continuity of the Dinka is often ascribed to their pride and ethnocentrism. A Dinka, for example, does not call himself "Dinka", but "Monyjang", which means "the man of men. This denotes that Dinka see themselves as the standard of what is normal for the dignity of man and assert their superiority over "the others" or "foreigners. "[108]

In character, the Dinka are highly socially conscious but individualistic people who share an aversion for organized government, at least in the modern sense of the word. They are gentle, witty, humorous, but sensitive people. A Dinka is "prone to violent reaction when his sense of pride and dignity is hurt – and that may not take too much. Determination and readiness to fight for one's honor and right against anyone of whatever strength merit high esteem in children and youth."[109]

The Dinka society is highly egalitarian. Only wealth in terms of cattle gives the impression of class structure. The only element of organization exists in the age set system where Dinka of certain age pass through phases of responsibility in their society. Each Dinka camp has a chief with no real authority except through persuasion and influence. Instead, the Dinka abide by rules passed on through the centuries within the clan or family.

The political system of the Dinka functions through lineages, with each descent group operating as an autonomous unit. The system revolves around a paramount chief, subordinate chiefs and elders. In this system, "political leadership is considered divine and is traced through religious legends that are continually retold to reinforce contemporary structure."[110] In it also, the person of the chief "is conceived as the father uniting the living members of his community among themselves and with their dead."[111] In the ceremonies of installation, the chief is lifted by representatives of various lineages in the community "so that the will of the tribe and divine acceptance are symbolized."[112]

The Dinka society is highly patriarchal, with the family serving as its most important unit. The Dinka believe that they are virtually worthless without the support of family, and hence, their morals stress exogamous marriage arrangements.

In their belief system, the family is the means through which a Dinka achieves immortality. The immortality for a person is contingent on fathering a son to carry on the line, as well as his name. "Every Dinka fears dying without a son 'to stand his head': to continue his name and revitalize his influence in this world. From the time a boy is born he is prepared for this role..."[113]

Through age-old ceremonies, the Dinka "ritualize the passage from boyhood to manhood." During these ceremonies "a number of boys of similar age undergo hardship together before abandoning forever the activity of milking cows, which had marked their status as children and servers of men."[114]

In their conception of things, "when a man dies leaving children behind, people mourn but are quick to add that his is not 'the bad death'. But a man who dies without issue is truly dead. Another word for death is 'perishing' (*riar*)."[115]

In order to avoid "true death", that is perishing, if a man dies without a son, the Dinka quickly designate one of the village boys to carry his name. In their view, procreational immortality is not a purely biological phenomenon. It is also a social phenomenon. It is an extension of this life into the hereafter, as well as "into this life through the memory of the dead. The closer the dead are to the living, biologically and socially, the greater the memory."[116] Clearly, the designation of one of the village boys to carry the name of a man who dies without issue demonstrates the generous aspect of the Dinka society. Virtually, every Dinka adheres to this view and tries to apply it, regardless of status or wealth.

Accordingly, what a Dinka father wants most is to perfect "his lineage through his posterity. The more children he has and from as many wives as he can afford, the more they complement and complete this idealized image."[117] By the same token, "a child who is handsome, courageous, courteous, intelligent, wise, well spoken, or otherwise worthy of praise gives his parents the joy of seeing themselves immortalized in virtue."[118]

Dinka religion is centered around one supreme God, *Nhialic*. Yet, everyday life centers around ancestor spirits that can influence common daily activities. "For a Dinka where he comes from, and where he goes to, are points in the cycle of life revitalized and continued through procreation. Despite the anxieties birth provokes, it is a cause for joy; but death is an end from which procreational immortality is the only salvation."[119]

Aside from being a means to one's immortality, marriage is also the most important means of acquiring wealth, or cattle, in their society. Bridewealth, or the practice of paying the bride's family for the right to marry, is the principal means of obtaining a wife in Dinka society. This leaves women extremely economically valuable, since the more daughters a family has the more cattle the family can obtain.

Cattle is the center of Dinka society. Dinka are socialized to highly revere cattle. A boy, for example, is given an ox with which he forms a very strong bond. A boy looks out for the ox's every-day needs, including "ornamenting" the ox by manipulating its horns. These manipulations give the ox an identity that will never leave it until death. The Dinka do not kill, trade or use their cattle as tools, they are accumulated for bridewealth (dowry, marriage price).

In their value system, cattle provide worldly needs and hence, help protect them against the evil forces of illness and disease. Cows provide dairy products that they "consider not only the best, but also the most noble, food..."[120] Moreover, the payment of cattle as "bridewealth" leads to the distribution of the "bridewealth" among a wide circle of relatives, a factor that not only contributes to cementing the network of human ties (which they highly regard in their society) but also guarantees the continuation of their race. Furthermore, cattle serve as a means to promote order and stability in society. They are used as "bloodwealth" in homicide and as compensation for a variety of possible wrongs within society. Additionally, cattle also address other basic needs. Their dried dung provides Dinka with fuel and fertilizer; their urine supplies them with disinfectants; their hides supply them with bedding skins and their horns furnish them with snuff boxes, trumpets and spoons. For all these reasons, cattle are considered indispensable to the welfare of the Dinka people. They explain why some Dinka speak of the cow or the bull as "the creator."[121]

The Dinka are very fastidious and adorn themselves with jewelry and ornamental painting. Men turn their hair bright red with cow urine, while women shave their hair, leaving just a small portion. The Dinka are also known to etch patterns on their skin using sharp blades which scar deeply.

Dinka art revolves around their bodies. Skin paintings are found to be very creative and beautiful. Also pottery making and basket weaving express Dinka women's artistic flare. Dinka men are fantastic blacksmiths and forge a multitude of cooking utensils and farm tools.

Since the sixteenth century, the Dinka traditional way of life, chieftainship system, culture, religious beliefs and sense of identity have been and continue to be threatened by foreign influences. Their exposure to different forms of foreign rule (Ottoman-Egyptian in the early part of the nineteenth century, Anglo-Egyptian Condominium between 1898 and 1956, and Sudan's rule since January 1, 1956) has already served to erode important aspects of their political, social and economic organization.

The Dinka are finding it more and more difficult to reconcile between the exigencies of their own cultures and those of the states to which they belong (Ethiopia and Sudan), as well as to foreign and/or modern cultures. Their acculturation is apparent in the way they are being governed. Their chieftainships, for example, have lost much of their divine character and are becoming more secular in their foundations and orientation. The transformation from divine-based chieftainships into secular-based ones is especially apparent among the Ngok Dinka, where reverence for their paramount chiefs or chiefs as secular-spiritual leaders was replaced by fear of secular punishment. "One by-product of the secularization of authority and control and the divine authority has been the intensification of power conflicts and the rise of modern political opposition."[122]

In an effort to contain the negative impact of acculturation on their societies, the Dinka have proposed and continue to advocate regionalism or autonomy within a federal system of government in the Sudan. The Dinka appear to believe that their proposal will help them maintain important aspects of their traditional way of life.

Failure to reach a working agreement with the Sudanese government to implement their proposal, however, seems to have incited some Dinka to resort to military struggle. Through the Anyanya, the army of the Southern revolt, they hope to achieve an autonomy status within the Sudan. In so doing, they joined the civil war that has been roaming southern Sudan since 1955. The choice of armed struggle, however, has not been without heavy cost. Hundreds of thousands of Dinka had to flee from their own country, The Sudan, to neighboring countries, especially to Congo, Uganda, Kenya, Ethiopia, and Central African Republic. Others sought refuge in northern Sudan. "For a people who had grown up thinking of themselves and their country as second to none, the indignities of refugee life brought lamentation and a feeling of isolation."[123]

DIOLA, see **DOULA**

DIOULA, see **DOULA**

DIPA, see **GURO**

DIR, see also **SOMALI**

One of the main Somali clans. The Dir live in the northwestern regions of Somalia. They speak Somali.

DIZI

An East African people. The Dizi are concentrated in highland areas south the Maji and Bero-Shasha provinces of the Kefa region in Ethiopia. Their neighbors include the Suri, Me'en, Murle, Mursi and Nyangatom peoples.

DJAGADA, see also **TOUBOU**

The Djagada are a Central African people. They are a Teda group, a Toubou people subgroup. The Djagada are concentrated in Chad, notably in the Kanem region. Their neighbors include the Azzas, Kokorda and Kreda peoples.

DJALLONKE, see **DIALONKE**

DJERMA, see **ZERMA**

DJERMIS, see **ZERMA**

DJOHEINA

The Djoheina, also Juhayna, are East Saharan Arab pastoralist people. They are concentrated in Chad.

DLAMINI

A Nguni-speaking people of pre-colonial Mozambique. They settled in Swaziland during the eighteenth century.

DODOTH

The Dodoth, also spelled Dodoz, are a Central and East African Eastern Nilotic-speaking pastoralist people. They are concentrated in Uganda and its neighboring countries. The Dodoth are related to the Iteso, Jie, Jiye, Topoza, Nyangatom and Turkana peoples.

DODOZ, see DODOTH

DOE

An East African people. The Doe are concentrated in the northeastern coastal regions of Tanzania. Their neighbors include the Kami, the Kutu, the Ndengereko, the Rufiji and the Wazaramo peoples.

DOGAN, see DOGON

DOGARA, see also KANURI

The Dogara, also known as Dagara, are a Kanuri people. They speak Kanuri. The Dogara are a Muslim people who live in Cameroon, Chad, Niger, Nigeria and other West African states. They are an essentially agricultural people.

DOGBA, see GUIZIGA

DOGOM, see DOGON

DOGON

The Dogon, also known as Dogan, Dogom, Dogono, Habbe, Hambee, Makbe, Tombo, Tommo, and Toro, are a West African people of the Middle Niger lands. They speak Dogon, a voltaic (or Gur) language which belongs to the Niger-Congo family of African languages and moreover, they comprise four major groups: the Arou, the Dyon, the Ono and the Domnu. The Dogon are located in southern Mali and northern Burkina Faso. In Mali, they are concentrated in the plateau region around Bandiagara and Douentza. Their neighbors include the Bobo, Bozo, Dyula, Fula, Mossi, Nono and Samo peoples. It is believed that they have lived in this region for at least five hundred years. Also, it is believed that they are the direct descendants of the Tellem peoples whose buildings, carving and textiles have been preserved from the fourteenth century.[124]

Historical evidence suggests that the Dogon are an ancient people who not only developed one of Africa's oldest cultures, but also always resisted outside influences upon it. Their whole life is governed by "a collection of myths that explain the structure of the universe and how the Dogon fit into that structure."[125] Virtually everything in their society is systemized from the layout of fields and villages to politics and the roles of the two sexes. According to Davidson, these people "conceive of life's development as the perpetual alteration of opposites – right and left, high and low, odd and even, male and female – reflecting a principle of twin-ness, which ideally should direct the proliferation of life."[126] In his view also, the Dogon are believed to consider "that creation began with an egg containing the elemental germs of the world's things: these germs developed first in seven segments of increasing length, representing the fundamental seeds of cultivation, which are to be found again in the human body, and which... indicate... the organization of the cosmos, of man, and of society."[127]

The masked society, *awa*, of the Dogon appears to play a vital role in preserving their elaborate mythology.[128] In their rituals, members of this male society use a secret language of their own known as *sigi so*.[129]

The Dogon support a hierarchically stratified society, the basic unit of which is "the patrilineage, or *ginna*. Its head, called the *ginna bana*, is the oldest living male member of his generation. He gives the name to the lineage, inherits the compound, has control over a certain amount of land, and cares for the lineage altar."[130] Their society is also divided into a series of occupational groups, age groups, and rituals' groups. Politically, each village or a group of villages is overseen by a chief, known as *hogon*, who has both religious and judicial functions. Relations between Dogon chiefs are normally coordinated by regional chiefs.

The Dogon people are essentially farmers and hunters. Their fields reflect their mythology. They are centered around three ritual fields which are laid out in the shape of a square. Their traditional religious system is highly ordered. It is centered on the belief in a creator-god, *Amma*, who made the earth from a lump of clay, as well as in spirits and reincarnation.[131] Like other West African peoples, the Dogon are famous for their wood carving, iron and leather works, pottery and weaving skills.

DOGONO, see **DOGON**

DOGORDA

The Dogorda are a Central African people. They are concentrated in the eastern vicinity of Lake Chad, Chad. Their neighbors include the Kanembou, Kecherda, and Koto peoples.

DOKO

The Doko are a West Central African people. They are concentrated in the Democratic Republic of the Congo (Zaire), primarily in its north central regions. Their neighbors include the Baloulou, Bombesa, and Mongo peoples.

DOM, see **AKAN**

DOMBE

A West Central African pastoralist people. The Dombe, also known as Ndombe, are concentrated in the southwest coastal areas in Angola. Their neighbors include the Cisanji, Hanya, and Kwisi peoples.

DOMNU, see **DOGON**

DONDO, see **KONGO**

DONGO

The Dongo are an East African people. They are concentrated in the northeastern regions of the Democratic Republic of the Congo (Zaire), primarily in the western vicinity of Lake Albert. Their neighbors include the Alur, Budu, Lugbara, Logo, Okebo, and Vonoma peoples.

DORIA, see KURA

DOROBO, see also OKIEK and KALENJIN

The Dorobo are an East African Okiek people, a Kalenjin people. Their main concentrations are in Kenya, Tanzania and Uganda. The Dorobo speak a dialect of Kalenjin, a Southern Nilotic language of the Eastern Sudanic family of African languages. They are essentially a semipastoralist people.

DOROSSIÉ, see also LOBI-DAGARTI

These are a West African people. The Dorossié, also spelled Dorosie, are concentrated in the Ivory Coast and adjoining countries. They are linguistically related to the Lobi-Dagarti people. They speak Lobi, a language that belongs to the Voltaic branch of the Niger-Congo family of African languages. The Dorossié neighbors include the Diam, Guin, Karaboro, Komono, Lobi and Tusyan peoples.

DOU MENIA

The Dou Menia are a North African people. They are concentrated in northwestern Algeria and northeastern Morocco. Their neighbors include the Ait Atta, Oulad Djerir, and Wad Yihya peoples.

DOULA, see also MANDE

The Doula, also Diola, Dioula, Diouala, Duala, Dyola, Dyula, Jola, Jula, Wangara and Yola, are one of the ethnic minorities in a number of West African states, especially Burkina Faso, Cameroon, The Gambia, Ivory Coast, Mali and the Senegal. They are Bantu-speaking Muslim people, who originally came from Equatorial Africa. They are a Mande group who speak dialects of Manding, a northern Mande language of the Niger-Congo family of African languages.

In the Cameroon, they account for about one-sixth of the total population. In The Gambia they constitute the fourth largest ethnic group, accounting for 10% of the country's total population or what amounts to about 80,000. In Ivory Coast, they live primarily in the northeastern region. In Senegal, they constitute the fifth largest ethnic minority, accounting for 9% of the population, or what amounts to about 0.7 million.

The word "Doula" is a Manding word that refers to "'traders' as a socioprofessional category, particularly to Muslim long-distance traders who speak one or another dialect of Manding. The name is used as an ethnic label by Manding-speaking minorities, particularly those living amid various Gur-speaking groups, such as the Senufo and Kulango."[132]

DOUROU

The Dourou, also known as Dui, Duru, Nyag Dii, and Zaa, are a West and West Central African people. They are concentrated in the Republic of Cameroon.

DOZA, see TOUBOU

DSCHAGGA, see CHAGGA

DUALA, see DOULA

DUI, see DOUROU

DUKA, see CONIAGUI and DUWAKA

DUKKALA

The Dukkala are a North African Berber people. They are concentrated in the mountainous regions along Morocco's Atlantic coast. Their neighbors include the Mzab and Shawya peoples.

DUMA

The Duma are a Southeast African-Malagasy Karanga subgroup. They live in Zimbabwe, notably in its central regions. Their neighbors include the Danda and Hlengwe peoples.

DUROP, see KOROP

DURU, see DOUROU

DURUMA

The Duruma people are an East African Mijikenda group. They are concentrated in Kenya, notably along its coast. Their economic activities focus on agriculture, fishing, and trading. The Duruma speak a dialect of Mijikenda, a language that belongs to the Northeast Coastal Bantu languages.

DUWAKA

A West African people. The Duwaka, also called Duka, Ethun and Hune, are concentrated in the northwestern regions of Nigeria. Probably, they are a Tenda group.

DWONG, see NUER

DYABARMA, see ZERMA

DYALO, see also FULANI

The Dyalo are a renowned Fulani clan which had control over the Kingdom of Macina during the early part of the nineteenth century. This clan was rivaled by another Fulani clan, namely, the Sangare.

DYALONKE, see DIALONKE

DYARMA, see ZERMA

DYE

These are one of Benin's and Togo's ethnic groups. The Dye are Voltaic (Gur)-speaking people. They are located in the northern areas of both countries.

DYERMA, see ZERMA

DYIMINI, see also SENUFO

These are a West African Voltaic (Gur)-speaking people. They speak Dyimini, a language belonging to the Gur branch of the Niger-Congo family of African languages. The Dyimini are a subgroup of the Senufo people who are highly concentrated in the northern parts of the Ivory Coast, the eastern and southeastern regions of the Republic of Mali and the northwestern regions of Burkina Faso.

DYOLA, see DOULA

DYON, see DOGON

DYULA, see DOULA

EASTERN NIGRITIC

This Eastern Nigritic people constitute one of Cameroon's ethnic minorities. They account for 7% of the country's total population.

EBIRA, see IGBIRA

EBOE, see EGBO

EBRIE

The Ebrie are a West African people. They are concentrated in the Ivory Coast, especially in the capital of this country, Abidjan, and speak the Kwa language. Their neighbors include the Abbe (Abe), Ajukru, Alagya, Anyi, Ari, Assini and Mekyibo peoples. The Ebrie engage in miscellaneous economic activities which include fishing and trading.

EBUNA, see **YUNGUR**

ECHIJITA, see **JITA**

EDDA, see **IGBO**

EDIBA, see **KOHUMONO**

EDO

The Edo, also called Bini, are a West African people. They are one of Nigeria's major ethnic groups, constituting the seventh largest group after the Hausa, Fulani, Yoruba, Igbo (Ibo) and Tiv. They speak a language of the Kwa branch of the Niger-Congo family of African languages and are concentrated in the southern parts of the country, notably in the state of Bendel. Their lands are located in the region west of the Niger river, extending from hilly areas in the north to swampy areas in the Niger Delta. The Edo neighbors include the Abua, Bassa-Nge, Igala, Igbirra, Igbo, Ijaw and Yungur peoples.

The Edo people were the founders of the Kingdom of Benin, which flourished between the fourteenth and the eighteenth centuries, stretching its control over territories lying between the Niger Delta and Lagos, additionally developing trading and diplomatic relations with the Portuguese. Its major exports were ivory, pepper and palm oil.

The rise of this kingdom sometime before 1300 is described in both Edo and Yoruba legends. According to these legends, the son of Oranmiyan, an Ife prince, from the daughter of a Bini chief, was the founder of the Benin empire.[134]

At the formative stage, *oba* – that is king – Eweka focused his attention on consolidating the internal power of the kingdom. Thereupon his attention, as well as those of his successors, was focused on expanding the kingdom. During the reign of *oba* Ewuare the Great (c. 1440-c. 1480), for example, the kingdom's influence was extended to Lagos in the west and the Niger in the East.[135]

The power, stability and prosperity of the kingdom during Ewuare's reign, as well as that of his son Ozolua (c. 1480-c. 1504) and their successors, was not only apparent in their wealth, divine attributes and command over commercial transactions, but also in the lavishness of their courts, the abundance of food in the kingdom, and their distinctive bronze and ivory artistic works.[136]

The Edo were among the first West African people to come into contact with European explorers. In 1485, they came into contact with the Portuguese who appeared at Benin in search of trade and converts. Initially, the impact of this contact was limited. Benin was a stable, established and prosperous state, and moreover, the Portuguese had little products to offer. In time, however, the impact started to spread more so when other European nations sent their own explorers, traders, slavers, political agents and manufactured goods, including firearms, to West Africa. Internal divisions within the kingdom regarding succession, *obas's* delegation of political and military authority to chiefs, uprisings of subjected peoples and foreign intrigues – all these factors contributed to the weakening of Benin and the eventual decline in the nineteenth century. In 1892, the kingdom was brought under British protection and five years later, it was seized and incorporated within Britain's Royal Niger Coast Company Protectorate. In the process, its capital, Benin City, was destroyed.[137]

In 1900, the territory of the Royal Niger Coast Company was assumed by the British government. Subsequently, the Kingdom of Benin and its people were placed under British imperial administration, incorporated into British Nigeria and more importantly, its economy was transformed into a primary producing economy to meet the economic interests of Britain.

Like in other countries of Africa, the British government ruled the Edo through the chiefly agency, which had lost much of its former independent decision-making power. This continued until October 1, 1960, when Nigeria was granted its independence, with the Edo, their *obas* and kingdom within it.

Currently, the Edo's *obas* retain limited traditional and advisory roles. Their main economic activities center on agriculture, animal husbandry, and bronze, ivory, wooden and brass craftsmanship, with villages being the cores of both their social and political socialization. The males of each village are divided into three main age groups (boys, adults and elderly), each group of which has assigned specific tasks. Boys are given light communal responsibilities, whereas adults are given executive and difficult tasks. The elderly form the village council which addresses issues relating to "tax collection, collective tasks, cult festivals, relations with central authorities, and other community concerns."[138]

Though Christianity and Islam have won many converts, some Edo people continue to be impacted by their traditional religion, which is based on the belief in a remote creator, lesser gods, mythical heroes and ancestors' spirits. The position of *oba* continues to exist but without its traditional powers.

EFE, see MBUTI

EFIK

These are the Nigerian people of the Bakassi peninsula at the borders of Nigeria and Cameroon. Their main economic occupation is fishing.[139] The Efik people are concentrated in the lower Cross River area in what is presently the Cross River State of Nigeria. They speak Efik-Ibibio dialect of the Kwa branch of the Niger-Congo family of African languages and share many common traits with the Igbo, one of Nigeria's major ethnic groups. Their dialect is currently the literary language of their educated people. Their neighbors include the Abua, Ibibio, Igbo, Ododop and Ogoni peoples.

The Efik are a subgroup of the Ibibio people. "They migrated down the Cross River during the first half of the 17th century and founded Creek town, Duke Town, and other settlements. Because of a European error in confusing their territory with that of the Kalabari Ijaw (known as New Calabar), the Efik area became known as Old Calabar."[140]

As a people engaged in fishing, the Efik were attracted to the slave trade and succeeded in developing Old Calabar into a major slaving center between the seventeenth and nineteenth centuries. They thrived on importing large numbers of slaves, especially from the Ibo interior, and selling most of them to European slavers in return for European manufactured goods, including firearms.[141] Later, they shifted their trade activity to the exportation of palm oil and kernels. This new activity drew some Efik to farming villages.

A great majority of Efik people live in villages that are built around central courtyards. Their villages are governed by councils representing the heads of their various households. In their turn, villages are bonded together by descent from same ancestors, as well as by their common tutelary spirits and totems. Socialization of men and women within villages was furthered through the initiation ceremonies and activities of secret societies. This entails religious rituals, exaltation of ancestral spirits and practice of magic, sorcery and various forms of wizardry.

The Efik society is patrilineal with households constituting its basic units. Traditionally, a household "consisted of a man, his several wives, and their children."[142] Normally, the eldest male served as the leader of the household and related households lived in wards, the units of their respective settlements.

The Efik are a patrilineal people. In their society, questions relating to descent, succession and inheritance are based on patrilineal lineages. The heads of their households continue to have ritual responsibilities, including the protection of ancestral shrines.

The leader, or chief, of the Efik people is elected by the representatives of various households. Known as *Obung*, he is the head of Ekpe (Egbo), or Leopard Society, a secret male society comprised of the leading men of the Efik community.[143] Traditionally, the Ekpe society, which continues to exist until today, was tasked with maintaining the unity and well-being of the Efik people through law enforcement and carrying out punishments against violators.

Though most Efik are Christian, their society is still being impacted by their traditional religion which rests on the belief in a supreme creator,

God, an ancestral cult, supranatural spirits and in the power of sorcery and magic. Like other West African peoples, they are renowned for their wood carving skills.

EGBA, see also YORUBA

A West African Yoruba subgroup of what is presently southern Nigeria. The Egba asserted their independence from the Youruba Oyo empire towards the end of the eighteenth century and established Abeokuta as one of their new cities. They engaged as middlemen in the arms and slave trade. Their relations with the British started to worsen in the 1860's, but were able to withstand British campaigns against them, as well as British encroachments on their independence until 1914. In 1918, they staged a protest against the indirect system of rule which the British had introduced to Egbaland.

EGBADO, see also YORUBA

This is a West African Yoruba subgroup of what is presently southwestern Nigeria. Like other Yoruba subgroups, the Egbado developed a kingdom of their own. During the later part of the eighteenth century they founded Ilaro, in what is presently western Ognun, southwestern Nigeria, as its capital and main trade center. Their kingdom however was a tributary of the state of Old Oyo. With the decline of the latter state early in the nineteenth century, the Egbado became a vulnerable people and were raided for slaves by the kingdom of Dahomey. In the 1840s, it fell to the Egba and was incorporated within their Kingdom. In 1890, Great Britain responded to their request for protection against the Egba and built a garrison in their capital.

Presently, the Egbado people are essentially agriculturalists and farmers. Their produce includes cocoa, palm oil and kernels, kola nuts, rice and miscellaneous fruits and vegetables. Ilaro, their original capital, serves as the seat of the Egbado South Local Government Council.

EGGAN, see EGGON

EGGON

A West African group. The Eggon, also known as Eggan, Egon, Egun, Mada Eggoni and Megong, are concentrated in the central regions of Nigeria. Their language belongs to the Benue-Congo branch of the Niger-Congo family of African languages.

EGON, see also **EGGON**

EGUN, see **EGGON**

EJAGHAM, see also **EKOI**

The Ejagham are a West African Bantu-speaking people. They speak a language belonging to the Benue-Congo branch of the Niger-Congo family of African languages and are related by language to the Ekoi people. The Ejagham are concentrated in the southeastern regions of Nigeria and the western regions of Cameroon.

EKET

The Eket, also called Southern Ibibio, are one of the main subgroups of the West African Ibibio people. They are concentrated in the southeastern areas of Nigeria, especially in the Cross River State.

Together with other Ibibio subgroups (Anang, Andoni-Ibeno, Efik, and Ibibio proper), they represent one of the ten largest ethnic minorities of Nigeria. With other Ibibio groups, their population ranks after those of the Hausa, Fulani, Yoruba, Ibo, Kanuri, Tiv, Edo and Nupe peoples.

The Eket speak a Kwa language of the Niger-Congo family of African languages and share many common traits with the Igbo, one of Nigeria's major ethnic groups.

A great majority of Eket people are engaged in agriculture and trade and live in villages that are built around central courtyards. Their produce includes palm oil and kernels.

The Eket villages are governed by councils representing the heads of their various households. In their turn, villages are bonded together by descent from same ancestors, as well as by their common tutelary spirits and totems. Socialization of men and women within villages is furthered through the initiation ceremonies and activities of secret societies, which entail religious rituals, exaltation of ancestral spirits and practice of magic, sorcery and various forms of wizardry.

The Eket are a patrilineal people. In their society, questions relating to descent, succession and inheritance are based on patrilineal lineages. The heads of their households continue to have ritual responsibilities, including the protection of ancestral shrines. Like other West African people, the Eket are renowned for their wood carving skills.

EKITI, see also YORUBA

These are a West African Yoruba subgroup. They are concentrated in southwestern Nigeria. They were Egba neighbors and had a kingdom of their own.

Presently, the Ekiti people are agriculturalists and farmers. Their produce includes cocoa, palm oil and kernels, kola nuts, rice, pumpkins and miscellaneous fruits and vegetables. The Ekitis' main center is Hawe Ekiti, which is the seat of the Ekiti Southwest Local Government Council.

EKOI

The Ekoi, also called Ekoid Bantu, are a West African people. They are concentrated in the southeastern parts of Nigeria and in adjacent areas along the Nigerian borders with Cameroon. Their neighbors include the Efik, an Ibibio subgroup. Their neighbors are the Boki, Ibibio, Ibo, Mbembe, Ododop, Tiv and Yako peoples.

The Ekoi are originally from the north, probably from areas around the lower end of the Nile Valley. They speak a Bantu language, and linguistically are related to the Atam, Boki, Ejagham, Mbembe, Ufia and Yako peoples. The Ekoi have a secret Nilotic script of their own called *nsibidi*.

The Ekoi are a semi-sedentary agriculturalists and hunters and traditionally, they were governed by councils of elders the decisions of which were implemented with the help of *egbo*, a secret society that enjoyed social and religious powers.

Traditionally, the Ekoi religion centered on Obassi Osaw, the sky god, and Obassi Nsi, the earth god, as well as on ancestral spirits and natural phenomena.

The Ekoi are noted for their traditional medicine, as well as utilization of plants to cure common diseases, including smallpox. They are also renowned for their "extensive knowledge of and aesthetic appreciation of flowers," as well as for their mural paintings on sanctuaries, pottery crafts and carving skills.[144]

EKONDA, see MONG

EKPOMA, see ISHAN

EKUMURU, see KOHUMONO

EL ARBAA

The El Arbaa are a North African people. They are concentrated in the central regions of Algeria. Their neighbors include the Chaamba, Hamiyan, and Mzab peoples.

ELGEYO, see also KEIYO and KALENJIN

The Elgeyo are an East African Keiyo people, a Kalenjin group. They are concentrated in Kenya, Tanzania and Uganda. The Elgeyo speak a dialect of Kalenjin, a Southern Nilotic language of the Eastern Sudanic family of African languages. They are a semipastoralist people.

ELGON, see also KONY and KALENJIN

An East African Kony people, a Kalenjin group. Their main concentrations are in Kenya, Tanzania and Uganda. The Elgon speak a dialect of Kalenjin, a Southern Nilotic language of the Eastern Sudanic family of African languages. They are essentially a semipastoralist people.

ELGONYI, see also KONY and KALENJIN

The Elgonyi are an East African Kony people, a Kalenjin group. They are concentrated in Kenya, Tanzania and Uganda. The Elgonyi speak a dialect of Kalenjin, a Southern Nilotic language of the Eastern Sudanic family of African languages. They are essentially a semipastoralist people.

ELGUMI, see ITESO

EMBU

The Embu are one of Kenya's eleven largest ethnic groups. They are a Bantu-speaking people. The Embu are concentrated in the east central regions of the country, notably in the Eastern Province. Their neighbors include the Kamba and Nyeri peoples.

EMU, see ISHAN

ENDO, see also KALENJIN

An East African Kalenjin group. Their main concentrations are in Kenya, Tanzania and Uganda. They speak a dialect of Kalenjin, a Southern Nilotic language of the Eastern Sudanic family of African languages. The Endo comprise several groups, including the Chebleng. They are a semipastoralist people.

ENIA, see GALLA

ENUGU, see IGBO

ENYONG, see also IBIBIO

The Enyong, also called Northern Ibibio, are one of the main groups of the West African Ibibio people. They are concentrated in the southeastern areas of Nigeria, especially in the Cross River State. Together with other Ibibio subgroups (Anang, Andoni-Ibeno, Efik, Eket, and Ibibio proper), they represent one of the ten largest ethnic minorities of Nigeria. With other Ibibio groups, their population ranks after those of the Hausa, Fulani,

Yoruba, Ibo, Kanuri, Tiv, Edo and Nupe peoples. The Enyong speak a Kwa language of the Niger-Congo family of African languages and share many common traits with the Igbo, one of Nigeria's major ethnic groups.

A great majority of the Enyong people are engaged in agriculture and trade and live in villages that are built around central courtyards. Their produce includes palm oil and kernels. Like other West African people, the Enyong are also renowned for their wood carving products.

The Enyong villages are governed by councils representing the heads of their various households. In their turn, villages are bonded together by descent from same ancestors, as well as by their common tutelary spirits and totems. Socialization of men and women within villages is furthered through the initiation ceremonies and activities of secret societies, which entail religious rituals, exaltation of ancestral spirits and practice of magic, sorcery and various forms of wizardry.

The Enyong are a patrilineal people. In their society, questions relating to descent, succession and inheritance are based on patrilineal lineages. The heads of their households continue to have ritual responsibilities, including the protection of ancestral shrines.

EOTILE, see MEKYIBO

EQUATORIAL BANTU

The Equatorial Bantu people constitute the second largest ethnic minority of the United Republic of Cameroon. They account for about 19% of the country's total population.

ERDIHA, see TOUBOU

ESA, see ISHAN

ESELE

The Esele are a Southwest Central African Bantu-speaking people. They are concentrated in Angola's northwestern coastal areas, neighboring the Csanji and Mbui peoples. The Esele are an Mbundu subgroup.

ESHIRA

The Eshira people constitute the second largest ethnic group in the Gabonese Republic. They are concentrated in the coastal areas of the country. The Eshira are tribally organized. They speak Eschira.

ESRÁELOTCH, see FALASHA

ETHUN, see DUWAKA

ETON

The Eton people are a Central African ethnic group. They are a Bati subgroup. The Eton are concentrated in southern Cameroon. Groups of them, however, can be found in Equatorial Guinea and Gabon.

ETSAKO

The Etsako, also known as Afenmai and Yekhee, are a West African cluster of people. They comprise several groups who live in the southern regions of Nigeria.

EWATTO, see ISHAN

EWE

The Ewe, pronounced Evvies, are a major Adja cluster of peoples in West Africa. They are highly concentrated in the southeastern areas of the Republic of Ghana, southern regions of Benin and the southern parts of the Republic of Togo. In Ghana, they constitute the third largest ethnic minority after the Akan (44%) and the Moshi-Dagomba (16%), accounting for 13% of the Ghanian population. In Togo, they represent one of the largest ethnic minorities. In Benin, they also represent an important ethnic minority. Their total population is estimated at over 3.3 million.

The Ewe people speak different dialects of Ewe (Evegbe), all of which belong to the Kwa branch of the Niger-Congo family of African languages. Known also as Dahomeans, they comprise many groups, including the Anlo, Abutia, Be, Kpelle and Ho. They also include other linguistically and culturally related groups such as the Adja, Oatchi and Peda peoples. Although their related languages are commonly incomprehensible, the Ewe and Fon people are often considered to belong to the same grouping.[145]

The original homeland of the Ewe is Oyo, in western Nigeria, where they supported several states. In the 17th century, for example, Old Oyo eyed Damomey. This objective was materialized between 1726 and 1730, during which time Dahomey fell to Oyo's control and became an Oyo vassal state.[146]

Late in the 19th century, the Ewe assisted the British in subduing the Ashanti to whom they formerly were paying tributes. As a result of European colonial deals, they were turned over to the Germans in 1899, and after World War I, their land was divided into three territories, namely: French Togoland, British Togoland and Gold Coast (later Ghana). Eventually, however, British Togoland was united with Ghana, whereas French Togoland became an independent state (1960).

The social and political organization of the Ewe people is patrilineal. The patrilineal kinship relation is most pronounced among the Anlo, an Ewe tribe that lives in coastal Ghana.

Ewe live in villages that are small and kin-based. The social order is set up through lineage. The lineage, or *frome*, is headed by a chief who is responsible for the lineages' spiritual and social life. This male elder also oversees justice and manages the property of the lineage. In their society all property belongs to the male lineage. "Not only does each community, as a rule, have a family from which the chiefs come; also they have what is called a 'stool family,' which is in some respects superior. There is a royal line and also a separate 'stool line,' the head of which is the 'stool father."[147]

The Ewe's traditional clothing consists of a multi-colored cloth called *pagne*, which is wrapped as a skirt around the waist.

The Ewe are sedentary people with agriculture as their main economic activity. They farm for both sustenance and for trade. In their society, men engage in farming and (in coastal areas) in small scale fishing, whereas women engage in commercial activities, trading of foodstuffs in markets located in adjacent towns or cities. Like other West African peoples, the Ewe are famous not only for their carved and sculptured wooden stools and drums, but also for their pottery, weaving, basketry, and blacksmithing skills.

Though some had converted to Christianity by European missionaries during the colonial period, most Ewe still adhere to their traditional religious beliefs. They worship their high god, *Mawa*, and the lesser spirits, *Trowo*, that are regarded intermediaries for both human beings and God. Ancestors are also worshiped and witchcraft is seen as the source of misfortunes in their life. In their beliefs, there is also the notion of a filial divine savior such as *Nummo*, the son of the High God *Mawa* who, in their view, was sent down to earth "to clear the forests and make tools."[148]

EWONDO, see FANG

FAJULU

These are one of Sudan's tribal people who live in the southern regions of the country. They speak an Eastern Sudanic language of the Chari-Nile branch of the Nilo-Saharan family of African languages.

The Fajulu support a relatively sedentary type of society. They live in scattered villages and their main economic activities center on farming, cattle raising, and hunting. Their social organization is essentially tribal and patrilineal.

FALASHA

The Falasha are the "Black Jews of Ethiopia." They reside in Northern Ethiopia and Israel.[149] They number, collectively, approximately 30,000 and speak Amharic, Tigrinya and Ge 'ez. Though most people in Ethiopia and around the world call Ethiopian Jews *Falashas*, these people see this term as derogatory, since this term means "landless ones." They prefer, instead, to be called Beta Esráel (Israel).

The Falasha are a pre-Talmudic Ethiopian Jewish ethnic group, whose legends claim descent from Menelik I, the son of the Ethiopian Queen of Sheba and the Jewish King Solomon. Another legend "claims that the tribe, Falasha, was founded when Moses married an Ethiopian princess."[150] Historical evidence, however, suggests that their ancestors are the Agau people, who have converted to Judaism, probably by Yemenite Jews, some time during the Second Commonwealth. According to <u>The New Encyclopaedia Britannica</u>, the "Jewish Falasha (or 'Black Jews') retain some of the old Agau words in their religious vocabulary."[151] In Israel, however, they are considered the descendants of one of the 10 lost tribes of Israel.

Known also as Esráelotch, Felasha and Kayla, the Falasha describe themselves as House of Israel, Beta Esráel (Israel). They have a Bible and a prayer book, both of which are related in Ge'ez, the ancient Ethiopian language. They observe Judaism the way it was practiced before the First Temple was destroyed some 2,500 years ago. Their religious books do not cover rabbinical teachings, Talmudic scholarship or other refinements that have been added to Judaism since then.

The Falasha base their Jewish faith on the Pentateuch, from which they receive their laws and religious ceremonies. Hence, they do not subscribe to all the Jewish holidays. In some respects, they also share similar customs with their Christian neighbors. Like their Christian neighbors, for example, they hold confessions and moreover, do not work for seven days after a relative's death.

Until the 17th century, the Falasha had their own independent province of Semyen, Ethiopia. They were driven out from their province by Emperor Susenyos and ever since, they lived north of Lake Tana.

Though small in number, about 30,000 of Ethiopia's 50 million population, the Falasha were the focus of media attention in 1985 and in May 1991. In 1985, about 7,000 of the Falasha were flown to Israel in a special operation (Operation Moses). On May 24-25, another group of the Falasha, numbering 14,500, were successfully flown to Israel in a 36-hour voyage. The forty flight operation, dubbed Operation Solomon, the preparation of which invoked extensive negotiations, involved special cooperation between Israel, the United States, the Sudan and remnants of the Ethiopian government, as well as the payment of an "extra" $35 million to unnamed Ethiopian elements. As a result of this operation, about half the Falasha population now lives in Israel and the other half in Ethiopia. Those that are still in Ethiopia live in villages and engage in miscellaneous farming activities.

In Ethiopia, the Falasha wear the customary Ethiopian toga, called a *shamma*, worn by Christian and Muslim Ethiopians. The languages spoken by them are the same as those of their Christian and Muslim neighbors, the Amhara and Tigrayans. Furthermore, the Falasha family is extremely close and duties are divided by sex: boys help their fathers at work and girls share the domestic duties with their mothers.

FALI

The Fali, also called Kirdi, are a West and Central African ethnic people. They are highly concentrated in the northern regions of Cameroon. Groups of them are also located in northeastern Nigeria. Their language belongs to the Chad-Adamawa group of African languages. They are composed of four major groups, namely: the Bossoum Fali, the Kangou Fali, the Peské-Bori Fali and the Tinguelin Fali. These divisions correspond to the territorial areas in which they live.

The Fali people trace their ancestry to the Ngomma who founded the city of Timpil and made it their capital in ancient times. Some accounts, however, trace the Fali's ancestry to the Sao people who prospered in the Lake Chad area from the tenth to the sixteenth centuries. The Sao people lived independently until their fall to German (1912), and subsequently, French (1916) rule. In 1960, they gained their independence within the state of Cameroon.

The Fali continue to adhere to their traditional religion which rests on the belief in one god, called *Faw*. They conceive of *Faw* not only as creator and organizer, but also as a just god who is undepictable by human intelligence.[152]

The economic activities of the Fali people focus on farming and hunting. Their society is made up of exogamous patrilineal clans, each clan of which is traced to a common ancestor and has a territory and a chief of its own. Their social and political organization is highly hierarchical in nature, consisting of noble clans, clans of free men and warriors, and clans of foreigners and serfs.

FAN, see FANG

FANG

The Fang, also Fàn, are one of West Africa's major ethnic groups, constituting important segments of the populations of Cameroon, Equatorial Guinea and Gabon. The Fang belong to the larger Pahouin group of Central Africa. Their total number is estimated at over 2.6 million.

The Fang are a Bantu-speaking peoples. Their languages are of the Bantu subgroup of the Niger-Congo family. Linguistically, they comprise three groups: the Beti language which is spoken by the Yaunde (Ewondo) and the Bene tribes; the Bulu which is spoken by the Bulu proper, the Fong, the Zaman and the Yelinda; and the Fang which is spoken by the Fang proper, the Ntumu and the Mvae. Their social system is strongly based on patrilineal lineages.

Historical evidence suggests that the Fang had evolved from various migrating peoples who originally lived in the rain forests of the northern areas of what is now modern Cameroon. In the later part of the eighteenth century they settled near European settlements, acquired the name Fang, started to grow in size (by absorbing other peoples they defeated), and got involved in miscellaneous trading activities with the Europeans.[153]

The Fang society is sedentary and relies on agriculture and fishing on its coastal territories. It is male dominated. Men have a prominent role in the family. Women are responsible for all duties within the house. Women also take a commanding role in the rearing of children, especially female offspring. In the village set-up, houses of men are positioned near the center, while the houses of women are positioned farther from the center. Each Fang village is headed by a chief.

Currently, the Fang peoples account for one fifth or 24% of the total population of Cameroon, where they are also known as Pangwe. They account for virtually all the population of Rio Muni, the mainland of Equatorial Guinea and they largest ethnic group of Gabon's four major ethnic minorities, accounting for over one third of the total population.

In Equatorial Guinea, the Fang comprise several groups, the most important of which are the Ntumu, Okak, Kombe, Mabea, Lengi and Benga. They are highly concentrated in the eastern regions of the country. In Cameroon, they are concentrated in the southern regions of the country. In Gabon they live in the northern regions of the republic.

The Fang society embraces a wide array of artistic history in painting, song and poetry. They have a, still vibrant, oral literature that is intertwined with traditional mythology and Christianity. A lot of Fang literature is printed in English, as well as in French.

Many Fang were converted by European missionaries during the centuries of colonization. Yet, many Fang still believe that there are spiritual causes of many illnesses and they still consult secret societies, or *bieri*, to fend off such evil.

FANTI

A West African people. The Fanti are concentrated in the southern coastal regions of Ghana. They speak a Kwa language which belongs to the Niger-Congo family of African languages. Their neighbors include the Akyem, Asante and Gā peoples. The Fanti engage in miscellaneous economic activities such as farming, fishing and trading.

FELASHA, see **FALASHA**

FELLAH, see **FULANI**

FELLAATA, see **FULANI**

FELLATA, see **FULANI**

FELUP

These are one of Guinea-Bissau's ethnic minorities. The Felup, also Felupe, people live in the western regions of the country in close proximity to the sea (Atlantic Ocean).

FELUPE, see FELUP

FERNANDINOS

The Fernandinos are an admixture of descendants of slaves liberated by the British government during the 19th century, who freed Africans from Sierra Leone and Cuba and immigrants from West African countries. Currently, they constitute the second largest ethnic group on the Bioko island of the Republic of Equatorial Guinea. However, they are a small minority compared to Bioko's predominantly Bubi population.

FEROUAN

The Ferouan are a West African people. They are a Taureg group. Like other Taureg groups, the Ferouan are semipastoralists.

FERTIT

These are one of the ethnic minorities of the Central African Republic. They are concentrated in the northeastern parts of the country.

FETRA, see MEDI

FILANI, see FULANI

FIPA

The Fipa, also known as Afipa and Wafipa, are an East Central African Bantu-speaking people, and one of Tanzania's ethnic groups. They are concentrated in the southwestern areas of the country, especially in the Mbeya administrative region. Their land, Ufipa, is bordered on the west by Lake Tanganyika and on the south by Lake Nyasa, Malawi and the Republic of Zambia. The Fipa's economic activities focus on agriculture, fishing, animal husbandry, and mining salt, gold, coal and mica in their region. Prior to the colonial era, they had important trading relations with Zanzibar merchants.

FIKA, see BOLEWA

FINGO, see MFENGU

FINGOES, see MFENGU

FO

A West African group. The Fo are one of Nigeria's and Benin's many ethnic minorities. They are concentrated in Benin's east central regions and across the border in west central Nigeria. Their neighbors include the Mahi and Yoruba peoples.

FOGNY, see KUJAMAAT

FOKENG, see also SOTHO

The Fokeng, also known as Bafokeng, are one of the major tribes of the Kwena, a subgroup of the Sotho people. They are concentrated in the Kingdom of Lesotho.

Like other Sotho, they are a southern African people, speak Sesotho, a Bantu language, and engage in agriculture and animal husbandry. Their settlements are characterized "by scattered hamlets of circular huts with mud and wattle or stone walls surmounted by a conical, thatched roof."[154] In their social patterns, most Kanga-Kone recognize patrilineal lineages and continue to be impacted by their traditional religious beliefs.

FON

The Fon – also known as Dahomean, Dahomey, and Fonn – are the largest group of Benin's four major ethnic minorities. Currently, they account for about 60% of the country's total population, and are predominant in its southern regions. The Fon people speak a dialect of Ewe, a language of the Kwa branch of the Niger-Congo family.

Historical evidence suggests that the Fon were once members of the Oyo Empire and that they migrated south from the Niger river basin because of famine and drought. It also suggests that they settled in present-day Benin during the 13th century. In the 16th century, they founded the Allada Kingdom in south Dahomey. This kingdom prospered as a result of its trading relations with Europeans. In 1625, however, the Allada Kingdom was succeeded by a new Fon kingdom, the Kingdom of Dahomey. This latter kingdom reached an imperial status during the 18th and 19th centuries. It flourished on the trade of human beings to Europeans including: French, Dutch and Portuguese.

The Kingdom of Dahomey was headed by a king whose responsibilities included the conduct of war, the administration of justice, the collection of tributes and the manning of political posts. He managed the kingdom through the tribal chiefs, who acted as his representatives. In addition, he was supported by a large standing army that was highly equipped with guns and uniforms. One third of this army was made up of the legendary corps of female warriors, called Amazons, who fought alongside male soldiers during the kingdom's wars and raids.[155]

The Kingdom of Dahomey retained its independence until 1894, at which time it fell to French rule. The Fon people remained under French colonial rule until 1960, the year in which France decided to grant them their independence as part of Dahomey (later Benin).

The Fon kinship system is based on patrilineal relations, with land inherited through the father's line. The village, headed by a hereditary chief, who rules over all aspects of its political existence. Polygamy is practiced only by the wealthy, since marriages are based on bridewealth.

Most Fon are involved in agriculture and raise a multitude of foodstuffs for trade and consumption. Fon who live on the coast of Benin are comparable fishermen, collecting the bounty of the sea for the same purposes as their agricultural brothers farther inland.

Though European dress is predominant these days, some traditional aspects of dress still exist in Fon society. For example, women may wear a "sarong-style dress of printed cotton fabric"[156] Men may be seen in a tunic top along with modern shorts. Chiefs can be seen with the traditional symbol of Fon political power, the parasols.

Fon artistic expression is widely varied. Like the Dinka in East Africa, the Fon beautify themselves by scarring. Painting and tapestry is also prevalent in Fon artistic culture, "many of them attest to epic battles and sacred scenes"[157] The Fon are famous for the production of statues made of wood.

Though Fon oral tradition has been difficult to translate, many portions of this have been recognized by scholars as legends or folk tales. A few famous writers from Benin have been Fon and their works were published in French.

Fon adhere to an animist concept of religion, where all objects possess a spirit. Many Fon gods are "symbolized as animals."[158] The Fon also recognize a number of lesser deities called *Vodu*, whose rituals espouse a significant sense of mystery and magic.

FONG, see FANG

FONGORO

An East Saharan and East and Central African people. The Fongoro, also known as Gelege, are a Muslim group of hunters-gatherers. They live in the regions lying along the Chadian-Sudanese borders.

FORDUNGA, see FUR

FORROS

The Forros people are descendants of freed slaves in Sâo Tomé and Principé. They constitute the third largest group in the country.

FOTA, see FUR

FOULAH, see FULANI

FRASE, see BAKA

FRENCH

People of French background and/or French expatriates or settlers who live in Francophone Africa or in African countries that formerly fell to French rule or influence. These people and/or their descendants are unevenly distributed in the following countries: Algeria, Benin, Burkina-

Faso, Cameroon, Central African Republic, Chad, Comoros, Congo, Djibouti, Egypt, Gabon, Guinea, Ivory Coast, Madagascar, Mali, Mauritania, Mayotte, Morocco, Niger, Reunion, Senegal, Togo, and Tunisia.

FUGON

A West Central African people. The Fugon are concentrated in Cameroon, primarily in its west central regions along the country's borders with Nigeria. Groups of them can also be found in east central Nigeria. Their neighbors include the Bum and Udam peoples.

FULA, see FULANI

FULANI

The Fulani, also known as Bororo, Bororo'en, Fellaata, Fellata, Fellah, Filani, Fula, Fulata, Fulbe, Foulah, Hilani, Peul and Toroobe, "form the largest pastoral nomadic group in the world," and are one of the largest Muslim groups in Africa.[159] These people are found in twenty different West and East African states, especially in Benin, Burkina Faso, Cameroon, Central African Republic, Chad, Ethiopia, The Gambia, Guinea, Guinea-Bissau, Kenya, Mali, Mauritania, Niger, Nigeria, Senegal, Sudan and Togo. The nomadic among them are estimated at over 8 million, and the settled at over 16 million. They speak the Fulani language, known also as Fulfulde, Fula, Peul and Poular (Pulaar), which falls within the West Atlantic branch of the Niger-Congo family of African languages. Their society is highly hierarchical.

Originally, the Fulani were a pastoral nomadic people and subsequently got involved in religious wars, which resulted in their developing an empire and establishing themselves as a ruling aristocracy in many parts of West Africa. Originally also, they were part of the Sultanate of Sokoto, during the reign of the Hausa-Fulani empire.

In the 14th century, they gradually expanded eastwardly from Fula Toro in Lower Senegal, reaching and controlling Mecina in the Niger Bend in the 16th century, including the Hausaland in what constitutes modern Nigeria in the 19th century. In the 1790s, Usman (Othman) Dan Fodio (1754-

1817), a Muslim scholar and one of their emirs in the northern Hausa state of Gobir, staged a *jihad*, campaign (holy war) aimed at purifying Islam of pagan beliefs and managed to control Adamawa, Nupe and Yorubaland. Ilorin, lying to the northeast of Hausaland, was established as the base of his emirate. Numerous emirates were also founded to ensure cohesiveness and stability in the Fulani conquered lands, including that of Kazaure in what is presently in northwestern Kano State, northern Nigeria. Kazaure, the seat of the Kazaure emirate, was founded in 1819 by Dan Tunku, one of the 14 flag bearers for the Fulani *jihad*.

The Fulani empire reached its zenith under Usman's son, Muhammad Bello, but subsequently it started to weaken, making possible its fall to the British at the end of the 19th century.

Currently, the Fulani people are partly pastoral and partly sedentary. "They may be nomadic pastoralists, semi-sedentary farmers and cattle owners, sedentary agriculturalists, or, in some northern Nigerian Emirates, members of a ruling class."[160] The pastoral among them are called Fulani Boro (cattle Fulani), whereas the sedentary are called Fulani Gida (house Fulani).

The Fulani Boro are nomadic and rely heavily on their cattle for food, trade, clothing and all around well-being. The Fulani Gida are agriculturalists who are sedentary and adhere vehemently to Muslim beliefs. Many Fulani Gida are better off due to greater educational opportunities and other advantages credited to living in more urban environments. There are also Fulani who are both herders and agriculturalists, who live on the savanna.

The Fulani people are involved in miscellaneous economic activities. They engage in raising cattle and sheep and long-distance trading activities, as well as in leather, silver, gold and iron works. Also, they engage in teaching, legal, real estate and financial activities. The Bororo'en among them, for example, are renowned not only for raising cattle, but also for contributing to Fulani control over the cattle market in West Africa. Likewise, the Fulbe Mbalu, or Sheep Fulani, specialize not only in raising sheep for their own livelihood, but also for the markets of West Africa. The Fulbe Laddi, or semisedentary Fulani, are providers of agricultural produce to the markets in which they are located. Finally, the urbanized Fulani, such as the Toroobe, are famous for supplying religious clerics, teachers, and government personnel, as well as for their involvement in real estate and trading activities. Because of their numbers, economic activities and presence in numerous countries, they continue to impact the individual and collective politics of most West African states.

In Benin, where they are known as Peul, the Fulani are concentrated in the northern parts of the country. In Chad, they live primarily in the semiarid tropical zone of the country. In Burkina Faso, they constitute the sixth largest ethnic group. In the Cameroon, they account for about 10% of the population, or what amounts to over one million, and are concentrated in the northern areas of the country, especially in the Adamawa Plateau region. In northern Chad, where they are known as the Fulbe, they constitute the third largest ethnic group. In The Gambia, where they are known as Fula, they constitute the second largest ethnic group after the Mandika (42%), accounting for 18% of the population or what amounts to about 150.000. In Guinea, they constitute the largest ethnic minority. In Guinea-Bissau, where they are known as Fula, they are the second largest ethnic minority after the Balanta (30%), accounting for 20% of the total population or what amounts to about 200,000. In Mali, where they are known as Peul, they constitute the second largest ethnic minority after the Mande (50%), accounting for 17% of the population or what amounts to over 1.5 million. In Mauritania, where they are known as Fula, they are also one of the major ethnic minorities. In Niger, where they are known as Fula, they constitute the third largest ethnic minority after the Hausa (56%) and the Djerma (22%), accounting for 8.5% of the population, or what amounts to over 0.6 million. In Nigeria they constitute the second largest minority after the Hausa and are concentrated in the states of Gongola, Plateau, Sokoto, Kaduna and Bauchi. In Senegal, where they are known as Peul, they constitute the second largest ethnic minority, accounting for 17% of the country's total population. In Togo, the Fulani constitute one of the ethnic minorities, living essentially in the northern regions of the country.

FULATA, see FULANI

FULBE, see FULANI

FULBE LADDI, see FULANI

FULBE MBALU, see FULANI

FULERO, see FURIIRU

FUMBU

The Fumbu are a West Central African people. They are concentrated in the Republic of Congo, primarily in its central regions. Their neighbors include the Achikouya, Dondo, Sise, and Teke peoples.

FUNJ

The Funj were a Muslim people of obscure origin.[161] In 1504-1505, they established a sultanate of their own, and subsequently succeeded in subduing the Abdullabi Arabs, who previously had taken over the Sudanic state of Alawa, and henceforth established their own hegemony over the Sudan. They, moreover, converted to Islam and established close ties with Mamluk Egypt.[162]

The Funj sultanate reached it zenith during the mid-seventeenth century, at which time it had control over a vast territory that included areas close to the third cataract and the White and Blue Nile.[163] It continued its reign until June, 1821 when it was subdued by Muhammad Ali Pasha, the new Ottoman governor of Egypt. Sultan Badi, its last ruler, had no other choice but to transfer the Funj sultanate to Muhammad Ali.

FUR

One of Central and East African groups. The Fur, also known as Fota, Fordunga and Konjara, are a Muslim farming people. They are concentrated in Sudan and Chad, primarily along the borderline that separated the two countries. Their neighbors include the Gimr, Meganin, and Midob peoples.

FURIIRU

The Furiiru, also known as Kifuliiru and Fulero, are an East Central African people. They live in the eastern highland regions of the Democratic Republic of the Congo (Zaire).

FURU

One of the ethnic groups of the Democratic Republic of the Congo (Zaire). The Furu are part of the Kivu cluster of peoples.

FYAM

One of West Africa's peoples. The Fyam are concentrated in the northwestern regions of Nigeria. Their neighbors include the Fyam, Kwanka, and Nga peoples.

GA, see also LOBI-DAGARTI

The Ga, spelled Gan or Gà, also known as Ga-Adangme and Ga-Adangbe, are a West African people. They speak a dialect of the Kwa branch of Niger-Congo languages. They are concentrated in the southeast coast of Ghana, where they constitute the fourth largest ethnic group, accounting for 8% of the total population. Groups of them, however, are also found in Togo and Ivory Coast. In Ghana and Togo, their neighbors include the Akan and Ewe peoples, whereas in the Ivory Coast, they include the Baule, Guro, Kulango and Senufo peoples.

The Ga migrated from the northern Niger river areas during the 17th century. They were organized into several towns including Accra, the present capital of Ghana. Subsequently, they founded a state of their own, which was surrounded by powerful Akan states, including Fanti. Originally, the Ga were farmers, but currently are engaged in farming, fishing and trading.

GA-ADANGBE, see GA

GA-ADANGME, see GA

GAAJOK, see **NUER**

GAALIEK, see **NUER**

GAÀN, see **LOBI-DAGARTI**

GAAWAR, see **NUER**

GABBRA

The Gabbra are an East African people. They are concentrated in the northwestern border regions that separate Kenya from Uganda, primarily east of Lake Rudolff. Their neighbors include the Elmolo and Gelubba peoples.

GABIBI

A West African group of hunters and farmers who used to live in the vicinities of the Niger river. These people are presumed to have been conquered by Aliman Za, the founder of the Za dynasty of Songhay, in the latter part of the eighth century.[164]

GABOU

The Gabou are a Central African people. Their main concentrations are in Chad, the Central African Republic and Sudan.

GACRKWE

A southern African people. The Gacrkwe are concentrated in Tanzania and the Democratic Republic of the Congo (Zaire).

GADE

The Gade are a West African Bantu-speaking people. They are concentrated in the central regions of Nigeria.

GADOA

The Gadoa people are one of Central African Bantu-speaking ethnic groups. They are concentrated in northern Chad. They are concentrated in the central regions of Nigeria.

GAEDA, see TOUBOU

GAGOU, see also MANDE

The Gagou, also Gagu and G'ban, are a West African Mande group. They are concentrated in the west-central regions of the Republic of the Ivory Coast. The Gagou speak a language of the Mande branch of the Niger-Congo family of African languages. Their neighbors include the Baule, Dida, Guro, Kulango and Senufo peoples.

GAGU, see GAGOU

GALLA, see also OROMO

The Galla, also known as Oromo, are an East African Eastern Hamitic people and one of the major ethnic groups in Ethiopia. They speak a Cushitic language, and are concentrated in the subtropical central and southern Highlands of Ethiopia. Groups of them, however, live in the Susan, notably south of the Blue Nile. Their neighbors in the susan include the Anwak, the Beir, the Kamn, and the Shilluk peoples. The Galla are divided into many groups and subgroups such as the Enia and the Raya. Their modern history is traced back to the sixteenth century, at which time they invaded southern Ethiopia from the west and managed to establish themselves there unopposed.[165]

Formerly, the Galla supported a highly complex system of social organization, aspects of which continue to exist until this day. Under this system, the people are divided into groups, called *gada*, arranged in pairs, with each man entering the group of his grandfather. Under the same system, each pair passed through five successive periods each of which consisted of eight years. The same system assigned those men who reach the fourth period the responsibility of ruling the society, as well as of electing an *Abba Boko*, father of the scepter, from among them.

The Galla people are mainly agriculturalists and cattle raisers. In their society, cattle is still considered one of the valued forms of wealth. Many Galla continue to cherish their traditional beliefs.

GALLAO

The Gallao are one of the Chadian Kuri subgroups. They speak Yedina, a Buduma dialect. Like other Kuri groups, they live along the eastern shores of Lake Chad.

GALLINA, see VAI

GAMAWA, see NGAMO

GAMERGU

These are a West African people and one of Nigeria's ethnic minorities. The Gamergu are concentrated in the Lake Chad region of northeastern Nigeria and eastern Niger. A large group of them are presently in the state of Borno (formerly Bornu). They are an essentially agriculturalist people.

GAMI-NUN

A Southwest African people. The Gami-Nun are concentrated in the south-central regions of the Republic of Namibia.

GAMO-GOFA

An East African agriculturalist people. The Gamo-Gofa are concentrated in the southern regions of Ethiopia, notably at the southwestern tip of Lake Abaya. Their neighbors include the Batutu peoples.

GAN, see also GA and LOBI-DAGARTI

A West African Ga group. The Gan are located in the Ivory Coast and speak Lobi, a Mande dialect of the Mande branch of the Niger-Congo family of African languages. Their neighbors include the Baule, Brong,

Kulango and Senufo peoples.

G//ANA, see also SAN

A southern African San group. The G//ana are a San-speaking people. They are concentrated in the central sand areas of Botswana and adjoining Namibia. Like other San-speaking peoples, they are essentially foragers, hunters and gatherers.

GANANWA, see PEDI

GANDA

The Ganda, also called Baganda, Luganda and Waganda, are Uganda's largest ethnic minority. They are Bantu-speaking people, accounting for about one fifth of the country's total population. Their language, known as Ganda and also Luganda, is a branch of the Benue-Congo group of African languages. The Ganda are concentrated in a region located to the west and north of Lake Victoria and south of the western shores of Lake Kyoga. Their territory is considered Uganda's richest and most fertile area. Their neighbors include the Lango, the Nyoro, the Nkole, the Soga and the Toro peoples. The Ganda are among the most literate and advanced people of Uganda.

The Ganda people trace their founding to Kintu – a legendary leader of the Binto people. The latter people lived in northern western Uganda during the fourteenth century. They were famous as skilled hunters and warriors. Subsequently, they moved eastwardly, settled northwest of Lake Victoria, and established the kingdom of Baganda. Their modern history, however, could be traced back to the sixteenth century, at which time they supported a small kingdom governed by a king called *kabaka* who served both as their political leader, as well as high priest and supreme judge.

In the eighteenth century, the Gandas' kingdom, Buganda, developed into a sophisticated, highly centralized, absolutist monarchy with a royal bodyguard responsible to the *kabaka*. In the kingdom, there was an efficient imperial administrative system run by royal administrators, not by hereditary chiefs, an export-oriented economy controlled by the crown and a well-organized military force capable of maintaining order and stability within the kingdom's domains and attaining the respect of neighboring peoples and nations. All these factors contributed to the expansion of Buganda's territory, as well as the extension of its effective control over the northwestern shoreline and hinterland of Lake Victoria from the Nile to the Kagera river. As a result, the Baganda kingdom became the largest kingdom in East Africa.

In the nineteenth century, Buganda's territory saw further expansion in the northwest, in the lands of the Nyoro (Bunyoro) people. Moreover, its trading activities were greatly enhanced through the intermediary of Arab traders (who first appeared in Buganda in the 1830's and its royal court in 1844) and later those of European nations.

Expanding trade under the reign of Kabaka Suna (d. 1856) and his successor Kabaka Mutesa (1856-1884) made possible the introduction of new products into Buganga, especially cotton cloth and guns. These were exchanged for slaves and the ivory were wrested from neighboring peoples. Henceforth, firearms were utilized by Buganda's military to supplement their spearmen, as well as to halt Bunyoros' resurgence, Egypt's thrust to extend its control over Buganda, the rising power of the Mahdists' movement in the Sudan and European imperialist penetration in the region.

As a direct result of openness to trade, European influence started to mount in the country, inviting more entrepreneurs, Protestant and Catholic missionaries (who were allowed to arrive in 1877 and 1879, respectively), as well as imperial rivalries. Eventually, the impact of this influence was Buganda's fall into an internal religious civil war and eventually to British rule.[166] Both phenomena took place during the reign of Mwanga (1884-1899), who succeeded his father Mutesa as Buganda's kabaka in 1884.

As a consequence of the Berlin Conference, Africa was partitioned among Europe's imperial powers. More importantly, it led to a British-German understanding (reached in 1890) that recognized Uganda as a British protectorate.

Following a series of military engagements in 1890 between Buganda forces on the one hand and those of the Imperial British East Africa

Company and Ganda Christian chiefs on the other, Kabaka Mwanga was captured and exiled in 1899. With this dramatic event, Buganda fell to British rule.[167]

Between 1900 and Uganda's independence from the United Kingdom on October 9, 1962, the Ganda people of Buganda like those of other traditional kingdoms that were incorporated within the Uganda Protectorate, such as Bunyoro, Toro, and Ankole, were governed by a British civil servants presided over by a British governor. These administrators exercised prerogatives indirectly through an African chiefly hierarchy.

After Uganda's independence on October 9, 1962, rivalry between Milton Obete, Prime Minister and President General of Uganda People's Congress and Sir Edward Metusa II, *kabaka* of Buganda and Uganda's head of state, resurfaced. The former leader wanted to establish a centralized welfare state, whereas the latter was committed to Buganda's particularism within a decentralized system of government. The conflict ended in Obote's suspension of the country's constitution and his ouster of Metusa II in February, 1966. As a result, Metusa II (who formerly threatened secession from Uganda) left for England where he died in 1969, whereas Obote quickly arranged for the adoption of a new constitution in 1967, abolishing Uganda's four traditional kingdoms (Buganda, Bunyoro, Toro, and Ankole). Obote's actions provoked several attempts on his life and eventually led to a series of coups and insurgency movements, the last of which was that of January 27, 1986, which brought Yoweri Museveni, head of the National Resistance Army (NRA), to power. On January 29, 1986, Museveni was sworn in as President of Uganda.

Seven years later (July 15, 1993) and upon Museveni's persuasion, Uganda's national Assembly passed a constitutional amendment canceling the abolition of traditional rulers. As a result, two of the country's traditional monarchies, Buganda and Batoro, were restored.[169]

In an official ceremony held at Kampala on July 31, 1993, Ronald Muwenda Mutebi was proclaimed *ssabataka* (leader) of Baganda clans and crowned 36th *kabaka* of Buganda. At the same time, Patrick Olimi Kaboyo was crowned as Batoro king.

The restoration of the Buganda monarchy was considered an important step towards furthering internal stability within the country.[170]

The Ganda are divided into a number of patrilineal clans, each of which is traceable to a male ancestor. Traditionally, their clans formed an integral part of the political organization of Baganda and were assigned specific responsibilities by its king, or *kabaka*. In most cases, heads of clans had to be confirmed in their positions by the *kabaka*. In his turn, the *kabaka* "was selected from the royal family, and the office went in direct descent from the father to one of his sons other than the eldest."[171] Normally, the naming of a new king was made "by the chief minister, or *katikiro*, and the official in charge of the king's fetishes."[172] The accession ceremonies symbolized the transfer of power and legitimacy from a deceased king to his successor. Additionally, they served as a reminder to the new king of his responsibility as a guardian of his people, protector of the land, and dispenser of justice in the kingdom.

Currently, the Gandas are still concentrated in the Buganda region of the republic of Uganda, constituting about 4,000,000 of the country's total population. They are engaged in farming, growing plantain (their staple food), cotton and coffee (their export-oriented products), as well as animal husbandry. Moreover, they observe patrilineal lineages in matters relating to descent, inheritance and succession.

Though a great majority of Ganda are Christian, many of them continue to practice aspects of their traditional beliefs. A number of their clans, for example, continue to have "principal and secondary totem animals that may not be killed and eaten."[173] Their traditional "recognized ancestors, past kings, nature spirits, and a pantheon of gods who were approached through spirit mediums."[174]

GANIN

A Southwest African people. The Ganin are concentrated in Namibia.

G/ANNA, see G//ANA, and SAN

GAO, see SONGHAI

GARAMANTIAN

These are an ancient people of the Fezzan region of what is presently in the modern state of Libya. Their territory was one of the trans-Saharan caravan routes. They were mentioned by Herodotus as people who used four-horse chariots to chase "Troglodyte Ethiopians." According to July, "Presumably, the troglodytes were the Tebu people of Tibesti."[175]

GARAP

The Garap are one of the Kim confederation groups. They live in Chad in the vicinities of the Longone River.

GARATI, see KONSO

GARO, see also SIDAMO

The Garo are an East African non-Galla Cushitic-speaking Muslim people. They live chiefly in southwestern Ethiopia, particularly in the Omo river and Rift Valley regions of the country. The Garo are a Sidamo group and hence are related to other Sidamo peoples, such as the Alaba, Hadya and Tambaro.

The Garo established a kingdom of their own between the tenth and twelfth centuries. During the same period, they absorbed Islam from coastal Arabs. Subsequently, however, their kingdom became a tributary of the Abyssinians (Amhara and Tigre), as well as the Galla.

The Garo are essentially an agricultural people. They specialize in the production of grains, cereals, fruits and spices, as well as in animal husbandry.

GAUWADA

A southern Ethiopian people. The Gauwada are concentrated in the Rift Valley region of Ethiopia. Their neighbors include the Konso, the Borana, the Gidole and the Burji.

GBAGYI

Also known as Gwari Matai, the Gbagyi are a West African farming people. They are concentrated in Nigeria. They are a Gbari subgroup.

GBAN, see GAGOU

GBANDA, see AVIKAM

GBANDE, see also NGBANDI

The Gbande are a West African Mande people. They are concentrated in Liberia. Groups of them, however, are also located in Central African Republic, as well as in northern Democratic Republic of the Congo (Zaire). Their language belongs to the Adamawa-Eastern subgroup of the Niger-Congo family of African languages. The Gbande neighbors in Liberia include the Gola, Kisi, Kpelle, Loma and Mende peoples.

GBANDI, see NGBANDI

GBANG, see BIROM

GBARI

The Gbari, also known as Gwari Yamma, are a West African people. They are concentrated in the western regions of Nigeria. The Gbari speak a Kwa language of the Niger-Congo family of African languages. Their neighbors include the Afo, Bassa, Gwandara, Idoma, Igbirra, Kadara, Kambari, Kamuku, Koro, and Nupe peoples.

GBAYA, see also MANDJIA and NGABAKA

The Gbaya, also known as Gbaya Mandjia, are an East Saharan and Central African agriculturalist Christian people. They are concentrated in Cameroon and the Central African Republic.

GBAYA MANDJIA, see GBAYA

GBUHWE, see LAMANG

GCOIKA

The Gcoika are a Southern African people. They are concentrated in the Republic of South Africa, primarily in its eastern coastal areas. Their neighbors include the Bomvana, Mpondomise, and Xhosa peoples.

GE

The Ge people are a West African group. They are among Benin's and Togo's ethnic minorities. They reside close to the coastal areas in both countries. Their neighbors include the Anlo and Watyi peoples.

GEBIET

A Southwest African people. The Gebiet, also known as Rehoboth Gebiet, constitute one of Namibia's small ethnic minorities.

GEIN

A Southwest African people. The Gein are concentrated in the south central regions of the Republic of Namibia.

GEIKHAUAN

A Southwest African Khoi people. The Geikhauan are concentrated in the northern regions of the Republic of Namibia.

GEIKHOIN

A Southwest African Khoi people. The Geikhoin are concentrated in the southwestern regions of Botswana.

GEININ

A Southwest African people. The Geinin are concentrated in the western regions of the Republic of Namibia.

GEIRIKU, see KAVANGO

GEKOYO, see KIKUYU

GELEBA, see DASANEC

GELEGE, see also FONGORO

GELUBBA, see DASANEC

GERAWA

The Gerawa are a West African people. They are concentrated in the northeastern regions of Nigeria. They speak a language that belongs to the Afro-Asiatic family of African languages. Their neighbors include the Auyokawa, Burum, Butawa, Fula (Fulani), Hausa, Jarawa and Warjawa peoples.

GERI, see SOMALI

GERMAN

People of German background and/or German expatriates or settlers who live in African countries that formerly fell to German rule and/or influence. These people and/or their descendants are unevenly distributed in the following countries: Burundi, Cameroon, Namibia, Rwanda, South Africa, and Togo.

GERSE, see KPELLE

GESINAN, see HARARI

GETUTU, see GUSII

GIAN, see LOBI-DAGARTI

GIDICHOSA

An East African Omotic-speaking people. The Gidichosa are one of the Koyra subgroups. They are concentrated in southern Ethiopia.

GIDOLE

A southern Ethiopian people. The Gauwada are concentrated in the Rift Valley region of Ethiopia. Their neighbors include the Konso, the Borana, the Gauwada and the Burji.

GIEN

The Gien are a West African people. They are concentrated in southwestern Guinea. However, groups of them can also be found in Liberia. Their neighbors include the Gio, Kara, and Kpelle peoples.

GIGUYU, see KIKUYU

GIKIKUYU, see KIKUYU

GILI

The Gili are a West African people. They are concentrated in eastern Nigeria. Their neighbors include the Afo, Angas, Arago, Gwandara and Mada peoples. The Gili speak a language that belongs to the Kwa branch of the Niger-Congo family of African languages.

GILIU

The Giliu are a Central African people. They are concentrated in the northeastern regions of Nigeria. Their neighbors include the Hausa and Koro peoples.

GIMA'A

A Central and East African people. The Gima'a are concentrated in both Chad and Sudan. They are primarily settled farmers.

GIMIRA

An East African people. The Gimira are concentrated in highland areas south of the Maji and Bero-Shasha provinces of the Kefa region in Ethiopia. Their neighbors include the Suri, Dizi, Me'en, Murle, Mursi and Nyangatom peoples.

GIMR

The Gimr are a Central and East African Tama and Arabic-speaking people. They are concentrated in western Sudan and eastern Chad, primarily along the border that separates the two countries. Their neighbors include the Bideyat, Fur, Midob, and Zaghawa peoples.

GINGWAK, see JARAWA

GIO, see DAN and also MANDE

GINGA

These are a Central African people and one of the ethnic minorities of Angola. They are concentrated northeast of Luanda, especially on the west bank of the Kwango river.

The modern history of the Ginga is traced back to the early part of the sixteenth century, at which time they had their own state, namely Matamba. Though an independent state, occasionally it paid a tribute to its northern neighbor the Kongo Kingdom.

Between the sixteenth and nineteenth centuries, the history of the Matamba kingdom was characterized by a constant conflict with the Portuguese colonists in Angola who were trying to colonize its territory. In the later part of the sixteenth century, it aligned itself with the Ndongo, Kongo and Jaga to repel Portuguese encroachments on its territory, as well as to capture their forts at Luanda and Massangano. The first objective was met but not the other.

In 1630, the Ginga people were conquered by Anna Nzinga, former queen of the Ndongo (whose kingdom fell to the Portuguese). Anna Nzinga used the Matamba territory as a base to sustain its struggle against the Portuguese.

The struggle culminated in the conclusion of a treaty between Matamba and Portuguese colonists in 1684. The treaty put an end to further Portuguese expansionist campaigns. In 1744, and again in the 1830s, however, the Portuguese resumed their expansionist activities and as a result, were able to capture parts of Matamba's territory.

Between 1870 and 1900, the Portuguese secured European recognition to their claim over the rest of the Gingas' territory. However, they failed to implement it and hence the Kingdom of Matamba retained its independence until the early part of the twentieth century, at which time it was occupied by the Portuguese. Hence, the Ginga fell to Portuguese colonial rule. They were unable to retrieve their independence until 1975 but as part of the Republic of Angola.

GIRIAMA

The Giriama, also called Agiryama, Kinyika, and Nika, are an East African agricultural people. Their economic activities focus on agriculture, fishing, and trading. They are the largest of all nine major Mijikenda groups. They are concentrated in Kenya, especially along its coastal areas. The Giriama speak a dialect of Mijikenda, a language that belongs to the Northeast Coastal Bantu languages.

GISIGA

A West African people. The Gisiga are concentrated in northeastern Nigeria, northern Cameroon, and western Chad. They speak a language that belongs to the Afro-Asiatic family of African languages. Their neighbors include the Gude, Kapsiki, Kotoko, Mandara, Matakam, Musgu and Paduko peoples.

GISO

These are one of Uganda's Bantu-speaking Luhya groups. The Giso, also known as Abagisu, Bagisu, Bamasaba, Bugisu, Gisu and Masaba, are a

Bantu-speaking people. Their language, Luluyia, is a Western Bantu language. The Gisu are concentrated in the eastern regions of the country east of Lake Kyoga and along the Ugandan-Kenyan borders, notably on the slopes and foothills of Mount Elgon. Groups of them, however, are also located in Kenya. Their neighbors include the Karamojong, the Teso and the Soga peoples. Politically and socially, the Giso are less cohesive than other Ugandan ethnic groups. They support segmentary lineage systems.

GISU, see **GISO**

GLAVDA

The Glavda, also known as Glavuda, are a West and West Central African Bantu-speaking people. They are concentrated in Cameroon and Nigeria.

GLAVUDA, see **GLAVDA**

GOBODA, see **TEDA**

GODABIIRSAY, see also **SOMALI**

An East African Somali group. The Godabiirsay, also known as Samanoan, are a subgroup of the Dir, one of the major Somali tribes. The Dir groups are concentrated in the northern regions of Somalia, as well as in southern Djibouti and eastern-central regions of Ethiopia.

GOFA

The Gofa are an East African people. They are concentrated in southern Ethiopia. They are part of the Omotic cluster of peoples.

GOGO

An Eastern Bantu-speaking people. The Gogo are highly concentrated in the central highlands of Tanzania. Groups of them, however, are also found in Mozambique. The Gogo constitute one of Tanzania's large ethnic groups.

GOLA, see also BADYARANKE

The Gola are a West African West Atlantic-speaking people. Their language belongs to the Niger-Congo family of African languages. The Gola constitute one of Liberia's ethnic minorities. Their neighbors include the Bassa, Gbande, Kpelle, Mende and Vai peoples.

GONAQUA

An extinct southern African people. The Gonaqua used to live in the southwestern regions of what is presently the Republic of South Africa.

GONJA, see GUANG

GORACHOQUA, see also KHOISAN

An extinct southern African Khoisan people. The Gorachoqua used to live in the southwestern regions of what is presently the Republic of South Africa.

GORINGHAIQUA, see also KHOISAN

An extinct southern African Khoisan people. The Goringhaiqua used to live in the southwestern regions of what is presently the Republic of South Africa.

GOROWA

The Gorowa are an East African people. They are concentrated in Kenya and Tanzania, notably in the border regions that separate the two countries.

GOULAYE, see also SARA

The Goulaye, also known as Gula and Gulay, are one of the major non-Muslim ethnic groups of the Republic of Chad. They are a Sara group. Like other Sara groups, they speak a Central Sudanic language that belongs to the Nilo-Saharan family of African languages. Like them also, they live primarily in the southern regions of the country, notably between Lake Iro in the east and the Logone river in the west.

GOUN

The Goun people, also known as Gun, are one of Benin's ethnic minorities. They are related to the Fon and like the Fon people, are concentrated in the southern regions of the country. Their neighbors include the Ewe, Fon, Popo, Yoruba peoples.

GOUNDA

The Gounda are a Central African and Saharan Teda group. They are concentrated in the Tibesti region of Chad. Groups of them are also found in the Fezzan region of Libya, as well as in the eastern areas of Niger.

GOURMA, see GURMA

GOURMANTCHE, see GURMA

GOURO, see GURO

GOUROA

A Central African people. They are concentrated in northern Chad, western Sudan, and southeastern regions of Libya.

GOUROUNSI, see also GURUNSI

The Gourounsi, also Gurunsi, are a West African people. They are concentrated in the Ivory Coast.

GOUROUS, see TOUBOU

GOWA

The Gowa are a Southeast African-Malagasy people. They live in Zambia. The Gowa are part of the Tonga cluster of peoples.

GREBO

The Grebo are a West African people and one of the Kru cluster groups. They are concentrated in the Ivory Coast and Liberia. The Grebo speak a language that belongs to the Kwa branch of the Niger-Congo family of African languages. Their neighbors include the Bakwe, Kran, Kru and Sapo peoples.

GREEK

People of Greek descent who are presently settled in several African states, notably Egypt. They are concentrated in Alexandria. A smaller Greek community, however, can also be found in Cairo, Egypt's capital.

GRIQUA

These are South African people of mixed Khoikhoi and European ancestry who, in the later part of the eighteenth century, fled discrimination around Cape town to settle in central South Africa north of Orange River.[176] There, they engaged in farming, raiding and hunting. Under a treaty concluded with the British Governor of Cape Colony, Sir Harry Smith, in 1848, they were granted an autonomous status over their new territory and moreover, their territory was declared a dependency of the Cape Colony.[177]

Following the establishment of the Orange Free State in 1854, however, the Griqua were faced with claims by the new state over the eastern parts of their territory. Unable to defend the claimed areas, they were forced to sell their lands to white trekkers. In 1861, the Griqua, under the leadership of Adam Kik III, decided to relinquish their land rights and to move to the southern foothills of the Drakensberg, where they established Griqualand East. The Griqua, who were farther west around Kimberely, did not face comparable threats to their lands until diamonds were discovered in their region. Under the leadership of Nicholaas Waterboer, they asserted their claim to Griqualand West and, with the help of the British, succeeded in preventing being taken over by the Orange Free State.[178]

In 1871, Great Britain recognized the Griqua as British subjects and annexed Griqualand West to the British crown. In 1879, both Griqualand East and Griqualand West were annexed to Cape Colony. This new arrangement, however, did not protect Griquas' land rights. The Griquas were again forced to sell their farms to white people. As a consequence, the Griqua of Griqualand West had to leave their territory which later developed into a prominent diamond mining center. Since 1963, this mining center has been under the De Beers Consolidated Mines, Ltd.. Those of Griqualand East had to face a different destiny. In 1903, their territory was established as a Black African council and incorporated within the Transkeian territories. In application of the latter-day policy of apartheid, in 1976, the eastern region of Griqualand East was incorporated in the state of Transkei (which became the main reserve for Africans), where its central regions were retained as part of Cape Province of South Africa. In 1978, they were transferred to the province of Natal.[179]

GRUNSHI

A West African Gur group and one of Ghana's ethnic minorities. The Grunshi are concentrated in the northern regions of the country and speak a language that belongs to the Voltaic branch of the Niger-Congo family of African languages. Their neighbors include the Builsa, Busa, Dagari, Guang, Gurensi, Nunuma and Wala peoples.

GRUSI

The Grusi are a West African Gur group. They are concentrated in Ghana, where they live in the central areas of the Northern Region. Their neighbors include the Dagaba, the Dagomba, the Gonja, the Mamprusi (Manprusi) and the Sisala peoples.

GU

The Gu, also known as Gun-Gbe and Kagu, are a West African people. They constitute one of Benin's and Nigeria's ethnic minorities.

GUAN, see GUANG

GUANG

The Guang, also known as Gonja, Ngbanya, Ngambaye or Guan, are a West African people. They speak Voltaic Gur and Guang languages, which belong to the Niger-Congo family of African languages. The Guang are concentrated in northern Ghana, notably in the Ahafo and Northern administrative regions, constituting one of Ghana's major ethnic groups. Their neighbors include the Builsa, Dagaba, Dagomba, Grusi, Krachi, Kulango, Lobi, Likpe, Nafana, Nanumba, Vagala and Wala peoples.

During the third quarter of the 16th century, the Guang founded a state of their own (Gonja) in what presently constitutes northern Ghana. In the 17th century, its ruler, Sumalia Ndewura Jakpa, established a dynasty and enlarged Gonja's territory. During his reign, Gonja supported a trading network that covered many areas of West Africa. Currently, the Guang have a chiefdom of their own, the rulers of which claim descent from Jakpa.

GUDE

A West African people. The Gude, also known as Cheke, Mubi and Mapuda, are concentrated in northern Cameroon and northeastern Nigeria. They speak a language that belongs to the Afro-Asiatic family of African languages. Their neighbors include the Bata, Gisiga, Fali, Fula, Kapsiki and Margi peoples.

GUDELLA, see **HAMER**

GUDJI, see **OROMO**

GUERE, see **DAN**

GUÉREP

The Guérep are one of the Kim confederation groups. They live in Chad in the vicinities of the Longone River.

GUERZE, see **KPELLE**

GUIDAR

The Guidar, also called Kada and Baynawa, are a West and West Central African farming people. They live in the Tandjilé Prefecture. In the Cameroon, they are located in the northern regions of the country, especially in the Bénoué Department.

GUIN

A West African people. The Guin are the descendants of Ga people who left the Gold Coast in the seventeenth and eighteenth centuries, to settle in the plain region between Lake Gbaga and the Mono river in Togo. Groups of them, however, are located in Ghana, Ivory Coast and Mali. Their language is closely related to that of the Ewe, and hence, belongs to the Kwa branch of the Niger-Congo family of African languages.

GUIZAGA, see GUIZIGA

GUIZIGA

Also known as Dogba, Guizaga, Mi Marva and Tchere, the Guiziga are a West and West Central African farming people. They are concentrated in northern Cameroon, southwestern Chad and southeastern Nigeria. The Guiziga are a Kirdi subgroup.

GULA, see BADYARANKE, GOULAYE and SARA

GULAY, see GOULAYE and SARA

GUMMA

The Gumma are an East African people. They are concentrated in the west central regions regions of Ethiopia. Groups of them, however, can also be found in Sudan and Chad. Their neighbors in Ethiopia include the Begemder, Berta, Galla, and Ingassana peoples.

GUMUZ

An East African Nilotic people. They are concentrated along the Blue Nile River region in eastern Sudan and western Ethiopia, adjoining the Anuak, Barya, Berti, and Kunama peoples.

GUN (Benin), see **GOUN**

GUN (Sudan), see **NUER**

GUNDA, see **TEDA**

GUN-GBE, see **GU**

GUNGAWA, see **RESHE**

GUNGUNCI, see **RESHE**

GURAGE

The Gurage people are one of the ethnic groups in Ethiopia. They are descendants of a mixture of Sidamo peoples with peoples from the Tigre province and the city of Harer. Their dominant language is Gurage, which belongs to the Semitic branch of the Hamito-Semitic family of African languages. They are essentially settled agriculturalists in the southwestern areas of Ethiopia. The Gurage are the seventh largest ethnic minority in Ethiopia, accounting for 2% of the country's total population.

GURENSI

A West African Gur group and one of Ghana's ethnic minorities. The Gurensi are concentrated in the northern regions of the country and speak a language that belongs to the Voltaic branch of the Niger-Congo family of African languages. Their neighbors include the Builsa, Busa, Grunshi, Moba and Mossi peoples.

GURMA, see also MOSSI

The Gurma people, also known as Gourma and Gourmantché, are a Voltaic (Gur)-speaking people. They are one of the Mossi groups. Currently, they are concentrated in Burkina Faso, Ghana, Niger and Togo. Their neighbors include the Borgu, Dendi, Fula, Moba, Somba, Songhai and Zerma. Together with Arabs and Toubou, the Gurma account for about 1.5% of Niger's total population.

GURO

The Guro or Gouro – also called Dipa, Kouen, Koueni, Kweni, Kweny, and Lo – are a West African people. They are concentrated in the Republic of Côte d'Ivoire (Ivory Coast), where they live in the valley of the Bandama river. They migrated to their present location during the second half of the eighteenth century, escaping Mande conquests of northern and northwestern areas of West Africa. The Guro speak a language of the Mande branch of the Niger-Congo family of African languages. Their neighbors include the Baule, Bete, Dan, Gagu, Senufo and Wobe peoples.

Originally, the Guro engaged in hunting. Currently, they are essentially agriculturalists. Villages constitute their primary social unit, with each village representing a distinct patrilineal lineage, and is governed by its own council of elders. Formerly, they recognized the position of a chief but did not allot its occupant real or centralized power.

Most Guros continue to adhere to their traditional religion, which is based on the belief in many gods, and like other West Africa peoples, they are renowned for their splendid ivory and wood carvings.

GURU, see KAGURU

GURUNSHI, see GURUNSI

GURUNSI

The Gurunsi, also known as Gurunshis, are a Voltaic people and one of the Mossi group. Currently, they constitute one of the sizable ethnic minorities of Burkina Faso.

GUSII

The Gusii, also known as Abagusii, Kisii, Kosova, Kossowa and Wakisii, are a Bantu-speaking people of the Atlantic (West Atlantic) groups. They are of Kenya's 11 largest ethnic minorities, accounting for 6% of the country's total population. They are concentrated in the Kisii and Nyamira districts of Nyanza Province, which is one of the heavily populated areas in western Kenya. The Gusii people are believed to have migrated to western Kenya from the Mt. Elgon region during the sixteenth century.

Currently, the Gussi are divided into numerous groups and subgroups, the most important of which are the Kitutu (Getutu), Mugirango, Majoge, Wanjare (Nchari), Bassi and Nyaribari.

The Gusii observe patrilineal relations and traditionally enjoyed decentralized forms of political organization. Their economic activities focus on agriculture, herding and hunting.

GWANDARA

The Gwandara are a West African people. They are concentrated in Nigeria and speak a language that belongs to the Afro-Asiatic family of African languages. Their neighbors include the Afo, Gbari, Gili, Kadara, Katab, Koro, Mada and Yesskwa peoples.

GWANGARA

The Gwangara are a subgroup of the Ngoni nation. The death of Zwangendaba, the leader of the Ngoni nation became the symbol of its unity. At Mapupo (about 1848), a successional conflict prompted them to move eastward to the eastern side of Lake Nyasa (Malawi), establishing their control over the southeastern areas of what is presently modern Tanzania. Subsequently, the Gwangara split into two separate kingdoms. Eventually, their kingdoms disappeared following the European conquest of their territory in the later part of the nineteenth century.

GWARI

A West African people. The Gwari are concentrated in Nigeria, especially in the state of Kaduna. They are a Gbari subgroup.

GWARI MATAI, see GBAGYI

GWARI YAMMA, see GBARI

GWE, see LUHYIA

An East Saharan, Central and East African Bantu-speaking people. The Gwe, also known as Abagwe, are a Luhya group. They speak Luluyia, a Western Bantu language. Like other Luhya groups, the Gwe are an agricultural people. They are concentrated in eastern Uganda.

GWEMBE TONGA, see TONGA

GWERE

One of Uganda's and Kenya's ethnic minorities. The Gwere are a Bantu-speaking people. They are concentrated in eastern Uganda and western Kenya.

G/WI, see also SAN

A southern African San group. The G/wi are a San-speaking people. They are concentrated in the central sand areas of Botswana and adjoining Namibia. Like other San-speaking peoples, they are essentially foragers, hunters and gatherers.

HA

One of Tanzania's large ethnic groups. They live in the northwestern regions of Tanzania, notably in the vicinity of lakes Tanganyika and Victoria. Their neighbors include the Buha, Jiji, Tongwe, and Vinza peoples.

HABAR-GIDER, see also SOMALI

An East African Somali group. The Habar-Gider are a subgroup of

Hawiya(e), a leading Somali tribe whose groups are concentrated in the southern regions of Somalia.

HABBANIA, see BAGGARA

HABBE, see DOGON

HABÉ, see DOGON

HADDAD

The Haddad are an East, Central and West African people. Their main concentrations are in Chad, Nigeria, and Sudan. The term "haddad" in Arabic means "Blacksmith." It correctly describes the profession of these people. Hence, they cannot be justifiably considered one ethnic group.

HADENDOWA, see also BEJA

The Hadendowa people are one of East Africa's Muslim groups. They are concentrated in the southeastern regions of the Sudan. Groups of them, however, are also found in Eritrea and Ethiopia. The Hadendowa speak Arabic, and are one of the four main Beja groups.

HADIMU, see also SHIRAZI

These are one of Tanzania's ethnic groups. The Hadimu are Bantu-speaking people and one of the Shirazi subgroups. They are concentrated in the island of Zanzibar, Tanzania.

HADIYA, see HAMER

HADJERAY

The Hadjeray people are one of Chad's ethnic groups. They are concentrated in the Guera-Massif area of the country.

HADYA, see also SIDAMO

The Hadya are an East African non-Galla Cushitic-speaking Muslim people. They live chiefly in southwestern Ethiopia, particularly in the Omo river and Rift Valley regions of the country. The Hadya are a Sidamo group, and hence are related to other Sidamo peoples, such as the Alaba, Garo and Tambaro. The Hadya are essentially an agricultural people. They specialize in the production of grains, cereals, fruits and spices as well as in animal husbandry.

Between the tenth and twelfth centuries, the Hadya established a kingdom of their own. During the same period, they absorbed Islam from coastal Arabs. Subsequently, however, their kingdom became a tributary of the Abyssinians (Amhara and Tigre), as well as the Galla.[180]

HADZAPI

The Hadzapi are an East African people. Like their neighbors the Iramba, Irangi and Iraqw, they are concentrated in the central border regions that separate Kenya from Tanzania.

HAI//OM, see SAN

HAKAVONA

The Hakavona are a Southwest African people. Their main concentrations are in Angola and Namibia, primarily along the border that separates the two countries. Their neighbors include the Herero, Himba, Kuvale, and Ngambwe peoples.

HALANGA, see HALENGA

HALENGA

The Halenga, also Halanga, are an East African ethnic group. Their main concentrations are located in the eastern regions of the Sudan, notably by the Red Sea. The Hamer are a Banna subgroup.

HALFAN, see **NUBIANS**

HAMAR

The Hamar are a Central and East African Arab nomadic people. They are highly concentrated in Chad and Sudan, notably in western Sudan. The Hamar are part of the Kawahla cluster of peoples.

HAMBA, see **AMBA**

HAMBBE, see **DOGON**

HAMBUKUSHU, see **MBUKUSHU**

HAMER

The Hamer, also known as Amar, Gudella, Hadiya and Haner-Banna, are an East African Muslim pastoralist people. They are concentrated in Ethiopia. The Hamer are one of the Banna subgroups. The Hamer are a Banna subgroup.

HAMITES

One of the four major racial/ethnic groups of which Africa is made. The other groups are the Negroes, Bantus and Bushmen. "Hamites are technically speaking white," and moreover, are speakers of Hamito-Semitic languages.[181] The latter languages are also called Semito-Hemitic, Erythraean, Afro-Asiatic, or Afrasian.[182] Broadly speaking, there are "10 principal Semitic languages, 47 Hamitic, 182 Bantu, and no fewer than 264 Sudanese."[183] Of African peoples, Ethiopians and Berbers are considered to be of Hamitic origin.

HAMIYAN

The Hamiyan are a North African people. They are concentrated in the west central regions of Algeria. Their neighbors include the Dou Menia and Mzab peoples.

HAMMADIDS, see also BERBER

The Hammadids, also known as Zirids, are a Berber clan. In the eleventh century they sought refuge in Monts du Hodna in Algeria.

HANCUMQUA

An extinct southern African people. The Hancumqua used to live in the southwestern regions of what is presently the Republic of South Africa.

HANER-BANNA, see HAMER

HANGAZA

An East African people. They are concentrated in the northwestern regions of Tanzania. The Hangaza are part of the Subi people.

HANYA

The Hanya are a Southwest African Ovimbundu group. They live in Angola, primarily in its northwestern regions. Their neighbors include the Cisanji, Esele, Ndombe, and Tyilenge-Muso peoples.

HAOUSSA, see HAUSA

HARARI

The Harari, also known as Adare, Gesinan and Hareri, are an East African Muslim people. They are concentrated in southern Ethiopia, especially in the city of Harar. The Harari are farmers and traders.

HARATIN, see MOOR and SAHRAWIS

HARERI, see HARARI

HARTI, see also SOMALI

An East African Somali group. The Harti people are made up of several clans, including the Dhulbahante, the Majeerteen and the Warsangali.

They are part of the Darod tribe, a major Somali tribe whose groups and subgroups are concentrated in the northeastern areas of Somalia, as well as in southern Somalia to the west of Juba river along the country's borders with Ethiopia.

HASSAOUNA, see also MOOR

A West Saharan and West African pastoralist people. The Hassaouna are concentrated in Mauritania and neighboring countries and are often regarded as Moorish people. Probably, they are related to the Hassouna of Chad.

HASSAUNA, see HASSOUNA

HASSOUNA

An East Saharan and Central African Arab pastoralist people. The Hassouna, also spelled Hassauna and Hassuna, are concentrated in Chad.

HASSUNA, see HASSOUNA

HAUKHOIN, see BERGDAMA

HAUSA

The Hausa people, also called Afnu, Afunu, Arna, Azna, Bunjawa, al-Hausin, Maguzawa, Aussa and Haoussa, form the largest ethnic group in West Africa. They do not only constitute the largest ethnic group in each of Niger and Nigeria, but also have minorities of varying sizes in other West African states. Because of extensive migration, they are found "in enclaves in various African cities as far south as the Atlantic coast."[184] In Niger, they account for 56% of the country's total population and in Nigeria, they represent the largest ethnic group and are concentrated in the states of Plateau, Sokoto, Kaduna, Bauchi and Kano. In Togo, where they are scattered throughout the country, they constitute a relatively small ethnic minority. In Chad, they are one of the major ethnic groups and live primarily in the northern regions of the country. In Burkina Faso, they comprise a small minority.

The language of the Hausa, called Hausa, belongs to the Chadic group of the Hamitic-Semitic family of African languages and includes many Arabic words. It is the most popular language in Sub-Saharan Africa. The Hausa language is the official language of northern Nigeria, and is widely used as a second language throughout a number of West African countries. Next "to Swahili, it is the most widely spoken African language."[185] Like Berber, Somali, and Galla, it is an 'advanced' language with grammatical rules of its own.[186]

The history of the Hausa can be traced back to some three thousand years ago, at which time they settled between Songhai and Kanem Bornu in what was later called Hausaland, and succeeded in adapting and/or developing deep-plowing techniques and irrigation systems, as well as in engaging themselves in animal husbandry, mining, ironworking, and trading.[187]

Originally, the Hausa were agriculturists. They thrived on cultivating the plains of the Hausaland to grow corn, barley, rice and cotton, as well as on animal husbandry. Originally also, they lived in small farming villages. Subsequently, however, the growing trade with North Africa across the Sahara desert signaled the emergence of walled towns like Kano and Katsina. In addition to their role as entrepôts, these towns served also as sedentary, religious, industrial, defense and trading centers, as well as nuclei of new states. As a result, Katsina and Kano became the major Hausa entrepôts, Zaria developed into a slaving center. Rano specialized in industrial products and Gobir focused its attention on military protection of the Hauseland, especially against raids staged by Sahara nomads.

The rise of Hausa states is covered in their legends, which note that a ruler called Bayajida (Abuyazidu), son of the king of Baghdad, came from the north to Hausaland where he married the local queen. Subsequently, their grandsons became the kings of the major Hausa states.[188] According to July, this legend probably refers to a series of "southward migrations of Saharan hunters and fisher folk" that Hausaland had experienced in the past, leading to a merger with indigenous groups.[189]

According to <u>Kano Chronicle</u> (1890s), however, the Kingdom of Kano "was founded as one of the Hausa Bakwai (seven True Hausa States) in 999 by Bagauda, a grandson of Bayajida (Abuyazidu), legendary progenitor of the Hausa people."[190] This view suggests that the history of the Hausa states (not people) is about one thousand years.

Between the fourteenth and the nineteenth century, the Hausa states developed into leading caretakers of a major political and trading empire ruled by great chiefs. This empire comprised seven states and seven outlying satellites, situated between the Songhai empire in the west and that of Bornu or Kanem-Bornu, to the east. The states included Biram, Daura, Gobir, Kano, Katsina, Rano and Zaria (Zazzau). The satellites included Zamfara, Kebbi, Yauri, Gwari, Nupe, Kororofa (Jukun) and Yoruba.

During the same period under consideration, most of the Hausa people gradually converted to Islam. Despite this development, their states continued to be linked together by loose alliances, which often shifted in light of inter-Hausa rivalries and conflicts.[191]

Historical evidence suggests that Malinke (Wangara) scholars from the Mali empire introduced Islam to the Hausa people, in general, and to those of Kano, in particular, in the 1340's. They also suggest that Kano King Yji, who reigned from 1349 to 1385 "was probably Kano's first Muslim Hausa king."[192]

During the fifteenth century, several Hausa states became tributaries of the Kanem-Bornu empire and in the sixteenth century, of the Songhai empire. Early in the 19th century, the Hausa states fell to the Sokoto *jihad*, led by a Fulani religious reformer, shehu Usuman dan Fodio (1754-1817). The success of the Sokoto campaign gave rise to the Fulani Empire. As a result, the Hausa were united by the Fulani and governed under the spiritual leadership Usuman dan Folio. Upon Usuman's death in 1817, the leadership of the Fulani empire devolved to his son, Muhammad Bello, Sultan of Sokoto (1817-1837).

Under the Fulani empire, the Hausaland was organized into emirates, each emirate of which was ruled by a Fulani ruler/commander called amīrs. Amīrs were assisted by a number of titled office holders who governed villages as fiefs.

The Fulani empire continued after Bello's death in 1837 and remained intact until it was occupied by the British during the early part of the twentieth century. Eventually, however, the British merged its emirates with Bornu to form the northern provinces and later, the region of the Protectorate of Nigeria.

Excepting a small minority of them, known as Maguzawa or Bunjawa (who are believed to be animists), the Hausa people are predominantly Muslim and are renowned for being strict Muslims. All men and women are expected to observe the tenets of their faith, privately and in public, as well as to apply Muslim *shar'ia* laws in whatever they do. Submission to God is the most important moral requirement, because through such submission one attains peace within himself or herself, within his or her family and with his or her community and all the human race at large.

The Hausa are predominantly a rural people (about 80%). Unlike the urbanized who live in cities and towns, the non-urban Hausa live in villages made up of households known as *gida*. The *gida* is the most important form of social organization. A *gida* is basically a conglomeration of dwellings for different members of an extended Hausa family. There is a house for the head of the family, a house for each of the head's wives or wife and one for each of his married sons. Most Hausa women marry young and normally move into their husbands' households immediately. They are responsible for a number of domestic chores, including the upbringing of children. Children are precious in Hausa society because they represent God's gifts, as well as one's hopes of the future. Many children are sent to schools and are encouraged to study the history of their religion, as well as the *Qur'an*, the Muslim Holy Book, in-depth.

HAUT-KATANGA

The Haut-Katanga are a West Central and East Central African people. They are concentrated in the southeastern regions of the Democratic Republic of the Congo (Zaire).

HAVU

One of the ethnic groups of the Democratic Republic of the Congo (Zaire). The Havu are part of the Kivu cluster of peoples.

HAWAWIR

The Hawawir are one of Central and North East African ethnic groups. They are concentrated in western Sudan. They are part of the Berber cluster of peoples in Sudan.

HAWAZMA, see BAGGARA

HAWIYA(E), see also SOMALI

One of the main Somali clans. The Hawiya, also spelled Hawiyah, Hawiye or Hawwiya, are based in and around Mogadishu, the capital of Somalia, as well as in the southern regions of Somalia and northeastern regions of Kenya.

HAWIYAH, see SOMALI

HAWIYE, see SOMALI

HAWWIYA, see SOMALI

HAYA, see also CHAGGA

The Haya, also known as Chaga or Chagga, are an East African people. They originated in the Taita region and currently represent one of Tanzania's large ethnic groups. Their main concentration is in the lakes' region of northern Tanzania.

HAZU, see SAHO

HAYO, see LUHYA

HEBA, see KILBA

HEEBO, see **IGBO**

HEHE, see **HEHET**

HEHET

The Hehet, also known as Hehe, are one of Tanzania's (formerly Tanganyika's) and Mozambique's large ethnic groups. They are concentrated in the Iringa region north of Lake Malawi (formerly Nyasa). The Hehet are an Eastern Bantu-speaking people.

The Hehet were once one of the most powerful peoples of East Africa. They excelled both as a trading and military power. In the mid-19th century, Munyigumba, head of the Muyinga family, succeeded in unifying the Hehet. Under his leadership and later that of his son, Mkwawa, they expanded their territory and resisted attempts to subdue them by their neighbors, the Sultanate of Muscat and Zanzibar, as well as the Imperial German government.

Despite their defeat in 1891, the Hehet continued their resistance to German encroachments on the Iringa region for almost a full decade. In 1898, however, they were subdued by German forces and placed under the full control of the colonial administration of the Imperial German government. In 1926, their chiefdom was restored under the headship of one paramount chief.

On the whole, the Hehet society is both patrilineal and exogamous. Though Christianity and Islam have won many converts, the great majority of Hehets continue to embrace their traditional religious beliefs, which center on the cult of ancestors. Many of them also continue to believe in witchcraft. In their values "no man must be too much in advance of his neighbours, or there is a danger that a jealous warlock will kill him by witchcraft." Hence, a "man must not wear clothes which differ too markedly from those of his neighbours, nor must he seek methods of gaining wealth or social superiority which involve too great a departure from traditional tribal life."[193]

The Hehet are primarily an agricultural people. They specialize in cereals including corn. They also engage in the raising of cattle.

HEHET NYAKYUSA, see HEHET

HEI/KUM, see also SAN

A Southwest African people. The Hei/Kum, also known as Heiom, are concentrated in the north central regions of Namibia.

HEIOM, see HEI/KUM

HELENGUE, see HLENGWE

HEMBA, see LUBA

HENGA, see TUMBUKO

HERERO

The Herero, also known as Dama and Damara, are a Southern Bantu-speaking people. Their language, Ovaherero or Herero, is a south-western Bantu dialect. The Herero constitute one of Angola's, Botswana's and Namibia's ethnic minorities. In Namibia, they account for about 8% of the total population. In Botswana, they are concentrated in the western areas of the country, notably on the northern edge of the Kalahari Desert. The Herero comprise several groups, which, apart from Herero proper, include the Himba, the Mbanderu and the Tjimba.

Originally, the Herero lived in eastern and central Africa. They migrated to Southwest Africa during the second half of the sixteenth century, and settled in what is currently northern Namibia. Subsequently, they expanded their territory southwardly at the expense of the Hottentots, the original inhabitants of Southwest Africa. The origin of the Herero people suggests that they are related to present-day East African Dama people.

The Herero have been extremely active through the years in defiance of European, especially German and later South African, rule over the state of Namibia (formerly Southwest Africa). This political activity led many Herero to join organizations, such as SWAPO, to fight against colonization. In effect, they were identified with the struggle for an independent Namibia – an objective that was achieved on March 21, 1990.

Traditional Herero political society consisted of a village chief, who answered to a centralized chief for all Herero villages. Today, the office of chief has become virtually symbolic. In fact, Herero chiefs, like Chief Kuaima Rimako, have outgrown their Herero roots to become overall political activists representing all the people of Namibia.

The traditional Herero social structure is both a matrilineal and patrilineal clan system. Both lineages have important functions in Herero society. The matrilineal clan is responsible for all the property of the person, while the patrilineal clan controls the spiritual affairs of the person. In Herero religion, Christianity is mixed with traditional Herero religious practices. Old Herero religious institutions still meet and practice. Even some Christian holidays are also used to recognize ancestor spirits.

Economically, the Herero continue to be predominantly engaged in cattle raising and herding. Some groups of them, however, are focusing greater attention on miscellaneous farming and trading activities.

HESSEQUA

An extinct southern African people. The Hessequa used to live in the southwestern regions of what is presently the Republic of South Africa.

HIECHWARE

The Hiechware are a South Central African people. They are concentrated in Zambia and Tanzania. Their neighbors include the Mahura, the Chekwe and the Bamangwato peoples.

HILANI, see FULANI

HIMA, see also NKOLE

The Hima are a Bantu-speaking Nkole people. Traditionally, they represented one of the two major Nkole subgroups, the other subgroup being the Iru. Unlike the agriculturalist Iru, the Hima were cattle pastoralists and were located in several East African states, especially Uganda. In Uganda, they were concentrated in the north and west of Lake Victoria.

The Hima's history is traced to the fifteenth century, at which time they settled to the north and west of Lake Victoria in what is presently modern Uganda and Rwanda. There, they established themselves over the Bantu farmers. There also the leaders of one of their clans, the Chwezi, organized themselves into the kingdom of Kitara between Lake Victoria and Lake Albert. Towards the end of the century, however, another Nilotic people, the Luo, poured into Uganda and western Kenya, subduing Kitara and reorganizing it as the kingdom of Bunyoro under the rule of the Bito dynasty. As a result, some Hima moved south, where they established a series of new kingdoms and principalities, the most important of which were the kingdom of Hinda and the kingdom of Buganda. The territories of these new kingdoms and principalities covered vast areas that stretched from south Lake Victoria to Lake Tanganyika.[194]

HIMBA, see HERERO

HINDA, see CHWEZI and NKOLE

HLAKWANA, see also SOTHO

The Hlakwana are one of the major tribes of the Kwena, a subgroup of the Sotho people. They are concentrated in the Kingdom of Lesotho.

Like other Sotho, the Hlakwana are a southern African people, speak Sesotho, a Bantu language, and engage in agriculture and animal husbandry. Their settlements are characterized "by scattered hamlets of circular huts with mud and wattle or stone walls surmounted by a conical, thatched roof."[195]

In their social patterns, most Kanga-Kone recognize patrilineal lineages and continue to be impacted by their traditional religious beliefs.

HLENGUE, see HLENGWE

HLENGWE

The Hlengwe, also known as Bahlengue and Hlengue, are a Southeast African-Malagasy people. They live in southern Mozambique, northern Transvaal in South Africa, and southeastern Zimbabwe.

HLUBI, see MFENGU

HO, see EWE

HODH

The Hodh people are a West African group. They have concentrations in both of Mauritania and Mali, primarily along the border that separates the two countries. Their neighbors include the Karago and Kassonke peoples.

HOGGAR, see TAUREG

HOLLI, see YORUBA

HOLO, see LUHYA

HOLOHOLO

The Holoholo are a West Central and East African people. They are concentrated in the Democratic Republic of the Congo (Zaire) and Tanzania, especially in the western vicinity of Lake Tanganyika. Their neighbors include the Bemba and Tumbwe peoples.

HONA

The Hona are a West African people and one of Nigeria's many ethnic groups. The Hona are concentrated in northwestern Nigeria and speak a language that belongs to the Afro-Asiatic family of African languages. Their neighbors include the Bata, Bura, Dera, Margi, Tera, and Yungur peoples.

HORUTSHE, see BANTU

A southern Bantu-speaking people. The Horutshe, also known as the Barutshe and Hurutshe, are concentrated in the southern central regions of Africa, notably in Botswana and South Africa. They are a Tswana group.

HOTNOT, see KHOISAN

HOTTENTOT, see KHOISAN

HUBA, see KILBA

HUININ

A Southwest African people. The Huinin are concentrated in the southern regions of the Republic of Namibia.

HUKWE BUSHMEN

The Hukwe Bushmen are a South Central African people. They are concentrated in southeastern Democratic Republic of the Congo (Zaire) and northwestern Zambia. Groups of them, however, can also be found in northeastern Angola. Their neighbors include the Mbukushu and Tawana peoples.

HULO, see MENDE

HUMA, see TOPOSA and ANKOLE

HUMR, see BAGGARA

HUNDE, see also KIVU

These are one of Democratic Republic of the Congo's (Zaire's) ethnic groups. The Hunde are part of the Kivu cluster of peoples. They are concentrated in the Masisi district, a fertile region of lakes and lush hills, located northeast of lake Kivu and the city of Goma along the country's eastern border with Rwanda. Since the late 1980's, their region has been witnessing an influx of Rwandan immigrants – both Tutsi and Hutu – and recurring tribal wars.[196]

HUNE, see DUWAKA

HURUTHSE, see also HORUTSHE

The Huruthse, also known as Hurutshe, are a Southwest and southern African people. They are concentrated in Botswana and South Africa.

HURUTHSHE, see also HURUTHSE

HUTU

The Hutu – also known as Abahutu, Bahutu and Wahutu – are a Bantu-speaking people. They speak Rwand, Rundi and Kirundi. The Hutu are concentrated in Rwanda, Burundi, the Democratic Republic of the Congo (Zaire) and Tanzania. They account for 85% of Burundi's total population and 90% of Rwanda's.

The Hutu are believed to have migrated around the second century AD to the area that presently constitutes Burundi and Rwanda from the Chad-Niger region of West Africa, forcing the Twa, pygmy hunter people who were the original inhabitants not only to retreat, but also to become serfs to them. Between the 14th and 18th century, the Tutsi people migrated from the Nile Valley or Ethiopia and settled in the same area, gradually subjugating the Hutu. The Tutsi established their hegemony "over the Hutu through military conquest, possession of their cattle, and assertion of divine origin."[197] As a result, a "feudal class system known as *ubuhake* developed whereby the Hutu were permitted the use of Tutsi cattle and land, and in exchange rendered personal and military service to the Tutsi."[198] This relation continued until the late 1890's, at which time the Germans colonized the Tutsi-Hutu territory. About fifty years later, the Belgians took over the area and established their control over Rwanda and Burundi under a League of Nations, and later United Nations, mandate. In the 1960s, the Hutu started to challenge the Tutsi's political domination.

In 1961, they asserted their authority in Rwanda, and in 1972, they staged an unsuccessful revolt against the Tutsi-controlled government in Burundi. Since then, ethnic conflict has been the norm in both countries. At the start of this decade, the conflict was transformed into a tragic civil war that led to the killing and plight of thousands of Hutu and Tutsi people.

Before the Tutsi infiltration and control, Hutu society was made up of clans ruled by kings, or *bahinza*. The Hutu society was and continues to be based on agriculture. The Hutu religion is a mixture of Christian and traditional animist practices.

HWADUBA

The Hwaduba are a southern African people. They are concentrated in Botswana and South Africa.

HWASO, see KPAN

HWAYE, see KPAN

IBIBIO

The Ibibio people are one of the ten largest ethnic minorities of Nigeria. They constitute the ninth largest group after the Hausa, Fulani, Yoruba, Ibo, Kanuri, Tiv, Edo and Nupe peoples. The Ibibio people share many common traits with the Ibo (Igbo), one of Nigeria's major ethnic groups. They are concentrated in the southeastern areas of Nigeria, especially in the Calabar and Owerri provinces of the Nigerian Cross River State. The Ibibio people speak a Kwa language of the Niger-Congo family of African languages.

The Ibibio are comprised of several major groups, the most important of which are the Anang, the Andoni-Ibeno, the Efik, the Eket, the Enyong and the Ibibio proper. The Anang are referred to as Western Ibibio, whereas the Andoni-Ibeno, the Eket and Enyong are referred to as Delta Ibibio, Southern Ibibio and Northern Ibibio, respectively. The Ibibio proper are referred to as Eastern Ibibio. In their turn, these groups are divided into subgroups that carry the names of their respective geographical localities.

They include such groups as the Aba, the Abak, the Ato, the Calabar, the Ikot Ekpene, the Kumba (Sate, Yofo), the Opopo and the Uyo.[199]

A great majority of Ibibio people are engaged in agriculture and live in villages that are built around central courtyards. Their villages are governed by councils representing the heads of their various households. In their turn, villages are bonded together by descent from same ancestors, as well as by their common tutelary spirits and totems. Socialization of men and women within villages is furthered through the initiation ceremonies and activities of secret societies, which entail religious rituals, exaltation of ancestral spirits and practice of magic, sorcery and various forms of wizardry.

The Ibibio are a patrilineal people. In their society, questions relating to descent, succession and inheritance are based on patrilineal lineages. The heads of their households continue to have ritual responsibilities, including the protection of ancestral shrines.

Like other West African people, the Ibibio are renowned for their wood carving skills.

IBO, see IGBO

IBOTENATEN, see TAUREG

IBUKWO, see KPAN

IBUQQUYEN, see also BERBER

The Ibuqquyen are a Moroccan Berber group. They are concentrated in the Rif region of Morocco, notably in El Hoceima, Nador and Taza provinces.

ICHIBEMBA, see BEMBA

ID AW-KANSUS, see also BERBER

A Moroccan Berber group. The Id aw-Kansus are concentrated in the

Ishilhayen region of Morocco, notably in the Western High Atlas, the Sus Valley, and the Anti-Atlas areas of the country.

ID AW-LTIT, see also **BERBER**

The Id aw-Ltit are a Moroccan Berber group. They are concentrated in the Ishilhayen region of Morocco, notably in the Western High Atlas, the Sus Valley, and the Anti-Atlas areas of the country.

ID AW-TANAN, see also **BERBER**

A Moroccan Berber group. The Id aw-Tanan are concentrated in the Ishilhayen region of Morocco, notably in the Western High Atlas, the Sus Valley, and the Anti-Atlas areas of the country.

ID AW-ZADDAGH, see also **BERBER**

The Id aw-Zaddagh are a Moroccan Berber group. They are concentrated in the Ishilhayen region of Morocco, notably in the Western High Atlas, the Sus Valley, and the Anti-Atlas areas of the country.

ID AW-ZKRI, see also **BERBER**

A Berber people in Morocco. The Id aw-Zkri are concentrated in the Ishilhayen region of Morocco, notably in the Western High Atlas, the Sus Valley, and the Anti-Atlas areas of the country.

IDAFAN, see **IRIGWE**

IDAKHO, see **LUHYA**

IDEMSIREN, see also **BERBER**

The Idemsiren are a Moroccan Berber group. They are concentrated in the Ishilhayen region of Morocco, notably in the Western High Atlas, the Sus Valley, and the Anti-Atlas areas of the country.

IDOMA

The Idoma are a West and Central African people. Their main concentrations are in the states of Benue and Gongola in Nigeria. The Idoma speak a Kwa language of the Niger-Congo family of African languages. Their neighbors include the Afo, Arago, Bassa, Igala, Igbo, Iyala, Orri and Tiv peoples.

IFE-ILESHA

The Ife-Ilesha are a West African people. They constitute one of Nigeria's ethnic groups. The Ife-Ilesha are concentrated in the west central regions of the country. Their neighbors include the Egba and Ora peoles.

IFOGHAS, see TAUREG

IFORA, see TAUREG

IGALA

The Igala, also called Igara, constitute one of Nigeria's ethnic minorities. They are concentrated in the west central areas of the country, particularly in the states of Benue and Kwara. Their neighbors include the Bassa, Bassa-Ege, Edo, Idoma, Igbirra, Igbo and Orri peoples. The Igala speak a Kwa language of the Niger-Congo family of African languages. They are predominantly Muslim, with agriculture being their main economic activity.

Traditionally, the Igala society was politically highly centralized around an absolute king who claimed divine powers. Moreover, it was class-structured and supported an elaborate administrative system comprised of nobility, high officials, serfs, slaves and eunuchs. Traditionally also, the Igala were a pagan people, who believed in human sacrifices and headhunting.

The Igala continue to have their own king, *ata*, but without his traditional attributes and powers. Their king is also the king of two neighboring peoples, namely the Bassa and the Bass Nkome.

IGARA, see IGALA

IGBIRA

The Igbira, also spelled Ebira and Igbirra, are West African peoples. They are essentially concentrated in the state of Kwara in central Nigeria, notably north and east of the confluence of the Niger and Benue rivers. Their language belongs to either a subgroup of the Kwa or the Nupe-Gbari language group and their society is based on patrilineal relation. Their neighbors include the Bassa, Bassa-Nge, Edo, Gbari, Igala, Nupe and Yoruba peoples. Currently, the Igbara are predominantly Muslim and agriculturalists who engage in farming.

The Igbira support two main chiefdoms: Panda and Koton Karifi. Both chiefdoms were independent prior to their falling to the Fulani empire in the late 19th century and subsequently to the British in the early 20th century.

IGBIRRA, see IGBIRRA

IGBO

The Igbo (more properly Ndi Igbo) who are wrongly called or referred to as Eboe, Heebo and Ibo, are one of Nigeria's major ethnic groups. They are concentrated in southeastern Nigeria, especially the Imo state, which is one of Nigeria's main onshore oil-producing areas, as well as in the state of Anambra. Their land, Ala Igbo or Ano Igbo, lies between the Niger river to the west and the Cross river to the east. The Igbo language, Igbo, belongs to the Kwa branch of the Niger-Congo family of African languages. The Igbo people are made up of over 200 separate groups, the most important of which are the Onitsha, the Owerri, the Ika and Abakaliki. In their turn, these groups are divided into subgroups such as the Adda (Edda), the Abam-Ohaffia, the Aro, the Awka, the Enugu, the Isu-Ama, the Isu-Item, the Kwale, the Nri-Awka, the Ogu Uku, the Ohuhu-Ngwa and the Oratta-Ikwerri. Currently, they constitute the fourth largest ethnic minority in Nigeria, after the Hausa, the Fulani and the Yoruba. Their economic activities focus on farming and trading.[200]

Traditionally, their society was divided into small democratically oriented settlements, each of which was ruled by a council of elders rather than a chief or a paramount chief. With the exception of two of their groups, such as Onitsha, they lacked centralized political authority.[201] On the whole, they are noted for their energy and individualism.

Prior to Nigeria's fall to British rule, the Igbo were not united under a single authority. Rather, they lived in autonomous local communities. After the country's independence in October 1960, they started to develop a feeling of ethnic identity, and between 1967 and 1970, they unsuccessfully tried, under the leadership of Lt. Col. Odumegwu Ojukwu, to secede from Nigeria as an independent state called the Republic of Biafra. The "Biafra crisis" resulted in over 1.5 million Igbo casualties.

The Igbo political and social organizations are based on patrilineal relations. Moreover, their society is very concerned with group achievement. Groups and secret societies pervade in every section of society. There are age-set societies made of boys of the same age that perform public duties, like building roads and policing Igbo villages. Wealthy Igbos are part of societies that initiate public projects for the nation, like road building. Women have more of a place in the economic aspect of society. They cultivate crops and sell them in the very competitive Igbo markets.

Marriage is very important in Igbo society. Though polygamy is an accepted practice, most men stay with one wife. Marriage negotiations in Ibo society are very arduous processes that include bridewealth. Husbands must supply the house and land for his new family; "if the marriage is outside of the village, the wife [cannot] inherit the property."[202] Igbo families have been known to have many children, but currently they are having smaller families. The wife controls all domestic duties and may call on the help of her female or male children.

Igbo literature has been well developed due to advanced education of the Igbo masses. Many fine writers have been published in Igbo, as well as many other languages. Dance, painting and sculpture are also fervent artistic expressions of the Igbo. Igbo art is mainly made for religious festivals where depictions of Igbo gods and goddesses predominate. Like other West African peoples, they are renowned for their splendid wood sculpture.

The Igbo combine traditional religious practices with Christian beliefs. In Igbo traditional religion, the spiritual world is ruled by one supreme God, that is known to have three names: *Chukwu, Cjomele,* and *Osebuluwa.* Each name represents the three different functions of God: an ever-immortal spirit, a creative spirit and an upholding spirit. Ancestors are also recognized and believed to be still active in everyday life.

In Igbo religious beliefs, a person's *chi* is analogous to the soul in Western religious thought. The Igbo still see traditional herbalists, or *dibia,* to cure many ailments and are tied to Igbo religious thought pertaining to illnesses.

IGEDE

One of Nigeria's small ethnic groups. The Igede are concentrated in the southwestern regions of the country and speak a language that belongs to the Kwa branch of the Niger-Congo family of African languages. Their neighbors include the Idoma, Igala, Igbo, Iyala, Orri and Tiv peoples.

IGEDMIWEN, see also BERBER

The Igedmiwen are a Moroccan Berber group. They are concentrated in the Ishilhayen region of Morocco, notably in the Western High Atlas, the Sus Valley, and the Anti-Atlas areas of the country.

IGLAWN, see BERBER

IGUNDAFEN, see also BERBER

The Igundafen are a Moroccan Berber group. They are concentrated in the Ishilhayen region of Morocco, notably in the Western High Atlas, the Sus Valley, and the Anti-Atlas areas of the country.

IGZINNAYEN, see also BERBER

A Moroccan Rifian Berber group. The Igzinnayen are concentrated in the northern Rif region of Morocco, notably in the El Hoceima, Nador and Taza provinces of the country.

IHAHAN, see also BERBER

The Ihahan are a Moroccan Berber group. They are concentrated in the Ishilhayen region of Morocco, notably in the Western High Atlas, the Sus Valley, and the Anti-Atlas areas of the country.

IHANSALEN, see also BERBER

A Moroccan Berber group. The Ihansalen are concentrated in the Imazighen region of Morocco, notably in the Middle Atlas, Central High Atlas, Saghro massif and the Presaharan oasis areas of the country.

'IISE, see also SOMALI

An East African Somali group. The 'Iise are a subgroup of the Dir tribe, one of the principal Somali tribes. The Dir people are concentrated in northern Somaliland, as well as in parts of Djibouti and Ethiopia.

IJAW

The Ijaw, or Ijo, are a West African people of the Niger River Delta. They are concentrated in what is presently southern Nigeria. They speak Ijaw, a language of the Kwa branch of the Niger-Congo family of African languages. The Ijaw people are one of the ten largest ethnic minorities of Nigeria. They constitute the tenth largest group after the Hausa, the Fulani, the Yoruba, the Ibo, the Kanuri, the Tiv, the Edo, the Nupe and the Ibibio. Their population is estimated at over 1 million. The Ijaw neighbors include the Abua, Edo, Igbo, Itsekiri and Ogoni peoples.

The Ijaw people "claim descent from a common ancestor."[203] Prior to falling to the British, they were engaged in fishing and slaving. Later, they got involved in palm oil trading and succeeded in establishing a few kingdoms. Generally, however, they lived in villages, where they were governed by councils of elders. Currently, their main economic activity is fishing. The western educated among them, however, swell the ranks of

Nigeria's professional and civil service sectors.

IJEBU, see also YORUBA

These are a West African Yoruba subgroup of what is presently southwestern Nigeria. Their capital, Ijebu, in what is presently Ogun State in Nigeria, was founded in the sixteenth century and was the seat of their kingdom, and of *awujale*, their political and spiritual king. According to their legends, it was founded by "one of the sons of Oduduwa, the Yoruba deity who is said to have spread earth on the primeval water at Ife-Ife."[204]

The geopolitical location of their kingdom enabled the Ijebu to command control over trade "between the ports of the Lagos Lagoon (including Lagos, 44 miles [70km] west-southwest) and the Yoruba hinterland (especially Ibadan, 38 miles [60km] north)."[205] This command, however, was later threatened by the outcomes of the Yoruba civil wars of 1820 to 1837, 1837 to 1878 and 1878 to 1893, which made Ibadan the most powerful of all Yoruba states.

In an effort to contain Ibadan's increasing power, the Ijebu aligned themselves with their neighbors the Egbu and jointly blockaded Ibadan. The main purpose of the blockade was to limit Ibandan's power by restricting its access to imported weapons. It forced Ibadan to seek other trading routes to meet its military needs, especially through Benin. At the same time, however, the blockade hurt British trading interests and provoked the British government to interfere militarily in support of Ibadan. The outcome of the confrontation was in favor of the British. In 1892, the Ijebu's *awujale* was defeated and its kingdom was placed under British colonial rule. As a by-product of the intervention, in 1893, Sir Gilbert Carter, Governor of Lagos and the commander of the expedition against the Ijebu was able to convince the various states of Yorubaland "to come to terms under British protection."[206]

Currently, the Ijebu kingdom continues to exist as part of the Republic of Nigeria and moreover, its *awujale* continues to be recognized as a traditional leader but without many of his former powers. However, the Ijebu's economic activities have diversified and presently focus on agriculture, trade and iron craftsmanship.

IJESHA, see also **YORUBA**

The Ijesha, also known as Ilesha, are a Yoruba subgroup, and are concentrated in the Ondo State of what is presently southwestern Nigeria. They were Egba neighbors and had a state of their own, which played an important part in the Yoruba civil wars of the nineteenth century.

Presently, the Ijesha people are essentially agriculturalists and farmers. Their produce includes cocoa, palm oil and kernels, kola nuts, rice, pumpkins and miscellaneous fruits and vegetables.

IJO, see **IJAW**

IK

A Central and East African Teuso (Tueso) group. The Ik are concentrated in Uganda, notably in the northeastern parts of the Karamoja region. They are an Eastern Nilotic-speaking people. Their neighbors include the Bari, Beir, and Lotuko peoples.

IKA, see **IGBO**

IKARAMOJONG, see **KARAMOJONG**

IKIKURIA, see **KURIA**

IKOKOLEMU, see **KUMAN**

IKOTA, see **KOTO**

IKOT EKPENE, see **IBIBIO**

IKPAN, see **KPAN**

IKWERE

The Ikwere, also spelled Ikwerri, are a West African Igbo people. Their main concentration is in the southern and southeastern regions of Nigeria.

IKWERRI, see **IKWERE**

ILA

Called also Baila, Shukulumbwe or Sukulumbwe, the Ila represent one of Zambia's ethnic minorities. They are concentrated in mountainous areas west of Lusaka, the capital of the country, especially around the town of Kasenga. The Ila are a Western Bantu-speaking people and are related to the Bichi, Lumbu, Lundwe, Mbala and Sala peoples.

Historical evidence suggests that together with the Lenje and Tonga peoples, the Ila had developed an important kingdom in the past. The territory "stretched from the Zambezi river north to the Lukanga Swamp of the Kafue river and from the contemporary Western Province (formerly Barotseland) to a great distance eastward."[207]

The Ila people are not organized around a centralized system. Instead, they function through an autonomous chief, called *mwami*, who "presides over each of a number of independent *shishi* (territories)."[208]

The economic activities of the Ila people focus on agriculture, animal husbandry, fishing and hunting. They live in villages which are governed by headmen and councils of elders. Their traditional religion was based on the belief in a supreme being, called Leza, as well as in the ancestor cult. Descent, succession and inheritance in their society are based on both patrilineal and matrilineal lineages.

ILESHA, see **IJESHA**

ILLALEN, see also **BERBER**

The Illalen are a Moroccan Berber group. They are concentrated in the Ishilhayen region of Morocco, notably in the Western High Atlas, the Sus Valley, and the Anti-Atlas areas of the country.

ILMAASAI, see **MASAI**

ILORIN, see also **YORUBA**

The Ilorin are a Yoruba subgroup and are concentrated in an area north of Ibadan and south of Old Oyo. Their state played an important part in the Yoruba civil wars of the nineteenth century.

ILTOROBBO, see **OKIEK**

IMAJEGHEN, see **BERBER**

IMAZIGHEN, see **BERBER**

IMBANGALA, see **MBANGALA** and **LUNDA**

IMERINA, see **MERINA**

IMRAGUEN

The Imraguen, also known as Hawata or Shnagla, are a West Saharan nomadic and seminomadic people. They are scattered all along the Atlantic coast of the Sahara. Their main concentrations, however, are in Senegal and its neighboring countries. In all probability, they are either of Berber or Arab origins. They speak a dialect of Arabic and engage in miscellaneous pastoral and fishing activities.

The Imraguen comprise many small and widely scattered semi-independent groups, each group of which is loosely governed by an elder headman.[209]

IMSFIWEN, see also **BERBER**

The Imsfiwen are a Moroccan Berber group. They are concentrated in the Ishilhayen region of Morocco, notably in the Western High Atlas, the Sus Valley, and the Anti-Atlas areas of the country.

IMTUGGAN, see also **BERBER**

A Moroccan Berber group. The Imtuggan are concentrated in the

Ishilhayen region of Morocco, notably in the Western High Atlas, the Sus Valley, and the Anti-Atlas areas of the country.

IMZABIYEN, see BERBER

IND AW-ZAL, see also BERBER

The Ind aw-Zal are Moroccan Berber group. They are concentrated in the Ishilhayen region of Morocco, notably in the Western High Atlas, the Sus Valley, and the Anti-Atlas areas of the country.

INDIAN

Descendants of persons from the Indian sub-continent who were brought to Africa by essentially British colonial concerns to work on plantations, or to assist in the construction of roads, ports and rail lines. These people are unevenly distributed in several East and Southern African countries. They are highly concentrated in East and South Africa.

INEME

The Ineme are a West African Edo-speaking people. They are concentrated in the southwestern areas of Nigeria.

INGASSANA

An East African Shilluk people. The Ingassana, also spelled Ingessana, are concentrated in Ethiopia and Sudan, notably in the mountainous areas of the Ethiopian-Sudanese border.

INGESSANA, see INGASSANA

INQUA

The Inqua are a Southern African Hottentot group. They are concentrated in the south central regions of South Africa.

IQAR'AYEN, see also BERBER

The Iqar'ayen are Moroccan Rifian Berber group. They are concentrated in the northern Rif region of Morocco, notably in El Hoceima, Nador and Taza provinces.

IRAMBA

The Iramba, also Nilamba, are an East African Bantu-speaking people. Their language is known as Kiniramba. The Iramba are concentrated in Kenya and Tanzania, notably in the central border region that separates the two countries.

IRANGI, see also RANGI

The Irangi are a Southeast and East African people. Like their neighbors the Iramba, they are concentrated in the central border region that separates Kenya from Tanzania.

IRAQ, see SOMALI

IRAQW

The Iraqw are an East African people. Like their neighbors the Iramba and Irangi, they are concentrated in the central border region that separates Kenya from Tanzania, notably in the Mbulu and Hanang districts of the Arusha region in northern Tanzania. Their language, Iraqw, belongs to the Cushitic group of African languages, but with some features that are common to both Hamitic and Semitic languages.

The Iraqw are essentially agriculturalist-pastoralist people. Their society is composed of numerous patrilineal clans, each clan of which is named after its founder. Though they recognize kinship units, their "most important social and political groups are based on age and gender and local spacial relations."[210]

Though Christianity and Islam have won converts, many Iraqwe continue to cherish their traditional religion which rests on the belief in Lo'a, a female deity and Netlangw, or earth spirits. Lo'a is "associated with the sky, the sun and the rain," whereas Netlangw is believed to "live in stream beds and springs."[211]

IRIFIYEN, see **BERBER**

IRIGWE

The Irigwe, also called Idafan, Kwoll and Miango, are a West African people. They are concentrated in the central regions of Nigeria.

IROB, see **SAHO**

IRREGUENATEN, see **TAUREG**

IRU, see **NKOLE**

IRUA, see **ISHAN**

ISA, see **ISHAN**

ISAAQ, see **ISHAAK**

ISAFFEN, see also **BERBER**

The Isaffen are a Moroccan Berber group. They are concentrated in the Ishilhayen region of Morocco, notably in the Western High Atlas, the Sus Valley, and the Anti-Atlas areas of the country.

ISEKSAWEN, see also BERBER

A Moroccan Berber group. The Iseksawen are concentrated in the Ishilhayen region of Morocco, notably in the Western High Atlas, the Sus Valley, and the Anti-Atlas areas of the country.

ISHAAK, see SOMALI

An East African people. The Ishaak, also Isaaq and more correctly Ishaaq, are one of the main Somali tribes. They are concentrated in the northern regions of Somalia along the Gulf of Aden shores, as well as in Djibouti.

ISHAAQ, see **ISHAAK**

ISHAN

The Ishan, also Esa and Isa, are a West African Kwa-speaking people. They comprise numerous groups and subgroups the most important of which are the Ekpoma, Emu, Ewatto, Irua, Ugun and Urhu. The Ishan are concentrated in the southern regions of Nigeria.

ISHAWIYEN, see **BERBER**

ISHEKIRI, see **ITSEKIRI**

ISHILHAYEN, see **BERBER**

ISHINDE, see **LUNDA**

ISOKO

The Isoko are a West African people and one of Nigeria's ethnic groups. They are concentrated in the northwestern areas of the Niger Delta and speak a language belonging to the Kwa branch of the Niger-Congo family of African languages.

The Isoko are essentially an agrarian people. Their economic activities center on farming and fishing. They live in highly autonomous villages, with extended families forming their basic units. Each Isoko village is structured on the basis of different gender and age groups and is governed by a council of elders.

The Isoko practice polygamy and moreover, they recognize patrilineal lineages in matters relating to descent, succession and inheritance. Historical evidence does not suggest that they ever had centralized social or political organizations of their own. Though Christianity has won many converts among them, the Isoko continue to be impacted by their traditional religion which is based on the belief in a supreme god and his messengers, as well as in spirits, including ancestral spirits. Diviners continue to be active and are often visited for consultation on occasions of illness or death.

ISSA

The Issa people are one of East Africa's ethnic Somali tribes. They have a Hamitic origin and language and are predominantly Muslim.

The Issa are essentially a nomadic people. They are divided into three main groups: namely the Abgals, the Dalols and the Wardiqs. In their turn, these groups are divided into several tribes. Their supreme chief, the *ougaz*, is elected for life from the Wardiqs and resides in Ethiopia. The Issa constitute the largest ethnic group in the Republic of Djibouti, accounting for 60% of the country's population. They are concentrated in the southern areas of the country. Moreover, they constitute the sixth largest ethnic minority in Ethiopia, accounting for 4% of the total population.

ISU-AMA, see IGBO

ISU-ITEM, see IGBO

ISUKHA, see LUHYA

ISUKTAN, see also BERBER

The Isuktan are a Moroccan Berber group. They are concentrated in the Ishilhayen region of Morocco, notably in the Western High Atlas, the Sus Valley, and the Anti-Atlas areas of the country.

ITALIAN

People of Italian background and/or Italian expatriates or settlers who live in African countries that formerly fell to Italy's rule and/or influence. These people and/or their descendants are unevenly distributed in the following countries: Ethiopia, Libya, and Somalia.

ITESEN, see TAUREG

ITESO, see also TESO

The Iteso – also known as Ateso, Elgumi, Itesyo, Teso, or Wamia – are a Southern Nilotic people. They speak Ateso, an Eastern Sudanic language of the Chari-Nile branch of the Nilo-Saharan family of African languages. They are one of Uganda's and Kenya's ethnic groups. In Uganda, they constitute the second-largest ethnic group, and are highly concentrated in the eastern-central regions north of Lake Kyoga. Their neighbors include the Ganda, the Giso, the Karamojong, the Lango and the Soga peoples.

In Kenya, the Iteso represent a large segment of the country's non-Bantu-speaking people, and moreover, are related to the country's Turkana people. The Iteso are essentially a people of farmers. They engage in the production of miscellaneous agricultural products, including millet and cotton.

Historical evidence suggests that the Iteso used to live in what is presently modern Sudan. A few centuries ago they migrated to their present locations. By the middle of the nineteenth century they were fully established in what came to be regarded as Itesoland. Eventually, however, they fell to British rule, and in 1902, part of Itesoland (Western Kenya) was transferred from Uganda to Kenya. Since then, the Iteso people were divided into northern and southern segments.

The Iteso have lost many important aspects of their traditional culture and social and political organization. Three factors have contributed to this loss: the first is Ganda's conquest of their territory in the nineteenth century which culminated in the destruction of their institutions. Second, missionary activity led to the replacement of their traditional beliefs by Christian beliefs. The third factor is Iteso's traditional lack of political cohesiveness.

Traditionally, their activities revolved around the clan and was determined by councils of elders. Both features have virtually disappeared. Traditionally also, their religion was based on the belief in a supreme god, called *Akuj*, and in a god of misfortune, called *Edeke*. This belief was replaced by Christian tenets.

ITESYO, see **ITESO**

ITSEKIRI

The Itsekiri, also known as Ishekiri, Jekri or Owerri, are a West African people. They are one of Nigeria's ethnic groups. They are concentrated in the Niger Delta area of the country. Their language is a dialect of Yoruba and culturally, they are related to the Yoruba peoples, as well as the Edo, the Ijaw and the Urhobo. Their neighbors include the Edo and Ijaw peoples.

Itsekiri legends suggest that their "founder and first *olu* (king), came from Benin," and that "subsequent kings [were] descendants of the Oba of Benin."[212]

Traditionally, the *olu* governed with the advice of a council of lesser chiefs. Moreover, their society recognized both patrilineal and matrilineal lines in matters relating to descent, succession and inheritance.

The Itsekiri were among the first ethnic groups in Nigeria to get into contact with Europeans and to establish trade relations with them. During the nineteenth century, they served as intermediaries between the Portuguese (the first Europeans to come in contact with them) and inland peoples. Later, they provided the same services to other European traders, especially the British.

Prior to the abolition of the slave trade, the Itsekiri were active in the slave traffic but later on, they shifted their activity to the export of palm oil. In 1891, their country was placed under a British Oil Rivers Protectorate. Henceforth, the Itsekiri people were given a measure of indirect rule. In 1914, they were incorporated within the Nigerian federation which upon its independence on October 1, 1960, became the Federal Republic of Nigeria.

Currently, the Itsekiri people are essentially in the fishing and trading businesses. The discovery of oil in the Niger Delta in the 1980's has incited some Itsekiris to get involved in the oil industry and its services.

Though Christianity has won converts among them, the Itsekiri people continue to be impacted by their traditional religion, which rests on the belief in a number of gods including: *Oritse*, the supreme god and creator, *Umale Okun*, the god of the sea and *Ogun*, the god of iron and war, as well as in ancestral spirits and powers.

ITU, see IBIBIO

ITTU

The Ittu are an East African people. They are concentrated in southern Ethiopia. Groups of them, however, are also found in neighboring countries. The Ittu's neighbors include the Afar, the Galla, the Saho, the Somali, the Wallo and the Yaju peoples.

IWA

The Iwa, also known as Mashulumbwe, are a Southeast African people. They are concentrated in Malawi and Zambia.

IYALA

The Iyala, also Yala, are a West African people. They are concentrated in the southeastern regions of Nigeria. Their neighbors include the Boki, Idoma, Igede, Orri, Mbembe and Tiv peoples. The Iyala speak Kwa dialect and hence their language belongs to the Niger-Congo family of African languages.

IZARGUIEN, see MOOR and SAHRAWIS

IZIYYAN, see also BERBER

A Moroccan Berber group. The Iziyyan are concentrated in the Imazighen region of Morocco, notably in the Middle Atlas, Central High Atlas, Saghro massif, and the Presaharan oasis areas of the country.

JAA, see LOBI-DAGARTI

JAAJOAH, see NUER

JABARTI

An East African Muslim farming people. The Jabarti are concentrated in both Eritrea and Ethiopia. They are a Tigrinya-speaking people.

JAGA

These are a people of the African interior, who left their original homelands towards the middle of the sixteenth century and in their search for a new home, invaded the kingdom of Kongo in 1568, routing the kingdom's army, sackings its villages, looting its supplies, and killing many of its people.[213]

The Jaga people were eventually ousted from the Kongo, but with the help of the Portuguese. In acknowledging Portuguese help, the Kongo king acknowledged Portugal's suzerainty over his own kingdom.[214]

In the latter part of the sixteenth century, however, the Jaga directed their campaigns against the kingdom of Ngola. In the 1590s, they aligned themselves with the Ginga, Ndongo and Kongo to battle the Portuguese.

JAGGA, see CHAGGA

JAGHNIM, see KOFYAR

JAHANKE, see DIAKHANKE

JANHANKA, see DIAKHANKE

JANJERO

The Janjero are an East African, Sadama people. They are concentrated in southern Ethiopia.

JAR, see JARAWA

JARAWA

A cluster of West and Central African people. The Jarawa, also called Jar, comprise such groups as the Bankal and the Gingwak. They are concentrated in the central and eastern regions of Nigeria, as well as in a number of East Saharan states. They speak a language that belongs to the Benue-Congo branch of the Niger-Congo family of African languages. Their neighbors include the Afusare, Birom, Burum, Fula (Fulani), Hausa and Jerawa peoples.

JARSO

The Jarso are an East African Galla group. They are concentrated in southern Ethiopia.

JEKRI, see ITSEKIRI

JEN

The Jen are a West African people. They are concentrated in eastern Nigeria. Their neighbors include the Bachama, Mbula, Tangale, Tera, Vere and Wurkum peoples. The Jen speak a language that belongs to the Adamawa branch of the Niger-Congo family of African languages.

JERAWA

A cluster of West and Central African people. The Jerawa are concentrated in the central and eastern regions of Nigeria, as well as in a number of East Saharan states. They speak a language that belongs to the Afro-Asiatic family of African languages. Their neighbors include the Afusare, Birom, Hausa, Jarawa, Katab and Kurama peoples.

JERE, see also NGONI

The Jere, also called Ngoni, are a South African Nguni-speaking people who, in the late 1820's, were forced out of their lands in northern Zululand by the Mfecane. Under the leadership of Zwangendaba, the Jere people's plight led them to southern Mozambique, the Shona country, Lunda areas and west Lake Nyasa before they settled at the southern tip of Lake Tanganyika. In the course of their northward monumental migration, they began to be called Ngoni.

Skilled in Zulu fighting tactics, the Jere people were not only able to protect themselves, but also to expand their numbers by assimilating their captives and other people they conquered into their own society. This eventually helped them to establish major kingdoms of their own.[215]

In the new homeland, Zwangendaba built a seat for his people, which he called Mapupo.[216] Moreover, political unity was maintained by retaining the Ngoni clan structures and cultural values, while at the same time involving conquered peoples in the various activities of the kingdom and its society.[217] In this new society, ultimate loyalty was given to the new Ngoni nation.[218]

The death of Zwangendaba, the leader of the Ngoni nation, became the symbol of its unity. At Mapupo (about 1848), a successional crisis occurred. As a consequence, the Ngoni people were split into several major groups, the most important of which were the Tuta, Gwangara, Mpezeni Ngoni, Mombera Ngoni and Maseko.

The first group, the Tuta, moved northward along the eastern side of Lake Tanganyika. There, they conquered the Nyamwezi people of south Lake Victoria and established their own kingdom.

The second group, the Gwangara, moved eastward to the eastern side of Lake Nyasa (Malawi), establishing their control over the southeastern areas of what is presently modern Tanzania. Subsequently, the Gwangara split into two separate kingdoms.

The third and fourth groups comprised the main body of the Ngoni people, but split into two subgroups: one led by Mpezeni which moved westwardly into Bemba lands and then eastwardly to the Fort Jameson area in what is presently modern Zambia; the other led by Mombera moved southwardly and settled in the highlands west of Lake Nyasa (Malawi). In its turn, the latter group, the Mombera, witnessed a split. One of its subgroups moved southwardly and settled in the Dowa uplands in what is presently the southern region of the state of Malawi.

The fourth group, the Maseko, moved southwardly and established themselves in the Shire lands south of Lake Nyasa (Malawi).

All these kingdoms continued to exist separately until the later part of the nineteenth century, at which time they fell to European conquerors.

JIBANA

The Jibana people are an East African Mijikenda group. They are concentrated in Kenya and Tanzania, notably along their coasts. Their economic activities focus on agriculture, fishing, and trading. The Jibana speak a dialect of Mijikenda, a language that belongs to the Northeast Coastal Bantu languages.

JIE

The Jie are an East African Eastern Nilotic-speaking people. They are concentrated in northeastern Uganda, and hence, constitute one of Uganda's ethnic minorities.

The Jie are closely related to the Ugandan Karamojong and the Kenyan Turkana peoples. Their neighbors include the Acholi, the Alur, the Lango, the Madi and the Paluo peoples.

JIENG, see DINKA

JIJI

The Jiji are an East African Bantu cluster of peoples. They are concentrated in the west-central regions of Tanzania. Groups of them, however, can be found in Uganda.

JIKANY, see NUER

JIMAC, see NUER

JINDU, see KAMAKU

JITA

The Jita, also Echijita, are an East African people. They are concentrated in the northern regions of Tanzania, notably south of Lake Victoria. Groups of them are also found in Burundi.

JIYE

The Jiye are an East African Eastern Nilotic-speaking people. They are concentrated in northern Uganda and southern Sudan. The Jiye are closely related to the Teso, Iteso, Jie, Dodoz, Topoza, Nyanggatom Turkana peoples of Kenya and Uganda.

JJU, see KAJE

JOAKWA, see NYAKWAI

JOLA, see DOULA

JOLANGO, see LANGO

JONAM

The Jonam are a western Nilotic-speaking agricultural people. They are concentrated in the north central regions of Uganda, neighboring the Acholi, Langi (Lango) and Alur peoples. The Jonam are related to the Luo people of Kenya.

JONGN

The Jongn are an East Central and East African people. They are concentrated in the northeastern regions of the Democratic Republic of the Congo (Zaire).

JOPADHOLA

The Jopadhola are an East African people. They are concentrated in the west central border region that separates Kenya from Uganda.

JORTU, see KOFYAR

JUHAYYNA, see DJOHEINA

JUKUN

The Jukun are a West African people. They speak a language of the Benue-Congo branch of the Niger-Congo family of African languages and are concentrated in areas around Ibi, a river port on the east side of the Benue river and the state of Gongola in east central Nigeria. Their neighbors include the Angas, Bolewa, Daka, Fula, Kam, Tangale, Tera, Tiv and Wurkum peoples.

The Jukuns are probably the descendants of the fifteenth century Sudanic kingdom of Kororofa, the seat of which was in an area northeast of the present Jukun's territory. "Many royal families of Nigerian tribes trace their ancestry to the [Kororofa] area and to the Jukun royal family."[219]

Though the Jukun society is composed of an admixture of people of different social structures and organizations, the extended family is their basic unit. Moreover, most of its people recognize or practice polygamy. Further, the great majority of them are agriculturalists, with agriculture being their main economic activity. Small groups of them also engage in trading and salt extraction.

The Jukuns have their own kingdom and their own royal family. Traditionally, their king, called *Aka Uku*, combined both political and religious responsibilities, and moreover, was considered to possess divine attributes. Probably, the Junkun's motions of divine kinship and centralized government were of eastern and northern origins, primarily from Egypt and Meroe.[220] This however presumably changed in 1947, when their king became a member of northern Nigeria's house of chiefs.

In its modern history, the Kingdom of Jukun was not able to amass the power or riches of other West African kingdoms. Often, it was a tributary of other neighboring powers, such as the renowned Kanem-Bornu empire.

JUWASI, see !KUNG and SAN

JULA, see DYULA

KABA, see also SARA

The Kaba are one of Chad's non-Muslim Sara groups. Like other Sara groups, they speak a Central Sudanic language that belongs to the Nilo-Saharan family of African languages.

Like the Sara also, they live primarily in the southern regions of the country, notably between Lake Iro in the east and the Logone river in the west.

KABABISH

The Kababish are a nomadic Arab people in East Africa. They are concentrated in the Kordofan (Kurdufān) province in northern Sudan. They support a population of over 70,000.

The Kababish are essentially pastoralists who specialize in animal husbandry and animal products, such as hides. They trade their animal products with their neighbors. Some of them, however, are also engaged in agricultural activities, growing cotton, wheat, barley, corn, date palms and sugarcane along both banks of the Nile River that passes through their lands.

KABBA, see BUNU

KABORDA, see TOUBOU

KABRAS, see LUHYA

KABRE

These are a West African people and one of the ethnic minorities of Togo. They are concentrated in the northern parts of the country, especially in the eastern la Kara region. Their neighbors include the Basila, Konkomba, Moba, Naudeba, Somba and Tem peoples. The Kabre are a Gur-speaking Voltaic people. They are predominantly engaged in farming and animal husbandry.

KABULA

The Kabula are an East African people. They are concentrated in the southwestern regions of Uganda, primarily between Lake Victoria and Lake Albert. Their neighbors include the Koki, Nyamb, and Toro peoples.

KABYE

The Kabye people are one of the three major ethnic minorities of the Republic of Togo. They constitute the third largest group after the Ewe and Mina.

KABYLE, see BERBER

KACHE, see KAJE

KADA, see GUIDAR

KADARA

A West African people. The Kadara are concentrated in the north central regions of Nigeria. They speak a language that belongs to the Benue-Congo branch of the Niger-Congo family of African languages. Their neighbors include the Gbari, Jerawa, Katab, Koro, Kurama and Hausa peoples.

KADO, see also SONGHAI

The Kado people are one of the important ethnic groups of the Republic of Chad, who once formed an aristocracy. They live primarily in the Ouaddai region of the country.

KAFA, see KAFFA

KAFFA

The Kaffa, also spelled Kafa, are an East African people. They are concentrated in southern Sudan and southwestern Ethiopia. The Kaffa are part of the Kaffa-Sadama cluster of Ethiopian peoples.

KAFFICHO, see **KEFE-MOCHA**

KAFFIR, see **XHOSA**

KAFIE, see **XHOSA**

KAFIMA

The Kafima are a Southwest African people. They are concentrated in Angola, primarily in its east central regions. Their neighbors include the Kung (!Kung), Kwankhala, Mbwela, Ngangela, Nyemba, Sekele, and Tyokwe peoples.

KAGORO, see also **MANDE**

A West African Mande group. The Kagoro are concentrated in Mali and adjoining countries. Their neighbors include the Fula, Khasonke, Malinke and Soninke peoples. They speak a language that belongs to the Mande group of African languages.

KAGU, see **GU**

KAGULU, see **KAGURU**

KAGURU

The Kaguru, also known as Guru, Kagulu, Northern Kiningo, and Sagala, are an East African people. They are concentrated west of the Mkundi and Chogoali rivers, in Kaguruland, known as Ukaguru, in the east central regions of Tanzania. Their neighbors include the Masai, the Ngulu, the Kwere, the Luguru, the Sagara and the Gogo peoples.

Their legends suggest that they migrated to their present land from the northwest. Kaguru land is partly lowlands, partly mountains and partly plateau. Historically, it served as a major caravan route between the Indian Ocean ports and the great inland lakes of Central Africa.[221]

The Kaguru are essentially agriculturalists. Their livelihood is directly from the land, which they classify into four general types: garden lands (*malulu*), valley lands (*malolo*), fields (*migunda*) and bushfields (*miteme*).

The rights to tracts of land are granted to Kaguru individuals by headmen. These rights are normally retained as long as the land is cultivated. Failure to use a tract of land for three consecutive years constitutes a cause for revoking these rights and returning the land to common holdings.[222]

The Kaguru people are divided into many exogamous matrilineal clans. Membership in these clans determines a Kaguru's "social life, including marriage, religious activity, and access to land and political [status]."[223]

In their belief system, the closest bond that exists between persons is that between a mother and her children. In their belief system also, children share common blood with their mother but not with their father.

The Kaguru are noted for their wood crafts and fine pottery works. Historical evidence suggests that they developed their own iron smelting techniques in the past.

KAJE

The Kaje, also called Jju and Kache, are a West African people. Their main concentrations are in the north central regions of Nigeria.

KAKA, see BAYA

KAKWA

These are one of Sudan's, Uganda's and Democratic Republic of the Congo's (Zaire's) tribal people. They speak an Eastern Sudanic language of the Chari-Nile branch of the Nilo-Saharan family of African languages.

In Sudan, they are concentrated in the Gondokoro area, near Juba, the southwestern region of the country. In Uganda, they live in the northwestern areas. In Zaire, they are located in the north eastern region of the country. The Kakwa are predominantly Muslim.

The Kakwa support a relatively sedentary type of society. They live in scattered villages and their main economic activities center on farming, cattle raising, and hunting. Their social organization is essentially tribal, patrilineal and non-hierarchical in nature.

KALABARI

The Kalabari are the people of the Niger delta. They are concentrated in Rivers State in Nigeria. The Kalabari are noted for their respect for their ancestral spirits.[224]

KALIA

The Kalia are one of the main Kuri subgroups in Chad. They speak Yedina, a Buduma dialect. Like other Kuri groups, they live along the eastern shores of Lake Chad.

KALLAMEIDA, see KURA

KALLAMIA, see YAKUDI

KALANGA, see also SHONA

A Southern Bantu-speaking Shona group. The Kalanga – also known as Bakalanga, Kalaka and Vakalanga – are one of Botswana's and Zimbabwe's ethnic minorities. They are concentrated in the southwestern areas of Zimbabwe and eastern regions of Botswana. Groups of them, however, live in Mozambique. Together with the Basarwa and Kgalagadi, they account for 4% of Botswana's total population. In Zimbabwe, they account for about 5% of the country's total population.

KALENJIN

The Kalenjin are a Nilo-Hamitic people of Kenya, Tanzania and Uganda. They are a Nilotic people, who are highly concentrated in the region lying between the Rift Valley and Lake Victoria. They speak an Eastern Sudanic language, called Kalenjin, which is of the Chari-Nile branch of the Nile-Saharan family of African languages. They comprise several related groups, the most important of which are the Endo, Keiyo, Kipsikis (Kipsigis), Kony, Marakwet, Nandi, Okiek, Sebei, Terik, Suk (also known as Pokot and Sukuma), Sabaot, Tatoga, Tenik and Tugen. The Kalenjin are concentrated in Kenya, Tanzania and Uganda.

The Kalenjin society is functionally divided into several groups including boys, warriors and elders, and moreover, it is supported by a well-developed system of age-sets. Though Christianity has won a foothold among them, many Kalenjin continue to uphold their traditional beliefs which center on a watchful but distant god.

Currently, the Kalenjin are Kenya's fourth largest ethnic minority, accounting for 11% of the country's total population. In Tanzania, where they are known as Sukuma, they are the largest ethnic group, accounting for 13% of the population.

KALIA

The Kalia are one of the main Kuri subgroups in Chad. They speak Yedina, a Buduma dialect. Like other Kuri groups, they live along the eastern shores of Lake Chad.

KALLAMEIDA, see KURA

KALLAMIA, see YAKUDI

KALUM, see BAGA

KAM

The Kam are a West African people. They are concentrated in eastern Nigeria and Western Cameroon. Their language belongs to the Adamawa branch of the Niger-Congo family of African languages. The Kam neighbors include the Daka, Jukun and Mumuye peoples.

KAMADJA, see MOOR and TOUBOU

KAMAKU

A West African people. The Kamaku, also known as Jindu, are concentrated in the Western regions of Nigeria.

KAMANGA, see TUMBUKO

KAMASIA, see also TUGEN and KALENJIN

An East African Tugen people, a Kalenjin group. They are concentrated in Kenya and Uganda, notably along escarpments in the Rift Valley region, and speak a dialect of Kalenjin, a Southern Nilotic language that belongs to the Eastern Sudanic family of African languages. The Kamasia are semipastoralist people.

KAMBA

The Kamba, also known as Akamba, are an East and Central African Bantu-speaking people who are closely related to the Kikuyu and the Kongo peoples. They speak Kikamba and Kiswahili and are highly concentrated in the highlands of the central Kenyan plateau between Mt. Kilimanjaro and Mt. Kenya, especially in the Machakos and Kitui districts of Kenya, the northern regions of Tanzania, and the eastern regions of the Congo. Groups of them are also located in Angola and the Democratic Republic of Congo (Zaire). In Kenya, they are the fifth largest ethnic minority, accounting for approximately 11% of the country's total population.

The modern history of the Kamba people can be traced back to the sixteenth century, at which time they lived in the Kilimanjaro plains. Threatened by the Masai, they migrated northeastwardly in the early part of the eighteenth century, and eventually, settled in their present areas. For many years, the Kamba engaged in trading ivory, medicines and food products. In the late nineteenth century they fell to British rule and in the 1960s acquired their independence within the modern states of Kenya and Tanzania.

Social organization in Kamba society is based on patrilineal clans (*mbae*), which are further divided into families (*muvia*). Each clan determines its own symbol or totem. A Kamba village is actually a village of extended families that are related in some way.[225] In their social structures there are no chiefs.[226] Individuals, however, are organized in age grades, with those in the eldest age grade forming their governing councils.

The Kamba are essentially agriculturists. Their main economic activities focus on farming and animal husbandry. In the past, however, they succeeded in monopolizing the coastal trade routes of what is presently modern Kenya.

Traditionally, the Kamba's religion was similar to that of the Kikuyu people. It was based on the belief in the existence of a high god, called *Ngai*, and ancestor spirits, or *aimu*. Though now predominantly Christian, they continue to incorporate some traditional religious thought into their Christianity.

The most famous artistic expression of the Kamba are their woodcarvings. Kamba are also fond of singing and poetry, which incorporates a mixture of traditional and Christian elements. Some of them "file a triangular space between their two upper middle teeth as a form of body decoration."[227]

KAMBARI, see **KAMBERI**

KAMBATA, see **KEMBAT**

KAMBATTA, see **KEMBAT**

KAMBE

The Kambe people are an East African Mijikenda group. They are concentrated in Kenya and Tanzania, notably along the coasts of both countries. Their economic activities focus on agriculture, fishing, and trading. The Kambe speak a dialect of Mijikenda, a language that belongs to the Northeast Coastal Bantu languages.

KAMBERI

The Kamberi, also called Kambari, are a cluster of West African ethnic groups. They are highly concentrated in the west central areas of Nigeria, particularly in the state of Kwara. Their major neighbors include the Bargu (Borgu), Busa, Dakarkari, Fula (Fulani), Gbari, Hausa, Kamuku, Nupe, Reshe and Yoruba peoples. The Kamberi speak a language belonging to the Benue-Congo branch of the Niger-Congo family of African languages.

KAMI

The Kami are an East African people. They are concentrated in the northeastern coastal lowland regions of Tanzania. Their neighbors include such ethnic groups as the Wazaramo, the Doe, the Kutu, the Kwere, the Ndengereko and the Rufiji.

KAMUKU

The Kamuku are a West African people. They are concentrated in the west central areas of Nigeria, particularly in the state of Kwara. Their major neighbors include the Dakarkari, Gbari, Hausa, Kamberi (Kambari) and Nupe peoples. The Kamuku speak a language belonging to the Benue-Congo branch of the Niger-Congo family of African languages.

KANA

The Kana, also known as Khana and Ogoni, are a West African people. They are concentrated in east central Benin and west central Nigeria. Their neighbors include the Ak Posso, Bono, Nanumba, and Wala peoples. The Kana are a Chadic-speaking people.

KANAM

The Kanam, also known as the Koenoem, are a West African people. They are concentrated in the Plateau State in Nigeria.

KANEMBA, see also KANURI

The Kanemba – also known as Beriberi, Boro, Bornu, Kanembou and

Kanembu – are a subgroup of the Kanuri people. They live primarily in Cameroon, Chad, Niger and Nigeria. Their main concentration is in the Lake Chad region, adjoining the Buduma, Kanuri, Kwayam, Mabar, Manga and Shuwa peoples. The Kanemba are a sedentary people of Arabic origin and are predominantly Muslim. They speak an original Saharan dialect of the Saharan group of African languages, as well as Arabic.[228]

The modern history of this people is traced back to the ninth century, at which time they established the Kanem kingdom with Saif as their first *mai* (king) and N'jimi as their capital. At the end of the eleventh century, the kingdom's royal family, the Saifawa, became Muslim, and moreover, its imperial territory expanded to cover the areas stretching from Kano in Nigeria to western Sudan.[229]

The Saifawa's adoption of Islam was initiated by *Mai* umme Jilne and later fostered by his successors. As a consequence, the kingdom's destiny was linked with that of the Muslim world.

Around the middle of the thirteenth century, the Kanem kingdom expanded southwest of Chad into Bornu. Following the fall of Kanem to the Bulala late in the fourteenth century, *Mai* Umar ibn Idris moved the capital to Bornu. Thereupon, the kingdom remained stagnant until the end of the fifteenth century, at which time it resurged (as the Kanem-Bornu Empire) under the leadership of Ali Ghaji (1472-1504) and his son, Idris Katakarmabi (1504-1526). It reached its zenith under *Mai* Idris Alooma (1571-1603).

The Kanem kingdom endured for about one thousand years. It started to decline in the eighteenth century. Its sustained decline, however, did not hinder its resistance to the Sokoto Fulani-led Islamic *jihad* of 1812. Under the leadership of al-Kanemi, its kingdom was able not only to check the Fulani expansion in the direction of Bornu, but also was able to sustain itself into the twentieth century. During this time, parts of its territory fell to British rule and subsequently incorporated within the modern state of Nigeria.

As in the past, the Kanemba continued to have a centralized political structure based in their "capital city" of Maiduguri in Nigeria. Their main economic activities focus on farming, animal husbandry and trading. Additionally, they continue to maintain close family and commercial connections with the Kanuri in Nigeria, as well as with their Arab, Boudouma and Toubou neighbors.

KANEMBOU, see **KANEMBA**

KANEMBU, see **KANEMBA**

KANGABA, see **MALINKE**

KANGA-KONE, see also **SOTHO**

The Kanga-Kone are a Sotho group of people. They are concentrated in the Lebowa, formerly one of the Black homelands in South Africa. Now, they are an integral part of the country.

Like other Sotho, they are a southern African people, speak Sesotho, a Bantu language and engage in agriculture and animal husbandry. Their settlements are characterized "by scattered hamlets of circular huts with mud and wattle or stone walls surmounted by a conical, thatched roof."[230] In their social patterns, most Kanga-Kone recognize patrilineal lineages and continue to be impacted by their traditional religious beliefs.

KANGO

The Kango are one of the many Pygmy people of equatorial Africa. Originally, they inhabited the tropical rain forest, in what is now within the Republic of Congo. Subsequently, however, they moved to other countries neighboring the Congo Basin, including the Burundi, Cameroon, Central African Republic, Democratic Republic of the Congo (Zaire), Equatorial Guinea, Gabon, Rwanda, Sudan and Uganda. They are essentially hunters, foragers and potters.

KANOA, see **YAKUDI**

KANONGESHA, see **LUNDA**

The Kanongesha are a Bantu-speaking people whose origin is traced back to the Congo, where they were part of the Lunda kingdom and later empire, which was founded in the later part of the fifteenth century and endured until late in the nineteenth century. Over time, they broke away from the central Lunda kingdom in the Kapanga district of the southern Congo to establish their own kingdom. Currently, the Kanongesha are among Angola's, Democratic Republic of the Congo's (Zaire's) and Zambia's ethnic groups.

Traditionally, the main economic activities of the Kanongesha people centered on food gathering, hunting and trading. Traditionally also, their religion rested on the belief in a supreme being, who was either a sky god or an earth god.[231]

KANOURI, see KANURI

KANTANA, see MAMA

KANUM

The Kanum are a Central African people. They are concentrated in Cameroon, Chad and Nigeria, primarily south of Lake Chad. Their neighbors include the Fulani, Kapsiki, Mandara, Matakam, and Shuwa peoples.

KANURI

The Kanuri people, known also as Kanouri or Beri Beri, are one of West Africa's Sudanic-speaking peoples. They live in several West African states, notably Chad, Cameroon, Niger and Nigeria. Their neighbors include the Bade, Bolewa, Bura, Hausa, Kanemba, Karekare, Kwayam, Mabar, Mandara, Manga, Margi, Ngizim, Tazarawa, Tera, Shuwa and Wakura peoples. The Kanuri are Sunni Muslims, adhering to the Malikite school of Muslim jurisprudence. Their language, Kanuri, is a Sudanic language, belonging to the Saharan branch of the Nilo-Saharan family of African languages.

The Kanuri are divided into numerous groups, the most important of which are the Dogara (Dagara), the Buduma, the Kanemba (Kanembu) and the Mober. They are mainly traders and agriculturalists with a centralized political structure based on an emirate and a hierarchical social structure. On top of the hierarchy is the *shehu* (Shaykh), the political and religious leader of all Kanuri. Below him are members of his royal court, notables and ordinary Kanuris. The structure of the Kanuri society "closely resembles that of the Hausa," but is a little more egalitarian than that of the Hausa.[232]

The Kanuri people developed their own kingdom, the kingdom of Bornu, during the eleventh century. The core of their kingdom was in what is presently the state of Borno (formerly Bornu) of Nigeria, and the name of their kingdom meant "Home of the Berbers."[233] Eventually, however, their kingdom became a tributary province of the renowned Kanem Empire. Seizing the opportunity of the decline of the Kanem Empire, they reasserted their independence in the later part of the fourteenth century. Under the leadership of the Saifawa family, they established a new empire, Bornu, southwest of Lake Chad. In the early sixteenth century, the Saifawa spread their control over the Kanem Kingdom, placing it under their protection. With this achievement, the Kanuri people signaled the rise of the Kanem-Bornu Empire, which dominated the political and commercial scene in West Africa, reaching its zenith in the second half of the sixteenth century during the reign of Mai Idris Alawma (1571-1603).

In 1808, Birni Ngazargamu, the capital of the Bornu Kingdom was captured by the renowned Fulani *jihad*. The event prompted the *mais* of Bornu to establish another capital at Kukawa in 1814. With the help of Muhammad al-Kanami, (also known as al-Amin), a member of the Bornu royal family and a renowned Muslim scholar, the Fulani assault was repelled in the 1820's. Henceforth, however, the Kanuri kingdom started to witness an accelerated decline caused by internal division and external assaults.

The internal division was exemplified in the succession crisis that faced the kingdom after the death of *Sefawa Mai* Ali Dalatami in 1846. The crisis was resolved when 'Umar bin Muhammad al-Kanami proclaimed himself

Shehu of Bornu.

The external assaults were exemplified by Bornu's failure to defend itself against the forces of Rabih al-Zubayr, a Sudanese militant. As a consequence, Kukawa was destroyed in 1893, forcing *Shehu* 'Umar to move his headquarters to Dikwa. Al-Zubayr's assault continued until he was killed in a battle with French forces in 1900. With the help of the French, *Shehu* 'Umar resumed his rule from Dikwa.

The external assaults were also exemplified in the partitioning of the Bornu kingdom by the French, British, and German governments. As a consequence of this partition, *Shehu* Bukar Garbai fled to Monguno, Northern Nigeria, in 1902, where he was recognized by the British colonial government as *Shehu* of British Bornu. In 1904, *Shehu* Bukar relocated the seat of the Kingdom of Bornu to Kukawa and in 1907 to Yerwa. With the partitioning of Bornu's territory between the British and French, the Bornu kingdom was incorporated within northern Nigeria and in 1967, it became part of the Borno state, Nigeria's largest state.

The Kingdom of Bornu is still in existence and its *shehu* is acknowledged as the most prominent Muslim leader in Nigeria second only to the Fulani's Sultan of Sokoto.

Currently, the Kanuri people account for 4.3% of Niger's total population and are highly concentrated in the southeastern areas of the country. Additionally, they are the fifth largest minority in Nigeria after the Hausa, the Fulani, the Yoruba and the Igbo (Ibo), constituting the largest portion of the population of Borno state in the northeastern part of the country. In Cameroon, they are concentrated in the Adamawa Plateau, whereas in Chad they live in the semi-arid tropical zone of the country.

The Kanuri people are essentially agriculturalists and traders. They are actively engaged in growing miscellaneous agricultural products, as well as in fishing, livestocks, and salt mining. Their main exports include cotton, peanuts, millet, sesame, corn, onions, gum arabic, cattle, hides, skins and leather products. Their society is based on the household. As Ronald Cohen observes, in the Kanuri society, the

> everyday business of getting a living is organized within a

household, and a series of households linked through their household heads can form larger economic organizations for productive or trading purposes. Family life, the crucible of human society, is of course centered within the household. Finally the modes of behavior that one requires in order to adapt to everyday social relationships in the society are learned within the household.[234]

KAOKOVELDER

The Kaokovelder are a Southwest African people. They constitute one of Namibia's small ethnic minorities.

KAONDE

The Kaonde – also referenced as Bakahonde, Bakaonde, Kaundi, Kawonde, Kunda and Luba Kaonde, are a Southwest and Southeast Bantu-speaking African people. They are concentrated in the Democratic Republic of the Congo (Zaire) and Zambia.

KAPCHEPKENDI, see OKIEK

KAPLELACH, see OKIEK

KAPSIGI, see KAPSIKI

KAPSIKI

The Kapsiki, also spelled Kapsigi, are a West African Kirdi group. They are concentrated in the northern regions of Cameroon and Nigeria, and speak a language that belongs to the Afro-Asiatic family of African languages. The Kapsiki neighbors include the Gisiga, Gude, Margi and Matakam peoples.

KAPUTIEI, see MASAI

KARA, see **BAYA** and **SARA**

KARABORO

A West African Senufo group. The Karaboro, also known as Karakora, are concentrated in the northern regions of the Ivory Coast, as well as in Southwestern Burkina Faso and southern Mali. Groups of them, however, are also located in adjoining countries.

The Komono speak a language that belongs to the Voltaic branch of the Niger-Congo family of African languages. Their neighbors include the Dorossié, Dyula, Guin, Komono, Tusyan and Wara peoples.

KARAGO

The Karago are a West African people. They are one of Mali's and Mauritania's ethnic groups. The Karago are concentrated in the border areas that separate the two countries. Their neighbors include the Hodh and Kassonke peoples.

KARAKORA, see **KARABORO**

KARAMOJONG

The Karamojong – also known as Bakaramoja, Ikaramojong, and Karimojon – are an East African southern Nilotic-speaking people. They are concentrated in the eastern plateau region of Uganda along the Ugandan-Kenyan borders, notably in the Karamoja region. Hence, they are one of Uganda's large ethnic minorities. Their neighbors include the Acholi, the Gisu, the Lango and the Iteso (Teso) peoples.

The Karamojong are closely related to the Ugandan Jie and the Kenyan Turkana peoples. They are essentially a pastoral people with cattle playing a key role in their culture. Their social and political structures are based on families, clans and age sets.

KARANGA, see also SHONA

A southern Bantu-speaking people. The Karanga, also known as Vakanga, are probably the ancestors of the modern Shona-speaking peoples of Mashonaland.[235] To all evidence, they originated in the Congo basin and subsequently contributed o Zimbabwe's civilization which is reflected in its stone walls, as well as to the establishment of the earliest states that appeared in it during the ninth century.[236] Currently, the Karanga are one of Zimbabwe's large ethnic groups. They account for about 22% of the country's total population. They are divided into some 15 subgroups.

KARE, see also TOPOSA

The Kare people are a Central and East African people. Their main concentrations are in Chad, Central African Republic, Ethiopia and Sudan.

KAREKARE

The Karebare are a West African Kanuri people and one of Nigeria's ethnic minorities. They are concentrated in the northeastern parts of Nigeria in what is presently the state of Borno (formerly Bornu). Their neighbors include the Auyokawa, Bolewa, Kanuri and Ngizim peoples. The Karekare speak a language that belongs to the Afro-Asiatic family of African languages. They are essentially an agriculturalist people.

KAREMBOLA

The Karembola, also known as Caremboules in French, are a Madagascaran people. Historical evidence suggests that they have been among the early inhabitants of the southwestern semiarid Androy region of Madagascar. Presently, Androy is considered a Tandroy land and is settled by Malagasy people of diverse origins, including the Bara, Mahafale, Sakalave, Tandroy proper and Tanosy peoples.

KARIA

The Karia are one of the Chadian Kuri subgroups. They speak Yedina, a Buduma dialect. Like other Kuri groups, they live along the eastern shores of Lake Chad.

KARIMOJON, see KARAMOJONG

KASAI

A West Central Bantu-speaking people. The Kasai are one of Democratic Republic of the Congo (Zaire's) ethnic groups. They are concentrated in the southwestern areas of the country, notably in the vicinity of the Kasai river basin and those of its tributaries.

KASONKE

A West African people. The Kasonke, also spelled Kassonke, are one of Mali's and Mauritania's major ethnic groups. They are concentrated in the border areas that separate the two countries. Their neighbors include the Hodh and Karago peoples.

KASOVA, see GUSII

KASSONKE, see KASONKE

KASSOWA, see GUSII

KATAB

The Katab, also called Atyap, are a cluster of West African peoples. They are concentrated in the north central regions of Nigeria, especially in the State of Kaduna. They speak a language that belongs to the Benue-Congo branch of the Niger-Congo family of African languages. Their neighbors include the Jerawa, Kadara, Koro, Kurama, Mada and Yeskwa peoples.

KAU-EN

A Southwest African Khoisan group. The Kau-en are concentrated in the northeastern regions of the Republic of Namibia.

KAUMA

The Kauma people are an East African Mijikenda group. They are concentrated in Kenya, notably along its coast. Groups of them, however, can also be found in Tanzania. Their economic activities focus on agriculture, fishing, and trading. The Kauma speak a dialect of Mijikenda, a language that belongs to the Northeast Coastal Bantu languages.

KAUNDI, see **KAONDE**

KAVANGA, see **KAVANGO**

KAVANGO

The Kavango, also known as Kavanga and Okavango, are a Bantu-speaking people. They constitute one of Namibia's ethnic minorities and live in the northern regions of the country. They account for about 10% of Namibia's population. The Kavango people are divided into a number of subgroups. Some of these groups live in Angola. Their major subgroups include the Kwangari, Kwangali, Geiriku, Mbukushu, Mbunza and Sambyu.

KAVIRONDO, see **LUO**

KAWAARA, see **SONGHAI**

KAWAHLA

The Kawahla people are one of Central and East African Arab groups. Their main concentrations are in the west central areas of Sudan. Kawahla groups are also found in adjoining countries, especially Chad.

KAWONDE, see **KAONDE**

KAYLA, see **FALASHA**

KAZEMBE, see also **LUNDA**

The Kazembe are a Bantu-speaking people whose origin is traced back to the Congo, where they were part of the Lunda kingdom and later empire. The kingdom was founded in the later part of the fifteenth century and endured until late in the nineteenth century. Over time, they broke away from the central Lunda kingdom in the Kapanga district of the southern Congo to establish their own kingdom.

Historical evidence suggests that the Kazembe kingdom was founded in the later part of the eighteenth century and endured until 1890, when it fell to eastern tribes. It was the largest and most organized of Lunda kingdoms.

Between 1740 and 1890, it was governed by kings carrying the title *mwata kazembe*. Aside from its founder, Kazembe I, its most important kings were Kazembe II, called Kaniembo, and Kazembe IV, called Kibangu. Under Kazembe II who ruled from 1740 to 1760, the kingdom's territory was expanded and conquered peoples were incorporated within the kingdom. On the other hand, under Kibangu, who ruled from 1805 to 1850, trading relations with the Portuguese in the Atlantic and the Arabs in East Africa and the Indian Ocean were encouraged and expanded.

The Kazembe kingdom reached its zenith towards the end of the nineteenth century, at which time it commanded control over the Shaba region in what is presently the modern state of Democratic Republic of the Congo (Zaire), as well as parts of northern Zambia.

Currently, the Kazembe are among Angola's, Democratic Republic of the Congo (Zaire's) and Zambia's ethnic groups.

Traditionally, the main economic activities of the Luvale people centered on food gathering, hunting and trading. Traditionally also, their religion rested on the belief in a supreme being, who was either a sky or an earth god.[237]

KE

A southern African people. The Ke are concentrated in the southern regions of Botswana.

KEAKA

These are one of Cameroon's over 100 ethnic groups. The Keaka are a Bantu-speaking people. They are concentrated in the Bamenda region of the country.

KEBBAWA

The Kebbawa are a West African people and one of the Hausa subgroups. They are concentrated in Nigeria.

KEBU (Togo and Ghana)

A West African people. The Kebu, also known as Akebu, are a Kwa-speaking group. They live primarily in the central areas of Togo. However, groups of them can also be found in Ghana. Their neighbors include the Akpose (Akposo), Krachi, Lefana and Tribu peoples.

KEBU (Uganda)

A Sudanic-speaking people. The Kebu are one of Uganda's ethnic groups. They live in the northern areas of the country.

KECHERDA, see TOUBOU

KEDE

The Kede are a Southwest African people. Their main concentration is in the Republic of Namibia.

KEDI

The Kedi are an East African Bantu-speaking people. They are highly concentrated in eastern Uganda and western Kenya. Their neighbors include the Gisu, Iteso, Karamojong and Soga peoples.

KEDJIM

One of Cameroon's ethnic minorities. The Kedjim are concentrated in the Northwest Province. Their economic activities center on farming.

KEEKONYUKIE, see MASAI

KEFA, see KEFA-MOCHA

KEFA-MOCHA

The Kefa-Mocha, also called Kafficho and Keffa, are an East African people. They are concentrated in southern Ethiopia, primarily in the Kefa Province.

KEFFA, see **KEFA-MOCHA**

KEFFICHO, see **KEFA-MOCHA**

KEIYO, see also **KALENJIN**

An East African Kalenjin group. Their main concentrations are in Kenya, Tanzania and Uganda, notably along escarpments in the Rift Valley system. They speak a dialect of Kalenjin, a Southern Nilotic language of the Eastern Sudanic family of African languages. The Keiyo comprise several groups, including the Elegyo. They are a semipastoralist people.

KEL ADRAR, see **TAUREG**

KEL AHAGGAR, see **TAUREG**

KEL AJJER, see **TAUREG**

KELANGI, see **RANGI**

KEL ANTESSAR, see **TAUREG**

KELE

The Kele are a West Central African people. They live in the central regions of Cameroon. Their neighbors include the Kota, Makaa, and Shake peoples.

KEL GERES, see **TAUREG**

KELIKO

A Central and Eastern African people. The Keliko are a Nilotic people. They speak Keliko, an Eastern Sudanic language which is closely related to those of their neighbors the Bale (Lendu), the Logo, the Lugbara and the Madi peoples. The Keliko are concentrated in Sudan, Uganda and the Democratic Republic of the Congo (Zaire).

KEL NAN, see TAUREG

KEL RELA, see TAUREG

KEL TADEMAKET, see TAUREG

KEL TAMAJAQ, see TAUREG

KEMBAT

The Kembat – also known as Kambata, Kambatta, Kembatta, and Kemata – are an East African agricultural people. Their main concentration is in Ethiopia, notably in its southwestern regions. The Kembat are a Sadama subgroup.

KEMBATA, see KEMBAT

KEMNANT

The Kemnant are an East African people. They are one of the Agaw subgroups. They live in the central and northern regions of Ethiopia.

KENE, see NUPE

KENGA

A Central and East African people. The Kenga are concentrated in the Hadjeray region of Chad. Groups of them, however, can also be found in neighboring countries, including Nigeria. They trace their origin to the Darfur region of Sudan.

KENGAWA

The Kengawa, also known as the Kiengawa, Kyengawa, and Tienga, are a West African Muslim people. They are concentrated in the northwestern regions of Nigeria.

KENUZE

The Kenuze are one of the Nubian Egyptian subgroups. They trace their origin to Beni Kanz, an Arab group. The Kenuze used to live in the vicinity of Aswan. The construction of the Aswan Dam led to their relocation to newly built cities.

KENYANG

A West Central African group. The Kenyang live in the Southwest Province of the Cameroon. Their neighbors include the Denya, Ejagham and Mundani peoples.

KENYI

An East African Bantu-speaking people. The Kenyi, also known as Lukenyi, live in the area of Lake Kyoga in central Uganda.

KERA

The Kera are one of Chad's many ethnic groups. They live to the east and south of Lake Tikun.

KERANG, see ANGA

KERERE, see KEREWE

KEREWE

The Kerewe, also called Kerere, are an East African people. They are concentrated in the northwestern regions of Tanzania, notably south of Lake Victoria.

KETE

The Kete are one of the Luba subgroups. They are concentrated in the Democratic Republic of the Congo (Zaire), primarily in the southeastern regions of the country.

KETO, see YORUBA

KETU, see YORUBA

KEYO

The Keyo, also known as the Elgeyo and Keiyu, are an East African people. They live in Kenya, notably in the Elgeyo-Marakwet District.

KGAFELA KGATLA, see KGATLA

KGAKGA, see PEDI

KGALAGADI

The Kgalagadi, also known as the Bakgalagadi, are a Sotho-Tswana speaking people. They are a cluster of ethnic groups which includes the Balaongwe (BaLaongwe), Kgwatheng (Bakgwatheng), Ngologa (Bangologa), Phaleng (BaPheleng), and Shaga (BaShaga) peoples. The Kgalagadi are concentrated in the Kweneng and Southern districts of Botswana. Together with the Kalanga and Basarwa, they account for approximately 4% of the country's total population. They are concentrated in the southwestern areas of the country, notably in the Kgalagadi administrative district.

KGATLA

The Kgatla are a Southwest African people. They are a Southern Bantu-speaking group. The Kgatla are concentrated in the south central regions of Africa, especially in Botswana, and are related to the Tswana people. They are divided into several groups, including the Kgafela Kgatla.

KGWATHENG, see KGALAGADI

KHANA, see KANA

KHARA

The Khara (!Kara) are a Southwest African people. They are concentrated in the southwestern regions of Botswana.

KHASONKE, see also MANDE

A West African Mande group. The Khasonke, also spelled Khassonké, are concentrated in western Mali and adjoining countries, notably Mauritania and Senegal. Their neighbors include the Fula, Kagoro, Malinke and Soninke peoples. They speak a language that belongs to the Mande group of African languages.

KHASSONKÉ, see KHASONKE

KHAU-GOAN

A Southwest African Khoisan group. The Khau-Goan are concentrated in the northwestern regions of the Republic of Namibia.

KHAYO

The Khayo are an East African Bantu-speaking people. They are one of the Luhya subgroups. The Khayo live in Kenya and Uganda, primarily north of Lake Victoria.

KHENI

The Kheni are a Southeast African-Malagasy people. They are concentrated in Mozambique, notably in its southeastern regions. However, some of their groups are also found in adjoining countries. Their neighbors include the Hananwa, Ndeble, Toka, and Venda peoples.

KHOEK-HOE, see **KHOISAN**

KHOI, see **KHOISAN**

KHOIKHOI, see **KHOISAN**

KHOIKHOIN, see **KHOISAN**

KHOISAN

The Khoisan, also called Auen, Khoek-hoe, Khoi, Khoikhoi, Khoikhoin, Hottentots and "Hotnot", are a southern African people. They are located in the southern African states of Botswana, Namibia, Angola and South Africa. They are the African people that Europeans first encountered in South Africa. They were given the name Hottentot and its abbreviated version "Hotnot" by early Dutch, and later other Europeans, who settled in South Africa, most probably for the clicks in their language. Both names, however, "have acquired derogatory connotations, and the preferred terms "Khoi" or "Khoikhoi"... are most commonly used in the literature today."[238]

The Khoisan are descendants of an ancient people who once inhabited a long stretch of land that ran from Ethiopia southward to the Cape of Good Hope. Their modern history, however, dates back to the fourteenth century, at which time they migrated from Ethiopia and settled in southern African areas that were suitable for their hunting and gathering tradition. In the sixteenth century, the Khoisan started to lose their new land and independence to European traders, especially the Dutch and British among them.[239]

Originally, the Khoisan were divided into numerous groups, each of which had its own distinctive name, namely that of its own clan. But whether they were Chochoqua, Goringhaiqua, or Gorachoqua, they all called themselves Khoikhoin, a term that means "men of men."[240]

Currently, however, they are divided into two main groups: namely, the Nama and the Orlams. They speak Khoikhoin languages, also known as Hottentot languages, which are closely related to the Central San languages. Most notable of these languages are the Nama (Naman) and

!Kora (Korana).

The Khoisan are nomadic hunters and gatherers, but their lifestyle is being threatened by excessive intermarriage and overpopulation by their neighbors. There is another part of the Khoisan nation that relies on herding and is heavily influenced by Europeans.

Khoisan families are nomadic most of the year and gather once a year with other nomadic families to celebrate entrances into adulthood, to tell stories and to arrange marriages. Families are led by the father and larger annual groupings are led by an elder. Yet Khoisan society is basically egalitarian. Men are responsible for hunting, while women are in charge of "packing" for travel and gathering roots and other edibles found around the camp. Women are also the primary caretakers of children.

Traditional dress and material culture is extremely meager, due to the climate and lifestyle of the Khoisan. Men wear simple leather loincloths and women wear leather aprons. Shelters made of grass and mats made of the same material are part of the Khoisan material culture, including simple hunting and cooking implements that can be easily packed and carried.

Koisan artistic expression includes music played with simple instruments like mouth organs, thumb pianos and the *gwashi*, "a five-stringed guitarlike instrument."[241] During festivals, body painting is prevalent, with women painting their faces with red paint in dots. Khoisan oral literature is dominated by stories and myths using objects from their environment.

Khoisan religion is mainly animist, giving everything in nature a soul. This helps the Khoisan maintain a special relationship with the harsh environment to which they are so well adapted.

KHOLIFA

A West African people. The Kholifa are one of the Temne subgroups. They live in Sierra Leone.

KHOZZAM

The Khozzam are a Chadian Arab group. They are one of Djoheina's large subgroups.

KHURUTSHE

The Khurutshe, also known as Bakhurutshe, are a Tswana Hurutshe subgroup. They live in Botswana.

KHUTE

The Khute are a Southern African people and one of the San Tshu-Kwe subgroups. They live in Botswana.

KHUZE

The Khuze are a Southern African people. They are concentrated in the Republic of South Africa, primarily in its southeastern coastal regions. Their neighbors include the Bhaca and Makhanya peoples.

KIBALA

The Kibala are one of the Mbundu subgroups. Like other Mbundu peoples, they are concentrated in Angola.

KIBALLO

The Kiballo, also known as the Kiwollo, are a West African people. They live in Mali and Nigeria. In Mali, they are concentrated in the Karta region, whereas in Nigeria, they are located in the State of Kaduna.

KIBBO, see BIROM

KIBERA, see AMBA

KIBET

A Chadian Tama-speaking people. The Kibet are concentrated in the southeastern regions of the country.

KIBO, see BIROM

KIBOMA, see BOMA-SAKATA

KIBULA

The Kibula are an Ovimbundu subgroup. Like many Ovimbundu groups, they live in the central highlands of Angola.

KIBUSHY, see SAKALAVA

KIBSI

The Kibsi are one of West Africa's ethnic groups. They belong to the Ninisi cluster of peoples and currently live in Burkina Faso.

KIBYEN, see BIROM

KIDIGO, see DIGO

KIFULIIRU, see FURIIRU

KIGA, see CHIGA

KIGE, see BERI

KIKUYU

The Kikuyu – also called Giguyu, Gekoyo or Agekoyo (Agikuyu) and Gikikuyu – are an East African Bantu-speaking people and one of the most politically active nations in Africa. They are concentrated in the highland region of south central Kenya, near Mt. Kenya, and in the northern areas of Tanzania. Their total population in Kenya is estimated at well over 6,000,000 people. The Kikuyu speak a dialect of the Bantu language called Kikuyu and they also speak English. They refer to themselves as Mugikuyu, singular of Agikuyu.

The Kikuyu have common historical lineage with the Kamba, Embu, Mbere, Tharaka and Meru peoples. "All these groups date back to a prototype population known as the Thagicu." [242] Their modern history is traced back to the thirteenth century, at which time they moved from the Shungwaya region in the north to their present concentration in the central Kenya plateau on the slopes of Kirinyaga (Mount Kenya). Shungwaya, an area lying between the Juba and Tana rivers in southern Somalia, was used in Bantu migration waves as a dispersal point to new and/or permanent settlements. Hence, they are the descendants of one of Thagicu's splinter groups. In time, they developed a clan structure, with each clan tracing its lineage to a female ancestor. In Kikuyu mythology,

> there were nine (or nine plus one) original clans. Two clans, the Acera and Agaciku, are thought to have formed through contact with neighboring Kamba. The largest clan is the Anjiru; its members were formerly renowned as great warriors and medicine men. The Aithaga clan was known for its ironworks, and its members were also thought to have the power to control rain. Other clans include the Ambui, Angari, Aithiegeni, Aithirandu, and Aiththanga. According to Kikuyu myths, Kikuyu and Mumbi were the male and female progenitors of the nine clan ancestors.[243]

Originally, the Kikuyu were hunter-gatherers. In their new homelands, however, they adopted horticultural practices and moreover, engaged in trade among themselves, as well as with their neighbors, especially the Masai and the Kamba. The goods they traded consisted essentially of agricultural and craft products.

Like other Bantu peoples, the family constituted the basic social unit. Next in importance to the family was the village, which constituted the Kikuyu's basic political unit. Each village was regulated by lineage or age groupings and governed by a chief who was assisted by a council of elders. Unlike other Bantu groups, however, their society was based on dispersed rather than compact homesteads.[244]

Despite the decentralized nature of their political, economic and social systems, the Kikuyu succeeded in retaining a highly coherent society. Its unity was maintained through a representative system based on the family, the clan, the community and the age group. Under their representative system, each family had its own council with the father serving not only as its head, but also as its representative in the village council, which consisted of the heads of the several families in the village. The same system provided for district councils composed of the district elders. In addition, it provided for a national council whose members were chosen from district elders and hence, represented the mature and wise members of the Kikuyu society. Furthermore, it represented young people in government. This was done through a special council with primary responsibility over the society's military affairs.

More importantly, traditional Kikuyu political power rested in age-sets, *mariika* (plural of *riika*) where male members of a particular generation become responsible for political decisions within the nation. In order to become part of the ruling age-set, a person had to go through rigorous initiation rites. The age-sets were based on date of circumcision and scheduled to rule for over 30 years, then they were replaced by the next generation of age-sets. Members of an age-set were circumcised at the same time. Moreover, all political positions were elective in nature, but graded by age. Furthermore, recall of elected personnel was recognized, primarily in cases involving violations of established rules.[245] The functioning of this system was closely tied to the Kikuyu's traditional religion, which centered on the belief in a supernatural world, a world of spirits, and a close bond between the living and ancestral spirits.[246] Broadly speaking, their system was based on cherishing collective responsibility and the primacy of the society's interest over those of its individuals.[247]

Furthermore, the unity of the Kikuyu people was fostered by their traditional system of land tenure and land use. Under this system, known as the *githaka* (land) system, every member of an *mbari*, an extended family or subclan, was entitled to cultivate a plot, *ngundu*, of the communally owned *githaka*, but not to sell it or lease it without the permission of the *mbari* leaders. Under the same system, upon the death of a user (developer), an *ngundu* was passed from father to son, thus establishing continuity in land utilization.[248]

The Kikuyu retained their political, social and economic systems virtually intact until 1895, at which time the British East Africa Protectorate was proclaimed. As a result, the Kikuyu not only lost their freedom and independence, but also were forcibly evicted and dispossessed of many of their ancestral lands to give way for white settlement. In addition, they were prohibited from farming on Kenya Highlands (later renamed White Highlands), subjected to a headtax, forced to work as laborers and treated as an inferior class to white British and South African Boer settlers. Like the Masai, the Nandi, the Kalanjin and other ethnic groups in what is presently modern Kenya, they were relegated to inadequate reserves and required to comply with "new oppressive and discriminatory measures hitherto unknown in the country."[249] Between 1903 and 1906, for example, large areas of their lands were appropriated by white settlers for nominal or no compensation.[250] In another example, in 1915, the Crown Lands Ordinance declared all lands in possession of Africans as Crown land.[251] The same ordinance granted authority to the British governor to sell parts of lands held in reserve.[252] In a third example, the Native Registration Ordinance of 1921 required all native men to carry an identification card contained in a metallic case and to tie it around the neck at all times. Failure to wear this identification plate, known as *Kipande* in Swahili, was considered an offense punishable with a fine or imprisonment or both.[253]

Naturally, these colonial measures (among many other comparable ones) aggrieved the Kikuyu and sparked their alienation against, and opposition to, British rule. Like many Africans, the Kikuyu viewed land "as the only real security, something sacred, eternally the possession of the people who once occupied it and depended upon it. Communally owned, the temporary abandonment of such land did not change the situation at all."[254] When the Kikuyu found their lands occupied by White settlers "it was, indeed, from their point of view, stolen."[255]

Kikuyu protest and resistance to British rule started as early as the 1920's. It was exemplified in the formation of several organizations such as the Kikuyu Association (KA), the East African Association (EAA), the Young Kiykuyu Association (YKA), the Young Kavirondo Association (YKA) and the Kikuyu Central Association (KCA). The first association was founded by Kiambu farmers in 1920, the second by Kikuyu leaders, including Jesse Kariuki and Harry Thuku, in 1921, the third by Harry Thuku in 1921, the fourth by James Beauttah in 1922, and the fifth by Joseph Kangethe in

1924. In 1925, the EAA was renamed, assuming KCA's name.

Of all these Kikuyu or Kikuyu-led organizations, the KCA was the most effective, more so, when Jomo Kenyatta became its General Secretary and editor of its journal in 1928, its representative in Britain between 1929 and 1946, and subsequently its leader, as well as the leader of the Kenya African Union (KAU) during Kenya's struggle for independence.

In the 1950s, the Kikuyu organized an armed rebellion against British rule. Militant campaigns staged by the Mau Mau, a Kikuyu underground organization, coupled with political resistance under the leadership of Jomo Kenyatta, culminated in granting Kenya its independence on December 12, 1963.

In Kenya's struggle for independence, over 11,000 Kikuyu were killed, and more than 20,000 others were detained and retained in detention camps.

Though foreign rule has drastically impacted their traditional way of life, the Kikuyu have nevertheless managed to keep their traditional religion alive. As mentioned, Kikuyu religion recognizes one supreme God, *Ngai*. Yet, there are a few Kikuyu who incorporate the teachings of Christianity with their traditional religious beliefs.

Presently, the Kikuyu's social organizations are patrilineal and hence, questions relating to descent, inheritance and succession in their society are determined according to patrilineal lineages. In other words, the father is the head of the family. Upon his death, the eldest son succeeds "him to the post of authority as head of the family group, unless it broke up."[256] Landownership is passed patrilineally down the family line. Members of the same extended family, live close together in the same village. If a husband decides to obtain many wives, each wife may have her own dwelling. Their society is divided into numerous clans and subclans.

The Kikuyu continue to be a sedentary people relying on agriculture for sustenance. Their economy is based on agriculture, which makes land extremely important for the Kikuyu nation. Vegetables are the main food source for the Kikuyu, with meat being secondary.

The Kikuyu have adapted Western styles of dress in all walks of life. Only on special occasions do the Kikuyu adorn themselves in traditional jewelry on their necks and arms, also donning elaborate headdresses and leather goods.

The Kikuyu have a vibrant literature of fiction and non-fiction published in English and Kikuyu. Traditional Kikuyu storytelling is primarily non-fiction in nature, describing historical events and conflicts with Kikuyu neighbors, particularly the Maasi.

Currently, the Kikuyu people constitute Kenya's largest and most outstanding ethnic minority. They account for 22% of the country's total population.

KILA

One of West Africa's peoples. The Kila are concentrated in the southeastern regions of Nigeria, notably in the Gongola State.

KILANG

The Kilang are one of the subgroups of the Ngambaye people, a Sara group. They live in the southern border areas of Chad.

KILANGA, see KILINGA

KILBA

The Kilba, also called Chobba, Haba, Huba, Ndirma and Xibba, are a West African people. They are concentrated in the southeastern regions of Nigeria, notably in the Gongola state.

KILEGA, see LEGA

KILENDU, see LENDU

KILENGI

An Angolan people. The Kilengi, also known as Twilenge and Tyilenge, live in the southwestern areas of the country. Their neighbors include Mwila and Vatwa peoples.

KILINDE

The Kilinde are one of Tanzania's ethnic groups. They are part of the Tanzanian Zigula cluster of peoples. The Kilinde are concentrated in the northeastern coastal areas of the country. Their neighbors include the Ngulu and Swahili peoples.

KILINGA

These are a West African people and one of the ethnic minorities of Togo. They are concentrated in the northern parts of the country, especially in the eastern la Kara region. Groups of them, however, are also located in Benin. Their neighbors include the Basila, Borgu, Naudeba, Somba, Tem and Yoruba peoples. The Kilinga, also known as the Kilanga, are a Gur-speaking Voltaic people. They are predominantly engaged in farming and animal husbandry.

KILLAKADA

The Killakada are one of the Chadian Kuri subgroups. They speak Yedina, a Buduma dialect. Like other Kuri groups, they live along the eastern shores of Lake Chad. Their neighbors include the Dogorda, Kanembou, and Koto peoples.

KIM

One of Chad's peoples. The Kim people emanated from a confederation of several peoples of the Longone River banks, namely the Garap, Guérep, Kolop, Kolobo and Kossope.

KIMANDA, see NYASA

KIMATUMBI, see MATUMBI

KIMBU

These are an East African people and one of Tanzania's ethnic groups. The Kimbu are concentrated in the southwestern areas of the country, especially in the Mbeya administrative region. Their lands are bordered on the west by Lake Tanganyika and on the south by Lake Nyasa, Malawi and the Republic of Zambia.

The Kimbu's economic activities focus on agriculture, fishing and animal husbandry. They are also engaged in salt, gold, coal and mica mining activities in their region.

KIMBUNDU, see MBUNDU

KINDIN, see also TEDA

A Saharan Goboda subgroup. The Goboda are a Teda group. They are an Arab nomadic and semi-nomadic people.

KINGA (Chad)

The Kinga, also spelled Kenga, are one of Chad's clusters of ethnic groups. They are Sudanic people whose origin is traced back to the Darfur region in the Sudan. Currently, the Kinga are concentrated in the Hadjeray region. Their neighbors include the Bidio, Dungal, and Junkun peoples.

KINGA (Tanzania)

The Kinga are an East African people. They are concentrated in the central regions of Tanzania, notably along the northeastern shore of Lake Malawi. The Kinga are part of the Nyasa cluster of peoples.

KINGBETU, see MANGBETU

KINGENGEREKO, see NDENGEREKO

KINGOLO

The Kongolo are an Angolan people. They are one of the Ovimbundu subgroups. The Ovimbundu are concentrated in the northwestern, central, and eastern parts of the country.

KINGULU, see **NGULU**

KINKOMBA

The Kinkomba, also known as Konkomba, are a West African Molé-Dagbane group. They live in northern Ghana. Their neighbors include the Dagomba, Gonja, Nanumba, and Tem peoples.

KINONGO, see **KONONGO**

KINUGY, see **KINUKU**

KINUKA, see **KINUKU**

KINUKU

The Kinuku, also known as the Kinuka and Kinugy are a West African people. They are concentrated in Nigeria, notably in the Kaduna State.

KINYASA, see **NYASA MANDA**

KINYIKA, see **GIRIAMA**

KIONG

A West African people. The Kiong, also known as Akayon, Akoiyang, Okonyong, and Okoyong, are concentrated in Nigeria, primarily in the Cross River State.

KIPCHORNWONEK, see **OKIEK**

KIPIRSI

The Kipirsi, known also as Kõ, are one of West Africa's ethnic groups. They belong to the Ninisi cluster of peoples. The Kipirsi are a Kibsi subgroup. They are concentrated in the southern regions of Burkina Faso.

KIPSIGIS, see **KIPSIKIS**

KIPSIKIS, see also **KALENJIN**

The Kipsikis (Kipsigis), also known as Lumwa, are an East African Kalenjin group. They are concentrated in the highlands of southwestern Kenya, notably in the Kericho District. Their language, Kipsikis (Kipsigis), is Nilotic, belonging to the Eastern Sudanic Branch of the Nilo-Saharan language family of African languages. They comprise several subgroups, including the Lumbwa and Sotek.

Originally, the Kipsikis people lived in the vicinity of Lake Baringo. Sometime between the seventeenth and early nineteenth century, they migrated southwardly to their present location where they pursued an agrarian type of life and engaged in livestock and cattle-raising.

As a result of the fall of East Africa to British rule in 1895, the Kipsikis, like other Kalenjin groups, lost their freedom, forcibly evicted of their lands and relegated to inadequate reserves. They were required to comply with suppressive and segregationist laws and compelled to be part of the white settlers colonial market economy.

The Kipsikis are polygamous and their social structures are based on patrilineal lineages and age-sets, *ipinda*, which apply to both males and females. They lack centralized political authority and more importantly, their society places great value on personal autonomy.[257] Currently, they support over 200 exogamous clans. Their population is estimated at about one million.

KIPSORAI, see also **SEBEI** and **KALENJIN**

An East African Sebei people, a Kalenjin group. They are concentrated in Kenya, Tanzania and Uganda, notably in western Kenya and eastern Uganda. The Kipsorai speak a dialect of Kalenjin, a Southern Nilotic language of the Eastern Sudanic family of African languages. They are a semipastoralist people.

KIPUNGU

The Kipungu are an Angolan group. They are part of its Nyaneka-Humbi cluster of peoples.

KIR, see **MANDARI**

KIR-BALAR

The Kir-Balar are one of West Africa's ethnic groups. They live in Nigeria, notably in the Bauchi State.

KIRDI, see also **SARA**

The Kirdi, also known as Sara, are one of the major ethnic minorities of Cameroon, Chad, Sudan and neighboring countries. The name Kirdi was given to them by their Muslim neighbors the Bagirmi people, probably to denote their non-Muslim status. In Cameroon, they account for 11% of the country's population, whereas in Chad they constitute the largest ethnic minority accounting for 23% of the total population. The Kirdi speak Sara, a Central Sudanic language that belongs to the Nilo-Saharan family of African languages.

KIRFI

The Kirfi are one of West Africa's ethnic groups. They live in Nigeria, notably in the Bauchi State.

KISA, see **LUHYA**

KISAMA

The Kisama are one of the Mbundu subgroups. They live in the north-central regions of Angola. Their neighbors include the Cisanji, Hanya, Kung (!Kung), and Ovimbundu peoples.

KISHAMBA

An East African Bantu-speaking people. The Kishamba are a Taita (Teita) subgroup. Their main concentrations are in Kenya, primarily in its southeastern coastal regions.

KISI, see **KISSI**

KISII, see GUSII

KISONKO, see MASAI

KISSI

A West African people. The Kissi, also spelled Kisi, are concentrated in the forest areas of Guinea and Liberia. Their neighbors include the Gbande, Kono, Konyanke, Loma, Malinke, Mende and Temne peoples. The Kissi speak a language that belongs to the West Atlantic branch of the Niger-Congo family of African languages.

KITARA, see NYORO

KITATA

The Kitata are one of the Ovimbundu subgroups. They are concentrated in Angola. The Ovimbundu are located in the northwestern, central, and eastern parts of the country.

KITIMI

A West African people. The Kitimi live in Nigeria, primarily in the State of Kaduna.

KITOSH, see LUHYA

KITURIKA

The Kiturika are one of Tanzania's ethnic groups. They are part of the Yao cluster of peoples.

KITUTU, see GUSII

KIVU

A cluster of ethnic groups in the Democratic Republic of the Congo (Zaire). It includes several groups including the Hunde, Nyanga, and Yira.

KIVWANJI, see WANJI

KIWOLLO, see KIBALLO

KIYAKA

A Bantu-speaking people. The Kiyaka, also known as Bayaka, are concentrated in the northern areas of Angola and the southwestern regions of the Democratic Republic of the Congo (Zaire). Their neighbors in both countries are the Kongo (Bakongo), Kusu (Bakusu), and Lunda (Balunda) peoples.

KIYANZI, see YANZI

!KO, see SAN

KOBA

The Koba are a Bantu-speaking people. They are concentrated in the Democratic Republic of the Congo (Zaire) and Zambia.

KOBCHI

The Kobchi are a West African Bantu-speaking people. They are concentrated in the central areas of Nigeria.

KOBE

The Kobe, also spelled Kobé, are a Zaghawa subgroup. They speak a distinct Saharan language along with Arabic. Their main concentrations are located along the Chadian-Sudanese borders. Their neighbors include the Bideyat, Daza, Gimr, Noarma, and Tama peoples.

KOCHOQUA

An extinct South African people. The Kochoqua used to live in the southwestern regions of what is presently the Republic of South Africa.

KODIA, see KOTROHOU

KODOI

The Kodoi, also known as the Kodoy, are a Maba subgroup. They live in Chad, primarily in its south central Ouaddai region of the country. Groups of them, however, can also be found in northeastern Nigeria.

KODOY, see KODOI

KOENOEM, see KANAM

KOFYAR

The Kofyar are a West African people. They are concentrated in the central regions of Nigeria, primarily in the Plateau State. Their major subgroups include the Jaghnim and the Jortu.

KOHUMONO

The Kohumono, also identified as the Bahumono, Ediba, and Ekumuru, are a West African people. Their main concentrations are in the Cross River State in Nigeria.

KOITOKITOK, see MASAI

KOKE, see KOKI

KOKI

The Koki, also spelled Koke, are an East African people. They are concentrated in the southwestern regions of Uganda, as well as in the Moyen-Chari and Guéré prefectures in Chad.

KOKOFU

The Kokofu are a West African people. They are one of the subgroups of the Asante people. Their main concentrations are in Ghana.

KOKORDA

A Central and East African people. The Kokorda are concentrated in Chad and Sudan. They are a Daza subgroup.

KOLA, see also KOLE

The Kola are one of the Chadian Kuri subgroups. They speak Yedina, a Buduma dialect. Like other Kuri groups, they live along the eastern shores of Lake Chad.

KOLE

The Kole, also spelled Kola, are a West and West Central African people. They are one of the many Pygmy people of Equatorial Africa. Originally, they inhabited the tropical rain forest, in what is now within the Republic of Congo. Subsequently, they moved to other areas. Of these groups, the Kole among them eventually settled in the southeastern coastal areas of Cameroon. They are essentially hunters, foragers and potters.

KOLELA

The Kolela–also known as the Clela, Chilala, Dakarkari, Dakkarari, Lalawa, Lela, and Lelau– are a West African Muslim people. They are located in Benin, Burkina Faso, Ivory Coast, Niger and Nigeria. The Kolela are one of the subgroups of the Songhai people.

KOLOBO

The Kolobo are one of the Kim confederation groups. They live in Chad in the vicinities of the Longone River.

KOLOLO, see also LOZI

One of the Southern African groups. The Kololo, also known as the Bakololo, are a subgroup of the Fokeng Sotho people. Their main concentrations are in Botswana and Zambia.

KOLOP

The Kolop are one of the Kim confederation groups. They live in Chad in the vicinities of the Longone River.

KOM

The Kom people are a Central and West Central African ethnic group. They are concentrated in central Cameroon and northeastern Democratic Republic of the Congo (Zaire). Groups ofthem are also found in other adjoining states. The Kom are one of the Tigar (Tikar) subgroups. Their neighbors in Zaire include the Bombesa, Mba, and Mbudja peoples, whereas in Cameroon they include the Bali, Bum, Nso, and Ibibio peoples.

KOMA (East Africa)

An East African pastoralist people. The Koma are found in Ethiopia, Sudan and Zambia. In Ethiopia, they are part of the Beni-Sciangul cluster of peoples. In Sudan, they live south of the Blue Nile, neighboring the Nuer, Burun, Beir, Malakel, Galla, Nuba, Shilluk, Anuak and Dinka peoples. In Zambia, they are part of the Luyana cluster of peoples.

KOMA (West Africa)

A West African people. The Koma, also called Kuma, are concentrated in Nigeria and Cameroon, especially in the border areas that separate the two countries.

KOMBA, see KOMKOMBA and KONKOMBA

KOMBE, see FANG

KOMKOMBA

The Komkomba, also Komba and Konkomba, are a West African Voltaic (Gur)-speaking people. They are highly concentrated in the northwestern areas of Togo and the northeastern areas of Ghana. Their neighbors include the Dagomba and the Mamprusi peoples. Groups of the

Kombomba peoples are also found in Burkina-Faso.

KOMO

The Komo are one of the Bantu-speaking ethnic minorities of the Democratic Republic of the Congo (Zaire). They live in the northeastern areas of the country.

KOMONO, see also LOBI-DAGARTI

A West African people. The Komono are concentrated in the northern regions of the Ivory Coast. Groups of them, however, are also located in adjoining countries. The Komono speak a language that belongs to the Voltaic branch of the Niger-Congo family of African languages. Their neighbors include the Dorossié, Dyula, Guin, Karaboro, Kulango, Lobi and Senufo peoples.

KONAGI

The Konagi–also known as the Coniagui, Koniagui, Konianke, and Konyanke –are a West African people. Their groups are found in Guinea, Guinea-Bissau, Senegal, and other West African states. Their neighbors in Guinea, Guinea-Bissau, and Senegal include the Bassari and Fulani peoles.

KONAMBEMBE

The Konambembe are a Central African Sangha subgroup. They are found in Cameroon, Congo, Central African Republic, and the Democratic Republic of the Congo (Zaire).

KONDA

One of the ethnic minorities of the Democratic Republic of the Congo (Zaire). The Konda are concentrated in the western areas of the country, especially north of Lake Ndombe.

KONDE, see also MAKONDE

The Konde, also known as Makonde, are an Eastern Bantu-speaking people. They are concentrated in Tanzania, Mozambique and the Republic of South Africa.

KONGURAMA, see NGADJI

KONE, see PEDI

KONGO

The Kongo – also called Bacongo, Badondo, Bakango, Bakongo, Bandibu, Congo, and Koongo – are Western Bantu-speaking people. Their language, Kikongo, belongs to the Benue-Congo branch of the Niger-Congo family of African languages. They are highly concentrated in West Central Africa, notably in Angola, Congo and Democratic Republic of the Congo (Zaire). The Kongo are a Kasai people. They are divided into numerous tribal groupings, the major ones of which include, apart from Kongo proper: the Bembe, Dondo, Kamba, Kougni (Kunyi), Lali, Manianga, Mboma, Mpangu, Ndibu, Ntandu, Sundi (Basundi, Sandi or Nsandi), Solongo, Vili and Yombe. KiLeta, a Kikongo dialect, is the lingua franca of these and other Kongo-related peoples.

The history of the Kongo people can be traced back to the last millennium B.C., at which time their ancestors inhabited the forests and woodland areas in the lower Zaire river region. Their modern history, however, dates back to the fourteenth century, at which time they developed their own kingdom, the Kongo Kingdom, which covered a great part of west central Africa. The kingdom was a loose confederation of local states. It stretched over large parts of the area between the Congo River and the Kwango River, and was headed by a paramount chief, called *manikongo*.[258]

The Kongo Kingdom was visited by the Portuguese in 1484, and in 1491, Nzinga Kuwu, its *manikongo*, developed an unusually good relationship with them, as well as the Vatican. As a consequence, both Portugal and Kongo exchanged ambassadors and through the intermediacy of Portuguese missionaries, Kongo kings, including Nzinga and his son

Afonso (who succeeded to the throne in 1506), willingly converted to Christianity.

With the help of the Portuguese, the *manikongos* converted their kingdom into a grand slave trading center, a development that led to their isolation from their people and neighbors. The decentralization of their powers led eventually to the fall of the Kingdom of Kongo to Portuguese direct colonial rule.

The Kongo Kingdom started to decline in 1570 and following the battle of Mbwila in 1665, it collapsed giving way to a number of small chiefdoms. In 1885, Belgium took control over the Kingdom's territory and placed it under its colonial rule. Subsequently, it renamed the territory as Belgian Congo, and continued to govern it until June 30, 1960, when Belgium granted it independence. Prior to renaming it the Democratic Republic of the Congo in 1997, the Belgian Congo witnessed several name changes, namely, Congo/Leopoldville, then Congo/Kinshasa, and later Republic of Zaire, and the Democratic Republic of the Congo.

The Bakango are extremely politicized, initiating political parties wherever they dwell. For example, the Zairean Bakango were involved in the formation of a political party in the former Belgian Congo and the Anolan Bakango made up the majority of the National Front for the Liberation of Angola (FNLA) during the independence movement. Probably, their political dispositions are a direct result of their highly structured hierarchical national formation.

The Kongo's social structure centers on a matrilineal organization. These clans are divided into *nzo*, or houses, which further divided into *futa*, or smaller lineages. The Kongo Kingdom is divided into towns and villages, or *mbanza* and *mabata*. Towns always have leeway over villages, since Kongo nobles reside in the towns. Villages are expected to give surpluses of crops to the towns. The village political structure is dominated by a headman, called *nkuluntu*, who is the middleman between the *mabata* and the *mbanza*.

There is a strict division of labor in Kongo family life. Women do most of the field work, while men are responsible for harvesting the many resources found in trees, as well as building the shelters for his family. Before men and women marry, there is a trial period in which the potential of compatibility of the man and woman is measured. Also, this period determines the amount of money that will be paid in bridewealth for the marriage to take place. Boys and girls are separated at around age 5 and raised by the parent of similar sex, in order to learn their places in Kongo society.

The Kongo are basically an agricultural people relying on staples such as maize and millets. This lifestyle has led to a sedentary life pattern that has fostered a hierarchical society where the nobles reside in dwellings built of stronger material which separates them from the "common Kongo" with dwellings of simpler material.

Kongo artisans are adept at ironworking, so much so that the skill "ranks them with chiefs and priests."[259] A major form of artistic expression among the Kongo is sculpture. Sculpture is used to express religious feeling, as well as political loyalty to *nkuluntus* and *nganga*.

Though many Kongo converted to Christianity, ancestor worship is still widespread. Houses still contain shrines directed toward the recognition of ancestors that are believed to take an active interest in everyday affairs. Also, Christian priests in Kongo society are known by the traditional name given to powerful priests in the past, *nganga*.

The Kongo are still superstitious concerning evil spells and curses espoused by witches; therefore, charms and amulets are still used for protection.

According to Davidson, however, their culture supports two tendencies: a balanced acceptance of reality, on the one hand, and a denial of necessity on the other. In his view, the denial of necessity is expressed by anti-witchcraft movements that they undertake now and then.[260]

The Kongo are involved in a variety of sustenance practices. With the exception of the Ashiluanda (a sub-group) in Angola (who are engaged in intensive open sea fishing), most of them are pastoralists.

Religiously, the great majority of Kongo are Roman Catholic due to Belgian influence in Democratic Republic of the Congo (Zaire) and Portuguese influence in Angola.

Currently, the Kongo people constitute the third largest ethnic minority in Angola after the Ovimbundu (37%) and the Kimbundu (25%). They account for about 15% of the country's total population. They speak Kikango and are subdivided into several groups, namely: the Bashikongo, Sosso and Pombo (who are situated in the East of Bakango territory); the Solango of the coastal plain; the Ashiluanda of the island of Luanda; and the Mayombe (Maiombe) in Cabinda. In the Republic of Congo, however, they constitute the largest ethnic minority, accounting for 48% of the total population. In Democratic Republic of the Congo (Zaire), they are concentrated in the western regions of the country.

KONGURAMA, see NGADJI

KONHAQUE

The Konhaque, also spelled Conhaque, are a West African people. They belong to the Senegambian cluster of peoples. Currently their groups are concentrated in the southeastern regions of Guinea-Bissau.

KONIAGUI, see KONYANKE

KONIANKE

The Konianke – also known as the Coniagui, Konagi, Koniagui, Konianke, and Konyanke – are a West African Mande-speaking people. They originated in Mali, but presently are highly concentrated in Guinea, Liberia, Sierra Leone, and other West African states.

KONIÉRÉ

A Central African people. The Koniéré are one of the Maba subgroups. They are concentrated in Chad. Groups of them, however, can also be found in Cameroon and Nigeria.

KONJARA, see **FUR**

KONJO, see **BAKONJO**

KONKOMBA, see also **DAGOMBA**

These are a West African people, and one of the ethnic minorities of Togo, Ghana, and Burkina Faso. In Togo, they are concentrated in the northern parts of the country, especially in the western la Kara region. Their neighbors include the Basari, Chakossi, Dagomba, Mamprusi, and Naudeba peoples. In Ghana, they live in the northern regions of the country. In Burkina Paso, they are found along the country's southern borders. The Konkomba – also called Komba, Kombomba and Konkombo – are a Gur-speaking Voltaic people. They are predominantly engaged in farming and animal husbandry.

KONKOMBO, see **DAGOMBA** and **KONKOMBA**

KONO, see also **MANDE**

The Kono, also known as the Konu and Kwono, are a West African Mande forest group. They are concentrated in eastern Sierra Leone as well as in Guinea, Ivory Coast, Liberia, Nigeria and Mali. Their neighbors include the Bullom, Limba, Loko, Kisi, Kuranko, Malinke, Mende and Temne peoples. The Kono speak a language that belongs to the Mande branch of the Niger-Congo family of African languages.

KONONGO

The Konongo, also called Kinongo, are one of Tanzania's ethnic groups. They live east of Lake Tanganyika. Their economic activities focus on farming and animal husbandry.

KONSO

The Konso are an East African people. They are highly concentrated in southern Ethiopia, notably south of Lake Shamo. Groups of them are also located in Uganda. These people speak a language that belongs to the

East Cushitic family of African languages. They are divided into three main groups, namely, the Garati, the Takadi and the Turo. Their neighbors include the Borana, the Guawada, the Gidole and the Burji.

The Konso are an ancient people. Historical evidence suggests that they were conquered by Ethiopian Emperor Menelik II, and eventually incorporated in Ethiopia in 1897.

Though essentially agriculturalists, the Konso are also noted for their engagement in miscellaneous trading and iron manufacturing activities.

The Konso's society is highly egalitarian. Moreover, it is based on patrilineal kinship relations with exogamous clans constituting its basic units. Though Christianity has won a foothold in their society, the Konso continue to cherish their traditional religion which is based on the belief in *Waga*, the sky God, who created and lived among humans in the beginning, but later "was offended by a woman and so went to live far away."[261] In their beliefs, *Waga* "is still concerned with human affairs," and "punishes sinners with sickness, sterility, and death."[262] According to the same beliefs, the elders of their society serve as *Waga's* deputies on earth.

KONTA

An East African people. The Konta live in the southern regions of Ethiopia.

KONU, see KONO

KONY, see also KALENJIN

An East African Kalenjin group. Their main concentrations are in Kenya, Tanzania and Uganda, notably in western Kenya and eastern Uganda. They speak a dialect of Kalenjin, a Southern Nilotic language of the Eastern Sudanic family of African languages. The Kony comprise several groups, including the Bong'om, Bok, Elgon Masai, Elgonyi and Sabaot. They are a semipastoralist people.

KONYAKA

The Konyaka are a West African Mande-speaking people. They live in the southern Mali, northwestern Ivory Coast, and eastern Guinea.

KONYANKE

The Konyanke – also spelled Coniagui, Konagi, Koniagui, and Konianke – are a West African people. They are concentrated in Liberia and neighboring states and speak a language that belongs to the Mande branch of the Niger-Congo family of African languages. Their neighbors in Liberia include the Dan, Kisi, Kpelle, Loma and Malinke peoples.

!KOŌ, see also SAN

A southern African San group. The !Koō, also known as !Xoō, are a San-speaking people. They are concentrated in the central sand areas of Botswana and adjoining Namibia. Like other San-speaking peoples, they are essentially foragers, hunters and gatherers.

KOONGO, see KONGO

KORANA

The Korana are a southern African people. They are concentrated in the Republic of South Africa, notably in its central regions between the Orange and Vaal rivers.

KORANKO, see KURANKO

KORARA, see UDUK

KOREKORE, see also SHONA

A Southern Bantu-speaking Shona group. They are concentrated in the northern regions of Zimbabwe, as well as in the Zambezi Valley. Large groups of them are also found in Mozambique. The Korekore account for about 12% of Zimbabwe's total population. The Korekore speak Shona.

Their neighbors include the Tonga, Rozwi, Zezuru, and Manyika peoples.

KORING, see ORRI

KORO

The Koro are a West African cluster of peoples. They are concentrated in the north central regions of Nigeria. They speak a language that belongs to the Benue-Congo branch of the Niger-Congo family of African languages. Their neighbors include the Gwandara, Kadara, Katab and Yeskwa peoples.

KOROBAT

An East African people. The Korobat live in the Sudan. They are a Berber group belonging to the Hawawir cluster of Berber peoples in the country.

KOROMBA

The Koromba people are a West African group. They are concentrated in the south central regions of Mali. Groups of them can also be found in the southwestern regions of Burkina Faso. Their neighbors include the Gourmantche, Dogon, Mossi, and Busani peoples.

KOROMBOYE, see KULERE

KOROP

The Korop, also known as Durop and Ododop, are a West African people. They speak a language that belongs to the Benue-Congo branch of the Niger-Congo family of African languages. The Korop are concentrated in the Cross River State in Nigeria. Groups of them, however, live in the western regions of Cameroon.

KOSA, see MENDE

KOSANKE

The Kosanke are a West African Mende-speaking people. They are highly concentrated in Mali. Groups of them, however, are also found in adjoining states.

KOSOVA, see GUSII

KOSSA, see MENDE

KOSSEDA

One of Chad's ethnic groups. The Kosseda are one of the subgroups of the Teda people. They are concentrated in the northern regions of the country. Their neighbors include the Ouria and Tomagra peoples.

KOSSO, see MENDE

KOSSOP, see KOSSOPE

KOSSOPE

The Kossope, also spelled Kossop, are one of the Kim confederation groups. They live in Chad in the vicinities of the Longone River.

KOTA, see also KOTO

The Kota people are one of Gabon's Koto groups. They are located south of the Ogooué river, notably in the western regions of the country. Groups of them can also be found in Cameroon. Their neighbors include the Fang, Kele, and Shake peoples.

KOTE

The Kote are one of the many ethnic groups of the Democratic Republic of the Congo (Zaire). They are concentrated in the northwestern regions of the country where they engage in miscellaneous farming activities.

KOTO

The Koto, also known as the Bakota, Ikota, and Kota, are a Central African people. They are a cluster of several ethnic groups such as the Bandjambi, Dambomo, Mahongwe, Mindassa, Shake, Shamaye, and Voumbou. The Koto live in Cameroon and Gabon.

KOTOKO

The Kotoko, also known as Mogori, are one of the Chad's ethnic groups. Groups of them, however, are also located in the northwestern regions of Cameroon as well as in northeastern Nigeria. The Kotoko are predominantly Muslim and live primarily in the northern regions of the country along the lower courses of the Logone and Chari rivers. They are the descendants of the ancient Sao (Sau) population, reputedly a nation of giants, that formerly inhabited the region. The Kotoko were impacted by the Kanuri culture and presently speak Kanuri. Their neighbors include the Gisiga, Mandara, Musgu and Shuwa peoples.

KOTOKOLI, see also TEM

The Kotokoli, also known as the Chaucho, Cotocoli, Tem, Temba and Timn, are a West African Tem-speaking people. Their main concentrations are in both Ghana and Togo.

KOTOKU AKYEM, see also AKAN and AKYEM

The Kotoku Akyem are one of the subgroups of the Akyem people, an Akan group. They live primarily in the Eastern Region of the Republic of Ghana.

KOTOPO

A West African people. The Kotopo – also known as Patapoke, Potopo, and Potopore – are concentrated in western Cameroon. Groups of them, however, are also located in eastern Nigeria. Their neighbors include the Chamba, Fula and Vere peoples. The Kotopo speak a language that belongs to the Adamawa branch of the Niger-Congo family of African languages.

KOTROHOU

One of the West African peoples. The Kotrohou, also known as Kodia, are part of the Kru cluster of ethnic groups. They are concentrated in the Ivory Coast.

KOUEN, see GURO

KOUENI, see GURO

KOUGNI, see also KONGO

The Kougni are one of the subgroups of the Kongo people. They speak Kikongo, a language that belongs to the Benue-Congo branch of the Niger-Congo family of African languages. The Kougni people live in Angola, Congo, and the Democratic Republic of the Congo (Zaire).

KOUKA

The Kouka, also spelled Kuka, are a Muslim sedentary people of central Chad. They make up less than 2% of Chad's multi-ethnic population and speak a language similar to Lisi as well as Arabic. The Kouka live in the plains of the Guéra-Massif, neighboring the Bilala people. They support a centralized political system and focus their economic activities on cattle raising and small-scale farming. Religion and education in the Kouka society are based on Islamic *shari'a*.

KOULANGO, see KULANGO

KOUNTA

The Kounta are a West African people. They are concentrated in Mali. Their neighbors include the Kel Ahaggar, Iforas, Berabiche and Kel Adrar peoples.

KOURANKO, see KURANKO

KOURI

The Kouri, also spelled Kuri, are one of Chad's and Nigeria's many ethnic groups. Their language is very similar to Buduma. The Kouri live south of Lake Chad.

KOUROUMBA, see KURUMBA

KOURTEY, see KURTEY

KOUSSASSI, see KUSASI

KOUYA

One of the West African peoples. The Kouya are part of the Kru cluster of ethnic groups. They are concentrated in the Ivory Coast.

KOUYOU, see UBANGI and KUYU

KOUZIÉ

One of the West African peoples. The Kouzié are part of the Kru cluster of ethnic groups. They are concentrated in the Ivory Coast.

KOVOU, see ALLADIAN

KOVU, see ALLADIAN

KOYAM

These are a West African people and one of Nigeria's ethnic minorities. The Koyam are concentrated in the northeastern parts of Nigeria in what is presently the state of Borno (formerly Bornu). Groups of them, however, are located in Niger. The Koyam are essentially an agriculturalist people.

KOYRA

An East African Omotic-speaking people. The Koyra are concentrated in southern Ethiopia.

KPA-MENDE

The Kpa-Mende are a West African Mende-speaking group. They represent one of the three principal groups of the Mende people. They are concentrated in Sierra Leone's south central coastal areas.

KPAN

One of West Africa's peoples. The Kpan, also known as the Abakan, Akpanzhi, Hwaso, Hwaye, Ibukwo, Ikpan, Kpanten, Kpanzon, Kpwate, Nyatso, Nyonyo, and Yorda, speak a language that belongs to the Benue-Congo branch of the Niger-Congo family of African languages. They are concentrated in the southeastern regions of Nigeria, notably in the State of Gongola.

KPANTEN, see KPAN

KPANZON, see KPAN

KPE

The Kpe are one of Central and West Central African Bantu-speaking Bakwere groups. They are concentrated in the southern forest region of Cameroon.

KPELLE, see also EWE and MANDE

The Kpelle – also known as Gerse, Guerse, Guersé, Kpese, Ngere, Nguerze, Pele, and Pessy – are an Ewe group of the Mande people. They constitute one of ethnic minorities of both Liberia and Guinea, as well as other adjoining West African states. In Guinea, they are known as Gerse, Guerze, and Guerzé. Their language, Kpelle, belongs to the Mande branch of the Niger-Congo family of African languages. The Kpelle are organized into several chiefdoms, each of which is headed by a paramount chief. In their turn, chiefdoms are divided into smaller localities. The Kpelle are a rural people who engage in farming a variety of agricultural produce, including rice and potatoes, and peanuts. Their neighbors include the Bassa, Dan, Gbande, Gola, Konyanke, Loma, Mano, and Mende peoples.

KPESE, see KPELLE

KPESHI, see KPESI

KPESI

The Kpesi, also called Kpeshi, are a West African group. They are part of the Guan people. The Kpesi are concentrated in southern Ghana.

KPILAKPILA, see PILA-PILA

KPLOH

The Kploh are one of West Africa's Bassa subgroups. They are concentrated in the northern coastal areas of Liberia. Their neighbors include the Gola, Kpelle, Kru, Sapo, and Vai peoples.

KPONG

The Kpong are one of West Africa's peoples. They are an Adangbe subgroup. They live in Ghana, especially in its southeastern regions.

KPORWEIN

The Kporwein are one of West Africa's Bassa subgroups. They are concentrated in the northern coastal areas of Liberia.

KPWATE, see KPAN

KRACHI

The Krachi, also known as Krakye, are a West African Guan people. They speak a Kwa language of the Niger-Congo family of African languages, and are concentrated in Ghana and Togo. Their neighbors include the Adele, Akyem, Asante, Atyuti, Dagomba, Ewe, Guang, Kebu, Leefana

peoples.

KRAHN, see also **KRU**

A West African people. The Krahn, also spelled Kran, are one of Liberia's many ethnic minorities. They belong to the Kru cluster of peoples. Their neighbors include the Bakwe, Bassa, Grebo, Kru and Ngere peoples. The Krahn speak Kwa language of the Niger-Congo family of African languages.

KRAKYE, see **KRACHI**

KRAYE, see **KRACHI**

KRAN, see **KRAHN**

KRAN PADEBU, see **KRU**

KRECH, see **KREISH** and **SARA**

KREDA, see also **TOUBOU**

A Chadian people. The Kreda are one of Chad's nomadic Arab tribes. They are a Daza subgroup and live in the vicinity of Bahr al-Ghazāl river. Groups of them, however, can also be found in Sudan.

KREISH, see also **SARA**

The Kreish, also known as Krech, are a Central and East African Sara group. Their language is a Central Sudanic language that belongs to the Nilo-Saharan family of African languages. The Kreish are concentrated in western Sudan and eastern Central African Republic.

KREPE, see **KREPI**

KREPI

The Krepi, also known as the Krepe and Peki, are a West African people.

They are one of the Ewe subgroups in both Ghana and Togo.

KRIM

The Krim, also known as Kimi and Kittim, are a West African people. They are concentrated in the northern regions of Sierra Leone, as well as along its eastern coast. The Krim are essentially immigrants from Guinea. They engage in miscellaneous farming, fishing and trading activities. The Krim are related to the Sherbro people.

KRIO, see also CREOLE

People of racially mixed backgrounds. The term is especially used in Sierra Leone to describe the Creole communities that developed after the abolition of slavery and the founding of the country as a home for freed slaves. The settlers in Sierra Leone were often of mixed African and European descent, and generally speaking, lacked an identifiable African culture. In Sierra Leone, the Krio, that is Creole, are concentrated in Freetown and its vicinity.

KROBOU

The Krobou, also known as the Klobi and Krobo, are a West African people. They represent one of the groups that make up the Lagoon cluster of peoples in Ghana and the Ivory Coast.

KRONG

An East African people. The Krong are concentrated in southern Sudan.

KROU, see KRU

KRU

The Kru – also known as the Crau, Grebo, Krao, Krou, Krumen, and Wané – are a group of kindred tribes and one of the ethnic minorities of both Liberia and the Ivory Coast. They are related to the Basa (or Bassa), De, Grebo, Sikon, Sapo and Kran Padebu (or Papedu). Together with these related peoples, they occupy virtually one third of Liberia. Their language, Kru, belongs to the Kwa branch of the Niger-Congo family of African languages. The Kru are famous as navigators and fishermen throughout the west coast of Africa. They have established colonies in most West African ports, especially those of Liberia and the Ivory Coast. They number over 100,000. The modern history of the Kru people dates back to the sixteenth century, at which time they engaged in miscellaneous trading activities with European traders. During the eighteenth century, they became actively engaged in the slave trade. Not only did they allow Europeans to transport slaves across their territory, many of their men also became "sailors on the slave ships...and acting as cooks and interpreters" for slave ship crews.[263] The banning of the slave trade in the nineteenth century ended their involvement in slaving, but definitely not in other maritime or trading activities.

The Kru society is based on patrilineal relations. Moreover, it is divided into numerous clans and subclans, the most important of which is the Bete tribe of the western banks of the Bandama river in the Ivory Coast. Their society supports "a well-marked system of age-grades," as well as secret societies that are "open to all males except the very young."[264] The latter societies play a religious-ritual function in society.

The Kru reside in their traditional villages that thrive on the West African coast. They are divided into clans, each clan of which is overseen by an hereditary chief, who in turn is part of an overarching council that addresses the needs of the Kru people.

Though Christianity and Islam have won converts, many Kru continue to cherish their traditional religion which recognizes ancestor worship, nature spirits and one supreme God. This Kru religion is passed on through their oral traditions of folklore and proverbs.

KUA, see also TSHU-KWE

The Kua are a Southern African people. They are a Tshu-Kwe people, a San group. The Kua live in Botswana.

KUALUTHI

A Southern African Ambo people. They are highly concentrated in the Republic of Namibia.

KUAMBI

A Southern African Ambo people. They are concentrated in the Republic of Namibia.

KUANYAMA, see **KWANYAMA**

KUBA (Nigeria), see **KUBI**

KUBA (DRC/Zaire)

The Kuba, also known as Bakuba, are a cluster of Bantu-speaking people in the interior of the Democratic Republic of the Congo (Zaire). They are highly concentrated in the south central regions of the country, notably in the areas between the Kasai and Lulua rivers in the southwest and the Sankura river in the north. The Kuba support several subgroups, the most important of which are the Bushongo and the Ngongo.

The modern history of the Kuba is traced back to the seventeenth century, at which time their various chiefdoms organized themselves into a federation under the king of the Bushongo group (who assumes his powers by divine right). The federation is supported by a royal army and serviced by a unified administration. In their turn, its constituent units, the chiefdoms, are autonomous with each having its own hereditary chief (or subking) who rules with the help of councils that represent the main classes in society.

During the nineteenth century, internal conflict between the Bushongo kings and those of the chiefdoms of the federation culminated in a civil war. This war persisted until 1910, at which time the Kuba lands were conquered by the Belgian Congo colonial administration. With Belgian help, the central authority of the Bushongo kings was restored. Subsequently, the kingdom was incorporated within the Belgian Congo and later on within Democratic Republic of the Congo (Zaire).

In matters relating to descent, inheritance and succession, the Kuba are matrilineal. They observe matrilineal lineages and apply them. Despite exposure to European thought, they continue to uphold their traditional religion which is based on the belief in nature spirits and the spirits of their dead kings. Also, they continue to observe the traditional cultural patterns of their society, including its division into different age groups and initiation ceremonies. Their lifestyles are traditional and their main economic activities continue to center on agriculture, hunting, fishing and the production of woodcrafts and handwoven cloth.

KUBI

The Kubi, also known as the Kuba, are a West African Chadic-speaking people. They are concentrated in the Bauchi State in Nigeria.

KUBONYE

The Kubonye are a Southern African Swazi people, and one of the principal Emakhandzambili subgroups. They live in Swaziland.

KUBRI, see also KANEMBA

A West African group. The Kubri are a Kanemba people, a Kanuri subgroup. They are concentrated in Chad. Groups of them, however, are also located in northern Niger and Nigeria.

KUDA-CHAMO

The Kuda-Chamo are a West African people. They live in the Bauchi State in Nigeria.

KUDAWA

A West African group. The Kudawa are a Hausa Muslim people. They are concentrated in northwestern Nigeria. Groups of them, however, live in the northern regions of Benin and Niger.

KUEK

An East African people. The Kuek are one of the Atuot main subgroups. They live in southern Sudan.

KUENA, see KWENA

KUGAMA

The Kugama, also known as the Wegam, are a West African people. They are concentrated in the southeastern regions of Nigeria, notably in the Gongola State.

KUGBO

A West African people. The Kugbo live in Nigeria, primarily in the Rivers State. They speak a language that belongs to the Benue-Congo branch of the Niger-Congo family of African languages.

KUJAMAAT

The Kujamaat, also known as the Fogny, are a West African Jola subgroup. They live in the Senegal, primarily along the Casamance river.

KUKA, see KOUKA

KUKAMBA, see AMBA

KUKELE

The Kukele, also known as the Bakele and Ukele, are a West African people. Their groups are found in both Nigeria and the Cameroon, notably in the Cross River and Anambra states in Nigeria.

KUKU

These are one of Sudan's tribal people who live in the southern regions of the country. Groups of them, however, can also be found in the northeastern parts of the Democratic Republic of the Congo (Zaire). The

Kuku speak an Eastern Sudanic language of the Chari-Nile branch of the Nilo-Saharan family of African languages.

The Kuku support a relatively sedentary type of society. They live in scattered villages and their main economic activities center on farming, cattle raising, and hunting. Their social organization is essentially tribal and patrilineal.

KUKURUKU

The Kukuruku are a West African Edo people. Their concentrations are along the coastal areas of Nigeria, Benin and Togo. Kukuruku groups, however, can also be found in southwestern Nigeria. They are closely related to the Edo people.

KUKWE

The Kukwe are an East African people. They are part of the Nyakyusa cluster of peoples in Tanzania.

KULAGO, see KULANGO

KULANGO, see also LOBI-DAGARTI

A West African people. The Kulango – also known as Babé, Koulango and Kulago, Kulano, Lorhon, Ngwela, and Nkoramfo – are concentrated in Ivory Coast, Burkina-Faso and Ghana. They speak a language that belongs to the Kwa branch of the Niger-Congo family of African languages. Their neighbors include the Anyi, Brong, Dyula, Gan, Guang, Komono, Likpe, Lobi, Nafana, Senufo and Vagala peoples.

KULANO, see KULANGO

KULERE

The Kulere, also known as the Korom Boye and Tof, are a West African people. They live in Nigeria, primarily in the Plateau State.

KULLO

An East African people. The Kullo live in the southern regions of Ethiopia.

KULUNG

The Kulung, also known as Bakulung, Bambur, and Wurkum, are a West African Bantu-speaking people. Their language belongs to the Benue-Congo branch of the Niger-Congo family of African languages. The Kulung are concentrated in the southeastern regions of Nigeria, notably in the Gongola State.

KULYA, see KURIA

KUMA, see KOMA (West Africa)

KUMAILAB

The Kumailab are an East African Beja group. They live in the southeastern coastal plains of Sudan.

KUMAM, see KUMAN

KUMAN

The Kuman, also known as Akum, Akokolemu, Ikokolemu and Kumam, are an East Saharan and Central and East African Nilotic-speaking people. They are concentrated in the north central areas of Uganda.

KUMASE, see KUMASI

KUMASI

The Kumasi, also spelled Kumase, are a West African people. They are one of the main Asante subgroups. The Kumasi live in Ghana.

KUMBA, see IBIBIO

KUMBO MEIN

The Kumbo Mein are a West African people. They are an Izon subgroup. These people live in Nigeria, primarily in the Rivers State.

KUMBU

The Kumbu people are a West African group. Their main concentrations are in Nigeria and Mali. Their neighbors include the Bariba, Lodagaba, Lowiili, and Tene peoples.

KUMRA

One of Chad's many ethnic groups. The Kumba are part of the Sara cluster of peoples.

KUMU

The Kumu are a Bantu-speaking people. They live in the Democratic Republic of the Congo (Zaire).

KUN, see !KUNG

KUNAMA, see KUNEMA

KUNDA, see KAONDE

KUNDU

The Kundu are one of the peoples of Equatorial and Central Africa. They live primarily in the western regions of the Democratic Republic of the Congo (Zaire).

KUNEMA

An East African agricultural people. The Kunema, also called Baden, Baza, Diila and Kunama, are concentrated in the northern regions of Ethiopia and Eritrea, primarily along their borders with Sudan. They are a Nilotic-speaking people. Their neighbors include the Anak, Barya, and Berti

peoples.

KUNFEL

One of East Africa's peoples. The Kunfel are concentrated in the vicinity of Lake Tana in Western Ethiopia. Groups of them, however, are also found in southern Sudan.

!KUNG, see also SAN

A Southwest African people. The !Kung, also known as the Zhu and Xhu, are concentrated in the northeastern regions of the Republic of Namibia and western Botswana. They are a San group.

KUNIKE

The Kunike are a West African Temne subgroup. They are concentrated in Sierra Leone. Groups of them, however, can also be found in neighboring states.

KUNTA

These are an Arab nomadic people of the southern Algerian desert and the northern banks of the Niger River.

The Kunta are the people that brought the teachings of the Qadiriyyah brotherhood, a sufi cult that flourished among the Fulani people during the nineteenth century, to the Sudan.[265] The Qadiriyyah disapproved of religious laxity and advocated recourse to the fundamental principles of Islam. Its members called for a total *jihad* to realize their goals.[266]

KUNYI, see KONGO

KUPSABINY

The Kupsabiny are an East African Nilotic-speaking people and one of Uganda's principal ethnic groups. They are concentrated in the northern regions of Uganda.

KUPTO

The Kupto are one of West Africa's ethnic groups. They are concentrated in Nigeria, primarily in the Bauchi State.

KURA

The Kura are one of the main Kuri subgroups in Chad. They speak Yedina, a Buduma dialect. Like other Kuri groups, they live along the eastern shores of Lake Chad. The Kura are divided into several clans, the most important of which are the Dagila, Doria, Maradalla, Kallameida, and Tojima.

KURAMA

The Kurama – also known as the Akurumia, Bagwama, Rurama and Tikurimi – are a West African people. They are concentrated in the east central regions of Nigeria and the Karta region of Mali. They speak a language that belongs to the Benue-Congo branch of the Niger-Congo family of African languages. Their neighbors include the Hausa, Kadara, Katab and Jerawa peoples.

KURANKO, see also MANDE

The Kuranko – also spelled Koranko, Kooranko and Kouranko – are a West African Mande forest group. They are concentrated in Sierra Leone, notably in the northern areas of the country. However, groups of them are also found in Guinea and Liberia. The Kuranko are related to the Mandingo. Their neighbors include the Bullom, Limba, Loko, Kono, Mende, Sherbro, Susu and Temne peoples.

KURFEI

A West African Hansa group. The Kurfei, also known as the Kurfey and Saudié, are concentrated in Niger and adjoining countries. They speak a language that belongs to the Afro-Asiatic family of African languages. Their neighbors include the Adarawa, Fula, Mauri and Zerma peoples.

KURFEY, see KURFEI

KURI

The Kuri are one of the many ethnic groups of which Chad is composed. They speak Yedina, a language that belongs to the Saharan group of African languages. The Kuri are concentrated in the Lake Chad region. They support several subgroups, including the Kalia (Kwallia), Kura, Medi, Ngadji and Yakudi.

KURIA

The Kuria – also called Ikikuria, Kulya and Tende – are an East African people. They are concentrated in Kenya and Tanzana, notably along the eastern shore of Lake Victoria, The Kuria are culturally and linguistically related to the Gusii people.

KURTEY

The Kurtey, also known as Kourtey, are one of Niger's, Benin's and Mali's Zerma subgropus. Groups of them, however, can also be found in Ghana. The Kurteyy live along the banks of the Niger river.

KURUMBA

The Kurumba, also known as the Akurumba and Kouroumba, are a West African people. They live in the central regions of Burkina-Faso. The Kurumba are part of the Ninisi cluster of ethnic groups.

KUSAE, see KUSASI

KUSAI, see KUSASI

KUSASE, see KUSASI

KUSASI

The Kusasi, also known as the Koussassi, Kusae, Kusai, and Kusase, are a West African people. Their main concentrations are in Burkina-Faso and Ghana.

KUSH, see CUSH

KUSU

One of the Bantu-speaking peoples of Equatorial and Central Africa. The Kusu are part of the Mongo cluster of peoples. They are concentrated in the Democratic Republic of the Congo (Zaire), notably in the western regions of the country.

KUTED

The Kuted, also known as the Kutep, Kutev, Jompre, Mbarike, and Zumper, are one of West Africa's peoples. They speak a language that belongs to the Benue-Congo branch of the Niger-Congo family of African languages. The Kuted live in the southeastern regions of Nigeria, notably in the Gongola State.

KUTEP, see KUTED

KUTEV, see KUTED

KUTIN

The Kutin are a West African people. They are concentrated in southeastern Nigeria, primarily in the Gongola State.

KUTSWE, see PEDI

KUTU

The Kutu are an East African Bantu-speaking people. They are concentrated in the northeastern coastal regions of Tanzania. Their neighbors include the Doe, the Kaguru, the Kami, the Kwere, the Luguru, the Ndengereko, the Ngulu, the Rufiji, the Sagara, the Vidunda, the Wazaramo (Zaramo) and the Zigua peoples. The Kutu are part of the

Zaramo cluster of peoples.

Historical evidence suggests that the Kutu used to live in the Ulugura Mountains region, which is located about 200 kilometers west of Dar es Salaam, the capital of what is presently Tanzania. In the nineteenth century they moved down onto the plains south of the mountains, and subsequently, they moved again east.[267]

The Kutu are organized in village groups that are politically, economically and religiously independent. Traditionally, they were not subject to a centralized political authority. In addition, they also supported a matrilineal society.

KUTUMBAWA

One of West Africa's peoples. The Kutumbawa are concentrated in Nigeria, notably in its northwestern regions.

KUTURMI

The Kuturmi, also known as the Ada, are one of Nigeria's, Niger's and Benin's many ethnic groups. They are part of the Hausa-Fulbe cluster of peoples.

KUVALE

The Kuvale are a Southwest African people. They are concentrated in Angola, primarily in its western regions. Their neighbors include the Hakavona, Herero, Ngambwe, and the Vatwa peoples.

KUVOKO, see LAMANG

KUWAA

The Kuwaa, also known as the Belle, are a West African Kraun-speaking people. They live primarily in Liberia.

KUYU

The Kuyu, also spelled Kouyou, are an Equatorial and Central African Mbochi subgroup. They are concentrated in Gabon, the Republic of Congo and the Democratic Republic of the Congo (Zaire).

KUZAMANI

The Kuzamani, also known as the Rishuwa, are one of Nigeria's many ethnic groups. They are concentrated in the Kaduna State.

KWA (Nigeria)

A Kwa-speaking people who live in the southeastern regions of Nigeria, notably in the Gongola state.

KWA (Togo)

The Kwa people constitute one of Togo's major ethnic minorities, accounting for about one half of the country's population. They are highly concentrated in the country's southwestern regions.

KWAHU

The Kwahu – also known as the Akwahu, Kwawu, and Quahoe – are a West African people. They constitute one of Ghana's many ethnic minorities and one of the Akan's major groups. They live in the eastern regions of the country.

KWAKA, see AVIKAM

KWALE, see IGBO

KWALLA

One of West Africa's peoples. The Kwalla live primarily in the Plateau State in Nigeria. They are closely related to the their neighbors the Bwal, Dimmuk, and Namu peoples.

KWALLIA, see **KURI** and **YAKUDI**

KWAMATWI

The Kwamatwi are a Southwest African people. They are concentrated in the northwestern regions of Namibia. Their neighbors include the Kwanyama, Ongona, Tyavikwa, and Zimba peoples.

KWAMI

The Kwami, also known as the Kwom, are a Nigerian people. They are concentrated in the Bauchi State.

KWANDA

An East African people. The Kwanda, also known as Kwandi, are highly concentrated in western Zambia. They are closely related to the Lozi people. They speak Kololo, the Lozi language, share many of Lozi customs, and are part of the Lozi-dominated Barotse Kingdom.[268] The Kwanda are part of the Luyana cluster of peoples.

KWANDI, see **KWANDA**

KWANGA, see **KWANGWA**

KWANGALI, see also **KAVANGO**

The Kwangali, also Kwangali-Gcikuru, are a Southwest African Kavango people. They are concentrated in Angola, Namibia, and Botswana.

KWANGARE, see also **KAVANGO**

The Kwangare, also called Kwangari, are a Southwest African people. They are one of the Kwango groups who live in Angola and in the northeastern regions of Namibia. Their neighbors include the Mashi and the Hukwe peoples.

KWANGARI, see **KAVANGO**

KWANGO

The Kwango are a West Central African Bantu-speaking people. They are concentrated in the Democratic Republic of the Congo (Zaire), primarily in its southwestern areas of the country.

KWANGWA

The Kwangwa, also known as Kwanga and Makwanga, are an Equatorial and Central African people. They are concentrated in southwest Zambia. They speak a Luyana language. Their neighbors include the Lumbu, Tonga, and Totela peoples.

KWANIM PA, see UDUK

KWANKA

One of West Africa's peoples. The Kwanka are concentrated in the northwestern regions of Nigeria.

KWANKHALA

The Kwankhala are a Southwest African people. Their main concentrations are in Angola and Namibia.

KWANKUA

The Kwankua are one of Angola's many ethnic groups. They are concentrated in the southwestern regions of the country.

KWANYAMA

The Kwanyama are a Southwest African people. They are an Ambo group. They live primarily in Angola as well as in the northwestern regions of Namibia. Their neighbors include the Kwamatwi, Ovambo, and Zimba (Wazimba) peoples.

KWARA

The Kwara are an East African Agaw people. They are concentrated in the central and northern regions of Ethiopia.

KWARRA, see MAMA

KWATAMA

The Kwatama are a West African people. They are concentrated in the northwestern regions of Nigeria, as well as in southwestern Niger and northern Benin. The Kwatama belong to the Hausa-Fulbe cluster of peoples.

KWAWU, see KWAHU

KWAYA (Ivory Coast)

The Kwaya are an Ivorian people and one of the Kru cluster groups. They live in the south central regions of the Ivory Coast.

KWAYA (Tanzania)

An East African Jiji people. The Kwaya are concentrated primarily in Tanzania.

KWAYAM

These are a West African Nilo-Saharan-speaking people. The Kwayam are concentrated in northeastern Nigeria, notably in the vicinity of Lake Chad. Their neighbors include the Buduma, Kanembu, Kanuri, Mabar and Manga peoples.

KWENA, see also SOTHO

The Kwena – also known as the Bakuena, Bakwena, and Kuena – are a Sotho group of people. They are a Southern Bantu-speaking people. The Kwena are concentrated in the Lebowa, formerly one of the Black homelands in South Africa, as well as in Lesotho and Botswana. Kwena subgroups comprise such tribes as Molibeli, Monaheng, Hlakwana, Kxwakxwa (Qwagwa) and Fokeng.

Like other Sotho, they are a southern African people who speak Sesotho, a Bantu language, and engage in agriculture and animal husbandry. Their settlements are characterized "by scattered hamlets of circular huts with mud and wattle or stone walls surmounted by a conical, thatched roof."[269] In their social patterns, most Kwena recognize patrilineal lineages and continue to be impacted by their traditional religious beliefs.

KWENI, see GURO

KWEPE

The Kwepe are a Southwest African people. They are concentrated in Angola, primarily in its southwestern coastal regions. Their neighbors include the Herero, Himba, and the Kwisi peoples.

KWERA

The Kwera are a Southwest African people. They are concentrated in Botswana. Their neighbors include the Ngwato, Ohekwe, and Tswana peoples.

KWERE

The Kwere, also known as Mwere, are an East African Bantu-speaking Muslim people. They are concentrated in the northeastern coastal regions of Tanzania. Their neighbors include such groups as the Doe, the Kaguru, the Kami, the Ndengereko, the Kutu, the Luguru, the Ngulu, the Rufiji, the Sagara, the Vidunda, the Wazaramo (Zaramo) and the Zigua peoples. The Kwere are organized in village groups that are politically, economically and religiously independent. Traditionally, they were not subject to a centralized political authority. In addition, they also supported a matrilineal society. They are an independent group within the Zarama cluster of peoples.

KWESE

A West Central African people. They speak Kwese, a Western Bantu language. The Kwese, also spelled Kwisi, are concentrated in Angola and the Democratic Republic of the Congo (Zaire). In the Democratic Republic of the Congo (Zaire), their neighbors include the Pende people of the Bandundu and Kasai administrative provinces. The Kwese are part of the Pende cluster of peoples living in Central Africa.

KWISI, see **KWESE**

KWITH, see **NUER**

KWOLL, see **IRIGWE**

KWOM, see **KWAMI**

KWONO, see **KONO**

KXOE, see also **SAN**

A southern African San group. The Kxoe, also known as Makwengo, are a San-speaking people. They live along the Okavango river in the Caprivi Strip of Namibia. Like other San-speaking peoples, they are essentially foragers, hunters and gatherers.

KXWAKXWA, see also **SOTHO**

The Exwakxwa, also called Qwagwa, are a Sotho group of people. They are one of the Kwena subgroups of the Sotho people. They are concentrated in the Kingdom of Lesotho.

Like other Sotho, they are a southern African people, speak Sesotho, a Bantu language, and engage in agriculture and animal husbandry. Their settlements are characterized "by scattered hamlets of circular huts with mud and wattle or stone walls surmounted by a conical, thatched roof."[270]

KYAMBA, see **BASARI (Togo** and **Ghana)**

KYEDYE, see **NUPE**

KYENGA, see **SHANGAWA**

KYEREPON, see **KYEREPONG**

KYEREPONG

The Kyerepong, also known as Cherepong and Kyerepon, are a West African people. They are concentrated in Ghana, notably in its eastern regions.

KYIBAKU

The Kyibaku, also known as Chibak, Chibbuk, Icibak, and Kikuk, are a West African people. They live in Nigeria, notably in the Borno State.

LABWOR

A small group of Central and East African people. The Labwor are concentrated in the Karamoja District in Uganda. Trade is their main economic activity.

LAGOON

A West African cluster of people. They are concentrated in the coastal lagoons of the Ivory Coast where they engage in fishing and trading activities.

LAHU, see **AVIKAM**

LAITAYOK, see **MASAI**

LAK, see **NUER**

LAKA

The Laka are one of the many ethnic groups of which Chad is composed. Their language belongs to the Niger-Congo family. They are concentrated in areas west of the Chari and Longone River basins.

LAKHSAS, see also BERBER

The Lakhsas are a Moroccan Berber group. They are concentrated in the Ishilhayen region of Morocco, notably in the Western High Atlas, the Sus Valley, and the Anti-Atlas areas of the country.

LALA

The Lala are a Southwest and Southeast African people. They are concentrated in Zimbabwe. Their neighbors include the Aushi, Chishinga, Luapula, and Swaka peoples.

LALAWA, see KOLELA

LALI, see KONGO

LAMA, see LAMBA

LAMANG

The Lamang, also known as Gbuhwe and Kuvoko, are a West African cluster of people. They are concentrated in Cameroon and Nigeria.

LAMBA

These are one of the ethnic minorities of Togo. The Lamba, known also as Namba, Nambane and Lama, are Bantu-speaking people. They speak Tem-Kabre. They are concentrated in the Kéran River Valley and Monts du Togo area. Their society observes patrilineal lines of descent.

LAMBYA

These are an East African people and one of Tanzania's ethnic groups. The

Lambya are concentrated in the southwestern areas of the country, especially in the Mbeya administrative region. Their lands are bordered on the west by Lake Tanganyika and on south by Lake Nyasa, Malawi and the Republic of Zambia.

The Lambya's economic activities focus on agriculture, fishing and animal husbandry. They are also engaged in salt, gold, coal and mica mining activities in their region.

LANDOGO, see LOKKO

LANDOUMA, see LANDUMA

LANDOUMAN, see LANDUMA

LANDUMA

The Landuma, also known as Landuman, Landouma, Landouman and Tyapi, are a West African people. They are related to the Baga. The Landuman are concentrated in Guinea-Bissau and speak a language that belongs to the West Atlantic branch of African languages. Their neighbors include the Baga, Biafada, Fula, Nalu and Susu peoples.

LANDUMAN, see LANDUMA

LANGI, see RANGI and LANGO

LANGO

The Lango people are one of Uganda's Nilotic-speaking minorities. Their language is an Eastern Sudanic language belonging to the Chari-Nile branch of the Nile-Saharan family of African languages. They are concentrated in the northern regions of the country, especially in those areas located northeast of Lakes Kwania and Kyoga. The Lango neighbors include the Acholi, Ganda, the Karamojong, the Nyoro and the Teso peoples. The main economic activities of the Lango focus on agriculture and animal husbandry. Their society observes patrilineal lineages in matters relating to descent, inheritance, and succession, as well as age-sets in political and social structures.

Currently, the Lango support a small principality of their own which is characterized by lack of cohesiveness. Traditionally, however, they were governed by non-hereditary senior chiefs called *rwot*, as well as hereditary chiefs. Each non-hereditary chief oversaw a group of hereditary chiefs.

Though Christianity and Islam have won many of them, the Lango continue to be impacted by their traditional religion, which centered on the belief in a supreme being called *Jok*, as well as in the ancestral cult. In their traditional beliefs, every individual has a guardian spirit, called *winyo*, "that [attends] him during life and that must be ritually liberated from the corpse. There [is] also a belief in a shadow self, or immaterial soul (*tipo*), that after death [is] merged into...*Jok*."[271]

LARIM, see LONGARIM

LATUKA

An Eastern Nilotic Sudanese people. The Latuka are concentrated in Sudan, notably in its southern central regions along Sudan's border with Uganda.

LEBANESE

Lebanese immigrants and/or their descendants who, since the later part of the nineteenth century, had settled in Africa. These people are unevenly distributed in essentially Francophone African countries. Their main concentrations are in Chad, Egypt, Gabon, Ghana, Ivory Coast, Kenya, Liberia, Mali, Nigeria, Senegal, Sierra Leone, and Sudan. Their economic activities focus on miscellaneous trading and industrial activities.

LEBOU

The Lebou, also spelled Lebu, are a West African Muslim people. They are concentrated in the Cape Verde peninsula, Senegal. The Lebou speak the Wolof language.

LEBU, see **LEBOU**

LECK, see **NUER**

LEFANA

A West African people. The Lefana are concentrated in Togo. Groups of them, however, are also located in adjoining countries. Their neighbors include the Akyem, Ana, Asante, Ewe, Kebu, Krachi and Tribu peoples. The Lefana speak a language that belongs to the Kwa branch of the Niger-Congo family of African languages.

LEGA

The Lega, also known as Kilega, Mwenga and Rega, are a Southeast African people. They are concentrated in the eastern regions of the Democratic Republic of the Congo (Zaire).

LELA, see **KOLELA**

LELAU, see **KOLELA**

LELE, see **KONGO**

A West Central Western Bantu-speaking people. They are concentrated in Angola and the Democratic Republic of the Congo (Zaire). In Zaire, their neighbors include the Pende people of the Bandundu and Kasai administrative provinces.

LEMTA

A Berber group of southern Libya. It is generally presumed that Aliman Za, the founder of the Za dynasty of Songhay that endured from the later part of the eighth century to 1492, originated from this group.[272]

LENDU

The Lendu, also known as Bale, Badha and Kilendu, are a West Central,

Southwest and Southeast African people. They are concentrated in the northeastern regions of the Democratic Republic of the Congo (Zaire), as well as in Uganda.

LENG, see NUER

LENGE

The Lenge, also spelled Lenje, are a Bantu-speaking people. They are concentrated in Zambia, where they represent one of its ethnic minorities. Historical evidence suggests that together with the Ila and Tonga peoples, the Lenge had developed an important kingdom in the past. Their territory "stretched from the Zambezi River north to Lukanga Swamp of the Kafue River and from the contemporary Western Province (formerly Barotseland) to a great distance eastward."[273]

LENGI, see FANG

LENGOLA

The Lengola are a West Central African people. They are concentrated in the eastern regions of the Democratic Republic of the Congo (Zaire), notably west of the Lualaba River.

LENJE, see LENGE

LEYA

The Leya people are a Southwest African ethnic group. They are concentrated in Zambia. Their neighbors include the Ndebele, Toka, and Subya peoples.

LIKOUALA, see UBANGI

LIKPE

These are a West African people. The Likpe are concentrated in the Ivory Coast and Ghana. Their neighbors include the Brong, Guang, Nafana,

Kulango and Vagala peoples. Their language belongs to the Kwa branch of Niger-Congo African languages.

LILSE

A West African Voltaic-speaking people. The Lilse are concentrated in Burkina Faso and adjoining countries. Their neighbors include the Bobo, Busa, Dogon, Dyula, Grunshi, Mossi, Nunuma and Samo peoples.

LIMBA, see also NGABAKA

The Limba are a West African people and one of the ethnic minorities of both Guinea and Sierra Leone. In Guinea, they are concentrated in the savanna surrounding the Fouta Djallon plateau in what is the western central areas of the country. In Sierra Leone, they inhabit the northern areas of the country and adjoin the Bullom, Loko, Kono, Kuranko, Malinke, Mende, Susu and Temne peoples. The Limba speak a language that belongs to the West Atlantic branch of the Niger-Congo family of African languages.

LISSAWAN, see TAUREG

LIYUWA

The Liyuwa are a Southwest and Southeast African people. They are concentrated in Angola, Namibia and Zambia.

LO, see GURO

LOBAIZU

The Lobaizu are a West African Kraun-speaking people. They live in Liberia, primarily in the Lofa County. The Lobaizu are a Kuwaa subgroup.

LOBEDU, see PEDI and LOVEDU

LOBI, see also MOSSI

The Lobi are one of West Africa's peoples. Their language is a Voltaic Gur language of the Niger-Congo family. Currently, they constitute one of the ethnic minorities of Burkina Faso (formerly Upper Volta), Ghana (formerly Gold Coast) and the Ivory Coast (Côte d'Ivoire), but have tribal affiliations with more numerous groups outside both countries. Their neighbors include the Birifor, Diam, Dorossié, Komono and Kulango peoples. The Lobi were noted for their effective use of poisoned arrows, a factor that hindered French attempts to subdue them until 1903.

LOBI-DAGARTI

The Lobi-Dagarti, also called Dagara, Dagara-Lobr, LoDagaa, LoWilisi and Dagarti, are a West African cluster of peoples who live in Burkina Faso, Ghana, Ivory Coast and other western African states. In Burkina Faso, they are concentrated in the Southwest department. In Ghana, they live in the Lawra, Wa and Bole districts. In the Ivory Coast, they are located in the Bonduku and Buna districts. Aside from Lobi proper, the cluster includes the Birifor (or LoBirifor), the Dagaa Wiili, the Dorossié, the Gan (Gaàn or Gian), the Komono, the Kulago (Kulango), the Lobiri, the LoPiel, the LoSaala, the LoWiili, the Mole-Dagbane, the Padoro, the Pwa (Pugula or Pougouli), the Teguessié (Tégué or Teésé) and Wala peoples. Of these groups, the Birifor speak Dagara, the Dorossié and the Gan speak Lobi, the Teguessié speak Kulango, the Pwa speak Crusi, and the Wala speak Dagaba.

The Lobi-Dagarti "are without any overarching tribal organization or, strictly speaking, any territory. They move not as large units, but as family groups, sometimes into other ethnic areas, where they may be absorbed into the local population."[274]

The Lobi-Dagarti people continue to adhere to their traditional beliefs which center on the worship of the Earth and the ancestors.

LOBIRI, see LOBI-DAGARTI

LODAGAA, see DAGARA and LOBI-DAGARTI

LODAGABA, see DAGARA and LOBI-DAGARTI

LOGBA

These are a West African people. They are concentrated in the northern areas of Togo. Groups of them, however, can also be found in Ghana. The Logba are a Kabré subgroup.

LOGO

A Central and eastern African people. The Logo are a Nilotic people. They speak Logo, an Eastern Sudanic language which is closely related to those of their neighbors the Bale (Lendu), the Keliko, the Lugbara and the Madi peoples. The Logo are concentrated in Sudan, Uganda and the Democratic Republic of the Congo (Zaire).

LOGOLI, see LUHYA

LOGWARI, see LUGBARA

LOITA, see MASAI

LOKKO, see LOKO

LOKO, see also MANDE

The Loko, also Lokko and Landogo, are a West African Mande people. They are located in Guinea, Liberia and Sierra Leone. In Sierra Leone, they live chiefly in the northern areas of the country. Their adjoining neighbors include the Bullom, Kono, Kuranko, Limba, Malinke, Mende, Susu and Temne peoples. The Loko speak a language that belongs to the Mande branch of the Niger-Congo family of African languages.

LOKOP, see SAMBURU

LOLO

A Southeast and East African people. The Lolo are concentrated in Malawi,

Mozambique and Tanzania.

LOMA, see also MANDE

The Loma people, also known as Buzi and Toma, are a Mande people. They are one of the ethnic groups of Guinea, Liberia and other West African states. In Guinea, they are concentrated in the Forest Region adjoining the Bassa, Gbande, Kissi, Konyanke, Kpelle, Malinke, Mano and Mende peoples. Their language belongs to the Mande group of the Niger-Congo branch of African languages.

LOMAMI

The Lomami people are a Central African people. They are concentrated in the Democratic Republic of the Congo (Zaire), primarily west of Lake Tanganyika. Their neighbors include the Bemba, Holoholo, Kuba, Moer, and Tumbwe peoples.

LOMONGO, see MONGO

LOMUE, see LOMWE

LOMWE

A Southeast and East African people. The Lomwe, also spelled Lomue, are one of the major ethnic groups of the Republic of Malawi. They are also located in Mozambique and Tanzania.

LONGARIM

An East African people. The Longarim, also called Boya and Larim, are concentrated in the southern regions of Sudan.

LONGUDA

The Longuda are a West African people. They are concentrated in eastern Nigeria. Their neighbors include the Bachama, Dera, Jen, Mbula, Tangale, Tera and Vere peoples. The Longuda speak a language that belongs to the

Adamawa branch of the Niger-Congo family of African languages.

LOODOKILANI, see **MASAI**

LOPIEL, see **LOBI-DAGARTI**

LORHON, see **KULANGO**

LOSAALA, see **LOBI-DAGARTI**

LOSO, see **NAUDEBA**

LOTILLA MURLE

An East African agricultural people. They are concentrated in the eastern regions of Sudan.

LOTUKO

The Lotuko are a Central African group. Their main concentrations are in southern Sudan. Groups of them, however, can also be found in Uganda and the Democratic Republic of the Congo (Zaire). Their neighbors include the Bari, Ik, and Lano peoples.

LOU, see **NUER**

LOVEDU, see also **SOTHO**

The Lovedu are a Sotho group of people. They are concentrated in the Lebowa, formerly one of the Black homelands in South Africa. Now, they are an integral part of the country.

Like other Sotho, they are a southern African people, speak Sesotho, a Bantu language, and engage in agriculture and animal husbandry. Their settlements are characterized "by scattered hamlets of circular huts with mud and wattle or stone walls surmounted by a conical, thatched roof."[275]

LOWIILI, see **LOBI-DAGARTI**

LOWILISI, see **LOBI-DAGARTI**

LOWWE

The Lowwe are a Southeast African-Malagasy people. They are concentrated in the east central regions of Mozambique. Their neighbors include the Makua and Yao peoples.

LOZI

The Lozi, also called Aluyi, Barotse, Barutsi, Barozi, Kololo, Luyi, Malozi, Marotse, Marutse, Rotse, Rozi, Rutse, Silozi, or Tozui, are a Western Bantu-speaking people. They comprise some 25 peoples of about six cultural groups. Currently, they are concentrated along the Zambezi River in the Western Province, formerly Barotseland, of the Republic of Zambia. They speak Kololo, a Benue-Congo language of the Niger-Congo family of African languages.

Prior to their present name, all Lozi people were called Barotse, the name of the Barotse tribe to which they belonged and whose clans lived in several provinces of Zambia, as well as in Angola and Namibia (formerly Southwest Africa). And prior to being called Barotse, they were known as Aluyi. They acquired the name Barotse upon their defeat by Sebetwane, the paramount chief of the southern African Kololo (formerly Sotho) people, in 1838. The name "Barotse" stood for "Aluyi" in the Koloko speech.

In an effort to win their support, Sebetwane encouraged intermarriage between his people and the Aluyi. Moreover, he recognized Aluyi's leaders and assigned to them prominent positions in the government. These enlightened policies helped to pacify the Aluyi, and more importantly, facilitated their eventual integration with the Kololo society.[276]

Sebetwane's death in 1851, however, led to a succession crisis, which was not resolved to the liking of the Barotse. Hence, in 1864, the Barotse overthrew the Kololo's chiefdom and assumed control over their own destiny and those of their new subjects, the Kololo. Additionally, they adopted a new name Lozi (Malozi) which refer to both their own people and the Kololo.

On the whole, the Lozi society is highly cohesive with authority hierarchically divided between three classes: nobility, commoners and serfs. At the apex of the hierarchy there is a paramount chief who is assisted by a council of chiefs. In their turn, chiefs attend to their respective clans, with each clan having its own council of elders.

The Lozi people are renowned farmers. Apart from agriculture, their main economic activities focus on animal husbandry and fishing.

LUANO

The Luano are a Southwest African people. They are concentrated in the central regions of Zambia. Their neighbors include the Ambo, Lenje, and Mbwera peoples.

LUAPULA, see also LUNDA

The Luapula people are a West Central and Southwest African Lunda group. They are concentrated in the Democratic Republic of the Congo (Zaire) and Zambia.

LUBA

The Luba, also known as Baluba, are a Western Bantu-speaking people. Their language, Kiluba, is a tonal language. The Luba constitute the second largest ethnic group in Democratic Republic of the Congo (Zaire), where they are concentrated in the south central parts of the country, notably in Shaba. They are historically and culturally related to other Congo peoples and in addition they are subdivided into several groups, the most important of which are: the Shankaji (Shankadi) of Katanga, the Bambo of Kasai and the Hemba of northern Katanga and southern Kivu.

Originally, the Luba people inhabited the central Benue River valley around the present border between the modern states of Cameroon and Nigeria. During the first century A.D., they moved to the Congo River basin, and from there, their migration led them to the Luba country of northern Katanga. With Luba country as their new base, they expanded in various directions, imparting their culture and civilization on other peoples.[277] By the eighth and ninth centuries A.D., they were able to develop an elaborate culture that was based on the exploitation of Katanga's copper fields, as well as on miscellaneous trading activities with their neighbors. Also, they were able to organize themselves into a series of small chiefdoms around Lake Kisale in northern Katanga to the west of the southern tip of Lake Tanganyika.

Their modern history, however, is traced back to the early part of the sixteenth century, at which time a conqueror called Kongolo started a process of unifying the Luba chiefdoms – a process that was continued under his son and successor, Kalala Ilunga. Eventually, the process culminated in the establishment of the kingdom of Luba.

Under this new kingdom, political unification was consolidated through a hierarchy of chiefdoms, which provided an intermediary between the central authority of the king who possessed divine and absolute powers and the villages which were the constituent units of the kingdom. Under the same kingdom, groups of chiefdoms formed territorial chiefdoms, which, in their turn, were joined together to form the larger territorial units or provinces of the kingdom.[278] Under it also, all chiefs with the exception of some local headmen, were members of the royal family–a factor that contributed to he enhancement of the kingdom's internal security and its unity.[279] With the consolidation of the kingdom, Kalala's successors embarked on expanding Luba's territory by conquering other kingdoms and ruling them as tributary states.

The Luba kingdom began to decline in the later part of the nineteenth century, and eventually it collapsed as a result of continued succession struggle, repeated attacks by Angolan slave traders, and frequent assaults by Tanzanian conquerors, and Belgian colonization.

At the start of the twentieth century, the Belgian colonizers divided the kingdom's "center into two large territories, the government of which was assigned to two rival heirs from the ancient dynasty: Kabongo and Kasongo Nyembo. Moreover, about twenty Luba chiefdoms were acknowledged as fully independent from those two rulers."[280] Foreign rule over the Luba continued until the independence of the Congo on August 15, 1960. Following the Congo's independence, the Luba people engaged in a war with their southern neighbors who aspired to establish Katanga as an independent state.

Traditionally, the Luba engaged in food gathering, hunting, agriculture, fishing and trading. Traditionally also, they believed in a supreme god and ancestral, as well as natural spirits. Additionally, they observed circumcision and supported a variety of initiation associations.

The Luba in general, and the Shankaji and Hemba among them in particular, are renowned for their artistic and wood-carving skills.

LUBA-BEMBA, see BANTU

LUBA-HEMBA, see BANTU and LUBA-LUNDA

LUBA-KAONDE, see KAONDE

LUBA-LUNDA, see also BANTU, LUBA and LUNDA

A Western Bantu-speaking people. The Luba-Lunda comprise several groups the most important of which are the Aushi, Bemba, Bisa, Luba-Hemba, Luluwa, Shila and Songe.

LUBALE LOZI

The Lubale Lozi are a Southwest African people. They speak a Benue-Congo language of the Niger-Congo family of African languages. The Lubale Lozi are concentrated in east central Angola and northwest Zambia, notably east of the Zambeze River. Their neighbors include the Ambuella, Ishinde, Luchazi, and Makoma peoples.

LUCHAZI, see LUNDA

The Luchazi are a Bantu-speaking people whose origin is traced back to the Congo, where they were part of the Lunda kingdom which later became an empire. This was founded in the later part of the fifteenth century and endured until late in the nineteenth century. Over time, they broke away from the central Lunda kingdom in the Kapanga district of the southern Congo to establish their own kingdom.

Currently, the Luchazi are among Angola's, Democratic Republic of the Congo's (Zaire's) and Zambia's ethnic groups.

Traditionally, the main economic activities of the Luvale people centered on food gathering, hunting and trading. Traditionally also, their religion rested on the belief in a supreme being, who was either a sky god or an earth god.[281]

LUENA, see LUVALE

LUGANDA, see GANDA

LUGBARA

The Lugbara, also known as Logwari, are a Nilotic farming people who have long inhabited a fertile region in the north of West Nile province in Uganda, northeastern regions of the Democratic Republic of the Congo (Zaire), and southern Sudan. They speak a Central-Sudanic language that belongs to the Sudanic group of African languages and moreover, are an agricultural people with a non-hierarchical social and political organization. The Lugbara are related to other Nilotic peoples, including the Bale (Lendu), the Logo, the Keliko and the Madi. Prior to their incorporation in the modern states of the Democratic Republic of the Congo (Zaire), Uganda and Sudan, they were subject to European colonial rule, notably Belgian (in Zaire) and British (in Uganda and Sudan).

The Lugbara trace their origins to two heroes, Jaki and Dribidu. In time, the sons of both heroes were divided into sub-clans and tribes with major, minor and minimal kinship relations. This phenomenon, however, did not alter the role of the family cluster as the basic reproductive, economic, and socialization unit of their society.[282]

The Lugbara support a tight social system that rests on the belief that the closer a person is to the family cluster, the more validated he is and the further he is from the family cluster, the more inverted he becomes.[283] Traditionally, the "family cluster was based on a minimal lineage. The head of the lineage acted as the head of the cluster. The composition of a family cluster was fluid. Members moved to other communities, where they became tenants, and members of other communities moved in and became tenants. As time passed and members multiplied, segmentation took place."[284]

In their ancient moral system, it is men who open the gate to Evil. They do so by harboring *Ole*. According to this system "'indignation'..., spite, jealousy, disappointed ambition, undue greed, aggressiveness: all these are the fruits of *Ole* and lead to socially destructive acts or wishes..."[285] According to the same system, the "sins" generated by giving one's self to *Ole* will be one's fault. They destroy "ties of kinship and neighbourhood, the 'ties that are necessary for the existence of any kind of orderly social life."[286]

LUGURU

The Luguru are an East African people. They are concentrated in the Ulugura Mountains region, which is located west of Dar es Salaam, the capital of what is presently Tanzania. Their neighbors include such groups as the Doe, the Kaguru, the Kami, the Ndengereko, the Kutu, the Ngulu, the Rufiji, the Sagara, the Vidunda, the Wazaramo (Zaramo) and the Zigua peoples. The Luguru are organized in village groups that are politically, economically and religiously independent. Traditionally, they were not subject to a centralized political authority. In addition, they also supported a matrilineal society.

LUHYA

The Luhya, also called Baluyia, Luyia, Abaluyia and Abaluhya, are an East African people. Though their name and the names of its groups and subgroups are southern Arabian, they speak Luluyia, a Western Bantu language called Luluyia. In Arabic, the words Aba, Abe, Ba and Bu refer to fatherhood, and luhyia refers to one's beard, meaning descendants of the person with the (presumably distinct) beard.

The Luhya people are concentrated in the Nyanza and western provinces of Kenya, notably in the vicinity of Lake Victoria's Kavirondo Gulf. They comprise numerous groups and subgroups, the most important of which are: the Bakhayo (Abakhayo), Basonga (Abasonga), Batsotso (Abatsotso), Bukusu (Babukusu, Kitosh, and Vugusu), Dakho (Idakho, Abetakho, Babetakho), Hayo, Holo, Isukha (Abesukha, Babesukha), Gisu (Abagisu, Bagisu, Bamasaba, Masaba), Gwe (Abagwe), Kabras (Abakabras), Kisa (Abakisa, Bakisa), Marachi (Abamarachi, Bamaraki, Marach), Maragoli (Abalogoli, Logoli), Marama (Abamarama, Bamarama), Nyala (Abanyala, Banyala), Nyole (Abanyole, Abanyuli), Abanyore, Banyore(l)), Samia (Abasamia, Basamia), Tadjoni (Abatachoni, Tachoni, Kitosh), Tiriki (Batiriki), Tsoto (Batsotso) and Wanga (Abawanga, Bawanga).

The Luhya constitute Kenya's second largest ethnic minority after the Kikuyu, accounting for 14% of the country's total population. Their respective societies are based on patrilineal lineages.

LUIMBE

The Luimbe are a Southwest African people. They are concentrated in Angola, primarily in its central regions. Their neighbors include the Chokwe, Luena, and Mbunda peoples.

LUKENYI, see also KENYI

LUKOLWE

An East African people. The Lukolwe are concentrated in western Zambia. Though they were incorporated within the Lozi-dominated Barotse Kingdom, they continue to have their own language and customs.[287]

LULUA

The Lulua, also called Luluwa, are a West Central African Western Bantu-speaking people. They are concentrated in the Democratic Republic of the

Congo (Zaire) and Zambia. In all probability, their name is derived from the Arabic word Lu'lua, meaning diamond. The Lulua neighbors include the Pende people of the Bandundu and Kasai administrative provinces.

LULUWA, see BANTU and LULUA

LUMBU

These are one of Zambia's ethnic minorities. The Lumbu are a Bantu-speaking people and are related to the Ila people. Their neighbors include the Ambo, Nsenga, Toka, and Totela peoples.

LUMBWA, see also KIPSIKIS and KALENJIN

An East African Kipsikis people, a Kalenjin group. They are concentrated in Kenya, Tanzania and Uganda. They speak Kalenjin, a Southern Nilotic language that belongs to the Eastern Sudanic family of African languages. The Lumbwa are a semipastoralist people.

LUNDA

These are a group of Western Bantu-speaking peoples whose origin is traced back to the Bantu heartland located in the Luba-Lunda region of the Congo. They comprise many groups, including the: Akosa, Aluunda, Aruund, Chokwe, Imbangala, Ishindi, Kanongesha, Kazembe (Cazembe), Luapula, Luchazi, Lunda proper, Luunda, Luvale (Luena, Balovale), Mbunda, Musokantanda, Ndembu, Ruund, Shinje and Songo. Over time, all these groups broke away from the central Lunda kingdom in the Kapanga district of the southern Congo.

Currently, the Lunda are among the ethnic groups of the states of Angola, Democratic Republic of the Congo (Zaire) and Zambia. In Angola, they are located in the northeastern areas of the country. In Democratic Republic of the Congo (Zaire), they are concentrated in the southern areas of the country, especially in the Musokantanda region. They are predominant in the Kwango River, where they exercise significant political influence over other peoples, including the Yaka. In Zambia, they live in the northern areas of the country.

The Lunda societies differ in their observance of descent, inheritance and succession lineages. Northern Zambian Lunda, for example are patrilineal, whereas southern Lunda, Luvale and Luchazi are matrilineal. A few, like the Kapanga Lunda, are both matrilineal and patrilineal.

Traditionally, the main economic activities of the Lunda peoples centered on food gathering, hunting and trading. Traditionally also, their religion rested on the belief in a supreme being, who was either a sky god or an earth god.[288]

The modern history of the Lunda peoples is traced back to the later part of the fifteenth century, at which time Cibinda Ilunga, a son of Kalala, who was the King of the Kingdom of Luba, conquered the Lunda kingdom and married its queen to become king of the Lunda. For unclear reasons Cibinda and his successors assumed the title *Mwata Yamvo* (the Lord of the viper), divorced themselves from further contact with the Luba kingdom and ruled the new Kingdom of Lunda as a separate and an independent state.

The Lunda kingdom was located in what is presently northwestern Angola and western Democratic Republic of the Congo (Zaire, the Shaba province), around the headwaters of the Kasai River. Eventually, it expanded its territory to cover large areas of the central Congo west of the kingdom of Luba. By the seventeenth century, it acquired an imperial status with a structure that "consisted of a centralized core, a ring of provinces closely tied to the capital, an outer ring of provinces that paid tribute but were otherwise autonomous, and a fringe of independent kingdoms that shared a common Lunda culture."[289]

The cohesiveness of the Lunda empire was secured through a kinship system that related chiefs of villages to each other and to the royal family, as well as allowed new chiefs to inherit not only the name but also the kinship relations of former chiefs.[290]

The most important of the autonomous states within the Lunda kingdom were Kasanje and Kazembe. The latter kingdom had its seat in the Luapula Valley (within the copper-bearing Katanga) in what is presently the state of Zambia and endured until it fell to the British towards the end of the nineteenth century.

The Lunda empire reached its zenith towards the middle of the nineteenth century. It engaged in trading relations with the Arabs in East Africa and the Indian Ocean and the Portuguese in the Atlantic Ocean. It started to decline as a result of internal dissension, the Lunda-Chowke periodic assaults against the central government (especially in the later part of the nineteenth century), as well as Portuguese and Belgian (from the Congo Free State) occupation of parts of its territory in 1884 and 1898, respectively. It collapsed in 1909 when its leaders were captured and executed by the Belgians.

LUNDA-NDEMBU

The Lunda-Ndembu are a Southwest African people. They are concentrated in the northwestern regions of Angola. Their neighbors include the Amahundu, Luena, and Lunda peoples.

LUNDWE

These are one of Zambia's ethnic minorities. The Lundwe are a Bantu-speaking people and are related to the Ila people. They are concentrated in the southwestern regions of the country.

LUNGU

These are a Congolese people. Their traditional country has been at the southern end of Lake Tanganyika adjacent to that of the Tabwa. Their modern history is traced to early nineteenth century, at which time they had a kingdom of their own.

LUNYOLE, see NYULI

LUO

The Luo (Lwo), also known as Dholuo and Kavirondo, are a Nilotic people. Their language belongs to the Chari-Nile branch of the Nilo-Saharan family of African languages. They are concentrated in the Kenyan province of Nyanza in western Kenya. Large groups of them are also located in northern Uganda, Tanzania and other East African states. Their neighbors include the Gusii, Kuria, Nandi and Masai peoples.

The history of the Luo in East Africa could be traced back to the 15th century, at which time they lived in the region of the Bahr al-Ghazal tributary to the White Nile. In their old lands, they specialized in cattle-raising and millet-farming. Towards the end of the century, they invaded the Hima kingdom of Uganda and western Kenya. They formed their own ruling Bito dynasty, reorganized Kitara as the kingdom of Bunyoro and successfully governed other peoples in the area (who outnumbered them). Additionally, they established a series of kingdoms north and west of Lake Victoria, namely, Buddu, Buganda, Buruli, Busoga and others. Most of these tributary kingdoms were governed by sub-dynasties of the Bito clan.

In their new lands, the Luo experimented with a wide range of new ideas. "They adopted variant forms of religion, helped to found prestigious dynasties of kings, lived repeatedly on the ideological as well as physical frontiers of 'somewhere else' and 'something different'."[291]   More importantly, they gave precedence to whatever enhanced the interests of their kingdom. Loyalty, for example, was focused on the crown, the symbol of the kingdom's unity and its central authority, rather than on kinship ties. The *kabaka* or king was divorced of his connection with the Bito clan and was given divine attributes and established as the source of political patronage. Additionally, chiefs were appointed by the king on non-hereditary grounds.[292]   Furthermore, the crown's authority was strengthened by a system of royal tours as well as by rotating the kingdom's seat.[293]

Eventually, however, these new techniques of government gave way to traditional kinship relations, as well as to old farming and pastoral cultures. As a consequence, the Liu kingdom and its tributary states weakened, and towards the end of the 19th century, fell to German and British rule. Later, a sizable group of them were integrated in British East Africa, which gained its independence from the United Kingdom on December 12, 1963, as the Republic of Kenya.

Like other Kenyan ethnic groups, the Luo were active in their struggle for Kenya's independence, producing such renowned national figures as Tom Mboya (1930-1969) who prior to his assassination in 1969, was a founder and member of the People's Convention Party, and later, the African National Union (KANU).

Currently, the Luo people are one of Kenya's eleven largest ethnic groups. They constitute Kenya's third largest ethnic minority after the Kikuyu (21%) and the Luhya (14%), accounting for 13% of the country's total population. In Uganda and Tanzania, they enjoy the status of small ethnic minorities.

LUSHANGE

The Lushange are a Southwest African people. They are concentrated in the central regions of Zambia. Their neighbors include the Ambo, Ila, Kaonde, and Tonga peoples.

LUUNDA, see LUNDA

LUVALE, see also LUNDA

The Luvale, also called Luena or Balovale, are a Bantu-speaking people whose origin is traced back to the Congo, where they were part of the Lunda kingdom and later, empire. It was founded in the later part of the fifteenth century and endured until late in the nineteenth century. Over time, they broke away from the central Lunda kingdom in the Kapanga district of the southern Congo, to establish their own kingdom. Currently, the Luvale are among Angola's, Democratic Republic of the Congo's (Zaire's) and Zambia's ethnic groups.

Traditionally, the main economic activities of the Luvale people centered on food gathering, hunting and trading. Traditionally also, their religion rested on the belief of a supreme being, who was either a sky god or an earth god.[294]

LUYIA, see LUHYA

LWO, see LUO

LYANGALILE

The Lyangalile are an East African people. Their main concentrations are in Tanzania, notably west of Lake Rukwa. Their neighbors include the Fipa and Mambwe peoples.

MAA, see **MASAI**

MAASAI, see **MASAI**

MAASI, see **MASAI**

MABA, see also **NGABAKA**

The Maba, also Ma'ba, are a North Central African people and one of the major ethnic groups of the Republic of Chad. They are predominantly Muslim and live primarily in the south central Ouaddai region of Chad. The Maba have been highly influential to all inhabitants of Chad, and speak Bora Mabang, a Nilo-Saharan language. Their total population is estimated at about 200,000.

The Maba are a semi-sedentary people, occupying their villages during the rainy season in order to cultivate their crops. The Maba are also involved in stock raising, which they primarily accomplish after the rainy season.

Maba are mainly Muslims, but adhere to the pre-Islamic age-grade institution which helps determine political leadership and socio-sexual rules of each individual in a particular generation.

MABAR

These are a West African people and one of Nigeria's ethnic minorities. The Mabar are concentrated in the Lake Chad region of northeastern Nigeria, notably in the state of Borno (formerly Bornu). Groups of them, however, are also located in Chad and Niger. Their neighbors include the Buduma, Kanembu, Kanuri, Kwayam and Manga peoples. The Mabar speak a Nilo-Saharan language. They are essentially an agriculturalist people.

MABEA, see **FANG**

MABIHA, see **MAWIA**

MABINZA

The Mabinza people are a West Central African people. They are concentrated in the Democratic Republic of the Congo (Zaire), primarily in its north central regions. Their neighbors include the Bali, Bapoto, Bongo, and Ngandi peoples.

MABISANGA

A Central African people. The Mabisanga are concentrated in the Democratic Republic of the Congo (Zaire), notably in its northeastern regions. Their neighbors include the Bangba, Barambo, Madi, Mangbetu, Mayogo, Mayvu and Makango.

MACHA, see **OROMO**

MACONDE, see **MAKONDE**

MACUA

A Southeast and East African people. Macua – also known as Alolo, Makwa, and Mukwa – are part of the Macua-Lomwe cluster of peoples who constitute the largest ethnic group in Mozambique and represent one of the ethnic minorities of both Malawi and Tanzania. In Mozambique, they are concentrated in areas north of the Ligonha River, as well as in the country's coastal regions. Their neighbors include the Makonde and Yao peoples.

MACUA-LOMUE, see **MACUA**

MACUA-LOMWE, see **MACUA**

MADA

The Mada are a West African group. They are concentrated in central Nigeria. Their neighbors include the Angas, Birom, Gili, Gwandara, Katab,

Nafana and Yeskwa peoples. The Mada speak a language that belongs to the Benue-Congo branch of the Niger-Congo family of African languages.

MADA EGGONI, see EGGON

MADI

Madi, also spelled Ma'di or Ma'adi, are one of Uganda's and Sudan's ethnic minorities. They are concentrated at both banks of the Nile River in Uganda and Sudan. Groups of them, however, are also located in the Democratic Republic of the Congo (Zaire), notably in its northeastern regions. The Madi speak a Central Sudanic language which belongs to the Chari-Nile branch of the Nilo-Saharan family of African languages. Their neighbors include the Bale (Lendu), the Keliko, the Logo and the Lugbara peoples.

The Madi are divided into many chiefdoms, each chiefdom of which is headed by a chief chosen from the dominant patrilineal clan. Their main economic activities center on agriculture, fishing, herding and animal husbandry.

MAGON

The Magon are a southern African people. They live in Botswana, Namibia, and the Republic of South Africa. In Botswana, they are concentrated in the country's southwestern regions. In Namibia, they are found in the country's southeastern regions. In South Africa, they live in its north central parts, close to the country's borders with Botswana and Namibia.

MAGUZAWA, see HAUSA

A West African Hausa group. The Maguzawa are concentrated in northern Nigeria. Their neighbors include the Auyokawa, Butawa, Hausa proper and Warjawa peoples. Like other Hausa, they speak Hausa, a language that belongs to the Afro-Asiatic family of African languages.

MAHAFALE

The Mahafale, also spelled Mahafaley, are a Malagasy people. They are concentrated on the Island of Madagascar, notably in its southern areas which are considered Tandroy lands. Groups of them, however, are found along the coastal areas of East Africa. The Mahafaly speak a Malagasy dialect that is shared by related groups, including the Bara, Sakalava, Tandroy, Tanosy and Vezo.

MAHAFALEY, see MAHAFALE

MAHI

The Mahi, also Maxi-Gbe, are a West African people. Their main concentrations are in Benin, Nigeria, and Togo. Their neighbors include the Fo, Ife-Ilesha, and Yoruba peoples.

MAHONGWE, see KOTO

MAHORANS, see MOHARAIS

MAHURA

The Mahura people are a Southwest African Khoisan people. They are concentrated in northern Botswana. Their neighbors include the Chekwe, the Hiechware, and the Bamangwato peoples.

MAIOMBE, see KONGO

MAJEERTEEN, see also SOMALI

An East African Somali group. The Majeerteen are one of the Hurti clans, a subgroup of the Darod tribe. Like all Somalis, they speak Somali.

MAJOGE, see GUSII

MAKA

This is one of Cameroon's more than 100 different ethnic groups, and hence, are a West Central African people. The Maka, also Makka and Makaa, are a Bantu-speaking people. Originally they settled in Cameroon.

MAKAA, see MAKA

MAKANGO

A Central African people. The Mabisanga are concentrated in the Democratic Republic of the Congo (Zaire), notably in its northeastern regions. Their neighbors include the Bangba, Barambo, Mabisanga, Madi, Mangbetu, Mayogo and Mayvu.

MAKATE

One of Southern Africa's peoples. The Makate are a subgroup of the Abarue, a Shona people. They live in Zimbabwe and Mozambique.

MAKHANYA

The Makhanya are a southern African people. They are concentrated in the Republic of South Africa, primarily in its southeastern coastal areas. Their neighbors include the Bhaca, Khuze, and Zulu peoples.

MAKKA, see MAKA

MAKKE, see DOGON

MAKO

The Mako are a West Central African ethnic group. They are concentrated in the central regions of Cameroon. Their neighbors include the Fang, Kaka, Pygmy, and Eton peoples.

MAKOA

The Makoa, also Makua, are speakers of Makoa, a Bantu language. They live in the northern regions of Mozambique, as well as in Madagascar and the Federal Islamic Republic of the Comoros. In Comoros they constitute one of the country's five major ethnic groups. In Madagascar, they constitute one of the country's ethnic groups and at times are regarded as Sakalava people.

The term "Makoa" is derived from the ethnic label "Makua" in Mozambique which denoted slave ancestry. In Madagascar, however, now it is applied to people the Sakalava assume to be of African origin, notably those laborers whose ancestors worked for the Sakalava royalty.[295]

MAKOMA

An East African people. The Makoma, also known as Bamakoma, are concentrated in western Zambia. They are closely related to the Lozi people. They speak Kololo, the Lozi language, share many of Lozi customs, and are part of Lozi-dominated Barotse Kingdom.[296]

MAKONDE

The Makonde, also Maconde, are a Bantu-speaking people. Their main concentrations are found in Mozambique, Tanzania, and Malawi.

The Makonde are essentially an agricultural and trading people. Their society observes polygamous marriages, as well as matrilineal lineages in matters relating to descent, inheritance and succession.

The Makonde live in independent settlements, each settlement of which is headed by a hereditary chief and an advisory council of elders. They lack a centralized political authority.

The Makonde were impacted by Arab traders and, in the past, the Lugala among them resisted repeated attempts by the German East African Company to conquer their homeland. Under the leadership of the Yao leader, Machembra, they were able to hold German assaults against their territory until 1899.

MAKOUA, see UBANGI

MAKUA, see MAKOA

MAKWA, see MACUA

MAKWANGA, see KWANGWA

MAKWENGO, see also SAN

A southern African San group. The Makwengo, also known as Kxoe, are a San-speaking people. They live along the Okavango River in the Caprivi Strip of Namibia. Like other San-speaking peoples, they are essentially foragers, hunters and gatherers.

MALAGASY

The Malagasy people are speakers of Malagasy languages, which are Austronesian languages. They are concentrated in Madagascar and its adjacent islands, including Reunion. Madagascar was known as Malagasy Republic in reference to its peoples' Malagasy languages.

The history of the Malagasy people is traced back to over two thousand years, at which time Madagascar was settled by Malayo-Indonesian people. In Madagascar, they organized themselves in several kingdoms, the most important of which at the turn of the sixteenth century (when Portuguese navigator Diogo Dias discovered the island) were those of the Antemore, Antesaka (Antaisaka), Betsileo and Merina.

Under the reign of King Andrianampoinimerina (1787-1810), the Merina kingdom of the Merina Malagasy people became the leading state in the island. Under his son, Radama I (1810-1828), the Merina kingdom gained command, with British help, over a large part of Madagascar.

In the 1860s, King Radama II resolved to open the kingdom to Europeans, and hence, granted a concession to a French trading company. The concession paved the way for placing Madagascar under French protection in 1885. In 1894-97, the French crushed the Kingdom's army, abolished the kingdom, exiled its Queen Ranavalona III to Algiers (1897) and set up a colonial administration.

Following World War II, the country became a French overseas territory, and in 1958, it was renamed the Malagasy Republic and became an autonomous state within the French community. Two years later (June 26, 1960), it became an independent member within the French Community.

Currently, the Malagasy people constitute the great majority of Madagascar's population. Their main economic activities focus on agriculture, animal husbandry, fishing and trade.

Though Christianity and Islam have won converts among them, the majority of Malagasy people (over 52%) continue to uphold their own traditional animist beliefs.

MALAKAL

One of Sudan's ethnic groups. The Malakal are concentrated in the areas southwest of the Blue Nile. Their neighbors include the Anuak, Burun, Beir, Dinka, Koma, Nuer, and Shilluk peoples.

MALI, see MANDE

MALINKE

The Malinke people, also known as Mali, Mandinga, Mandinka and Mandingo, Maninka or Manding, are one of the major ethnic groups in West Africa. They are a Mande people, and predominantly Muslim. Their large concentrations are in The Gambia, Guinea, Guinea-Bissau, Ivory Coast, Mali and Senegal. They speak a Mande (Mandekan) language of the Mande branch of the Niger-Congo family of African languages.

The Malinke people are divided into numerous groups, each with its own hereditary nobility. The most important of these groups is the Kangaba, the bearers of the Mali Empire, the most powerful and most renowned of all West African states. Their dynasty was one of the world's oldest dynasties. Founded in the seventh century with Kangaba as its seat, its descendants continued to rule in some independent Malinke states until relatively recent times.

The modern history of the Malinke dates back to the tenth century, at which time they lived along the Niger river in what is presently the Republic of Mali. There, they established the state/kingdom of Kangaba, which subsequently developed into the renowned Mali empire.

Under the Mali empire, the Malinke people assumed the role of middlemen in the gold trade. Under the leadership of Sundiata, they revolted in 1230 against Sumaguru (Sumanguru), the Soso (Susu) chief and ruler of the Ghana Empire. After defeating and killing Sumaguru in 1235, Sundiata established his own Malinke kingdom in Kangaba, absorbed the Susu people and their allies and cultivated traditional relationships within clans and lineage groups to build the administration of the new state. Subsequently, the Kangaba state controlled the salt, gold, copper and ivory caravans within its territory and developed into a powerful empire covering many portions of the West African region, including Mali, Mauritania and Senegal. It flourished from the 13th to the 16th century with Timbuktu as one of its leading cultural and commercial center. The empire started its downfall with successive revolts staged against its rule by the Gao (1400), the Taureg (1431), the Wolof and the Mossi peoples. By 1550, it lost much of its stature and started to splinter into small states and principalities. In the nineteenth century, these entities were overwhelmed by the Fulani *jihad*.

The Malinke are sedentary peoples living off the land using their farming, fishing, livestock or trading skills, depending on which environment they are living. They use their crops or catches for food or for trade with their neighbors, particularly the Berber and/or Fulani peoples.

The Malinke mostly reside in independent areas ruled by hereditary kings. Kinship is important in their society, as kin share the same name and even taboos. Kin groups live together in Malinke villages. Each group is led by the eldest male, which is usually the grandfather. The eldest male makes all decisions and arrangements for the group and is consulted on all decisions including marriage.

The Malinke have a stringent class structure based on heredity. The lowest class entails artisans, followed in rank by the commoners, then the nobles. The highest is the old royal class.

Currently, the Malinke constitute 42% of the Gambian population or what amounts to about 350,000. They are known as Mandinka. In Guinea, they constitute the largest ethnic group. In Guinea-Bissau, where they are known as Mandinga, they constitute 13% of the population. In the Ivory Coast, the Mande people are represented by the Malinke and Dyula (Dioula) peoples. They constitute the fourth largest ethnic minority, accounting for 11% of the total population or what amounts to about 1.3 million. Moreover, they are highly concentrated in the west central part of the country, but have tribal affiliations with more numerous groups living outside the Ivory Coast. In Mali, they constitute together with other Mande peoples (Bambara and Sarakole) about 50% of the country's population. They are concentrated in the southwest regions of the country. In Senegal, where they are known as Mandingo, they constitute the sixth largest ethnic group, accounting for 9% of the population or what amounts to about 0.7 million.

MALLUMIA, see YAKUDI

MALOZI, see LOZI

MALUAL, see DINKA

MAMA

The Mama, also known as Kantana and Kwarra, are a West African cluster of the Arum, Barrku, Burruza and Upie people. They are concentrated in central Nigeria. Their neighbors include the Angas, Birom, Gili and Mada peoples. The Mama speak a language that belongs to the Benue-Congo branch of the Niger-Congo family of African languages.

MAMBERE, see MAMBILA

MAMBETTO, see MANGBETU

MAMBILA

A West African people. The Mambila – also known as Bang, Mambere, Nor Tagrbo and Tongbo – are concentrated in the southeastern regions of Nigeria. Groups of them, however, can also be found in Cameroon.

MAMBOE

An East African people. The Mamboe, also known as Mbowe, are concentrated in western Zambia. They are closely related to the Lozi people. They speak Kololo, the Lozi language, share many of Lozi customs, and are part of the Lozi-dominated Barotse Kingdom.[297]

MAMBWE

The Mambwe are a Southeast and East African-Malagasy people. They are concentrated in Zimbabwe and Tanzania.

MAMPRUSI

The Mamprusi (Manprusi), or Dagbamba as they used to call themselves, are a West African people. They are concentrated in the East and West Mamprusi districts of northern Ghana. Their name is derived from "Mamprugu", the kingdom with which they are associated. They opted for the new name, Mamprusi, to distinguish themselves from their southern neighbors, the Dagomba. In addition to the Dagomba, the Mamprusi neighbors include the Builsa, Chakossi, Grusi, Guang, Gurensi, Konkomba, Moba and Sisala peoples. The Mamprusi speak Mampruli, a Voltaic language that belongs to the Mole Dagbani languages of Ghana, Burkina Faso and Togo.

Mamprusi legends suggest that Na Gbewa was the founder of their kingdom in an indeterminate time in the past. Their kingdom continued its independent existence until the turn of the twentieth century, at which time it was invaded by European troups. As a result of the Treaty of Vienna of 1902, their kingdom's territory was partitioned by the British, the French and the Germans, to allow for the establishment of the modern states of Burkina Faso, Ghana and Togo.

The Mamprusi society is based on patrilineal kinship relations with clans serving as its basic units. Their economic activities focus on agriculture and animal husbandry. Traditionally, their kingdom was a theocracy. It supported both religious and political functions, and moreover, kings were required to adhere to their traditional religion which rested on the exaltation of ancestral spirits. Now, however, the Mamprusi are either

Christian or Muslim and hence, it is common to see them having either Christian or Muslim kings.

MANALA, see NDEBELE

MANCAGNE

The Mancagne, also known as Bola and Brame, are a West African people. They are concentrated in Guinea-Bissau and Senegal.

MANDA, see also NYASA

The Manda are an East African people. They are concentrated in Tanzania, notably on the eastern shores of Lake Rukwa in the Ruvuma Province. Their neighbors include the Bungu, Kimbu, Nyiha, and Manda peoples.

MANDARA

The Mandara, also known as Montagnard, Ndara and Wandala, are a West African people. They are concentrated in Cameroon and Nigeria. The Mandara are a Muslim people who were impacted by various aspects of Kanuri culture. They speak Kanuri and are essentially an agricultural people.

Their neighbors include the Gisiga, Musgu, Kanuri, Paduko, Shuwa and Wakura peoples.

MANDARI

The Mandari, also called Kir and Shir, are an East African Beri people. They are concentrated in the southern regions of Sudan.

MANDE, see also MALINKE

The Mande, also known as Mali, Manding, Mandingo or Mandingue, are a West African people. They comprise numerous groups, the most important of which are the Bambara (Bamana), Busansi, Dyula (Diouala), Malinke (Maninka), Marka, Samo, Senufo and Soninke. Less prominent groups and subgroups include the Bozo, Kagoro, Khasonke, Kono,

Kuranko, Mandinko, Somono, Susu, Wasuluka and Yalunka. The Mande speak varying dialects of the Mande language, which belongs to the Niger-Congo family of African languages.

The Mande peoples are acknowledged among the earliest people to engage (as early as 4000 B.C.) in the independent development of deep-plowing techniques. They were the founders of the Soninke state of Ghana and subsequently, the Mali Empire.

The Mande people are scattered throughout West Africa, with large concentrations in Burkina Faso, The Gambia, Guinea, Guinea-Bissau, the Ivory Coast, Mali, Liberia, Senegal and Sierra Leone. Those located in Guinea, Liberia, Mali, Sierra Leone and Senegal are known as Mande-tan. Prominent among the Mande are the Malinke, whereas those located in Burkina Faso, The Gambia, Guinea-Bissau, the Ivory Coast and Senegal are known as Mande-fu. The latter group comprises the Buzi (also known as Loma and Toma), Gbande, Gio, Kpelle, Loko, Mano, Mende and Vai tribes.

In Mali, the Mande people (Bambara, Malinke, and Sarakole) account for about 50% of the country's population. In Sierra Leone, they are concentrated in the eastern and southern regions of the country.

The economic activities of the Mande focus on agriculture, animal husbandry and trade. Their society is patrilineal, with the oldest male serving as lineage head. In addition, it is highly structured and hierarchical, comprising a royal class, a class of hereditary nobility, a class of commoners, a class of artisans and a class of former slaves.

MANDENYI, see **MMANI**

MANDING, see **MANDE** and **MALINKE**

MANDINGA, see **MALINKE**

MANDINGO, see **MALINKE**

MANDINGUE, see **MANDE**

MANDINKA, see MALINKE

MANDINKO, see MANDE

MANDJA, see MANJIA

MANDJIA

The Mandjia people, also known as Mandja and Manja, are one of the six major ethnic minorities of the Central African Republic. They live essentially around Sibut.

Currently, the Mandjia account for 21% of the country's total population, constituting the third largest minority after the Baya (34%) and the Banda (27%).

MANDYAKO, see MANJACA

MANDJAK, see MANJACA

MANGA (Nigeria)

These are a West African people and one of Nigeria's ethnic minorities. The Manga are concentrated in the Lake Chad region of northeastern Nigeria, notably in the state of Borno (formerly Bornu). Groups of them, however, are also located in Chad and Niger. Their neighbors include the Bade, Hausa, Kanuri, Kwayam and Mabar peoples. The Manga speak a Nilo-Saharan language. They are essentially an agriculturalist people.

MANGA (Tanzania)

These are one of the ethnic groups of Tanzania. The Manga are people of Arab Omani descent. They are located on the island of Zanzibar, part of the Republic of Tanzania.

MANGATI, see TATURU

MANGBELE

The Mangbele are a Central African people. They are concentrated in the Democratic Republic of the Congo (Zaire), notably in its north eastern regions. Their neighbors include the Bangba, Barambo, Mabisanga, Madi, Makango, Mangbetu, Mayogo and Mayvu peoples.

MANGBETU

The Mangbetu, also called Amangbetu, Kingbetu, Mambetto, Monbuttu and Nemangbetu, are a Central African people. They comprise a mixture of Nigritic and Bantu peoples of different cultural and linguistic backgrounds. Their language, Kere, also known as Mangbetu, is a Central Sudanic language belonging to the Chari-Nile branch of the Nilo-Saharan family of African languages.

Originally, the name Mangbetu referred to the aristocracy which founded a number of powerful centralized kingdoms in Central Africa during the 19th century. Presently, however, it covers the cluster of peoples they used to rule.

The Mangbetu support patrilineal societies governed by local headmen and councils of elders. Extended families constitute the basic units of their respective societies. Their economic activities center on agriculture, fishing, hunting and gathering.

Traditionally, some of their groups were renowned for practicing cannibalism, as well as for "deforming the heads of babies by binding them tightly so that they retained through life a curiously elongated form."[298]

The Mangbetu are renowned for their artistic skills, especially wood carving, iron crafts, pottery works and sculptures.

Currently, the Mangbetu peoples constitute one of Democratic Republic of the Congo's (Zaire's) ethnic minorities. They are highly concentrated in areas falling to the south of the Azande in northeastern Democratic Republic of the Congo (Zaire).

MANGBETU-AZANDE (AZENDE), see MANGBETU

MANIANGA, see KONGO

MANINKA, see MANDE and MALINKE

MANJA, see also MANDJIA

A Central African people. The Manja, also spelled Mandja and Mandjia, are concentrated in the central regions of the Central African Republic. Their neighbors include the Dakwa, Laka, Ndere, and Ngapou peoples.

MANJACA

The Manjaca people are one of Guinea-Bissau's five major ethnic groups. They constitute the third largest minority after the Balanta (30%) and the Fula (20%), accounting for 14% of the country's total population. They are noted for their experience in growing palm trees and in fishing.

MANO, see also MANDE

The Mano are a Mande people. They constitute one of the ethnic minorities of the Liberia and Guinea. Their language belongs to the Mande group of the Niger-Congo family of African languages. The Mano neighbors include the Bassa, the Kpelle, the Loma and the Mende peoples.

MANPRUSI, see MANPRUSI

MANSA

The Mansa people are an East African ethnic group. They are concentrated in Eritrea.

MANYIKA, see also SHONA

These are a group of Western Bantu-speaking peoples from the extreme eastern parts of Zimbabwe, particularly north of the Lundi River, as well as adjacent areas in Mozambique, especially south of the Púnguè River. They are a Shona subgroup and like other Shona subgroups such as Karanga,

Ndau, Tonga-Korekore, Rozwi and Zezuru, they speak Shona. Currently, the Shona people constitute the largest ethnic group in the state of Zimbabwe, accounting for 71% of the country's total population. The Manyika group, however, accounts for about 13% of the same population.

The Manyika people observe patrilineal lineages in matters relating to descent, inheritance and succession. Moreover, they support several kingdoms, the most important of which are Mutasa and Makoni. The historical roots of the kingdoms of Mutasa and Makoni are traced back to the later part of the sixteenth or the early part of the seventeenth centuries. Traditionally, their kingdoms were governed by hereditary chiefs, assisted by family heads.

The Manyika are predominantly farmers who engage in miscellaneous agricultural activities, as well as in cattle raising. They live in villages comprised of interrelated families. Currently, however, many of them also work in the gold, chromium and tungsten mines, or in the lumber and/or other industries, located in their region. Currently also, many Manyika are successful and well-educated civil servants and politicians. Some of their leaders, such as Herbert Chitepo, were active participants in Zimbabwe's struggle for independence.

Though Christianity has won many converts among them, many Manyika continue to be impacted by their traditional religion which rests on the belief in a creator-god, called *Mwari*, as well as in ancestral spirits, magic, witchcraft and sorcery.

MAOURI

A West African Hausa-speaking people. The Maouri constitute one of Niger's ethnic groups. They are highly concentrated along the Niger River.

MAPOÊRS, see **NDEBELE**

MAPOGGERS, see **NDEBELE**

MAPOUNOU

The Mapounou are a West Central African people. They are concentrated in the coastal areas of Gabon of the Republic of Congo. Their neighbors include the Nkomi and Punu peoples.

MAPUDA, see GUDE

MAPUTA

The Maputa are a southern African people. They are concentrated in the southeastern regions of the Republic of South Africa. Their neighbors include the Konde, Ngomane, and Tembe Tonga peoples.

MARABOUTS, see MOOR

MARACH, see LUHYA

MARACHI, see LUHYA

MARADALLA, see KURA

MARAGOLI, see LUHYA

MARAGWETA, see also MARAKWET and KALENJIN

An East African Marakwet people, a Kalenjin group. They are concentrated in Kenya, Tanzania and Uganda, notably in the Rift Valley region. The Marakwet speak Kalenjin, a Southern Nilotic language that belongs to the Eastern Sudanic family of African languages. They are a semipastoralist people.

MARAKWET, see also KALENJIN

An East African Kalenjin group. They are concentrated in Kenya, Tanzania and Uganda, notably along escarpments in the Rift Valley region. They speak Kalenjin, a Southern Nilotic language that belongs to the Eastern Sudanic family of African languages. The Marakwet comprise several groups, including the Cherang'any, Maragweta and Sengwer. They are a semipastoralist people.

MARAMA, see LUHYA

MARAVI

The Maravi, also known as Chewa and Cewa, are people living in Zambia, Zimbabwe and Malawi. They are concentrated in the extreme eastern region of Zambia and the northwestern regions of Zimbabwe. In Malawi, they constitute the largest ethnic minority.

The Maravi are divided into nine groups, the two largest of which are the Chewa and the Nyanja.

The Maravi are a Bantu-speaking people. They speak Chewa, also known as Chinyanja and share many cultural features of the Bemba, another Bantu people who occupy the western areas of Malawi. They are matrilineal, observing matrilineal lineages in matters relating to descent, inheritance, and succession. Polygamy is popular in their society.
The people live in villages, each of which is headed by a hereditary headman supported by an advisory council of elders. Agriculture, hunting, fishing and livestock represent their main economic activities.

Though Christianity and Islam have won Maravi converts, the people still believe in sorcery.

According to Marwick, the Maravi support the notion of a socio-moral order based on a divine force in the distant past. Those who comply with this order are considered to be possessed with righteousness, whereas those who willfully oppose it are possessed with evil.[299] In Davidson's view, sorcery provided the Maravi people with means to dramatize social norms. In their moral order, God may use Evil to straighten or punish those who stray, that is, sinners.[300]

The Maravi people developed their own empire (Confederacy) in South Africa about 1480. The empire was headed by a *karonga* (king), who ruled through the leaders of each of the Maravi clans. The empire reached its zenith in the 17th century due to its trade with the Portuguese and Arabs.

Its territory stretched "north of the Zambezi River to the Dwangwa River, west to the Luangwa River, and east to the Mozambique coast."[301] It started to decline when its clans' leaders became increasingly independent of the Confederation's central authority. By 1720, the Maravi Confederacy broke down into several small entities.

MARAZIG

The Marazig are a West Saharan North African people. They are concentrated in the southern areas of Tunisia.

MARBA, see BANDA

MARCUDIA

The Marcudia are one of the Chadian Kuri subgroups. They speak Yedina, a Buduma dialect. Like other Kuri groups, they live along the eastern shores of Lake Chad.

MAREEHAAN, see SOMALI

MARESIONIK, see OKIEK

MARGHI, see MARGI

MARGI

These are a West African people and one of Nigeria's ethnic minorities. The Margi, or Marghi, are concentrated in the northeastern parts of Nigeria, notably in the Damboa district in what is presently the state of Borno (formerly Bornu). The Margi are a Muslim people who were impacted by various aspects of Kanuri culture. They speak Kanuri and are essentially an agricultural people. Their neighbors include the Bata, Bura, Hona, Kanuri, Kapsiki, Matakam and Wakura peoples.

MARKA, see also MANDE

The Marka are a Voltaic Bambara-speaking people. They are a group of the Mande peoples. They are concentrated in Burkina Faso and Mali.

MAROTSE, see LOZI

MARUNGU

The Marungu are an East African people. Their main concentrations are in the east central regions of the Democratic Republic of the Congo (Zaire). The Marungu live on the western shores of Lake Tanganyika. Their neighbors include the Bwile and Tabwa peoples.

MARUTSE, see LOZI

MASABA, see LUHYA

MASAI

The Masai, also known as Ilmaasai, Maa, Maasai or Maasi, are an East African Nilotic-Hamitic people who speak Maasai, an Eastern Sudanic language of the Chari-Nile branch of the Nilo-Saharan family of African languages. Their main concentrations are found in Kenya and Tanzania. Throughout the nineteenth century, they were an extremely feared warrior-like nation. In the past, they commanded control over large areas of pastoral land all over East Africa, and exacted tribute from other peoples who wanted to pass through it. Though they lost much of their former power and influence, the Masai continue to be a highly proud and independent people.

The history of the Masai people dates back to about 500 B.C., at which time they lived along the Nile River. Subsequently, they migrated to their present locations. Throughout their history, the Masai were resistant to outside intrusions on their society.

The Masai are essentially a nomadic pastoralist people who continue to maintain their traditional pastoral lifestyle. They wander along the Great Rift Valley of Kenya and Tanzania, the Samburu region of Kenya and the Arusha and Baraguyu (Kwafi) lands of Tanzania in search of pastures. They subsist on the blood and milk of their herds. Currently, some Masai clans are engaged in miscellaneous agricultural activities in addition to raising livestock, notably cattle which occupy a central importance in their diet. They "live almost exclusively on milk and blood from their cattle," and are often regarded as the "[best] cattle people in the world."[302]

The Masai comprise many groups and subgroups, the most important of which are the Purko and Kisonko. Less prominent groups include: the Arusha, Dalalekutuk, Damat, Kaputiei, Keekonyukie, Koitokitok, Laitayok, Loodokilani, Matapato, Moitanik, Parakuyu, Salei, Samburu, Serenket, Siria, Tiamus and Uasinkishu. Because each of these groups "is effectively autonomous, both economically and socially, there is a considerable diversity in custom between [them]."[303] The Parakuyu, Samburu and Tiamus groups, for example, have their own age sets and hence, their own age-sets customary rituals.

Masai society is based on kinship. A typical Masai village, known as *boma*, is based on kinship, and broadly speaking supports several families. (From Afar to Zulu, 119) In their society, life is an accumulation of stages, each stage of which invokes a set of responsibilities, particularly for Maasai men. These stages lead up to the highly prized warrior stage, which establishes a person's worth and respectability in society.

Extended families constitute the basic units of Masai patrilineal clans and society. Their society is highly egalitarian. Its main formal structures are based on age groups, each group of which is assigned special functions and responsibilities. The age groups include junior warriors, senior warriors, junior elders and senior elders. Of all these groups, only senior elders are empowered to participate in making decisions for the whole tribe.[304]

The Masai are polygamists and observe wife lending between men of same age groups. Additionally, they practice circumcision in special ritual initiation ceremonies that signal a child's advent into adulthood. Ritual ceremonies are conducted by the religious head of the tribe, called *oloiboni*. An *oloiboni's* responsibilities are strictly religious. One of their main celebrations is the *E Unoto*. This celebration is devoted to the initiation of new warriors, that is *morans*. It occurs when a person becomes fifteen years old, and features the shaving of his head by his mother to signify his attainment of *murani* status.

Masai arts are dominated by ritual dancing and a very long and impressive oral storytelling tradition. Descriptive singing is also a very admired artistic tradition in their society. Most topics deal with ancient warriors, ancestors' bravery, cattle and women's beauty. "By many the Masai are thought to be the most 'romantic' tribe in Africa."[305]

Under the pressure of modernization, the Masai people are losing some aspects of their traditional cultural patterns. Moreover, they are being increasingly encouraged by the governments of Kenya and Tanzania to live in permanent agricultural settlements.

MASARWA, see also SAN

A southern African Bushmen-related people. The Masarwa, also known as Basarwa, are concentrated in Botswana. Their neighbors include the Barolong, the Bakalahari, the Bakwena and the Bangwaketse peoples. The terms Masarwa and Basarwa refer to all San-speaking peoples in Botswana.

MASEKO

The Maseko are a subgroup of the Ngoni nation. The death of Zwangendaba, the leader of the Ngoni nation, became the symbol of its unity. At Mapupo (about 1848), a successional conflict prompted them to move southward and settle in the Shire lands south of Lake Nyasa (Malawi). There, they established a kingdom of their own. Eventually, the Maseko kingdom disappeared following the European conquest of their territory in the later part of the nineteenth century.

MASHI

The Mashi are a Southeast and Southwest African people. They are a Lozi group. Their main concentrations are in Angola, Namibia and Zambia.

MASHUKULUMBWE, see IWA

MASSA

The Massa, or Bonana, are a Muslim sedentary people found in Chad, as well as in northeastern Cameroon. They represent one of the major Chadian ethnic groups.

The Massa support political and social institutions akin to those of the Fulani people. Their economic activities center on extensive farming, cattle raising, and trading.

MASSA LIT

The Massa Lit are a sedentary Muslim people who live in eastern Chad and southwestern Sudan. They number over 70,000 and speak a language very similar to Bora Mabang. Their economic activities focus on small-scale subsistence farming.

MASSAESYLI, see NUMIDIAN MASSYLI

MASSALAT

Centered in central Chad, the Massalat are a semi-sedentary people who number, approximately 30,000. The Massalat are a Muslim people. They speak Arabic and culturally resemble their Dadjo neighbors.

MASSYLI, see NUMIDIAN MASSYLI

MATAKAM

The Matakam, also known as Mafa and Mofa, are a West African people. They are concentrated in Cameroon and Nigeria and speak a language that belongs to the Afro-Asiatic family of African languages. Their neighbors include the Gisiga, Kapsiki, Paduko and Wakura peoples.

MATAPATO, see MASAI

MATEBELE, see NDEBELE

MATENGO

The Matengo, also known as Chimatengo, are a Southeast African-Malagasy people. They are concentrated in the southwestern regions of Tanzania.

MATLALA, see PEDI

MATHABATHE, see PEDI

MATO

A Southeast and East African people. The Mato are concentrated in Malawi, Mozambique and Tanzania.

MATUMBI

The Matumbi, also known as Kimatumbi, are a Southeast and East African people. They are concentrated in Mozambique and Tanzania, notably in the border area between these two countries.

MAU

The Mau are a West African people. They live in Mali and Guinea-Bissau. They are highly concentrated west of Bamako in Guinea-Bissau where their neighbors include the Kono and Tura peoples.

MAUR

A West African people. The Maur are concentrated in Mauritania. The term Maur, like the term Moor, is derived from the Latin word Mauri, designating the people of the Roman Province of Mauritania. In ancient times, this comprised the western areas of modern Algeria and the northeastern parts of modern Morocco. Currently, it refers to essentially Mauritania's Arab-Berber population.

The Maur constitute 30% of the Mauritania's total population, whereas the mixed Maur-black make up 40%.

MAURES, see also MAUR

The Maures people constitute one of the small ethnic groups of the Republic of Senegal. They live chiefly in the northern regions of the country.

MAURI

A West African people. The Mauri are concentrated in Niger and speak a Nilo-Saharan language. Their neighbors include the Adarawa, Fula and Zerma peoples.

MAWIA

The Mawia, known also as Chimaviha and Mabiha, are a Southeast and East African people. They are concentrated in Mozambique and Tanzania.

MAXINJE

The Maxinje are a Central and Southern African people. They live in Angola, the Democratic Republic of the Congo (Zaire) and Zambia. Their main concentration, however, is in the southern regions of Zaire, neighboring the Bangala, Bayaka, and Lunda peoples.

MAYOGO

A Central African people. The Mayogo are concentrated in the Democratic Republic of the Congo (Zaire), notably in its northeastern regions. Their neighbors include the Bangba, Barambo, Mabisanga, Madi, Makango, Mangbele, Mangbetu and Mayvu.

MAYOMBE, see KONGO

MAYVU

The Mayvu are a Central African people. They are concentrated in the Democratic Republic of the Congo (Zaire), notably in its northeastern regions. Their neighbors include the Bangba, Barambo, Mabisanga, Madi, Makango, Mangbele, Mangbetu and Mayogo.

MAZHI

The Mazhi are an East African people. They are concentrated north of Lake Rudolf in southern Sudan and southwestern Ethiopia. Their neighbors include the Chara, Kambatta, Galla, and Toposa peoples.

MBA

The Mba are a West Central African ethnic group. They are concentrated in the north central and eastern regions of the Democratic Republic of the Congo (Zaire) and the northwestern regions of Zambia. In Zaire, their neighbors include the Babali, Baboa, Eso, Lombi, and Wagenia peoples, whereas in Zambia they include the Iwa, Tambo, and Senga peoples.

MBAI, see also SEBEI and KALENJIN

An East African Sebei people, a Kalenjin group. They are concentrated in Kenya and Uganda, and speak Kalenjin, a Southern Nilotic language that belongs to the Eastern Sudanic family of African languages. The Mbai are a semipastoralist people.

MBAKA, see also BAKA

The Mbaka are a Central African people and one of the Mbundu subgroups. They are concentrated in the Ubangi region of the Central African Republic, as well as in the north central regions of Angola. In the Central African Republic, they represent one of the six major ethnic groups, accounting for 4% of the country's total population and constituting the fifth largest group after the Baya (34%), the Banda (27%), the Mandjia (21%) and the Sara (10%). In Angola, together with other Mbundu peoples, the Mbaka account for about 25% of the country's total population. The Mbaka are essentially a tribal people engaged in trading and fishing.

MBALA

The Mbala are a West Central African Bantu-speaking people. They are concentrated in Angola, the Democratic Republic of the Congo (Zaire), and Zambia. Their neighbors include the Mbun (Mbunda) and Pende peoples. The Mbala are related to the Ila people.

MBAM

The Mbam are a Central African Bantu-speaking people. They are concentrated in the Cameroon, the Republic of Congo, and the Democratic Republic of the Congo (Zaire). Their neighbors in Cameroon include the Eton, Fang, Mum and Ndop peoples.

MBANDERU, see HAUSA

MBANGALA, see also JAGA

Mbangala, also known as Imbangala and Jaga, is one of Angola's ethnic minorities. Their modern history is traced back to the fifteenth century, during which a leader, entitled kinguri, and his followers left the Lunda state of Shaba to settle in what is presently eastern Angola. Around the middle of the sixteenth century, the Mbangala established contacts with the Portuguese and exchanged trade with them. In the early part of the seventeenth century, they aligned themselves with the Portuguese slaving business.

In 1618, they established a kingdom of their own, the Kingdom of Kasanje, between the Kwango and Kwanza rivers and prospered as an intermediary between the Lunda kingdoms of Mwata Yamvo and Mwata Kazembe on the one hand and the city of Luanda on the other. By the eighteenth century, they managed to monopolize trading activities of the business centers of these kingdoms and became the virtual client of Portuguese traders.[306]

The Mbangala's relation with the Portuguese started to deteriorate in the latter part of the nineteenth century, especially when the Portuguese tried to penetrate their territory. Eventually, their kingdom of Kasanga was conquered by the Portuguese military between 1911 and 1913.

MBANJA

These are a South Central African Banda-speaking people. They are concentrated in the Central African Republic, as well as in the northern regions of the Democratic Republic of the Congo.

MBARIKE, see KUTED

MBATA

The Mbata people are one of West Central African ethnic groups. They are concentrated in the Democratic Republic of the Congo (Zaire). Their neighbors include the Bali, Ndibu, and Teke peoples.

MBATO

A West African people. The Mbato are concentrated in the Ivory Coast. They are part of the Ivorian Lagoon cluster of peoples.

MBAY, see MBAYE and SARA

MBAYE, see also SARA

The Mbay, also pronounced Mbaye, are one of Chad's non-Muslim Sara groups. Like other Sara groups, they speak a Central Sudanic language that belongs to the Nilo-Saharan family of African languages. Like them also, they live primarily in the southern regions of the country, notably between Lake Iro in the east and the Logone River in the west.

MBEERE, see also SHONA

The Mbeere—also spelled Mbire—are a Bantu-speaking, East African people. They speak Kimbeere, a language which is closely related to the other Bantu languages of the Mount Kenya periphery.[307] The Mbeere are concentrated in the Embu District in the Eastern Province of Kenya. Their neighbors include the Embu, Kamba, Kikuyu and Chuka peoples.

The Mbeere were originally living around the Lake Tanganyika region. In the fourteenth century they migrated to the south of the Zambezi. Historical evidence suggests that they had developed an advanced system of government as well as special skills in metallurgical and masonry works.[308] It also suggests that they played a distinctive role in helping the

Shona kingdom achieve an imperial status.[309]

The Mbeere came into contact with Europeans in 1851, at which time the German missionary Johann Ludwig Krapf visited their territory. Subsequently, they fell to British rule and in 1895, they were incorporated within the protectorate that Britain established over Kenya.

The Mbeere are essentially agriculturalists and traders. Their society is based on patrilineal lineages with exogamous clans constituting its basic units.

Though Christianity has won numerous converts, many Mbeere continue to adhere to their traditional religious beliefs. Their religion is based on the belief in a High God, *Nagai*, who is presumed to live on top of Mount Kenya.

MBEMBE

The Mbembe are a West African Bantu-speaking people. Their language belongs to the Benue-Congo branch of the Niger-Congo family of African languages and they are related by language to the Ekoi people of southeastern Nigeria and western Cameroon. The Mbembe are concentrated along the middle Cross River and hence are one of Nigeria's many ethnic minorities. Their neighbors include the Boki, Ekoi (Ekoid), Igbo, Iyala, Orri and Yako peoples.

The Mbembe's society observes both matrilineal and patrilineal lines of descent, and moreover, is structured along age-groups. Broadly speaking, movable property is inherited matrilineally, whereas nonmovable property is inherited patrilineally.

The people are essentially agriculturalists. They live in villages composed of a number of kin families. Each village is governed by a village chief, who is selected by a village association, known as *okwa*, which functions as a vehicle of control and socialization.

Though Christianity has won many converts, the Mbembe people continue to be impacted by their traditional religion which is based on the belief in a creator god and spirits. In their religion, spirits provide a continuing link between the living and dead.

MBENZELE

The Mbenzele are a West and West Central African people. They are one of the many Pygmy people of equatorial Africa. Originally, they inhabited the tropical rain forest, in what is now within the Republic of Congo. Subsequently, they moved to other areas, including Cameroon, Central African Republic and Gabon. The Mbenzele are essentially hunters, foragers and potters.

MBERENZABI

The Mberenzabi are an Equatorial and a West Central African people. They are concentrated in the Republic of Congo and adjoining states. Their neighbors include the Bakere, Bayaka, and Punu peoples.

MBIRE, see MBEERE

MBO

The Mbo people are a Central African people. Their main concentrations are in eastern Central African Republic, western Sudan, and north central Zaire. Their neighbors include the Balese Ndake and Basiri peoples.

MBOCHI

The Mbochi are an Ubangi people. They constitute one of the major ethnic groups of the Republic of Congo, accounting for 12% of the country's total population. The Mbochi can also be found in the Democratic Republic of the Congo (Zaire) and the Republic of Gabon.

MBOKO

The Mboko are a West Central African people. They are concentrated in the northwestern coastal areas of Cameroon. Their neighbors include the Agoi, Kole, Kpe, and Mungo peoples.

MBOLE, see MONGO

MBOMA, see KONGO

MBONDO, see MBUNDU

M'BORORO

The M'Bororo are an East Saharan people. They are a Toubou subgroup. They are concentrated in Chad and neighboring countries, especially Niger.

MBOUM

The Mboum, also spelled Mbum, are one of the many ethnic groups of Chad, the Central African Republic and Cameroon. Their language belongs to the Niger-Congo family. In Chad, they are concentrated to the west of the Chari and Longone River basins. In the Central African Republic they live in the northeast regions and account for 4% of the country's total population, constituting the fifth largest minority after the Baya (34%), the Banda (27%), the Mandjia (21%) and the Sara (10%).

MBOWE

An East African people. The Mbowe, also known as Mamboe, are concentrated in western Zambia. They are closely related to the Lozi people. They speak Kololo, the Lozi language, share many of Lozi customs, and are part of the Lozi-dominated Barotse Kingdom.[310]

MBUDJA

The Mbudja are a West Central African people. They are concentrated in the Democratic Republic of the Congo (Zaire).

MBUGWE

A Bantu-speaking farming people of northern and central Tanzania. Traditionally, sorcery was widely used in their society to maintain the political structures of their chiefdoms.[311] Many Mbugwe are now Muslim.

MBUI

The Mbui are a South Central and Southwest African people. They are concentrated in the western coastal regions of Angola. The Mbui are related to the Ovimbundu people. Their neighbors include the Chokwe, Esele, and Ovimbundu peoples.

MBUKUSHU

The Mbukushu, also known as Hambukushu, are a Central, Southwest and Southeast African people. They are concentrated in Angola, Botswana, Namibia and Zambia. Their neighbors in these countries include the Hukwe Bushmen and the Lozi peoples.

MBULA

A West African people and one of Nigeria's small ethnic minorities. The Mbula are concentrated in the eastern regions of the country and speak a language that belongs to the Benue-Congo branch of the Niger-Congo family of African languages. Their neighbors include the Bachama, Bata, Dera, Longuda, Vere and Yungur peoples.

MBUM, see MBOUM

MBUN, see MBUNDA

MBUNDA, see also LUNDA

The Mbunda, also known as Mbun, are a Bantu-speaking people whose origin is traced back to the Congo, where they were part of the Lunda kingdom and later empire. This was founded in the later part of the fifteenth century and endured until late in the nineteenth century. Over time, they broke away from the central Lunda kingdom in the Kapanga district of the southern Congo to establish their own kingdom. Currently, the Mbunda are among Angola's Democratic Republic of the Congo's (Zaire's) and Zambia's ethnic groups.

MBUNDU

The Mbundu people, also called Kimbundu, are a Central African people and the second largest ethnic group in Angola. They are concentrated in the northern central regions of Angola, accounting for about 25% of the country's total population. Groups of them, however, are also found in the Democratic Republic of the Congo (Zaire). The Mbundu speak Kimbundu, a Bantu language. Linguistically, they are related to the Ovimbundu, their southern neighbors. Culturally, however, they are related to the Bakongo, their northern neighbors. The Mbundu support numerous subgroups, the most important of which are the Mbaka, Ndongo and Mbondo.

The modern history of the Mbundu is traced back to the sixteenth century, at which time they "were organized into small tribal groups that maintained loose political connections."[312] Alarmed by the growing power of the Kongo Kingdom, they aligned themselves with the ngola, the king of the Ndongo people. In the period between the late 16th to the late 17th centuries, however, this alignment together with all other native centers of power, were destroyed by the Portuguese, inciting warfare and slaving among the Mbaka, Mbondo, Ndongo and other peoples of the region.

Due to the regional position of the Mbundu, in northwest Angola, they have been the most influenced indigenous group by Portuguese advancement into Africa. For example, many Portuguese words have been incorporated into their Kimbundu dialect. Also, the urban nature of the Mbundu, no doubt caused by Portuguese colonization, has led to the development of an urban Mbundu class known as Ambundu (or Akwaluada), in contrast to the conservative Mbundu peoples of the interior who are known as Dembo (Ndembo).

During the late twentieth century, most Mbundu have been totally immersed in the Portuguese lifestyle (i.e. intermarrying with Portuguese settlers and accepting Roman Catholicism). An entirely new class of mestizos, or mixed race people, has developed who have access to formal education. In fact, such mestizos, along with their Mbundu brethren have been the most fervent supporters of the current MPLA regime.

MBUNGA

The Mbunga are a Southeast African Bantu-speaking people. They are concentrated in Tanzania, primarily in the vicinity of the Kilombero and Rufiji rivers. Their neighbors include the Gogo, Kutu, and Pogoro peoples.

MBUNZA, see KAVANGO

MBUTI

The Mbuti, also known as Bambuti, are a Central African group of Pygmies who inhabit the Ituri Forest of northeastern Democratic Republic of the Congo (Zaire). Their total population is estimated at little over 55,000. They are people of very short stature and are considered the shortest group of Pygmies in Africa, "averaging under 4 feet 6 inches (137 cm)."[313] They are brown skinned, and hence, "much lighter in [color] than their Bantu and Sudanic [neighbors]." They also differ from their neighbors "in blood type and other physical characteristics..."[314]

The Mbuti are the original inhabitants of the northeastern Democratic Republic of the Congo (Zaire) and probably the earliest inhabitants of the African rain forests who were mentioned in ancient Egyptian records.

The Mbuti are divided into several groups, the most important of which are the Efe people. All of them are essentially nomadic hunters and gatherers, with each group of them having its own territory. They live in small bands comprised of several families for easy movement throughout the forests and speak a multitude of Bantu languages and dialects from Mbuti to Efe, as well as a number of other indigenous Congo languages.

Their society is highly egalitarian, with no chiefs, councils of elders, class structure, hierarchy or formal political organizations. Decisions are made through debates and disputes among them are resolved through general discussions.

The Mbuti family structure is nuclear, with a monogamous couple and their children. Marriage is by mutual consent or is arranged by brothers. Sister-exchange is practiced, where bands exchange women for marriage. Matrimonial unions may be dissolved if both partners do not get along.

Patrilineal relations in matters of descent and inheritance are predominant in their society.

Men and women are considered equals in Mbuti society. The men hunt and the women gather the fruit from the forest. Mbuti families have relationships with bigger villages, where men trade their bounty from hunting for agricultural and cooking utensils for their wives.

The Mbuti's religion is dominated by the belief in a supreme deity, called *Molimo*, the one Mbuti God, who rules the forests. It is tied to their practices of justice and their religious rituals center on the exaltation of the forest.

According to Moss and Wilson (1991), the Mbuti believe that punishment is delivered by the supernatural, in the form of disease or damage to one's home. A band may, however, collectively punish the culprit through beatings. Lesser offenses are dealt with between the people involved in a hand to hand combat.[315]

Mbuti artistic expression is mainly found in their music, which is dedicated to their God, *Molimo*. Dancing is also extremely important during religious celebrations. Body painting is very depictive and done only during religious observances. There is no known written tradition of the Mbuti.

MBWELA

The Mbwela are a Southwest African Bantu-speaking people. They are concentrated in southern Angola where they are part of the Ngangela cluster of peoples. Their neighbors include the Ndunduhe and Simaa, two of the Lozi subgroups.

MBWERA

Southwest African Bantu-speaking people. The Mbwera are a Lozi subgroup. They live in southeastern Angola. Their neighbors include the Lenje, Luano, Nkoya, and Nyaturu peoples.

MEBAN

The Meban are an East African people. They are concentrated in east central Sudan and west central Ethiopia. Their neighbors include the Berta, Burun, Ingassana, and Uduk peoples.

MEDI

The Medi are one of the main Kuri subgroups in Chad. They speak Yedina, a Buduma dialect. Like other Kuri groups, they live along the eastern shores of Lake Chad. The Medi people are divided into two principal clans, namely, the Dalla and Fetra.

MEDOGO

One of Chad's small ethnic minorities. They speak a central Sudanese language, locally known as Lisi. They also speak Arabic. The Medogo are a strict Muslim sedentary agricultural people. They have a centralized political culture that maintains amicable relationships with their Arab, Bilala and Kouka neighbors.

MEDZAN

The Medzan are one of the many Pygmy people of equatorial Africa. Originally, they inhabited the tropical rain forest, in what is now within the Republic of Congo. Subsequently, they moved to other areas neighboring the Congo Basin. Of these groups, the Medzan among them settled in the forest and wet savanna region of central Cameroon. The Medzan are essentially hunters, foragers and potters.

ME'EN

The Me'en are a Surmic (formerly Surma)-speaking people. Their language belongs to the East Sudanic group of the Nilo-Saharan family of African languages. They are concentrated in southern Ethiopia and Sudan. The Me'en are related to the Suri, Mursi and Murle peoples of southern Ethiopia and Sudan.

MEGANIN

The Meganin are a Central and East African people. Their main concentration is in the west central areas of Sudan. Groups of them, however, can also be found in Chad. The Meganin's neighbors include the Fur, Kawahla, Midob, and Hamar peoples.

MEGONG, see EGGON

MEIDOB

Central and East African Muslim pastoralist people. The Meidob (Midob), also known Tiddi, are concentrated in the western regions of Sudan. Groups of them, however, also live in Chad. Their neighbors include the Baggara (Kababish), Fur, Gimr, and Meganin peoples.

MEKWA

The Mekwa are a Southern African people. They are concentrated in the northern regions of Botswana. Their neighbors include the Kgatla, Kwena, and Rolong peoples.

MEKYIBO

The Mekyibo, also known as Eotile and Vetere, are a small West African people. They are concentrated in the Ivory Coast, notably in its southern forest region. Their neighbors include the Anyi, Assini, Attie, and Ebrie peoples. The Mekyibo speak a language that belongs to the Kwa branch of the Niger-Congo family of African languages. Their economic activities focus on farming, fishing and trading.

MENDE, see also MANDE

The Mende, also known as Boumpe, Hulo, Kosa, Kossa and Kosso, are a Mande people. They are one of the ethnic minorities of Sierra Leone, Liberia, Guinea and other West African states. In Sierra Leone, they account for about 30 percent of the country's population. Their neighbors include the Gbande, Gola, Kissi (Kisi), Kono, Sherbro and Vai peoples. The

Mende language belongs to the Mande branch of the Niger-Congo family of African languages.

The Mende society observes patrilineal relations in matters relating to descent, inheritance and succession. It is headed by a paramount chief who is the eldest male descendant of the founder of the chiefdom. The chiefdom is divided into subgroups, each of which is headed by a subchief, chosen from the male line of the founder of the subgroup.

The Mende are essentially an agriculturalist people. Currently, their activities cover both cash crops and shifting agriculture, producing, among other things, rice, yams, cassava, cocoa, palm oil and kernels, peanuts and ginger. Like other West Africa peoples, they are renowned for their splendid wood sculpture and masks.

Though now predominantly Muslim or Christian, some Mende continue to be impacted by their traditional religion which centered on the belief in a supreme creator god, as well as in nature deities and ancestral spirits. Traditionally, religious rituals were overseen and applied by diviners. Their observance was maintained by a secret male society known as *poro* and a secret female society known as *sande*.

MENING

Central and East African Nilotic-speaking people. The Mening are concentrated in the border area between Uganda and Sudan.

MERCA

The Merca are a small ethnic minority in Somalia. They are presumed to be of either Arab or Persian descent.

MERDU, see MURSI

MERILE, see DASANEC

MERINA, see also MALAGASY

One of Madagascar's ethnic groups. Also known as Imerina, the Merina people are of Malayo-Indonesian origin. They are related to the Betsileo, another Malayo-Indonesian group on the island. Their language is Malagasy (Merina dialect). Currently, they account for about 14% of Madagascar's population.

MERITU, see MURSI

MERU

The Meru are an East African Bantu-speaking people. They are concentrated in the Arusha region in Tanzania and the central eastern regions of Kenya. In Kenya, they account for approximately 6% of the country's total population.

MERULE, see MURLE

MESSIRIYA, see BAGGARA

MESTIÇO

The Mestiço are peoples of mixed foreign and native African ancestry. They are found in a number of African states. In Angola, for example, they constitute the fourth largest ethnic group after the Ovimbundu (37%), the Kimbundu (25%) and the Bakongo (13%), accounting for 2% of the country's total population. In São Tome and Principe, they constitute the largest ethnic group. In Guinea-Bissau, where they are known as Mulattos, they form a small minority, which, together with the European minority, accounts for less than 1% of the country's total population.

METOKO

South Central African people. The Mekoto are concentrated in the eastern regions of the Democratic Republic of the Congo (Zaire).

MFENGU

Known also as Fingo and Fingoes, the Mfengu are a Bantu Xhosa-speaking South African people of essentially Hlubi, Bhele and Zizi origin. They were uprooted by the White from Mfecane, their original lands in

Natal during the nineteenth century, and hence became refugees. Subsequently, the British government granted them Xhosa lands in both Transkei and Ciskei. This was partly in recognition of their support to the British forces against the Xhosa in the wars of 1835, 1846 and 1851-53, and partly to contain further Xhosa invasions of the Cape Colony. In 1879, the new Mfengu lands were incorporated in the Cape Colony.

Upon their uprooting from Natal, the Mfengu lost much of their traditional social, economic, religious and political tribal institutions, and hence, they became receptive to Christianity and Western education. This helped to generate a class of Western educated Mfenfu professionals who are employed "as businessmen, civil servants, lawyers, and teachers in large cities."[316] The great majority of the Mfengu, however, continue to engage in farming and herding cattle.

During the Whites' rule of South Africa, Transkei and Ciskei, whose populations are predominantly Mfengu, were established as independent African homelands.

MI MARVA, see GUIZIGA

MIANGO, see IRIGWE

MIDOB, see MEIDOB

MIDOGO

The Midogo people are one of the many ethnic groups of which Chad is composed. They are concentrated in the plains of the Guéra-Massif and are essentially sedentary people.

MIHAVANE

Southeast and East African people. The Mihavane are concentrated in Malawi, Mozambique and Tanzania.

MIJIKENDA

The Mijikenda, also known as Nika, are an East African people. They speak Mijikenda, a language that belongs to the Northeast Coastal Bantu languages. The Mijikenda are concentrated in Kenya and Tanzania, notably along the coasts of both countries. They comprise several groups, the most important of which are the Chonyi, Digo, Duruma, Giyamair, Jibana, Kambe, Kauma, Nyika, and Rabai. Currently, they constitute one of Kenya's eleven largest ethnic groups. Their economic activities focus on agriculture, fishing, and trading.

MIJURTEIN, see SOMALI

MIKHIFORE

The Mikhifore are a West African Mandika people. They are concentrated in Guinea, Liberia and Sierra Leone.

MIMA

A Central and East African Muslim pastoralist and semi-pastoralist people. They are concentrated in Uganda and Sudan, notably in the Darfur and Kerdofan provinces of the latter country.

MIMI

A Central and East African Muslim agricultural people. The Mimi are concentrated in Chad, Uganda and Sudan. They are a semi-sedentary people and speak a language which is related to Bora Mabang, as well as Arabic, Zaghaura and Tama. Their culture and customs are akin to those of the Maba people.

MINA

The Mina people – known also as Ana, Ane and Fante-Ane – are one of the ethnic minorities of the Republic of Togo. They constitute the second largest group after the Ewe. The Mina people are members of the GE Group and speak a variant of the Ewe language. They are the descendants of Fanti people who left the Gold Coast in the seventeenth and eighteenth centuries to settle in Aneho, a seat which they founded for themselves, in what is presently modern Togo.

MINANGENDE, see NGABAKA

MINDASSA, see KOTO

MINIANKA

One of Mali's Voltaic ethnic groups. The people speak a language of the Voltaic (Gur) branch of the Niger-Congo family and are essentially a sedentary agricultural people. Together with other Voltaic peoples, they account for 12% of the country's total population. They are concentrated in the eastern and southeastern areas of the country. Their neighbors include the Bambara, Bobo, Karaboro, Senufo, Sia, Tusyan and Wara peoples.

MINIFERE, see SAHO

MINYAL, see NUER

MIRIFLE, see SOMALI

MISHULUNDU

An East African people. The Mishulundu are concentrated in western Zambia. They are closely related to the Lozi people. They speak Kololo, the Lozi language, share many of Lozi customs, and are part of the Lozi-dominated Barotse Kingdom.[317]

MJJAT, see also BERBER

The Mjjat are a Moroccan Berber group. They are concentrated in the Ishilhayen region of Morocco, notably in the Western High Atlas, the Sus Valley, and the Anti-Atlas areas of the country.

MMALEBOGO, see PEDI

MMAMABOLO, see PEDI

MMANI

The Mmani, also called Mnami and Mandenyi, are a West African people. They are concentrated in Guinea. Groups of them, however, can also be found in adjoining states.

MNAMI, see MMANI

MOBA

The Moba people are one of Togo's ethnic minorities. They are a Voltaic (Gur)-speaking group who live in the northern areas of the country. Their neighbors include the Chakossi, Gurensi, Gurma, Mamprusi (Manprusi), Naudeba and Somba peoples.

MOBBER, see MOBER

MOBER, see also KANURI

The Mober are a West African Kanuri people who live in Cameroon, Chad, Niger and Nigeria. The Mober, or Mobber, are concentrated in the Lake Chad region of northeastern Nigeria and eastern Niger. A large group of them are presently in the state of Borno (formerly Bornu). They are essentially an agriculturalist people.

MOER

The Moer are a South Central and East African people. They are concentrated in the Democratic Republic of the Congo (Zaire) and Zambia. The Moer live on the southwest shores of Lake Tanganyika. Their neighbors include the Bemba, Holoholo, Kuba, and Lungu peoples.

MOFOU

A West and West Central African people. The Mofou, also called Douvangar and Mofu, are concentrated in the northern regions of Cameroon, primarily in the Diamaré department of the country.

MOFU, see MOFOU

MOGOBOYA, see PEDI

MOGORI, see KOTOKO

MOGWANDI, see NGBANDI

MOHARAIS

The Moharais are a people of Malagasy origin who live on the island of Mayotte, also called Mahoré, a southeastern island of the Comoros archipelago in the Indian Ocean.

The Moharais, also known as Mahorans, are Muslim people, but highly influenced by the French culture. They speak a Malagasy dialect, Comorian, a language closely related to Swahili and French.

The Moharais are essentially agriculturalists, but some of them are also engaged in trading services. Currently, they represent the great majority of Mayotte's population.

MOINJAANG, see DINKA

MOITANIK, see MASAI

MOLE-DAGBANE, see LOBI DAGARTI

MOLE-DAGBANI, see DAGOMBA

MOLET-E, see PEDI

MOLIBELI, see also SOTHO

The Molibeli are one of the major tribes of the Kwena, a subgroup of the Sotho people. They are concentrated in the Kingdom of Lesotho.

Like other Sotho, they are a southern African people, speak Sesotho, a Bantu language, and engage in agriculture and animal husbandry. Their settlements are characterized "by scattered hamlets of circular huts with mud and wattle or stone walls surmounted by a conical, thatched roof."[318] In their social patterns, most Kanga-Kone recognize patrilineal lineages and continue to be impacted by their traditional religious beliefs.

MOMBERA

The Mombera are a subgroup of the Ngoni nation. The death of Zwangendaba, the leader of the Ngoni nation became the symbol of its unity. At Mapupo (about 1848), a successional conflict prompted them to move southwardly and settle in the highlands west of Lake Nyasa (Malawi). There, they established a kingdom of their own bearing the name of their leader, Mombera. Soon after, however, the Mombera witnessed a split. One of its subgroups moved southwardly and settled in the Dowa uplands in what is presently the southern region of the state of Malawi. Eventually, both Mombera kingdoms disappeared following the European conquest of their territories in the later part of the nineteenth century.

MONAHENG, see also SOTHO

The Monaheng are one of the major tribes of the Kwena, a subgroup of the Sotho people. They are concentrated in the Kingdom of Lesotho. Like other Sotho, they are a southern African people, who speak Sesotho, a Bantu language, and engage in agriculture and animal husbandry. Their settlements are characterized "by scattered hamlets of circular huts with mud and wattle or stone walls surmounted by a conical, thatched roof."[319] In their social patterns, most Monaheng recognize patrilineal lineages and continue to be impacted by their traditional religious beliefs.

MONBUTTU, see MANGBETU

MONDARI

The Mondari are one of Sudan's tribal people. They speak an Eastern Sudanic language of the Chari-Nile branch of the Nilo-Saharan family of African languages and are concentrated in the southern region of the country.

The Mondari support a relatively sedentary type of society. They live in scattered villages and their main economic activities center on farming, cattle raising and hunting. Their social organization is essentially tribal and patrilineal in nature.

MONGO

The Mongo, also known as Lomongo, are a cluster of Bantu-speaking people, who live in the equatorial forest area of central Democratic Republic of the Congo (Zaire), south of the Congo River and north of the Kasai and Sankuru rivers. They speak different dialects of Mongo or Nkundo languages, which belong to the Benue-Congo branch of the Niger-Congo family of African languages, and moreover, they comprise several groups, the most important of which are: the Bolia, Bokoto, Bongandu, Boyela, Ekonda, Mbole, Ndengese, Nkutu, Ntomba, Sengele, Songomeno and Tetela-Kusu. Currently, the Mongo constitute Zaire's largest ethnic group and are highly concentrated in the central areas of the country.

The Mongo society is patrilineal and patriarchal. It is composed of numerous villages, each village of which is grouped on lineages traced back to single ancestors and ruled independently by a village council made up of lineage heads.

In the Mongo society, property is governed by a system called *etuka* that places property under the control of the oldest male of the oldest lineage and provides for its distribution by lineages. This system is fostered by the Mongo's religion which is based on the belief in a supreme god, also known as Mongo, ancestral and nature spirits, as well as the power of magic, sorcery, and witchcraft.

The economic activities of the Mongo focus on agriculture, food gathering, hunting and fishing.

The Mongos are noted for their artistic talents, but their art is essentially oral. The people "have developed such epics as the highly aesthetic Lianja, which relates the origin of the Mongo. Talking-drum literature and songs also show a rich artistic content."[320]

MONTAGNARD, see MANDARA

MOOR, see also MAUR

The term Moor, also known as *Beidan*, refers to Muslim peoples of mixed Arab-Berber ancestry in the northwestern countries of Africa, especially Mauritania, Morocco and Mali. In Mauritania, the Moors constitute the overwhelming majority of the people. In Mali, the Moors, together with the Tauregs, account for about 5% of the total population and inhabit the Sahelian zone in the central region of the country. The Moors speak Hassaniyah, an Arabic dialect with Berber vernaculars.

The Moors are divided into many groups, including the Chaamba, Hassaouna, Haratin (also known as Kamadja), Imraguen, Ouled Tidrarin, Ouled Delim, Ait Lahsen, Izarguien, Marabouts, and Rguibat. The basic unit of their society is the patrilineal clan.[321]

MOOSE, see MOSSI

MOR, see NUER

MORMOREA, see TEDA

MORU

An Eastern Nilotic Sudanese people. The Moru are concentrated in Sudan's southern central equatorial regions, notably in the vicinity of Bahr al-Ghazal. Their neighbors include the Belanda, Jur, Kederu, Luo, Mittu, and Thuri peoples.

MOSHI-DAGOMBA, see also DAGOMBA and MOSSI

The Moshi-Dagomba, also Mossi-Dagomba, are a West African people. They speak a Voltaic (Gur) language akin to the Moré language of the Mossi people. They constitute the second largest ethnic group in Ghana, accounting for 16% of the total population. The Moshi-Dagomba are related to other groups within and outside the country, including the Mamprussi of Ghana and the Mossi of Burkina Faso.

MOSI, see MOSSI

MOSSI

The Mossi, also Moose, Mosi, Moshi and Moussei, are one of West Africa's Voltaic peoples. They speak Moré, also known as Molé, Moore, Mooré and Mossi, is a Voltaic (Gur) language. Their economic activities focus on agriculture, animal husbandry and trade.

The Mossi support numerous groups, the most important of which are the Gurma (Gourma), Grunshis (Gurunsi), Bobo, Lobi and Yarsé. Their neighbors include the Busa, Deforo, Dogon, Fula, Lilse, Moba, Nunuma and Samo peoples.

The Mossi society observes patrilineal lineages and is organized as a feudal kingdom composed of several classes: royalty, nobles, commoners and servants. The kingdom is headed by a paramount chief known as *morho naba*, that is "big lord." Second to the king are divisional chiefs, the chiefs and then the commoners. Members of the Mossi royalty trace their origin to northern Ghana, where they are related to several of its groups, like the Mamprussi and Moshi-Dagomba.

In the early 16th century, the Mossi developed a number of independent kingdoms in what presently constitutes Burkina Faso and Ghana, the most important of which were Dagomba, Fada Ngourma (Fada N'Gurma), Mamprussi, Nanumba, Tenkodogo (Tankudugu), Wagadugu (Wogodogo, Ouagadougou) and Yatenga. These kingdoms not only withstood the expansion of the empires of Mali and Songhay, but also sustained their independence until late in the 19th century, when they fell to either French or British conquests.

Currently, the Mossi people primarily live in Burkina Faso, Ghana, Ivory Coast and Togo. They are highly concentrated in Burkina Faso, where they constitute the principal tribe and account for about 28% of the country's total population or what amounts to over 2.5 million.

In Ghana, the Moshi-Dagomba constitute the second largest ethnic group, accounting for 16% of the population. In Ivory Coast, they are the second largest ethnic group. In Togo, where they constitute one of the country's ethnic minorities, they live in the northern areas.

MOUADHI, see CHAAMBA

MOUBI

The Moubi reside in central Chad, where they make up less than 1% of the state's population. They are a sedentary people who grow a wide range of agricultural staples. They are also involved in small-scale cattle raising. "Their language is related to the Dadjo."[322]

The Moubi are split into two groups, the Moubi Hadaba and Moubi Zarga. Both groups maintain good relations with each other, as well as other neighboring ethnic groups. Yet, they do not maintain an amiable relationship with the central government of Chad.

MOUDANG

A Central and East African people. The Moudang are one of the major ethnic groups of the Republic of Chad. They live essentially in the northern and central regions of the country.

MOUDIA, see TOUBOU

MOUNDAN

The Moundan reside in southwestern Chad, as well as Cameroon. They speak a dialect belonging to the Congo-Kordofanian language family.

Moundan farm for subsistence, as well as for trade. They also raise cattle, which is used for marriage payments and religious observations.

The Moundan have been heavily influenced by the Fulani in terms of political and social organization, as well as clothing. The Moundan have also incorporated the Islamic religion through contact with the Fulani.

MOURDIA, see also TOUBOU

The Mourdia are a Central and East African people. They are concentrated in the west central areas of Sudan. Their neighbors include the Ankaza, Bideyat, and Ounie peoples.

MOUSGOUM

The Mousgoum, also known as Mulwi, Munjuk and Musuk, are an East Saharan, Central and West African people. They are concentrated in Chad and Cameroon. The economic activities of the Mousgoum center on farming and fishing.

MOUSSEI

A Central and East African people. The Moussei are one of the major ethnic groups of the Republic of Chad. They live essentially in the northern and central regions of the country.

MPANGU, see KONGO

MPEZENI

The Mpezeni are a subgroup of the Ngoni nation. Upon the death of Zwangendaba, the leader of the Ngoni nation and the symbol of its unity, at Mapupo (about 1848), a successional conflict prompted them to move westwardly into Bemba lands and then eastwardly to the Fort Jameson area in what is presently modern Zambia. There, they established a kingdom of their own bearing the name of their leader, Mpezeni. Eventually, the Mpezeni kingdom disappeared following the European conquest of its territory in the later part of the nineteenth century.

MPHAHLELE, see **PEDI**

MPONDO

The Mpondo, also Pondo, are a South African Bantu-speaking people. They speak Nguni. Since the sixteenth century, they have inhabited Pondoland, a region on the Indian Ocean between Mtamvuna and Umtata (Mtata) rivers. In 1828, they were defeated by Shaka Zulu warriors and were forced to flee their lands to areas across the Mzimvubu River. There, they reorganized their state, formed a new army on the Zulu model, focused their attention on producing and selling grains, as well as rebuilding their cattle stocks. In 1847, they were uprooted of their lands in application of British Governor Harry Smith's decision to annex Xhosa areas between the Fish and Keiskamma rivers, and Keiskamma and Kei rivers, to Cape Colony and the colony of British Kaffraria, respectively. The final annexation of Pondoland, however, did not take place until 1894 at which time the Cape government under Cecil Rhodes annexed their territory.

Like other peoples, such as the Fingoes and Griquas, they were later resettled north to Natal in Transkei, which eventually became the main reserve for Africans in South Africa during the Apartheid era.[323]

Traditionally, the Mpondo shared many cultural patterns of the Ngoni people. Their society observed patrilineal lineages in matters relating to descent, inheritance and succession, and recognized exogamous marriages. Politically, it consisted of several chiefdoms which were subject to a central chieftaincy governed by a royal lineage.

Traditionally also, the Mpondo were agriculturists, with women attending to agriculture and men attending to cattle.

As a result of the seizure of their lands, uprooting, diaspora and displacement, many Mpondo were forced to become migrant workers in the gold mines at Witwatersrand and elsewhere.

MPONDOMISE

The Mpondomise are a southern African people. They are concentrated in the Republic of South Africa. Their neighbors include the Bhaca, Bomvana, and Thembu peoples.

MPONGWE

The Mpongwe are a West Central African people. They are concentrated in the western coastal areas of Cameroon, Equatorial Guinea, and Gabon. Their neighbors include the Adyamba, Fang, and Yasa peoples.

MUBI, see GUDE

MUCATU

One of Southern Africa's peoples. The Mucatu are a subgroup of the Abarue, a Shona people. They live in Zimbabwe and Mozambique.

MUENYI

An East African people. The Muenyi, also known as Mwenyi, are concentrated in western Zambia. They are closely related to the Lozi people. They speak Kololo, the Lozi language, share many of Lozi customs, and are part of the Lozi-dominated Barotse Kingdom.[324]

MUGIRANGO, see GUSII

MUKWA, see MACUA

MULATTO, see MESTIÇO

MULLUMTCHILLOUM

The Mullumtchilloum are one of the Chadian Kuri subgroups. They speak Yedina, a Buduma dialect. Like other Kuri groups, they live along the eastern shores of Lake Chad.

MULWI, see MOUSGOUM

MUM, see BAMUN

MUMUYE

A West African people. The Mumuya are concentrated in central eastern regions of Nigeria and speak a language of the Adamawa branch of the Niger-Congo family of African languages. Their neighbors include the Bachama, Chamba, Daka, Jukun, Kam, Vere and Wurkum peoples.

MUNCHI, see TIV

MUNGO

The Mungo are a Central and West Central African people. They are concentrated in the western coastal areas of Cameroon and adjoining states. Their neighbors include the Duala and Kpe peoples.

MUNJUK, see MOUSGOUM

MUNSHI, see TIV

MUPUN, see SURA MWAGHAVUL

MURD GUACHEY

The Murd Guachey are a West Saharan African group. They are found in Mauritania, Mali, Morocco, Senegal, and Western Sahara. They are highly concentrated in the Canary Islands.

MURLE

An East African pastoralist people. The Murle, also known as Ajibba, Beir, Boma-Murle, Omo-Murle and Merule, are a Surmic (formerly Surma)-speaking people. Their language belongs to the East Sudanic group of the Nilo-Saharan family of African languages.

The Murle are concentrated in southwestern Ethiopia and southeastern Sudan, notably east of the White Nile. Their neighbors include the Suri and Dizi peoples of the Maji and Bero-Shasha provinces of the Kefa region in Ethiopia as well as the Galla, the Dinka, the Nuer, the Anuak peoples of the

Sudan.

MURSI

The Mursi, also known as Merdu and Meritu, are an East African farming and fishing people. They are concentrated in the Kefa region in Ethiopia. Like their neighbors the Suri, Me'en and Murle, they speak a Surmic (formerly called Surma) language.

MUSGU

The Musgu are a West African people. They are concentrated in the northern regions of Cameroon and speak a language that belongs to the Afro-Asiatic family of African languages. The Kapsiki neighbors include the Gisiga, Koloko and Mandara peoples.

MUSOKANTANDA, see LUNDA

MUSUK, see SUK

MUTANDA, see LUNDA

MVAE, see FANG

MVUBA

A small East Saharan and Central African people. The Mvuba are concentrated in the Republic of Chad. Groups of them, however, can also be found in the Democratic Republic of the Congo (Zaire) and Sudan. The Mvuba are essentially an agricultural people.

MWAGHAVUL, see SURA

MWANGA

An East African people. The Mwanga are concentrated in western Zambia. They are closely related to the Lozi people. They speak Kololo, the Lozi language, share many of Lozi customs, and are part of the Lozi-dominated

Barotse Kingdom.[325]

MWELA, see MWERA

MWENGA, see LEGA

MWENYI

An East African people. The Mwenyi, also known as Muenyi, are concentrated in western Zambia. They are closely related to the Lozi people. They speak Kololo, the Lozi language, share many of Lozi customs, and are part of the Lozi-dominated Barotse Kingdom.[326]

MWERA

The Mwera – also known as Chimwera, Mwela and Mwere – are a Southeast African people. They are concentrated in Tanzania. Groups of them, however, can also be found in Malawi and Mozambique.

MWERE, see KWERE

MWERE, see MWERA

MWILA

The Mwila people are a Southwest African ethnic group. They are concentrated in the southwestern areas of Angola. Their neighbors include the Ngambwe, Twilenge-Humbi, Vatwa, and Zimba peoples.

MZAB

The Mzab are a West Saharan North African group. They are concentrated in the north central regions of Algeria. Their neighbors include the Chaamba, Dou Menia, El-Arbaa and Hamiyan peoples.

NAFANA

The Nafana are a West African people. They are concentrated in Ghana and Ivory Coast. Their neighbors include the Brong, Guang, Kulango and Likpe peoples. The Nafana speak a language that belongs to the Kwa branch of the Niger-Congo family of African languages.

NALU

These are one of Guinea-Bissau's ethnic minorities. The Nalu people live in areas close to the sea. They speak Nalu. Their neighbors include the Baga, Landuma and Susu peoples.

NAMA

A Southwest African Khoisan-speaking people. The Nama, often called Hottentots, a name they dislike, are concentrated in the southern regions of Namibia. They account for about 5% of the country's population.

NAMAQUA

The Namaqua are a southern African Hottentot group. They are concentrated in the northwestern regions the Republic of South Africa. Their neighbors include the Chariguriqua, Tswana, and Xam peoples.

NAMBA, see LAMBA

NAMBANE, see LAMBA

NAGO, see YORUBA

NAGOS, see SURI

NAGOT, see YORUBA

NALU

A West African people. The Nalu are concentrated in Guinea. Their neighbors include the Baga, Biafada, Landuma and Susu. They speak a language that belongs to the West Atlantic branch of the Niger-Congo family of African languages.

NAMOOS

The Namoos are a West African Voltaic people. They are concentrated in the basin of the Volta rivers in Ghana. Their neighbors include the Tallensi people.

NAMU

One of West Africa's peoples. The Namu live primarily in the Plateau State in Nigeria. They are closely related to the their neighbors the Bwal, Dimmuk, and Kwalla peoples.

NANDE

The Nande are one of the ethnic groups of the Democratic Republic of the Congo's (Zaire's) ethnic groups. They are concentrated in the Masisi district, a fertile region of lakes and lush hills, located northeast of lake Kivu and the city of Goma along the country's eastern border with Rwanda. Since the late 1980's, their region has been witnessing an influx of Rwandan immigrants – both Tutsi and Hutu – and recurring tribal wars.[327]

NANDI, see also KALENJIN

The Nandi are one of Kenya's ethnic minorities. They are concentrated in the southwest corner of the Uashin Gishu Plateau. Their land begins a few miles to the northeast of the Kavirondo Gulf of Lake Victoria and much of it is forested.[328] Prior to their settlement in the Uashin Gishu Plateau, the Nandi used to live in the vicinity of Lake Baringo. They migrated to their present land sometime between the seventeenth and early nineteenth centuries.

The Nandi are related to the Kipsikis and Okiek peoples both culturally and linguistically. Like the Kipsikis and Okiek peoples, they speak Kalenjin, a language that belongs to the southern Nilotic group of African languages. Including the Nandi, the Kalenjin-speaking peoples of Kenya account for about 11% of the total population. The Nandi comprise several groups, including the Chemwal and Teng'wal.

Until recently, the Nandi were essentially a pastoral people with their main interest, if not existence, focused on cattle. Their cattle, which provided them with milk, blood and meat, the main sources of their diet, was also the principal means for generating respect and prominence in their society. In their traditional values, those who did not own cattle were not only subject to great contempt, but also deprived of significant social or political privileges, including the right to speak in council meetings. "Cattle was the only form of property that mattered. A man could not sell the cattle which he inherited, only the cattle which he acquired by himself."[329] In addition, the "payment of cattle was essential for bridewealth and, hence, marriage."[330] Furthermore, cattle "were used for gifts between relatives and for compensation for offenses. Milk, grass, and dung had a sacred quality because of their connection with cattle. The hides of cattle were used for clothing and covering in sleep. The dung was used for building and medicinal purposes. The Nandi were, in short, absorbed in cattle."[331] In their traditional values also, land was cherished primarily for cattle grazing. Because of this reason, land was considered a common property, held by the whole Nandi people.

The Nandi society was originally composed of scattered homesteads, every group of which constituted a *koret*, their basic political unit. The word *koret* is probably derived from the Arabic words *qaryah* and *qurah*, meaning village and villages, respectively. Every *koret* "had its own governing and judicial council of elders called the *kokwet*."[332] This council met under the leadership of the most important old man who takes counsel in the presence of all men of a *koret* who could attend the meeting. The next level in their political organization was represented by a territorial council of warriors called *pororiet*. The main concern of this council was to address the security issues of the Nandi society, including war. The third and highest level was composed of a regional grouping called *emet*, the primary function of which was to address Nandi regional concerns. Originally, the Nandi supported six *emets*. Now they have only five of them.[333]

The Nandi were also organized on the basis of their respective clans. Unlike many other African peoples, however, their clans were not "segmented into lineages. Clans were patrilineal and totemic. They had an exogamous significance and provided a link among their members, which were dispersed throughout the country."[334]

The Nandi had their own religion which rested on the belief in one supreme god and Creator, named *Asis*, and a Thereafter of spirits. In their religious beliefs, God not only regulated the balance between human beings and nature, but also provided for harmony and order in the world. The Nandi are noted for developing the belief that when law cannot retrieve one's rights then that person could resort to the spirits for help.[335]

NANGIA-NAPORE

A Central and East African people. The Nangia-Napore are concentrated in Uganda.

NANUMBA

The Nanumba are a West African Voltaic people. They are a Mossi group. Their concentrations are primarily in Burkina Faso, Ghana and Togo. In Ghana, they live essentially in the Northern and Volta administrative regions, neighboring the Akan, the Dagomba and the Gonja peoples. In the early 16th century they established an independent kingdom of their own, the Nanumba.

NAR, see also SARA

The Nar are one of Chad's non-Muslim Sara groups. Like other Sara groups, they speak a Central Sudanic language that belongs to the Nilo-Saharan family of African languages. Like them also, they live primarily in the southern regions of the country, notably between Lake Iro in the east and the Logone River in the west.

NARA

The Nara, also known as Barea and Barya, are an East African Nilo-speaking people. They are concentrated in the northwestern regions of Ethiopia. The Nara are a Muslim people.

NARENE, see PEDI

NARIM

An East African people of southern Ethiopia and Sudan. The Narim speak Narim, a Surmic (formerly Surma) language which belongs to the East Sudanic group of the Nilo-Saharan family of African languages. They are related to the Suri, Me'en, Mursi and Murle peoples of southern Ethiopia and Sudan.

NARO, see NARON and SAN

NARON, see also SAN

A southern African San (Khoisan) people. The Naron, also known as Nharo and Naro, are concentrated in the eastern central regions of Botswana, notably in the limestone karst zone of the Ghansi District. Their neighbors include the Amraal Hoteentot, the Bakalahari, the Kau-en and the Tsaukwe peoples. Like other San-speaking peoples, they are essentially foragers, hunters and gatherers.

NAATH, see NUER

NATH, see NUER

NATIMBA

The Natimba are one of Benin's and Togo's Somba subgroups, and hence, they are Voltaic (Gur)-speaking people. They are located in the northern areas of both countries.

NAUDEBA

These are a West African people and one of the ethnic minorities of Togo. They are concentrated in the northern parts of the country, especially in the eastern la Kara region. Their neighbors include the Kabre, Kilinga and Somba peoples. The Naudeba, also known as Loso, are a Gur-speaking Voltaic people. They speak Moré, the language of the Mossi. They are predominantly engaged in farming and animal husbandry.

NBOMBE

The Nbombe are an Equatorial, West Central and Southwest African people. They are concentrated south of the Zaire River in the north central regions of the Democratic Republic of the Congo (Zaire). Their neighbors include the Baloulou (Kongo), Ekonda, Ngbaka, and Tswa peoples.

NBULE, see BABOUTI

NCHARI, see GUSII

NDALI

The Ndali are a Southeast African ethnic group. They are concentrated in the northeastern areas of Zambia, as well as in northern Malawi, primarily west of Lake Nalawi. Their neighbors include the Henga, Iwa, Ngonde, and Nyakyusa peoples.

N'DAM

A Central and East African people. The N'Dam are concentrated in Chad. However, some groups of them can also be found in Cameroon and Nigeria.

NDARA, see MANDARA

NDAU, see also SHONA

The Ndau are a Southern Bantu-speaking Shona group. They speak Shona, a tonal Bantu language. The Ndau are concentrated in the southeastern regions of Zimbabwe and span down to the coast in Mozambique. They account for about 3% of Zimbabwe's total population. Their neighbors include the Karanga, the Manyika, the Rozwi, the Shangaan and the Zezuru peoples.

NDEBELE, see also ZULU

The Ndebele people, known as the Amandebele by the nation itself and also identified as Matabele, are a southern African Western Bantu-speaking people. They speak IsiNdebele, an Nguni language, and Sepedi, a Northern Sotho language. Many of them, however, also speak Afrikaans and/or English. The Ndebele are divided into two major groups: the Ndzundza and the Manala. A third group, the Mhwaduba, ceased to exist because of its integration with neighboring Sotho-speaking communities. "During the colonial era, White settlers derogatively referred to the Ndzundza-Ndebele as 'Mapoggers' or 'Mapoêrs," after their ruler Mabohoko, called 'Mapog' or 'Mapoch' by Whites."[336]

The Ndebele are concentrated in southwestern Zimbabwe and northeastern South Africa. In Zimbabwe (where they are also known as Matebele), they constitute the second largest ethnic minority after the Shona (71%), accounting for about 16% of the total population. In South Africa, they comprise virtually the total population of the former KwaNdebele homeland. Their total population is about 3 million.

The Ndebelle people are an offshoot of the Zulus. The word Ndebele means "strangers" in the Sotho tongue. It originated when in the 1820s, Mzilikazi, an officer in the army of the renowned Zulu leader Shaka, committed the gross mistake of refusing to turn to his overlord Shaka a number of cattle seized in a military raid. Mzilikazi and a few of his followers had no choice but to defect and seek refuge in northeastern South Africa (Transvaal). Run-ins with the Zulu fighters, and later with the Boer trekkers, resulted in their flight farther north into western Zimbabwe. There, the group became identified with the land they occupied (Matabeleland) translated to Ndebele, a land which had once been the domain of the Changamire. There also, they subdued the Shona and other tribes living in the area and, moreover, established a small empire that lasted until the late 1800s.[337]

In 1868, Lobengula succeeded his father, Mzilikazi,as king of the Ndebelle. Because his succession was the result of a civil war, Lobengula sought to consolidate his rule by cultivating external friendships.[338]

In 1887, King Lobengula concluded a treaty with his neighbors, the Boers. The treaty, known as the Grobler Treaty, provided special privileges for Boers traveling and trading within Matabeleland, effectively placing

Matabeleland under Transvaal's protection. The British government's reaction to this treaty was immediate. In February, 1988, it concluded its own treaty, the Moffat Treaty, with King Lobengula, which bound Lobengula to consult the British South African high commissioner prior to entering into external engagements with external parties entailing territorial commitments. For all practical purposes, this treaty neutralized, if not abrogated, the Grobler Treaty.[339]

Henceforth, the Ndebele started to fall to British rule. In October of 1888, Cecil Rhodes persuaded Lobengula to sign the Rudd Concession which provided Rhodes with exclusive mineral rights throughout Matabeleland and Mashonaland (which was regarded under the effective sovereignty of the Ndebele). In return, Rhodes agreed to supply Lobengula with "one thousand breech-loading rifles" as well as a monthly subsidy of £100.[340] In the autumn of 1889, he was also persuaded to grant Rhodes' company, the British South Africa Company, limited prospecting rights in his territory.

These concessions proved to be the Trojan horse that Rhodes used to penetrate both the Matabeleland and the Mashonaland. When Lobengula realized that the concession entailed the establishment of white settlements, resulting in more than a few miners who would always be under his control. It became too late to reverse the colonists' penetration effort or to halt their occupation of Ndebele lands.

At first, Lobengula reacted to these developments by repudiating the Rudd concession as contrary to his understanding, as well as by condemning the occupation of areas not covered by his authorization. When these reactions failed to halt the colonists' penetration, Lobengula ordered his troops to raid European settlements in July 1893, a measure that provoked a war with the British South Africa Company.

The results of the war were in favor of the British South Africa Company troops and in October of the same year, Lobengula and his defeated forces had to retreat toward the Zambezi. There, Lobengula fell to smallpox and died in January, 1894. Both Matabeleland and Mashonaland were declared the property of the British South Africa Company by right of conquest.

Thereupon, the British South Africa Company assigned the Ndebele two reserves and additionally, it formed an African police force to recruit Ndebele for mining work. Subsequently, the 1895 ordinance that established the two Ndebele reserves was modified in 1902 and 1920. As a result of the amendments, about 23 percent of the Matabeleland was designated as African reserves, 32 percent for Europeans, and 45 percent for the British crown.[341]

The Ndebele's uprising against the 1895 measures (March to October 1896) ended with their capitulation and resulted in the adoption of a series of new ordinances under which terms Ndebele (and Shona people who supported them) were required to pay taxes – a factor that indirectly compelled them to seek work in European enterprises and hence become wage earners.[342] Moreover, more of Ndebele's lands were seized.[343] An ordinance issued in 1902, for example, required African workers to be permanently at their posts. Another ordinance issued in 1904, introduced a head tax. The purpose of which were to pressure more Africans to work for European farming and mining enterprises.[344]

Subsequent ordinances tied franchise to property and literacy, practically restricting political activity to the European population. Thus, when South Rhodesian electors rejected their incorporation in the Union of South Africa in 1922, the decision was made strictly by Europeans. The African people had no say in the decision. In South Rhodesia, they continued a marginal existence until April 18, 1980, when the country acquired its independence as the Republic of Zimbabwe. In South Africa, they also continued a marginal existence within strictly Black homelands until the adoption of an interim constitution on April 27, 1994 that ended former segregationist laws in the country.

Within the Republics of South Africa and Zimbabwe, the Ndebele continue to retain basic features of their traditional, strict social hierarchy that was made up of original Zulu descendants and conquered peoples. Zulu descendants are called the *Zani*, and occupy the highest rank. *Enhla* is the middle class that contains conquered Sotho and Tswana peoples. The lowest class is made up of former small tribes in Matabeleland most recently absorbed and is called *Holi*. Political control rests completely in the *Zani* class.

In Ndebele society, men have the most influence in the family. A man can have many wives and adultery on his part risks only a mild retribution. Adultery on the woman's part leads to the confiscation of her children and divorce. Children have two mothers in society: the biological mother called "little mother" and the stand-in mother when needed, called a "big mother". This arrangement suggests that Ndebele parents normally have responsibilities that call on them to be away from their kids and hence, seek the help of big mothers in upbringing their kids. In fact, Ndebele husbands and wives often live separately, with men tending the cattle and women living close to the agricultural land.

In traditional Ndebele society, men hunted and the women farmed. Now, men tend to work in the southern African mining industry or large farms owned by Europeans, whereas women still farm but on much smaller plots of land.

Most Ndebele still adhere to their traditional religion that centers on the worship of their high God, *Nkulunkulu,* and their ancestor spirits. A priestess, or *igoso,* serves as the main intermediary between the Ndebele and their ancestors. Also traditional medicine still popular, due to active *nganga,* or medicine men. A great percentage of Ndebele continue to visit these native doctors for both spiritual and physical treatments.

Economic development in South Africa and Zimbabwe has dissolved many important aspects of Ndebele culture, including political authority over their own affairs. Yet, at the same time, it entailed greater access to education among all Ndebele. This has led some Ndebele to aspire to greater occupations in the bigger cities and lowered the illiteracy rate among older Ndebele.

NDEMBA, see also **LUNDA**

The Ndemba are a Bantu-speaking people whose origin is traced back to the Congo, where they were part of the Lunda kingdom, and later empire. This empire was founded in the later part of the fifteenth century and endured until late in the nineteenth century. Over time, they broke away from the central Lunda kingdom in the Kapanga district of the southern Congo to establish their own kingdom.

Currently, the Ndemba are among Angola's, Democratic Republic of the Congo's (Zaire's) and Zambia's ethnic groups.

Traditionally, the main economic activities of the Luvale people centered on food gathering, hunting and trading. Traditionally also, their religion rested on the belief in a supreme being who was either a sky god or an earth god.[345]

NDEMBO, see LUNDA

NDEMBU, see also LUNDA

Democratic Republic of the Congo (Zaire) and Zambia. Their language is a West Central Bantu language. They are an agricultural people.

NDENGEREKO, see NDEREKO

NDERE

The Ndere people are a Central African ethnic group. Their main concentrations are in southeastern regions of Chad and the north central areas of Central African Republic. Their neighbors in both countries include the Bwaka, Dakwa, Laka, Mandja, and Yanghere peoples.

NDEREKO

The Ndereko, also known as Kingengere and Ndengereko, are a Southeast African people. They are concentrated in the northeastern coastal regions of Tanzania. Their neighbors include the Wazaramo, the Doe, the Kami, the Kutu, the Kwere and the Rufiji peoples.

NDENGESE, see MONGO

NDEROBO, see OKIEK

NDI ANIOMA, see **IGBO**

NDI AWKA, see **IGBO**

NDI IGBO, see **IGBO**

NDIBU, see also **KONGO**

The Ndibu are a Central and Southwest African Western Bantu-speaking people. They are concentrated in the Republic of Congo and the Democratic Republic of the Congo (Zaire). The Ndibu are a Kongo group.

NDIRMA, see **KILBA**

NDJEM

The Ndjem are one of Cameroon's more than 100 different ethnic groups. The Ndjem are Bantu-speaking people. They settled in the Cameroons from Equatorial Africa.

NDOMBE

The Ndombe are a Southwest Bantu-speaking African people. They live in the western coastal areas of Angola. Their neighbors include the Cisanji, Hanya, Kwisi, and Tyilenge-Muso peoples.

NDONGO

These are a Central African people and one of the ethnic minorities of Angola. Their modern history is traced back to the early part of the sixteenth century, at which time they had their own state, namely Ndongo.

Between the sixteenth and nineteenth centuries, the history of the Ndongo kingdom was characterized by a constant conflict with the Portuguese colonists in Angola who were trying to colonize its territory. In the 1590s, it aligned itself with the Ginga, Kongo and Jaga to battle against the Portuguese.

NDOP

The Ndop are a Central African people. They are concentrated in the western regions of the Cameroon. Their neighbors include the Bafia, Bali, Kom, Mum, Nso and Tikar peoples.

NDOROBO, see OKIEK

NDU LENDU

The Ndu Lendu are a Central and East African people. They live in the Sudan, Uganda and Democratic Republic of the Congo (Zaire). The Ndu Lendu's major concentration is on the northern shore of Lake Rudolf, neighboring the Kakwa, Kuku, and Nuer peoples.

NDUKA, see SARA

NDUNDULU

An East African people. The Ndundulu are concentrated in western Zambia. They are closely related to the Lozi people. They speak Kololo, the Lozi language, share many of Lozi customs, and are part of the Lozi-dominated Barotse Kingdom.[346]

NDZUNDZA, see NDEBELE

NEGROES

One of the four major racial/ethnic groups of which Africa is made. The other groups are the Hamites, Bantus and Bushmen. The term negro, however, is "an extremely imprecise and unsatisfactory term. There are hundreds of different types of Negro, Negroid, and Negrillo peoples. Speaking roughly, the Negroes are those who occupy parts of Central Africa and most of the West Coast."[347]

NEMADI

These people are a West Saharan North African group. The Nemadi, also known as Nemedai, speak a dialect of Arabic Hassania and are essentially inland hunters. They are concentrated in Senegal and its neighboring states, where they constitute very small ethnic groups.[348]

NEMEDAI, see NEMADI

NEMENCHA

The Nemencha are a North African people. They are concentrated in the west central mountainous regions of Tunisia. Their neighbors include the Chaamba and Marazig peoples.

NEMANGBETU, see MANGBETU

NGA

One of West Africa's peoples. The Nga are concentrated in the northwestern regions of Nigeria. Their neighbors include the Fyam, Kwanka, and Saya peoples.

NGABAKA

The Ngabaka, also known as Gbaya, Limba, Ma'ba and Minangende, are a Central African people. They are concentrated in the Central African Republic, the Democratic Republic of the Congo (Zaire) and the Republic of Congo.

NGADJI

The Ngadji are one of the main Kuri subgroups in Chad. They speak Yedina, a Buduma dialect. Like other Kuri groups, they live along the eastern shores of Lake Chad. The Ngadji people are divided into several subgroups the most important of which are the Batuma, Bellerama, Issia, Kongurama, and Tchukulia.

NGALA, see UBANGI

NGAMA, see SARA

NGAMBAY, see also **SARA**

The Ngambay are one of Chad's non-Muslim Sara groups. Like other Sara groups, they speak a Central Sudanic language that belongs to the Nilo-Saharan family of African languages. Like them also, they live primarily in the southern regions of the country, notably between Lake Iro in the east and the Logone River in the west.

NGAMBAYE, see **GUANG**

NGAMBWE

The Ngambwe are a Southwest African Bantu-speaking people. They are concentrated in the southwestern regions of Angola. Their neighbors include the Hakavona, Kuvale, Mwila, and Zimba peoples.

NGAMO

The Ngamo are a West African people and one of Nigeria's ethnic minorities. The Ngamo, also known as Gamawa, are concentrated in the Lake Chad region of northeastern Nigeria and eastern Niger. A large group of them are presently in the state of Borno (formerly Bornu). They are essentially an agriculturalist people.

NGANGELA

The Ngangela are a Southwest African ethnic group. They are concentrated in the south central regions of Angola. Their neighbors include the Nyemba and Ovimbundu peoples.

NGANGUELA

The Nganguela or Ganguela is a pejorative term used by the Ovimbundu to describe their neighbors residing east and southeast of their territory. The Nganguela are actually an independent conglomeration of peoples that include the Lwena, or Lavale, Mbunda and Luchazi. The combination of these peoples account for under 6% of the population of Angola. These groups are essentially pastoral. Some of them, however, engage in minimal cultivation and fishing. All Nganguela groups speak a language extremely similar to the Lunda-Chokwe.

During the slaving era, the Nganguela were raided mercilessly. As a result, they were marginalized and more importantly, lost the opportunity to develop centralized political and social organizations to oversee their affairs and/or protect their interests. During the Angolan civil war, for example, they were split among the fighting factions and moreover, many of them sought refuge in Zambia and Democratic Republic of the Congo (Zaire).

NGANYAGATAUK, see TURKANA

NGAPOU

A Central African people. The Ngapou are highly concentrated in the southeastern regions of Chad, as well as in the north central areas of the Central African Republic. Their neighbors include the Gabou, Laka, Mandja, and Ndere peoples.

NGATUNYO, see TURKANA

NGBAKA

The Ngbaka people are one of West Central African ethnic groups. They live in the Democratic Republic of the Congo (Zaire), Republic of Congo, and Central African Republic. They are highly concentrated in the north central areas of Zaire, neighboring the Baloulou (Mongo), Bangala, Binga, Kaka, Pomo, and Tswa peoples.

NGBANDI, see also MAND

The Ngbandi, also known as Gbande, Gbandi and Mogwandi, are a Mande people of southern parts of the Central African Republic, as well as northern Democratic Republic of the Congo (Zaire). A group of them, however, live in Liberia. Their language belongs to the Adamawa-Eastern subgroup of the Niger-Congo family of African languages.

Originally, the Ngbandi were inhabitants of the southern region of what is presently modern Chad and The Sudan. In the 18th century, one of their clans, Bandia, conquered the Azande regions, and subsequently, established several Ngbandi states.

Traditionally, the Ngbandi were renowned warriors and craftsmen. They lived in small villages, observed patrilineal lineages in matters relating to inheritance and succession, tolerated polygamy and gave their chiefs both political and religious functions. Their religious beliefs centered on the ancestral cult. Currently, the Ngandi are essentially agriculturalists.

NGBANYA, see **GUANG**

NGERE, see also **DAN**

A West African, Mande-speaking people. The Ngere are concentrated in the states of Liberia and the Ivory Coast. Their neighbors include the Bassa, Bete, Dan, Kpelle, Kran, Sapo and Wobe peoples.

NGINDO

The Ngindo are a Southeast African Bantu-cluster of peoples. They are concentrated in the south central regions of Tanzania, west of Lake Malawi. Their neighbors include the Mwera, Pogoro, and Yao peoples.

NGIBELAI, see **TURKANA**

NGIBOTOK, see **TURKANA**

NGIBOCHEROS, see **TURKANA**

NGICHORO, see **TURKANA**

NGIGAMATAK, see **TURKANA**

NGIJIE, see **TURKANA**

NGIKAJIK, see **TURKANA**

NGIKUNIYE, see TURKANA

NGIKWATELA, see TURKANA

NGILUKUMONG, see TURKANA

NGIMAMONG, see TURKANA

NGIMAZUK, see TURKANA

NGIMONIA, see TURKANA

NGISETO, see TURKANA

NGISIGER, see TURKANA

NGISONYOKA, see TURKANA

NGISSIR, see TURKANA

NGITURKAN, see TURKANA

NGIWOYAKWARA, see TURKANA

NGIYAPAKUNO, see TURKANA

NGIZIM

The Ngizim are a West African people and one of Nigeria's ethnic minorities. The Ngizim are concentrated in the Lake Chad region of northeastern Nigeria and eastern Niger. A large group of them live in the Bade emirate within the state of Borno (formerly Bornu) in Nigeria. In addition to Bade, their neighbors include the Auyokawa, Bolewa, Kanuri and Manga peoples. The Ngizim speak a language that belongs to the Afro-Asiatic family of African languages. They are essentially an agriculturalist people.

NGOIKA

The Ngoika are a southern African people. They are concentrated in the southeastern coastal areas of the Republic of South Africa. Their neighbors include the Bomvana, Mpondomise, and Xhosa peoples.

NGOK, see DINKA

A Dinka clan that is renowned for its acculturation under Arab, Ottoman-Egyptian and later British influences. As a result, the power structure within its society became more hierarchical, the legacy of 'living by the arm' was abandoned, and the authority of their chiefs was entrenched and recognized. Because of the same influences, the Ngok chieftainship "is losing its religious sanctity, and reverence for the Chief as a secular-spiritual leader is now being replaced by fear of secular punishment."[349]

NGOLOGA, see KGALAGADI

NGOMANE

The Ngomane are a Southeast and Southern African people. They are concentrated in the coastal areas near the border between the Republic of South Africa and Mozambique. Their neighbors include the Konde, Maputa, Nkosi, and Pai peoples.

NGONDE, see also NYAKYUSA

An Eastern Bantu-speaking people. The Ngonde are concentrated in Zambia and around Lake Nyasa (Malawi), Malawi. Groups of them, however, can also be found in Tanzania. Their neighbors include the Iwa, Kamanga, Lambya, Ndali, Nyakyusa, and Phoka peoples.

NGONGO, see KUBA

NGONI, see also JERE

The Ngoni, also Angoni and Nguni, are a Southern Bantu-speaking peoples. They live throughout the eastern African region and are scattered between Malawi, Zambia, Tanzania and South Africa. They constitute one of Malawi's nine major ethnic groups.

Originally, the Ngoni lived in what is presently called Zululand. Upon the rise of the Zulu Empire in the early 19th century, they were forced to retreat northwardly. Zwangendaba, their king, led his party to Lake Tanganyika. Upon Zwangendaba's death in 1845, the Ngoni kingdom split into five major groups, the most important of which was headed by Mpezeni (1830-1900), one his sons. Mpezeni led his group to what is now souther Zambia. The other four Ngoni groups were headed by Zwangendaba's other sons. They settled in adjacent regions.

The Ngoni people were militarily organized. This factor gave them an advantage over other peoples in East Africa which eventually placed them in a position of predominance. At the end of the 19th century, however, their new settlements were fancied by the Portuguese, the British and the Germans. "Mpezeni tried to play off the European powers against each other," but under pressure from his people, he reluctantly consented to an attack on British settlements in the Nyasaland Protectorate (now Malawi) in 1897. The British counterattacked in force, and in February 1898 Mpezeni was forced to surrender."[350] Between 1903 and 1905, the Ngoni staged a rebellion against German rule. This rebellion, known as the Maji Maji rebellion, however, was quelled by German forces. By 1910, all their new settlements fell to foreign European rule.

NGUERZE, see **KPELLE**

NGULU

The Ngulu – also known as Kingulu, Nguru, and Nguu – are an East and Southeast African people. They are concentrated in Malawi, Mozambique and Tanzania. Traditionally, they lived in village groups that were politically, economically, and religiously not subject to a central authority. In addition, they also supported a matrilineal society.

NGUMBO

The Ngumbo are a Southeast African people. They are concentrated in northeastern Zambia. The Ngumbo are part of the Aushi cluster of peoples. Their neighbors include the Bemba, Lungu, Mambwe, Mba, and Ushi peoples.

NGUNI, see NGONI

NGURU, see NGULU

NGUU, see NGULU

NGWAKETSE

The Ngwaketse are a Bantu-speaking Southwest and South Central African group. They are concentrated in Botswana and the Republic of South Africa. Their neighbors in both countries include the Kgatla, Kwena, Kwera, Rolong and Tswana peoples.

NGWATO

The Ngwato are a Southwest African people. They are a Southern Bantu-speaking group. They are concentrated in the south central regions of Africa and are related to the Tswana people.

NGWELA, see KULANGO

NHARO, see NARON and SAN

NHLANGWINI

The Nhlangwini are a southern African people. They are concentrated in the eastern areas of the Republic of South Africa, primarily between Lesotho and Swaziland. Their neighbors include the Kwena and Yesibe peoples.

NIAM-NIAM, see AZANDE

NIELLIM

A Central and East African people. The Niellim are a Sara group. They are concentrated in southern Chad. Groups of them, however, can also be found in neighboring countries, especially Cameroon and Central African Republic.

NIKA, see NYIKA and GIRIAMA

NILAMBA, see IRAMBA

NINZAM

The Ninzam are a Central African people. They are concentrated south of Lake Chad in east central Nigeria and across Nigeria's border with Cameroon. Their neighbors include the Awe, Bolewa, Fali, and Jukun peoples.

NJEMBE

A Central and Southwest African people. The Njembe are concentrated in the Democratic Republic of the Congo (Zaire).

NKANSI

The Nkansi are an East African people. Their main concentrations are in Tanzania, notably in the areas between Lake Tanganyika and Lake Rukwa. Their neighbors include the Bende, Fipa, Lyangalile, and Ukonongo peoples.

NKOLE

The Nkole, also known as Ankole, Ankore, Banyankole, Nkore, Nyankole and Nyankore, are one of Uganda's Bantu-speaking ethnic minorities. They are concentrated in the southwestern areas of the country between Lakes Edward and George and the Tanzania border. Their neighbors include the Ganda and the Toro peoples. The Nkole are agriculturalists, cattle growers and traders. Their territory is a trading route between the western hinterland and the East African highlands.

The Nkole people observe patrilineal relations and traditionally were divided into two groups: namely, the Hima, also Huma, and the Iru. The Hima were pastoral people, whereas the Iru were agricultural. The Nkole had a kingdom of their own, ruled by a despotic divine *mugabes* or kings, and governed through an elaborate hierarchy of court officials and provincial chiefs.[351] Their kingdom was located in what is presently the Mbarara administrative district of southwestern Uganda.

NKOMI

The Nkomi are a West Central African people. They are concentrated in the western coastal areas of Gabon. Groups of them, however, can be found in adjoining countries. Their neighbors include the Adyumba, Bakele, and Mapounou peoples.

NKONDE, see NYAKYUSA

NKORAMFO, see KULANGO

NKORE, see Nkole

NKOSI

The Nkosi are a southern African people. They are concentrated in the southeastern coastal areas in the Republic of South Africa as well as in the southwestern coastal areas in Mozambique. Their neighbors include the Maputa, Ngomane, and Pai peoples.

NKOYA

The Nkoya people are a Southwest African Lozi group. They are concentrated in the south central areas of Zambia. Their neighbors include the Lozi and Mwenyi peoples.

NKUMBI

The Nkumbi are a Southwest African people. They are concentrated in south central Angola. Their neighbors include the Kung (!Kung), Kede, Vale, Twa, and Zimba peoples.

NKUTU, see MONGO

NNGA, see ANGA

NOARMA, see also TOUBOU

The Noarma people are one of the Central and East African ethnic groups. They are concentrated in north central Chad and west central Sudan. Their neighbors include the Anakazza, Daza, Tama, Wadai, and Zaghawa peoples.

NOK

An ancient West African people who lived in the central regions of what is presently Nigeria between 500 B.C. and A.D. 200. Evidence suggests that the Nok were agriculturalists and that they supported a highly prosperous society. Recovered artifacts such as statues, iron, gold and tin jewelry, and murals painted on cave walls also suggest that they had a strong interest in art. According to Haskins and Biondi, "archaeologists have unearthed lifelike terra-cotta Nok statues that resemble the artwork of present-day Nigeria. These statues have elongated ears and heads that are three times larger than the bodies, a distortion which historians believe symbolized the Nok belief that the eyes and the ears were the most important parts of the human being."[352] In their view, around 100 B.C. the Nok region started to be infiltrated by hunting and herding societies that by A.D. 200, the Nok people were completely assimilated in the new societies and their respective cultures.[353]

NOLE

The Nole are an East African Afran Qalla people, one of the Oromo subgroups. They are concentrated in southern Ethiopia.

NONO

These are a West African people of Burkina Faso, Mali and Niger. Their neighbors include the Bambara, Bozo, Dogon, Dyula and Samo peoples. They speak a language that belongs to the Mande branch of the Niger-Congo family of African languages.

NOR TAGRBO, see MAMBILA

NORTHERN KININGO, see KAGURU

NORTHERN SOTHO, see also SOTHO

The Northern Sotho, also called Transvaal, represent one of the three Sotho major groups. The other two are Western (or Tswana), and Southern (or Basuto, Lesotho) Sotho. Like other Sotho people, they occupy the high grasslands of southern Africa and speak Sesotho, a Bantu language.

The great majority of Northern Sotho engage in agriculture, relying both on cultivation and animal husbandry. But males among them often seek work as laborers. Their settlements are characterized "by scattered hamlets of circular huts with mud and wattle or stone walls surmounted by a conical, thatched roof."[354] In their social patterns, most Sotho recognize patrilineal lineages and traditionally they allowed polygamy.

NORTHWESTERN BANTU

The Northwestern Bantu people are one of the ethnic minorities of the United Republic of Cameroon. They account for 8% of the country's total population.

NQUA

An extinct southern African people. The Nqua used to live in the southern regions of what is presently the Republic of South Africa.

NSANDI, see KONGO

NSENGA

The Nsenga, also Senga, are an Eastern Bantu-speaking people. They are concentrated in the Luangwa Valley region of eastern Zambia and are linguistically related to other Mozambican peoples.

The Nsenga's origins are traced back the Luba people of Democratic Republic of the Congo (Zaire). They migrated to their present dwellings in the early parts of the nineteenth century.

The Nsenga fell to the Ngoni towards the middle of the 19th century and hence their kingdom became a tributary of the Ngoni. Eventually, however, the Ngoni settled among the Nsenga, intermarried with them and acquired their language and culture. The Nsenga influence on the Ngoni was so effective that the Ngoni people are occasionally called Nsenga.

Traditionally, the Nsenga's chiefdoms lacked a centralized political hierarchy. This changed when Zambia fell to the British in the later part of the nineteenth century. Traditionally also, the Nsenga observed matrilineal lineages in matters relating to descent, inheritance and succession.

Currently, the main economic activities of the Nsenga people focus on agriculture, hunting and trading. Some Nsenga people, however, seek work in Zambia's copper mines or in adjacent countries, especially Malawi.

NSO

The Nso are a Central African Bantu-speaking people. They are concentrated in the northwestern areas of Cameroon. Their neighbors include the Bum, Kom, Tigar (Tikar), War, and Wiya peoples.

NSULA

The Nsula are a West Saharan North African people. They are concentrated in the mountainous regions of the Algerian-Moroccan borders.

NTOMBA, see **MONGO**

NTOMBA TWA, see **TWA**

NTWANE, see **PEDI**

NTUMU, see **FANG**

NUBA, see **NUBIANS**

NUBI, see also **NUBA**

These are one of the ethnic minorities of Uganda. The Nubis trace their ancestry back to Emin Pasha's troops of the old Equatoria Province. They were recruited by the British government and taken to Kampala to secure its control over Buganda following the religious wars of 1892-95 and thereupon settled in Uganda.

NUBIANS

These are an eastern non-Arab Muslim Sudanic people who are highly concentrated in the Nuba hills in the southern Kordofan province of modern Sudan. Their country is known as Nubia, a geographical region parts of which are in southern Egypt as well as in northern Sudan. In 1964, Nuba Egyptian groups were relocated to Komombo in the governorate (muhaafazat) of Aswan to allow for building the Aswan High Dam Lake. The Nubians are essentially settled agriculturalists.

The Nubians, also known as Nuba and Nubi, are composed of four major groups, namely, Kenuz, Arab, Fadija and Halfan. These groups are physically and culturally different. Of all of them, the Halfan, or southern Nubians, live in Sudan. Unlike the other groups, the Halfan are matrilineal. Additionally, those that live along the banks of the Nile River, mainly between the first and fourth cataracts, speak one of three Nile Nubian languages: Northern or Kenuzi, Central or Mahas, and Southern or Dongola. Those that live in areas within the Nuba Hills of Western Sudan speak one of two Hill Nubian languages: Midobi or Birked.

Clans constitute the basic units of the Nubian society, with each clan having its own chief. Economically, their activities center on agriculture, herding and livestock.

Historical evidence suggests that the Nubians had supported an advanced culture in the past. Also, it suggests that they were converted to Christianity in the sixth century and to Islam in the fourteenth century.[355] Presently, Islam is the religious belief of most Nubians. Despite this fact, however, the Nubian society continues to be tribe-centric. Also, some Nubians continue to adhere to their traditional beliefs that rest on the exaltation of ancestral spirits.

NUER

The Nuer, or Nath (Naath) as they call themselves, are a Nilotic eastern Sudanic pastoral people. They are concentrated in the regions between the Sudd (Sadd) and the White Nile in southern Sudan. More specifically, they "live in the swamps and open savannah that stretch on both sides of the Nile south of its junction with the Sobat and Bahr el Ghazal, and on both banks of these two tributaries."[356] Their language is an Eastern Sudanic language of the Chari-Nile branch of the Nilo-Saharan family of African languages, and is closely related to that of the Dinka. Culturally, they are similar to the Dinka, who are also a Nilotic group. The Nuer people are divided into many groups such as the Atwot (Atuot), the Bor, the Buldok, the Dwong, the Gaajok, the Gaaliek, the Gaawar, the Gun, the Jaajoah, the Jikany, the Jimac, the Kwith, the Lak, the Leek, the Leng, the Lou, the Mor, the Minyal, the Nuong, the Nyarkwac, the Nyathol, the Rengyan, the Rumjok, the Thiang, the Thiur, the Wang, the Wangkac, the Yol and the Zeraf.

The Nuer are preeminently pastoralists and only secondarily agriculturalists. Cattle were their dearest possession. They are not only their criterion of wealth, but also a main source of their diet. In fact, the

> care and use of cattle dominated their patterns of life. They loved their cattle, identified themselves with their cattle, sought to acquire cattle, and preserved them as their most highly prized possession. Cattle were the source of their bridewealth, the means for ritual sacrifice, and a source of food, though they were not kept to provide meat for regular food consumption.[357]

The patrilineal clan is the basic territorial, social, and political unit in the Nuer society. Their clans are autonomous and as such, they are not answerable to a centralized authority. Unlike other societies, they lack governmental organs and organized political life. Nevertheless, their society is highly egalitarian and democratic, marked by "recognition of the independence and dignity of the individual."[358]

As Evans-Pritchard observes, the prominent features of a Nuer tribe include: "(1) a common and distinct name; (2) a common sentiment; (3) a common and distinct territory; (4) a moral obligation to unite in war; and, (5) a moral obligation to settle feuds and other disputes by arbitration."[359]

The Nuer society observes age-groups which define an individual's status in relation to other Nuers in terms of seniority, equality, or juniority. Belonging to an age-group, however, does not entail any administrative, juridical, military or specific political functions. In addition, it provides for initiation ceremonies for boys to mark their passage from boyhood to manhood. These ceremonies are organized independently in each tribe, and moreover, they involve the cutting of a boy's brows to the bone in six long cuts from ear to ear, leaving a Nuer identification scar that remains for life.

Religiously, the Nuers believe in one god who is the creative spirit. Though God is located in the sky, he also makes his presence felt by humans on earth. In their religious beliefs, God is "the guardian of the established norms of behavior in relations with others in that their breach would bring misfortune."[360]

NUKULO

The Nukulo are a Southwest African Bantu-speaking people. They are concentrated in the north central areas of the country, as well as across the border in the Democratic Republic of the Congo (Zaire). Their neighbors include the Aushi, Chishinga, and Luapula peoples.

NUMIDIAN

These are semi-nomadic North African tribes from what is presently modern Tunisia. Their kingdom, known as the kingdom of Numidia, was an ally of Rome in the last years of the Second Punic War with Carthage (218-201). Masinissa, ruler of Massyli, a Numidian tribe, assisted Rome in its invasion of Carthage in 201. As a reward, Rome recognized his claim to the Numidian throne which was contested by Syphax, ruler of the Massaesyli, another Numidian tribe. Henceforth, Masinissa became king of both Massyli and Massaesyli.

NUNUMA

The Nunuma are a West African people. They are concentrated in Burkina Faso and adjoining countries. Their neighbors include the Dagari, Dyula, Grunshi, Lilse and Mossi peoples. The Nunuma speak a language that belongs to the Voltaic branch of the Niger-Congo family of African languages.

NUONG, see NUER

NUPE

The Nupe people are one of the ten largest ethnic minorities of Nigeria. They constitute the eighth largest group after the Hausa, the Fulani, the Yoruba, the Ibo, the Kanuri, the Tiv and the Edo, and are concentrated in the Niger River Valley in the west central areas of the country, particularly in the states of Niger and Kwara. Their neighbors include the Busa, Gbari, Igbira (Igbirra), Kamberi (Kambari), Kamuku and Yoruba peoples. The Nupe population is estimated at about 100,000. They are a Muslim people. They were converted to Islam by their Fulani neighbors in the 1800s.

The Nupe speak a language of the Kwa branch of the Niger-Congo family of African languages. Their society is hierarchical in nature and supports numerous groups, the most important of which are Batache (Bataci), Beni, Kede (Kyedye) and Zam.

The Nupe people have their own kingdom, headed by a king, within which the Beni and the Kede have their own kingdoms. Their kingdom is traced back to the 18th century. At its inception, it "resembled that of the Yoruba states," and occasionally, it fell to the influence of neighboring dynasties.[361]

In the last quarter of the 18th century, the Nupe kingdom asserted its independence from the Oyo empire. It fell to British colonial influence following Britain's intervention in Yorubaland in 1893.[362]

The old political structure of the Nupe kingdom remains relatively the same as in the past. Though now an integral part of Nigeria, the kingdom continues to have its own ruling class and a centralized political structure. Interactions with the Nigerian government are controlled by an *Imviate*.

The Nupe are an enterprising people and are primarily agricultural, relying on grain crops. Their traditional crafts (which are made up of mainly glass and brasswork), however, continue to be popular.

NYAG DII, see DOUROU

NYAKWAI

The Nyakwai, also known as Akwa and Jo Akwa, are a Central and East African pastoralist people. They are concentrated in the northeastern areas of Uganda.

NYAKYUSA

The Nyakyusa, also known as Ngonde, Nkonde or Sokile, are an East African Bantu-speaking people. They constitute one of Malawi's as well as Tanzania's and Zambia's ethnic minorities.

In Tanzania, the Nyakyusa are concentrated in the southwestern areas of the country, especially in the Mbeya administrative region. Their lands are bordered on the west by Lake Tanganyika and on the south by Lake Nyasa (Malawi), Malawi and the Republic of Zambia. Their economic activities focus on agriculture, fishing and animal husbandry. They are also engaged in salt, gold, coal and mica mining activities in their region.

The Nyakyusa are organized into age-villages which are formed when a group of young men of roughly the same age join together to develop their own settlement. "All villages thus formed [retain] the quality of contemporaneity of the male heads of the constituent households."[363]

NYALA, see LUHYA

NYAMB

The Nyamb are an East African Bantu-speaking people. They live in Burundi, Rwanda, Tanzania and Uganda. Their major concentrations, however, are in Tanzania and Uganda, primarily to the west of Lake Victoria. Their neighbors include the Haya, Kabula, Koki, and Rwanda peoples.

NYAMWEZI

The Nyamwezi people, also known as Banyamwesi(zi), are one of Tanzania's ethnic minorities. They are concentrated in the western areas of the country, notably south of Lake Victoria in what they call Bunyamwezi or Unyamwezi, their homeland. Their neighbors include the Sukuma people with whom they share many characteristics.

The Nyamwezi are a Bantu-speaking people. Their language, Nyamwezi, is akin to that of the Sukuma people.

Until the middle of the nineteenth century, the Nyamwezi people had highly organized chiefdoms, which were supported by a large aristocracy. Prior to European colonial rule, their capital Tabora, served as one of the most important trade links and centers between the harbors of the Southeast African coast and the Congo basin. Towards the middle of the nineteenth century, the Nyamwezi were conquered by the Tuta people, a subgroup of the Ngoni nation. The latter people established their own kingdom, which continued to exist until its fall to German rule in the later part of the nineteenth century. In 1890, they became part of the German colony of East Africa, and in 1919, they fell to British rule as part of World War I settlements. British rule continued until 1961, at which time the Nyamwezi became part of independent Tanzania.

The Nyamwezi people are essentially agriculturalists, traders and cattle-raisers. Their economic activities focus on miscellaneous agricultural and trading pursuits, as well as on cattle-keeping activities. They are famous for their traditional crafts which include ironwork, pottery and stool carving.

NYANEKA

Southwest and West Central African Bantu-speaking people. They are concentrated in the southwestern regions of Angola.

NYANGA, see also KIVU

The Nyanga are one of West Central African ethnic groups. The Nyanga are part of the Kivu cluster. They are concentrated in the Democratic Republic of the Congo (Zaire), notably in the vicinity of Lake Kivu. Their neighbors include the Lendu and Nande peoples.

NYANGATOM

The Nyangtom are an East African people. They speak a Nilotic language which is very close to Turkana, and are concentrated in Uganda, Ethiopia and Sudan, notably in the Omo Valley and Kefa regions of Ethiopia. Their neighbors are the Suri and Dizi peoples. The Nyangtom are an offshoot of the Karamojong cluster, and moreover, are related to the Iteso, Jie, Jiy, Topoza, Nyangatom proper and Turkana peoples. Historical evidence suggests that they have always been in conflict with their Suri neighbors.

NYANGBARA

These are one of Sudan's tribal people's who live in the southern region of the country. They speak an Eastern Sudanic language of the Chari-Nile branch of the Nilo-Saharan family of African languages.

The Nyangbara support a relatively sedentary type of society. They live in scattered villages and their main economic activities center on farming, cattle raising and hunting. Their social organization is essentially tribal and patrilineal in nature.

NYANG'ORI, see also TERIK and KALENJIN

An East African Terik people, a Kalenjin group. They are concentrated in western Kenya, and speak Kalenjin, a Southern Nilotic language that belongs to the Eastern Sudanic family of African languages. The Nyang'ori are a semipastoralist people.

NYANGURU

One of Southern Africa's peoples. The Nyanguru are a subgroup of the Abarue, a Shona people. They live in Zimbabwe and Mozambique.

NYANJA

The Nyanja are an Eastern Bantu-speaking people. They are one of Malawi's nine major ethnic minorities. They constitute the second largest group after the Chewa.

NYANKOLE, see NKOLE

NYANKORE, see NKOLE

NYARIBARI, see GUSII

NYARUANDA, see also BANYARWANDA

The Nyaruanda, also known as Banyaruanda and Banyarwanda, are a Central and East African people. They are concentrated in the Bifumbira County in Uganda. The Nyaruanda include many people who were originally Rwandans, notably Hutu and Tutsi groups.

NYARKWAC, see NUER

NYASA

The Nyasa are an East and Southeast African people. They are also known as Kimanda, Kinyasa and Manda. The Nyasa are concentrated in Malawi and Tanzania. Large groups of them live along the northeastern shore of Lake Malawi.

NYATHOL, see NUER

NYATSO, see KPAN

NYATURU

The Nyaturu are an East and Southwest African people. Their main concentrations are in north central regions of Tanzania, notably in the Singida District.

NYEMBA

The Nyemba are a Southwest African Bantu-speaking people. They are concentrated in Angola. Their neighbors include the Kafima, Kede, and Tyokwe peoples.

NYENGO

The Nyengo people are a Southwest and Central African ethnic group. They are a Lozi group. The Nyengo are found in eastern Angola and western Zambia. Their neighbors include the Makoma, Mbunda, Mwenyi, and Ndundulu peoples.

NYEPU

These are one of Sudan's tribal people who live in the southern region of the country. They speak an Eastern Sudanic language of the Chari-Nile branch from the Nilo-Saharan family of African languages.

The Nyepu support a relatively sedentary type of society. They live in scattered villages and their main economic activities center on farming, cattle raising and hunting. Their social organization is essentially tribal and patrilineal in nature.

NYERI

The Nyeri are an East African people. They are concentrated in central Kenya. Their neighbors include the Embu, Kamba, and Kikuyu peoples.

NYGENGO

An East African people. The Nygengo are concentrated in western Zambia. They are closely related to the Lozi people. They speak Kololo, the Lozi language, share many of Lozi customs, and are part of the Lozi-dominated Barotse Kingdom.[364]

NYIHA

The Nyiha, also known as Shinyiha and Nyixa, are an East and Southeast African people. They are concentrated in Tanzania and Zambia.

NYIKA

The Nyika people are an East African Mijikenda group. They are concentrated in Kenya, notably along its coast. Their economic activities focus on agriculture, fishing, and trading. The Nyika speak a dialect of Mijikenda, a language that belongs to the Northeast Coastal Bantu languages.

NYIKORÒMA, see SURI

NYIXA, see NYIHA

NYOLE, see NYULI and LUHYA

NYONYO, see KPAN

NYORO, see also NYULI

The Nyoro, known also as Banyoro, Bunyoro and Kitara, are an East Central African Bantu-speaking people. They call themselves Banyoro (singular Munyoro), and speak Lunyoro. The Nyoro are concentrated in Bunyoro country in the west central regions of Uganda between Lake Albert and Lake Kyoga, notably in the uplands of west central Uganda. Groups of them, however, are also located in the Congo. The Nyoro's neighbors include the Acholi, the Ganda, the Lango and the Toro peoples.

Prior to the colonial era, the Nyoro established one of the most powerful of a number of kingdoms in Bunyoro. Their kingdom, Bunyoro, was ruled by kings who were the direct male descendants of their ancient rulers. Until the 18th century it "dominated the surrounding peoples, holding an empire over much of what is now Uganda. In the 18th and 19th centuries, however, the kingdom declined owing to several wars of succession and other internal conflicts, and it surrendered its preeminence to the [neighboring] Ganda (Buganda) kingdom."[365] In the 1890s, however, the Bunyoro kingdom, fell to British forces, and eventually, was incorporated within the Uganda Protectorate.

The Nyoro's society is based on patrilineal kinship relations as well as on a highly hierarchical system of chiefs.

In precolonial times, the Nyoro developed iron smelting skills and currency exchange systems. Currently, however, it is primarily made up of small-scale rural farmers.

NYTUK, see SAMBURU

NYULI

An East African people. The Nyuli, also known as Lunyole, Nyole and Nyore, are highly concentrated in Kenya and Uganda, notably in the border areas that separate the two countries.

NZAKARA, see AZANDE

NZEBI

These are one of Gabon's largest ethnic groups. They are concentrated in areas south of the Ogooué River.

NZIMA, see AKAN

OATCHI, see EWE

OBANEN

An extinct Southwest African people. The Obanen used to live in the northwestern regions of what is presently the Republic of South Africa.

ODODOP, see also KOROP

These are a West African people. The Ododop are concentrated in Nigeria's southeastern coastal regions and speak a language that belongs to the Benue-Congo branch of the Niger-Congo family of African languages. The Ododop neighbors include the Ekoi (Ekoid), Igbo, Efic-Ibibio and Yako peoples.

OGAADEEN, see also SOMALI

An East African Somali group. The Ogaadeen are concentrated in the southeastern regions of Ethiopia, notably in the Province of Ogaden which was subject to a dispute between Ethiopia and Somalia.

OGADEIN, see also SOMALI

The Ogadein are an East African Somali people. They are concentrated in the northeastern areas of Kenya. Their territory was formerly claimed by Somalia.

OGIEK, see also OKIEK and KALENJIN

An East African Okiek people, a Kalenjin group. They are concentrated in Kenya, Tanzania and Uganda, and speak Kalenjin, a Southern Nilotic language that belongs to the Eastern Sudanic family of African languages. The Ogiek are a semipastoralist people.

OGONI, see also KANA

These are a West African people. The Ogoni are concentrated in Nigeria's southeastern coastal regions and speak a language that belongs to the Benue-Congo branch of the Niger-Congo family of African languages. Their neighbors include the Abua, Igbo, Ijaw and Efic-Ibibio peoples.

OGOWE, see also BANTU

The Ogowe are a Western Bantu-speaking people. They are concentrated in the southwestern regions of Africa.

OGU UKU, see IGBO

OHEKWE

The Ohekwe are a southern African people. They are concentrated in Botswana. Their neighbors include the Bamangwato, the Mahura, the Hiechware and the Tserekwe peoples.

OHINDO

The Ohindo are one of West Central African ethnic groups. They are concentrated in the Democratic Republic of the Congo (Zaire), primarily in its central eastern regions. Their neighbors include the Kuba, Lengola, Luba, and Ndenge peoples.

OHUHU-NGWA, see IGBO

OIMATSAHA

The Oimatsaha people are one of the five major ethnic groups of the Federal Islamic Republic of the Comoros.

OKAK, see FANG

OKAVANGO, see KAVANGO

OKEBO

The Okebo are an East African people. Their main concentration is in the northeastern regions of the Democratic Republic of the Congo (Zaire), primarily west of Lake Albert. The Okebo neighbors include the Alur, Bale, Dongo, Jongn, Lendu, Logo, and Lugbara peoples.

OKIEK, see also **KALENJIN**

The Okiek, also known as Athi, Athie, Dorobo, Il Torobbo, Ndorobo, Torobbo and Wandorobo, are a Nilotic-speaking, East African people. They speak Okiek, a language that belongs to the Kalenjin group of southern Nilotic languages. The Okiek comprise many groups, including the Akie (Akiy), Digiri, Dorobo, Kapchepkendi, Kaplelach, Kipchornwonek, Ogiek and the Omotik. Excepting the Akie of Tanzania, all other Okiek groups live within the Rift Valley Province in Kenya. Originally, the Okiek "lived by hunting game, making beehives, and gathering and trading honey."[366] Subsequently, they engaged in farming and herding. Currently, they "rely on maize and other crops, supplementing agriculture with trading, hunting, and honey gathering."[367]

The Okiek society recognizes patrilineal lineages. The units of their social organization comprise lineage as well as clans, local groups and age sets. Though Christianity has won some converts, the majority of Okiek people continue to adhere to their traditional religion which rests on the belief in one beneficent God called *Torooret* or *Aiista*.

OKONYONG, see **KIONG**

OKOYONG, see **KIONG**

O-KUNG

A Southwest African Khoisan people. The O-kung are concentrated in the southern regions of Angola. Their neighbors include the Ova Mbo and the Kung peoples.

OMETO, see **WOLAYTA**

OMO-MURLE, see **MURLE**

OMYÈNÈ

These are one of the small ethnic groups in Gabon. The Omyènè people speak Myènè, a Bantu language. They are located on the Atlantic coast of the country.

ONDO

The Ondo are a Yoruba subgroup and are concentrated in the Ondo State of what is presently southwestern Nigeria. They were Egba neighbors and had a state of their own, which played an important part in the Yoruba civil wars of the nineteenth century. Presently, the Ondo people are essentially agriculturalists and farmers. Their produce includes cocoa, palm oil and kernels, kola nuts, rice, pumpkins and miscellaneous fruits and vegetables.

ONGONA

The Ongona are a Southwest African people. They are concentrated in Angola and Namibia. Their neighbors in both countries include the Kade, Kwamatwi, Tyavikwa, and Vale peoples.

ONITSHA, see IGBO

ONO, see DOGON

OPOPO, see IBIBIO

ORA

These people are a West African group. They constitute one of Nigeria's ethnic minorities. The Ora are an Edo subgroup. They live in the southern areas of the country.

ORATTA-IKWERRI, see IGBO

ORLAMS, see also NAMA

A Southwest African people. The Orlams, also spelled Oorlams, are a Nama group. Originally, they lived in the Cape Colony in what is now the Republic of South Africa. Under pressure from white colonial expansion in the early 19th century they moved north and finally settled in Namibia.

ORO, see **ORON**

OROMO

The Oromo, also known as Galla, are the largest ethnic minority in Ethiopia. They call themselves Ilm Orma, account for about 40% of the total population and live essentially in most of the subtropical central and southern highlands of the country. Some of them, however, are also found in Kenya where they live along the Tana river basin, as well as in western areas of Eritrea. The Oromo speak Gallinya, a language of the Cushitic branch of the Hamito-Semitic family of African languages. There are several subgroups of the Oromo, the most important of which include the Arusi, the Boran (Borana), the Gudji, the Macha, the Tulama and the Wello (Welo).

The Oromo are descendants of Cushite peoples in southern Ethiopia. In the middle of the sixteenth century, they moved northward occupying the emirate, spreading in Shoa, and eventually penetrating Amhara and Lasta.[368] Unable to militarily stop them, the Amhara and Tigre were forced to move north and eventually had no choice but to share their country with the Oromo. Though greater in number, the Oromo were unable to unify the country under their own rule. They were too divided among themselves to achieve such a goal. In 1755, for example, a half-Galla king mounted the Ethiopian throne. This event led to the unification of the Oromo people around the new king and incited Oromo leaders to exercise a role apart from that of mercenaries that were occasionally invited to help weak Amhara monarchs. Until recently, their role in Ethiopia's politics remained relatively indirect, if not marginal. More importantly, the Amharan-Tigrayan leadership in Ethiopia made sure to limit any significant role for the Oromo in the Ethiopian society. They were aware of the Oromos' demographic advantage, and hence, made sure to limit the Oromos' political and social development.

The Ethiopian revolution of 1974, and subsequently, the Ethiopian civil war of 1991, have provided the Oromo with an opportunity to assert their political power and to secure an important role in the management of Ethiopia's domestic and international affairs.

Currently, the Oromo people are represented in the country's government, Federal Council and parliament. Moreover, they have their own political parties, the most important of which are the Oromo People's Democratic Union and the Oromo Liberation Front (OLF). The latter party was formed on January 12, 1995, upon the merger of the United Oromo People's Liberation Front and the Islamic Front for the Liberation of Oromia.[369]

The Oromo society is patrilineal and observes patrilineal lineages in matters relating to descent, succession and inheritance. Its traditional lifestyle is essentially pastoralist, but now a great number of Oromo have become metropolitan.

Unlike those of the northern and eastern provinces of Ethiopia who have converted to Coptic Christianity or to Islam, the Oromo people of the southern regions continue to adhere to their traditional religion, which is based on the belief in a sky god. Also, they continue to apply the *gada* system, which structures society on the basis of age groups.

ORON

A West African people. The Oron, known also as Oro or Oru, are concentrated in the southeastern regions of Nigeria, notably in the Cross River State.

OROPOI, see OROPOM

OROPOM

The Oropom, also known as Oropoi, are a Central and East African people. They are concentrated in Uganda.

ORRI

The Orri, also known as Koring and Orringorrin, are a West African people. They are concentrated in the southern regions of Nigeria and speak a language that belongs to the Benue-Congo branch of the Niger-Congo family of African languages. Their neighbors include the Boki, Igbo, Igedo, Iyala and Mbembe peoples.

ORRINGORRIN, see ORRI

ORU, see ORON

OTHAN, see UDUK

OUARSENIS

The Ouarsenis are a West Saharan North African people. They are concentrated in the mountainous regions overseeing Algeria's western Mediterranean coast.

OUASSOULOUNKE

A West African people. The Ouassoulounke, also known as Wasulunka, are a Malinke group. They are concentrated in Mali and Guinea.

OUATCHI

These are a West African people. They are concentrated in the southern Maritime region of the Republic of Togo.

OUBI

A West African Krou group. The Oubi, also known as Ouobe and Wobe, are concentrated in the Ivory Coast. Their neighbors include the Bete, Dan, Guro and Ngere peoples. The Oubi speak a language of the Mande branch of the Niger-Congo family of African languages.

OULAD BOU SBAA, see SAHRAWIS

OULAD DELIM, see SAHRAWIS

OULAD DJERIR

These are a West Saharan North African people. They are called after one of their founding ancestors, Djerir. The word *oulad* in Arabic means sons and daughters or offsprings of, pointing to Djerir. Oulad Djerir are concentrated in the mountainous regions along the Algerian-Moroccan borders.

OULAD HAMAYD, see BAGGARA

OULAD SLIMAN

These are an East Saharan Arab pastoralist people. They are called after one of their founding ancestors, Sliman. The word *oulad* in Arabic means sons and daughters of offsprings of, pointing to Sliman. Oulad Sliman are concentrated in Chad.

OULAD TIDRARIN, see SAHRAWIS

OULED ABD-EL-KADER, see CHAAMBA

OULED HANICH, see CHAAMBA

OULED AICHA, see CHAAMBA

OULED ALLOUCH, see CHAAMBA

OULED DELIM, see MOOR

OULED FREDJ, see CHAAMBA

OULED TIDRARIN, see MOOR

OULED TOUAMEUR, see CHAAMBA

OULOF, see WOLOF

OUNIA, see TOUBOU

OUNIE

The Ounie are a Central and East African pastoralist and semi-pastoralist people. They are concentrated in western Sudan. Groups of them, however, can also be found in Chad and Uganda.

OUOBE, see OUBI

OUOLOF, see WOLOF

OURIA

The Ouria people are a Central and East African ethnic group. They are concentrated in northern Chad, western Sudan, and southeastern regions of Libya.

OUROUBOUE

A West African Krou group. They are concentrated in the Ivory Coast.

OUTENIQUA

An extinct southern African people. The Outeniqua used to live in the southern regions of what is now the Republic of South Africa. Their neighbors include the Bergdama, the Kau-en and the Amraal Hottentot peoples.

OVAHERERO, see also HERERO

The Ovaherero, also known as Herero, are a Southwest African Bantu-speaking people. They are concentrated in Angola, Botswana, and the Republic of Namibia.

OVAMBO, see AMBO

OVIMBUNDU

The Ovimbundu people, also known as Umbundu, are the largest ethnic minority of the Republic of Angola, comprising about 37% of the country's total population. They speak Umbundu, a Bantu language. They are concentrated in the west central and southern areas of Angola, especially in the Benguela Highlands.

Before the Portuguese domination of the country in the 1500s, the Ovimbundu comprised over twenty-two kingdoms (chiefdoms), each of which was headed by a paramount chief and was supported by a council and subchiefs. The chiefdoms flourished as a result of their engagement in trade with other African peoples and subsequently, with the Portuguese. They raised cattle, relied on small-scale cultivation and collected and marketed ivory.

During Portuguese rule, the Ovimbundu served as intermediaries in the slave trade. When slave trade was abolished in the late nineteenth century, the Ovimbundu shifted their economic activity to the production of rubber and continued this profitable activity until it was completely taken over by the Portuguese in the early twentieth century. Their economy in general, and trading activities (which were based on caravans) in particular, suffered another major blow upon the construction of the Benguela railway in 1904. Right before Angola's independence in 1975, the Ovimbundu were heavily involved in the development and cultivation of cash crops, especially coffee. Because of the pastoral nature of the Ovimbundu society, the competition of Portuguese plantation owners, as well as the Portuguese confiscation of valuable lands and the precarious economic nature of cash-crops resulted in the failure of their cash crop experiments.

The Ovimbundu are predominantly a Christian nation. The Portuguese exposed them to Catholicism beginning in the 16th century. In the late 1940s, North American missionaries exposed them to other Christian faiths, including Protestantism. The latter group succeeded in setting up a network of schools, churches, and hospitals in the country, the impact of which is being felt to this day.

During the Angolan civil war (1975-1994), many Ovimbundu supported the National Union for the Independence of Angola (UNITA) effort to overthrow the socialist regime of the Popular Movement for the Liberation of Angola (MPLA).

OWERRI, see IGBO and ITSEKIRI

OYOKO, see also **AKAN**

An Akan royal clan, under the leadership of the Ashanti kingdom, was founded and led to an imperial status in the later part of the seventeenth century. Under the leadership of its first three kings, Obiri Yeboe, Osei Tutu and Opoku Ware, the Ashanti kingdom rose against the Denkeyera state. In a series of campaigns against the Denkeyera state in the 1670s, they succeeded in not only crushing the Denkeyera state, but also in establishing their control over the area between the Komoé River in the west to the Togo mountains in the east. As a result, the Ashanti kingdom became the paramount military and commercial power in the whole Gold Coast region, in what is presently modern Ghana. Moreover, the supremacy of the Oyoko clan was recognized by Akan and non-Akan peoples in the Kumasi region, as well as by other Akan ruling lineages.

Under Obiri Yeboe, the first of the Oyoko kings who was killed in battle during the campaigns of the 1670's, the foundation of the Amanto states of Ashanti-Kumasi, Bekwai, Juaben, Kokofu and Nsuta was placed. This foundation was consolidated under Osei Tutu, the second Oyoko king, who established Kumasi as his capital, instituted the golden stool as the Achantis' sacred symbol, and adopted a constitution that highlighted his supremacy as head of the kingdom.[370]

In further consolidation measures, member kingdoms were integrated into the new union by having their respective kings serve as commanders of the army of the Ashanti state, as well as members in a council of advisers to the *asantehene*. Also, member kingdoms were required to supply the Ashanti army with troops as needed and to participate in Ashanti state celebrations. Responsibility for kingdoms' domestic affairs was retained by their respective kings.

Upon these achievements, the newly structured state embarked on expanding its territory and incorporating defeated kingdoms (such as Denkyira, Akyem, Akwapim, and Akwamu) within the Ashanti union. By 1750, Opoku Ware, the third Oyoko king, died. The Ashanti empire became virtually an unchallenged power in the whole Gold Coast region. It maintained its supremacy until the middle of the nineteenth century, at which time it started to decline. Several factors contributed to the decline, including internal divisions and revolts and failures to thwart repeated British campaigns against its territory.

On January 1, 1902, the British government formally declared Ashanti a crown colony and in a separate declaration, established the Northern Territories of the Gold Coast a British Protectorate. Ashanti King Prempeh I, had no choice but to accept the partition of his country and direct British rule. In the 1930's, however, the British government established an Ashanti Confederacy Council and more importantly, restored the position of *asantehene*, but only as a symbolic figurehead.

PABIR, see **BURA**

PADEBU, see also **KRU**

A West African people. The Padebu are a Kru group. They constitute one of Liberia's many ethnic minorities.

PAI, see also **PEDI**

The Pai are a southern African Bantu-speaking people. They speak a Sotho dialect and are concentrated in northern Transvaal of the Republic of South Africa.

PADHOLA

An East Saharan Central and East African cattle-raising people. The Padhola, also known as Adhola and Dhopadhola, are concentrated in Uganda.

PADORO, see **LOBI DAGARTI**

PADUKO

The Paduko are a West African people. They are concentrated in the northern regions of Cameroon and speak a language that belongs to the Afro-Asiatic family of African languages. The Paduko neighbors include the Gisiga, Mandara, Matakam and Wakura peoples.

PAHOUIN, see also **FANG**

West and West Central African Bantu-speaking people. The Pahouin are concentrated in the southern regions of the Cameroon and neighboring Equatorial Guinea and Gabon. They support many subgroups, including Beti, Beti-Pahouin, Boulous, Fang, Pamue and Pangwe.

PAJADE, see **BADYARANKE**

PAKOT, see also **POKOT** and **KALENJIN**

An East African Pokot people, a Kalenjin group. They are concentrated in Kenya, Tanzania and Uganda, and speak Kalenjin, a Southern Nilotic language that belongs to the Eastern Sudanic family of African languages. The Pakot are a semipastoralist people.

PALAKA, see also **SENUFO**

These are a West African Voltaic (Gur)-speaking people. They speak Palaka, a language belonging to the Gur branch of the Niger-Congo family of African languages.

The Palaka are a subgroup of the Senufo people who are highly concentrated in the northern parts of the Ivory Coast, the eastern and southeastern regions of the Republic of Mali, and the northwestern regions of Burkina Faso. They "separated from the main Senufo stock well before the 14th century AD."[371]

PALUO

East Saharan, Central and East African cattle-raising people. The Paluo are concentrated in Uganda and its neighboring countries. They are a Luo-speaking people. Their neighbors include the Acholi, the Alur, the Jie, the Karamojong, the Lango and the Madi peoples.

PAMBILA

The Pambila are a Central and East African people. Their main concentrations are in southern Sudan, primarily in the areas between Bahr al-Ghazal and Jur rivers. Their neighbors include the Azande and Kreish peoples.

PAMUE, see PAHOUIN

PANDE

The Pande are a Central and West Central African people. They live in Cameroon, Central African Republic, Chad, Gabon, and the Republic of Congo. Their neighbors in these countries include the Bandza, Binga, and Kaka peoples.

PANGWE, see also FANG and PAHOUIN

A western Bantu-speaking people. The Pangwe are a Pahouin subgroup. They live in Cameroon, Equatorial Guinea, and Gabon.

PAPEDU, see PADEBU

PAPEL

A West African people and one of the major ethnic groups of the Republic of Guinea-Bissau. The Papel, also spelled Pepel, account for 7% of the country's total population and speak a language that belongs to the West Atlantic branch of the Niger-Congo family of African languages. Their neighbors include the Balante, Banyun, Biafada and Dyola peoples.

PARAKUYU, see MASAI

PARE

The Pare are an East African people. They are concentrated in the vicinity of Mt. Kilimanjaro in southern Kenya and northern Tanzania. Their neighbors include the Chagga, the Kamba and the Maasai peoples.

PATAPORI, see KOTOPO

PEDA, see also EWE

The Peda, also known as "Popo" and Xwla, are a West African people. They speak a language which is closely related to that of the Ewe people. They are concentrated in Togo, notably in the area between Lake Gbaga and the Mono River. Their neighbors include the Ewe, Fon and Guin people. The Peda were named "Popo" by the Portuguese of the fifteenth century.

PEDI, see also BAPEDI and SOTHO

Traditionally, the term Pedi referred to all Sotho-speaking people who lived in the northern Transvaal of South Africa. More recently, however, "the term 'Northern Sotho' has replaced 'Pedi' to characterize this loose collectivity of groups."[372] Currently, the term is used in a narrower sense to refer to only one group of the Northern Sotho-speaking people, and more specifically, to one group of the high-veld Sotho, one of the two subdivisions of Northern Sotho-speaking peoples. In contrast to the low-veld Sotho "who combine immigrants from the north with inhabitants of longer standing", the high-veld "are comparatively recent immigrants mostly from the west and southwest."[373] On the one hand and aside from the Pedi, the high-veld Sotho include such groups as the Batlokwa, Dikgale, Gananwa (Mmalebogo), Kone, Mathabathe, Matlala, Mmamabolo, Molete, Mphahlele, Ntwane, Roka, Tau and Thwene. On the other hand, the low-veld Sotho include such groups as the Kgakga, Kone, Kutswe, Lobedu, Mogoboya, Narene, Pai, Phalaborwa and Pulana. As it is presently used, the term Pedi "refers more to a political unit than to a cultural or linguistic one: the Pedi polity included the people living within the area over which the Maroteng dynasty established dominance during the eighteenth and nineteenth centuries."[374]

The Pedi people speak Sepedi, also known as "Sesotho sa Leboa" or Northern Sotho. Sepedi is a southern Bantu language. Traditionally, they engaged in miscellaneous agricultural pursuits, as well as cattle keeping. Because of colonial and white rule, however, many Pedi were forced to work as laborers in white-owned farms, mines and industrial plants.

PEKI, see **KREPE**

PELE, see **KPELLE**

PEMBA, see also **SHIRAZI**

The Pemba are one of Tanzania's ethnic groups. The Pemba are a Bantu-speaking people and one of the Shirazi main subgroups. They are concentrated in the islands of Pemba and Zanzibar. The Pemba are a Shirazi subgroup and hence of Persian background.

PENDE

A Central African Bantu-speaking people. The Pende are one of Democratic Republic of the Congo's (Zaire's) ethnic groups. Groups of them, however, are also located in neighboring countries, notably Angola. They are concentrated in the Bandundu and Kasai administrative provinces. Their homeland stretches from the banks of the Lutshima river, a tributary of the Kwilu, to those of the Kasai river. Their neighbors include the Cokwe, Kwese, Lele, Luba-Kasai, Luluwa, Lunda, Mbala, Mbun (Mbunda), Sonde and Wongo peoples.

The Pende engage in miscellaneous farming and animal husbandry pursuits. Their society is organized around matrilineal clans and lineages. Though Christianity has won converts, many Pende continue to cherish their traditional religion which rests on the belief in one God known as Nzambi, Kalunga and Mawese, as well as on the exaltation of ancestral spirits.

PEPEL, see **PAPEL**

PEPPLE

These are a West African people of what is presently Nigeria. They supported a kingdom of their own, which flourished during the reign of Opubu the Great between 1792 and 1830. In recognition of Opubu's achievements in 1870, Jubo Jubogha (called Chief Jaja by Europeans), a former Ibo slave and ruler of the Anna Pepple House of Bonny, founded the Kingdom of Opobo at Ikot Abasi (also called Opobo, and formerly called Egwanga), a port in southern Nigeria. The new kingdom continued to prosper as a prominent center for oil-palm trade until 1887, at which time the British founded their own center at Opobo town and deported Jubo.

PEUL, see also **FULANI**

The Peul are a Fulani people. They constitute one of the major ethnic groups of the Republic of Mali. They account for 17% of the country's total population.

PHALABORWA, see **PEDI**

PHALENG, see **KGALAGADI**

PHOKA

The Phoka are a Southeast African people. They are concentrated in northern Malawi. Groups of them, however, also live in Tanzania and Zambia. The Phoka are part of the Tumbuka cluster of peoples.

PIIKAAP OOM, see **OKIEK**

PILA, see **PILA-PILA**

The Pila people are one of Benin's Pila-Pila groups. They are concentrated in the northern regions of the country. The Pila are a Voltaic-speaking people.

PILA-PILA

The Pila-Pila, also known as Kpilakpila and Yom, are a West African Voltaic-speaking people. They are concentrated in the northern areas of Benin. Groups of them, however, can also be found in Ghana.

PINDE

The Pinde people are a West Central African ethnic group. They are concentrated in the Democratic Republic of the Congo (Zaire).

PIYA, see WURKUM

PLATEAU TONGA, see TONGA

PLAWI

The Plawi people are a West African ethnic group.

PODZO

The Podzo are a Southeast African ethnic group. They are concentrated in Mozambique.

POGOLO, see POGORO

POGORO

The Pogoro, also known as Chipolgolo and Pogolo, are a Southeast African people. They are concentrated in Tanzania.

POJULU

A Central and East African people. Their main concentrations are in the Sudan, Uganda and the Democratic Republic of the Congo (Zaire). The Pojulu live close to the northern shores of Lake Rudolf.

POKO

The Poko are a South African people who were conquered in 1864 by the Boer settlers in Transvaal with the help of Mswati, king of the Swazi people. As a result, the Poko were uprooted from their lands.

POKOMO

The Pokomo are an East African Bantu-speaking people. They are concentrated in the eastern regions of Kenya, notably along the banks of the Tama River. Their neighbors include the Agiryama, Embu, and Kamba peoples.

POKOT, see also KALENJIN

An East African Kalenjin group. They are concentrated in Kenya, Tanzania and Uganda, and speak Kalenjin, a Southern Nilotic language that belongs to the Eastern Sudanic family of African languages. The Pokot comprise several groups, including the Pakot and Suk. They are a semipastoralist people.

POMBO, see KONGO

POMO

The Pomo people are one of West Central African ethnic groups. They are concentrated in the Republic of Congo. Their neighbors include the Kaka and Ngbaka peoples.

PONDO, see MPONDO

PONGO

The Pongo are a Central African ethnic group. They live in the coastal areas of Cameroon. Their neighbors include the Bali, Duala, Ibibio, Mungo and Kpe peoples.

POPO, see PEDA

PORTUGUESE

People of Portuguese background and/or Portuguese expatriates or settlers who live in African countries that formerly fell to Portugal's rule and/or influence. These people and/or their descendants are unevenly distributed in following countries: Angola, Cape Verde, Guinea-Bissau, Mozambique, and Sâo Tomé and Principé.

POTOPO, see **KOTOPO**

POTOPORI, see **KOTOPO**

POUGOULI, see **LOBI-DAGARTI**

PUGULA, see **LOBI-DAGARTI**

PULANA, see **PEDI**

PUNU

The Punu people are one of the largest ethnic groups of the Gabonese Republic. They are concentrated in areas south of the Ogooué River. Their neighbors include the Bayaka, Mberenzabi, and Mapounou peoples.

PURKO, see **MASAI**

PWA, see **LOBI-DAGARTI**

PYGMY

The Pygmy are a West Central African people. They are concentrated in the Cameroon, Central African Republic, Republic of Congo, the Democratic Republic of Congo (Zaire), and Gabon. Smaller groups of them are located in Rwanda and Burundi. They support many groups, including the Aka, Binga, and Twa (Gwa).

QUAHOE, see **KWAHU**

RABAI

The Rabai people are an East African Mijikenda group. They are concentrated in Kenya, notably along its coast. Their economic activities focus on agriculture, fishing, and trading. The Rabai speak a dialect of Mijikenda, a language that belongs to the Northeast Coastal Bantu languages.

RAHANWAYN, see **RAHANWIN**

RAHANWIN, see also **SOMALI**

One of the main Somali clans. The Rahanwin, also Rahanwayn, are based in the southern regions of Somalia, notably between Shibel (Shabeelle) and Juba rivers.

RANGI

The Rangi, also known as Irangi, Kelangi and Langi, are a Southeast and East African Nilotic-speaking people. They are closely related to the Luo people. The Rangi are concentrated in Kenya, Uganda, Tanzania and neighboring countries. They are mixed agriculturalists and support their own chiefdom.

RAYA, see **GALLA**

REENDIILE

A Cushitic-speaking East African people. The Reendiile, also called Rendille, are concentrated in Kenya, primarily on the southeastern shore of Lake Rudolf. Their neighbors included the Elmolo, Samburu and Suk peoples.

REGA, see also **LEGA**

Central African Bantu-speaking people. The Rega, also known as Lega, are one of Zaire's ethnic groups.

REGEIBAT, see also **MOOR** and **SAHRAWIS**

The Regeibat, also spelled Reguibat, are a Sahrawi Moorish people. This group is concentrated in Algeria, Mali, Mauritania and Western Sahara.

Currently, they constitute a numerical majority of the Sahrawi population. The Regeibat are *Shorfa (Shurafa')*, a noble title for Muslims who claim descent from Prophet Muhammad.

REGUIBAT, see **REGEIBAT**

REHOBOTH BASTER, see **BASTER**

REHOBOTH GEBIET, see **GEBIET**

REIZEGAT, see **BAGGARA**

REK, see **DINKA**

RELA

These are a West Saharan people. Their concentrations are located in Niger and neighboring countries.

RENDILLE, see also **REENDIILE**

An East African cattle-raising people. The Rendille, also called Reendiile, are concentrated in Kenya, notably in the Marsabit District. Their neighbors include the Elmolo, Samburu, and Suk peoples.

RENGAYAN, see **NUER**

RER HAMAR

An East African people of the Horn of Africa. The Rer Hamar are a small ethnic minority in Somalia. They are either of Arab or Persian descent.

RESHE

The Reshe, also called Gungawa or Gungunci, are one of West Africa's ethnic groups. Their main concentration is in the west central areas of Nigeria, particularly in the state of Kwara. Their major neighbors include the Bargu, Boko, Busa, Dakarkari, Fula (Fulani), Hausa, Kamberi, Tienga and Yoruba peoples. The Reshe language belongs to the Benue-Congo branch of the Niger-Congo family of African languages.

RIBE

The Ribe people are an East African Mijikenda group. They are concentrated in Kenya, notably along its coast. Their economic activities focus on agriculture, fishing, and trading. The Ribe speak a dialect of Mijikenda, a language that belongs to the Northeast Coastal Bantu languages.

RIF, see also BERBER

The Rif, also Rifian, are a West Saharan North African Berber group. They are concentrated in the Rif Atlas regions of Morocco. Their neighbors include the Ben Guil and Zemmur peoples.

RIFIAN, see RIF and BERBER

RIMAIBE, see FULBE

RISHUWA, see KUZAMANI

RIZEGAT

The Rizegat are a Central African people. Their main concentrations are in the west central regions of Sudan. However, groups of them live in Chad. Their neighbors in Sudan include the Bederiat, Hamar, Humr, Kreish, and Shilluk peoples.

ROKA, see PEDI

ROLONG

The Rolong are a Southern Central Bantu-speaking people. They are concentrated in Botswana and South Africa. Their neighbors include the Kgatta, Kwena, and Mekwa peoples.

RONGA, see BANTU

A Southeastern Bantu-Speaking people. The Ronga are related to the Tsonga people who live in the southern coastal areas of Mozambique.

ROTSE, see LOZI

ROZI, see LOZI

ROZWI, see also SHONA

A Southeast African Bantu-speaking people. They speak Shona and are concentrated in the central regions of Zimbabwe where they account for about 9% of the country's total population. Their neighbors include the Karanga, the Korekore, the Ndau, the Ndebele, the Tonga and the Zezuru peoples.

RUFIJI

The Rufiji are a Southeast African people. They are concentrated in the northeastern coastal regions of Tanzania. Their neighbors include the Wazaramo, the Doe, the Kami, the Kutu, the Kwere and the Ndengereko peoples.

RUKIYA, see CHIGA

RUKUBA

A West African farming people. The Rukuba, or Bache as they call themselves, speak Rukuba, a language that belongs to the Niger-Congo family of African languages. Their main concentration is in central Nigeria, notably on the High Plateau west of Jos, the capital of Plateau State.

Originally, the Rukuba lived in Ugba, an area about 50 miles north of their present location. They migrated to their present territory sometime during the eighteenth century. Traditionally, they engaged in iron smelting. This activity, however, disappeared after the British conquest of their territory in 1905. Currently, they are essentially a farming people.

The Rukuba society is patrilineal. Their villages are divided into patrilineal clans. Under this system of social and political organization each village has a chiefdom of its own. In their turn, chiefdoms are linked together by a loose federation.

RUMJOK, see **NUER**

RUNDI

The Rundi are the people of the Republic of Burundi, who speak Rundi. They are divided into three ethnic groups: namely, the Hutu, the Tutsi and the Twa.

RUNGA, see **BANDA**

RUNGU, see **TABWA**

RURAMA, see **KURAMA**

RUTSE, see **LOZI**

RUUND, see **LUNDA**

SAB, see **SOMALI**

SABAOT, see also **SEBEI** and **KALENJIN**

The Sabaot are an East African Kalenjin people. They are concentrated in Kenya and Uganda, notably in the Mount Elgon region, and speak a dialect of Kalenjin, a Southern Nilotic language that belongs to the Eastern Sudanic family of African languages. The Sabaot are a semipastoralist people.

SACLAVE, see **SAKALAVA**

SADAMA, see also **SIDAMO**

An East African people. The Sadama are a Sidamo group. They are concentrated in Ethiopia. Groups of the Sadama, however, can also be found in neighboring countries.

SAFWA

The Safwa are an East African people and one of Tanzania's ethnic minorities. They are concentrated in the southwestern areas of the country, especially in the Mbeya administrative region. Their lands are bordered on the west by Lake Tanganyika and on the south by Lake Nyasa, Malawi, and the Republic of Zambia. Their economic activities focus on agriculture, fishing and animal husbandry. They are also engaged in salt, gold, coal and mica mining activities in their region.

SAGALA, see KAGURU

SAGARA

The Sagara are a Southeast African Bantu-speaking people. They are concentrated on the east coasts of Tanzania and Mozambique. Traditionally, they lived as village groups that were politically, economically, and religiously not subject to a central authority. In addition, they also supported a matrilineal society.

SAGHALA, see SAGARA

SAHO

Saho, also Afar-Saho, Sao, Shaho, Shiho and Shoho, are peoples of the coastal plains of southern Eritrea. They speak Saho, an Eastern Cushitic branch of the Hamito-Semitic (or Afro-Asian) language family of African languages. They are nomadic shepherds and are mostly Muslim. The Saho comprise several groups, the most important of which are the Asaorta, the Debri-Mela, the Hazu, the Irob, the Minifere and the Teroa. Their neighbors include the Afar, the Galla, the Ittu, the Somali, the Wallo and the Yaju peoples.

SAHRAWIS

A West African subgroup of the Moors, or *Beidan*, nomads. The Sahrawis are a people of mixed Berber, Arab and black African descent who speak a dialect of the Arabic language known as Hassaniya Arabic. They are concentrated "in a swathe of desert from the Oued Draa in southern Morocco to the valleys of the Niger and the Senegal."[375] Historically, these people "are the result of the fusion, through [trade], wars, subjucation, alliances and inter-marriage, of Sanhaja Berbers (who first migrated into this region in the first millennium BC and acquired the camel in about the first century AD), Bedouin Arabs known as Beni Hassan (who began arriving at the end of the thirteenth century), and black African [peoples]."[376] Because they lived close to the Atlantic Ocean, they were called *ahl al-Sahel*, which means (in Arabic) the people of the littoral or the coast.

Traditionally, the Sahrawis supported a highly stratified society. At the apex were *ahel mddafa (ahl al-Mad-fa')*, people of the canon and the gun, and the *Shorfa (Shurafa')*, descendants of Prophet Muhammad. Next in line, were the *znaga*, vassal people and tribes. The third group in the social structure of the Sahrawi society were the *maalemin (mu'alemin)*, that is craftsmen, and *iggawen*, bards. These were followed by the *haratin*, freed-slaves, and the *abid ('abid)*, servants and non-freed slaves.

The *ahel mdafa* included such groups as Oulad Delim, the Izarguien and the Ait Lahsen, whereas the *Shorfa* included "the Reguibat (who today constitute a numerical majority of the Sahrawi population), the Arosien and the Oulad Bou Sbaa."[377] The main Znaga tribe is that of Oulad Tidrarin. According to Hodges, there "were very few *maalemin, iggawen, haratin* and *abid.*"[378]

SAID ATBA

The Said Atba are a North African people. They are concentrated in the central eastern regions of Algeria along the Algerian-Tunisian borders.

SAKAKUYE, see also **SAKUYE**

SAKALAVA, see also **MALAGASY**

The Sakalava, also spelled Saclave, Sakalave and Séclave, are one of the five major ethnic groups of the Federal Islamic Republic of the Comoros and also one of Madagascar's principal ones.

The Sakalava are a Malagasy people of mixed African, Malayo-Indonesian and Arab ancestry. They speak a dialect of Malagasy.

In Madagascar, the Sakalava developed a kingdom of their own in the late 16th century, which split into two allied kingdoms towards the middle of the seventeenth century. Their kingdoms reached their zenith during the eighteenth century due to trading with the Europeans. Towards the end of the 18th century, however, they fell to the Merina Kingdom. In the 1890s, both the Sakalava and the Merina were conquered by the French, and thereupon, became part of a French colony.

In Comoro Islands where they are called Kibushy, they are the descendants of Sakalava who fled from western Madagascar following the fall of their kingdom to the Merina towards the end of the eighteenth century. They are concentrated in Mayotte.

Traditionally, the Sakalava society was organized into clans, each of which had separate responsibilities towards the royalty. Traditionally also, it was hierarchical in nature. It consisted "of royalty *(ampanjaka)*, the "people" *(vahoaka)* or "commoners" *(vohitry)*...; those who [served] royalty at ceremonial occasions (most notably the *Sambarivo*); and slaves *(andevo)*..."[379]

Currently, the Sakalava account for nearly 6 percent of Madagascar's population and moreover, engage in miscellaneous economic activities such as farming, fishing, animal husbandry, and trading.

SAKALAVE, see **SAKALAVA**

SAKUYE

The Sakuye, also known as Sakakuye, are an East African people. They are concentrated in the northeastern areas of Kenya, neighboring the Somali people. The Sakuye speak an Oromo language.

SALA

The Sala are one of Zambia's many ethnic minorities. The Sala are a Bantu-speaking people who are related to the Ila people. They speak Tonga. The Sala live to the north of Lake Kariba, and are highly concentrated near Lusaka, the capital of Zambia.

SALAMAT, see BAGGARA

SALEI, see MASAI

SAMAROAN, see also SOMALI

A Somali people. The Samaroan, also known as Godabiirsay, are a subgroup of the Somali Dir clan. Like other Somalis, they speak Somali.

SAMBAA, see also SHAMBAA

The Sambaa are an East African people. They are concentrated in the southeastern areas of Kenya. Their neighbors include the Bondei, Digo, Pare, and Swahili peoples.

SAMBARA, see BANTU

The Sambara are an Eastern Bantu-speaking people. They are concentrated on the east coasts of Tanzania and Mozambique.

SAMBURU, see also MASAI

The Samburu, also known as Burkeneji, Lokop, Nytuk and Sampur, are an East African Masai pastoralist people. Like other Masai people, they speak Maa (Maasai), a Paranolotic language. The Samburu are concentrated in Kenya.

SAMIA, see **LUHYA**

SAMO, see also **MANDE**

The Samo are a West African Voltaic people. They are a group of the Mande peoples and speak a language that belongs to the Mande branch of the Niger-Congo family of African languages. The Samo are concentrated in Burkina Faso. Their neighbors include the Bobo, Dogon, Dyula, Lilse and Mossi peoples.

SAMPUR, see **SAMBURU**

SAN

The San, also known as Bushmen and Sarwa, are the original inhabitants of many parts of Central and Southern Africa. They are nomadic people, related to the Khoikhoin, or Hottentots. Historical evidence suggests that they were pushed by other tribes, especially the Bantu-speaking ones, as well as European settlers to the areas in which they are presently located.

The San are considered the least mixed of African peoples, and moreover, presumed to be the "most direct descendants of the late Stone Age population of southern Africa."[380] They speak San, or Khoi, languages that make use of "click" consonants, and are difficult for outsiders to learn. The San languages are regarded as part of the Khoisan family of African languages.

Originally, the San people were foragers, hunters and gatherers, and eventually, they also became herders. As in the past, they continue to live in rock shelters, as well as "in small bands under the leadership of the most skillful hunter, and move from place to place in search of antelope, giraffe, ostrich, and other game that they hunt with spears, bows, and arrows."[381]

The band constitutes the San's basic social and political unit. It consists of a number of families and moreover, it is led by a band leader according to a complex of inherited customs and taboos.

Religiously, the San believe in an omniscient being called N!odima who created the world, and is good. Also, they believe in an evil being called G//aua or G//awama who tries to destroy the work of the good god, N!odima.[382]

Currently, the San's chief concentration is in the Kalahari desert in Botswana, where they are collectively known as Basarwa, Sarwa or Masarwa. Small concentrations of the San, however, are located in Angola and Namibia. Their groups include the Anikhoe, Auen, BaKalagadi, Deti, G//ana, G/anna, G/wi, Hai//om, Hei-Kum (Heiom), Kxoe (Makwengo), Nharo (Anharo, Naro, Naron), !Ko, !Koõ (!Xoõ), !Kung (Zhu/õasi), and !Xu (Kxoe) groups. All these groups are San-speaking peoples. The San's population is estimated at about 125,000.

SANDAWE

The Sandawe are an East African people. They are concentrated in north central Tanzania. Their neighbors include the Arusha, Barabaig, Burungi, Iramba, Irangi, and Nyaturu people.

SANDI, see KONGO

SANGA, see SANGHA

SANGARE, see also FULANI

The Sangare are a West African people. They represent one of the powerful Fulani royal clans. Historically, they were rivals of the Dyalo clan.

SANGHA

The Sangha people, also Sanga, are a Bantu-speaking people. They constitute one of the major ethnic groups of the Republic of Congo, accounting for about 20% of the country's total population. They are concentrated in Katanga, especially in the Sangha region of northern Congo and along the Sangha River, a tributary of the Congo River.

Historically, they were part of the Mwata Kazembe tributary state system. In 1856, they were subdued by a Nyamwezi, known as Misri. With the help of his Yeke warriors who were well armed with guns, he managed to maintain his new realm, to engage in the then popular copper, ivory and slaving trade and to impose heavy taxes on the Sangha people. In 1886, the Sangha revolted against his rule, and a few years later (1891), Misri was shot by a member of an expedition sent by the Belgian king Leopold II's Congo Free (Independent) State to occupy the Katanga region. The death of Misri, however, did not put a halt to the Sanghas' revolt, which continued until its final suppression by Congo (Free) Independent Forces in the early 1900's. Thereupon, the Sangha fell to Belgian rule.

SANGO

The Sango are an Eastern Bantu-speaking people. Their language belongs to the Adamawa-Eastern subgroup of the Niger-Congo family of African languages. Their groups are located in Tanzania, Mozambique, the Central African Republic and the Democratic Republic of the Congo (Zaire). They are concentrated in the Upper Ubangi (Oubangui) River region of southern Central African Republic and northern Zaire. The Sango are essentially a tribal agriculturalist people, but also engage in trading and fishing.

SANGU

The Sangu are an East African Bantu-speaking people and one of Tanzania's ethnic groups. Together with their neighbors the Bena and Hehe people, they live north of Lake Malawi (formerly Nyasa).

They are concentrated in the southwestern areas of the country, especially in the Mbeya administrative region. Their lands are bordered on the west by Lake Tanganyika and on the south by Lake Malawi and the Republic of Zambia. Their economic activities focus on agriculture, fishing and animal husbandry. They are also engaged in salt, gold, coal and mica mining activities in their region.

Prior to colonial rule, the Sangu supported a strong kingdom that was able to withstand encroachments by the Ngoni people and Arab traders on their lands. Additionally, they mastered the Ngoni superior military tactics, adopted firearms and centralized political authority. In this way, they managed to sustain their independence until late in the 1880's, at which time they fell to German rule. After the First World War, they fell to British rule under a League of Nations mandate.

SANHAJA

These are a West African Berber people who commanded control over Awdoghast, west of Ghana Kingdom, which was one of the main trading centers during the tenth century. The Sanhaja were powerful enough to check Ghana's imperial expansion in the direction of their state. Seizing the opportunity of internal dissension among the Sanhaja, the Soninke of Ghana managed to capture Awdoghast in 990 A.D. In the eleventh century, however, the Sanhaja witnessed a profound religious revival led by a puritanical Muslim movement, the Almoravids. Religious zest was soon transformed into a *jihad* with repercussions as far as North Africa and the Iberian Peninsula. In West Africa, the *jihad* led to the recapture of Awdoghast in 1055, and Kumbi, Ghana's capital, in 1076.[383] As a consequence, Ghana's imperial status started to crumble and by 1203, its kingdom ceased to exist.

Currently, the Sanhaja are concentrated in Western Sahara and neighboring countries. Hence, they are essentially a Sahrawi people.

SANYE

The Sanye are an East African people. They are concentrated in the east central and coastal areas of Kenya. However, groups of them can also be found in Tanzania. Their neighbors in Kenya include the Jibana, Pokomo, and Swahili peoples.

SAO

The Sao are an ancient Sudanic-speaking people. Their main concentrations are in Chad and Cameroon. In the Cameroon, they live primarily in the Adamawa Plateau of the country. In precolonial times, the Sao people were highly engaged in the trans-Saharan trade.[384] In addition, they developed "a brilliant civilization on the periphery of Lake Chad from the tenth to the sixteenth centuries... Their influence is proven by numerous necropolises composed of very characteristic tomb jars."[385] Historical evidence suggests that the Sao dispersed in the region following the destruction of their villages and centers by the ruler of Bornu.

SAPEI, see SEBEI

SAPING', see also SEBEI and KALENJIN

The Saping' are an East African Sebei people, a Kalenjin group. They are concentrated in Kenya and Uganda, and speak a dialect of Kalenjin, a Southern Nilotic language that belongs to the Eastern Sudanic family of African languages. The Saping' are a semipastoralist people.

SAPO, see also KRU

The Sapo are a West African ethnic group. They form part of the Kru cluster of peoples in Liberia. The Sapo live in the central regions of the country. Their neighbors include the Grebo, Kran, Siken, and Tewi peoples.

SAR, see also SARA

The Sar are one of Chad's non-Muslim Sara groups. Like other Sara groups, they speak a Central Sudanic language that belongs to the Nilo-Saharan family of African languages. Like them also, they live primarily in the southern regions of the country, notably between Lake Iro in the east and the Logone River in the west.

SAR, see WARJAWA

SARA

The Sara, also known as Kirdi, are the most numerous group in Chad, and one of the main ethnic groups of the Central African Republic and the Sudan. They speak Sara, a language that belongs to the Chari-Nile family of African languages and is widely spoken in southern Chad. They comprise several groups, which apart from Sara proper, include the Gula (Goulaye, Gulay), Kaba, Kara, Kreish, Nduka, Mbay (Mbaye), Nar, Ngama, Ngambay and Sar.

The Sara are the largest ethnic group in Chad, accounting for about one-quarter of the country's population. They are concentrated in the central parts of the Chari and Logone river basins, notably between Lake Iro in the east and the Logone River in the west. They share the Saraland with the related Bagirmi and Bongo.

In the Central African Republic, the Sara account for 10% of the population, constituting the fourth largest ethnic group after the Baya (34%), the Banda (27%) and the Mandjia (21%).

Sara are extensive farmers. Due to European influence, cotton has become one of their cash crops. Due to the same influence, many Sara people were converted to Christianity. During the colonial period, Sara males were utilized by the French army, as well as the French colonial administration.

Sara society is a rigid hierarchy based on age and sex. A clear delineation is presented in the Sara male initiation rite called *yoindo*. The *yoindo* is described as a "painful and humiliating ordeal."[386] The rite may last up to ten years and includes intervals of confession of past sins, learning historical traditions, customs and a special language. Today, the rite of *yoindo* has been heavily affected by the mass of Sara Christian converts.

Sara religious life revolves around the maintenance of equilibrium between the real and supernatural through ritual sacrifice.

The Sara are fairly egalitarian and are ruled by the *mbai-e* or village chiefs. An *mbai-e* can be replaced if others feel he is not circulating the wealth throughout the village.

Sara social organization is patrilineal. In Sara society, polygamy is practiced, but wives have the power to divorce their husbands. Marriage is accomplished by payment of bridewealth in the "form of livestock, cloth, money, or services from the groom to bride."[387]

SARAKOLE, see **SONINKE**

SARUA

A Central and East African people. The Sarua are concentrated in Chad and Sudan.

SARWA, see **BASARWA, MASARWA** and **SAN**

SASI, see **SHASHI**

SATE, see **IBIBIO**

SAU, see **SAO**

SAWSA, see **BERBER**

SAYA

One of West Africa's peoples. The Saya are concentrated in the northwestern regions of Nigeria. Their neighbors include the Fyam, Kwanka, and Nga peoples.

SAYAWA

The Sayawa, also Seiyara and Seya, people are a West African ethnic group. They are concentrated in the northeastern regions of Nigeria.

SEBEI, see also **KALENJIN**

The Sebei, also Sapei, are an East African Kalenjin group. They are concentrated in Kenya and Uganda, notably in eastern Uganda and the Mount Elgon region, and speak a dialect of Kalenjin, a Southern Nilotic language that belongs to the Eastern Sudanic family of African languages. The Sebei comprise several groups, including the Kipsorai, Mbai, Sabaot, Saping' and Sor. They are a semipastoralist people.

SECLAVE, see **SAKALAVA**

SÉCLAVE, see **SAKALAVA**

SEIYARA, see **SAYAWA**

SEKELA, see **SEKELE**

SEKELE, see also **TSWANA**

The Sekele, also spelled Sekela, are a Southwest African Tswana group. They are a Bantu-speaking people and share the historical and cultural heritages of other Tswana groups. The Seleke are concentrated in Angola.

SEMITES

People who speak Semitic languages like Arabic and Hebrew. The Semites trace their origin to Sam, son of Noeh. These people, especially the Arabs among them, have crossed with Hamitic, Bantu, and Negroid peoples of Africa. Historical evidence suggests that in ancient times Semites entered Africa from the Red Sea and Sinai Peninsula. Also it suggests that they continue to mingle with indigenous African groups until this day. Semitic African peoples include many Arab and Jewish groups in North, Central, West and East Africa.

SENA

An Eastern Bantu-speaking people and one of Malawi's nine major ethnic groups. The Sena are related to the Nyanja people. They live in the southern areas of Malawi and across the border in Mozambique.

SENARI, see also SENUFO

These are a West African Voltaic (Gur)-speaking people. They speak Senari, a language belonging to the Gur branch of the Niger-Congo family of African languages. The Senari are a subgroup of the Senufo people who are highly concentrated in the northern parts of the Ivory Coast, the eastern and southeastern regions of the Republic of Mali and the northwestern regions of Burkina Faso.

SENGA, see NSENGA

SENGELE, see MONGO

SENGWER, see also MARAKWET and KALENJIN

An East African Marakwet people, a Kalenjin group. They are concentrated in Kenya and Uganda, notably along escarpments in the Rift Valley region. The Sengwer speak a dialect of Kalenjin, a Southern Nilotic language that belongs to the Eastern Sudanic family of African languages. They are semipastoralist people.

SENOUFOU, see SENUFO

SENUFO

These are one of the major ethnic groups in West Africa. The Senufo, or Senoufou, are a Voltaic (Gur)-speaking people. They speak several languages of the Gur branch of the Niger-Congo family of African languages, the most important of which are: Dyimini, Palaka, Senari and Suppire. The Senufo are highly concentrated in the northern parts of the Ivory Coast and the eastern and southeastern regions of the Republic of Mali. A sizeable group of them are also found in Burkina Faso. Their neighbors include the Bambara, Baule, Dyula, Gan, Guin, Komono, Malinke, Minianka and Wara peoples.

Currently, the Senufo account for about 5% of the total population of the Ivory Coast, constituting the third largest ethnic minority in the country after the Baoule and the Bete.

The Senufo have tribal affiliations with more numerous groups living outside the Ivory Coast. Thus, in Mali, together with other Voltaic peoples, they account for about 12% of the country's total population. In Burkina Faso, they constitute one of the sizeable ethnic groups.

The economic activities of the Senufo focus on the production of agricultural products, including corn and millet. Their farms are located in villages; each village supports a cluster of extended families. In their society, descent, inheritance and succession are based on matrilineal lineages. Initiation ceremonies for adults continue to be observed as important means to assuming tribal responsibilities.

Like other West African peoples, the Senufo are renowned for their splendid wood sculpture, as well as for their musical talents and musical instruments. Their musical instruments include marimbas, iron guns and a wide range of drums and flutes.

SERACULEH, see **SONINKE**

SERAHULI, see **SONINKE**

SERENKET, see **MASAI**

SERER

The Serer are a West African people found primarily in The Gambia and the Senegal. They speak Serer, a language that belongs to the West Atlantic branch of the Niger-Congo family of African languages. Their neighbors include the Dyola, Fula, Malinke and Wolof peoples.

Traditionally, the Serer had a highly centralized kingdom, the king of which was elected by the nobility. The kingdom, moreover, availed ample opportunities for women of the royal clans to exercise political, economic, and judicial powers.[388]

Traditionally also, the Serer society was highly hierarchical in nature. It was organized into about six classes, namely the royalty, nobility, warriors, peasants, crown servants, and artisans.[389] Additionally, it supported a class of slaves divided into several groups: those who were "pawned for debt, hereditary house servants and true slaves acquired through war or purchase."[390]

Many aspects of the traditional features of Serer society have eroded in face of modern political developments, including the introduction of electoral systems based on equal representation and universal suffrage, as well as modern legal systems providing for the equality of citizens before the law and the abolishment of tribal laws.

Currently, the Serer are one of Senegal's seven major ethnic groups. They constitute the third largest group, accounting for about 17% of the total population. In The Gambia, however, they constitute a small minority. The people are essentially settled agriculturalists.

SERVICAIS

These are contract laborers from Angola, Mozambique and Cape Verde in Sâo Tome and Principe. They constitute the fourth largest ethnic group in the country after the mestiço, the Agolares, and the forros.

SESE

The Sese are a Central and East African people. They are concentrated in Uganda, primarily on the northwestern shores of Lake Victoria. Their neighbors include the Bukuli peoples.

SESEJU

These are an East African Bantu-speaking people, whose migration led them to settle in the Shungwaya district between Juba and Tana rivers in Somalia. In the thirteenth century they migrated again to settle in the Great Lakes areas of East Africa.

The Seseju are renowned for defeating the Zimba, a people implicated with cannibalism in the past. The Zimba, in the later part of the sixteenth century (1587-1589), attacked a number of East African coastal cities, including Kilwa and Malindi, "killing and eating every living thing, men, women, children, dogs, cats, rats, snakes, lizards, sparing only those who joined them in their insane orgy."[391]

SESOTHO, see SUTO

SEWA

The Sewa are a Southwest African people. They live in Zambia, primarily in its north central regions. Groups of them, however, can also be found in the Democratic Republic of the Congo (Zaire). Their neighbors in Zambia include the Luapula, Nukulo, and Temba peoples.

SEYA, see **SAYAWA**

SEYCHELLOIS

These are natives of Seychelles, who are a mixture of Asians, Africans and Europeans. The mother tongue of most Seychellois is a creole vernacular, although English and French are the official languages in their country.

SHAGA, see **KGALAGADI**

SHAKE

The Shake people are a West Central African ethnic group. They are part of a cluster that includes the Koto and Bandjami peoples. The Shake are concentrated in Cameroon and Gabon, primarily along the banks of the upper Ogooué River. Their neighbors include the Bakere, Fang, and Koto peoples. The Shake are a Bakota-speaking people.

SHAKIYYA

These are an eastern Sudanic people of the Sudanese Nile basin. Though renowned as distinguished warriors, the Shakiyya proved to be no match for the guns of an Egyptian-Turkish expedition that was dispatched to their region in 1820. As a consequence, many of the Shakiyya people were killed or taken as captives.[392]

SHAMAYE, see **KOTO**

SHAMBAA, see also **SAMBAA**

These are an East African Bantu people. Together with the Chagga, they originated in the Taita region.[393] The Shambaa, also known as Sambaa, are concentrated in the southeastern areas of Kenya and across the border in Tanzania. They are a Bantu-speaking people.

SHAMKELLA

The Shamkella are an East African people. They are concentrated in the northeastern regions of Sudan. However, groups of them live across the border in northwestern Ethiopia. Their neighbors include the Gumma and Besharin peoples.

SHAMVI

An East African people. The Shamvi are concentrated in Tanzania.

SHAMYA, see SINYAR

SHANGAAN

These are a South African people. The Shangaan, also known as Shangana, are concentrated in Gazankulu, a formerly non-independent black homeland in the Republic of South Africa, as well as in Zimbabwe.

Together with the Tsonga people of Gazankulu, the Shangaan support a population of over 0.7 million, growing at the rate of 4.0% per year. In Zimbabwe, they live in the southeastern regions of the country and account for about 1% of the Zimbabwean total population. The Shangaan people migrated from Mozambique to their present areas when their kingdom, Gaza, fell to the Portuguese in 1898.

SHANGANA, see SHANGAAN

SHANGAWA

The Shangawa, also known as Kyenga and Shonga, are a West African people. They are concentrated in Nigeria, notably in the vicinity of the city of Shanga. The Shangawa's main economic activities center on farming, fishing and trading.

SHANJO

An East African people. The Shanjo are concentrated in western Zambia. They are closely related to the Lozi people. They speak Kololo, the Lozi language, share many of Lozi customs, and are part of the Lozi-dominated Barotse Kingdom.[394]

SHANKADI, see LUBA

SHANKAJI, see LUBA

SHANKELLA

The Shankella are the fourth largest ethnic minority in Ethiopia. They account for approximately 6% of the country's total population.

SHASHI

The Shashi, also Sizaki and Sasi, are an East African people. They are concentrated in Kenya and Tanzania. The Shashi speak Nubian languages, which are Eastern Sudanic languages belonging to the Chari-Nile branch of the Nilo-Saharan family of African languages.

SHAWIA, see SHAWIYA

SHAWIYA, see also BERBER

The Shawiya, also spelled Chaouia, Shawia and Shawya, are a North African Berber people. They speak Shawya, one of the Berber languages, and are concentrated in the Algerian Aurès mountains, especially in the *wilāya* (province) of Tébessa. The latter *wilāya* was formed in 1974 from parts of the *wilāyats* of Batna and Annaba.

SHAWYA, see SHAWIYA

SHENABLA

The Shenabla are a Central and East African people. They are concentrated in west central regions of Sudan. Groups of them are also found in Chad. The Shenabla are camel nomads.

SHERBRO

The Sherbro are a West African people. They are concentrated in the southern regions of Sierra Leone. Their neighbors include the Bullom, Kono, Kuranko, Limba, Loko, Mende, Susu, Temne and Vai peoples. The Sherbro speak a language that belongs to the West Atlantic branch of the Niger-Congo family of African languages.

SHI

One of the ethnic groups of the Democratic Republic of the Congo (Zaire). The Shi are part of the Kivu cluster of peoples.

SHILA

The Shila are a Western Bantu-speaking people. They are concentrated in the southwestern and southeastern regions of Africa, notably in Zimbabwe, Zambia and Angola.

SHILLUK, see also FUNJ

The Shilluk, also known as Collo, are an eastern Sudanic Nilotic people. They are concentrated along the White Nile and Sobat rivers in what is presently modern Sudan. They speak an Eastern Sudanic language of the Chari-Nile branch of the Nilo-Saharan family of African languages. Their language is closely related to that of the Anuak people.

The Shilluk people are partly sedentary farmers and rtly pastoralists. Both men and women engage in agricultural activities, but hunting, herding and attending to livestock is essentially undertaken by men. Their society is segmented into hamlets, each of which is governed by a head who represents a dominant lineage. It is governed by a headman, who is elected by a council of hamlet heads.

Traditionally, the Shilluk had a highly structured kingdom of their own composed of a royal class, commoners and slaves. The kingdom was governed by a divine king, called *reth*, who was elected from descendants of former kings – a class the members of which traced their descent to Nyikang (Nyikango), the first Shilluk king.

The Shilluk support some one hundred patrilineal and exogamous clans, the most important of which are the Funj who established a Sudanic sultanate of their own at the start of the sixteenth century. The sultanate's seat was at Sennar on the Blue Nile.[395]

In more recent times, the Shilluk people are known to have been among the Sudanic tribes that resisted the expedition in 1839 that was dispatched by Muhammad Ali, governor of Egypt, to explore the upper reaches of the White Nile.

SHINGE, see also LUNDA

The Shinge are a Bantu-speaking people whose origin is traced back to the Congo, where they were part of the Lunda kingdom, which was founded in the later part of the fifteenth century, developed into an empire, and endured until late in the nineteenth century. Over time, they broke away from the central Lunda kingdom in the Kapanga district of the southern Congo to establish their own kingdom.

Currently, the Shinge are concentrated in Angola, Democratic Republic of the Congo (Zaire) and Zambia.

Traditionally, the main economic activities of the Shinge people centered on food gathering, hunting and trading. Traditionally also, their religion rested on the belief in a supreme being, who was either a sky god or an earth god.[396]

SHINYIHA, see NYIHA

SHIR, see MANDARI

SHIRAZI

The Shirazi are one of Tanzania's ethnic groups. The Shirazis are descendants of Persian peoples who settled in the islands of Zanzibar and Pemba, and in areas south of Somalia during the 10th century. Currently, the Afro-Shirazi people constitute the largest ethnic group in Zanzibar and Pemba. They are divided into three major groups, namely Hadiman,

Pemba and Tumbatu.

SHLEUCH, see also BERBER

The Shleuch, also Chleuh, Chleuch and Shluh, are a North African Berber people. They speak Shluh, one of the Berber languages and are concentrated in Morocco, notably in the High Atlas and the Sous region.

SHLUH, see SHLEUCH and BERBER

SHONA

These are a group of Southern Bantu-speaking peoples of the eastern parts of Zimbabwe, particularly north of the Lundi River. They comprise several tribal groups, the most important of which are Kalanga, Karanga, Korekore, Manyika, Ndau, Tavara, Tonga-Korekore and Zezuru. They all speak Shona, a tonal Bantu language. Currently, the Shona constitute the largest ethnic group in the state of Zimbabwi accounting for over 70% of the country's total population. In addition, they support several chiefdoms that are overseen by hereditary chiefs.

The Shona are essentially farmers who live in villages comprised of interrelated families. Excepting a group of them who is matrilineal, most Shona people observe patrilineal lineages in matters relating to descent, inheritance and succession.

Though Christianity has won many converts among them, many Shona continue to be impacted by their traditional religion which rests on the belief in a creator-god, called *Mwari*, as well as in ancestral spirits, magic, witchcraft and sorcery.

Prior to Portuguese colonization of Zimbabwe in the sixteenth century, the Shona had a prosperous kingdom of their own. Their kingdom, Munhumutapa or Monomotapa, reached an imperial level under Mutota and then his son Matope of the Rozwi dynasty that assumed power over the Shona towards the middle of the fifteenth century. Both kings managed to extend the territory of their kingdom from the Indian Ocean in the east to the Kalahari Desert in the west.[397]

The prosperity of the empire was derived from the Shona's active engagement in gold mining, an industry that was highly guarded and controlled by the Rozwi dynasty. This prosperity arrested the attention of the Portuguese and incited them to occupy the coastal town of Sofala in 1505, and subsequently other parts of the empire to lay hand on the gold mines of the Shona's kingdom. In 1629 they managed to reduce the Shona kingdom into a vassal state. The Shona kingdom remained a vassal of the Portuguese until the end of the seventeenth century, at which time the Changamire kingdom succeeded in conquering most of its territory. [398]

The Shona people are renowned for their architectural and artistic talents, as well as for their decorated pottery, copper, bronze, ironcrafts, gold ornaments and musical instruments.

SHONGA, see SHANGAWA

SHORFA, see SAHRAWIS

SHUKULUMBWE, see ILA

SHUWA

These are a West and Central African Arab people and one of Nigeria's ethnic minorities. The Shuwa are concentrated in the Lake Chad region of northeastern Nigeria and eastern Niger. A large group of them are presently in the state of Borno (formerly Bornu). The Shuwa's neighbors include the Buduma, Kanuri, Koloko and Mandara peoples. They are essentially a tribal people engaged in herding and livestocks.

SIA

These are a West African people. They are concentrated in Burkina Faso and adjoining countries. Their neighbors include the Bambara, Bobo, Diam, Minianka and Tusyan peoples. The Sia speak a language that belongs to the Mande branch of the Niger-Congo family of African languages.

SIDAMA, see SIDAMO

SIDAMO

The Sidamo, also spelled Sidama, are an East African non-Galla Cushitic-speaking Muslim people. They live chiefly in southwestern Ethiopia, particularly in the Omo River and Rift Valley regions of the country. The Sidamo comprise several groups, which include the Alaba, Doaro, Hadya and Tambaro.

The Sidamo founded their own kingdom of Kefa between the tenth and twelfth centuries. This kingdom absorbed Islam from coastal Arabs and rose to prominence during the fifteenth century. Subsequently, however, their territory was contained and moreover, their kingdom became a tributary of the Abyssinians (Amhara and Tigre), as well as the Galla.[399]

Currently, the Sidamo constitute Ethiopia's third largest ethnic group, accounting for about 9% of the country's total population.

The Sidamo are essentially agriculturalists. They specialize in the production of grains, cereals, fruits and spices, as well as in animal husbandry.

SIHANAKA

The Sihanaka are a Southeast African-Malagasy people. They are concentrated on the Island of Madagascar. The Sihanaka live on the northeastern side of the island, neighboring the Betsimisaraka and the Bezanozano peoples.

SIKON

A West African ethnic group. The Sikon are part of the Kru cluster of peoples in Liberia. They live in the country's coastal areas, neighboring the Bassa, Grebo, and Sapo peoples.

SILOZI, see LOZI

SIMAA

An East African people. The Simaa are concentrated in western Zambia. They are closely related to the Lozi people. They speak Kololo, the Lozi language, share many Lozi customs, and are part of the Lozi-dominated Barotse Kingdom.[400]

SIMBA

These are one of Democratic Republic of the Congo's (Zaire's) ethnic groups. They are also known as "Muletists."

SINGO

The Singo are a Central and East African people. They are concentrated in Uganda.

SINYAR

A Central and East African Muslim agricultural people. The Sinyar, also called Shamya, are concentrated in Chad and Sudan, notably in the border area that separates the two countries.

SIRA

These are one of the largest ethnic groups of Gabon. They are concentrated in areas south of the Ogooué River.

SIRIA, see MASAI

SISALA

A West African people. The Sisala are concentrated in the northern areas of Ghana, notably in the Upper Region. Their neighbors include the Dagaba, the Grusi and the Mamprusi peoples.

SISE

The Sise are a West Central African ethnic group. They are concentrated in the Republic of Congo, north of the merging point between the Zaire and Kasai rivers. However, groups of them can also be found in the Democratic Republic of the Congo (Zaire). Their neighbors in both countries include the Achikouya, Bali, Fumbu, and Teke peoples.

SIZAKI, see SHASHI

SO

These are an African people of central Sudan, and the original inhabitants of the Lake Chad area or what is also known as the Kanem region, in what is presently part of modern Nigeria and Chad. Between the seventh and ninth centuries, their territory was infiltrated by other peoples, including the Zaghawa under whose impetus the Kanuri-speaking state of Kanem was subsequently established.

The So people supported a number of individual tribal units which were loosely interrelated by language and culture. Their traditional political system was highly hierarchical in nature and was based on the principle of divine kingship.[401]

SOBO, see also ISOKO and URHOBO

The term Sobo is used by ethnographers to refer to the Isoko and Urhobo peoples of Niger Delta in Nigeria. Though neighbors, both peoples "remain distinct from one another."[402]

SOGA

The Soga, also Busoga, are one of Uganda's Bantu-speaking agriculturalist peoples. They constitute the fourth largest ethnic minority in the country. They live chiefly in the area lying between Lakes Victoria and Kyoga along the Ugandan-Kenyan borders. Groups of them, however, are also located in Kenya. The Soga's neighbors include the Bukedi, Ganda, the Giso (Gisu), the Lango and the Teso peoples.

SOKILE, see NYAKYUSA

SOKORO

A West African people. The Sokoro, also known as Sorko, are one of Nigeria's ethnic minorities. They live on the banks of Lake Chad and primarily engage in fishing.

SOLANGO, see KONGO

SOLI

The Soli are a Southwest African Tonga-speaking people. They live in Zambia, primarily on the southeastern edge of Lake Kariba. Their neighbors there include the Nkoya, Nsenga, and Tonga peoples. The Soli observe matrilineal lineages.

SOLONGO, see KONGO

SOMALI

They are one of East Africa's peoples. They occupy all of Somalia, a part of Djibouti, the Ethiopian eastern province of Ogaden and part of the northwestern region of Kenya, known as the Wajir District. They speak Somali, a language that belongs to the Cushitic branch of the Hamito-Semitic family of African languages.

Originally, the Somali people lived in the Arabian peninsula. They migrated to their present locations over 1000 years ago, displacing "the ethnically related Galla peoples and small bands of Bantu, known to the early Arab geographers as the Zanj. The Zanj were concentrated along the banks of the Giuba and Shebelle and in fertile pockets between them. As the Somali swept south, pushing the Galla and Zanj before them, Yemenite Arabs set up coastal city states such as Zeila, Berbera, Mogadishu, and Brava."[403] Like other East African peoples, the Somalis engaged in entrepôt trade between the markets of the African interior on the one hand, and those of Arabia and the Indian subcontinent, Burma, Thailand, Malaysia, Singapore and Indonesia on the other. By the tenth century the Somali people converted to Islam. In the sixteenth century, their littoral cities were occupied by the Portuguese. In the seventeenth century, however, they were recaptured by Muslim forces, especially those of the Imamate of Muscat. Thereafter, they fell to Ottoman, Egyptian, and Sultanate of Zanzibar. By the end of the nineteenth century, however, Somaliland fell to French, British and Italian rule. As a result, Somaliland was partitioned and continued to be ruled by European powers until the 1960s and 1970s, at which time Somalia and Djibouti gained their independence, respectively.

Somalians are relatively homogeneous people physically, culturally and religiously. They support distinct features that make it easy to distinguish them from other African peoples. They are tall, with slender shapes and delicate facial features. In addition, they are predominantly pastoral and Muslim people.

Despite their homogeneity, however, they are often split by patrilineal clan loyalties and affiliations.

The Somali people are divided into several principal tribes, namely, Darod (Daarood, also known as Geri), Dighil (Digil, also known as Sab), Dir, Hawiya (Hawiye), Ishaak (Isaaq), Mareehan, Mirifle (also known as Mijurtein or Majeerteen), Rahanwayn (Rahanwin) and Ogaadeen. In turn, these principal tribes are divided into numerous subtribes, clans, and subclans.

The Harti clans of Dhulbahan and Warsangali, for example, are part of the Darod tribe, whereas the Abgaal and Habar-Gidir are part of the Hawiya, and the Godabiirsay, or Samaroon, and the 'Iise of the Dir.

Currently, they constitute 85% of the population of Somalia and 60% of that of Djibouti. Moreover, they constitute the fifth largest ethnic minority in Ethiopia, accounting for 6% of the country's total population.

SOMBA, see also TAMBERMA

The Somba, also known as Tamberma, are a Voltaic-speaking people. They are concentrated in the northern regions of Benin, where they, together with the Bariba and other related groups, constitute about one-fifth of the country's total population. Their neighbors include the Borgu, Chakossi, Gurma, Kabre, Kilinga, Moba and Naudeba peoples. Significant groups of Somba people can also be found in both Ghana and Togo.

SOMONO, see also MANDE

The Somono are a West African Mande group. They constitute one of Mali's important ethnic minorities. The Somono people live along the banks of the Niger River in Mali.

SOMRAI

A Central and East African pastoralist people. The Somrai live in both Chad and Sudan. In Chad, they are concentrated in the Moyen-Chari Prefecture.

SONDI

A West Central African Western Bantu-speaking people. The Sondi are concentrated in Angola and the Democratic Republic of the Congo (Zaire). In Zaire, their neighbors include the Pende people of the Bandundu and Kasai administrative provinces.

SONGHAI

The Songhai, known also as Gao, Songhoi, Songhay, Songhrai, Sonrhai, Djerma, Zabrama, and Zerma, are a West African Negroid people with probable Caucasoid mixture. They are chiefly concentrated in the area lying between the Niger River in Mali and the Sokoto River in Nigeria, notably in eastern Mali, western Niger, and northern Benin. Groups of them are also found in Ghana, Nigeria, Togo and Ivory Coast. In Ghana, they are known as Zabrama or Gao. The Songhai are predominantly Muslim, speak Songhai, a Nilo-Saharan language, and comprise numerous groups, the most important of which are the Zerma (Djerma). Their neighbors include the Deforo, Fula (Fulani), Gurma, Kurfei, Mauri and Taureg peoples.

The Songhai established themselves in the city of Gao in the latter part of the eighth century. In the 11th century, their kingdom started to develop into a powerful and prosperous empire. Upon gaining control of the Mali empire in the fifteenth century, they stretched their domains from the coast of the Atlantic Ocean in what is now Guinea eastward into parts of modern Nigeria and Niger. With Gao and Timbuktu as its leading commercial and cultural centers, their empire saw its zenith during the reign of Sunni (Sonni) Ali Ber (1464-1492). Despite internal power struggles, the Songhai empire sustained its expansionary course until the 1590's, when it was defeated by the forces of Sultan Ahmad Al-Mansur of Morocco which were equipped with guns and cannons. Descendants of the Askia Muhammad Toure dynasty that was established upon the death of Sunni Ali in 1492, however, continued to rule a unified state in what is presently the modern state of Niger until 1660. Thereafter, succession rivalries led to the parceling of this unified state into five principalities, namely: Anzuru, Dargol, Garuol, Kokoro and Tera. These Songhai principalities sustained their independence until 1898, at which time they fell to French rule.

Currently, the Songhai are essentially farmers, fishermen, shipbuilders and traders. Some of them, however, are engaged in politics, especially in the Niger where they constitute the second largest ethnic group, accounting for about 22% of the country's total population.

SONGHAI-ZERMA, see SONGHAI

SONGHAY, see SONGHAI

SONGHOI, see SONGHAI

SONGHRAI, see SONGHAI

SONGO, see also LUNDA

The Songo are a Bantu-speaking people whose origin is traced back to the Congo, where they were part of the Lunda kingdom and later empire. This kingdom was founded in the later part of the fifteenth century and endured until late in the nineteenth century. Over time, they broke away from the central Lunda kingdom in the Kapanga district of the southern Congo, to establish their own kingdom. Currently, the Songo are concentrated in Angola where they live in the north and south central areas of the country. However, groups of them can also be found in the Democratic Republic of the Congo (Zaire) at Zambia. Their neighbors in Angola include the Bayaka, Mbala, Ovimbundu, and Yanzi peoples.

Traditionally, the main economic activities of the Songo people centered on food gathering, hunting, and trading. Traditionally also, their religion rested on the belief in a supreme being, who was either a sky god or an earth god.[404]

SONGO-MENO, see **MONGO**

SONIAKE, see **SONINKE**

SONINKE

The Soninke, also known as Sarakole, Seraculeh, Serahuli and Soniake, are a West African Mande people. They are primarily located in The Gambia, Mali, Senegal and Mauritania. Their neighbors include the Bambara, Fula, Kagoro, Khasonke, Malinke and Tukulor peoples. The Soninke speak a Mande language of the Niger-Congo family of African languages. They are predominantly Muslim.

The Soninke are agriculturalists and are the descendants of the founders of the ancient Ghana Empire, which was destroyed by Muslim invasions in the 10th century.

Currently, they account for 9% of the population of The Gambia and 6% of Mali's. They are also one of Senegal's seven major ethnic groups, constituting the seventh largest minority. In Mauritania, they are located in southern regions of the country.

SONRHAI, see **SONGHAI**

SOR, see also **SEBEI** and **KALENJIN**

An East African Sebei people, a Kalenjin group. They are concentrated in Kenya and Uganda, and speak a dialect of Kalenjin, a Southern Nilotic language that belongs to the Eastern Sudanic family of African languages. The Sor are semipastoralist people.

SORKO, see **SOKORO**

SORONGO

The Sorongo are a Central and Southwest African people. They are concentrated in Angola and the Democratic Republic of the Congo (Zaire).

SOSO, see **SUSU**

SOSSO, see **KONGO**

SOTEK, see also **KIPSIGIS** and **KALENJIN**

An East African Kipsigis people, a Kalenjin group. They are concentrated in Kenya and Uganda, and speak a dialect of Kalenjin, a Southern Nilotic language that belongs to the Eastern Sudanic family of African languages. The Sotek are semipastoralist people.

SOTHO

The Sotho, also called Suthu, Suto or Basuto, are a southern African group of peoples who are linguistically and culturally similar. They occupy the high grasslands of the region and speak Sesotho, a Bantu language. They comprise three major groups: northern (or Transvaal), western (or Tswana) and southern (or Basuto, Lesotho) Sotho peoples. They are concentrated in the Kingdom of Lesotho, as well as in Lebowa and QwaQwa, which until recently represented two of the black homelands in the Republic of South Africa. In QwaQwa, they are called Basuto.

Lebowa and QwaQwa are essentially Sotho. Lebowa's population is over 2.6 million, growing at the rate of 3.9% per year, whereas QwaQwa's is about 0.8 million, growing at the rate of 2.5%. Lesotho's population is 99.7% Sotho, growing at the rate of 2.7% per year.

The Sotho comprise numerous groups. The most important of these groups are: Pedi, Lovedu, Kanga-Kone in Lebowa and Kwena in Lesotho. The Kwena subgroup comprises such tribes as Molibeli, Monaheng, Hlakwana, Kxwakxwa (Qwagwa) and Fokeng.

The modern history of the Sotho is traced back to Mshweshwe I (Moshoeshoe I, 1786-1870), the first paramount chief of the Sotho kingdom, Basutoland, in which he founded with Thaba Bosiu as its capital. In 1833, Mshweshwe welcomed French missionaries to his territory and sought their advice in dealing with European powers. In order to safeguard the independence of his kingdom, he "played off British and Boer against one another, until 1843, when he allied himself with the British."[405] In 1848, however, most of his lands were annexed by the British, a measure that provoked a war between the two parties, the results of which ended in his favor. Subsequently, he got into a war with the Orange Free State. Having realized that the balance was tipping in favor of the Orange Free State, in 1868, he persuaded the British to annex his country. Henceforth, Basutoland came under British protection, and between 1884 and 1966, it was governed by a British high commissioner. In 1966, Basutoland was granted its independence within the Commonwealth as the Kingdom of Lesotho, with Mshweshwe (Moshoeshoe) II, the country's paramount chief as its king. Following a military intervention and a constitutional crisis, the monarch's powers were curtailed and reduced to nominal powers. Now the kingdom is headed by Mshweshwe's son Letsie III.

The great majority of Sotho are agricultural, relying both on cultivation and animal husbandry. But males among them often seek work as laborers. Their settlements are characterized "by scattered hamlets of circular huts with mud and wattle or stone walls surmounted by a conical, thatched roof."[406] In their social patterns, most Sotho recognize patrilineal lineages, and traditionally, they allowed polygamy.

SOUDIÉ, see KURFEI

SOUNGOR

The Soungor are an East Saharan Central African pastoral and semi-pastoral people. They are concentrated in western Sudan and eastern Chad. In Chad, they are located east of Lake Chad. Their neighbors there include the Karranga, Kreda, and Wadai peoples.

SOUNINKE, see SONINKE

SOUSOU, see **SUSU**

SOUTHERN SOTHO, see also **SOTHO**

The Southern Sotho, also called Basuto or Lesotho, represent one of the three Sotho major groups. The other two are Northern (or Transvaal) and Western (or Tswana) Sotho. Like other Sotho people, they occupy the high grasslands of southern Africa and speak Sesotho, a Bantu language.

The great majority of Southern Sotho engage in agriculture, relying both on cultivation and animal husbandry. But males among them often seek work as laborers. Their settlements are characterized "by scattered hamlets of circular huts with mud and wattle or stone walls surmounted by a conical, thatched roof."[407] In their social patterns, most Sotho recognize patrilineal lineages, and traditionally, they allowed polygamy.

SPANIARD

People of Spanish background and/or Spanish expatriates or settlers who live in African countries that formerly fell to Spain's rule and/or influence. These people and/or their descendants are unevenly distributed in the following countries: Equatorial Guinea, Morocco, and Western Sahara.

SRAGHNA

The Sraghna are a West Saharan North African people. They are concentrated in the central mountainous regions of Morocco. The Sraghna are a Berber people.

SUBI

The Subi are an East African people. They live in Tanzania, primarily west of the southern edge of Lake Victoria. Their neighbors include the Ankole (Banyanhkole), Burundi, and Sumbwa peoples.

SUBIA, see **SUBYA**

SUBYA

An East African people. The Subya, also Subia, are concentrated in western Zambia. Though they were incorporated within the Lozi-dominated Barotse Kingdom, they continue to have their own language and customs.[408]

SUK, see also POKOT and KALENJIN

An East African Pokot people, a Kalenjin group. The Suk, also Musuk, are concentrated in Kenya, Tanzania and Uganda, notably in Kenya's West Pokot District which is located along the Ugandan border. Their language, *ng'ala Pokot,* is a dialect of Kalenjin, a Southern Nilotic language that belongs to the Eastern Sudanic family of African languages. The Suk are semipastoralist people. Their economic activities focus on cattle keeping, grain growing and trading.

SUKU, see also YAKA

The Suku – formerly called Yaka – are a Bantu-speaking, Central African people. They are concentrated in the Kwango subregion of the Bandundu region in the Democratic Republic of the Congo (Zaire). The Suku, also known as Basuku and Bayaka, are essentially agriculturalists. Their economic activities focus on farming and trading.

The Suku came into contact with the Portuguese in the 1890s. Subsequently, however, they fell to the rule of the Congo Free State (later the Belgian Congo).

The Suku society is matrilineal. This feature is evident in their property and inheritance systems, as well as in their social and political organizations.

The Suku kingdom is pyramidal in nature with the royal lineage standing at the apex, whereas other specific lineages govern their respective chieftainces and subchieftainces. Traditionally, all "lineage heads performed the basic lineage rituals (such as marriage, burials, appeals to dead elders, curses), and all political chiefs performed the basic chiefly rituals (harvest, hunts, installation of chiefs and villages)."[409]

Though Christianity has won converts, many Suku continue to be impacted by their traditional religion which rests on the notion of one supreme Creator.

SUKULUMBWE, see **ILA**

SUKUMA

The Sukuma people, also known as Basukuma, are one of Tanzania's ethnic minorities. They are concentrated in the western areas of the country, notably south of Lake Victoria in what they call Busukuma or Sukumaland, their homeland. Their neighbors include the Nyamwezi people with whom they share many characteristics. The Sukuma are a Bantu-speaking people. Their language, Sukuma, is akin to that of the Nyamwezi people. In addition to Sukuma, they also speak Swahili.

Historical evidence suggests that the Sukuma settled in their present areas sometime during the seventeenth century. Also it suggests that they established their own chiefdoms which came into contact with Indian and Arab traders. In the later part of the nineteenth century they fell to German influence and rule and became part of the German colony of East Africa in 1890. In 1919, the administration of this colony was taken over by the British as part of World War I settlements. British rule continued until 1961, at which time the Sukuma became part of independent Tanzania.

The Sukuma people are essentially agriculturalists, traders and cattle-raisers. Their economic activities focus on miscellaneous agricultural and trading pursuits, as well as on cattle keeping activities. They are famous for their traditional crafts which include ironwork, pottery and stool carving.

SUMBWA

The Sumbwa are an East and Southeast African people. They are concentrated in Tanzania, primarily west of the southern edge of Lake Victoria. Their neighbors include the Ankole, Nyamwezi, Subi and Vinza peoples.

SUMBYU, see **KAVANGO**

SUNDI, see **KONGO**

SUPPIRE, see also **SENUFO**

These are a West African Voltaic (Gur)-speaking people. They speak Suppire, a language belonging to the Gur branch of the Niger-Congo family of African languages. The Senari are a subgroup of the Senufo people who are highly concentrated in the northern parts of the Ivory Coast, the eastern and southeastern regions of the Republic of Mali and the northwestern regions of Burkina Faso.

SURA

A West African people. The Sura, also known as Mwaghavul and Mupun, are concentrated in Nigeria, notably in Plateau State.

SURI

The Suri, formerly Nagos, are an East African agro-pastoralist people. They are concentrated in southwestern Ethiopia and southeastern Sudan, notably in the Kefa region, and are related to their neighbors the Ethiopian Mursi, Murle and Me'en peoples. They speak Surmic, formerly Surma, a language presumed to belong to the East Sudanic group of the Nilo-Saharan family of African languages. The Suri people comprise several major groups, including the Bale, Chai, Nyikoròma, and Tirma. All these groups live in the southern regions of Ethiopia and the Sudan.

Historical evidence suggests that the Suri people had never fallen "to any overarching state structure–neither colonial nor indigenous."[410] Though their area of Shulugui and Tirma were penetrated by the imperial troops of the Ethiopian emperor Menileck II (r. 1889-1913) in 1897, and subsequently by Italian (1932), British (1940-1941) and Ethiopian (1941-1997) troops, nevertheless the Suri managed to retain their own political and administrative control and hence, enjoy their own laws and way of life.

The Suri society is patrilineal. It recognizes patrilineal lineages in their personal, social and political systems. These lineages are supported by their own religious beliefs and veneration to ancestral traditions. The Suri people believe in a supreme God, *Tumu*, which is conceived as the source of all power and wealth.

SUSU, see also MANDE

The Susu, also Sousou or Soso, are a West African Mande forest group. They are concentrated in Guinea, Guinea-Bissau, and Sierra Leone. Their neighbors include the Baga, Biafada, Bulom, Fula, Dyalonke, Landuma, Limba, Loko and Nalu peoples. The Susu language, Susu-Yalunka, is a Mande language of the Niger-Congo family of African languages. The Susu people have their own chiefdoms, each of which is headed by a paramount chief. They constitute the third largest ethnic group after the Fulani and the Malinke in the Republic of Guinea.

SUTHU, see SOTHO

SUTO, see also SOTHO

A southern African people. The Suto, also known as Sesotho, are concentrated in Lesotho.

SWAHILI

The name Swahili refers to a people that live along the coastlines of East African countries lying between southern Somalia in the north and northern Mozambique in the south, as well as in the islands of Amoros, Zanzibar, Pemba, Mafia and northwestern areas of Madagascar. They speak KiSwahili, a language that "belongs to the Sam Family of Northeastern Bantu and has many loanwords from Arabic."[411] The name is derived from the Arabic word sawāhili, meaning the people living along the coast. The Swahili people have always played the role of intermediaries in long-distance trade between the countries of the Indian Ocean and subsequently European and non-European countries on the one hand, and the African interior on the other. They are sedentary people and predominantly Muslim.

SWAKA

The Swaka are a Southwest African Lala group. They live in the eastern areas of Zambia. Their neighbors include the Lala, Lamba, Luano, and Mbwera peoples.

SWAZI

The Swazi are a Southern-Eastern Bantu-speaking people. Speakers of their language, siSwati, are found in Swaziland, South Africa and Mozambique. SiSwati is a tonal language of the Ngoni group of African languages. It is closely related to Zulu. The Swazi derived their name from one of their prominent leaders Mswati II. They are an Ngwane group, "a derivative of the Zulus, but are less warlike in background, and have their own highly individual characteristics."[412] They are concentrated in South Africa. Swazi, or what presently constitutes KaNgwane and Swaziland, was their traditional homeland.

The Ngwane people were organized into a kingdom by Sobhuza, one of their greatest kings. Upon his death in 1840, the reign devolved to his son and successor Mswati (1820-1868), who succeeded in expanding the kingdom northward into Zimbabwe (formerly Rhodesia), reorganizing the Ngwane society into age-regiments and developing his kingdom into one of the most powerful in the region. In 1860, he extended his influence into southern Rhodesia and Mozambique. His policy of befriending the Boers of Transvaal (by ceding lands to them and supporting them in their assault against the Poko people), however, proved detrimental to his kingdom in the future. During the reign of King Mbandzeni (d. 1899), also spelled Umbandine, the entire land of the Swazi people came under white rule. In 1895, the Boer South African Republic, later the Crown Colony of the Transvaal, took over KaNgwane, whereas the other portion of the country (Kingdom of Swaziland) fell to British protection (1902). Henceforth, KaNgwane was ruled directly by South Africa, whereas the Kingdom of Swaziland was ruled indirectly by the British.

After a period of regency under his mother, in 1921, Sobhuza II, as a member of the royal Dlamini clan, assumed the kingly title of Ngwenyama (lion) and became paramount chief of the Swazi people. Under his leadership, the Kingdom of Swaziland acquired its independence from the United Kingdom on September 6, 1968.

The independence of Swaziland incited South Africa to assign eastern Transvaal for the Swazi people that were under its rule and in 1977, it designated the area as KaNgwane.

The Swazi people are predominantly agriculturalists. They specialize in the production of corn, cotton, tobacco and fruit, as well as in cattle husbandry.

Currently, the Swazi are divided between the Kingdom of Swaziland and KaNgwane. In KaNgwane, the Ngwane population is over 0.5 million, growing at the rate of 3.6% per year. The nucleus of the Swazi nation, however, is in the Veld region, Swaziland.

TAABWA, see TABWA

TA'AISHA, see BAGGARA

TABOU

A West African Krou group. The Tabou are concentrated in the Ivory Coast.

TABWA

The Tabwa, also known as Taabwa and Rungu, are one Democratic Republic of the Congo's (Zaire's) and Zambia's ethnic groups. They live on the southwestern shores of Lake Tanganyika in southeastern Zaire and in the northeastern areas of Zambia.

The Tabwa are a Bantu-speaking people. Their language is akin to those of the Luba people of Zaire and the Bemba people of Zambia.

The Tabwa comprise several clans and numerous subclans, which developed independently from each other. This explains their lack of cohesiveness. During the nineteenth century, both Nsama and Tumbwe, two of their chiefs, tried to unify them. Their attempts however were thwarted by internal dissension, as well as external assaults.

Traditionally, their society observed matrilineal lineages in matters relating to descent, inheritance and succession.

Traditionally also the Tabwas' activities focused on producing iron and copper products, salt and smoked fish, as well as on trading with neighboring nations. In more recent times, their focus has slightly shifted to cattle raising, farming, industrial fishing and copper mining.

Since the 1890s, the Tabwa were serviced by Catholic missionary schools. Between 1960 and 1962, several of their people assumed political leadership positions in Moise Tshombe's secessionist movement, but suffered as a result of the civil war and the eventual downfall of the separationist Katanga state that they helped to establish.

TACHONI, see LUHYA

TADJAKANT

A West African people. The Tadjakant are concentrated in the northwestern regions of West Africa, notably in Mauritania.

TADJUNI, see LUHYA

TAHOU

A West African Krou group. They are concentrated in the Ivory Coast.

TAIMORO

The Taimoro are a Southeast African people. They are concentrated on the Island of Madagascar, primarily in its southeastern coastal areas. Their neighbors include the Tambahoaka, Tanala, and ZaFisoro peoples.

TAISAKA

The Taisaka are a Southeast African people. Like the Taimoro, they are concentrated on the Island of Madagascar. They live in the southeastern regions of the country, neighboring the Tanosy and Timanambondro peoples.

TAITA, see also **BANTU**

An Eastern Bantu-speaking people. They are concentrated in the northern areas of East Africa, notably in Kenya north of Mombasa. Their neighbors include the Masai people.

TAITOQ, see **TAUREG**

TAKADI, see **KONSO**

TALLENSI

The Tallensi are a West African Voltaic people. They are concentrated in the basin of the Volta rivers in Ghana, and are essentially a farming people. They support a patrilineal society whose basic economic and jural unit is the nuclear or extended family. Traditionally, "the father was the manager of the family unit, its authoritative decision maker, and its ritual head. He controlled, managed, and allocated its economic resources."[413] Traditionally also, the religious beliefs of the Tallensi people rested on the exaltation of spiritual forces, notably ancestral spirits.

The Tallensi people had no temporal chiefs or councils of elders. They relied on intermediaries between the temporal and the spiritual worlds to address their problems and/or conflicts.

TAMA

The Tama people are one of Chad's and Sudan's ethnic groups. They are concentrated in Ouaddai region in eastern Chad, as well as in the western regions of The Sudan. Their population is estimated at over 40,000. The Tama speak a dialect of the Nilo-Saharan language.

The Tama are a Muslim people who developed an independent sultanate of their own in the past. The capital of their sultanate was at Niere, the ruins of which still stand. They are a sedentary people with agriculture as their main economic activity. Their educational system is based on Qur'anic schools.

TAMBAHOAKA

The Tambahoaka are a Southeast African people. They are concentrated on the Island of Madagascar. The Tambahoaka live in the south central areas of the country, neighboring the Taimoro and Tanala peoples.

TAMBARO, see also SIDAMO

The Tambaro are an East African non-Galla Cushitic-speaking Muslim people. They live chiefly in southwestern Ethiopia, particularly in the Omo River and Rift Valley regions of the country. They are a Sidamo group and hence are related to other Sidamo peoples, such as the Alaba, Garo and Hadya.

The Tambaro established a kingdom of their own between the tenth and twelfth centuries, which absorbed Islam from coastal Arabs. Subsequently, however, their kingdom became a tributary of the Abyssinians (Amhara and Tigre), as well as the Galla.[414]

The Tambaro are essentially agriculturalists. They specialize in the production of grains, cereals, fruits and spices, as well as in animal husbandry.

TAMBERMA, see also SOMBA

The Tamberma, also known as Somba, are a West African people. They are concentrated in Benin and Togo. Groups of them, however, can also be found in Ghana. The Tamberma speak Moré, the language of the Mossi.

TAMBO

The Tambo are a Southeast African people. They are concentrated in Malawi, Tanzania, and Zambia, notably west of Lake Malawi. Their neighbors include the Kamanga and Mba peoples.

TANAKA

A West African people. The Tanaka, also known as Tongba, are concentrated in Benin.

TANALA

The Tanala are a Southeast African people. They are concentrated on the Island of Madagascar. The Tanala live in the southwestern areas of the country, close to the Taimoro and Tombahoake peoples.

TANDROY

A Malagasy people. The Tandroy are concentrated in "the Androy", a semiarid land of thorny bush in south Madagascar. Their name is derived from this land. It means the people of the thorny bush. Groups of the Tandroy people, however, are also found on the East African coastal areas.

The Tandroy speak a dialect of the Malagasy language, and are considered one of the twenty-I've officially recognized ethnic groups in Madagascar. They form a composite ethnicity that comprises clans of diverse origins, including the Sakalava, Bara, Mahafale and Tanosy. The economic activities of the Tandroy people are based "upon a mixture of pastoralism and horticulture, supplemented by gathering."[415]

TANG

The Tang are a West Central African people. They are concentrated in the central regions of Cameroon. Their neighbors include the Adamaua, Bum, War, and Wiya peoples.

TANGA

The Tanga are a West Central African people. They live in the southwestern areas of Cameroon, neighboring the Banen, Fang, Limba, and Mungo peoples.

TANGALE

These are a West African people and one of Nigeria's ethnic minorities. They are concentrated in the northeastern regions of the country. Their neighbors include the Jen, Jukun, Longuda and Wurkum peoples. The Tangale speak a language that belongs to the Afro-Asiatic family of African languages.

TANGULE

The Tangule are one of the many ethnic groups of which Chad is composed. They are concentrated along the banks of the Chari and Logone rivers.

TANKARANA

The Tankarana are a Southeast African-Malagasy people. They are concentrated on the Island of Madagascar. The Tankarana live in the northern coastal areas of the country.

TANNEKWE

A southern African people. They are concentrated in Botswana. Their neighbors include the Tsaukwe, the Tserekwe, the Hukwe and the Galikwe peoples.

TANOSY

The Tanosy are a Malagasy East African Tandroy people. They are concentrated on the Island of Madagascar, notably in its southern semiarid regions. Groups of them, however, are found along the coastal areas of East Africa. The Tanosy speak a dialect of Malagasy and are closely related to other Tandroy groups, including the Bara, Mahafale, Sakalave, and Tandroy proper peoples.

TAPOSA

An Eastern Nilotic Sudanese people. The Taposa, also spelled Toposa, are concentrated in the equatorial regions of southern Sudan. Their neighbors include the Beir, Chara, Didinga, and Mazhi peoples.

TARA-BAAKA, see **BAKA**

TAROK, see **YERGAM**

TASSILI, see **TAUREG**

TATOGA, see **KALENJIN** and **TATURU**

TATURU

A Southeast African people. The Taturu, also known as Datog, Mangati and Tatoga, are concentrated in Tanzania.

TAU, see **PEDI**

TAUREG

The Taureg, also Targui, Touareg and Tuareg, are an Arab-Berber-speaking pastoralist people of West Africa. They live in a number of North and West African states primarily in Algeria, Burkina Faso, Chad, Libya, Mali, Mauritania, Niger and Senegal. They speak the Tomahaq (Tamaheq, Tamacheq) and dialects of the Arabic language. The Taureg are a Muslim people comprised of shifting confederations and alliances. In their turn, these are made up of many tribal and subtribal groups, the most important of which are the Adrar, Ahaggar (Hoggar, also Kel Ahagger), the Asben (Kel Aïr), the Aulliminden, the Azjer (Ajjer, also Kel Ajjer), the Ibotenaten, the Iforas, the Ifoghas, the Itesen (Kel Geres), the Kel Rela, the Kel Tademaket, the Tassili, the Tégéhé Mellet, and the Taitoq. Their total population is estimated at about 1.0 million.

Like other North African peoples, the Taureg are believed to be of Caucasoid origins. They migrated from the north in two waves: the one during the closing millennia of the Paleolithic period (which were marked by a wet phase in the Sahara), and the other in the period between approximately 5500 and 2500 B.C.[416] Subsequently, when the Sahara water supply receded, the Taureq decided not to leave the area. In time, they successfully adapted themselves to its new condition.[417] In addition, they also succeeded in exacting an important role in trans-Saharan trade.[418]

Evidence suggests that the Taureg were also involved in the trade of, among other things, the salt of the north with the gold, copper, spices, ivory and ostrich feathers of the south of the Sahara – a trade that was widespread since ancient times. Aside from their control of the Taghaza salt mines in the northern sector of the Sahara, evidence also suggests that they were the founders of Timbuktu about 1000 A.D. as a communication center in the caravan trade between the north and the south of Sahara regions and beyond. Subsequently, this outpost became the political, economic, social and educational capital of the Mali empire.[419]

The Taureg society continues to be highly structured, with nobles, religious notables, vassals, artisans and laborers representing its constituent parts. Despite this feature, it remains without an overall centralized authority. Each tribe continues to have its own paramount chief, or *amenokal*, who is selected from the noble clan with which it shares a common name. The Kel Rela, the Tégéhé Mellet and the Taitoq for example, are not only the names of Taureg tribes from which paramount chiefs are selected, but also the names of their respective noble clans.[420]

Presently, the Taureg are partly semi-nomadic herders and partly village-dwelling agriculturalists. Politically, they are divided between a number of states. In Niger, where they account for 8% of the population, they live in the regions of Azbine (Aïr), Azaouak, Imanan, and Tagazart. In Mali, together with the Moors, they account for 5% of the country's population. In Burkina Faso, where they are known as Bella, they constitute one of the country's important ethnic minorities.

TAVARA, see also SHONA

The Tavara are a Southern Bantu-speaking Shona group. They speak Shona, a tonal Bantu language, and are concentrated in the Zambezi

Valley in Mozambique and in the northeastern regions of Zimbabwe. Their neighbors include the Karanga, the Manyika, the Rozwi, the Shangaan and the Zezuru peoples.

TAVETA

The Taveta are an East African Bantu-speaking people. They are concentrated in the south central areas of Kenya. Groups of them, however, can also be found in Tanzania.

TAWANA, see also BATAWANA and TSWANA

The Tawana, also known as Batawana, are a Southwest African people. They are concentrated in Ngamiland, Botswana. The Tawana are an offshoot of the Ngwato, a Tswana subgroup.

TAWARA

The Tawara are a Southeast African people. They are concentrated in Zimbabwe. Groups of them, however, can also be found in Mozambique. Their neighbors in both countries include the Shona, Teve, and Zimba peoples.

TAZARAWA

A West African people. The Tazarawa are concentrated in Niger and speak a language that belongs to the Afro-Asiatic family of African languages. Their neighbors include the Adarawa, Hausa and Kanuri peoples.

TCHAMAN, see AKAN

TCHAMBA, see BASARI (Togo and Ghana)

TCHARIGIRIA

The Tcharigiria are one of the Chadian Kuri subgroups. They speak Yedina, a Buduma dialect. Like other Kuri groups, they live along the eastern shores of Lake Chad.

TCHERE, see **GUIZIGA**

TEBELE, see **BANTU** and **NDEBELE**

A Southern Bantu-speaking people. The Tebele are an Ngoni group. They are concentrated in the eastern parts of southern Africa.

TEBOU, see **TEDA**

TEBU, see also **TEDA**

These are an ancient people presumed to be originally from Tibesti. According to July, they are presumably the "Troglodyte Ethiopians" who, according to Herodotus, were often chased by the Garamantian people of Fezzan (now in modern Libya) in ancient times.[421] The Tebu may also be the ancestors of present-day Teda (Toubou) people of Chad.

TEDA

The Teda (pronounced Tedah), also known as Teda-too (Teda-tou), Tebou, Tebu, Tibbu, Tibou, Toda, Todaga, Todga, Toubou, Tubu, Tuda, Tudaga and Tudu, are presumably an Arab nomadic and semi-nomadic people of the states of Chad, Libya, Niger and Sudan. They are concentrated in the southeastern central Sahara, notably in the Tibesti Massif in northern Chad, and are known to frequent the Ténéré region of the Sahara which is renowned for its inhospitable, hot and sandy environment. Their total population is estimated at about 200,000. A great number of them live in the mountainous plateaus of the Tibesti and represent one of the major Chadian groups. Together with Arabs and Gourmantche, they account for 1.5% of Niger's total population. The Teda are predominantly Muslim and hence, apply Muslim *shari'a* in their personal and communal relations, as well as in their business transactions. Their name suggests that they originally came from Tibesti. It means, "man from Tibesti".

Depending on dialect spoken, the Teda are divided into two main groups: The Teda and the Dazaga. The Teda reside above the eighteenth parallel of the African continent and encompass four major groups: the Teda-Too,

Gourous, Arna and Mourdia. Their clans are almost totally nomadic and specialize in raising camels. The Dazaga encompass over fourteen major groups including: the Kreda, Daza, Charfarda, Kecherda, Djagada, Doza, Annakoza, Kaborda (Goboda), Kamadja, Noarma (Mormorea), Ounia, Gaeda and Erdiha. They generally live below the eighteenth parallel, are semi-nomadic and specialize in raising a variety of livestock, including cattle.

Broadly speaking, however, the "Teda of Tibesti are believed to be divided into some forty clans, and there are indications that these may be loosely organized into broader tribe-like groupings within some kind of unstable and ill-defined confederation."[422] Of these clans, the Tomaghera (or Tomagra), the Gunda, the Arna and Derdekishia are recognized as noble clans. Of the noble clans, the Tomaghera are presumed to have come from the Sudan and to have intermarried with Arabs.[423]

Due to their nomadic and semi-nomadic lifestyle, centralized authority really did not develop among the Toubou. However, each clan chooses a knowledgeable elder, or a *boui*, to oversee the proper application of both *shari'a* and customary laws, as well as to resolve conflicts between members of the clan. Conflicts between clans are normally resolved through arbitration during clan meetings or *cafonas*.

Formerly, the Teda "used to be great raiders, operating over a tremendous area that extended from the Nile Valley to the Niger Bend and from the heart of the eastern central desert southward far into the Sudan."[424] In addition, they "used to derive most of their revenue from a far-flung caravan trade of their own, from protection fees extracted by them from the caravans of others, and from raiding..."[425] These activities, however, were before their power was contained by the Ottoman authorities and their Sannusi allies in Libya, and subsequently by the French and Italian colonial administrations, during the nineteenth century. Currently, their nomadic ways are being restricted by state boundaries and administrative divisions, as well as by increased intrusions on their independence by the central Chadian, Libyan, Niger and Sudanese governments.

TEDA (Mauritania), see MOOR

TEDA-TEBOU, see TOUBOU

TEDA-TEBU, see TOUBOU

TEDA-TOO, see TEDA

TEÉSÉ, see LOBI-DAGARTI

TÉGÉHÉ MELLET, see TAUREG

TEGUÉ, see LOBI-DAGARTI

TEGUESSIÉ, see LOBI-DAGARTI

TEITA

The Teita are an East African people. They are concentrated in the southeastern areas of Kenya. Their neighbors include the Burungi, Digo, Isangi, Pare, Sambaa, and Segeju peoples.

TEKE

The Teke (Téké) people, also known as Bateke or Bateki, are one of Gabon's and Congo's ethnic minorities. Groups of them, however, are also found in the Democratic Republic of the Congo (Zaire) as well as in Chad. They are a Western Bantu-speaking people. Their language is Bateke.

The Teke people developed a kingdom of their own on and north of the Congo (now Zaire) River, known as the Kingdom of Anziku and also as the Kingdom of Teke and the Kingdom of Tyo. The kingdom had control over the lower Congo River, and moreover, it extended northwest to the upper KouilouNari basin. These two features enabled Anziku to establish control over trade with the hinterland, especially with the Kingdom of Loango. By 1600, this kingdom was a rival to the Kongo Kingdom, which was located south of the Congo River. Both kingdoms were involved in the slave trade.

In 1875 French explorer and colonialist Pierre Savorgnan de Brazza explored the Congo area. Five years later, he capped his explorations by the treaty of 1880 with the Bateke king, Makoko, which set the basis for France's claims to the Gabon hinterland as far as the site of Brazzaville. Three years later, he concluded a treaty with Makoko's successor, King Iloo, which placed Teke lands and people under French protection. Thereupon, the kingdom fell to French rule. In 1891, the French renamed the kingdom French Middle Congo.[426]

In 1905, Middle Congo became part of French Equatorial Africa, which also included Chad, Gabon and Ubangi-Chari (Central African Republic). The four territories reported to a governor-general at Brazzaville. In 1910, they were merged together to form the Federation of French Equatorial Africa. In 1958, the constituent territories of the Federation became fully autonomous states within the French Community. The Middle Congo was renamed the Republic of the Congo and on August 15, 1960, it acquired its independence from France.

Currently, the Teke people account for 17% of the Congo's total population and are concentrated in the central regions of the country. Moreover, they constitute the fourth largest tribal grouping in the Gabon after the Fang, the Eshira and the Bapounou. Furthermore, they represent an important ethnic minority in the Democratic Republic of Congo (Zaire).

TEKNA

The Tekna people are a West Saharan North African group. They are concentrated in the southwestern mountainous regions of Morocco, overseeing the Moroccan Atlantic coast.

TEM

These are a West African people and one of the ethnic minorities of Togo. They are concentrated in the northern parts of the country, especially in the eastern la Kara region. Their neighbors include the Atyuti, Basari, Basila, Dagomba, Kabre, Kilinga and Yoruba peoples. The Tem, also known as Cotocoli (Kotokoli) and Temba, are a Gur-speaking Voltaic people. They are predominantly engaged in farming and animal husbandry.

TEMBA, see TEM

TEMBE TONGA

The Tembe Tonga are a southern African Bantu-speaking people. They are concentrated in South Africa, Zimbabwe and Mozambique.

TEMBO

One of Southern Africa's peoples. The Tembo are a subgroup of the Abarue, a Shona people. They live in Zimbabwe and Mozambique.

TEMBU

The Tembu – also spelled Thembu – are a South African Bantu-speaking people. Their language is a dialect of Xhosa, a language of the Nguni group which is closely related to Zulu. Originally, they inhabited the Xhosa areas between the Fish and Keiskamma rivers, as well as the Keiskamma and Kei rivers. In 1857, they were uprooted from their lands in application of British Governor Harry Smith's decision to annex their lands to Cape Colony and the colony of British Kaffraria, respectively. Like other peoples, such as the Fingoes, Griquas, Pondos and Xhosa, they were later resettled north to Natal, in Transkei, which eventually became a major reserve for Africans in South Africa during the Apartheid era.[427] Currently, they inhabit the upper areas of the Mzimvubu River, which form part of Transkei in South Africa.

Traditionally, the Tembu people shared many of the cultural patterns of other Nguni-speaking groups.[428] Since the middle of the nineteenth century, however, they started to lose these patterns which formerly provided the bases of cohesiveness within their society and gave them a distinctive sense of identity[428]

Many factors had contributed to the destruction of their original cultural patterns, including: their uprooting from Tembuland, repeated European and non-European assaults against the people and the periods of starvation that they faced (especially after the cattle-killing episode of 1857, which occurred in response to a young girl's prophecy that foretold the end of the European presence in the area if the people killed their cattle and destroyed their foodstuffs). Other important factors also included: the introduction of British magistrates to their territory in 1857 (a measure that weakened the authority of their traditional chiefs), the activities of European missionaries which resulted in weakening their traditional values, raising doubts about their validity and inciting dissension within their society, as well as British tax laws which forced them to seek employment as wage laborers. Among others, all these factors have not only weakened the cultural patterns of the Tembu people, but also forced them to lose their prior self-reliance and eventually to join in "the [labor] migrations that have characterized the South African economy since the establishment of the gold mines in the Witwatersrand in 1886. The people living in the areas of Tembuland have thus become increasingly dependent upon remittances sent home by migrant [laborers] for their survival."[429]

TEMEN, see TEMNE

TEMNE

The Temne people, also known as Temen, Tene, Timanee, Timmannee and Timni, are one of the largest ethnic minorities of the Republic of Sierra Leone. They are concentrated in Sierra Leone's Northern Province, notably in the districts of Bombali, Kambia, Karene, Port Loko and Tonkolili. Their neighbors include the Bullom, Kuranko (Kooranko), Kono, Limba, Loko, Mende, Sherbro and Susu peoples. The Temne speak a language belonging to the West Atlantic branch of the Niger-Congo family of African languages. They comprise several groups, including the Ansasa.

The Temne society observes patrilineal lineages in matters of descent, inheritance and succession. Moreover, it supports secret male *(ragbene* and *poro)* and female *(bundu)* societies, the primary responsibilities of which are the socialization of members into the Temne's way of life, the protection of Temne's values and (in some southern groups) appointment of chiefs.

The Temne people are divided into numerous subgroups, each subgroup of which supports its own chiefdom and its own paramount chief. In their turn, chiefdoms are subdivided into sections composed of one or more villages. Traditionally, a village was governed by a headman who was a descendant of its founder. Now, however, this has changed. The position of headman is filled by an elected official.

Traditionally, the Temne chiefs carried both political and religious responsibilities. Now, however, their former roles have weakened and devolved into mere ceremonial functions.

Though Christianity and Islam have won many converts, the Temne people continue to be impacted by their traditional religion which is based on the belief in an omnipotent god, nature deities and ancestral spirits.

Currently, the Temne account for about 30% of Sierra Leone's total population, and are concentrated in the northern areas of the country. They are essentially farmers who engage in the production of such products as rice, peanuts, cotton, cassava and millet, as well as in animal husbandry.

TENDA

These are a West African people. The Tenda are concentrated in Mali and adjoining countries and speak a language that belongs to the West Atlantic branch of the Niger-Congo family of African languages. Their neighbors include the Dyalonke, Fula (Fulani) and Malinke peoples.

TENDE, see **KURIA**

TENE, see **TEMNE**

TENG'WAL, see also **NANDI** and **KALENJIN**

An East African Nandi people, a Kalenjin group. They are concentrated in Kenya and Uganda, and speak a dialect of Kalenjin, a Southern Nilotic language that belongs to the Eastern Sudanic family of African languages. The Teng'wal are semipastoralist people.

TENIK, see **KALENJIN**

TEPES, see TEPETH

TEPETH

The Tepeth, also known as Tepes, are a Central African people. They are concentrated in areas close to the southwest tip of Lake Rudolf in Uganda, notably in the Karamojong region. Their neighbors include the Karamojong, Suk, Rendille, and Turkana peoples.

TEPO

A West African Krou group. They are concentrated in the Ivory Coast. Their language belongs to the Kwa branch of the Niger-Congo family of African languages.

TERA

These are a West African people and one of Nigeria's ethnic minorities. They are concentrated in the northeastern regions of the country. Their neighbors include the Bolewa, Bura, Dera, Fula, Hona, Jukun, Kanuri, Longuda and Tangale peoples. The Tera speak a language that belongs to the Afro-Asiatic family of African languages.

TERIK, see also KALENJIN

An East African Kalenjin group. The Terik are concentrated in Kenya and Uganda, and speak a dialect of Kalenjin, a Southern Nilotic language that belongs to the Eastern Sudanic family of African languages. They comprise several groups, including the Tiriki and Tugen. The Terik are semipastoralist people.

TEROA, see SAHO

TESO, see ITESO

TETELA, see also MONGO

The Tetela people are a group of the Mongo cluster of Bantu-speaking peoples who live in the equatorial forest area of Democratic Republic of the Congo (Zaire), south of the Congo River and north of the Kasai and Sankuru rivers. They speak a language that belongs to the Benue-Congo branch of the Niger-Congo family of African languages. Other peoples who belong to their cluster include the Bolia, Bokoto, Bongandu, Boyela, Ekonda, Mbole, Ndengese, Nkutu, Ntomba, Sengele, Songomeno and Tetela-Kusu. The economic activities of the Tetela focus on agriculture, food gathering, hunting, fishing and trading.

In the 1860's, the Tetela's chieftaincy in the area of the Lualaba and Lomani rivers fell to the acclaimed Tippu Tib, who embarked on consolidating and expanding his power. In the 1860's he staged a series of campaigns in the Bemba and Lungu lands, using armed retainers.[430] These campaigns culminated in defeating Nsama, chief of the Tabwa people. Later, he claimed and assumed a chieftaincy among the Tetela people and in 1875, he established his seat in Kasongo and reigned as a paramount chief.[431] By 1883, he expanded his territory as far as Stanley Falls, (which were under the control of the International Association of the Congo, and hence part of the Congo Independent State). [432]

In 1890, Tippu left Kasongo to visit Zanzibar but never to return. A few years later, the lands over which he ruled fell to the Congo Independent State and a few years later (1905) were incorporated in this state. In 1905, Tippu died in Zanzibar.

Like other Mongo peoples, the Tetela support a patrilineal and patriarchal society composed of numerous villages, each village of which is grouped on lineages traced back to single ancestors and ruled independently by a village council made up of lineage heads.

TETELA-KUSU, see MONGO

TEUSO

The Teuso are a Central African people. They are concentrated in the northeastern regions of Uganda.

TEVE, see TIV and IK

TEWI

The Tewi people are a West African ethnic group. They are concentrated in Liberia, primarily in its south central areas. Groups of them can also be found in the Ivory Coast. Their neighbors include the Bakwe, Grebo, Kran, and Ngere peoples.

THARAKA

The Tharaka are an East African Bantu-speaking people. They are concentrated in the south central regions of Kenya. Their neighbors include the Hawiyah, Meru, and Ogadein peoples.

THEMBU, see TEMBU

THIANG, see NUER

THIMSAMAN, see also BERBER

The Thimsaman are a Moroccan Rifian Berber group. They are concentrated in the northern Rif region of Morocco, notably in El Hoceima, Nador and Taza provinces of the country.

THIUR, see NUER

THWENE, see PEDI

TIAMUS, see MASAI

TIBBU, see TEDA

TIDDI, see MEIDOB

TIENGA

A West African people. The Tienga are concentrated in Benin, Niger and Nigeria. Their neighbors include the Busa, Dendi, Fula, and Zerma (Zarma) peoples. They speak a language that belongs to the Mande branch of the Niger-Congo family of African languages.

TIGAR

The Tigar, also spelled Tikar, are a West and West Central African people. They are one of the many Pygmy people of equatorial Africa. Originally, they inhabited the tropical rain forest, in what is now within the Republic of Congo. Subsequently, they moved to other areas. Of these groups, the Tigar eventually settled in the western areas of Cameroon. They are essentially hunters, foragers and potters.

TIGRAY, see TIGRE

TIGRE

The Tigre, also known as northern Tigray, are peoples of distinct backgrounds living in northern portions of the Ethiopian Plateau, Eritrea and The Sudan. They are a mixture of South Arabian peoples and local African Cushite-speaking stock. The Tigre represent one of the largest ethnic groups in both Ethiopia and Eritrea. In Ethiopia, they are highly concentrated in the provinces of Tigray, Gonder and Welo. In Eritrea, they live in the southern highland areas of the country. In Sudan, they are located in the southeastern regions. The Tigre speak Tigreñña (Tigré, Tigrinya), a Semitic language, which is related to Tigrinya (Tigrai), the language of the southern Tigre, as well as of the Amharic. Their language is closely related to the ancient liturgical Ge'ez language and its modern version Tigrinya.

Historical evidence suggests that the Tigre "have been in their present location since before the time of Christ and began converting to Christianity in the fourth century."[433] Also, it suggests that they may have originally migrated to their present areas from the Arabian peninsula.

The Tigre have a similar political organization as the Amhara. For centuries, both groups have enjoyed a favorable political status in Ethiopia. Together with the Amhara people with whom they intermarried and mixed, they share an "imperial" legacy. Both peoples are regarded the "coinheritors" of the Aksumite Kingdom. This kingdom, which subsequently became the Ethiopian Empire, had its seat (Mekelle/Maqelle) in Tigre territory. More importantly, both "Tigray as well as Amhara were eligible for the emperorship, the last [Tigre] emperor being Yohannes [IV] (1872-1889)."[434]

The Tigre are comprised of a number of federations, the most important of which are Beni Amer, Bet-Asgade, Maria and Mensa. Their society is primarily patrilineal. These kingroups are the primary social organization. Their most important function is the allocation of arable land. They also prescribe barriers to marriage by forming degrees of status for each clan.

The Tigre people are essentially agriculturalists. Some of them, however, engage in miscellaneous commercial pursuits, including trading activities.

Religiously, some Tigre are Muslim while others are Christian or animist. This difference in religious affiliation, however, has not been a cause of any serious friction in the Tigrean society.

TIGRAYAN, see **TIGRE**

TIKAR, see **TIGAR**

TIKURIMI, see **KURAMA**

TIMANAMBONDRO

The Timanambondro are a Southeast African people. They are concentrated on the Island of Madagascar, primarily along its southeastern coastal areas. Their neighbors include the Taisaka and Tanosy peoples.

TIMBARO

An East African people. The Timbaro are concentrated in Ethiopia.

TIMANEE, see **TEMNE**

TIMMANNEE, see **TEMNE**

TIMN, see KOTOKOLI

TIMNI, see TEMNE

TIO

A South Central African people. The Tio are concentrated in the southern regions of the Republic of Congo and the southwestern regions of the Democratic Republic of the Congo (Zaire). They live along the southern banks of the Zaire river.

TIRIKI, see also LUHYA, TERIK and KALENJIN

The Tiriki are an East African Tirik people, a Kalenjin group. They are concentrated in Kenya and Uganda, notably in western Kenya. The Tiriki speak a dialect of Kalenjin, a Southern Nilotic language that belongs to the Eastern Sudanic family of African languages. They are semipastoralist people.

TIRIS

The Tiris are a West African people. They are highly concentrated in Mali and neighboring countries.

TIRMA, see also SURI

The Tirma are a Surmic (formerly Surma)-speaking East African pastoralist people. They are a Suri group and live in the southern regions of Ethiopia and Sudan.

TIV

The Tiv (Teve), also known (in Hausa) as Munchi or Munshi, are one of Nigeria's large ethnic minorities. They constitute the sixth largest group after the Hausa, Fulani, Yoruba, Ibo and Kanuri. They live in northwestern Nigeria along the Benue River and are concentrated in the states of Benue and Gongala. Their neighbors include the Angas, Arago, Boki, Idoma, Igede, Iyala and Jukun peoples. The Tiv language, Tiv, is a semi-Bantu language belonging to the Benue-Congo branch of the Niger-Congo family of African languages.

Originally, the Tiv people had no chiefs and supported a highly decentralized society. Their society was completely unstructured and more importantly, highly egalitarian. Additionally, their affairs were conducted by elderly leaders who were descendants of their common ancestor. In their society, consensus, "rather than binding authority, was the means for dispute settlement."[435] Furthermore, they had "no significant offices of a political and jural nature above the minimal *tar*, or lineage group, and the *jir*, or court."[436] In 1948, the British colonial administration tried to rectify this problem by establishing a position of paramount chief to facilitate the representation of the Tiv people as a group.

The Tiv people are essentially hunters and farmers, mainly relying on cash crops. They support kinship relations that are based on patrilineal lineages. Their population is estimated at over 2 million people.

TJIMBA, see HAUSA

TOF, see KULERE

TOJIMA, see KURA

TLHAPING

The Tlhaping are a southern African people. They are concentrated in the central areas of the Republic of South Africa.

TLHARA

The Tlhara are a Southern African people. They are concentrated in the Republic of South Africa, primarily in its central regions. Their neighbors include the Korona, Tlhaping, and Xam peoples.

TODA, see TEDA

TODAGA, see TEDA

TOGBO, see **BANDA**

TOGUESSIÉ, see **LOBI-DAGARTI**

TOKA, see **TONGA**

TOKA-LEYA, see **TONGA**

TOMA, see also **MANDE**

The Toma, also known as Buzi and Loma, are a Mande people. They are located in Liberia, as well as in a number of other West African states.

TOMAGHERA, see also **TEDA**

The Tomaghera, also spelled Tomagra, are a Central African Teda people. They are concentrated in the northern regions of Chad. The Tomaghera are a pastoralist and semi-pastoralist people.

TOMAGRA, see **TEDA**

TOMBO, see **DOGON**

TOMMO, see **DOGON**

TONGA

The Tonga are a Bantu-speaking people. Their language, ciTonga, is a Central Bantu language. They are highly concentrated in Malawi, Zambia and Zimbabwe. In Zambia, they are concentrated in the Southern Province. In Zimbabwe, they live in the eastern regions of the country. Based on the administrative districts in which they live in Zambia, they are divided into three main groups: the Toka (or Toka-Leya), Plateau Tonga, and Gewmbe Tonga. They are settled agriculturalists, living in scattered villages.

Historical evidence suggests that together with the Lenge people, the Tonga had developed an important kingdom in the past, the territory of which "stretched from the Zambezi River north to the Lukanga Swamp of the Kafue River and from the contemporary Western Province (formerly Barotseland) to a great distance eastward."[437]

The Tonga are among the African people who welcomed missionary assistance to their areas as a means to neutralize the victimization by the Mombera (Ngoni).[438]

Prior to their colonization by the British, the Tonga were organized into matrilineally-based clans without leaders or politically defined posts. To ensure effective control over the Tonga, the British colonial administration appointed village chiefs, and subsequently, developed for them a hierarchy of chiefs.

Currently, the Tonga constitute Zambia's second largest ethnic group. They account, together with related Tonga-speaking peoples, for about 16% of the country's total population. In Zimbabwe, they account for about 2% of the total population.

TONGA-KOREKORE, see also SHONA

The Tonga-Korekore are a southern African Bantu-speaking Shona group. They speak Shona, a tonal Bantu language. The Tonga-Korekore are concentrated in the northern regions of Zimbabwe. Their neighbors include the Karanga, the Manyika, the Rozwi, the Shangaan and the Zezuru peoples.

TONGAS

The Tongas people are descendants of servicais born in Sâo Tome and Principe. They constitute the fifth largest ethnic group after the Metiço, the Angolares, the Forros and the Servicais.

TONGBA, see TANAKA

TONGBO, see MAMBILA

TONGWE

The Tongwe are a Southeast African people. They are concentrated in the northwestern areas of Tanzania.

TOPOSA

A Central and East African Nilotic-speaking nomadic people. The Toposa, also known as Abo, Akeroa, Huma, Kare and Topoza are concentrated in Chad, Central African Republic, Ethiopia, Sudan, Uganda and Zaire. The Toposa are related to the Iteso, Jie, Jiye, Topoza, Nyangatom and Turkana peoples.

TOPOZA, see TOPOSA

TORO, see also DOGON

The Toro, also known as Batoro, are one of Uganda's ethnic minorities. They are concentrated in the southwestern regions of the country between Lake Albert and Lake Edward. Groups of them, however, are also located in the Congo and neighboring countries. The Toro are a Bantu-speaking people. Their neighbors include the Ganda, the Nkole and the Nyoro peoples. The social and political structures of the Toro society are centralized in nature. Traditionally, they were governed by Toro royal families. Currently, the Toro are essentially an agricultural people.

TOROBBO, see OKIEK

TOROOBE, see FULANI

TOTELA

The Totela are a Bantu-speaking people. They are concentrated in Zambia, where they represent one of its ethnic minorities. The Totela live in the southern regions of the country. Their neighbors include the Kwandi, Kwangwa, Lumbu, Shanjo, and Subya peoples.

TOUAREG, see TUAREG

TOUBAURI

The Toubauri are a Chadian sedentary people. They speak the Chadian dialect of Toubauri. Their economic activities center on farming and cattle-raising and currently they represent about 3% of Chad's total population. The political life of the Toubauri is dominated by a theocracy ruled by a high chief, *avandoulou*, who oversees the management of their political and religious affairs.

TOUBOU, see TEDA

TOUBOURI

A West and West Central African people. The Toubouri are concentrated in the northeastern regions of Cameroon.

TOUCOULEUR

The Toucouleur, also Tukulor, Tukolor and Turkylor, are a West African Muslim people. Their name is a perversion of the name of their former kingdom of Tekrur. Their largest concentration is in Sénégal, where they constitute the fourth largest of the country's seven major ethnic groups. They account for about 9% of the country's total population and live primarily in the Sénégal River Valley.

Minorities of Toucouleur people are also found in states adjacent to Sénégal, especially Mali and Mauritania. In Mauritania, they are concentrated in the Sénégal River Valley.

The people are akin to the Serer and the Wolof and were highly influenced by the Fulani. They speak a Fulani language, called Fulfulde (also known as Fulah, Peul and Poular), which belongs to the West Atlantic branch of the Niger-Congo family of African languages.

The Toucouleur established the kingdom of Tekrur in the 10th century. In the 11th century they embraced Islam. Their kingdom developed into an empire under al-Hajj 'Umar (1795-1864), who launched a *jihad,* holy war, subduing the Bambara chiefdoms, the Bambara kingdom of Kaarta, Macina and subsequently Timbuktu. In 1864, al-Hajj 'Umar was succeeded by his son, Ahmadu Seku, who continued resistance to French attempts that aimed at penetrating Tekrur's domain and at rallying the support of rival neighbors. In 1890, the French staged an invasion against Tekrur, and by 1893, managed to control it and eventually incorporate it into French overseas territory. As a consequence to the French occupation, many of the Toucouleur people migrated to Mali.

TOURA, see also **TURA**

TOUYO

A West African Krou group. They are concentrated in the Ivory Coast and speak a language that belongs to the Kwa branch of the Niger-Congo family of African languages.

TOZUI, see **LOZI**

TRANSVAAL SOTHO, see also **SOTHO**

The Transvaal Sotho, also called Northern, represent one of the three Sotho major groups. The other two are Western (or Tswana), and Southern (or Basuto, Lesotho) Sotho. Like other Sotho people, they occupy the high grasslands of southern Africa and speak Sesotho, a Bantu language.

The great majority of Northern Sotho engage in agriculture, relying both on cultivation and animal husbandry. But males among them often seek work as laborers. Their settlements are characterized "by scattered hamlets of circular huts with mud and wattle or stone walls surmounted by a conical, thatched roof."[439] In their social patterns, most Sotho recognize patrilineal lineages, and traditionally, they allowed polygamy.

TREKKERS, see **AFRIKANERS**

TREPO

A West African Krou group. They are concentrated in the Ivory Coast. Their language belongs to the Kwa branch of the Niger-Congo family of

African languages.

TRIBU, see TRIBUOE

TRIBUOE

A West African Krou group. The Tribuoe, also spelled Tribu, are concentrated in the Ivory Coast. Their neighbors include the Adele, Akpose, Ana, Kebu, Kranchi, Lefana and Yoruba peoples. Their language belongs to the Kwa branch of the Niger-Congo family of African languages.

TSAUKWE

The Tsaukwe are a southern African people. They are concentrated in Botswana. Their neighbors include the Tannekwe, the Tserekwe, the Hukwe and the Galikwe peoples.

TSEREKWE

The Tserekwe are a Southern African people. They are concentrated in Botswana. Their neighbors include the Tannekwe, the Tsaukwe, the Hukwe and the Galikwe peoples.

TSHIDI, see also TSWANA

The Tshidi are a South African Tswana group. They are a Bantu-speaking people and share the historical and cultural heritages of other Tswana groups. The Tshidi are concentrated in Botswana.

TSHU-KWE

A Southern African San subgroup. The Tshu-Kwe are concentrated in central Botswana. They are divided into several groups the major ones of which include the G//ana, G/wi, Khute, and Kua peoples.

TSIMIHETY, see also MALAGASY

These are a Malagasy seminomadic mountainous people. They live in the central northeastern areas of Madagascar, constituting one of the country's ethnic groups. The Tsimihety people are of mixed African, Malayo-Indonesian and Arab ancestry. They speak a dialect of Malagasy, the Austronesian West Indonesian language, which is common to all Malagasy peoples. In the 1820s, they fell to the native Merina Kingdom and at the turn of the century to French rule. Currently, they are part of independent Madagascar, accounting for about 4% of its total population. Though Christianity has won converts, the great majority of the Tsimihety continue to cherish their traditional religion which rests on the belief in a Supreme Being, Andriamanitra, who oversees a spiritual world made up of ancestral spirits.

TSONGA

The Tsonga, also spelled Thonga, are a South African Bantu-speaking people. They are concentrated in Gazankulu, a non-independent black homeland in the Republic of South Africa, as well as in the southern coastal areas of Mozambique and in parts of Swaziland and Zimbabwe. Their total population is estimated at over 3.2 million. In Gazankulu, they, together with the Shangaan people, support a population of over 0.7 million, growing at the rate of 4.0% per year.

The Tsonga were the original inhabitants of what presently constitutes Gazankulu. They were joined by the Shangaan people of Mozambique when the Shangaan's kingdom (Gaza) fell to the Portuguese in 1898.

TSOTO, see LUHYA

TSWA

The Tswa are a West Central African ethnic group. They are concentrated in the Democratic Republic of the Congo (Zaire) and the Republic of Congo. Their neighbors include the Nbombe and Ngbaka peoples.

TSWANA

The Tswana, or Batswana (formerly Bechuana), are a South African agro-pastoralist people. They are an independent subgroup of the Sotho and are concentrated in the states of Botswana ("land of the Tswana"), South Africa and Namibia. Their language, Setswana, is closely related to western Sotho. They are highly concentrated in Botswana where they constitute about 95% of the total population, and in South Africa, notably in Bophuthatswana. In Namibia, they constitute one of the country's small ethnic minorities. The Tswana comprise a number of groups, the most important of which include the Bahurutshe, Bakaa, Bakgatla, Bakwena, Bamelete, Bangwaketse, Bangwato, Barolong, Barolong Sekela (Sekele), Barolong Tshidi, Batawana, Batlhaping, Batlharo and Batlokwa.

The Tswana settled in Botswana and Bophuthatswana (in South Africa) around 1600. There, they established powerful chiefdoms based on four classes: the "royals *(dikgosana)*, commoners *(badintlha)*, immigrants absorbed into the tribe *(bafaladi)*, and non-Batswana clients *(bolata)*."[440] In the nineteenth century, these chiefdoms suffered from war launched against them by Shaka, the founder of the Zulu empire, as well as from famine (between 1822 and 1837). In 1837, they fell to the Boer states.

In 1884, the territory of what presently constitutes Botswana became the British Bechuanaland Protectorate. It continued to be ruled by the British until September 30, 1966, at which time it was granted independence as Republic of Botswana. However, the territory of what until recently constituted Bophuthatswana homeland became part of South Africa. In the 1960s, South Africa designated Bophuthatswana as a Tswana "homeland", and in December 1977, proclaimed it as an independent republic. Following major constitutional developments, Bophuthatswana lost its status as a black homeland and became an integral part of South Africa.

Division of labor in Tswana's traditional society is extremely strict. Men are mainly responsible for the livestock and hunting, whereas women are mainly responsible for most farm labor and domestic responsibilities. Though Christianity has won converts, many Tswana continue to cherish their traditional religion which is based on the belief in a Supreme Being, Badimo, and the exaltation of ancestral spirits. They also allow the practice of polygamy.

TUAREG, see **TAUREG**

TUBU, see **TEDA**

TUDA, see **TEDA**

TUDAGA, see **TEDA**

TUDU, see **TEDA**

TUESO, see **IK**

TUGEN, see also **KALENJIN**

The Tugen are an East African people. They are concentrated in Kenya's west central borders with Uganda north of Lake Victoria. Their neighbors include the Kikuyu, the Luhya and the Luo peoples. The Tugen are a Kalenjin subgroup.

TUKKONGO

The Tukkongo people are a West and South Central African ethnic group. They are concentrated in the Democratic Republic of the Congo (Zaire) and Zambia.

TUKOLOR, see **TOUCOULEUR**

TUKU

The Tuku, also Batuku, are a Central and East African people. They are concentrated in southeastern Tanzania, notably in the vicinity of Rufiji River. Their neighbors include the Gogo, Mbunga, Ndereko, and Rufiji peoples.

TUKULOR, see **TOUCOULEUR**

TUKYLOR, see **TOUCOULEUR**

TULAMA, see **OROMO**

TUMAK

The Tumak people are one of the ethnic groups of the Republic of Chad. They are concentrated in the Goundi area.

TUMBATU, see also **SHIRAZI**

These are one of Tanzania's ethnic groups. The Tumbatu are a Bantu-speaking people and one of the Shirazi subgroups. They are concentrated in the island of Zanzibar.

TUMBOKA, see **TUMBUKO**

TUMBUKA, see **TUMBUKO**

TUMBUKO

The Tumbuko, also known as Henga, Kamanga, Tumboka and Tumbuka, are a Bantu-speaking people living primarily in Malawi and Zambia. The people are an admixture of peoples of different origins, including the Ngoni. They speak Tumbuka.

In 1879, Scottish Presbyterian missionaries established the Livingstonia Mission in their territory, which made possible the spread of education among the Tumbuko. In the early 20th century, they were subjected to British colonial rule. In the 1940s, Tumbuka-speaking nationalist leaders, including Levi Mumba and Charles Chinula, formed the Nyasaland African Congress, whose struggle paved the way for Malawi's and Zambia's independence in 1964. Currently, the Tumbuko constitute Malawi's third largest ethnic group after the Chewa and the Nyanja.

TUMBWE

The Tumbwe are a West Central African ethnic group. They are concentrated in the southeastern areas of the Democratic Republic of the Congo (Zaire), notably west of Lake Tanganyika. Their neighbors include the Holoholo and Lomami peoples.

TUNGUR, see TUNJUR

TUNJUR

The Tunjur, also spelled Tungur, are one of the ethnic groups of the Republic of Chad. Their language belongs to the Saharan group of languages and are concentrated in the Lake Chad region. They are sedentary settled farmers of Arabic origin. The Tunjur are predominantly Muslim.

TURA

The Tura, also spelled Toura, are one of West Africa's ethnic groups. They are concentrated in Guinea and the Ivory Coast. The Tura are a Manding group.

TURKANA

The Turkana, or Ngiturkan as they call themselves, are an East African Nilotic-speaking people. They speak a Teso language that belongs to the Ateker Group of the Eastern Nilotic family of African languages which was formerly known as the "Karamojong Cluster," "Central Paranilotes," or the "Iteso-Turkana Group." In addition to Turkana, the Ateker Group includes the Dodoth, Donyiro (Ngiyengatom), Iteso, Jiye, Karamojong, Ngijie and Taposa languages.[441] The Turkana are concentrated in the equatorial regions of southern Sudan, as well as in northwestern Kenya, where they live in an arid, sandy desert area stretching from Lake Rudolf (Lake Turkana) to Uganda's borders. They refer to their land as Eturkan. Presently, they constitute one of Kenya's 11 largest ethnic groups.

The Turkana are divided into two major groups: the Ngimonia and the Ngichoro. In their turn, these two groups are divided into territorial subgroups. The Ngimonia subgroups include: the Nganyagatauk, Ngatunyo, Ngibocheros, Ngijie, Ngikajik, Ngikuniye, Ngikwatela, Ngimamong, Ngimazuk, Ngiseto, Ngisonyoka, Ngissir, Ngissiger and Ngiyapakuno. Those of the Ngichuro include: Ngibelai, Ngibotok,

Ngigamatak, Ngilukumong and Ngiwoyakwara.[442]

Originally, the Turkana lived in northeastern Uganda. Late in the eighteenth century, however, they migrated to their present location. They are closely related to the Ugandan Jie and Karamojong peoples.

Polygamy is recognized and widely practiced by the Turkana, and moreover, the extended family is their basic unit of social organization. "[A] father, his wives, and their sons and wives [normally] live together or in adjacent homesteads."[443]

The Turkana society is divided into different age groups, but leadership is recognized as a prerogative of the oldest individual in an extended family.

The Turkana are a semi-pastoralist people. Their economic activities focus on animal husbandry, fishing, seasonal farming and woodcrafts. They are renowned for their past resistance to repeated British attempts to penetrate their territory. It was not until the Second World War that they fell to British rule.

TURO, see **KONSO**

TUSSI, see **TUTSI**

TUSYAN

A West African Voltaic-speaking people. The Tusyan are concentrated in northern Ivory Coast, as well as in adjoining countries. Their neighbors include the Bobo, Diam, Dorossié, Guin, Karaboro, Minianka, Sia and Wara peoples.

TUTA, see also **NGONI** and **JERE**

The Tuta are a subgroup of the Ngoni nation. The death of Zwangendaba, the leader of the Ngoni nation, became the symbol of its unity. At Mapupo (about 1848), a successional conflict prompted them to move northward along the eastern side of Lake Tanganyika. There they captured and assimilated the Nyamwezi people of south Lake Victoria, and established their own kingdom. Eventually, the Tuta kingdom disappeared under pressure from European conquest of their territory in the later part of the nineteenth century.

TUTSI

The Tutsi people, known also as Batusi, Batutsi, Tussi, Watusi, Watousi and Watutsi, are one of East Africa's ethnic groups. Their original and correct name is Abatutsi. They are related to the Galla (Oromo) people of Ethiopia and are of Nilotic stock. The Tutsi are descendants of Cushitic-speaking herdsmen, and are essentially cattle raisers and pastoralists.

The Tutsi people, which are estimated at over .5 million, are divided between the states of Burundi, Rwanda and Democratic Republic of the Congo (Zaire). They account for 14% and 9% of Burundi's and Rwanda's total populations, respectively. In Zaire, they are concentrated in the Kivu region.

Between the 14th and 18th century, they migrated from the Nile Valley, or Ethiopia, to what presently constitutes Burundi and Rwanda, and settled among the Hutu people, adopting their Bantu languages of Rwanda and Rundi. Through a system of forced cooperation called *ubuhake*, they gradually subdued the Hutu, establishing themselves as the ruling aristocracy with a king, *mwami*, that was considered to be of divine origin. The Hutu were given cattle and protection by the Tutsi in exchange for labor. The Tutsi still owned the cattle and collected taxes from the Hutu for the *mwami*. This unequal relationship has resulted in Hutu-Tutsi animosity that thrives to this day. The Tutsi continued their expansion until they fell to European colonialism in the late 19th century.

The Tutsi retained their control over the Hutu in Rwanda until 1961, when Rwanda's Tutsi royalty was overthrown. However, in 1996, the Tutsi were able to retrieve their control over Rwanda. In Burundi, the Tutsi are still in control, facing periodic attempts by the Hutu to end their rule.

The Tutsi maintain an extremely strict class structure that permeates the lives of Tutsi neighbors, like the Hutu and Twa. The family is the main component of these nations' lives. Villages are divided among extended families called *inzu*. These units are patrilineal and contain very strong bonds.

Bridewealth is practiced in Tutsi society with cattle as the prime commodity. Males are responsible for teaching younger males their place and responsibilities in society, while females are responsible for teaching younger females their responsibilities. Overall instruction is given at Western-style schools.

In the past, the Tutsi were governed by a theocracy, which was ruled by the *mwami*, a person who was believed to be a vassal of God. The *mwami* was aided by lesser chiefs who settled local problems and collected taxes. His divine power gave credence to the aggressive nature of the Tutsi military, who conquered all they could in the name of God. Today, the *mwami* is mainly a figurehead, but many Tutsi males still belong to ancient warrior units. Today, with the modernized Hutu destroying vestiges of the old Tutsi system in Rwanda, the Tutsis have periodically been involved in extremely violent clashes that have killed thousands.

Tutsi men have contributed heavily to Tutsi oral tradition with their brilliant speech making and vibrant storytelling. Tutsi women are known for making fabulous jewelry and headdresses, along with woven artwork. Tutsi religion is Christian mixed with traditional Bantu beliefs.

TWA (Pygmoid), see also PYGMY

The Twa, also known as Batwa and Gwa, are one of the many Pygmy people of equatorial Africa. Originally, they inhabited the tropical rain forest in what is now within the Republic of Congo. Subsequently, they moved to other areas including the areas surrounding lake Kivu in Burundi, Rwanda and Democratic Republic of the Congo (Zaire). Currently, the Rwanda and Burundi Twa live in the western regions of both countries, whereas those of Zaire, known as Ntomba Twa and Kasai Twa, live in the vicinity of Lake Tumba as well as in the forest-wet savanna areas of the central and southern areas of the country, respectively. The Twa are essentially hunters, foragers and potters.

TWILENGE-HUMBI

The Twilenge-Humbi people are a Southwest African Bantu-speaking people. They are concentrated in Angola, notably in its northwestern regions. Their neighbors include the !Kung, Mwila, Ngambwe, Vatwa, and Zimba peoples.

TYAPI, see LANDUMAN

TYAVIKWA

The Tyavikwa are a Southwest African Bantu-speaking people. Their main concentrations are in south central Angola and north central Namibia. Their neighbors include the Kwamatwi, Kwankhala, Ongona, and Twa peoples.

TYILENGE-MUSO

The Tyilenge-Muso people are a Southwest African Bantu-speaking people. They live in Angola, primarily in its north western areas. Their neighbors include the Hanya, Twilenge-Humbi, and Vatwa peoples.

TYOKWE

The Tyokwe are a Southwest African people. They are concentrated in Angola, especially in its eastern central regions. Their neighbors include the Kafima, Ngangela, Nyemba, and Sekele peoples.

UALAMO, see WOLAYTA

UASINKISHU, see MASAI

UBA, see WOLAYTA

UBANGI

These are one of Congo's and Democratic Republic of the Congo's (Zaire's) ethnic minorities. They are divided into numerous groups, the most important of which are the Bonga, Kouyou, Likouala, Makoua, Mboshi and Ngala.

UDAM

The Udam are a West and Central African people. They are concentrated in Nigeria's east central border with Cameroon. Their neighbors include the Agoi and Chamba peoples.

UDUK

The Uduk, also known as Burun, Korara, Kwanim Pa and Othan, are an East African people. They are concentrated in the border mountain areas between Ethiopia and Sudan. The Uduk speak a Nilo-Saharan language.

UFIA

The Ufia people are a West African Bantu-speaking people. They speak a language belonging to the Benue-Congo branch of the Niger-Congo family of African languages and are related by language to the Ekoi people of southeastern Nigeria and western Cameroon.

UGUN, see ISHAN

UKELE, see KUKELE

UKONONGO

The Ukonongo are an East African people. They are concentrated in the west central areas of Tanzania, primarily north of Lake Rukwa and east of Lake Tanganyika. Their neighbors include the Bende, Kimbu, Nyammezi and Tongwe peoples.

ULAD YIHYA

These are a West Saharan North African people. They are called after one of their founding ancestors, Yihya. The word *ulad* in Arabic means sons and daughters or offsprings of, pointing to Yihya. Ulad Yihya are concentrated in the mountainous regions along the Algerian-Moroccan borders.

UMBUNDU, see OVIMBUNDU

UNGA

The Unga are a West Central African Bantu-speaking ethnic group. They are concentrated in the Democratic Republic of the Congo (Zaire) and Zambia, notably on the southern shores of Lake Bangwedu. Their neighbors include the Bisa, Bwile, and Kuba peoples.

UPIE

A West African people. They are concentrated in central Nigeria. The Upie are one of the groups in the Mama cluster of peoples.

UPILA

The Upila are a West African Edo people. They constitute one of Nigeria's ethnic groups. The Upila are concentrated in the central regions of the country to the west of the Niger River. Their neighbors include the Igbira and Nukuruku peoples.

URAREN

The Uraren are a West Saharan Taureg people. Their main concentrations are in Algeria and Niger.

URHOBO

The Urhobo are a West African people. They are highly concentrated in the northwestern areas of the Niger Delta and represent one of Nigeria's small ethnic groups. The Urhobo speak a language belonging to the Kwa branch of the Niger-Congo family of African languages.

Like their neighbors the Itsekiri, the Urhobo people are essentially in the fishing, trading and farming businesses. Relations between the two peoples were characterized by rivalry and at times (as in the 1950s) by violent conflicts.

The Urhobo people live in villages and towns with extended families being their constituent units. Their society recognizes patrilineal lineages in matters of descent, succession and inheritance.

Christianity has won converts among them, but a great majority of the Urhobo continue to be impacted by their religion, which is based on both the belief in a Supreme Creator called *Oghene,* and ancestral spirits and powers.

Like many West African people, the Urhobo are skilled artists. They are renowned for their "sacred mud sculptures, masks, figures, bronze jewelry, and their stilt and masquerade dances."[444]

URHU, see ISHAN

USHI

The Ushi are a Southeast African Bantu-speaking people. They are concentrated in Zambia.

USUKUMA

The Usukuma are an East African people. They are concentrated in the north central areas of Tanzania, primarily south of Lake Victoria. Their neighbors include the Iramba, Nyaturu, and Sumbwa peoples.

UYO, see IBIBIO

VAGALA

A West African people. The Vagala are concentrated in northwestern Ghana and speak a language that belongs to the Voltaic branch of the Niger-Congo family of African languages. Their neighbors include the Guang, Kulango and Likpe peoples.

VAI, see also **MANDE**

The Vai, also known as Vei and Gallinas, are a Mande forest group. They are located in Liberia, Sierra Leone, and other West African states. The appellation "Gallinas", meaning chickens, was given to them by early Portuguese writers. They speak a Mande language of the Niger-Congo family of African languages and are predominantly Muslim. Historically and culturally, they are related to the Mandingo people. Their neighbors include the Bassa, Gola, Mende and Sherbro peoples.

VAKALANGA, see **KALANGA**

VAKARANGA, see **KARANGA**

VALE

The Vale people are a Southwest African people. Their main concentrations are in south central Angola and north central Namibia. Their neighbors include the Onengo and Tyavikwa peoples.

VALUNKA

The Valunka are a West African people. They are concentrated in Sierra Leone and adjoining countries. Their neighbors include the Bullom peoples.

VATWA

The Vatwa people are a Southwest African people. They are concentrated in Angola, primarily in its northeastern regions. Their neighbors include the Kuvale, Mwila, Ngambwe and Twilenge-Humbi peoples.

VEI, see **VAI**

VENDA

The Venda, also known as Bavenda, are a South African Bantu-speaking people. They speak Venda and are currently concentrated in the formerly black homeland of the non-independent republic of Venda in northern Transvaal in South Africa, as well as in the southeastern regions of Zimbabwe.

The Venda people migrated into what is now their country in the early 1700, from what presently constitutes Zimbabwe. They established several kingdoms of their own. In the latter part of the 19th century they came into conflict with the expanding Transvaal Republic. Their leader Chief Mphephu was defeated and as a consequence, the Venda territory was annexed by the Transvaal Republic in 1898. Thereupon, Venda fell to Transvaal Republic, and was subsequently incorporated in South Africa. In 1962, the government of South Africa designated the area as a homeland for the venda-speaking people. In 1973, Venda was granted a measure of self-government. On September 13, 1979, South Africa proclaimed Venda an independent republic. The measure was condemned by the United Nations Security Council as an attempt by the government of South Africa to formalize and consolidate apartheid.

Currently, the Venda people in South Africa comprise a population of over 0.6 million, growing at the rate of 3.8% per year. In Zimbabwe, they account for about 1% of the total population.

VERE

A West African people. The Vere, also known as Were, are concentrated in northwestern Cameroon and northeastern Nigeria. Their neighbors include the Bachama, Bata, Fula, Chamba, Mbula, Mumuye and Yungur peoples. The Vere speak a language that belongs to the Adamawa branch of the Niger-Congo family of African languages.

VETERE, see MEKYIBO

VEZO, see also MALAGASY

The Vezo are one of Madagascar's ethnic minorities. They are related to the Sakalava and at times considered Sakalava people. They speak a dialect of Malagasy that is shared by related groups, including the Tandroy, Bara and Mahafale.

VIDUNDA

The Vidunda are an East African people. They are concentrated in Tanzania. Their neighbors include such groups as the Doe, the Kaguru, the Kami, the Ndengereko, the Kutu, the Ngulu, the Rufiji, the Sagara, the Wazaramo (Zaramo) and the Zigua peoples. The Vidunda are organized in village groups that are politically, economically and religiously independent. Traditionally, they were not subject to a centralized political authority. In addition, they also supported a matrilineal society.

VILI, see KONGO

VINZA

The Vinza are an East African people. They are concentrated in the northwestern areas of Tanzania, primarily east of Lake Tanganyika. Their neighbors include the Burundi, Ha, Nyamwazi, Sumbwa, and Tongwe peoples.

VOLTAIC

The Voltaic people are people speaking Voltaic (Gur) languages, a branch of Niger-Congo languages. They are concentrated in Burkina Faso, Benin, Ghana, Ivory Coast, Mali and Togo.

VONOMA

The Vonoma are a Central and East African people. They are concentrated in northeastern regions of the Democratic Republic of the Congo (Zaire), as well as in Uganda.

VOUMBOU, see KOTO

VOUTERE, see BABOUTI

VUGUSU, see LUHYA

VUTE, see BABOUTI

WA

The Wa are a West African people. They live in Burkina Faso and Ghana. Their neighbors include the Bariba, Grusi, Dagati, Mamprusi, and Tallensi peoples.

WAARUSHA, see also ARUSHA

An East African people. The Waarusha's main concentrations are in Kenya and Tanzania. In Tanzania, they live on the lower southwestern slopes of Mt. Maru. Their neighbors include the Nyaturu and Sandawe peoples.

WA-CAGA, see CHAGGA

WADAI

The Wadai are a Central African people. They are concentrated in western Sudan and eastern Chad. In the later part of the nineteenth century they supported an imperial kingdom that matched that of the Bagirmi people.

WADJIRIMA

The Wadjirima are one of the Chadian Kuri subgroups. They speak Yedina, a Buduma dialect. Like other Kuri groups, they live along the eastern shores of Lake Chad.

WAFIPA, see FIPA

WAGERA

The Wagera are a Central African people. They are concentrated in the Democratic Republic of the Congo (Zaire), primarily west of Lake Kivu. Their neighbors include the Twa and Wazimba peoples.

WAGGA, see WAJA

WAHUTU, see HUTU

WAJA

The Waja, also Wagga and Wuya, are a West African people. They are concentrated in northwestern Nigeria, notably in the Bauchi State. However, groups of them are also found in Benin and Nigeria.

WAKISII, see GUSII

WAKURA

The Paduko are a West African people. They are concentrated in the northern regions of Cameroon and speak a language that belongs to the Afro-Asiatic family of African languages. The Paduko neighbors include the Gisiga, Mandara, Matakam and Wakura peoples.

WALA, see also LOBI-DAGARTI

The Wala are a West African people. They are a Lobi-Dagarti group. Their main concentrations are in Burkina-Faso and Ivory Coast. The Wala speak Dagaba, a Voltaic language of the Niger-Congo family of African languages. Their neighbors include the Birifor, Builsa, Dagari, Grunshi, Guang and Kulango peoples.

WALLO

An East African people of the Horn of Africa region. Their neighbors include the Afar, the Galla, the Ittu, the Saho, the Somali and the Yaju peoples.

WAMIA, see ITESO

WANDA

The Wanda are an East African people. They are concentrated in the west central region of Tanzania, notably on the southern shores of Lake Rukwe. Their neighbors include the Bungu, Mambwe, Nyiha, and Safwa peoples.

WANDALA, see MANDARA

WANDOROBO, see OKIEK

WANG, see NUER

WANGA, see LUHYA

WANGARA, see DYULA

WANJARE, see GUSII

WANJI

A Southeast African people. The Wanji, also known as Kivwanji, are concentrated in Tanzania. They are part of the Nyasa cluster of peoples.

WANGKAC, see NUER

WANYAMWEZI

An East African Bantu-speaking people. The Wanyamwezi live in the vicinity of Lake Tanganyika, notably in Tanzania. Their neighbors include the Sumbwa, Tongwe, Ukonongo, and Vinza peoples.

WAR

The War people are a Central African ethnic group. They are concentrated in central Cameroon. Their neighbors include the Tikar, Nso, Tang, and Wiya peoples.

WARA

A West African people. The Wara are concentrated in Mali. Their neighbors include the Guin, Karaboro, Minianka, Tusyan and Senufo peoples. The Wara speak a language that belongs to the Voltaic branch of the Niger-Congo family of African languages.

WARJAWA

The Warjawa, also known as Warji and Sar, are a West African people. They are concentrated in the northeastern regions of Nigeria, notably in the Bauchi State. Their neighbors include the Auyokawa, Butwana, Gerawa and Maguzawa peoples. The Warjawa speak a language that belongs to the Afro-Asiatic family of African languages.

WARJI, see WARJAWA

WARSANGALI, see also SOMALI

An East African Somali group. The Warsangali are one of the Hurti clans, which are part of the Darod tribe.

WASCHAGGA, see CHAGGA

WASUKUMA, see SUKUMA

WASULUNKA, see OUASSOULOUNKE

WASONGOLA

The Wasongola are a West Central African people. They are concentrated in the Democratic Republic of the Congo (Zaire), primarily northwest of Lake Kivu. Their neighbors include the Lendu, Twa, and Wagera peoples.

WASULUKA, see MANDE

WATUTSI, see TUTSI

WATUSI, see TUTSI

WATYI

The Watyi people are a West African group. They constitute one of Nigeria's ethnic minorities. They are concentrated in the western areas of the country.

WAZARAMO

The Wazaramo, known also as Zalamo, Zalamu, Zaramo and Zaramu, are an East African people. They speak Kizaramo as well as Swahili, the lingua franca of East Africa. The Wazaramo are highly concentrated in the coastal areas of Tanzania, notably in the vicinity of Dar es Salaam, the capital of the country. They are related to other groups in Tanzania, including the Luguru and the Kutu.

Originally, the Wazaramo lived in the Ulugura Mountains region, which is located about 200 kilometers west of Dar es Salaam. In the later part of the 18th and early part of the twentieth centuries they moved to their present location.

The Wazaramo are essentially agriculturalists. Their economic activities center on farming and trading.

Traditionally, the Wazaramo society recognized both patrilineal and matrilineal lineages. Under this system, biological descent followed the line of the mother, whereas spiritual descent followed that of the father. Now, however, the Wazaramo are predominantly Muslim and hence, apply Muslim *shari'a* in whatever relates to marriage, divorce, and inheritance.

WAZIMBA, see also ZIMBA

The Wazimba are a West Central African people. They are concentrated in the Democratic Republic of the Congo (Zaire).

WEIYA, see DAGOMBA

WEGAM, see KUGAMA

WELAMO, see WOLAYTA

WELLO GALLA, see GALLA

WEMBA, see BEMBA

WERE, see VERE

WERIGHA

The Werigha people are a West Saharan North African group. They are concentrated in the central mountainous regions of Morocco.

WESTERN SOTHO, see also SOTHO

The Western Sotho, also called Tswana, represent one of the three Sotho major groups. The other two are Northern (or Transvaal) and Southern (Basuto or Lesotho) Sotho. Like other Sotho people, they occupy the high grasslands of southern Africa and speak Sesotho, a Bantu language.

The great majority of Western Sotho engage in agriculture, relying both on cultivation and animal husbandry. But males among them often seek work as laborers. Their settlements are characterized "by scattered hamlets of circular huts with mud and wattle or stone walls surmounted by a conical, thatched roof."[445] In their social patterns, most Sotho recognize patrilineal lineages and traditionally they allowed polygamy.

WETAWIT, see BERTA

WIDEKUM

A West Central African people and one of Cameroon's over 100 ethnic groups. The Widekum are Bantu-speaking people. They are concentrated in the Bamenda region of the country. Their neighbors include the Bali people.

WITBOUIS

The Witbouis are a Southwest African people. Their main concentration is in Namibia.

WIYA, see DAGOMBA

WOBE, see OUOBE

WOGO, see WOKO

WOKO

The Woko people, also known as Wogo, are one of Mali's, Nigeria's and Niger's ethnic minorities. They live along the banks of the Niger river.

WOLAMO, see WOLAYTA

WOLAYTA

An East African people. The Wolayta, also known as Borodda, Ometo, Ualamo, Uba, Welamo and Wolamo, are concentrated in the southern regions of Ethiopia.

WOLOF

The Wolof, also Ouolof or Oulof, are one of West Africa's peoples. Their population is estimated at over 1.5 million. They are highly concentrated in The Gambia, Sénégal and Mauritania. In the Sénégal, they constitute the largest ethnic group, accounting for 36% of the total population. In The Gambia, they account for about 16% of the country's population. In Mauritania, they represent a small minority and live primarily in the vicinity of Rosso in the southwestern areas of the country. The Wolof speak a language that carries their own name, Wolof, which belongs to the West Atlantic branch of the Niger-Congo family of African languages. Aside from Wolof, however, many of them also speak either French, English or Spanish. They are a kindred people to the Serer. Their neighbors include Fula (Fulani), Malinke, Serer and Tukulor peoples.

The Wolof developed a kingdom of their own around 1200 in what is presently inland Senegal. By the 14th century, their kingdom expanded into an empire with several satellite states, including the state of Cayor. The empire reached its zenith during the 15th century, and the Wolof were able to resist Portuguese attempts to penetrate their domains. In 1556, however, the Cayors rose against the Wolof and established their own state. With no access to the sea, the Wolof empire started to decline. In 1673, the Wolof fell to the Fulani, and in 1895, their territory became a colony of French West Africa.

Traditionally, the Wolof society was rigidly hierarchical. At the top was the king, followed in order by the nobility, the peasants and the artisan groups.[447] In their society, the king was elected by the mobility.[448]

The Wolof are, basically, an agricultural people but a magnanimous number of them are entirely urbanized. They are predominantly Muslim, and hence in their society, male and female roles are highly defined, with men working in the fields and women tending the children, while performing innumerable domestic duties. The Wolof are known for their artistic works and craftsmanship. Their gold and silver jewelry are renowned, and so are their clay bowls, pots, and jars and colorful woven cotton clothes.

WONGO

The Wongo are a West Central African Bantu-speaking people. They are concentrated in the central areas of the Democratic Republic of the Congo (Zaire), notably on the southern banks of the Sankuru river. Their neighbors include the Bunda and Kuba peoples.

WURKUM

A West African people. The Wurkum, also known as Kulung and Piya, are concentrated in Nigeria, notably in the Gongola State. Their neighbors include the Bachama, Jen, Jukun, Mumuye and Tangale. The Wurkum speak a language that belongs to the Benue-Congo branch of the Niger-Congo family of African languages.

WUTE

The Wute are a Central African people. They are concentrated in the northeastern areas of the Cameroon. Groups of them, however, can also be found in the Central African Republic and Chad. Their neighbors include the Eton and Tikar peoples.

WUYA, see WAJA

XAM

The Xam are a southern African people. They are concentrated in the central regions of the Republic of South Africa, notably on the northern banks of Orange river. However, groups of them can also be found in Botswana. Their neighbors include the Tlhaping and Tswana people.

XHOSA

The Xhosa, also Xosa, are a group of related South African Bantu-speaking peoples. They speak Isixhosa, a language that they share with the Pondo and Tembu peoples. Formerly, they were known as Caffre, Cafre, Kaffer, Kãffir or Kãfir, names that mean infidel in Arabic.

The Xhosa comprise numerous culturally related groups and subgroups, the most important of which are the Bhaca, Bomvana, Dushane, Gcaleka, Gqunkhwebe, Hlubi, Mfengu, Mpondo, Mpondomise, Ndlamba, Ngika, Ntinde, Qayi, Thembu, Xesibe and Xhosa proper. Currently, they are highly concentrated in the Ciskei and Transkei republics, formerly black homelands, in South Africa. Their population in Ciskei is over 1.0 million, growing at the rate of 2.89%. In Transkei, it is over 4.1 million, growing at the rate of 4.2%. Other Xhosa groups, however, are scattered in other parts of South Africa.

Traditionally, the Xhosa were hunters and herdsmen. They migrated to track wild game and to search out better grazing for their sheep and goats. As in the past, they continue to be essentially a pastoral people.[448] Traditionally also, the Xhosa society allowed polygamy, cherished large families, regarded fertility as a blessing, organized initiation ceremonies to signal a person's attainment of manhood and exalted ancestral spirits.

During the 18th and 19th centuries, the Xhosa resisted European encroachments on their domains. The wars between them and the European settlers, however, ended in their defeat, and eventually in their subjection to South Africa's rule.[449] In the 1960s, the government of South Africa designated both Ciskei and Transkei as homelands for them.

XIBBA, see KILBA

!XOŌ, see also **SAN**

A southern African San group. The !Xu are a San-speaking people. They are concentrated in the open woodlands of southern Angola. Like other San-speaking peoples, they are essentially foragers, hunters and gatherers.

XOSA, see **XHOSA**

!XU, see also **SAN**

A southern African San group. The !Xu are a San-speaking people. Like other San groups, they are essentially foragers, hunters and gatherers.

XHU, see **!KUNG**

XWALA, see **PEDA**

YADSI

The Yadsi are a West African group. They are concentrated in the north central regions of Mali. Their neighbors include the Berabiche and Kel Antessar peoples.

YAJU

An East African people. The Yaju are concentrated in the Horn of Africa region. Their neighbors include the Afar, the Galla, the Ittu, the Saho, the Somali and the Wallo peoples.

YAKA

The Yaka people are one of Democratic Republic of the Congo's (Zaire's) ethnic minorities. They are a Bantu-speaking people, who are concentrated in the area lying between the Kwango and the Wamba rivers in southwestern Zaire.

YAKÖ

The Yakö people, also Yakurr, are a West African Bantu-speaking people.

They speak Luko (Kö), a language belonging to the Benue-Congo branch of the Niger-Congo family of African languages, and are related by language to the Ekoi (Ekoid) people of southeastern Nigeria and western Cameroon. The Yakö represent one of Nigeria's ethnic minorities. They are concentrated in the Cross River region of the country and are primarily an agricultural people. Their neighbors include the Ekoi, Igbo, Mbembe and Ododop peoples.

YAKOMA

The Yakoma people are one of the ethnic minorities of the Central African Republic and Democratic Republic of the Congo (Zaire). Their language belongs to the Adamawa-Eastern subgroup of the Niger-Congo family of African languages.

The Yakoma are essentially a tribal people engaged in trading and fishing. They are concentrated in the Upper Ubangi (Oubangui) River region of southern Central African Republic and northern Zaire.

YAKUBA, see DAN

YAKUDI

The Yakudi are one of the main Kuri subgroups in Chad. They speak Yedina, a Buduma dialect. Like other Kuri groups, they live along the eastern shores of Lake Chad. The Yakudi people are divided into several subgroups the most important of which are the Kallamia, Kanoa, Kwallia, and Mallumia.

YAKURR, see YAKO

YALA, see IYALA

YALUNKA, see also MANDE

The Yalunka are one of Sierra Leone's Mande forest groups. They are concentrated in the northern areas of the country.

YANGHERE

The Yanghere are a Central African people. They are concentrated in southern Chad and north Central African Republic. However, groups of them can also be found in west central Sudan. Their neighbors include the Bwaka, Ndere, and Pande peoples.

YANS-MBUN, see YANZI

YANZI

A West Central and Southwest African people. The Yansi, also known as Yans-Mbum Kiyanzi, are a cluster of peoples in Angola and the Democratic Republic of the Congo (Zaire).

YAO

The Yao are a cluster of Eastern Bantu-speaking people. They are concentrated in Malawi, Tanzania and Mozambique, and are predominantly Muslim. The Yao believe themselves to have descended from the same stock as the Nyanja and that they originally inhabited the mountains between Lake Nyasa and the Mozambique coast.[450] Prior to falling to European powers at the turn of the 20th century, they had prosperous trading relations with the Arabs and inland African tribes. Currently, they are primarily engaged in farming and agriculture.

YARSE, see MOSSI

YASA

The Yasa people are a West Central African ethnic group. They are concentrated in the southwestern coastal areas of Cameroon. However, Yasa settlements can also be found in Equatorial Guinea. Their neighbors include the Bosyba and Tanga peoples.

YAUNDE, see FANG

YEKE

The Yeke are a Central and Southeast African, Bantu-speaking people. They are concentrated in the Democratic Republic of the Congo (Zaire) and Zambia.

YEKHEE, see ETSAKO

YELINDA, see FANG

YERGAM

The Yergam, also known as Appa, Tarok and Yergum, are a West African people. They are concentrated in northeastern Nigeria. Their neighbors include the Angas, Burum and Fula peoples. The Yergam speak a language that belongs to the Benue-Congo branch of the Niger-Congo family of African languages.

YERGUM, see YERGAM

YERIMA

The Yerima are one of the Chadian Kuri subgroups. They speak Yedina, a Buduma dialect. Like other Kuri groups, they live along the eastern shores of Lake Chad.

YESIBE

The Yesibe are a southern African people. They are concentrated in the east central regions of the Republic of South Africa. Their neighbors include the Kwena and Nhlangwini peoples.

YESKWA

The Yeskwa are a West African people. They are concentrated in the central regions of Nigeria and speak a language that belongs to the Benue-Congo branch of the Niger-Congo family of African languages. Their neighbors include the Gwandara, Katab, Koro and Mada peoples.

YIHUDI, see **AWI**

YIRA

One of the ethnic groups of the Democratic Republic of the Congo (Zaire). The Yira are part of the Kivu cluster of peoples.

YOFO, see **IBIBIO**

YOL, see **NUER**

YOLA, see **DOULA**

YOM, see **PILA-PILA**

YOMBE, see **KONGO**

YOOBA, see **DAGOMBA**

YORDA, see **KPAN**

YORUBA

The Yoruba are one of West Africa's largest contingents, numbering over 20 million. They speak Yoruba, a language belonging to the Kur (Gur) branch of the Niger-Congo family of African languages. They are concentrated in Nigeria, but have sizable minorities in both Benin and Togo. In Nigeria, they constitute one of the ten largest ethnic minorities of the country. They are the third largest group after the Hausa and the Fulani and are concentrated in the states of Lagos, Ogun, Oyo, Ondo and Kwara. In Benin, where they are known as Nago (Nagot) and include other smaller groups such as the Holli and Ketu (Keto), they constitute the third largest group after the Fon and Adja of the country's four major ethnic minorities. They account for one tenth of the total population. In Togo, they belong to the Ana group. Like the Hausa and Fulani peoples, the Yoruba have ancient connections with the Middle East.

About A.D. 1000, the Yoruba founded the city of Oyo, which became the seat of a kingdom in the 11th century and subsequently of an empire that was known as the Oyo empire. The Oyo empire lasted until the 19th century, when it declined as a result of internal squabbles, as well as Fon and Fulani invasions.

The Yoruba support numerous kingdoms, each of which is headed by a king (*oba*), who attends to the affairs of his kingdom and people with the consent and support of a council of chiefs. An *oba* is normally selected from a single royal lineage group.

In the past, the Yoruba relied on agriculture and extensive trading across the Atlantic, as well as with their eastern African neighbors. Today, agriculture in the form of cash crops continues to be one of their major economic activities. Though considered urbanized people, the Yoruba produce most of the cacao beans in Nigeria.

Yoruba have been known to live in two establishments: the *ilu* or permanent village, and the *aba*, the farming village. The *ilu* has its own government, ruled by a chief. *Aba* is a temporary settlement where farmers live when their farms are just too far away from the *ilu*.

Yoruba women are economically independent. Yet, men can have a number of wives in Yoruba society. Children inherit land through their father's line with the oldest son given the lineage's land. Because of land shortages in Yoruba territory, conflicts among brothers over lands that produce cash crops have increased.[451]

Traditional Yoruba male clothing consists of a long gown worn to the ankle with trousers. Traditional women's attire consists of a long piece of cloth stretching from the neck to the ankle. Both men's and women's attire are usually multi-colored.

Like other West Africa peoples, the Yoruba are renowned for their splendid wood sculpture. Their art, especially their stone and metalwork, has been and continues to be famous around the world. Their prosperity allowed artists to thrive using techniques such as the lost-wax method of metal casting. Artistic expression is also found in intricate woodcarving, which "portrays life on the farms, in the villages, in the cults, and the palaces."[452]

Recently, Yoruba literature has been internationally recognized with famous writers such as Wole Soyinka.

Though most Yoruba are either Christian or Muslim, there are an innumerable number of Yoruba who still adhere to traditional religious beliefs. Traditional Yoruba religion contains a main god, *Ogun*, lesser gods and ancestor spirits or *orisa*. A number of cults still worship these traditional entities like the *Ifa* and the *Egungun* cults. Witches are also feared in the Yoruba culture and can only be subdued by the cult of *Gelde*, who "perform healing dances with movements like those made by women in their daily chores."[453] The supernatural is still seen as a dominant force in Yoruba daily life.

YUNGUR

The Yungur, also known as Binna and Ebuna, are a West African people. The are concentrated in the eastern regions of Nigeria. Their neighbors include the Bata, Dera, Hona, Kurama and Vere peoples. The Yungur speak a language that belongs to the Adamawa branch of the Niger-Congo family of African languages.

ZAA, see DOUROU

ZABARMA, see **ZERMA**

ZABERMA, see **ZERMA**

ZABIRMAWA, see **ZERMA**

ZABRAMA, see **ZERMA** and **SONGHAI**

ZABRIMA, see **ZERMA**

ZAFISORO

The Zafisoro are a Southeast African people. They are concentrated on the Island of Madagascar, notably in the southeastern coastal areas of the country. Their neighbors include the Taimoro and Taisaka peoples.

ZAGHAURA

The Zaghaura, or Bideyat, are a semi-sedentary Beri people who speak a distinct Saharan language along with Arabic. They live along the Chadian border with Sudan. Their population is estimated at about 50,000. The Zaghaura are predominantly Muslim. They have a centrally organized sultanate, headed by a sultan who governs their affairs with the assistance of notables. Their semi-sedentary lifestyle allows them to cultivate their crops during the wet season.

ZAGHAWA

These are a central Sudan Beri people. Between the seventh and ninth centuries they infiltrated the Lake Chad area and successfully established themselves as a ruling aristocracy over many people within its vicinity. Eventually they sparked the rise of the Kanuri-speaking state of Kanem.[454] Presently, the Zaghawa are settled farmers, comprised of several groups, including the Berti people.

ZALAMO, see **WAZARAMO**

ZALAMU, see **WAZARAMO**

ZAM, see **NUPE**

ZAMAN, see **FANG**

ZANDE, see **AZANDE**

ZANJ

An East African Bantu people who together with the Galla used to occupy parts of what is presently Somalia. As a result of Somalian migration from the Arabian peninsula to the Horn of Africa region over 1000 years ago, the Zanj were pushed south. According to Arab geographers, "the Zanj were concentrated along the banks of the Giuba and Shebelle and in fertile pockets between them."[455]

ZARAMO, see **WAZARAMO**

ZARAMU, see **WAZARAMO**

ZARMA, see **ZERMA**

ZAYR

The Zayr people are a West Saharan North African group. They are concentrated in the northwestern mountainous regions of Morocco. Their neighbors include the Shawya, Werigha, and Zemmur peoples.

ZEGUA, see **ZIGULA**

ZEMMUR

The Zemmur are a North African people. They are concentrated in the north western mountainous regions of Morocco. Their neighbors include the Ban Guil and Werigha peoples.

ZERAF, see **NUER**

ZERMA

The Zerma, also called Djerma, Djermis, Dyabarma, Dyarma, Dyerma, Zabarma, Zaberma, Zabirmawa, Zabramas, Zabrima and Zarma, are a West African Muslim people. They speak a dialect of Songhai, a language that belongs to the Nilo-Saharan, also called Nilo-Sahelian, family of African languages, and are considered a branch of the Songhai people. Their language has also been regarded as a Congo-Kordofanian language. The Zerma people are highly concentrated in the Niger where they constitute about 22% of the country's population. They are primarily located in the western areas of Niger, notably in the Dosso Department, the traditional seat of their chieftaincy. Small groups of them, however, live also in Burkina Faso, Ghana, and Nigeria. The Zerma neighbors include the Dendi, Fula, Gurma, Kurfei, Mauri, Songhai and Tienga peoples.

The Zerma people are essentially a rural people. They live in villages where they engage in different agricultural pursuits. Groups of them, however, are sedentary. They live in urban centers and engage in miscellaneous trading activities. Their society is based on patrilineal relations. Like other West African peoples, they are renowned for their iron, wood, and leather crafts.

ZEZURU, see also SHONA

The Zezhru are a Southern Bantu-speaking people. They are a Shona subgroup, and are concentrated in the north southwestern regions of South Africa, as well as in the central plateau of Zimbabwe. In the latter country, they account for about 18% of the total population. Their neighbors include the Karanga, Korekore, Manyika, Ndau and Rozwi peoples.

ZHU/ÕASI, see also SAN

A southern African San group. The Zhu/Õasi, also known as !Kung, are a San-speaking people. They are concentrated in Ngamiland, a semiarid savanna in northwestern Botswana and adjoining areas in Namibia. Like other San-speaking peoples, they are essentially foragers, hunters and gatherers.

ZIGALU, see ZIGULA

ZIGUA, see ZIGULA

ZIGULA

The Zigula – also known as Zegua, Zigalu, or Zigua – are an East African Muslim people. They are concentrated in the eastern border areas that separate Kenya from Tanzania. Their neighbors include such groups as the Doe, the Kaguru, the Kami, the Ndengereko, the Kutu, the Ngulu, the Rufiji, the Sagara and the Wazaramo (Zaramo) peoples. Traditionally, the

Zigula were organized in village groups that were politically, economically and religiously independent and hence, were not subject to a centralized political authority. In addition, they also supported a matrilineal society. Presently, however, they apply the Muslim *shari'a* in matters of lineage.

ZIMBA

The Zimba are a Southwest and Southeast Bantu-speaking African people. Their groups are concentrated in Angola, Namibia, Zimbabwe and Mozambique.

Traditionally, these people were practicing cannibals. Around 1580, a band of about five thousand of Zimba staged a militant campaign that led to the devastation of the East African coast.[456] They first attacked the coastal trading posts of Tete and Sena, consuming their inhabitants. Then in 1587, they attacked Kilwa, killing many of its people.[457] In 1589, they moved to Mombasa, where they also consumed its people. In the same year, they succeeded in besieging Malindi, readying themselves to stage their final assault on the city. At Malindi, however, they were faced by a warlike Segejy people, who not only managed to defeat them but also to chase and crush them. Only about one hundred of the Zimba were able to escape.

ZIMMUR, see also BERBER

The Zimmur are a Moroccan Berber group. They are concentrated in the Imazighen region of Morocco, notably in the Middle Atlas, Central High Atlas, Saghro massif, and the Presaharan oasis areas of the country.

ZINZA

The Zinza are an East African people. They are concentrated in the northwestern regions of Tanzania, notably on the southern shores of Lake Victoria. Their neighbors include the Banyanhkole (Ankole) and Kerewe peoples.

ZIRIDS, see HAMMADIDS

ZIZI, see **MFENGU**

ZNAGA, see **SAHRAWIS**

ZOMBO

The Zombo are a West Central African ethnic group. They are concentrated in Angola and the Democratic Republic of the Congo (Zaire). In Zaire they live in the vicinity of the eastern lower stretches of the Congo river. Their neighbors include the Bayaka, Kongo, and Ndibu peoples.

ZULU

The Zulu, or AmaZulu as they like to call themselves, are a famous warrior nation that reside mainly in South Africa. They are concentrated in KwaZulu in the heart of Natal east of the Drakensberg Escarpment in the Republic of South Africa. The Zulu are an Nguni-speaking people. Apart from their native language, they also speak Afrikaans and English. In Nguni, the word Zulu means sky, whereas the word Ama means people. Hence, AmaZulu means "The People of the Sky." Like many other African peoples, the Zulu are divided into many clans, which still constitute their basic units of social and political organization. Their nation is highly patrilineal.

The Zulu are descendants of the Nguni peoples of southeast Africa. Their modern history is traced back to the 14th and 15th centuries when they migrated southward and settled in what is presently South Africa. There, the leadership of the people devolved to Luzumane, who is presumed to be the father of Malandela (about b1597-d1691). Oral history of the Zulu people suggests that Malandela was a nomad "until he settled with his wife Nozinja at Mandawe Hill near present Eshowe," and that he had "two known sons, Qwabe and Zulu."[458] In addition, it suggests that upon Malandela's death in 1691, Qwabe left his tribe to form his own clan, whereas Zulu (about b1627-d1709) remained with his mother, and in time, "gave his name to the family line and became founder of the famous Zulu clan."[459] Thereafter, chieftaincy successively devolved to Zulu's heirs as follows: Punga (about b1657-d1727), Mageba (about b1660-1745), Ndaba (about b1697-d1763), Jama (about b1727-d1781), Senzangakona (about b1757-d1816), Sigujana (about b1790-d1816), and Shaka (b1787-d1828). Under Shaka's leadership, the Zulu nation reached its political zenith.

The Zulu established their own empire in the 19th century. The empire, known as the Mtetwa Empire, was founded by Mtetwa king Dingiswayo in northern Zululand at the end of the eighteenth century. Dingiswayo reigned between 1809 and 1817. Under his leadership major military and administrative reforms were introduced, including the system of age-regiments. All these reforms were introduced with the help of Shaka, who was brought up, trained, and launched as a military leader under the supervision of Dingiswayo. In 1817, Shaka succeeded Dingiswayo as head of the Mtetwa empire, and in no time, he absorbed this empire by the Zulu empire. The latter empire was expanded, establishing Zulu dominance over their neighbors, as well as over what presently constitutes Natal. During Shaka's reign, the Zulu empire supported about 50,000 warriors.

In 1828, Dingane (Dingaan) succeeded Shaka. His efforts focused on resisting Boer attempts to penetrate the Zululand. In 1840, however, Dingane was deposed by his brother Mpande, who entered into an alliance with the Boers. During Mpande's reign (1840-72), the empire lost parts of its territory to the Boers, and in 1838, it lost Natal to the British. In 1872, Cetshwayo succeeded Mpande. In 1878, he rejected a British demand that called on him to disband his army and to accept British protection. As a consequence, the British forces invaded Zululand and upon defeating the Zulu, placed the country under their control and then divided it into 13 small kingdoms. Eventually, Zululand became part of South Africa.

Traditionally, the Zulu people had a highly hierarchical centralized form of political and military organization. This organization was headed by an autocratic king supported by an advisory council of chiefs and subchiefs. The Zulu king was the paramount chief and all clan chiefs were kinsmen or married to women of the royal family. Presently, the authority and influence of the king, chiefs and military system have considerably weakened. Additionally, the king's authority has greatly diminished and many Zulu leaders maintain regular or elected positions in the government of South Africa.

Zulu dwellings, called *kraal*, are quite small, with the village arranged in a horseshoe-shape formation surrounded by fences made of wood with the chief living in a separate house that is much bigger than those of the rest of the tribe. The dwellings are dome-shaped and made of straw and grass. Villagers are members of an extended family network.

The father continues to be the dominant figure in the Zulu family, and moreover, he is highly respected and allowed (by Zulu law) to have as many wives as he can afford. The mother is much less influential. On the whole, however, Zulu women are responsible for raising crops, tending the children, building the dwellings and producing domestic utensils. Today, men work in the South African mines and rarely have time to see their families, giving their wives even more responsibility.

Artistic expression in Zulu society is through song and dance performed during ceremony. *Izibongo* songs are the most popular and express praise toward their leaders' accomplishments.

Traditional Zulu religion is mainly composed of the worship of ancestor spirits or *amaDlozi*. *AmaDlozi* are expected to be involved in almost all aspects of earthly individual life. Graves of *amaDlozi* are well kept and any disturbance of these graves is believed to bring great hardship to all people. Sacrifices are made to the *amaDlozi* before every event of importance. The Zulu worship a supreme God named, *Unkulunkulu*, yet this entity is believed not to interfere too much in earthly matters.

Currently, KwaZulu is the most populous of South Africa's black provinces. It has a population of over 5.1 million, growing at the rate of 3.2% per year.

ZUMPER, see **KUTED**

PART SIX

ENDNOTES

ENDNOTES

1. *Encyclopedia of World Cultures, Africa and the Middle East.* Volume IX. Volume Editors: John Middleton and Amal Rassam (Boston: G.K. Hall & Co., 1995), p. 161.

2. *Ibid.,* p. 6.

3. *Ibid.,* p. 6.

4. Seligman, C.G. *Races of Africa* (New York: Oxford University Press, 1966), p. 79.

5. Moss, Joyce, and George Wilson. *Peoples of the World: Africans South of the Sahara* (Detroit: Gale Research, 1991), p. 30.

6. *Ibid.,* p. 31.

7. July, Robert. *A History of the African People,* Fifth edition, (Prospect Heights, IL: Waveland Press, Inc., 1988), p. 95.

8. *Ibid.,* p. 96.

9. Banks, Arthur S., ed. *Political Handbook of the World.* Published for the Center for Education and Social Research of the State University of New York at Binghamton and for the Council on Foreign Relations (Binghamton, New York: CSA Publications, 1986), p. 497.

10. Jackson, Richard H, and Lloyd E. Hudman. *Cultural Geography: People, Places and Environment* (St, Paul, New York, Los Angeles, San Francisco: West Publishing Company, 1990), p. 312.

11. July, *op. cit.,* p. 451.

12. Garraty, John A., and Peter Gay, eds. *The Columbia History of the World* (New York, Evanston, San Francisco, London: Harper & Row, Publishers, 1981), p. 930.

13. July, *op. cit.,* p. 93.

14. *Ibid.,* p. 93.

15. *Ibid.,* p. 94.

16. *The New Encyclopædia Britannica.* 26 volumes. Editor in Chief: Philip W. Goetz (Chicago: Encyclopædia Britannica, 1988 edition), Vol. I, p. 143.

17. *Ibid.,* Vol. I, p. 143.

18. *Ibid.*, Vol. I, p. 143.
19. *Ibid.*, Vol. I, p. 143.
20. July, *op. cit.*, p. 109.
21. *Encyclopædia Britannica*, Vol. II, p. 366.
22. *Ibid.*, 1988, Vol. II, p. 366.
23. *Ibid.*, 1988, Vol. I, p. 195.
24. *Ibid.*, 1988, Vol. IV, p. 680.
25. July, *op. cit.*, p. 125.
26. *Encyclopædia Britannica*, Vol. I, p. 185.
27. Seligman, *op. cit.*, p. 41.
28. *Encyclopædia Britannica*, Vol. I, p. 185.
29. *Encyclopedia of World Cultures*, Vol. IX, p. 12.
30. Davidson, Basil. *The African Genius* (Boston, New York, Toronto, London: Little, Brown and Company, 1969), p. 38.
31. *Ibid.*, p. 130.
32. *Ibid.*, p. 147.
33. July, *op. cit.*, pp. 94-95.
34. *Encyclopedia of World Cultures*, Vol. IX, p. 13.
35. Carlston, Kenneth S. *Social Theory and African Tribal Organization* (Urbana: University of Illinois Press, 1968), p. 242.
36. *Encyclopedia of World Cultures*, Vol IX, p. 15.
37. *Encyclopædia Britannica*, Vol. VI, p. 256.
38. *Encyclopedia of World Cultures*, Vol. IX, p. 84.
39. *Social Theory and African Tribal Organization*, p. 316.
40. *Ibid.*, p. 313.
41. *Ibid.*, p. 313.
42. *Ibid.*, p. 315.
43. *Social Theory and African Tribal Organization*, p. 126.
44. Haskins, Jim, and Joann Biondi. *From Afar to Zulu, A Dictionary of African Cultures* (New York: Walker and Company, 1995), p. 18.
45. *Social Theory and African Tribal Organization*, p. 128.

46. Haskins and Biondi, *op. cit.*, p. 24.
47. *Encyclopædia Britannica*, Vol. I, p. 754.
48. Moss and Wilson, *op. cit.*, pp. 77-78.
49. Gunther, John. *Inside Africa* (New York: Harper, 1953), p. 287.
50. July, *op. cit.*, p. 437.
51. Gunther, *op. cit.*, pp. 709-710.
52. *Ibid.*, p. 648.
53. Davidson, *op. cit.*, p. 39.
54. *Ibid.*, p. 39.
55. July, *op. cit.*, pp. 13-14.
56. *Encyclopædia Britannica*, Vol. I, p. 855.
57. *Ibid.*, p. 855, and Murray, Jocelyn, ed. *Cultural Atlas of Africa*. Fifth Reprint (New York: Facts on File, Inc., 1981), p. 98.
58. *Encyclopædia Britannica*, Vol. I, p. 855.
59. Gunther, *op. cit.*, p. 285.
60. *Encyclopædia Britannica*, Vol. I, p. 876.
61. Gunther, *op. cit.*, p. 286.
62. *Ibid.*, p. 285.
63. *Ibid.*, p. 286.
64. *Ibid.*, p. 286.
65. *Ibid.*, pp. 289-295.
66. *Encyclopædia Britannica*, Vol. XI, p. 23.
67. *Ibid.*, Vol. I, p. 896.
68. *Ibid.*, Vol. I, p. 896.
69. *Ibid.*, Vol. I, p. 896.
70. *Ibid.*, Vol. I, p. 896.
71. *Ibid.*, Vol. I, p. 896.
72. *Encyclopedia of World Cultures*, Vol. IX, p. 158.
73. *Encyclopædia Britannica*, Vol XI, p. 23.
74. *Encyclopedia of World Cultures*, Vol IX, p. 320.

75. Holt, P.M. *A Modern History of the Sudan* (New York: Grove Press, 1961), p. 10.

76. July, *op. cit.*, p. 43.

77. *Ibid.*, p. 93.

78. Niblock, Tim. *Class and Power in Sudan: The Dynamics of Sudanese Politics, 1898-1985* (New York: State University of New York Press, 1987), pp. 147-148.

79. O'Fahey, R.S. and J. L. Spaulding. *Kingdoms of the Sudan* (London: Menthuen, 1974), p. 80.

80. Seligman, *op. cit.*, p. 84.

81. *Encyclopedia of World Cultures,* Vol. IX, p. 48.

82. Seligman, *op. cit.*, p. 87.

83. Uku-Wertimer, Skyne. *Africa Changes and Challenges* (Acton, MA: Tapestry Press, 1990), p. 438.

84. *Ibid.*, p. 438.

85. Nelson et al, *op. cit.*, 1972:54.

86. *Ibid.*, p. 54.

87. *Cultural Atlas of Africa,* p. 161.

88. Seligman, *op. cit.*, p. 39.

89. *Encyclopædia Britannica,* Vol. I, p. 388.

90. July, *op. cit.*, p. 28.

91. *Ibid.*, p. 29.

92. Briggs, C.L. *Tribes of the Sahara* (Cambridge: Harvard, 1967), p. 190.

93. *Ibid.*, p. 201.

94. *Ibid.*, p. 202.

95. July, Robert, *A History of the African People* (New York: Charles Scribner's Sons, 1970), p. 135. Will be referred to in subsequent notes as the (1970 edition).

96. Moss and Wilson, *op. cit.*, p. 108.

97. July, *op. cit.*, p. 143.

98. *Cultural Atlas of Africa*, p. 137.

99. Garraty and Gay, *op. cit.*, p. 297.

100. Haskins and Biondi, *op. cit.*, p. 184.

101. *Encyclopædia Britannica*, Vol. III, p. 809.

102. Haskins and Biondi, *op. cit.*, p. 186.

103. *Ibid.*, p. 186.

104. Seligman, *op. cit.*, pp. 59-60.

105. *Encyclopædia Britannica*, Vol. III, p. 870.

106. *Ibid.*, Vol. IV, p. 103.

107. Deng, Francis Mading. *The Dinka of the Sudan* (New York, NY: Holt, Rinehart & Winston, Inc., 1972), p. 6.

108. *Ibid.*, p. 2.

109. Deng, *op. cit.*, p. 6.

110. *Ibid.*, p. 111.

111. *Ibid.*, p. 112.

112. *Ibid.*, p. 112.

113. *Ibid.*, p. 9.

114. *Encyclopædia Britannica*, Vol. IV, p. 103.

115. Deng, *op. cit.*, p. 9.

116. *Ibid.*, p. 10.

117. *Ibid.*, p. 10.

118. *Ibid.*, p. 10.

119. *Ibid.*, p. 3.

120. *Ibid.*, p. 3.

121. *Ibid.*, p. 3.

122. *Ibid.*, pp. 141, 144.

123. *Ibid.*, p. 139.

124. *Cultural Atlas of Africa*, p. 79.

125. Haskins and Biondi, *op. cit.*, p. 49.

126. Davidson, *op. cit.*, p. 39.

127. *Ibid.*, p. 39.

128. *Cultural Atlas of Africa*, p. 97.

129. *Encyclopedia of World Cultures*, Vol. IX, p. 71.

130. *Ibid.*, Vol. IX, p. 72.

131. Haskins and Biondi, *op. cit.*, pp. 53-55.

132. *Encyclopedia of World Cultures*, Vol. IX, p. 75.

133. July, *op. cit.*, p. 119.

134. *Ibid.*, p. 119.

135. *Ibid.*, p. 120.

136. *Ibid.*, p. 120.

137. *Encyclopædia Britannica*, Vol. II, p. 103.

138. *Ibid.*, Vol. IV, p. 372.

139. "Nigeria and Cameroon." *The Economist*, March 12, 1994, p. 50.

140. *Encyclopædia Britannica*, Vol. IV, p. 384.

141. July, *op. cit.*, p. 168.

142. *Encyclopædia Britannica*, Vol. IV, p. 384.

143. *Ibid.*, Vol. IV, p. 384.

144. *Ibid.*, Vol. IV, p. 411.

145. *Encyclopedia of World Cultures*, Vol. IX, p. 83.

146. July, *op. cit.*, p. 264.

147. Gunther, *op. cit.*, p. 840.

148. Davidson, *op. cit.*, p. 40.

149. Moss and Wilson, *op. cit.*, p. 128.

150. Haskins and Biondi, *op. cit.*, p. 62.

151. *Encyclopædia Britannica*, Vol. I, p. 143.

152. *Encyclopedia of World Cultures*, Vol. IX, p. 93.

153. Haskins and Biondi, *op. cit.*, p. 67.

154. *Encyclopædia Britannica*, Vol. XI, p. 23.

155. Haskins and Biondi, *op. cit.*, pp. 72-73.

156. Moss and Wilson, *op. cit.*, p. 149.

157. *Ibid.*, p. 151.
158. *Ibid.*, p. 150.
159. *Encyclopedia of World Cultures*, Vol. IX, p. 101.
160. Seligman, *op. cit.*, p. 96.
161. July, *op. cit.*, p. 102.
162. *Ibid.*, p. 102.
163. *Ibid.*, pp. 102, 212.
164. *Encyclopedia of World Cultures*, Vol. IX, p. 319.
165. Seligman, *op. cit.*, p. 76.
166. July, *op. cit.*, p. 376.
167. *Ibid.*, p. 377.
168. *Ibid.*, p. 377.
169. *Keesing's Record of World Events*, 1994, Vol. 39, No. 07, pp. 39546-39547.
170. *Ibid.*, Reference Supplement, 1994, Vol. 40, p. 28.
171. *Social Theory and African Tribal Organization*, p. 248.
172. *Ibid.*, p. 248.
173. *Encyclopædia Britannica*, Vol. V, p. 108.
174. *Ibid.*, Vol. V, p. 108.
175. July, *op. cit.*, p. 40.
176. *Ibid.*, pp. 91-92.
177. *Ibid.*, pp. 262, 372.
178. *Encyclopædia Britannica*, Vol. V, p. 505.
179. *Ibid.*, Vol. V, p. 505, and July, *op. cit.*, p. 385.
180. July, *op. cit.*, p. 94.
181. Gunther, *op. cit.*, p. 5.
182. *Encyclopædia Britannica*, Vol. V, p. 663.
183. Gunther, *op. cit.*, p. 6.
184. *Encyclopedia of World Cultures*, Vol. IX, p. 111.
185. *Ibid.*, IX:112.

186. Gunther, *op. cit.*, p. 78.

187. July, *op. cit.*, pp. 51-54, 76.

188. *Ibid.*, p. 76.

189. *Ibid.*, p. 76.

190. *Encyclopædia Britannica*, Vol. VI, p. 730.

191. July, *op. cit*, p. 77.

192. *Encyclopædia Britannica*, Vol. VI, p. 730.

193. Brown, G.C., and A. McDonald B. Hutt. *Anthropology in Action* (Oxford, UK: Oxford University Press, 1935), p. 182.

194. July, *op. cit.*, p. 142.

195. *Encyclopædia Britannica*, Vol. XI, p. 23.

196. McKinley Jr., James C. "Stoked by Rwandans, Tribal Violence Spreads in Zaire," *The New York Times International*, June 16, 1996, p. y3.

197. Best, A., and H.J. de Blij. *African Survey* (N.Y.: Wiley, 1977), p. 467.

198. Lemarchand, 1970, in *Ibid.*, p. 467.

199. *Encyclopedia of World Cultures*, Vol. IX, p. 119.

200. *Ibid.*, Vol. IX, p. 121.

201. *Social Theory and African Tribal Organization*, p. 190.

202. Moss and Wilson, *op. cit.*, p. 178.

203. *Encyclopædia Britannica*, Vol. VI, p. 252.

204. *Ibid.*, Vol. VI, p. 253.

205. *Ibid.*, Vol. VI, p. 253.

206. *Ibid.*, Vol. VI, p. 253, and July, *op. cit.*, pp. 363-364.

207. *The New Encyclopædia Britannica*, Vol. VI, p. 256.

208. *Ibid.*, Vol. 6, p. 256.

209. Briggs, *op. cit.*, pp. 113-115.

210. *Encyclopedia of World Cultures*, Vol. IX, p. 126.

211. *Ibid.*, Vol. IX, p. 126.

212. *Encyclopædia Britannica*, Vol. VI, p. 636.

213. July, *op. cit.*, pp. 89, 135, 156, 603.

214. *Ibid.*, p. 156.

215. *Ibid.*, pp. 233-234.

216. *Ibid.*, p. 234.

217. *Ibid.*, p. 234.

218. *Ibid.*, p. 234.

219. *Encyclopædia Britannica*, Vol. VI, p. 645.

220. July, *op. cit.*, p. 36.

221. Beidelman, T. O. *The Kaguru: A Matrilineal People of East Africa* (New York, NY: Holt, Rinehart and Winston, 1971), p. 11.

222. *Ibid.*, p. 18.

223. *Ibid.*, p. 32.

224. Davidson, *op. cit.*, p. 147.

225. Moss and Wilson, op. cit.

226. Seligman, *op. cit.*, p. 142.

227. Haskins and Biondi, *op. cit.*, p. 98.

228. Nelson, Harold D. *South Africa: A Country Study* (Washington D.C.: U.S. G.P.O. 1972), p. 56.

229. July, *op. cit.*, p. 74.

230. *Encyclopædia Britannica*, Vol. XI, p. 23.

231. *Ibid.*, Vol. VII, pp. 560-561.

232. Nelson et al., *op. cit.*, p. 116.

233. *Encyclopædia Britannica*, Vol. II, p. 391.

234. Cohen, Ronald. *The Kanuri of Bornu* (New York, NY: Holt, Rinehart & Winston, Inc., 1967) p. 111.

235. July, *op. cit.*, p. 130.

236. *Ibid.*, p. 130.

237. *Encyclopædia Britannica*, Vol. VII, pp. 560-561.

238. *Encyclopedia of World Cultures*, Vol. IX, p. 157.

239. Haskins and Biondi, *op. cit.*, p. 100.

240. Schapera, I. *The Khoisan Peoples of South Africa, Bushmen and Hottentots* (London, UK: Routledge & Kegan Paul LTD, 1965), p. 44.

241. Moss and Wilson, *op. cit.*, p. 195.

242. *Encyclopedia of World Cultures*, Vol. IX, p. 161.243. *Ibid.*, Vol. IX, p. 161.

244. July, *op. cit.*, p. 145.

245. *Ibid.*, p. 145.

246. *Ibid.*, (1970 edition), p. 140.

247. *Ibid.*, p. 145.

248. Taylor, D.R.F., "Agriculture Change in Kikuyuland," in Thomas N. F. and A.W. Whittington (eds.), *Environment and Land Use in Africa* (London, UK: Methuen & Co., Ltd., 1969).

249. Abuor, C. Ojwando. *White Highlands No More* (Nairobi, Kenya: Pan African Researchers, 1970), p. 21.

250. July, *op. cit.*, pp. 386-387.

251. *Ibid.*, pp. 385-386.

252. *Ibid.*, p. 386.

253. Abuor, *op. cit.*, pp. 21-22.

254. Best and Blij, *op. cit.*, p. 440.

255. *Ibid.*, p. 440.

256. *Social Theory and African Tribal Organizations*, p. 282.

257. *Encyclopedia of World Cultures*, Vol. IX, p. 165.

258. July, *op. cit.*, p. 154, and *From Afar to Zulu*, p. 109.

259. Moss and Wilson, *op. cit.*, p. 211.

260. Davidson, *op. cit.*, pp. 130-131.

261. *Encyclopedia of World Cultures*, Vol. IX, p. 171.

262. *Ibid.*, Vol. IX, p. 171.

263. Moss and Wilson, *op. cit.*, p. 213.

264. Seligman, *op.cit.*, p. 39.

265. July, *op. cit.*, p. 190.

266. *Ibid.*, pp. 188-190.

267. *Encyclopedia of World Cultures*, Vol. IX, p. 400.

268. *Ibid.*, Vol. IX, p. 187.

269. *Encyclopædia Britannica*, Vol. XI, p. 23.

270. *Ibid.*, Vol. XI, p. 23.

271. *Ibid.*, Vol. VII, p. 146.

272. *Encyclopedia of World Cultures*, Vol. IX, p. 319.

273. *Encyclopædia Britannica*, 1988:6:256)

274. *Encyclopedia of World Cultures*, Vol. IX, p. 183.

275. *Encyclopædia Britannica*, Vol. XI, p. 23.

276. July, *op. cit.*, p. 237, and *Encyclopædia Britannica*, Vol. VII, p. 528.

277. July, *op. cit.*, pp. 135-136.

278. *Ibid.*, (1970 edition), p. 141.

279. *Ibid.*, (1970 edition), p. 141.

280. *Encyclopedia of World Cultures*, Vol. IX, p. 191.

281. *Encyclopædia Britannica*, Vol. VII, pp. 560-561.

282. *Social Theory and African Tribal Organization*, pp. 263, 275.

283. Davidson, *op. cit.*, p. 132.

284. *Social Theory and African Tribal Organization*, p. 263.

285. Davidson, *op. cit.*, p. 132.

286. *Ibid.*, pp. 132-133.

287. *Encyclopedia of World Cultures*, Vol. IX, p. 187.

288. *Encyclopædia Britannica*, Vol. VII, pp. 560-561.

289. *Ibid.*, Vol. VII, p. 561.

290. July, *op. cit.*, (1970 edition), p. 141.

291. Davidson, *op. cit.*, p. 31.

292. July, *op. cit.*, (1970 edition), p. 143.

293. *Ibid.*, (1970 edition), p. 143.

294. *Encyclopædia Britannica*, Vol. VII, pp. 560-561.

295. *Encyclopedia of World Cultures*, Vol. IX, p. 294.

296. *Ibid.*, Vol. IX, p. 187.

297. *Ibid.*, Vol. IX, p. 187.

298. *Encyclopædia Britannica*, Vol. VII, p. 772.

299. Marwick, 1965:15.

300. Davidson, *op. cit.*, pp. 135-137.

301. *Encyclopædia Britannica,* Vol. VII, pp. 815-816.

302. Gunther, *op. cit.*, p. 401.

303. *Encyclopedia of World Cultures,* Vol. IX, p. 207.

304. *Encyclopædia Britannica,* Vol. VII, p. 906.

305. Gunther, *op. cit.*, p. 400.

306. July, *op. cit.*, p. 156.

307. *Encyclopedia of World Cultures,* Vol. IX, p. 220.

308. July, *op. cit.*, (1970 edition), p. 124.

309. *Ibid.,* (1970 edition), p. 124.

310. *Encyclopedia of World Cultures,* Vol. IX, p. 187.

311. Davidson, *op. cit.*, p. 147.

312. *Encyclopædia Britannica,* Vol. VII, 986.

313. *Ibid.,* Vol. VII, p. 986.

314. *Ibid.,* Vol. VII, p. 986.

315. Moss and Wilson, *op. cit.*.

316. *Encyclopæaedia Britannica,* Vol. VIII, p. 87.

317. *Encyclopedia of World Cultures,* Vol. IX, p. 187.

318. *Encyclopædia Britannica,* Vol. XI, p. 23.

319. *Ibid.,* Vol. XI, p. 23.

320. *Ibid.,* Vol. VIII, p. 255.

321. Briggs, *op. cit.*, pp. 211-236.

322. Nelson et. al., *op. cit.*, p. 54.

323. July, *op. cit.*, p. 359.

324. *Encyclopedia of World Cultures,* Vol. IX, p. 187.

325. *Ibid.,* Vol. IX, p. 187.

326. *Ibid.,* Vol. IX, p. 187.

327. McKinley, *op. cit.*, p. y3.

328. *Social Theory and African Tribal Organizations,* p. 294.

329. *Ibid.*, p. 295.

330. *Ibid.*, p. 295.

331. *Ibid.*, p. 295.

332. *Ibid.*, p. 298.

333. *Ibid.*, p. 298.

334. *Ibid.*, p. 298.

335. Davidson, *op. cit.*, p. 149.

336. *Encyclopedia of World Cultures*, Vol. IX, p. 235.

337. July, *op. cit.*, pp. 237-239, 364-366.

338. *Ibid.*, p. 239.

339. *Ibid.*, p. 364.

340. *Ibid.*, pp. 364-365.

341. *Ibid.*, p. 367.

342. *Ibid.*, p. 367.

343. *Ibid.*, (1970 edition), p. 395.

344. *Ibid.*, (1970 edition), p. 395.

345. *Encyclopaedia Britannica*, Vol. VII, pp. 560-561.

346. *Encyclopedia of World Cultures*, Vol IX, p. 187.

347. Gunther, *op. cit.*, p. 5.

348. Briggs, *op. cit.*, p. 108.

349. Deng, *op. cit.*, p. 142.

350. *Encyclopædia Britannica*, Vol. VIII, p. 386.

351. Best and Blij, *op. cit.*, p. 73.

352. Haskins and Biondi, *op. cit.*, pp. 186-187.

353. *Ibid.*, pp. 186-187.

354. *Encyclopædia Britannica*, Vol. XI, p. 23.

355. *Encyclopedia of World Cultures*, Vol. IX, p. 245.

356. Evans-Pritchard, E.E. *The Nuer* (New York and Oxford: Oxford University Press), p. 3.

357. *Social Theory and African Tribal Organization*, p. 358.

358. *Ibid.*, p. 364.

359. Evans-Pritchard, *op. cit.*, p. 122.

360. *Social Theory and African Tribal Organization*, p. 358.

361. Nelson et. al., *op. cit.*, p. 116.

362. July, *op. cit.*, pp. 119, 339.

363. *Social Theory and African Tribal Organization*, p. 338.

364. *Encyclopedia of World Cultures*, Vol. IX, p. 187.

365. *Encyclopædia Britannica*, Vol. VIII, p. 843.

366. *Encyclopedia of World Cultures*, Vol. IX, p. 258.

367. *Ibid.*, Vol. IX, p. 259.

368. July, *op. cit.*, p. 96.

369. *Keesing's Record of World Events*, Reference Supplement 1996, No. 42, p. R13.

370. July, *op. cit.*, p. 125.

371. *Encyclopædia Britannica*, Vol. X, p. 640.

372. *Encyclopedia of World Cultures*, Vol. IX, p. 268.

373. *Ibid.*, Vol. IX, p. 268.

374. *Ibid.*, Vol. IX, p. 268.

375. Hodges, Tony. *The Western Saharans*, The Minority Rights Group Report #40, 1994, 4)

376. *Ibid.*, p. 4.

377. *Ibid.*, p. 4.

378. *Ibid.*, p. 4.

379. *Encyclopedia of World Cultures*, Vol. IX, p. 297.

380. Stephen, David. *The San of the Kalahari*, The Minority Rights Group Report #56, 1982, p. 4.

381. Best and Blij, *op. cit.*, p. 61.

382. Schapera, I. *The Khoisan Peoples of South Africa: Bushmen and Hottentots* (London: George Routledge and Sons Ltd., 1930).

383. July, *op. cit.*, p. 66.

384. *Cultural Atlas of Africa*, p. 157.

385. *Encyclopedia of World Cultures*, Vol. IX, p. 94.

386. Nelson et. al, *op. cit.*, p. 70.

387. *Ibid.*, p. 68.

388. July, *op. cit.*, p. 109.

389. *Ibid.*, (1970 edition), pp. 105, 107.

390. *Ibid.*, (1970 edition), p. 107.

391. *Ibid.*, p. 89.

392. *Ibid.*, p. 210.

393. *Ibid.*, (1970 edition), p. 135.

394. *Encyclopedia of World Cultures*, Vol. IX, p. 187.

395. July, *op. cit.*, p. 102.

396. *Encyclopædia Britannica*, Vol. VII, pp. 560-561.

397. July, *op. cit.*, p. 131.

398. *Ibid.*, p. 131.

399. *Ibid.*, p. 94.

400. *Encyclopedia of World Cultures*, Vol. IX, p. 187.

401. July, *op. cit.*, p. 74.

402. *Encyclopædia Britannica*, Vol. VI, p. 417.

403. "Somalia: Irredentism in the 'Horn'" in Best and Blij, *op. cit.*, p. 497.

404. *Encyclopædia Britannica*, Vol. VII, pp. 560-561.

405. *Ibid.*, Vol. VIII, p. 387.

406. *Ibid.*, Vol. XI, p. 23.

407. *Ibid.*, Vol. XI, p. 23.

408. *Encyclopedia of World Cultures*, Vol. IX, p. 187.

409. *Ibid.*, Vol.IX, p. 322.

410. *Ibid.*, Vol.IX, p. 324.

411. *Ibid.*, Vol. IX, p. 327.

412. Gunther, *op. cit.*, p. 579.

413. *Social Theory and African Tribal Organization*, p. 103.

414. July, *op. cit.*, p. 94.

415. *Encyclopedia of World Cultures*, Vol. IX, p. 336.

416. July, *op. cit.*, (1970 edition), p. 11.

417. *Ibid.*, (1970 edition), p. 51.

418. *Ibid.*, (1970 edition), p. 51.

419. *Ibid.*, pp. 56, 58.

420. Briggs, *op. cit.*, p. 126.

421. July, *op. cit.*, pp. 38, 40.

422. Briggs, *op. cit.*, p. 168.

423. *Ibid.*, p. 187.

424. *Ibid.*, p. 167.

425. *Ibid.*, p. 180.

426. July, *op. cit.*, (1970 edition), p. 477, and *Encyclopædie Britannica*, Vol. I, p. 473.

427. July, *op. cit.*, p. 359.

428. *Encyclopædia Britannica*, Vol. XI, p. 620.

429. *Ibid.*, Vol. XI, p. 621.

430. July, *op. cit.*, p. 288.

431. *Ibid.*, p. 288.

432. *Ibid.*, p. 289.

433. *Encyclopedia of World Cultures*, Vol. IX, p. 346.

434. *Ibid.*, Vol. IX, pp. 346-347.

435. *Social Theory and African Tribal Organization*, p. 233.

436. *Ibid.*, p. 233.

437. *Encyclopædia Britannica*, Vol. VI, p. 256.

438. July, *op. cit.*, p. 372.

439. *Encyclopædia Britannica*, Vol. XI, p. 23.

440. *Encyclopedia of World Cultures*, Vol. IX, p. 363.

441. *Ibid.*, Vol. IX. p. 370.

442. *Encyclopedia of World Cultures*, Vol. IX, p. 370.

443. *Encyclopædia Britannica*, Vol. XII, p. 56.

444. *Ibid.*, Vol. XII, p. 205.

445. *Ibid.*, Vol. Xi, p. 23.

446. July, *op. cit.*, p. 109.

447. *Ibid.*, p. 109.

448. Elliot, Aubray. *The Magic World of the Xhosa* (New York, NY: Charles Scribners' Sons, 1970), p. 40.

449. *Cultural Atlas of Africa*, p. 206.

450. Seligman, *op. cit.*, p. 147.

451. Moss and Wilson, *op. cit.*, p. 282.

452. *Ibid.*, p. 284.

453. *Ibid.*, p. 284.

454. July, *op. cit.*, p. 73.

455. "Somalia: Irredentism in the 'Horn'." in Best and Blij, *op. cit.*, p. 497.

456. July, *op. cit.*, pp. 89-90, 137.

457. *Ibid.*, p. 90.

458. Firebrace, James. *Sons of Zulu* (Johannesburg, South Africa: William Collins Sons & Co., Ltd., 1978), p. 195.

459. *Ibid.*, p. 195.

PART SEVEN

BIBLIOGRAPHY

BIBLIOGRAPHY

Abrahams, Ray G. *The Nyamwezi Today* (Cambridge: Cambridge University Press, 1981).

Abuor, C. Ojwando. *White Highlands No More* (Nairobi: Pan African Researchers, 1970).

Achebe, Chinua. *The Trouble with Nigeria* (Reading: Cox & Wyman, 1983).

Adamu, Mahdi. *The Hausa Factor in West African History* (London: Oxford University Press, 1978).

Afigbo, A.E. *Ropes of Sand: Studies in Igbo History and Culture* (Ibadan and Oxford: Ibadan University Press and Oxford University Press, 1981).

Ajayi, J.F. Ade, and Ian Espie. *A Thousand Years of West African History* (London: Ibadan University Press and Nelson, 1969).

Allen, William D., and Jerry E. Jennings. *Africa* (Grand Rapids: Fideler, 1986).

Apter, David E. *The Political Kingdom of Uganda: A Study in Bureaucratic Nationalism* (Princeton: Princeton University Press, 1967).

Ardener, Edwin. *Coastal Bantu of the Cameroons* (London: International African Institute, 1956).

Argyle, W.J. *The Fon of Dahomey* (Oxford: Clarendon Press, 1966).

Ashkenazi, M., and A. Weingrod, eds. *Ethiopian Jews and Israel* (New Brunswick and Oxford: Transaction Books, 1987).

Atkinson, Ronald R. *The Roots of Ethnicity: The Origins of the Acholi of Uganda before 1800* (Philadelphia: University of Pennsylvania Press, 1994).

Balmer, W.T. *A History of the Akan Peoples* (The Atlantic Press, 1926).

Barnard, Allan. *Hunters and Herders of Southern Africa: A Comparative Ethnography of the Khoisan Peoples* (Cambridge: Cambridge University Press, 1992).

Barth, Fredrik, ed. *Ethnic Groups and Boundaries* (London: Allen & Unwin, 1970).

Basden, G.T. *Niger Ibos* (London: Frank Cass, 1966).

Baxter, P.T.W., and A. Butt. *The Azande and Related Peoples of the Anglo-Egyptian Sudan and the Belgian Congo* (London: International African Institute, 1953).

Beach, David N. *The Shona and Zimbabwe, 900-1850* (Gweru, Zimbabwe: Mambu Press, 1980).

Beattie, John. *Bunyoro: An African Kingdom* (New York: Holt, Rinehart & Winston, Inc., 1960).

Becker, Peter. *Traits and Tribes in Southern Africa* (London: Hart Davis, MacGibbon, 1975).

Beidelman, Thomas O. *The Kaguru: A Matrilineal People of East Africa* (New York: Holt, Rinehart & Winston, 1971).

_____. *The Matrilineal Peoples of Eastern Tanzania* (London: International African Institute, 1956).

Berghe, Pierre van den. *South Africa, A Study in Conflict* (Berkeley: University of California Press, 1967).

Best, Alan, and Harm J. de Blij. *African Survey* (New York: John Wiley & Sons, 1977).

Biobaku, Saburi O. *The Egba and their Neighbors, 1842-1872* (Oxford: Clarendon, 1928).

Birmingham, David, and Phyllis M. Martin, (eds.). *History of Central Africa.* 2 volumes. (New York: Longman, 1983).

Blackburn, Roderic. *Okiek* (London, UK: Evans Brothers, 1982).

_____. "In the Land of Milk and Hony." In *Politics and History in Band Societies,* edited by Eleanor Leacock and Richard Lee, 283-305 (Cambridge: Cambridge University Press, 1982).

Bohannan, Laura, and Paul Bohannan. *The Tiv of Central Nigeria* (London: International African Institute, 1953).

Bohannan, Paul, and Philip Curtin. *Africa and Africans* (Prospect Heights: Waveland Press, 1988).

Bourdillon, M.F.C. *The Shona Peoples* (Gweru, Zimbabwe: Mambu Press, 1987).

Bradbury, R.E. *The Benin Kingdom and the Edo-Speaking Peoples of South-Western Nigeria* (London: International African Institute, 1957).

Briggs, Lloyd Cabot. *Tribes of the Sahara* (Cambridge: Harvard University Press, 1967).

Brown, G.C., and A. McDonald B. Hutt. *Anthropology in Action* (Oxford: Oxford University Press, 1935).

Bustin, Edouard. *Lunda under Belgian Rule: The Politics of Ethnicity* (Cambridge: Harvard University Press, 1975).

Butt, Audrey. *The Nilotes of the Anglo-Egyptian Sudan and Uganda* (London: International African Institute, 1952).

Central Intelligence Agency. *The World Factbook 1995-96* (Washington, DC; London: Brassey's, 1995).

Cerulli, Ernesta. *Peoples of Southwest Ethiopia and Its Borderlands* (London: International African Institute, 1956).

Champion, Arthur M. *The Agiryama of Kenya* (London: Royal Anthropological Institute of Great Britain and Ireland, 1967).

Chapelle, Jean. *Nomades noirs du Sahara* (Paris: Librairie Plon, 1957).

Chendu, Victor C. *The Igbo of Southeast Nigeria* (New York: Holt, Rinehart & Winston, 1965).

Cohen, Ronald. *Africa: Its People and their Cultural History* (New York, NY: McGraw-Hill, 1959).

_____. *The Kanuri of Bornu* (New York: Holt, Rinehart & Winston, Inc., 1967).

_____. *The Structure of Kanuri Society* (Ann Arbor: University Microfilms, 1960).

Colson, Elizabeth, and Max Gluckman. *Seven Tribes of British Central Africa* (Manchester: Manchester University Press, 1951).

Covell, Maureen. *Madagascar: Politics, Economics, and Society* (London: Frances Pinter Publishers, 1987).

Crazzolara, J.P. *The Lwoo*. 3 volumes (Verona: Editrice Nigrizia, 1950-1954).

Cunnison, Ian. *The Baggara Arabs: Power and Lineage in a Sudanese Nomad Tribe* (Oxford: Clarendon Press, 1966).

_____. *The Luapula Peoples of Northern Rhodesia* (Manchester: Manchester University Press, 1959).

Cureau, D. Ad. *Les societes primitives de L'Afrique Equatoriale* (Paris: Librairie Armand Colin, 1912).

Davidson, Basil. *Africa in History* (New York: Macmillan, 1974).

_____. *The African Genius* (Boston, New York, Toronto, London: Little, Brown & Company, 1969).

_____. *The Lost Cities of Africa* (Boston: Little, Brown & Company, 1987).

Deng, Francis Mading. *The Dinka of the Sudan* (New York: Holt, Rinehart & Winston, 1972).

Doke, C.M. *The Lambas of Northern Rhodesia* (London: Harrap, 1931).

Driberg, Jack H. *The Lango: A Nilotic Tribe of Uganda* (London: T. Fisher Unwin, 1923).

Du Bois, W.E. Burghardt. *The World and Africa* (New York: International Publishers, 1972).

Dwyer, John O. *The Acholi of Uganda: Adjustment to Imperialism* (Ann Arbor: University Microfilms International, 1972).

Dyson-Hudson, Neville. *Karimojong Politics* (Oxford: Clarendon Press, 1966).

Eades, J.S. *The Yoruba Today* (Cambridge: Cambridge University Press, 1980).

Egharevba, Jacob U. *A Short History of Benin* (Ibadan: Ibadan University Press, 1968).

Elliot, Aubray. *The Magic World of the Xhosa* (New York: Scribners, 1970).

Ellis, A. B. *The Ewe-Speaking Peoples of the Slave Coast of West Africa* (Benin, 1965).

_____. *The Yoruba-Speaking Peoples of the Slave Coast of West Africa* (Benin, 1964).

Emley, E.D. "The Turkana of Kolosia District," *Journal of the [Royal] Anthropological Institute of Great Britain and Ireland*, 1927, 57:157-201. Esterman, Carlos. *The Ethnography of Southwestern Angola* (New York: Africana, 1976).

Evans-Pritchard, E. E. *The Azande* (Oxford: Clarendon Press, 1971).

_____. *The Nuer, A Description of the Modes of Livelihood and Political Institutions of a Nilotic People* (New York and Oxford: Oxford University Press, 1972).

_____. *Man and Woman Among the Azande* (New York: Free Press, 1974).

_____. *The Sanusi of Cyrenaica* (Oxford: Clarendon, 1949).

Fage, J.D. *An Atlas of African History* (London: Edward Arnold, 1978).

Fahim, Hussein M. *Egyptian Nubians: Resettlement and Years of Coping* (Salt Lake City: University of Utah, 1983).

Fallers, Margaret Chave. *The Eastern Lacustrine Bantu* (London: International African Institute, 1978).

February, Vernon. *The Afrikaners of South Africa* (London: Kegan Paul International, 1991).

Firebrace, James. *Eritrea & Tigray* (London: The Minority Rights Group, Report #5, 1983).

_____. *Sons of Zulu* (Johannesburg: William Collins Sons, 1978).

Forde, C. Daryll. *The Ethographic Survey of Africa* (London: International African Institute, 1988).

_____. *Marriage and the Family Among the Yako in Southwestern Nigeria* (London: International African Institute, 1951).

_____. *The Yoruba-Speaking Peoples of Southwestern Nigeria* (London: International African Institute, 1951).

_____. *Yako Studies* (London: Oxford University Press for the International African Institute, 1964).

Forde, C. Daryll, ed. *African Worlds* (London: Oxford University Press, 1954).

Forde, D., and G.I. Jones. *The Ibo and Ibibio-Speaking Peoples of South-Eastern Nigeria: Ethnographic Survey of Africa* (London: Stone & Cox, 1962).

Fortes, Meyer, and E. E. Evans-Pritchard, eds. *African Political Systems* (London: Oxford University Press, 1940).

Fraenkel, Peter, and Roger Murray. *The Namibians* (London: The Minority Rights Group, Report #19, 1985).

Frazer, James George. *The Native Races of Africa and Madagascar* (London: Percylund Humphries, 1938).

Gaily, Harry A. *The History of Africa in Maps* (Chicago: Denoyer-Geppert, 1967).

Gamble, David P. *Ethnographic Survey of Africa: The Wolof of Sengambia* (London: International African Institute, 1967).

Garraty, John A., and Peter Gay, eds. *The Columbia History of the World* (New York, Evanston, San Francisco, London: Harper & Row, 1981).

Gauthier, J. G. *Une population traditionnelle du Nord Cameroun: Les fali* (Bordeaux: Institut Pédagogique, 1963).

_____. *Les fali de Ngoutchoumi, montagnards du Nord Cameroun* (Oosterhout: Anthropological Publications, 1969).

Gellner, Ernest, and Charles Micaud, (eds.). *Arabs and Berbers: From Tribe to Nation in North Africa* (London: Duckworth, 1973).

Gibbs, J. L., Jr., ed. *The Peoples of Africa* (New York: Holt, Rinehart & Winston, 1965).

Gluckman, Max. *The Judicial Process Among the Barotse of Northern Rhodesia* (Manchester: Manchester University Press, 1955).

Goldschmidt, Walter. *The Culture and Behavior of the Sebei* (Berkeley and Los Angeles: University of California Press, 1976).

Goldthorpe, J.E., and F.B. Wilson. *Tribal Maps of East Africa and Zanzibar* (Uganda: East African Institute of Social Research, 1960).

Graf, William D. *The Nigerian State: Political Economy, State, Class, and Political System in the Post-Colonial Era* (London: James Currey, 1988).

Greenberg, J. H. *Studies in African Linguistic Classification* (New Haven: Compass, 1955).

_____. *The Languages of Africa* (Bloomington: Indiana University Press, 1962).

Griaule, Marcel. *Masques Dogons*. Second edition (Paris: Institut d'ethnologie, 1963).

Gulliver, Philip H., and Pamela Gulliver. *The Central Nilo-Hamites* (London: International African Institute, 1953, 1968).

Gunn, Harold D. *Pagan Peoples of the Central Area of Northern Nigeria* (London: International African Institute, 1956).

_____. *Peoples of the Plateau Area of Northern Nigeria* (London: International African Institute, 1953).

Gunther, John. *Inside Africa* (New York: Harper & Brothers, 1953).

Gunn, Harold D. *Pagan Peoples of the Central Area of Northern Nigeria* (London: International African Institute, 1956).

_____. *Peoples of the Plateau Area of Northern Nigeria* (London, UK: International African Institute, 1953).

Hall, H.U. *The Sherbro of Sierra Leone* (Philadelphia: University of Pennsylvania Press, 1938).

Hallpike, C.R. *The Konso of Ethiopia: A Study of the Values of a Cushitic People* (Oxford: Clarendon Press, 1972).

Hambly, W. D. "Culture Areas of Nigeria," *Field Museum Anthropology Series*. Vol. 21, no. 3 (Chicago: Field Musuem of Natural History, 1935).

_____. "The Ovimbundu of Angola," *Field Museum Anthropology Series*. Vol. 21, pp. 89-362 (Chicago: Field Musuem of Natural History, 1934).

Hammond-Tooke, W.D., ed. *The Bantu-Speaking Peoples of Southern Africa* (London: Routledge & Kegan Paul, 1974).

Harwood, Alan. *Witchcraft, Sorcery and Social Categories Among the Safwa* (London: Oxford University Press, 1970).

Haskins, Jim, and Joann Biondi. *From Afar to Zulu: A Dictionary of African Cultures* (New York: Walker and Company, 1995).

Herskovits, Melville J. *Dahomey: An Ancient West African Kingdom* (Vols. 1,2) (Evanston: Northwestern University Press, [1938] 1967).

Hiernaux, Jean. *The People of Africa* (New York: Scribner, 1975).

Hill, Polly. *Rural Hausa: A Village and a Setting* (Cambridge: Cambridge University Press, 1972).

Hitchens, Christopher, and David Stephen, eds. *Inequalities in Zimbabwe* (London: Minority Rights Group, Report #8, 1981).

Hodges, Tony. *The Western Saharans* (London: The Minority Rights Group, Report #40, 1994).

Holas, Bohumil. *Les Senoufo* (Paris: Presses Universitaires de France, 1957).

Hollis, Alfred C. *The Nandi: Their Language and Folklore* (Westport: Negro Universities Press, 1969).

Holt, P.M. *A Modern History of the Sudan from the Funj Sultanate to the Present Day* (New York: Grove Press, 1961).

Hooper, Ed, and Louise Pirovet. *Uganda* (London: Minority Rights Group, Report #66, 1989).

Hopen, C. Edward. "Fulani." In *Muslim Peoples: A World Ethnographic Survey*. 2nd edition, revised and expanded by Richard V. Weekes, 257-261 (Westport: Greenwood Press, 1984).

Hrbek, Ivan. "A List of African Ethnonyms," in *African Ethnonyms and Toponyms*, pp. 141-186 (Paris: Imprimerie des presses universitaires de France, 1984.

Huntingford, G.W.B. *The Galla of Ethiopia, the Kingdom of Kafa and Janjero* (London: International African Institute, 1955).

_____. *The Nandi of Kenya: Tribal Control in a Pastoral Society* (London: Routledge & Kegan Paul, 1953).

_____. *The Northern Nilo-Hamites* (London: International African Institute, 1953).

_____. *The Southern Nilo-Hamites* (London: International African Institute, 1953).

Iliffe, John. *A Modern History of Tanganyika* (Cambridge: Cambridge University Press, 1979).

Imperato, Pascal James. *Buffoons, Queens & Wooden Horsemen: The Dyo & Gouan Societies of the Bambara of Mali* (New York: Kilma House Publications, 1983).

_____. *Historical Dictionary of Mali* (Metuchen: Scarecrow, 1977).

Isichei, Elizabeth. *A History of the Igbo People* (New York: St. Martin's Press, 1976).

Jaenen, Cornelius J. "The Galla or Oromo of East Africa," *Southwestern Journal of Anthropology*, 1956, Vol. 12, pp. 171-190.

Jaspan, M.A. *The Ila-Tonga Peoples of North-Western Rhodesia* (London: International African Institute, 1953).

Johnson, Douglas H. *The Southern Sudan* (London, UK: The Minority Rights Group, Report #78, 1988).

July, Robert W. *A History of the African People* (New York: Charles Scribner's Sons, 1970).

_____. A History of the African People (Prospect Heights, IL: Waveland Press, 1998).

Karp, Ivan. Fields of Change Among the Iteso of Kenya (London: Routledge & Kegan Paul, Ltd., 1978).

Keesing's Record of World Events 1994, Reference Supplement, 1996, No. 40.

Kelly, Raymond. The Nuer Conquest: The Structure and Development of an Expansionist System (Ann Arbor: University of Michigan Press, 1985).

Kennedy, J.G. Nubian Ceremonial Life (Berkeley: University of California, 1978).

Kenyatta, Jomo. Facing Mount Kenya: The Traditional Life of the Gikuyu (London: Heinemann, 1979).

Klima, George J. The Barabaig: East African Cattle-Herders (New York: Holt, Rinehart & Winston, 1970).

Kottak, Conrad. The Past in the Present: History, Ecology and Cultural Variation in Highland Madagascar (Ann Arbor: University of Michigan Press, 1980).

Krige, Eileen Jensen. The Social System of the Zulus (London: Longman, Green, 1936).

Krige, Eileen Jensen, and J.D. Krige. The Realm of a Rain Queen: A Study of the Pattern of Lovedu Society (London: Oxford University Press, 1943).

Kuper, A. The Pedi (Pretoria: J.L. van Schaik, 1975).

Kuper, Hilda. An African Aristocracy: Rank Among the Swazi (London: Oxford University Press, 1947).

Kwamena-Poh, M.J. Tosh et al. African History in Maps (Essex: Longman, 1982).

La Fontaine, Jean S. The Gisu of Uganda (London: International African Institute, 1959).

Lambert, H.H. Kikuyu Social and Political Institutions (London: Oxford University Press, 1956).

Langley, Myrtle. *The Nandi in Kenya: Life Crisis Rituals in a Period of Change* (New York: St. Martin's 1979).

Leach, Graham. *The Afrikaners: Their Last Great Trek* (London: Macmillan, 1989).

Lebeuf, Annie M.D. *Les Populations du Tchad* (Paris: Presses universitaires de France, 1959).

Legum, Colin. *Eritrea & Tigray* (London: Minority Rights Group, Report #5, 1983).

Leonard, Arthur Glyn. *The Lower Niger and Its Tribes* (London: Frank Cass, 1968).

Lewis, Ioan Myrddin, ed. *Peoples of the Horn: Somali, Afar, and Saho* (London, UK: International African Institute, 1955).

Lienhardt, R.G. *Divinity and Experience: The Religion of the Dinka* (Oxford: Clarendon Press, 1961).

_____. "The Shilluk of the Upper Nile." In *African Worlds*, edited by D. Forde, 138-163 (London: Oxford University Press, 1954).

Little, Kenneth L. *The Mende of Sierra Leone* (London: Routledge & Kegan Paul, 1951).

Lystad, Robert A. *The Ashanti: A Proud People* (Greenwich: Greenwood Press, 1968).

MacGaffey, Wyatt. *Custom and Government in the Lower Congo* (Berkeley and Los Angeles: University of California Press, 1970).

MacMichael, Harold Alfred. *The Tribes of Northern and Central Kordofan* (London: Frank Cass, 1967).

Magnant, J.P. *La terre sara, terre tchadiene* (Paris: l'Harmattan, 1987).

Manoukian, Madeline. *The Akan and Ga-Adangme Peoples* (London: International African Institute, 1950).

_____. *The Ewe-Speaking People of Togoland and the Gold Coast* (London: International African Institute, 1952).

_____. *Tribes of the Northern Territories of the Gold Coast* (London: International African Institute, 1951).

Martin, Phyllis M. *Historical Dictionary of Angola* (Metuchen: Scarecrow, 1980).

_____, and Patrick O'Meara. *Africa* (Bloomington: Indiana University Press, 1977).

Marwick, Brian Allan. The Swazi: *An Ethnographic Account of the Natives of Swaziland Protectorate* (London: Frank Cass, 1940).

Marwick, M.G. *Sorcery in its Social Setting: A Study of the Northern Rhodesian Cewa* (Manchester: Manchester University Press, 1965).

McCaskie, T.C. *State and Society in Pre-Colonial Asante* (Cambridge and New York: Cambridge University Press, 1995).

McCulloch, Merran. *The Ovimbundu of Angola* (London: International African Institute, 1952).

_____. *Peoples of Sierra Leone* (London: International African Institute, 1950).

_____. *The Southern Lunda and Related Peoples* (London: International African Institute, 1951).

_____, M. Littlewood and I. Dugast. *Peoples of the Central Cameroons* (London: International African Institute, 1954).

McEvedy, Colin. *The Penguin Atlas of African History* (Hong Kong: Penguin Books, 1980).

McKinley Jr., James C. "Stoked by Rwandans, Tribal Violence Spreads in Zaire," *The New York Times International*, June 16, 1996, p. y3.

Meek, C. K. *A Sudanese Kingdom: An Ethnological Study of the Jukan-Speaking Peoples of Nigeria* (London: Trench, Trubner & Co., 1931).

_____. *Tribal Studies in Northern Nigeria* (London: K. Paul Trench, Trubner & Co., 1931).

Messing, Simon D. *Highland Plateau Amhara of Ethiopia.* Edited by Lionel M. Bender. 3 vols. (New Haven: HRAFlex Books, 1985).

Meyerhoff, Elizabeth. "The Threatened Ways of Kenya's Pokot People." *National Geographic*, 1982:161:120-140.

Meyerowitz, E. L. R. *Akan Traditions of Origin* (London: Faber & Faber, 1950).

_____. *The Sacred State of the Akan* (London: Faber & Faber, 1951).

Middleton, John. *The Lugbara of Uganda*. Rev. ed. (New York: Holt, Rinehart & Winston, 1992).

_____. *Lugbara Religion* (London: Oxford University Press, 1960).

_____. "The Yakan or Allah Water Cult Among the Lugbara," *Journal of the Royal Anthropological Institute of Great Britain and Ireland*, 1963, Vol. 93, No. 1, pp. 80-108.

_____, and Greet Kershaw. *The Kikuyu and Kamba of Kenya* (London, International African Institute, 1965).

_____, and Amal Rassam, (eds.). *Encyclopedia of World Cultures, Vol. IX, Africa and the Middle East* (Boston: G.K. Hall & Co., 1995).

_____, ed. *Peoples of Africa* (New York: Arco, 1978).

Montagne, Robert. *The Berbers: Their Social and Political Organization*. Translated from French by David Seddon (London, UK: Frank Cass, 1973).

Morton, Fred, et al. *Historical Dictionary of Botswana* (Metuchen, NJ: Scarecrow, 1989).

Murdock, George Peter. *Africa: Its Peoples and Their Culture History* (New York, Toronto, and London: McGraw-Hill, 1959).

Muriuki, Godfrey. *People Round Mount Kenya: Kikuyu*. Second edition (London, UK: Evans, 1985).

Murray, Jocelyn, ed. *Cultural Atlas of Africa* (New York: Facts on File, Inc, Fifth Reprint, 1993).

Nachtigal, Gustav. *Sahara and Sudan; The Chad Basin and Bagirmi* (London, UK: C. Hurst & Co., 1987).

Nadel, Siegfried F. *A Black Byzantium: The Kingdom of Nupe in Nigeria* (London: Oxford University Press, 1942).

_____. *The Nuba: An Anthropological Study of the Hill Tribes of Kordofan* (London: Oxford University Press, 1947).

Nai'ibi, Malam S., and Alhaji Hassan. *Gwari Gade and Koro Tribes* (Ibadan: Ibadan University Press, 1969).

Nelson, Harold D. et. al. *The Nuba: An Anthropological Study of the Hill Tribes of Kordofan* (London: Oxford University Press, 1947).

The New Encyclopædia Britannica (Chicago: Encyclopædia Britannica, Inc., 15th edition, 1988).

Niblock, Tim. *Class and Power in Sudan: The Dynamics of Sudanese Politics, 1898-1985* (New York: State University of New York Press, 1987).

"Nigeria and Cameroon." *The Economist,* March 12, 1994:50.

Nsugbe, Philip. *Ohaffia, A Matrilineal Ibo People* (Oxford: Clarendon Press, 1974).

Ntara, S.J. *The History of the Chewa* (Wiesbaden: Franz Steiner Verlag, 1973).

Nzimiro, Ikenna. *Studies in Ibo Political Systems* (Berkeley and Los Angeles: University of California Press, 1972).

Ocholla-Ayayo, A.B.C. *The Luo Culture: A Reconstruction of a Traditional African Society* (Wiesbaden: Steiner, 1980).

O'Fahey, R.S., and J.L. Spaulding. *Kingdoms of the Sudan* (London: Menthuen, 1974).

Ohadike, D.C. *Anioma* (Athens: Ohio University Press, 1994).

Ojany, Francis F., and Reuben B. Ogendo. *Kenya: A Study in Physical and Human Geography* (Nairobi: Longman, 1973).

Oliver, Ronald, and Michael Crowder, ed. *The Cambridge Encyclopedia of Africa* (Cambridge: Cambridge University Press, 1981).

Olivier de Sardan, J. P. *Concepts et conceptions songhay-zarma: Histoire, culture, société* (Paris: Nubia, 1982).

_____. *Sociétés songhay-zarma* (Paris: Karthala, 1984).

Onwuejeogwu, M.A. *An Igbo Civilization: Nri Kingdom and Hegemony* (London, Ethiope Publishing, 1981).

Orchardson, Ian Q. *The Kipsigis*. Abridged from the original manuscript by A.T. Matson (Nairobi: East African Publishing House, 1961).

Ottenberg, Simon, and Phoebe Ottenberg. *Cultures and Societies of Africa* (New York: Random House, n.d.).

Palau Marti, Montserrat. *Les Dogon* (Paris: Presses Universitaires de France, 1957).

Paques, Viviana. *Les Bambara* (Paris: Presses universitaires de France, 1954).

Paul, A. *A History of Beja Tribes of the Sudan* (London: Cambridge University Press, 1954).

Père, M. *Les lobi: Tradition et changement (Burkina Faso)*. 2 vols. (Laval: Siloë, 1988).

Price, David H. *Atlas of World Cultures, A Geographical Guide to Ethnographic Literature* (Newbury Park, London, New Delhi: Sage Publications, 1990).

Prins, A. H. J. *The Swahili Speaking Peoples of Zanzibar and the East African Coast* (London: International African Institute, 1961).

Radcliffe-Brown, A.R., and D. Forde. *African Systems of Kinship and Marriage* (London: Oxford University Press, 1950).

Rattray, R.S. *The Tribes of the Ashanti Hinterland* (Oxford: Oxford University Press, 1932).

Ray, Donald I. *Ghana: Politics, Economics, and Society* (Boulder: Lynne Rienner Publishers, Inc., 1986).

Richards, Audrey Isabel. *Chisungu: A Girls' Initiation Ceremony Among the Bemba of Northern Rhodesia* (New York: Grove, 1956).

_____. "The Ganda." In *East African Chiefs: A Study of Political Development in Some Uganda and Tanganyika Tribes*, edited by Audrey I. Richards, 41-77 (London: Faber & Faber for the East African Institute of Social Research, 1960).

_____. *The Multicultural States of East Africa* (Montreal, Canada: McGill-Queen's University Press, 1969).

Rigby, Peter. *Cattle and Kinship Among the Gogo, A Semi-Pastoral Society of Central Tanzania* (Ithaca: Cornell University Press, 1969).

Roscoe, The Reverend John. *The Baganda* (London: Frank Cass, 1965).

Rouch, Jean. *Les Songhay* (Paris: Presses universitaires de France, 1954).

Salim, A.I. *The Swahili-Speaking Peoples of Kenya's Coast 1895-1965* (London, East African Publishing House, 1973).

Samatar, Said S. *Somalia-A Nation in Turmoil* (London: The Minority Rights Group, 1991).

Schapera, I. *The Bantu-Speaking Tribes of South Africa* (London: Routledge & Kegan Paul, 1937).

_____. *The Ethnic Composition of Tswana Tribes* (London: London School of Economics and Political Science, 1952).

_____. *The Khoisan Peoples of South Africa* (London: Routledge & Kegan Paul, 1965).

_____. *The Tswana* (Plymouth: Clark, Doble and Brendon, 1976).

_____, ed. *The Bantu-Speaking Tribes of South Africa: An Ethnographical Survey* (London: Routledge & Kegan Paul, 1937).

Seligman, C.G. *Races of Africa* (New York: Oxford University Press, 1966).

Shack, William A. *The Central Ethiopians Amhara, Tigerina, and Related People* (London: International African Institute, 1974).

Sheddick, V.G.J. *The Southern Sotho* (London: International African Institute, 1953).

Skinner, Elliott P. *The Mossi of the Upper Volta: The Political Development of a Sudanese People* (Stanford, CA: Stanford University Press, 1946).

Smith, Edwin W. *The Ila-Speaking Peoples of Northern Rhodesia* (London: Macmillan, 1920).

Smith, M.G. "The Hausa of Northern Nigeria." In *Peoples of Africa*, edited by J.L. Gibbs, Jr., 119-155 (New York: Holt, Rinehart & Winston, 1965).

Sousberghe, Léon de. *Les pende: Aspect des structures sociales et politiques.* Annales du Musée Royal de l'Afrique Centrale. Sciences Humaines, No. 46 (Tervueeren, 1963).

Southall, Aidan. *Social Change in Modern Africa* (New York: Oxford University Press, 1969).

Southwold, Margin. "The Ganda of Uganda." In *Peoples of Africa,* edited by James L. Gibbs, Jr., 81-118 (New York: Holt, Rinehart & Winston, 1965).

Spencer, Paul. *The Maasi of Matapato: A Study of Rituals of Rebellion* (Manchester: Manchester University Press, 1988).

Spiro, Herbert J. *Politics in Africa: Prospects South of the Sahara* (Englewood Cliffs: Prentice-Hall, Inc., 1962).

Stephen, David. *The San of the Kalahari* (London: The Minority Right Group, Report #56, 1982).

Stevenson, R.C. *The Nuba People of Kordofan Province* (Khartoum: University of Khartoum, 1984).

"Stoked by Rwandans, Tribal Violence Spreads in Zaire," *The New York Times International,* June 16, 1996:Y3.

Swantz, M-L. *Ritual and Symbol in Transitional Zaramo Society* (Uppsala: Scandinavian Institute of African Studies, 1986).

Tait, David. *The Konkomba of Northern Ghana* (London: Oxford University Press, 1961).

Thairu, Kihumbu. *The African Civilization* (Kampala, Nairobi, Dar Es Salaam: East African Literature Bureau, 1975).

Thornton, John K. *The Kingdom of Kongo* (Madison: University of Wisconsin Press, 1983).

Thornton, Robert J. *Space, Time, and Culture among the Iraqw of Tanzania* (New York: Academic Press, 1980).

Trout, Frank E. *Morocco's Saharan Frontiers* (Geneva: Libraire Droz, 1969).

Turnbull, Colin M. *The Mbuti Pygmies: An Ethnographic Survey.* *Anthropological Papers of the American Museum of Natural History,* 1965, 50, Pt. 3.

Turner, Victor W. *The Lozi Peoples of Northwest Rhodesia* (London: International African Institute, 1952).

Uchendu, Victor C. *The Igbo of Southeast Nigeria* (New York: Holt, Rinehart & Winston, 1965).

Uku-Wertimer, Skyne. *Africa, Changes and Challenges* (Acton: Tapestry press, 1990).

UNESCO. *African Ethnonyms and Toponyms* (Paris: Imprimerie des presses universitaires de France, 1984).

_____. *Nomades et Nomadisme au Sahara* (Paris: Fountenoy, 1963).

Urvoy, Y. *Histoire des populations du Soudan Central* (Paris: Larose, 1936).

Van Geluwe. *Les Bali* (London: International African Institute, 1960).

_____. *Les Bira* (London: International African Institute, 1957).

Van Warmelo, N. J. *Contributions Towards Venda History, Religion and Tribal Ritual* (Pretoria: Union of South Africa, Department of Native Affairs, 1932).

_____. *Notes on the Kaokoveld and Its People* (Pretoria: Republic of South Africa, Department of Bantu Administration, 1951).

Vansina, J. *Les Tribus Ba-Kuba* (London: International African Institute, 1954).

Vincent, Joan. *Teso in Transformation* (Berkeley and Los Angeles: University of California Press, 1982).

Vivelo, Frank Robert. *The Herero of Western Botswana: Aspects of Change in a Group of Bantu-Speaking Cattle Herders.* American Ethnological Society. Monograph 61 (St. Paul: West Publishing Co., 1977).

Wagner, Gunter. *The Bantu of Western Kenya.* 2 vols. (London: Oxford University Press, 1949-1956).

Wallerstein, Emmanuel. "Ethnicity and National Integration in West Africa," *Cahiers d'Etudes Africaines,* 1960, Vol. 1, No. 3, pp. 129-139.

Walter, Bob J. *Territorial Expansion of the Nandi of Kenya 1500-1950* (Athens: Ohio University, Center for International Studies, 1970).

Were, Gideon S. *A History of the Abaluhyia of Western Kenya c. 1500-1930* (Nairobi, Kenya: East African Publishing House (1967).

Westermann, D., and M.A. Bryan. *The Languages of West Africa* (London: International African Institute, 1952).

Whiteley, Wilfred et al. *Bemba and Related Peoples of Northern Rhodesia* (London: International African Institute, 1950).

Wilks, Ivor. *Assante in the Nineteenth Century* (London, New York: Cambridge University Press, 1975).

Willis, Justin. *Mombasa, the Swahili, and the Making of the Mijikenda* (Oxford: Clarendon Press, 1993).

Willis, Roy G. *The Fipa and Related Peoples of Southwest Tanzania and Northeast Zambia* (London: International African Institute, 1966).

Wilson, Godfrey. *The Constitution of Ngonde* (Manchester, UK: Manchester University Press, 1968).

Wilson, Monica. *Reaction to Conquest, Effects of Contact with Europeans on the Pondo of South Africa* (London: Oxford University Press, 1979).

_____. "Nyakyusa Kinship." In *African Systems of Kinship and Marriage,* edited by A.R. Radcliffe-Brown and D. Forde, 111-139 (London, UK: Oxford University Press, 1950).

PART EIGpT

INDEX OF ENTRIES

INDEX

AFRICAN PEOPLES AND NATIONS